Carl Rogers' Helping System

Carl Rogers' Helping System

Journey and Substance

Godfrey T. Barrett-Lennard

SAGE Publications
London • Thousand Oaks • New Delhi

First published 1998

SAGE Publications Ltd
6 Bonhill Street
London EC2A 4PU

SAGE Publications Inc.
2455 Teller Road
Thousand Oaks, California 91320

SAGE Publications India Pvt Ltd
32, M-Block Market
Greater Kailash – I
New Delhi 110 048

British Library Cataloguing in Publication Data

A catalogue record for this book is available from the British Library

ISBN 0 7619 5676 X
ISBN 0 7619 5677 8 (pbk)

Library of Congress catalog card number 98–61269

Typeset by Mayhew Typesetting, Rhayader, Powys
Printed in Great Britain by The Cromwell Press Ltd, Trowbridge, Wiltshire

Contents

Preface

Writing this book was often like an extended inner conversation with varied imagined readers: student and teacher companions, colleagues with theoretical and research interest, practitioner-helpers in counselling and related disciplines, and inquiring individuals of other backgrounds. The work itself is the outcome of a search, of a long unfolding journey which began under a more modest aim than its conclusion reflects. In the period since I started on the 'smallish' book as first conceived, two decades ago, there have been ups and downs in my own life/career situation, periods in which the manuscript was wholly set aside, important further contributions within the approach in focus, and evolution in my own thought.

The 'journey' in this book's title is the evolutionary course of a human science and helping system, rooted in the field of psychotherapy and counselling. My leaning toward exploration of the whole becoming of this approach was soon evident in what I found myself doing. The directional pull has been like a gravitational force, drawing me to an adventure in fresh learning and a revisiting of familiar landmarks in new depth. My belief is that when a system of ideas, inquiry and practice is seen in motion, through its whole span from germination to maturity, much fuller understanding is possible than can come from a view confined to current end-products of this evolution.

My own acquaintance with the approach spans almost half a century, and includes memorable years with Rogers and others at the University of Chicago, in the 1950s. As with other international students, it was no mean task to gain this opportunity and actually get there, in the first place. For me, the culminating step was a long sea voyage, with my wife and infant son. After reaching our destination, a multi-level and far deeper journey followed. By another leap, some four years later, I joined a university in the 'deep south' of the United States – finding scope for student-centred teaching (and even a group workshop), and building on the research already reported for my PhD. From there our path led back to Australia and other new steps, but in a place still far from our roots in the West. After a time I was drawn back to North America, and spent many years in Canada before finally settling again in Perth. What I did in these varied settings is at some points a visible element in the far wider journey this book works to illuminate.

I have brought together the contributions of *many* people, in addition to Carl Rogers himself, within a fresh perspective. The first large question addressed is that of how the innovation, reflected in Rogers' thought and the new therapy, came so vigorously into being in the time and place that it did. Chapters 2 and 3 tackle this issue in a previously untravelled path of exploration. A vigorous new system of thought and practice is likely to pass through a cohesive 'school' phase, and then become more pluralistic. Chapter 4 is a bird's eye view of main steps in the development of ideas, practice and research through the first quarter century of the new school; and Chapter 5 articulates its basic stance, constructs and theoretical vision, as evolved during this phase. The big six-chapter third part of the book, 'Principles in Practice', spans areas of process from individual therapy to large groups and community, and speaks in descriptive and studied vein to the many areas and interests now represented in the approach.

The fourth group of chapters focuses on the story and contributions of research in psychotherapy and other fields that this system has spawned, from earliest beginnings to current challenges. The final, two-chapter part of the book articulates long-term continuities, present activity, and aspects of new thought. It includes a many-sided chapter on 'training', culminating in a review of the current international span of extended or full programs of study and training in this approach. The ending chapter includes my own view of continuities and core features of thought over the long haul, and maps ways of further growing our theory and range of practice.

Most often in the detailed writing of the book I saw myself as a careful reporter and synthesizer, and worked hard in an effort to do feasible justice both to individual contributions and their interconnection within larger themes or strands of development. By the time eight or nine chapters were written, and the rest mapped out, my vision had shifted somewhat. I could see that the book itself might be an addition to the journey and the substance that it is about. I also felt that the movement Rogers began and spearheaded for so long was faltering, and in considerable danger of declining in substantiality as a system of thought and inquiry as well as practice. It seemed to me that what he had set in train both needed and deserved the best creative and integrative infusions that others could contribute. This became part of my incentive in completing the long enterprise of this work.

I began writing about a system of psychotherapy, and this remains a primary axis, in keeping with the interest of perhaps the majority of readers to whom I have inwardly spoken along the way. There are other axes as well. New developments in ways of responding to human need, particularly those which take hold rapidly, do not arise *de novo*. I hope that readers who share a leaning toward the social-contextual understanding of such innovations will find food for thought in my tracing of pertinent features of the larger milieu in which Rogers' direction took form and became so quickly influential.

Another axis is the close exploration of varied areas of application and development beyond one-to-one therapy – group encounter and therapy, teaching and parenting, experiences in community, and peace processes, to name some. In searching into each area, issues, principles and practice are in interwoven focus. The three-chapter sequence on the story and substance of research breaks new ground in its scope and approach. My inquiry into training complements in distinctive ways Mearns' fine new book *Person-Centred Counselling Training*. The last chapter pleases *me* in that it directly expresses growing edges in my own thought and perspective, all evolved or furthered through this project.

The whole work obviously covers a large canvas and I expect any reader will draw on it selectively, especially to start with. Each chapter begins with mention of its scope, and usually ends by opening a door to what follows next. Where topics of immediate interest are found rewarding, less familiar areas may beckon with invitation. I realize that some readers will be drawn first to what is novel to them and from there, perhaps, wish to explore areas already in their sights. My sources are closely documented throughout, although this impedes the flow a little. I have tended to judge others by myself, imagining the reader will be tempted here and there to mine the further riches of original sources and, in any case, wish to know what they are. Similarly, my cross-referencing, unnecessary if one reads from start to finish, is meant as an aid to the reader actively navigating his or her own individual course through the book.

Curiosity, thoughtfulness, capacity for suspension of belief, interest in checking or discovery through research, all seem to me entirely compatible with responsive openness and attention to feeling-emotional life. Persons *can* use one side of their potential while neglecting another, but those more fortunate in their functioning call readily on all sides. A 'left-brain' tendency in the wider intellectual culture has perhaps contributed to a later reaction of mistrust of probing inquiry and intellectual interest by some members of the humanistic movement, even some who identify with person-centred work. This reaction has worried me; it might be personally freeing at first but is then limiting unless transcended – and it would please me if my work contributes to such transition.

Achieving a particular effect is not, however, my deepest motivation. The fact is that this work has grown from absorbed interest and a career-long involvement in the approach itself and in reaching for an expanded frame of understanding. Extended engagement with Rogers himself and a community of other vital contributors has nourished my search. I am directly indebted to a good many of these colleagues for encouragement, information and materials, and critical feedback at times, as well as for their primary contributions. Given the long time-span and varied circumstance of my writing, I will not single anyone out here. My references to their work are the important testimony.

I have not forgotten that way back near the beginning of this project, a Private Scholar research award from the Social Sciences and Humanities Research Council of Canada was a most valuable boost. Without that moral and practical assistance, the foundling enterprise might not have survived my transition from career academia and then back to Australia. Greatest of all in importance is the long companionship and support (and tolerance of my 'work marriage') of my wife and life-partner, Helen; and the ambient nurture of our children and my wider family.

If you as reader have a sense of being in company with me, in parts of this book, I would welcome direct contact and sharing of ideas or reactions. This could be by letter (c/o School of Psychology, Murdoch University, WA, Australia 6150) or perhaps by Email (present address: <lennard@central.murdoch.edu.au>). This preface is a kind of letter to reader-companions, and it comes with my good wishes – and the hope that my book honours the trust of your interest.

Godfrey Barrett-Lennard,
Perth

PART I

CARL ROGERS AND HIS MILIEU

1

The Beginnings of Client-Centred Therapy

> The word 'therapy' has no verb in English, for which I am grateful; it cannot do anything to anybody, hence can better represent a process going on, observed perhaps, understood perhaps, assisted perhaps, but not applied. The Greek noun from which therapy is derived means 'a servant', the verb means 'to wait'.
>
> Jessie Taft, 1933

In 1939, as World War II began in Europe, a book titled *The Clinical Treatment of the Problem Child* was published by a clearly talented but, until then, largely unknown clinical psychologist in Rochester, upper New York State. Based on over a decade of field experience working with children, parents and families in difficulty, in an era that included the Great Depression and Roosevelt's New Deal, the book was an original and substantial resource to other workers in its field. It is evident from many details of the book that the author's interest and thought were influenced by innovative sources in social work and other fields as well as psychology. In his opening chapter entitled 'A point of view' the writer, Carl R. Rogers, proceeds at once to a firm and revealing expression of his outlook:

> In this book we shall deal with the child, not with behavior symptoms. One will look in vain for a chapter on stealing, thumb-sucking, or truancy, for such problems do not exist, nor can they be treated. . . . [In] each instance it is the child with whom we must deal, not the generalization which we make about his behavior. (Rogers, 1939: 3–4)

Thirty-five years later, Rogers was to emphasize that seeing 'the unique, subjective, inner person as the honored and valued core of human life' was one of the main enduring features of the client-centred orientation (Rogers, 1974c: 9). While client-centred therapy as a distinct new approach was not yet born in 1939, its precursors are vividly apparent in Rogers' first book. This work itself was a convergent outcome of several major streams of influence. The most evident of these are the background and person of the founder, his professional experience and influences, and the larger social-ideational climate in which his thought and practice took form. I invite you as reader to join me, to start with, in inquiring into the origins of the client-centred system. My belief is that this can lead to a deeper understanding than would result from simply viewing the end product. This 'system', under Rogers' tillage and in the soil of the times, grew in its founder's lifetime into an approach to therapy and human relations of global import.

The 'growing' of the founder of client-centred therapy

Rogers was a middle child in a large, middle-class, religiously strict and socially conservative, close-knit family. He has described his strongly family-centred parents as 'masters of the art of subtle and loving control' (Rogers, 1967a: 344). They both were well-educated for their time, energetic and very practical in bent, with a strong belief in self-reliance and in the virtue and efficacy of hard work. Rogers' father was a civil engineer and contractor, with his own business, and he later took up scientific farming as a sideline. His mother cared for her large family and household, evidently taking the lead, both through example and her fundamentalist religious beliefs, in her children's moral education. The boy Carl had learned to read well before he started school at age 7. He remembers himself as a dreamy youngster and omnivorous reader, although somewhat conflicted by this absorption as opposed to being up and about 'working'. As a child and youth, he had relatively little social life outside his immediate family. The family itself included a variety of relationships and companionship with older and younger brothers. Humour with a cutting edge or in the form of 'unmerciful teasing' is mentioned as a feature of the family interaction (ibid.).

About the time Carl finished elementary school, his parents bought a farm away from their former home in the Chicago suburb of Oak Park. His father and mother both liked productive outdoor activity. Most of all, they wished to remove their large family, then aged 6 to 20, away from 'the temptations and evils of suburban and city life' (ibid.). The woods and country provided a rich setting for play and fantasy that connected with Carl's adventure story reading, and for his blossoming serious interest in nature and in natural science. Two examples seem to stand out. One included his fascinated study and diligent rearing, through the caterpillar-larval and cocoon-pupal stages, of various species of great night-flying moth. The second example was Carl's growing involvement in his father's interest in scientific agriculture, often via projects and ventures which he made his own. An important instance he remembered was, as a 14-year-old, ploughing determinedly through a large book describing exacting experimental procedures in agricultural science, and gaining his first learnings about control groups, randomization, hypothesis testing and the generally painstaking process of scientific inquiry in an applied field (ibid.: 347, and Rogers, 1961a: 6).

In all, Rogers' upbringing was rather narrow *and* it was spacious. The family climate was both judgemental and supportively valuing of its members. On the one hand, Carl was confined pretty much to his family in a kind of preventive 'house arrest' situation and, on the other side, he was given fertile opportunity for very important dimensions of exploration and growth. The opportunity included favourable conditions for imaginal and intellectual development, for learnings around the forming of beliefs and values, for keen experience both of connection and apartness from others, and for the growth of a strong sense of self. There was room in his bounded world to dream, and the inner and outer conditions for a rich fantasy life existed side by side with a family emphasis on pursuits of a very practical nature. Especially, there was space and general encouragement, to playfully explore, seriously study and directly investigate phenomena that interested him, in the 'safe' areas of natural history and agriculture.

Carl took his formal schoolwork in his stride, excelling in English, where he could be personally expressive, and in science. Experiences of significant failure or defeat seem to have been almost non-existent, and the young Carl grew up in an atmosphere of generally taken-for-granted confidence in his basic ability, potential to succeed, and 'specialness' – in himself and as a member of his family. Although there were social/interpersonal ways in which he felt unsure of himself, his family and school experience would have supported the assumption that he could continue to develop and achieve what he wanted to, in directions he *felt free* to take. To discover and freely move along a growthful and fulfilling path some constraining personal walls would almost certainly need to come down. Vivid new experiences away from home were catalysts in this direction.

After finishing high school, Carl joined his next older brother at the University of Wisconsin, taken for granted as the place members of his family would go to college, and opted for agricultural science as his primary field. Soon his religious inclinations led to association with a band of classmates in a Sunday-morning group nondirectively facilitated by one of his professors. In this voluntary open situation, both self-initiation and interpersonal bonding developed strongly. For the first time, outside his family, Carl experienced 'real closeness and intimacy'; and he reports that 'the friendship and companionship which developed in this group of about twenty-five young men was an exceedingly important element in my life. We came to know each other well and to trust each other deeply' (1967a: 349). Many particular activities and learning experiences ensued. About midway in his second year Carl took part in an evangelistic conference of Student Volunteers (a kind of religion-based 'Peace Corps') where he experienced strong inspiration to change his life goal and go into Christian work. One consequence was to shift from agriculture to history as his major undergraduate field.

The following year, another profoundly influential episode occurred, beginning with selection as one of ten students from the United States to take part in a World Student Christian Federation Conference, in Peking. Rogers speaks of the six-months-long experience, including the leisurely voyages by sea and the intellectual and personal stimulus of his student companions and the gifted professional staff, as probably the most formative transition period in his undergraduate years. Even the conference itself centred on intercultural relations and was not evangelical in tone. Carl kept a journal record of the trip and of his developing thought and outlook, and sent a copy of this ahead to his family. By the time he returned home, the effect of his mailed communications and evident 'radical' change was an emancipating breaking of ties with his parents, in terms of religious and intellectual perspective (1967a: 350–351).

A concurrent development in Rogers' life was his movement into a deeply sharing, love relationship with the young woman who was to become his wife, and who was already his sweetheart by his second university year. His later years in college strongly carried forward his maturing intellectual development – the main influences including particular teachers, the work of historical figures to whom he resonated, and the opportunities for searching, creative engagement and independent achievement. Another significant new activity was involvement in the University debating team. This was a demanding but also exciting and confirming experience, yielding new skills and mastery (ibid.: 351). Gone was the outward dreaminess of Carl's early youth, and in its place was a still-visionary but highly active, energetic pattern of roving exploration and achievement.

By no means was it all plain sailing in these liberating but also personally stretching years. About the time that his most critical steps toward independence from his family were being taken, after his return from China, Carl was diagnosed as having a duodenal ulcer. Indications are that this condition had been incubating since his mid-teens, and it seems likely that inner stresses around breaking away from the confining security of his family for a changing, risky, separate identity were contributing causes. His rehabilitation, away from University, included the family cure-all of hard physical work. Between the six-month trip to China, and this further time out, coupled with his earlier shift from agriculture to history, Carl's pathway through college did not synchronize with that of a class or year group and contributed to a lack of continuous friendships. The most notable exception was with Helen, his bride-to-be, whom he married soon after graduating and just before he headed for New York to begin the next phase in his educational life, a phase which became the transition to another major shift in career direction.

The immediate destination was Union Theological Seminary, a leading intellectual centre in religious work, with a reputation for liberalism. While a new world opened in terms of the quality of philosophical inquiry and teaching, and his first exposure to 'pastoral' studies with a clinical-human relations emphasis, the climate was a heady freedom of rising expectations. Carl and others sought and gained permission to organize an official, credit seminar where there would be no instructor and the curriculum would consist of the participants' own questions and searching.

Most members of this special seminar 'in thinking through the questions they had raised, thought their way right out of religious work' (1967a: 354). For Carl, the key issues seemed to be those of sustaining a hard-won freedom of belief and a growing attraction to the personality and person-helping field.

He was already taking courses at Teachers College, Columbia University; and made the decision to transfer, after his second year at Union Seminary, into doctoral studies in clinical and educational psychology. In keeping with an earlier mentioned area of confidence, he was sure that he could take the formal requirements in his stride. 'Preparation for examinations [he wrote] was a well-organized affair for me. It never gave me any trouble because it never entered my head that I would not be successful' (ibid.: 355).

Next year, Carl obtained a fellowship at the new Institute for Child Guidance where the emphasis on personality and emotional dynamics in the context of an 'eclectic Freudianism' was sharply at variance with the objective measurement-oriented ethos dominant in the Teachers College program. His subsequent doctoral research, focusing on the development of a test for measuring personality adjustment in children, reflected an emergent synthesis of learnings and attitudes from these two influential contexts.

Rogers was 26 when his eventful year at the Institute for Child Guidance ended, the requirements for his doctorate evidently complete except for the dissertation. With his wife, Helen, and their 2-year old child to support, he secured his first regular job, as a psychologist in the Child Study Department established by the Rochester Society for the Prevention of Cruelty to Children. Looked at by usual criteria, the position was not impressive: professionally isolated; without academic connection; modest in salary even by the standards of the day (1967a: 358). These limiting features seem not to have weighed in Rogers' thinking at the time. The most important thing was that there appeared to be an opportunity, realized increasingly over the twelve professionally formative years that followed, to do work that interested him, with people.

Two years later, as Rogers was winding up his doctoral thesis part-time, just getting a job would have been a major achievement. By this time, the New York stock market had crashed and the Great Depression was beginning in earnest. The fallout in human terms of these crises would have accentuated the need for agencies such as the one Rogers was helping to staff, although conditions were scarcely conducive to the availability of resources during the agonizing pre-Roosevelt period. Remarkably, the Depression, Roosevelt's New Deal and associated transformations in American life, pass unmentioned in Rogers' autobiographies and receive virtually no attention in his professional writing. (I intend, in the next chapters, to establish the vital importance for his work of the wider context and climate of the times.)

Appraising problem children and families in difficulty, and arranging or providing remedial assistance; working in a relatively independent multidiscipline setting; trying out alternative methods in practice, and learning from errors and success; building programs and teams and growing in leadership resources; moving into new spheres of activity, such as writing his first book, and a summer session of teaching at Columbia University – all of these were part of the mix of Rogers' experience. All helped to prepare him for what lay ahead: leading counselling practice and thought into a new era, blazing fresh trails in the human service and educational fields, and opening his work to touch the lives and thought of people from many other callings.

The context of Rogers' Rochester years was one of immersion in working and learning with people from all walks of life, wanting always to know more, to become more effective, to expand his repertoire. His daughter grew from infancy and his son to adolescence, and in all his family provided a wellspring of learning, challenge, support and growth opportunity. Rogers' whole life, not just the phases viewed here, is a striking example of continuity within change, the unfolding process itself still sustained and visible in the last years of his life. One of his papers 'Growing older: or older and growing' (Rogers, 1980c, written in 1977) provides vivid testimony to the eventful and creative decade of his life from his mid-sixties to mid-seventies. His own becoming, in the period before and after the emergence of client-centred therapy, has a great deal to do with its fertility and bears on its emphases. Particular, main steps and qualities in Rogers' work, in the Rochester period and time immediately following it, which clearly included the gestation and 'birth' of non-directive client-centred therapy, call for closer description.

Early professional challenges: steps, direction, style

Rogers' river of publications has as its starting source his earlier-mentioned 'test of personality adjustment' in children (Rogers, 1931a, 1931b). Interestingly, many of the items in this test hinge on obtaining (with slight disguise) the child's view or picture of self compared point by point with the way the child would like to be. Two decades later, client-centred investigators were making pivotal use of a parallel approach in therapy outcome research. Discrepancy between a person's self-picture and their desired or ideal self was a principal criterion of disturbance and, conversely, congruence between self and ideal was an index of adjustment (see Rogers and Dymond, 1954). Rogers' first serious research, including his test for children, expressed a humanistic empiricism that was to characterize his work throughout his scientific career, a career that came fully of age after his Rochester years ended. Aside from his doctoral study, Rogers' formal research during the Rochester phase was very limited. However, for one of his drive and resourcefulness, the potential was there for other forms of significant inquiry and contribution. Of this period he writes, in a personal biographical statement:

> For at least the first eight of these years [to *c*. 1936/37] I was completely immersed in carrying on practical psychological service, diagnosing and planning for the delinquent and under-privileged children who were sent to us by the courts and agencies, and in many instances carrying on 'treatment interviews'. It was a period of relative professional isolation, where my only concern was in trying to be more effective with our clients. . . . There was only one criterion in regard to any method of dealing with these children and their parents, and that was 'Does it work? Is it effective?' (Rogers, 1967a: 358)

Among the several elements conveyed in this excerpt, is the highly pragmatic emphasis on getting results, on effectiveness in practice, which carried over strongly into the development of client-centred therapy itself. One expression of this emphasis in the Rochester phase was the focus on diagnosis and associated planning of remedial-treatment pathways. Such activity formed perhaps three-quarters of the service work of the Child Study Department (Rogers, 1937) and its *modus operandi* is strongly reflected in Rogers' first book in ways that merit comment.

Titled *The Clinical Treatment of the Problem Child* (Rogers, 1939), this book gives extensive attention to diagnosis, and to treatment by changing a child's environment. Personality test instruments in vogue at the time are informatively described and broadly appraised in terms of practical value. Rogers' finding is that their discriminating usage can *contribute* valuable information. However, he is concerned that 'in the enthusiasm for personality tests it has been supposed by some that they were . . . a sufficient means of diagnosis', and he warns that 'we shall not be most helpful in the treatment of children's problems if we regard diagnosis in any such mechanical light' (1939: 26). Rogers advanced an alternative working method in which a wide range of information is organized by the clinician to yield a profile of the child's functioning and potentiality across a spectrum of eight 'component factors', each rated on a scale from –3 to +3. The spectrum included, for example, a hereditary factor, the factor of 'mentality' (broadly, IQ), family environment and influence, social experience and skills, education, and 'self-insight'. Test results could be pertinent information in some areas, not in others. Although some of the areas are value-laden in terms of prevailing social norms, Rogers' functional intention and empiricism is unequivocal. In a typical statement, he asserts that:

> Diagnostic procedures such as we have described bring our thinking into a conscious framework which can be criticized, checked, improved. They avoid the smugness of an 'intuitive' diagnosis which cannot be confirmed or denied by another observer. . . . Improvement in diagnostic thinking can only come about as we objectify our methods and thus allow for continual study and correction of our basic procedures. (1939: 58)

Well over half of his book is devoted by Rogers to intensive practical consideration of the helping treatment of children via feasible changes in their life situation. Two broad levels of environmental alteration are distinguished: that of literally moving the child to a new life setting, particularly a foster home or an institution,[1] and the alternative of modifying the child's existing environment – at home, at school and through recreational learning contexts.

Illustrative of the author's thought is his firmness in pointing out 'that the

---

1 Rogers notes, in summary: 'Three chapters have been given over to a consideration of the question "Where shall the child live?" Although on the face of it this seems to be a simple question, the facts brought out indicate clearly that the selection of the child's total environment has tremendous importance especially in dealing with delinquent and problem behaviour' (1939: 175). The author's style visibly fluctuates from a child-centred quality to that of an expert in the treatment of child deviance in the service of the larger community. The direction of his journey is clear but there still is a long road ahead to the full unfolding of a child-/person-centred viewpoint.

institution which relies on mass treatment, whose work ends as the child is released, has little if any place in the realm of treatment techniques' (ibid.: 144). On the other hand, when an institution does adapt its program to respond to the needs of individual children, and works toward effective placement of these children back into the community, it may in particular situations be the best avenue of treatment. Later, with tough practicality, the author acknowledges:

> As a mode of treatment the selection of a place of residence which will have therapeutic effect does not necessarily appeal to the imagination. Such a choice has about it none of the mysterious elements or technical verbiage which makes some types of therapy so alluring. . . . Too often we find agencies and schools wasting precious remedial and therapeutic effort on children who cannot possibly make a normal adjustment in their present home setting. (1939: 175–176)

It is not surprising, perhaps, that during most of the Rochester phase of his career there was little in common between Rogers' work and interests and those, for example, of the psychology faculty at the University of Rochester or, for that matter, the professional establishment in psychology as represented at that time in the American Psychological Association. Between this fact, the nature of his work, and his response to the innovative developments in therapy coming, especially, from the Pennsylvania School of Social Work and Philadelphia Child Guidance Clinic, Rogers' identification with psychology attenuated. In his own words:

> The psychiatric social workers, however, seemed to be talking my language, so I became active in the social work profession, moving up to local and even national offices. Only when the American Association for Applied Psychology was formed [1937–38] did I become really active as a psychologist. (1961a: 12)

Rogers' first close, focused description and discussion of intensive personal therapy is finally also to be found in his 1939 book; embedded initially in his examination of environmental modification, under the heading of 'Means of changing parental attitudes' (1939: 184–220). Both here and in his separate discussion of 'Deeper therapies' with children, the author writes much more as a careful reporter than a strong advocate, seeking to present the central ideas and operational features of the main existing approaches to therapy. The deep therapy approaches he distinguishes are 'interpretive therapy' (psychoanalysis) and 'relationship therapy'.

A personal leaning toward relationship therapy is visible not so much through differences in the attention given to the two broad approaches as in the relative discrimination and 'warmth' of Rogers' discussion in the cases he presents, and by his appreciative references to the work, particularly, of Otto Rank (on his treatment approach), Jessie Taft and Frederick Allen. In retrospect, Rogers' exposition of relationship therapy *directly foreshadows most of the therapeutic principles he set forth and elaborated over the next several years.* His discussion of this therapy with parents, includes these points:

> 1 It applies only to those parents who have a desire to be helped. . . .
> 2 The relationship between the worker and the parent is the essential feature. . . . The worker endeavors to provide an atmosphere in which the parent can come freely to experience and realize his own attitudes. . . .
> 3 The effect of this relationship upon the parent may be characterized by the terms 'clarification of feelings' and 'acceptance of self'. . . .
> 4 . . . another characteristic of this viewpoint is its reliance on the parent himself to determine independently the manner of dealing with the child. (1939: 197–199)

Thus the significant aim is 'to bring about a higher degree of integration and self-realization in the parent' not to coach parents nor seek to train them to be more effective. Although he finds much to welcome in relationship therapy, Rogers also expresses some concern around the lack of evidence for its effectiveness. 'Enthusiasts claim much for it', he writes, but 'we find no mention of [demonstrated] degree or proportion of success, and it is probably unlikely that such a study will be made[!]'. Accompanying this voice of the empiricist-practitioner looking for concrete evidence is another train of thought, reflecting the author's more visionary radar: 'Indeed', he goes on, 'it seems likely that [relationship therapy's] major value might be, not in the percentage of cases assisted, but in the fresh viewpoint of non-interference and reliance upon the individual's own tendency toward growth which it has emphasized' (ibid.: 200). This comment singles out a feature which was to become a cornerstone of client-/person-centred thought. Also in keeping with subsequent client-centred emphases is another mentioned distinction:

> [Relationship therapy] deals entirely with present situations and makes no attempt to interpret or explain past reactions. Furthermore it is primarily those feelings which center on the worker which are the core of the process. . . .
>
> Because the child has learned to live successfully in one segment of his experience, the treatment relationship, it is expected that he can adapt himself more successfully in other segments of his life. (ibid.: 343–344)

The author emphasizes that the last point is a hypothesis not an established truth. He also stresses that relationship therapy depends on a certain viewpoint and philosophy in regard to others, 'and cannot therefore be picked up or laid down as a mechanical tool of treatment' (ibid.: 347); again foreshadowing a ramifying emphasis of the client-centred system.

Although Rogers' book was very important in its field and in his own career, such writing was not what his job was about. He became director of the Child Study Department prior to local initiatives to expand this unit into a full-fledged community guidance centre. It was by no means the case that he automatically would be head of this new centre (a psychiatrist was usually appointed to such positions) but after much work and a resourceful fight, the Rochester Guidance Center was established under Rogers' direct leadership. After publication of his book, added to his now rich professional background and fast growing standing, the need for another major career choice arose. Hard on the heels of winning an important battle for the position he held, he was offered, and finally accepted, appointment as full professor at Ohio State University (Rogers, 1967a: 360–361).

Nondirective client-centred therapy is born

Rogers took up his appointment at Ohio State in January, 1940. In December of that year he gave an invited talk at the University of Minnesota entitled 'Newer concepts in psychotherapy', later revised to form Chapter 2 of his swiftly following second book, *Counseling and Psychotherapy* (Rogers, 1942a). The Minnesota experience was a turning point – the birth of a new system of therapy:

> I was totally unprepared for the furor the talk aroused. I was praised, I was attacked, I was looked on with puzzlement. By the end of my stay in Minneapolis it struck me that perhaps I was saying something new that came from *me*. . . . I began to believe that I might personally, out of my own experience, have some original contribution to make to the field of psychotherapy. (Rogers, 1974c: 8)

In the published version of his Minnesota talk (1942a: 19–45), the author includes essentially the same points in characterizing the 'Newer Psychotherapy' as in his earlier account of Relationship Therapy (1939 – as previously cited). The therapeutic relationship as direct medium and vehicle for growth and change is emphasized. Within this relationship, effective movement is seen as generated by the individual's own drive toward growth and health. There is direct focus on the emotional-feeling aspects of the client's experience while intellectual or abstract considerations are not seen as profitable to pursue in therapy. The immediate situation rather than analysis of the past is stressed.

A further, complementary view and account of the therapy process is now added by Rogers. This new feature is a portrayal of the course of therapy – specifically the way overall qualities of relationship and client motivation translate into characteristic steps in the treatment process. In barest outline, the crucial first step is that of the individual making up his or her mind to come for help, and finding at once that this responsibility carries over into counselling where it is recognized and affirmed by the counsellor. Once in counselling, the therapy client is visibly encouraged in free expression of her/his feelings, with negative feelings usually coming to the fore first, followed by more positive ones. The expressive-responsive dialogue with the therapist produces clarification of the client's feelings. This leads on to instances of fresh insight and self-understanding, followed in turn by the choice and testing of new courses and modes of action. Typically, the client then feels a diminished need for help and a recognition that the therapy relationship must end (1942a: 30–44).[2]

---

2 A fuller summary of Rogers' early account of the steps of therapy, and of the research this led to, is given in another place by the present writer (Barrett-Lennard, 1990: 123–128).

Unlike his earlier statements, Rogers expresses sharp advocacy of the new approach he presents, as against 'older methods'. This quality, and the substance of Rogers' more detailed discussion of the therapy relationship in a later chapter, is well conveyed in his own summary:

> The counseling relationship is one in which warmth of acceptance and absence of any coercion or personal pressure on the part of the counselor permits the maximum expression of feelings, attitudes, and problems by the counselee. The relationship is a well-structured one, with limits of time, of dependence and of aggressive action which apply particularly to the client, and limits of responsibility and of affection which the counselor imposes on himself. In this unique experience of complete emotional freedom within a well-defined framework the client is free to recognize and understand his impulses and patterns, positive and negative, as in no other relationship. (1942a: 113–114)

Rogers' founding statement of the new therapy does not reveal originality on a conceptual plane so much as vividly describing a new, wholly distinctive mode of practice. The originator had not literally invented reflection and clarification of feeling but his development and systematic usage of these processes was without precedent.

Seen as a how-to-do-it manual, in the best sense, for counselling practitioners and students, as a documentary resource for research workers and others interested in studying the actual phenomenon of therapy, and also as a lucid, demystifying, educative and humanly encouraging statement in its field for intelligent lay readers, the 1942 volume was without peer or serious rival. A particularly innovative and strikingly effective feature was Rogers' extensive use of illustrative documentation from actual transcripts of recorded therapy interviews, including the famous verbatim record of a complete eight-interview therapy case![3] He also was able to draw on the first of the formal therapy research studies stimulated by his work, of which a notable example is E.H. Porter's doctoral dissertation, which focused on systematic analysis and comparison of the interview behaviour of counsellors independently classified as clearly directive or as non-directive in orientation (Porter, 1941).

Several other students completed graduate thesis studies with Rogers, during his Ohio State period, each study typically a discovery in method, technique or theoretical formulation in the previously uncharted field of empirical research on psychotherapy. Victor Raimy's work (1943 and 1948) on the self-concept in counselling and personality organization helped to initiate the development of self-theory as a central axis in Rogers' forming theoretical

---

3 Jessie Taft, in her classic work *The Dynamics of Therapy in a Controlled Relationship* (1933) had pioneered in reporting the interview-by-interview development of therapy with two child clients, the longer case running to thirty-one interviews. While the therapist must have been excellent in her note-taking and recall, selected parts only of the interaction could have been verbatim. By the time that Rogers (himself the non-identified therapist) interviewed 'Herbert Bryan', sound-recording of full-length interviews had become possible, and these were transcribed and reproduced, word for word. A usefully specific commentary, critically relating particular responses to the principles advanced, appears in footnote form throughout (Rogers, 1942a: 261–437).

system. William Snyder's research on 'the nature of nondirective psychotherapy' was another foundation stone (1945). Papers on a variety of topics and in various journals flowed from Rogers' own pen: for example, on the use of sound recordings of interviews as a learning medium (Rogers, 1942b); a new paper in his earlier field of interest, therapy in guidance clinics (Rogers, 1943); a report supported by direct empirical data on insight in the counselling process (Rogers, 1944a); papers on adjustment problems and counselling with returning servicemen (Rogers, 1944b, 1945a); and a discussion of the potential of nondirective interviewing as a method of gathering unbiased information in social research (Rogers, 1945b).

Altogether, Rogers' Ohio State phase was a period of meteoric further development of his work and swiftly growing visibility: in the academic world, in the sphere of professional affairs in psychology, and in his contribution to the development of counselling resources for returning war veterans in the United States. A result of critical consequence was an invitation to a summer teaching position at the University of Chicago in 1944, ending with an offer of permanent appointment there. Accompanying a senior faculty appointment in a top-flight university was the explicit opportunity to design and establish a counselling centre in an urban academic setting.

The position at Chicago could have been taken up immediately but Rogers opted to begin a full year later since he was already 'committed to aid the war effort by teaching simple counselling methods to the staff members of USO [United Services Organization], whose staff were being besieged by servicemen with personal problems' (Rogers, 1967a: 363). This statement is significant partly in being the only direct mention in Rogers' autobiographical reports that World War II was an important factor in his working career and life. This paucity of mention, as will be seen later, bears no relation to the actual importance of war-related circumstances in the development of client-centred therapy. Leaving this aside for the moment, with Rogers' move to the University of Chicago in 1945, nondirective client-centred therapy was effectively recognized as a new school and Rogers as an outstanding leader in his field.

A major aid to the cited 'teaching of simple counselling methods', no doubt in preparation in 1944/45, was a further book, co-authored by John Wallen and titled *Counseling with Returned Servicemen* (1946). This work clearly is designed for use in teaching/training contexts other than specialized professional degree programs, and the authors refer to Rogers' 1942a book as providing a more complete, in-depth presentation of the approach. The term 'client-centred' did not appear in the 1942a book but is now used side by side with 'non-directive'. The term suited the strong emphasis on the client's frame of reference and motivation toward recovery and growth, and fitted the ethic of client self-responsibility in counselling. The reader of the book is advised at the start to expect something sharply different from traditional approaches to counselling. It is claimed that the viewpoint advanced is highly practical, and that it embodies a safer as well as more effective way of proceeding, especially for newcomers to formal helping practice, than previous methods do.

In a word, 'counseling is presented as a way of helping the individual to help himself' – an enduring precept that came to be widely adopted, in theory at least, in the newer helping approaches. Further expressed, 'the function of the counselor is to make it possible for the client to gain emotional release in relation to his problems and, as a consequence, to think more clearly and more deeply about himself and his situation' (Rogers and Wallen, 1946: 5). This distinctive view, not out of keeping with current Rogerian thought and practice, implies that feelings have first priority and that changes in the person's feeling life work as an entry to cognitive reorganization and behaviour change. As the authors go on to say:

> It is the counselor's function to provide an atmosphere in which the client, through this exploration of his situation, comes to see himself and his reactions more clearly and to accept his attitudes more fully. On the basis of this insight he is able to meet his life problems more adequately. . . . He has experienced psychological growth. (1946: 5–6)

An atmosphere for growth is fostered by the 'counsellor attitudes' that constitute a nondirective helping stance: respect for the integrity and autonomy of the client; belief in the person's (inherent) capacity for adjustment and growth; respect for the other's different and distinctive qualities; and desire to facilitate the client's own *self*-understanding and acceptance. The singling out of counsellor attitudes as a priority issue foreshadowed a long interest in and evolving conception of the necessary ingredients of a helping relationship, as will be apparent throughout this volume.

Interestingly, the authors give explicit attention also to 'The relation between client-centered counseling and democracy.' In a rare statement, Rogers (with Wallen, in this case) alludes broadly to a likely relationship between his therapy and the societal context in which it was developing. World War II was wholly different from any war in which the United States has been embroiled since. Her enemies, in the totalitarian extremity of their regimes and their visions of world conquest, were predatory anti-democracies in a very different place as systems from the US , on most political, social and value dimensions. Generally, Rogers believed strongly in the main institutions, traditions and aspirations of his country, and in this war context he was, like nearly all others, a patriot. One sentence explicitly suggests the link of vital interest here: '*It is perhaps no accident that this emphasis in counseling has reached its fruition in America*' (Rogers and Wallen, 1946: 23; italics added). I will return later to this passage.

My next two chapters search into the sociopolitical and cultural context in which the client-centred approach incubated and had its flourishing beginning. Exploration of this crucial milieu begins with the 1920s, focuses especially on the thirties and includes the cataclysmic period of World War II. The course, nature and impact of Franklin Roosevelt's presidency is studied in juxtaposed relation to Rogers' directions, steps and style. Should you as reader lack immediate interest or time to accompany me in this social and psycho-historical analysis, an option is to proceed directly to Chapter 4, with no great loss in continuity so far as the interior substance of client-centred thought and practice is concerned. But my hope is that you will return to Chapters 2 and 3, which break new ground in the search for contextual understanding of Rogers' innovation. Through such inquiry, I believe it is possible to see more deeply into the nature and underpinnings of any organized approach to understanding and working with people. And the chase itself was to me exciting and illuminating in unexpected ways.

2

A Time of New Pathways

Twenties Dissonance to New Deal Dawn

> The possibility of freedom is deeply grounded in our very beings. It is one with our individuality, our being uniquely what we are and not imitators and parasites of others. But like all other possibilities, this possibility has to be actualized: and, like all others, it can only be actualized through interaction with objective conditions. The question of political and economic freedom is not an addendum or afterthought . . . in the problem of personal freedom. For the conditions that form political and economic liberty are required in order to realize the potentiality of freedom each of us carries with him in his very structure.
>
> John Dewey, 1928

Client-centred therapy was conceived and fathered by an immensely energetic, determined and resourceful parent-innovator. By the middle forties, this lusty offspring was also surrounded by the growing adoptive family of Carl Rogers' associates and students, who increasingly influenced and contributed to its further development. The elements uniquely combined and developed in the early phase of client-centred therapy did not of course arise *de novo*. As already implied, they drew inspiration from the work of other pioneers, especially contributors to 'relationship therapy', and reflected a wealth of first-hand practice learning; all vivified and carried forward in Rogers' thought during the Rochester phase of his career.

This whole trajectory of learning and development on Rogers' part fell within a larger context involving massive human dislocation and suffering, and momentous changes in the working of encompassing political, social and economic systems. With the onset of World War II, the forms of dislocation and suffering shifted; and there developed a union of resolve and effort in the United States probably without precedent since the Revolution.

While Rogers was an active agent in his own crucially formative years in New York and Rochester, and his direct role was pivotal in the flourishing early development and specific nature of client-centred therapy, these things all occurred in an influential context. This chapter and the next explore this historical setting to discover features bearing on the opportunities, encouragement and challenges Rogers faced, and currents that would have supported and fed into his developing thought.

My exploration begins with a focus on the 1920s and conditions that fuelled the Great Depression, examines (albeit briefly) the social/human trauma and course of the Depression itself, goes on to outline the pathway and character of Roosevelt's administration and the 'New Deal' he inaugurated, and looks at authors and themes in serious literature of the 1930s. This chapter sets the stage for the next, which advances an original perspective on the fertilizing effects of the times for the germination and flourishing early growth of the client-centred system.

The twenties, and fuelling of the Great Depression

In the broad sphere of social welfare and health care, and in keeping with the dominant ethos of the time, most needs were considered to be the responsibility of the individual. Private charitable organizations and programs were the principal source of assistance to indigent families, homeless and neglected children, elderly people with no other means of support, and others who could pay little or not at all for essential needs. Direct government welfare and medical care assistance still were virtually non-existent, except in the case of war veterans.

In 1921, the federal government began a program of limited grants-in-aid to the states, for maternal and child care (Carleton, 1963). The usage of these grants was extremely uneven, at best providing marginal living allowances and advisory help to 'worthy' fatherless families. Community welfare schemes sponsored by charitable organizations – such as the Rochester Society for the Prevention of Cruelty to Children, Rogers' first employer – naturally differed greatly from one community to another in resources and services, were variably influenced in their policies by attitudes of the donors or subsidizing authorities, and typically were quite vulnerable to changing economic conditions. Historically, charitable and volunteer aid associations had often led the way in bringing social injuries and human need to public view, and in providing tangible and sometimes crucial large-scale assistance as, for example, in the case of the American Red Cross in World War I (Bornet, 1960). The first schools of social work had been sponsored by citizen charity and philanthropic associations (Trattner, 1974: ch. 11).

The predominant attitude was that voluntary giving to help those less fortunate than oneself was morally and practically superior to any public assistance programs. President Hoover (who succeeded Coolidge in 1929) with strong credentials as a humanitarian in the traditional mode, epitomized this view in declaring that 'personal feeling and personal responsibility of men to their neighbors is the soul of genuine good will; it is the essential foundation of modern society'. From this it naturally followed to him that 'charity which puts out its sympathy only through the tax collector yields a very meagre dole of unloving and perfunctory relief' (Bornet, 1960: 13). As late as 1931, he spoke even more strongly: 'No governmental action, no economic plan or project, can replace the God-imposed responsibility of the individual man and woman to their neighbors. That is a vital part of the very soul of the people. . . . The trial . . . is here and now. It is a trial of the heart and conscience of individual men and women' (ibid.).

The twenties became a time of cumulatively massive challenge to the ethos and mores that still held official sway; a time of heightening disparity and tension between the image (so far as one can generalize) that the nation had of itself as a people and the actuality of prevalent social patterns and life-styles of altered or radically new form. On a national level, the situation was analogous to a self-concept much out of keeping with experience, and increasingly vulnerable to any radical disturbance that would bring the discrepancy unmistakably to view.

One of the clearest indications of the developing societal neurosis was the extraordinary phenomenon of prohibition against the production and use of any alcoholic beverages. No sooner had 'prohibition' become law, by will of the people via national referendum, than it was flouted widely, often openly, in all classes and levels of society. Alcoholism remained a significant social problem while the new laws were in force.[1] The folk-musical rebellion of jazz, spreading via the gramophone record and new medium of radio, although distasteful perhaps to the majority, was exhilarating and liberating to many others. 'Speakeasy' night-club involvement, modern dancing, and massive response to the movie industry's magnetic new kind of entertainment, were some of the expressions of shifting social behaviour and mores (cf. Allen, 1931: ch. 5). Home and family diminished as the centre of activity and outlook of the young. The generation gap was born or, at least, underwent a growth spurt of major proportion.

Americans became a significantly more educated people, women as well as men, under the new conditions of universal suffrage and its side-effects. New sociopolitical ideologies, portrayals of life by contemporary prose writers and dramatists, the revolutionary Freudian thought, and the impact of science as an approach to knowing through observation rather than precept, all contributed to far more questioning, sceptical and experimental modes of thought and action. Most of Carl Rogers' tertiary educational journey, and the significant wayside experiences and emergent shifts earlier described, took place during the twenties. His family background was a strong version of the traditionalist pole and his development in that period swung to a distinctly opposing, liberal direction.

There is a remarkable congruence between values ascribed to Rogers' parental home and President Coolidge's concurrent outlook expressed, for example, in his remark that:

> The success which is made in any walk of life is measured almost exactly by the amount of hard work that is put into it. . . . There is only one form of political strategy in which I have any confidence, and that is to try to do the right thing and sometimes be able to succeed. . . . If society lacks learning and virtue it will perish. . . . The nation with greatest moral power will win. (cited in Allen, 1931: 182)

---

1 Prohibition remained federal law until 1933, when the repeal amendment was approved by Congress (at the height of the Depression) and rather quickly ratified by the states. Another phenomenon of differently bizarre nature was the lush resurgence (and then decline), in the twenties, of the racially terrorizing secret order of the Ku Klux Klan (Allen, 1931: 65–69).

Writing as an astute contemporary observer, Allen goes on to affirm that this philosophy 'of hard work and frugal living, and piety crowned with success' was 'so old that it looked new; . . . so exactly what uncounted Americans had been taught at their mother's knee that it touched what remained of the pioneer spirit in their hearts; and Coolidge set it forth with refreshing brevity' – and with great effectiveness in winning the votes and support of the majority of his countrymen. Although Coolidge appealed so strongly to an inheritance of thought and sentiment, this legacy was out of keeping with the new-born values and folkways of his time. It stood in opposite polarity to the already mentioned wave-fronts of attitude and life-style, and of much contemporary thought. In up-to-date intellectual circles 'no longer was it possible to say with any positiveness, This is right, or This is wrong. . . . The certainty had departed from life. And what was worse still, it had departed from science itself. . . . Einstein and the quantum theory introduced new uncertainties and new doubts. Nothing then, was sure' (ibid.: 240–241).[2] The same author continues prophetically:

> Yet in all this uncertainty there was new promise for the intellectual life of the country. With the collapse of fixed values went a collapse of the old water-tight critical standards in the arts, opening the way for fresh and independent work to win recognition. Better still, the idea was gaining ground that this fresh and independent work might as well be genuinely native, that the time had come when the most powerful nation in the world might rid itself of its cultural subjection to Europe. (ibid.: 241)[3]

By the late twenties a 'revolutionary' wind was blowing, the beginning of a major shift in outlook; visible in a kaleidoscopic mix of part changes rather than integrative development of the culture at large. The immediate state of affairs, as the end of the decade approached, amounted to a state of unstable equilibrium. The conditions that appear to have made the nation so vulnerable to the ensuing, profound economic and social convulsion of the Great Depression, may be drawn into brief outline as follows:

Working of the economy

◇ The enormous concentration into relatively few individual and corporate hands of most of the nation's wealth left the large majority of families and working individuals with their whole income in the form of wages. Thus, most people were in the risky position of being entirely dependent on

---

2 For a deeper, fuller view of dilemmas faced by intellectuals of the time see, for example, Joseph Wood Krutch's *The Modern Temper* (especially, ch. 8: 'The end of certitude') and Walter Lippman's *A Preface to Morals*, both books first published in 1929.

3 It can scarcely be entire coincidence (i) that Rogers (1967a) acknowledges the influence on his intellectual development of his history professors at Wisconsin, and (ii) that passages in Allen's work so strikingly anticipate Rogers' later style of thought and expression. The reader might, for example, find it interesting to note the very similar ring to this statement and the quotations from Rogers and Wallen cited earlier (p. 13).

wage-earning opportunities. Those who were 'owners' had a priority concern to maintain if not enhance their assets. To this end, an adjustable variable was that of labour utilization and cost.

- Industry's centre of gravity (and of buoyancy) lay in the huge manufacturing sector; and heavy industry, especially, depended on its overseas as well as domestic markets. Thus, change in outside demand had major effects.
- The apparently flourishing, diversifying economy drew over-speculation on the stock market especially through the purchase of securities on very narrow margins – effectively, very small down-payments. It reached the point of an escalating runaway system feeding largely on itself.
- Although most workers were somewhat better off, their modest increase in cash-in-hand buying power did not keep pace with increases in production.
- An effect of the last two aspects was that a large proportion of the American people was vulnerably in debt, through credit/loan purchasing.
- As both direct and spin-off effects of economic growth, very wide popular use of automobiles, of radio, and of movie entertainment was becoming in itself a substantial force toward major social transition.

Organized labour and employment security

- Organized labour was weak and discredited, had hardly any voice or support in political and government circles, and could provide little buffering protection to the needs of the working person *vis-à-vis* centres of economic power under threat. Public unemployment insurance or related benefit or relief programs, for practical purposes did not exist, apart from scattered outdoor work-relief schemes in some states.

Social-family welfare and security

- Assistance from public welfare systems was undeveloped and wholly inadequate for all social groups potentially at risk, besides war veterans and some 'deserving' widows. This paucity of resources and programs on federal and even state levels included most of the field of health care. Private charity systems were relatively strong and well-developed but dependent on the financial resources and value-systems of the donor communities. Volunteers were usually middle-class and inadvertently patronizing to those they assisted. Their resources could be expected to dwindle, as needs increased, under conditions of severe, widespread recession.

The national mind and character: image and actuality

- The traditional image of 'rugged individualism', with its ethic of responsibility of the individual for success or failure and virtue or vice, and its emphasis on hard work, 'clean living' and measured frugality, was ingrained in the consciousness of the majority although increasingly at variance with the reality of their own lives, and repudiated as an anachronism by an articulate minority.[4]

- ◇ The conflict between fixed or absolute belief systems based on religion and folk values, and relativistic changing assumptive beliefs based on an ethos of science and open inquiry, was at minimum confusing for a people traditionally professing a religious faith. More intense expressions involved bitter conflict between and within social groups and fed into the personal disillusionment many felt with the perceived hypocrisy of their culture. The Church shifted to increased polarization between fundamentalist and liberal denominations, and corresponding factions within the same denominations.
- ◇ Developing from these changes and other conditions, the nation was divided and unstable not only along economic lines but in ways that had to do with the basic character, outlook and inner life of its peoples and institutions. The symptoms were interpretable as an acute *societal* neurosis.

These then were among the principal conditions fuelling the Great Depression, a 'depression' directly of an economic but even more significantly of a psycho-social nature. The New York stock market, known as the 'Big Bull Market' in its boom time, had become the single most publicly compelling barometer of business morale and well-being. The Market amounted to a central depository of assets of companies, many banks and other financial institutions, and of private investors drawn from nearly all classes of society. The growing and then dizzying escalation of stock values peaked in early September 1929 (six months after Hoover's inauguration as President). The inevitable down-turn began in alarming but wavering form, soon changing to a nerve-racking downward slide in stock values generally. The slide became a horrifying, unstoppable series of plunges and within two months the ruinous great crash of late October/early November 1929 marked a shattering entry to the Depression era. Rising unemployment and many symptoms of suddenly increased human stress, reflected the domino-like chain of economic effects. Most politicians and economists still failed to see that a perilously difficult, extended and major transition had begun. Exceptions included the author of *Only Yesterday*, who in summing up his perspective at the time, wrote:

---

4 The residual strength of this umbilical creed – appropriate to frontier life and a far simpler society – was mirrored for example in the extraordinary popular excitement and outpouring toward Charles Lindbergh in 1927, following his achievement of the first solo non-stop overseas flight, from New York to Paris. This single-handed feat and qualities of Lindbergh's unassuming personal style had the strong–quiet ring of authentic traditional heroism. The response literally was overwhelming; when the aviator came home, the public celebration in New York and other major cities exceeded even that which followed news of the armistice signalling the end of World War I (Allen, 1931: 216–222 and frontispiece photograph).

> Prosperity is more than an economic condition; it is a state of mind. . . . There was hardly a man or woman in the country whose attitude toward life . . . was not now affected by the sudden and brutal shattering of hope. . . . Americans were soon to find themselves living in an altered world which called for new adjustments, new ideas, new habits of thought, a new order of values. (Allen, 1931: 338)

The Depression era, Roosevelt, and reform

The events and whole course of the Great Depression were a traumatic experience in American national life wholly different in form but with resemblance in human impact to the Civil War, seventy years earlier. The grandparents of many adults who fought the Depression had been caught up in the earlier internecine conflict and its aftermath, and would have passed on vivid images from direct experience and the witness of others. Features of attitude, custom and industry carried over from the Civil War period were still vividly reflected in the South and, more indirectly, in the North. Serious fiction of the time often reflected this near memory, weaving together issues rooted in the past and vivid in the present. I will return to focus on this literary voice after tracing the lengthening black shadow of the Depression itself, and its eventual fading in the new leadership and remarkable dawn that followed.

Injury, suffering, and hope: from the crash to FDR's *election*

President Hoover's prompt response to the stock market crash sought to restore business morale and public confidence. Believing the bedrock of the economic-social system to be sound, he felt that maintaining this belief in the public mind was justified and necessary to resolving the crisis. Hoover's stand and his assurance were not without effect; and within six months a principal spokesman of his administration declared that 'the spring of 1930 marks the end of a period of grave concern. . . . American business is steadily coming back to a normal level of prosperity' (Allen, 1931: 340).

While some 3 million persons already had lost their jobs, some of these had obtained employment again. The still magnetic stock market and its luminous barometer were active and rising again, appearing to be well on the road to recovery as leading stocks gained more than half the ground lost during the crash period (1931: 340). The respite, however, proved very brief. Stock values tumbled again, and the various signs of extreme recession mounted day by day even as the government physicians continued their campaign of optimism, with messages that the worst was past, business and employment conditions would shortly improve, tangible signs of recovery were evident, etc.

Such a campaign, like trying to put Humpty-Dumpty together again after the shell had broken and the contents spilt, could not possibly succeed. Conditions giving rise to the Depression, and the symptoms that resulted, required imagination and interventions of an altogether different order than a recycling of the practised repertoire of the existing national leadership. By mid-1931, the economic situation was desperate, and the economic depression was paralleled by intense, growing psychological stress and depression among millions of Americans. Brought up to believe that success and failure in life, sound and faulty judgement, moral virtue or vice, were matters of personal character and responsibility, the predominant response was to internalize what is seen in retrospect as systemic societal failure. In the words of one veteran observer, drawing on first hand knowledge and remarkable published interviews with survivors of the Depression:

> The suddenly-idle hands blamed themselves, rather than society. True, there were hunger marches and protestations to City Hall and Washington, but the millions experienced a private kind of shame when the pink slip came. No matter that others suffered the same fate, the inner voice whispered, 'I'm a failure.'
>
> True, there was a sharing among many of the dispossessed, but at close quarters, frustration became, at times, violence, and violence turned inward. Thus, sons and fathers fell away, one from the other. And the mother, seeking work, said nothing. Outside forces, except to the more articulate and political rebels, were in some vague way responsible, but not really. It was a personal guilt. (Terkel, 1970: 19–20)

Among other disasters with cruel repercussions, more than 1,000 US banks failed in 1930. Unemployment rocketed, some 10,000 additional persons becoming jobless each day. By mid-1931 'stock prices [had] faded until the panic levels of November 1929, looked lofty by comparison' (Allen, 1931: 345). Immigration virtually ceased and, for the first time on record, more people left the country in 1931 than came in. Of Americans at home, by year's end over 9,000,000 persons who had depended on week-by-week wages or regular salaries, no longer had such income (Boardman, 1967: 30–31).

Movies had become by far the most popular form of mass entertainment and escape, with attendances rising beyond belief in the Depression years. Reportedly, *100 million tickets per week* were sold in 1930 (ibid.: 43). Radio often served a similar, more economical function at home, but was also to become a medium for a quite new form of political communication, one that would be a factor in turning the Depression tide. In the meantime, the nightmare engulfing much of the nation reached its most formidable proportions.[5]

---

5 In 1932, with unemployment approaching 13 million, jobless families across the nation faced a winter of desperate hardship. One reporter-observer noted in his diary 'I see on the streets filthy, ragged desperate-looking men, such as I have never seen before.' In Seattle, jobless families, with utilities cut off, spent evenings in cold darkness. In Los Angeles, such families cooked what food they had over wood fires in vacant lots. In the mid-Southern coal fields, evicted family groups shivered in tents in midwinter, near starvation and without medical aid. In many cities, flimsy shanty settlements ('Hoovervilles') replaced unaffordable housing. A Commissioner in Salt Lake City 'disclosed that scores of people were slowly starving . . . and hundreds of children were kept out of school because they had nothing to wear'. In New York, visiting nurses found children literally on the edge of starvation. Of workers in New England mill towns, an observer wrote: 'There was something dead in them, as from exhaustion or perhaps too much idleness, without any personal winsomeness or power of demand . . .' (Leuchtenburg, 1963: chs 1 and 2).

By the end of Hoover's presidency in March 1933, *15 million* people had lost their jobs (Leuchtenburg, 1963: 14). This was at least one-fourth of the US labour force and it is plausible to infer that 30 million or more, not less than a quarter of all people in the land, were without benefit of earned or inherited income. The needs of those on charity or relief were out of all proportion to resources available, although the amount of such support in diverse forms had much increased. In Middletown (Lynd and Lynd, 1937), the township costs for relief rose from $21,000 in 1928 to nearly $300,000 in 1932, with every fourth family on relief in the latter case. In this small but industrially active mid-west city only one family was very rich and became more wealthy still;[6] most were and remained politically and socially conservative, and virtually all were affected adversely. Using vivid imagery, unlike most of their sober documentary reporting, and in a generalization applicable in most American cities, the Lynds observed that:

> The great knife of the depression had cut down impartially through the entire population cleaving open lives and hopes of rich as well as poor. The experience has been more nearly universal than any prolonged recent emotional experience in the city's history; it has approached in its elemental shock the primary experiences of birth and death. (Lynd and Lynd, 1937: 295–296)

This passage from the Lynds includes the phrase 'more nearly universal'. In fact, the exceptions were very numerous as applied to individuals and groups in the nation as a whole. Some two-thirds of those with jobs did not lose them, or quickly obtained or created alternative employment. A few, proportionately, fattened during the Depression. Many retained and experienced a comfortable standard of living for themselves, while variably troubled about others and/or obvious deficiency in the system or values they had believed in. Still others tightened their belts, hung on, and rode out the storm without being pitched from their heaving craft. And the vast majority of those who lost their jobs, or slid down without losing hold, changed in circumstances much more than in character or fundamental belief.

Certainly this estimation of continuity in outlook is in keeping with the Lynds' picture of Middletown dwellers, and is consistent with reflections in the mirrored past recorded by Studs Terkel in his *Hard Times: An Oral History of the Great Depression* (1970). One of his interviewees, a waitress, begins her recorded story as a ten-year-old in an orphan home in 1933. She

---

6 This family in fact helped to cushion the Depression for many others in the town. They are a case study in kind, of actual people whom Hoover had believed would counter the Depression. Originally, there were five brothers who came to the city. In their follow-up report, the Lynds record that 'Two of the brothers remain today, both men in their seventies, alert, capable, democratic Christian gentlemen, trained in the school of rugged individualism, patrons of art, education, religion and a long list of philanthropies. . . . In their conscientious and utterly unhypocritical combination of high profits, great philanthropy, and a low wage scale, they embody the hard-headed ethos of Protestant capitalism with its identification of Christianity with the doctrine of the goodness to all concerned of unrestricted business enterprise' (Lynd and Lynd, 1937: 75–76).

remembers walking from the home to school through a park. Men would be waiting there as the children went by with their paper-bag lunches, and every Friday at least, these lunches would be given freely to the waiting men. She continues:

> Today I tell my daughters: be careful of people. . . . Then we didn't have any fear. You'd never think that if you walked by people, even strangers: Gee, that person I got to be careful of. . . . These were guys who didn't have work. . . . I don't know how they got where they were going or where they ended up. They were nice men. They weren't bums. These were hard luck guys. (Terkel, 1970: 99)

Among occupational groups who tended to maintain their jobs or self-employment, even gaining ground in income, were practitioners in the mental health and social-welfare fields. Stress, guilt, failure, depression, fear, confusion, already were drawing a good many people, often educated and still with means, to seek help through psychotherapy or other counselling. A veteran New York psychiatrist, who has just been asked by Terkel whether his patients were not financially affected, replies:

> Not very much. They paid fairly reasonable fees. I just came across a bankbook that I had between 1931 and 1934, and, by God, I was in those days making $2,000 a month, which was a hell of a lot of money. Then in 1934, 1935, 1936 they began coming in droves, when things began to ease up. People were looking for help. (Terkel, 1970: 181)

People were seeking and needing help on many levels. In many cases, however, psychiatric psychotherapy of the time (even without the fees) would have been futile or irrelevant. Terkel quotes Nathan Ackerman, referring to the mid-thirties:

> In those days, psychiatry was quite removed from social problems. Almost ivory tower. For one thing, the really poor didn't go to psychiatrists. It was in no way concerned with poverty and reform. There was no connection seen between social health and mental health. (ibid.: 228)[7]

Besides their overt focus, Ackerman's words speak on another level, reflecting the contrast between the old politics and the new approach of another president confronting the national crisis and need for social and economic healing. The electors' choice of Franklin Delano Roosevelt, to follow Hoover, was a step not only toward resolving the Depression but one resulting in a revolutionary turn in substance and style of government action at the federal level, of new and linked economic and social policy, of the

---

7 Another veteran from the mental health and social welfare field spoke out plainly in related vein: 'In '33, I'd just been hired as a social worker by the United Charities. Social work at that time was beginning to get psychiatric. I got taken by some of my clients in a way that made me keenly aware of how stupid were some of our approaches. . . . It was my first contact with poverty. I found out the hard way' (Terkel, 1970: 440).

institution of centralized regulatory powers designed to extend the security, actual freedoms and well-being of the large majority of citizens, and of the *evolution of a personalized presidency in direct communication and felt relationship with the American people.*

Born of a well-to-do, long-established New York family, Roosevelt 'had enjoyed a singularly happy and privileged youth, culminating in his schooling at Groton and graduation from Harvard in 1904. His father, twenty-six years older than his mother . . . died when Roosevelt was eighteen.' 'Thus', writes the same author, in his searching account of the impact of the New Deal on American life, 'Roosevelt did not suffer the competition of a dominating or highly successful father. At the same time, however, he enjoyed the full attention and love of his mother, Sara Delano Roosevelt, a woman of great force and driving personality' (Ekirch, 1969: 73). Roosevelt went on from Harvard to graduate in the Columbia Law School and enter practice. At 23, while still completing his law studies, he married Eleanor (a distant cousin, as both were, of Theodore Roosevelt), who was to be companion and increasingly powerful ally throughout the rest of his life.

A successful move into politics in 1910 launched Roosevelt's main career; which continued strongly through World War I, to the point where he was vice-presidential nominee (with James Cox) in 1920. The next year a virulent attack of polio drastically changed his life, as he emerged from the disease physically crippled but personally matured. 'The evidence', a biographer wrote, 'is that Roosevelt's illness did not alter but strengthened already existent or latent tendencies in his personality.' Further, it seemed that 'Roosevelt's tragic blow even became a political asset, enhancing his appeal to those who suffered, who had calamities, and who aspired to overcome them' (see Ekirch, 1969: 74). The future president clearly brought exceptional inner resources to his own rehabilitation, a central, consistent occupation for at least the next six years. He learned to walk a little, with heavy braces, and to live with full and extraordinary energy. He made a full-fledged comeback into politics in 1928, to become governor of New York, presiding in that office through the worst period of the Depression, effectively serving a most salient further apprenticeship for the presidency.

A dramatic indication of Roosevelt's style came on the eve of his nomination by the Democratic Party, as their presidential candidate. Violating precedent, he appeared at the meeting in person to acknowledge publicly his nomination and candidacy. This action, he said, symbolized the setting aside of traditions: 'I pledge you', he concluded, 'I pledge myself to a new deal for the American people.' The term 'new deal' picked up by an alert cartoonist and highlighted by the press, originated fortuitously as the term for the hallmark of Roosevelt's program (Leuchtenburg, 1963: 8).

The New Deal for people: planning and implementation

Even before his nomination, Roosevelt had reached into the academic and professional community and formed a small close group of consultants and co-strategists, popularly known as the 'brain trust' during his campaign. Members of this group and many others from similar ranks were to serve later in his administration. Following the landslide election victory, little in substance was heard from the president-elect during the cruel, ever-worsening four months before his inauguration. Contrary to appearances, Roosevelt 'was quietly going about the business of building a legislative program – sifting memoranda, conferring with advisers, wearing out whole teams of experts with his amazing energy, and impressing skeptics with his ability to grasp the crux of an argument or to retain . . . details of economic data' (Leuchtenburg, 1963: 32).

The men and women the new president called and relied on, in central roles, included a whole cluster of professionals from the social welfare and helping field; social workers, for the main part, experienced in innovative developments with structurally disadvantaged groups. Frances Perkins, 'the first woman ever to serve in the cabinet, had been schooled at Hull House, Harry Hopkins [to become literally a right-hand man of the President] at Christadora House; Adolf Berle, Henry Morgenthau Jnr., and Herbert Lehman had all worked at Henry Street [New York]'. All shared 'John Dewey's conviction that organized social intelligence could shape society' for human benefit (Leuchtenburg, 1963: 33). Carl Rogers came in contact with John Dewey's 'pragmatist' philosophy and views on education and human development during his graduate studies in the mid-twenties, initially through a course with William Kilpatrick at Columbia University (Rogers, 1967a: 355). Given the nature and influence of Dewey's thought, it almost certainly was an enabling factor in the formation of Rogers' own viewpoint and path (Van Belle, 1980: 19–23).

In his inaugural address (March 3, 1933), in now famous rhetoric, the new President declared that 'The only thing we have to fear is fear itself – nameless, unreasoning, unjustified terror that paralyses needed efforts to convert retreat into advance.' Further, 'The people of the United States have not failed. In their need they have registered a mandate that they want direct, vigorous action.' The speaker's harshest words were for the banking system and, especially, its managers. Like Hoover, Roosevelt wished to instil hope and confidence again. The means he used, and their consequences, were radically different.

Since the beginning of the Depression, more than 4,000 banks had failed. Two days after assuming office, on March 3, the President issued emergency edicts proclaiming a national bank 'holiday' (all banks were closed for a week) and recalling Congress into special session. Meeting in a crisis atmosphere reminiscent of wartime, legislation was advanced, passed, and signed at once, validating the steps already taken and authorizing others, including provisions for assisted reorganization of banks and their selective reopening on a reliable footing. On Sunday evening, March 12, some 60 million people listened to their president by radio in the first of his 'fireside chats', warmly assuring them that this crisis was over and they now could safely deal with the banks that would open again, beginning the next day. An index of the quality of Roosevelt's contact with his audience, given the legacy of bank collapse and ruin, was that in each major city immediate deposits exceeded withdrawals.[8]

Further president-initiated fiscal and other steps followed in rapid succession. In two weeks, the mood of the nation as a whole had changed and was charged with a sense of positive expectancy and movement. A few days later, in the British House of Commons, Neville Chamberlain remarked: 'Today, thanks to the initiative, courage, and wisdom of the new President, a change has taken place which might almost be called miraculous. A new sense of hope and anticipation for the future is coming back to the American people, and that confidence is being reflected over here in the city of London.'[9]

The same essential pattern, ever widening in scope, complexity, and cross-currents of interest, continued for the 100-day period that Congress remained in session. Fifteen major laws passed at the President's urging – of which the development and broad overseeing was only part of Roosevelt's activity. One summing up, from an observer living through the time and stressing the dimension of national mood and attitude, is that of Walter Lippman: 'At the end of February we were a congeries of disorderly panic-stricken mobs and factions. In the hundred days from March to June we became an organized nation confident of our power to provide for our own security and to control our own destiny' (cited in Boardman, 1967: 66).

One of the new laws established the Civilian Conservation Corps (CCC), designed jointly as a job-creation and nature conservation measure. By August 1933, 300,000 young men were enrolled, in 1,500 camps. In the ensuing seven years, a million and a half young people served in CCC, planting trees by the hundreds of millions, aiding in forest and park preservation and development, building fire towers, wildlife shelters, canals and bridges, and effectively aiding redevelopment of farming areas. The Agricultural Adjustment Act (AAA) assisted farmers in various ways, including payments under the then new principle of subsidized non-production. The Tennessee Valley Authority was established, as a remarkable regional planning and development program almost uniquely participatory in its working. Other measures included the Federal Emergency Relief Administration, headed by Harry Hopkins, and industry-centred legislation expressed in the National Recovery Administration (NRA), through which codes were developed for protective regulation of labour relations and conditions.

Not long afterward, and with vast numbers of people still (in late 1934) on non-work relief, Roosevelt proposed a huge program of emergency public employment to provide genuine work to three and a half million jobless persons. Workers would be paid more than the dole but somewhat less than

8 Information drawn from Leuchtenburg, 1963: 42–45.

9 (i) Chamberlain as quoted by Leuchtenburg, 1963: 47, footnote 16. (ii) Adolf Hitler became Chancellor of Germany at the same time as Roosevelt's presidency began, taking the fate of the German people into his hands in a crisis of similar depth but sharply differing historical context. For a dozen years the two leaders would be dominant opposites in increasingly incompatible systems of world import, for whom coexistence finally would cease altogether as an option.

the prevailing wage, so that private employment would remain more attractive. Union leaders strenuously opposed the below-prevailing-wage concept, while conservatives balked at the huge cost. Finally the President had his way, with the power of 'discretionary control' over most wage levels. The resulting 'Emergency Relief Appropriation Act of 1935 authorized the greatest single appropriation in the history of the United States' (Leuchtenburg, 1963: 124–125).

Hopkins again headed the new agency, called the Works Progress Administration. While restricted from direct competition with private industry, the WPA spawned a wide spectrum of projects and employed men and women from unskilled labourers to highly qualified artists, actors and writers. Projects of a physical nature included the building or improvement of a very large number and distribution of human service, educational and other public facilities, including some 13,000 playgrounds. The WPA's Federal Theater Project made a major contribution to the cultural entertainment of the nation, presenting classical and contemporary drama to an audience of some 30 million people in four years. The Federal Writer's Project supported informational and quality fiction writing and publication. The Art Project, through teaching and original mural and art works, regenerated mural painting in particular and gave a fresh new life to the appearance of many public buildings across the land.

Unemployable persons, the aged, crippled and sick, were not directly assisted by these programs, their needs being left up to state governments often very ill-equipped to meet them. This gap provided part of the motive and ammunition for Roosevelt's historic request, early in 1935, for social security legislation. Much of the substance of the proposed act had been worked out by a cabinet committee headed by Frances Perkins, Roosevelt's Labor Secretary – and a former social worker, as was Hopkins. Sharply differing views were strenuously argued but, by mid-1935, congressional action was complete. Critical ingredients of the Social Security Act were (i) a national compulsory system of old-age insurance, financed by wage and payroll taxes, (ii) provision for the federal government to share equally with states in the care costs of destitute persons over 65 and outside the scope of the new insurance scheme, (iii) a system of unemployment insurance and (iv) federal matching assistance to the states, to provide support and care for dependent mothers and children, for crippled and blind persons, and for public health services.[10]

The spectrum of remedies and new development entrained by the New Deal, even including the employment aid (under WPA) to literary and other artists, addressed issues and needs that echoed in the work of social fiction

10 The Social Security Act was probably the *most* important lasting development in federal social policy and law during Roosevelt's first term. Although its intended permanence, and the embodiment of a more collectivist vision of responsibility, acted to constrain its scope, the long-range consequences overshadowed most other steps in the New Deal saga. The legislation and its provisions were viewed by Roosevelt himself as the cornerstone of his program of rehabilitation and reform (see, for example, Leuchtenburg, 1963: 132–133).

writers of the time. Carl Rogers read extensively and was part of a culture in which creative literature partly arose from, and fed back into, the general consciousness. To understand the culture of ideas, social vision and values surrounding Rogers, some attention to the voice of serious writers in the period under scrutiny is called for.

Literary voices of the thirties: envisioning human and societal nature

The first writer selected is William Faulkner, foremost Southern literary artist of his time if not of this century. With stories from a living past that also had vivid implication for the writer's contemporary world, Faulkner's work came to full flower in the 1930s. His major writings are connected by their setting in an invented Mississippi county and by the extraordinary, intertwined caste of human characters, from all classes and conditions of life, who dwell and come and go in this place. The longer works often take the form of narrations by one or more of the principal characters, each from his or her own perspective. The serious reader is drawn – much as therapists are with their clients – into intense, participatory engagement with invented/real people in worlds they inherit, create and struggle against.

For Faulkner, most humans are expressing and playing out, also in combat with and sometimes breaking free from, the programming of their lives. He implies, in the words of one observer-critic, that: 'The man who has adapted to modern human society is a kind of human cash register. He has lost his natural, "feeling" response to life; his religion is an empty formalism; he is incapable of love' (Volpe, 1974: 21). Contemporary society is seen as the enemy working against humanistic values and tending to destroy the individual's integrity. A return to the past is not a solution, however: 'The tragic plight of the Faulkner hero is that he is a prisoner of the past, of society, of social and moral taboos, and of his own introspective personality' (ibid.: 24).

The same observer describes Faulkner as presenting 'social man as the end-product of a process of psychological conditioning that practically eliminates his chance of responding naturally to the experiences of his existence' (ibid.: 24). But a positive antithesis, of a non-imprisoned 'primitive' or natural man and woman, also appears among Faulkner's living characters. Such persons '*are open to experience*; they are *spontaneous* and natural. Because man is part of the natural world, his natural or unconditioned responses are in harmony with nature' (ibid.: 26, italics added). The natural environment, human community, and the depth dimension of time, are powerfully invoked and interwoven in the world Faulkner brings to life. Always, there is motion, activity, process, usually on multiple levels, and quite often in spite of his characters' attempts to hold back time, or change, or new awareness. As expressed by another advocate-critic:

> The first characteristic that distinguishes . . . Faulkner's major works from most other literature is that, in the whole and in the parts, down to the smallest details of

> matter and of method, it moves. . . . It comes to us as highly compressed vital energy, which we can release, if we take it rightly, to make our own lives move more widely and deeply than they otherwise might. Faulkner's greatness is that he has added life to life and a world of richly imagined motion to the moving world in which we live. (Adams, 1968: 115)

Faulkner was five years older than Carl Rogers, living in an outwardly very different world, in Mississippi, and employing a contrasting medium for the enlargement of self and social consciousness inspired by his best writing. However, his penetrating interest in the inner lives, struggles and selfhood of his characters, and important features of his view of human possibilities and values, show kinship with unfolding emphases in Rogers' work.[11] While it is no doubt highly influential for his craft and vision that Faulkner's critical development as a writer (and inner-directed adult) occurred in the 1920s, and came to flower in the 1930s, his major work in that period is timeless in nature, and does not point specifically to the human situation in the Depression/New Deal era. Given Rogers' interest in reading and literature (Rogers, 1967a), direct contact with Faulkner's work is likely. More importantly, both men were part of a larger movement in psycho-social consciousness, to which Faulkner was actively contributing in his own medium.

Another influential feature of the 1930s was a distinctive genre of literary writing set in present time and focusing on the lives and conditions of life of ordinary men, women, families, and underprivileged social groups. The authors wrote from strong, at times passionate human and social concern, typically in powerfully descriptive or near documentary style. Agee and Evans' (1941) *Let Us Now Praise Famous Men*,[12] based on commissioned observation and study in 1936, focuses on three cotton sharecropping, tenant farmer families, and also touches briefly but with power on some of their black neighbours. The setting is Alabama and the reader has vivid occasion at times to think of Civil War legacies. Agee's style includes powerful, etched description, and a direct dialogical sharing with the reader of his own personal and interpretive thoughts. There is room here to mention only a single striking passage from Agee's text, one that could almost be found in subsequent Rogerian writing:

> I believe that every human being is potentially capable, within his 'limits', of fully realizing his potentialities; that this, his being cheated and choked of it, is infinitely the ghastliest, commonest, and most inclusive of all the crimes of which the human world can accuse itself; and that the discovery and use of 'consciousness', which has

11 In his Nobel Prize acceptance speech, Faulkner spoke concisely of his values and human potentiality. Young writers, he said, have 'forgotten the problems *of the human heart in conflict with itself* which alone can make good writing because that is worth writing about, worth the agony and the sweat'. Also, human *possibilities* are uniquely positive: The human person 'is immortal, not because he alone among creatures has an inexhaustible voice, but because he has a soul, a spirit capable of compassion and sacrifice and endurance' (Faulkner, 1950; italics added).

12 The text, written by James Agee, was first published as a whole in 1939.

> always been and is our deadliest enemy and deceiver, is also the source and guide of all hope and cure, and the only one. (Agee and Evans, 1941: 307)

John Steinbeck was a highly influential social fiction writer by the mid to late 1930s, standing out among those whose work centred on North American settings in present time. He was born and grew up over the same period as Rogers, and with resemblances in family background. His novels *In Dubious Battle* (1936), *Of Mice and Men* (1937), and *The Grapes of Wrath* (1939), powerfully brought into wider view the humanity, plight and unevenly heroic struggles of migrant agricultural workers and poor farmers. When the first of these books appeared, the author was living among the migrant workers whose worlds he so vividly brought to life in short stories and newspaper articles as well as in his books. The humanistic 'person-centredness' and advocacy of Steinbeck's work was another concordant voice in the intellectual milieu surrounding Rogers' path.[13]

Ernest Hemingway, like Rogers, was born in suburban Oak Park, Illinois, and they both attended the same elementary school in overlapping time. In Hemingway's case, his life and career from one angle of view, was 'a never ended rebellion against the prudery and conventionalism of both father and mother and the place of his birth'.[14] His work was to reach fruition in the late 1920s, particularly with his powerful individualist novel of love and war, *A Farewell to Arms*. His Depression-era novel, *To Have and Have Not* (1937) most resembles the special literary genre of the thirties, strongly reflecting social concerns and the importance and meaning of collective human action.[15] In *For Whom the Bell Tolls* (1940), these features reach a new level in the context of a comradeship in arms that transcends national/ethnic boundaries – the Spanish Civil War setting. The author's vision and plea for the brotherhood of man is introduced at the start of the book, with John Donne's timeless words: 'No man is an *Iland*, intire of it selfe . . . every man is . . . part of the *maine* . . . any man's *death* diminishes *me*, because I am involved in *Mankinde*; And therefore never send to know for whom the bell tolls; It tolls for *thee*.'

Full attention to relevant literary influences of the thirties would include focusing on left-wing social dramatists, such as Clifford Odets and John Howard Lawson. One of Odets' early militant plays *Waiting for Lefty* (1935a)

---

13 Steinbeck's *earlier* writing is a rebellious break-out from the traditional ethos, and tends to centre on dramatic individual activity. By the mid-thirties, however, the theme of collective action, with its dangers and positive potentialities, had replaced this earlier thrust. Character, action and social message were in balance and strongest conjunction in his writing, by the end of the decade. A brief example of this depth follows, in which the characters clearly recognize and speak from their differing personal realities and frames of reference:

> Pa said, 'S'pose he's tellin' the truth – that fella?' The preacher answered, 'He's tellin' the truth awright. The truth for him. He wasn't makin' nothin' up.' 'How about us?' Tom demanded, 'Is that the truth for us?' 'I don' know', said Casy. (Steinbeck, 1939: 261)

14 See *Encyclopaedia Britannica*, 1979, 8: 757.

15 As one illustration, the character Henry Morgan, fatally wounded and desperately struggling to articulate his thought, finally says: 'No matter how, a man *alone* ain't got no bloody . . . chance' (Hemingway, 1937: 225, italics added).

lends its name as a chapter title in Leuchtenburg's (1963) searching and scholarly history of the Roosevelt/New Deal period.[16] Published soon afterward, his full-length work *Awake and Sing* (Odets, 1935b) is a compassionate study of a Jewish family wrestling with poverty. Themes of human possibility and individual dignity in the face of adversity recur in Odets' work, especially as it softens from the pounding messages of his early writing into a deepening development of character and a more full-bodied humanism. J.H. Lawson's drama of social protest was well-established in the 1920s, and gathered further strength in an artistically versatile advocacy of Marxist aims and perspective during the Depression era. Sympathetically portrayed individuals and groups are positioned against the 'they' forces of corrupted bureaucracy and an exploitative socio-economic system. Lawson evidently did not evolve a full-bodied positive vision but his work contributed to the pressure for changes to reduce inequality, deprivation and powerlessness, and provide opportunities for shared self-realization, all envisioned through a revolutionary renewal of the social order.

Finally, in this too-brief outline, it warrants mention that there were major American poets also contributing to the temper and social direction of the times. As a single example, Archibald MacLeish – both poet and dramatist – was among those with overt, practical social-political concern. His active interest in the swirling forces and issues of the time came to a head in the thirties, particularly around the development of totalitarianism in Europe, which he saw in advance as an oncoming threat to American democracy. His writing included such verse plays as *Panic* (1935), for the stage; and *The Fall of the City* (1937) and *Air Raid*, for radio production. In World War II, he held senior US Government positions, while at the end of the war he was active in the United Nations and a major contributor to the development of UNESCO.[17] Years later, Rogers directly cited MacLeish as expressing a viewpoint close to his own heart. The quoted passage reads:

> We do not feel our knowledge. Nothing could better illustrate the flaw at the heart of our civilisation. . . . Knowledge without feeling is not knowledge and can lead only to public irresponsibility and indifference, and conceivably to ruin. (Rogers, 1974a: 105/MacLeish)

As visionary and pragmatist, scholar and administrator-statesman, MacLeish combined qualities valued by the Roosevelt Administration in the emergencies of war and of organization for peace; qualities not unlike the combination that propelled Rogers in his own course of innovation and leadership.

My focus here has been literature of the 1930s, not on direct comparison of work before and after that time. However, some major directions of shift in

16 In *Waiting for Lefty* 'a meeting of cab drivers waits for a leader who never appears. As they wait, the hackies rise to explain why they want to strike. On opening night in January, 1935, when the question was finally put, the audience, caught up in the drama, roared Strike! Strike! . . .' (cited in Leuchtenburg, 1963: 112, footnote).

17 See, for example, *Encyclopedia Americana*, 1977, 18: 78.

perspective from the previous decade, and penetrating into the 1940s, are discernible. These include movement away from classic American individualism toward a new spirit of collectivism, a growing awareness that complete freedom of enterprise and human/social well-being do not reliably go hand-in-hand, and that an overhaul of the relations between persons and the institutions and systems they create was needed. All of these features were reflected in the aspirations and reforms of the New Deal. The effects of anti-democratic and anti-humanistic 'reforms' in the totalitarian systems were to come into cruel relief with the advent of World War II.

The next chapter continues the story of Roosevelt's times and presidency, from the mid-thirties to the President's death and the end of the war. Carried forward from the ground laid in the present chapter, some principal threads emerge in sharper relief. These broad but distinct patterns, including qualities of Roosevelt's own approach, work as a lens through which to see in fuller view particular developments that have their roots in that era. My own interest has widened through this inquiry. Its impetus, however, remains the search to identify and distil features of Carl Rogers' broader milieu which plausibly supported, encouraged, and contributed opportunity for his own directions and course of innovation.

3

New Paths in Step

Roosevelt's Way/Rogers' Advance

> All the characteristics of this type of counseling are also tenets of democracy. The client's participation is voluntary, self-initiated. The counseling atmosphere is built upon respect for the person, tolerance, and acceptance of differences, faith in the person's ability to accept responsibility for his own conduct, and freedom for growth toward maturity. It is perhaps no accident that this emphasis in counseling has reached its fruition in America.
>
> Carl Rogers and John Wallen, 1946

President Roosevelt's reform drive continued, although more unevenly, to the late thirties. By then, international affairs and response to the danger of war, especially given the strongly isolationist sentiment at home, had become his overriding concern. The shift was in matters claiming attention, not in his basic outlook and style. His way of being President, the measures and ethos he fostered, the decisions he made, undoubtedly had direct or indirect bearing on many specific innovations. The relevance of this context became strikingly visible to me in the case of Carl Rogers and the therapy he parented. I will sum up the principal connections I see after first tracing Roosevelt's course through the further development of the New Deal to the thunderous approach of war. The story itself, through the war years to the ending of Roosevelt's life, is continued later in the chapter, revealing added features conducive to the advance of Rogers' work.

Roosevelt as leader: peacetime management and preparation for war

Biannual federal elections in the Fall of 1934 had yielded an even bigger Democratic Party majority than before, in the House and Senate, interpretable as a further vote of public confidence in Roosevelt's administration and the New Deal programs. Ensuing advances already mentioned include the employment relief legislation, leading to the WPA, and the historically pivotal Social Security Act. Another main development in 1935 was the National Labor Relations Act, also named after Robert Wagner, its principal originator.

The Wagner Act arguably was the most important piece of legislation of the New Deal *not* initiated by the Roosevelt administration, and the President's response was revealing of his style and leadership. He at first opposed the bill, but other concurrent events led him increasingly to distrust the employment intentions and still largely unbridled power of big business. Further, the radically labour-supportive Wagner bill turned out to draw strong and then massive favour from Congress. Roosevelt brought opponents within his administration into consultation with Wagner, thereafter announcing his wholehearted support for the bill, and embracing it as 'must' legislation. Positively viewed, this turn-about by Roosevelt reflects (i) a willingness to shift position in light of new evidence and opinion that he valued, (ii) a facility in bringing divergent viewpoints and viewers into accommodation, (iii) a readiness to give influence to others who sponsored reform, and (iv) a concern in this case to sustain momentum and, finally, to share in 'ownership' of the powerful new legislation.[1]

Others in high office might have wilted at the pace and pressure of events, the clash and struggle of opposing views, the enormous demands of implementing or of having to end far-reaching programs,[2] and the emotional strains of heavy responsibility. Roosevelt, however, seemed to be tireless, to function as though great weight flowed through him rather than resting on him, and to possess quite rare inner resources. 'Both friend and foe marvelled at his serenity', Leuchtenburg reports, also citing his White House physician's testimony that 'more than any person I have met, he had an equanimity, poise, and serenity of temper that kept him on the most even of keels' (Leuchtenburg, 1963: 168). In mid-1936, another keen observer wrote:

> On none of his predecessors has the office left so few marks as on Mr. Roosevelt. He is a little heavier, a shade greyer; otherwise he looks harder and in better health than on the day of his inauguration. His face is so tanned that his eyes appear lighter, a cool Wedgwood blue; after the four grilling years since the last campaign they are as keen, curious, friendly and impenetrable as ever. (McCormick, 1936: 2–3)

The impression of impenetrability seems to have been linked to Roosevelt's ability to switch the whole orientation of his response as though he had different personalities he could shift to 'with such speed that you often never knew where you were or to which personality you were talking' (see Leuchtenburg, 1963: 167). A likely key to the shifting complexity of his personality, to those not close to him, and perhaps quite different in their own ways of being, is given by Frances Perkins:

---

1 Another major economic measure of this time was the Holding Company Act, designed to sharply reduce and regulate distant or layered combine ownership and control of operating companies – especially electric power and other utility empires, which often operated in ways flagrantly against the public interest (Leuchtenburg, 1963: 154–156).

2 Including the dismantling of the industry-centred NRA, in the wake of the Supreme Court's upset verdict of unconstitutionality.

> He was a man of high intelligence but he used *all* his faculties when he was thinking about a subject. He had to have feelings as well as thoughts. His emotions, his intuitive understanding, his imagination, his moral and traditional bias, his sense of right and wrong – all entered into his thinking, and unless these flowed freely through his mind . . . he was unlikely to come to any clear conclusion or even to a clear understanding. (Perkins, 1947: 124–125)

Perkins attributes to this quality, an organismic way of functioning in Rogerian terms, a great part of the basis of Roosevelt's tremendous rapport with ordinary people. In any case, the qualities that inspired confidence in Roosevelt as person and national leader were again of critical importance as he faced election in late 1936 for his second term as President. Although a master of radio communication, he wanted to see and be seen in person, to hear and learn from people directly, and he seemed to draw nourishment from a pace of contact exhausting to others. The re-election was another landslide victory for the President and for his Party.

During 1936, threats to world peace from Nazi Germany, Italy and even Japan had been a growing reality in Roosevelt's mind. He was beginning to search for politically feasible ways to express his concern, within the context of overriding isolationist sentiment. One such forum was the Inter-American Conference for maintenance of peace, held in Argentina just after his re-election. While focusing strongly on hemispheric issues, he also sounded the alarm in regard to dangers from without:

> Beyond the ocean we see continents rent asunder by old hatreds and new fanaticisms. We hear the demand that injustice and inequality be corrected by resorting to the sword. . . . We hear the cry that new markets can be achieved only through conquest. . . . We know, too, that vast armaments are rising on every side. . . . A great war in other parts of the world would affect us and threaten our good in a hundred ways. (Zevin, 1946: 75)

By the Fall of 1937, Roosevelt decided to begin to speak out at home, via his famous 'quarantine speech' carefully questioning isolationism: 'There is a solidarity and interdependence about the modern world, both technically and morally, which makes it impossible for any nation completely to isolate itself from economic and political upheavals in the rest of the world.' In particular, '*war is a contagion. . . . It can engulf states and peoples remote from the original scene of hostilities*'. From this followed the metaphor of quarantine, which should be imposed on the aggressors, isolating them from normal interchange and trade. He argued that 'positive endeavors' are necessary to preserve peace. The speech provoked an uproar and the President was bitterly attacked. Internally, his concern mounted (Fitzsimmons, 1945: 289–291, italics added).

In spite of his stunning re-election victory and huge Party majority, 1937 was a time of setback for Roosevelt. Difficulties came into view of another order than those to which bold initiatives and legislated reform had been appropriate. Central, on the domestic front, was the Supreme Court's invalidation of some major New Deal measures, and the threat of a similar fate to others.[3] The balance of judgement among the life-tenured Chief Justices had remained conservative. In considered desperation, Roosevelt launched a court reform proposal. The nuclear feature was to open the Supreme Court up to additional appointees, one for each justice continuing to serve past the age of 70.

Popularly known as the court-packing bill, Roosevelt met opposition head-on, arguing that it was vital to change the composition of the Court, to restore not alter its enshrined role. As usual, taking the issue to the people, his speeches included a famous 'fireside chat' (March 9, 1937) in which he traced the events and outlined the principles that formed his case for the proposed measure. Given passage of the bill, he declared 'I will appoint Justices who will act as justices and not as legislators! If the appointment of such Justices can be called "packing the courts" then I say that I, and with me the vast majority of the American people, favor doing just that – now.' For once there was serious doubt whether the vast majority agreed; and more than on any other legislative initiative, his action was deeply divisive within his own Party.

As it turned out, the Supreme Court itself took much of the steam out of Roosevelt's aggressive drive to reform it. The balance and pattern of its decisions unexpectedly changed, in a direction that led to upholding major pieces of New Deal legislation and related law, notably including the Wagner Act and contested features of the Social Security Act. Internal recentring had occurred, and the ensuing decisions reflected movement away from the long dominant conservative stance of the Court (Leuchtenburg, 1963: 236). A quietly encouraged resignation from the Court opened the way for a liberal replacement, and limited 'face-saving' legislation, usefully reforming aspects of Court procedure, was passed.[4]

Organized labour, turbulently empowered during Roosevelt's first term, but with little foothold in the very large manufacturing companies, was moving strongly with well-planned strike tactics, as 1937 began. The main new technique was the 'sit-down', where employees refused to leave the plants, improvising temporary living arrangements. First, General Motors capitulated, then US Steel; and other big companies and industries throughout the land followed suit in the face of strikes and precedents. An enormous transfer

---

3 In his second inaugural address (January 20, 1937) Roosevelt stressed that the New Deal goals of conditions for human well-being were very far from accomplished. 'I see one-third of a nation ill-housed, ill-clad, ill-nourished' was an echoing phrase and theme, powerfully amplified in later speeches related to his drive for judicial reform (see, e.g., Burns, 1956: 299).

4 A new law that did pass in 1937 led to formation of the US Housing Authority, through which federal help was provided to lowest income earners to make tenancy possible in public housing projects (Rauch, 1963: 289–292). Elizabeth Wood points out that a limitation of the projects was that 'it never occurred to anybody that the people might make their own decisions about playgrounds, housing design or management policies'. She goes on: 'sometimes these people have awfully good ideas, better than ours. We're just beginning to learn. Tenants have a right to make their own decisions.' At the time, Ms Wood was Chief of Social Services in the Housing Assistance Administration. She felt that 'the New Deal was an enormous step . . . forward' but that failure to treat tenants as resourceful, active agents in their worlds brought on welfare dependency (Terkel, 1970: 441–445).

of social power was taking place, with coercion and legality conjoined, and little serious violence.

In mid-1937, under conditions of broadened prosperity, and fearing adverse consequences of prolonged 'pump-priming', Roosevelt turned off or scaled down a great portion of the federal employment/relief assistance programs. However, in the wake of the court-packing episode and in the face of large-scale militant unionization, business and middle-class confidence waned. In the late summer another wave of recession struck suddenly and hard, and by early 1938 the situation was again critical. Roosevelt's 'fireside chat on economic conditions', of April 14, 1938, on the heels of once more submitting work-relief and pump-priming proposals to Congress, is a masterpiece of educational and softly persuasive communication; ending with a distinctly person-centred sharing. 'I try always to remember', he said, that the American people's 'deepest problems are human. I constantly talk with those who come to tell me their own points of view. . . . And constantly I seek to look beyond the door of the White House . . . into the hopes and fears of men and women in their homes.' Finally, he speaks even more directly to the listeners present to his inner eye: 'I can hear your unspoken wonder as to where we are headed in this troubled world' (see Zevin, 1946: 142–143).[5]

Early in 1938, as Hitler annexed Austria, and Japan opened new campaigns in China, Congress supported Roosevelt's 'Two Ocean Navy' Act, with appropriations to substantially increase naval defence capacity. From an early hobby of naval studies, and his ardent, vigorous service as Assistant Secretary of the Navy before and during World War I, the navy was Roosevelt's first love among the military services. A naval cruise, such as one to the Galapagos Islands in the summer of 1938, was a favourite recreation; and he saw the navy as a 'strong shield held before the vulnerable heart of America' (Hatch, 1948: 192). Politically, it was the only medium through which to increase military strength as he foresaw the looming prospect of major war.[6] On the home front, refinement and extensions to the Social Security Act were achieved, and changes made in the Executive Branch, but the birth period of New Deal reforms was over.

Over the next long three years, before the US itself was catapulted directly into war, Roosevelt was to face enormous further challenges and tests as a political leader; as an educator in democratic mode in the open school of his

5 In June 1938, the Fair Labor Standards Act was passed, viewed as the last important enactment of the New Deal as such. Centrally, the law was concerned with establishing some minimum basic wage and a maximum hourly work week. However, 'the most memorable provision forbade the employment of child labor in interstate commerce' (Leuchtenburg, 1963: 262). Weak in many ways, the law was a foundation stone for later building, and a long step forward in the interests of non-union workers, who were still the large majority (Rauch, 1963: 307).

6 In September, 1938, war in Europe was narrowly averted, for the moment, by the capitulation to Hitler's demands, at Munich. Roosevelt's next annual message to Congress (January, 1939), dubbed 'a warning to dictator nations' but more a plea for realistic awareness at home, ended on a note of high eloquence and meaning to those disposed to listen: 'Once I prophesied that this generation of Americans had a rendezvous with destiny. That prophecy comes true. To us much is given; more is expected. This generation will "nobly save or meanly lose the last best hope of earth" . . .' (Zevin, 1946: 172).

nation; as a statesman increasingly on centre stage in a world in extraordinary peril; as the fallible top manager in a relatively loose-knit, highly pluralist society; and as a 'process' person with his own sense of responsibility, judgement, ambition and needs, in continuous interaction. Unlike the majority of his countrymen, by 1939 he no longer saw any realism or security in the policy of isolationism. Further, for many Europeans, he had come, more than their own heads of state, to represent democratic resistance to fascism (Leuchtenburg, 1963: 286).

The next moves in the war-approaching crisis, were Italy's overpowering of Albania, and Nazi Germany's flagrant violation in Czechoslovakia of the recent Munich agreements. On ending a visit to Warm Springs shortly after these events, Roosevelt openly remarked to those around him 'I've had a fine holiday here with you all. I'll be back in the Fall, if we do not have a war.' Again, a storm of reported abuse and cries of 'warmonger' ensued. In mid-1939, as vilification of Poland in the Nazi press gave warning of Hitler's next target, strenuous efforts to achieve partial repeal of the US Neutrality Act were made, initially to no avail. Within weeks, the awesome news of the predicted German invasion of Poland, and resulting British and French declarations of war with Germany, followed. Finally, Congress agreed to amend the Neutrality Act to allow 'cash-and-carry' sale of munitions to the Allies.

After a long winter lull, the military machine of Germany exploded again, storming across Europe with lightning speed and unstoppable power; and by late June its dark shadow blanketed mainland Europe. Suddenly, the effective perimeter of Nazi Germany was just across the Atlantic, with Britain alone in the pathway. During this crushing of one nation after another, with scarcely believable day-by-day news of the methods and advance of the war, the acrid smell of danger reached and shook most Americans for the first time; and the President was seen in altered vision. In mid-May, he addressed a now responsive Congress on needs and plans in the area of defence build-up (Burns, 1956: 419). By year's end (1940), he had (i) taken the risky plunge of sending fifty reconditioned US warships in response to Britain's plea for crisis assistance (Burns, 1956: 437–440), (ii) presided over the massive building up and disposition of defence forces, with Japan now formally an Axis power, (iii) been nominated and then re-elected to an unprecedented third term as President, (iv) kept in informative contact with the American people, and visible to the world, as a foremost symbol and exponent of the human value issues at stake, and (v) formulated his simple but powerful 'four freedoms' concept: 'The first is freedom of speech and expression – everywhere in the world. . . . The second is freedom of every person to worship God in his own way – everywhere. . . . The third is freedom from want . . . everywhere. . . . The fourth is freedom from fear . . . everywhere' (Zevin, 1946: 258–267).

Tracing the Roosevelt–Rogers 'connection'

The climactic ending of Roosevelt's second term and start of his third, in which highly pragmatic action was fused with continued affirmation of democratic and humanistic values, coincided in time with the microcosm of the birth of client-centred therapy. Although not linked in simple cause and effect, the intersection of these developments was no mere coincidence. The tracing that follows sums up key features of Roosevelt's time and presidency seen as conducive in varied ways for the philosophy and advance of Rogers' work. Some features are at a level implying broadly fertile soil for such innovation, while others are concordant in substance and suggestive of more distinct connection. First in my listing are aspects of the former kind.

1 *Scholars, human service professionals, and others of social-intellectual bent and talent, played an almost unprecedented role in Roosevelt's administration.* The President drew and relied heavily on liberal intelligentsia and professionals, in a variety of fields, individuals who were both inventive and down-to-earth, visionary *and* socially and politically aware. Established and younger scholars (including faculty from Columbia University), and persons from the human service professions, became involved in large numbers, and were highly influential in most branches of government and as presidential advisors and assistants. As vividly summed up by Hofstader (1966): 'The New Deal brought the force of the mind into closer relation with power than it had been within the memory of any living man – closer than it had been since the days of the Founding Fathers.'

2 *A central priority of the New Deal was to bring about practical improvement in the circumstances and life quality of ordinary people.* Improvements encompassed an immediate 'rescue' level, longer-range measures to enhance opportunity and security, and changes to create or strengthen structures designed to empower many categories of people who formerly had been weak, dependent, insecure or disenfranchised. Many changes were experimental and there was much greater openness to new thought, new perspectives on the working of economic systems, new vision and priority in the area of social and human well-being. In the emergencies of the time, it was not a *laissez-faire* openness but an active, evolving search. This thrust promoted opportunity, challenge and encouragement for innovative response to actual human circumstance and need and was thus fundamentally supportive of (among others) Carl Rogers' directions.

3 *The New Deal was highly pragmatic in character.* From conservation to public works and housing construction, unemployment relief to rural electrification, from public health and medical care to strengthening the hands and rights of workers through legally protected unionization, from banning child labour to getting former US warships to England in time to help avert invasion, the emphasis was on the achievement of concrete objectives – on getting results. According to Frances Perkins, on economic, welfare and other issues Roosevelt's question always was 'Will it work, will it do some good?' Carl Rogers' self-acknowledged pragmatism is an exactly congruent expression of this feature of the Roosevelt/New Deal ethos. Of course, pragmatism did not originate in the New Deal, but its expression assumed a new centrality and many new forms. Rogers' emphasis was one such new form.

4 *Unprecedented priority was given to programs on behalf of the more vulnerable and needy groups in society.* Among the beneficiaries were working children, persons in marginal employment or unemployed, people over retirement age, those with educational and other handicaps, sustenance farmers and miners, and temporarily or permanently dependent individuals. Social workers doubled in number during the 1930s (Trattner, 1974: 243), and demand greatly increased in the other helping professions, largely under the impact of social security reform. Americans became much more sensitized during the Depression to psychological stress and saw the corrosive effects on the individual's self-image and personal relationships of deeply felt failure, fears around intense privation, of humiliating dependency, of guilt and depression, and of bottled-up targetless or reactive anger. This awareness, coupled with the further social provisions, comprises another feature of context in basic accord with the values and thrust of Rogers' community-based work in Rochester.[7]

5 *A distinct shift in balance occurred, away from traditional forms of individualism and toward a social outlook and a network of arrangements that were more 'collectivist' in quality.* The collectivist concept implied a reciprocal relationship between the community-of-the-whole, or the state, and the individual, each responsible to the other. The society or state was seen as responsible for ensuring wide-ranging institutionalized provision for the security and well-being of its constituent members, self-supporting or not, employed or unemployed. Equally, individuals, especially voting adults, together supported and broadly guided the state in the exercise of these responsibilities. Specifically implied was the view that 'the individual can function best, both in his own interest and as a contributor to society, in a secure rather than an insecure environment' (Fusfeld, 1959: 67).

From the first, Rogers emphasized the importance in effective therapy of the client's responsibility and choice *and* of psychological safety (Rogers, 1942a: 31–32 and ch. 4; 1951: 71–75). He implied that the exercise and experience of such active choice was uniquely consistent with non-impositional forms of personal therapy. Such assistance should be available to those needing it, regardless of whether they could pay for it. His own work exemplified this principle, with each person paying according to their means (Rogers, 1942a: 244–246; 1977a: 153–156). Implied is an underlying

---

7 In his summing-up, Leuchtenburg (1963: 332) cites the view that 'During the ten years between 1929 and 1939, more progress was made in public welfare and relief than in the three hundred years after this country was first settled.' On a more philosophical level: 'The New Dealers inwardly recognized that what they were doing had a deeply moral significance however much they eschewed ethical pretensions . . . [and] they felt themselves part of a broadly humanistic movement . . . a movement that might someday even achieve a cooperative commonwealth. Social insurance, Frances Perkins declared, was "a fundamental part of another great forward step in that liberation of humanity which began with the Renaissance"' (ibid.: 345–346). Both in practical directions and moral quality, the permeating influence of the New Deal movement was an influential backdrop in Rogers' world during his professionally formative Rochester years.

consistency between the principle of collectivism in the New Deal sense and the philosophy advanced and practised by Rogers.

6 *Participation in appraisal and decision-making, by those directly affected by the decisions, became much more widespread under the New Deal.* The country became significantly more democratic in practice. As expressed by a specialist on the period:

> The Roosevelt administration spun an intricate web of procedures to permit the will of different interest groups to be expressed. Millions of farmers voted in AAA crop referendums, including thousands of southern Negroes who had never before cast a ballot, and . . . production-control associations [were] manned by more than 100,000 committee-men. . . . [The] TVA raised the principle of local participation to a fine art. . . . Millions of workmen cast ballots at Labor Board collective bargaining elections . . . local advisory committees were consulted in the national youth and art projects. (Leuchtenburg, 1963: 85)

The list could go on. Naturally, practice fell short of the ideal but, on the whole, along with federal 'centralization' came increased local participation built in by law and by a ferment of involvement in issues of the time. There was a loss of the sense of powerlessness that had come to a head during the Depression. Client-centred therapy practices, particularly as these became manifest in teaching and in group and organizational contexts, were an innovative expression of a broader ethos, one in which values of self-direction, choice and responsibility were alive in a 'laboratory' of national scale.[8]

7 *It was in Roosevelt's style to surround himself with people of distinct and varying viewpoint, to encourage debate, and inquiry, and to welcome the airing of hot differences of opinion and cooler variation in judgement.* His own thought involved roving exploration and 'lateral thinking' and, at moments, brilliant improvisation and synthesis. Elaborate theorizing, or problem-solving by formula, were not his forte. He encouraged and accepted divergent thinking in and between others to the point of seeming disorder, but with an accompanying vitality, release of creative energy, and mobilization of effort to 'impractical' orders of achievement.[9] He often pressed for what amounted to a synergistic integration of seeming opposites. According to Frances Perkins:

> [Roosevelt] administered by the technique of friendship, encouragement and trust. This method of not giving direct and specific orders . . . released the creative energy

---

8 Einaudi (1959: 73) expresses the view that 'the central notion of Roosevelt's doctrine of democracy was community. His efforts were aimed at demonstrating the compatibility, indeed the essential identity, between the community's concern for the general welfare and the survival of the traditions of individual freedom and dignity.' The same theme was implicit in Rogers' direction and leadership in Chicago, and is transparently evident in his later work, for example on the person-centred approach with large groups (see Rogers, 1977a: ch. 8).

9 Roosevelt's unorthodox approach in this sphere led to competition not simply among people but among ideas (he would tend to listen and take in the person and idea together – implied in Perkins, 1947; Leuchtenburg, 1963). His sometimes frustrating 'procrastination' was a way of arriving at a sense of national consensus and/or 'reaching a decision by observing a trial by combat among rival theories' (Leuchtenburg, 1963: 328–329).

> of many men. They looked to him for courage, for strength . . . [and genuine] leadership. . . . His free system involved . . . a recognition of the value and capacity of every individual. (1947: 305)

This syndrome of qualities and of attitudes in action bears extraordinary resemblance to Rogers' own style and values, both in my direct experience of him and as seen in his writing and views expressed by other colleagues (for example, Farson, 1974b). It is also in keeping with Gordon's (1955) concept of 'group-centred leadership', and the early leadership and flowering of the client-centred approach as others have described it (Kirschenbaum, 1979: 171–177).

8 *The term 'responsive initiator' describes another basic feature of Roosevelt's style and make-up, with counterpart in Rogers.* FDR clearly took profoundly influential initiatives and decisions, directly affecting millions of his countrymen and, as time went by, of global consequence. Yet, while a reformer, he did not adopt the ultimate convictions or role of a crusader; although a 'teaching president' with the whole nation as his classroom, and a devotion to inform, explain and influence, his approach was more to foster new awareness than to try to mould his audience or sell truths-without-question. Certainly, in the political arena, calculated manipulation and frontal attack were both within his repertoire, and he probably enjoyed a skilful fight. Yet these were resources he evidently used quite selectively as, for example, with powerful adversaries and systems that thwarted reforms he strongly believed in. More than most, he seemed to have the capacity to separate the means necessary to make a large difference from the kinds and qualities of difference he sought to make. All in all, he seemed to endeavour less to govern than to strongly guide, less to demolish and build anew than to foster *re*newal and development, more to serve from strength than to make servants of others, and (not least) to listen almost as well as he spoke.

The responsive-initiator feature applies also to Carl Rogers and, granted differences in balance of component elements and the very different theatres of action of the two men, there is a remarkable degree of concordance in this further crucial aspect of Rogers' and Roosevelt's styles. Given their respective orbits and impact at the time, one might infer that Rogers was indirectly encouraged in the development of his own potent integration of responsive and initiating elements. Plausibly, there was 'permission' in the culture for the pattern described, which Roosevelt personified and probably strengthened.

9 *People to an extraordinary degree and scale experienced an actual relationship with Roosevelt, as became true also of Carl Rogers.* As mentioned, Franklin himself felt a vivid personalized awareness of his audience even in radio addresses, especially his fireside chats. Although speaking perhaps to 50 million people, there was no sense of a mass audience in his bearing, tone or natural expressive movements. In Frances Perkins' (1947: 61) observation: 'His face would smile and light up as though he were actually sitting on the front porch or in the parlor with them. People [listening] felt this and it bound them to him in affection.' Leuchtenburg (1963: 331) notes the view that people responded to the President with 'the kind of trust they would normally

express for a warm and understanding father who comforted them in their grief, or safeguarded them from harm. . . . From his first hours in office, Roosevelt gave people the feeling that they could confide in him directly.'[10] In the same passage, Mrs Roosevelt is cited as recalling later that people would stop her in the street to say they missed his conversations with them about *their* government, while Justice William Douglas observed that he made people feel they shared the Presidency.

Frances Perkins (1947: 6) mentions a young soldier standing outside the White House after news came of Roosevelt's death, who said in soliloquy, in her hearing, '"I felt as if I knew him". (A pause) "I felt as if he knew me – and I felt as if he liked me".' The same author's richly documented chapter entitled 'He liked people' includes the observation: 'With few exceptions, even people who regarded themselves as Roosevelt haters felt agreeable toward him in his presence. They could not resist his contagious fondness for people – all kinds of people' (1947: 68). In a generally more critical portrayal, Burns (1956: 477) speaks of his 'courage, joyousness, responsiveness, vitality, faith and above all, concern for his fellow man'.[11]

My contact with Rogers spanned a period of thirty-five years. Before meeting him, I felt a distinct sense of personal engagement through his books; finding later that this seemed to apply to most readers. Through the sharing quality of expression of his ideas and experience, illustrated by excerpts from many actual therapy encounters, I recall feeling some of my own experience more distinctly. In direct conversation with him, it seemed rare for people *not* to feel a special clarity of warmth and quality of meeting and of being met. His capacity also to make contact with a big audience usually was high. Two of my strongest early impressions of him were first, of remarkable congruency between the person-in-action and what he wrote and espoused, and second, of his capacity (in common with Roosevelt) to change gears and completely refocus his attention and corresponding communication, almost instantly. More broadly, he also came to be experienced as a facilitating father figure–friend by great numbers of people. By his own life's end, either in person or through his contacts and writing, he had touched the lives of countless individuals, and large numbers of people worldwide felt a connection or relationship with him.

Again, the qualitative parallelism between Rogers and the New Deal/World War II President is striking, although not presumed to be simple in its basis. The fact that Roosevelt's extraordinary influence and luminosity, and the

---

10 A secondary bit of evidence, both in keeping with the blend of responsive and initiating elements referred to, and reflecting the sense of actual relationship so widely felt, was the huge and sustained outpouring of letters received by Roosevelt, from people in all walks of life. In Hoover's time, one person handled the letters from constituents; while under Roosevelt the staff required for this purpose increased to fifty! (Leuchtenburg, 1963: 331).

11 Hatch's book *Citizen of the World* (1948) and Perkins' work *The Roosevelt I Knew* (1947) are studded with vignettes of his interaction with people, indicative of an unusually consistent friendliness and warmth, a rare keenness of personal perception, and a remarkable capacity for person-to-person contact over a wide range of individual styles and contexts.

climate of viewpoint and values he furthered, were so prominent within the larger environment in which the incubation and early development of Rogerian client-centred therapy occurred, suggest an influence in some form. One might speculate that the younger Carl, without sharp awareness of it, took heart from such a notable example of qualities in accord with his ideals and ambition. Put another way, the likely mechanism was a kind of osmosis, in which Rogers absorbed and built on the strongest example(s) in his milieu of qualities in keeping with his own tendency.

10 *Roosevelt, as well as Rogers, held an essentially optimistic view of human nature.* In the words of one biographer, Roosevelt believed 'in the ultimate goodness and reasonableness of all men' (Burns, 1956: 476). His natural inclination was to expect well of people, to trust them as individuals and, where he had some doubt, to believe that to treat them as reasonable and trustworthy would bring out and enhance their potentials in these ways. He was sharply conscious that the inherent divinity or goodness he believed in could be and frequently was deflected, distorted, or even warped beyond recognition – but seldom beyond retrieval (as I understand him), if only the way could be found.[12]

Rogers' correspondingly optimistic views of human nature and potential are visible throughout his writing and practice. A great part of his work can be interpreted as a search to identify and bring to ever-wider application basic conditions that are both healing to troubled or damaged individuals *and* ingredients for natural human growth and actualization. Already in his 1942 book, drawing on the 1940 paper which he identified as marking the birth of client-centred therapy, he wrote that the new approach, in contrast to earlier ones, 'relies much more heavily on the individual drive toward growth, health and adjustment. Therapy is not a matter of doing something *to* the individual. . . . It is instead a matter of freeing him for normal growth and development, of removing obstacles so that he can again move forward' (Rogers, 1942a: 29). Roosevelt's concordant attitude need not have influenced Rogers directly. More likely, it both expressed and supported a wider trend in the culture, part of the climate in which his viewpoint could and did vigorously flourish.

These ten aspects include the most distinct features of concordance I see between qualities of the New Deal or its primary architect, on the one hand and, on the other, basic aspects of Rogers' direction and style as his new

---

12 A heritage of liberal religious faith was part of Roosevelt's personal make-up. He was open to others holding different faiths or, like Hopkins, having no avowed religious convictions. Rogers both differed from him, in religious background, and was alike first, in his active acceptance of others holding different beliefs and, second, in his commitment to a value-system rooted in a Judeo-Christian ethic. The concern of both men, each from a privileged family and educational background, contained also a *noblesse oblige* element, through which any patronizing elements were largely washed out in the course of their respective developmental crises and journeys.

therapy clarified and took hold. There are numerous channels, as already suggested, through which the broad contextual support and more particular congruencies revealed could have worked. Overall, the indications of conducive influence on Rogers' advance, during the incubation and flourishing beginning of client-centred therapy, seem to me beyond reasonable doubt. The war years further challenged and opened the way for Rogers and furnish fascinating added evidence for what I have ventured to call the 'Roosevelt–Rogers connection'.

War for peace: vision and process; special needs and the new therapy

At his third inauguration as President, in January 1941, Roosevelt talked in simple depth and potent affirmation about democracy, stirring thoughtful listeners and readers across his own country and in many others. Citing him is irresistible:

> A nation, like a person, has a body – a body that must be fed and clothed and housed, invigorated and rested. . . .
>
> A nation, like a person, has a mind – a mind that must be kept informed and alert, that must know itself, that understands the hopes and needs of its neighbors.
>
> And a nation, like a person, has something deeper, something more permanent, something larger than the sum of its parts.

The 'something deeper', Roosevelt felt, was fundamentally a spirit and faith; especially, a search for freedom and faith in the way of democracy:

> The democratic aspiration is no mere recent phase in human history. It permeated the ancient life of early peoples. It blazed anew in the middle ages. It was written in Magna Carta.
>
> In the Americas its impact has been irresistible. . . . America has been the New World in all tongues, to all peoples . . . because those who came here believed they could create a new life – a life that should be new in freedom.
>
> That spirit – that faith – speaks to us in our daily lives. . . . It speaks to us from other nations of the hemisphere, and from those across the sea – the enslaved as well as the free. . . .
>
> In the face of great perils . . . our strong purpose is to protect and to perpetuate the integrity of democracy. (Zevin, 1946: 267–271)

Before 1941 was over, the United States was a combatant on a full war footing, and events had moved to lend even greater weight to Roosevelt's words. On a still-minor stage, Rogers was writing *Counseling and Psychotherapy* (1942a) and, in the opening chapter, relating his counselling approach to wartime needs – and to the preservation of democracy:

> Military morale, like industrial morale, rests to an important degree on satisfactory adjustments and satisfying human relationships. . . . Thousands of draftees and recruits find themselves facing new situations which are difficult for them to meet –

> new adjustments to authority, new social grouping, . . . and uncertainties regarding the future. (Rogers, 1942a: 9)

Rogers goes on to point out that while the majority can successfully adapt, 'many are unable to do so and become the disgruntled, the neurotic, the malcontent', with costly and destructive influences on morale. However, 'counseling could do much to help such individuals face their difficulties, assimilate them, and find integrating purposes which they might wholeheartedly follow' (ibid.: 9). As for the impact on those who participate in or face attack, he notes that:

> The psychological organization of the individual recoils in the face of the terrific stresses which are part of the present war, with its two added strains in the shape of mechanized warfare and 'the war of nerves'. Psychological counseling has much to offer in the reorientation and cure of many of these victims of mankind's war against itself. (ibid.: 10–11)

Rogers also mentions another level of hazard. Many characteristics of a democratic society are temporarily laid aside during war, and there is always some risk that the structures adopted may not be reversible. A substantial counselling program in accord with the new therapy would, he proposes, 'be a force in preserving the concept of personal integrity, and a significant symbol of the value which democracy puts on the fundamental importance and worth of each citizen' (1942a: 11). It was some four years later that Rogers and Wallen (1946: 23 – see head of this chapter) described client-centred therapy virtually as a child of American democracy – by implication, still intact.

Rogers had no role analogous to that of commander-in-chief in a great nation being drawn inexorably into a vast war, and could pursue a far more unified course than was possible for the President. The latter held in his own way to steady themes, however, one being to see the war as a route to a peace whose quality was his ultimate concern. In August 1941, Roosevelt left on a surprisingly timed 'fishing vacation' and he and Churchill finally met in person off Newfoundland. For the President, the principal achievements were the strong development of direct understanding and relationship between the two men, and the main document they jointly forged. This 'Atlantic Charter' expressed basic common aims and principles of an implicit partnership, principles encompassing Roosevelt's four freedoms concept, in the war-for-peace context. The language was concise: 'First, their countries [the US and UK] seek no aggrandizement, territorial or other'; and the substance far-sighted – 'Fifth, they desire to bring about the fullest collaboration between all nations . . . with the object of securing, for all, improved labor standards, economic adjustment and social security'; and, 'Eighth, they believe that all of the nations of the world, for realistic as well as spiritual reasons, must come to the abandonment of the use of force' (cited in Hatch, 1948: 30).

The Atlantic Charter gave form to purposes with which most allied nations could identify, and further clarified American intent in the now almost certain event of being formally at war. The turning point came with devastating suddenness and destruction, via the Japanese surprise attack on Hawaii on 7

December, coupled with new Japanese offensives in half a dozen other crucial centres in the Pacific region. Congress endorsed a declaration of war with Japan the next day and, a few days later, the US was officially at war with Germany and Italy. Accounts, studies and memoirs focusing on military actions and conduct of this war, without parallel in its total scale of destruction, are legion. I will touch on additional developments in the war itself and on preparations for peace, both to keep Roosevelt's role in view and because of their relevance to conditions at home; conditions that formed the matrix of need and opportunity within which Rogers' work and the new therapy moved swiftly through continued development and into prominence.

That Christmas, Churchill and Roosevelt met again. In the context of Pearl Harbor and other US losses and retreats, and the momentum and scale of the then invincible Japanese offensive in the Pacific, Churchill was astonished to find the President agreeing at once that Nazi Germany was the greater danger to the United States, too, and that he was ready to begin planning major counter-offensive action. A prepared-for step taken during this conference was that of linking the many countries, and governments in exile, now at war with the Axis powers, via a common declaration of principles in direct sequel to the Atlantic Charter. The new statement and grouping, by Roosevelt's inspiration, was called the Declaration of the *United Nations* (see Hatch, 1948: 234–238; *Encyclopaedia Britannica*, 1979, 19: 992).

Until mid-1942, powerful Japanese advances continued, to the point of occupation of virtually all countries and islands of the Western Pacific/South-East Asia region, north of Australia. Japan also held a huge area of Eastern China. Then in June, a very large-scale attack on the Midway Islands failed, at great loss to the Japanese attackers and navy. Later that year, Allied counter-offensives began to build up. Gradually, through innumerable battles and engagements at sea, on land and in the air, the invaders were forced step-by-step to retreat from particular territories and strongholds and most areas of ocean dominance. Frightful losses of life and an enormous toll of casualties through physical and psychic injuries occurred on both sides over an agonizing three-year period, a period that culminated in two of the bloodiest and most costly localized battles of the war, for the island bases of Iwo Jima and Okinawa.[13]

Notwithstanding the scope and ferocity of the Pacific War, and major differences that surfaced among Allied leaders and military commanders about how best to pursue the war against Germany and Italy, Roosevelt remained firmly committed to his Europe-first position and dominant in his capacity to resolve differences, or at the least to discover positions of acceptable compromise. Roosevelt and Churchill staged a meeting in Casablanca (Morocco) as soon as that area was firmly in Allied hands, dramatically indicating to the world an unexpected freedom of movement and degree of

13 More than 120,000 combatants were killed in Okinawa and there were immense material losses (Wish, 1966: 576-577). The consequences also were fateful in weighing the odds toward final use of the atomic bomb and against land invasion of mainland Japan. These decisions, and most of the Okinawa battle, occurred after Roosevelt's death.

security, within a region until then associated with Nazi dominance. After a year (1942) which had seen huge American losses through submarine attacks in the Atlantic, frequent throttling of Allied supply convoys elsewhere, and deadly German advances into the heartland of Russia, the new year conference was as tough and serious as it was dramatic.

Just before the Casablanca meetings, Roosevelt had delivered his annual State of the Union message to Congress and to his worldwide audience beyond. For the times, his picture was open and informative, ranging from factual aspects of the enormous gearing-up for total war in the previous year to some of the bureaucratic frustrations and other effects of this great transition – including an increase up from *two* to *seven* million persons in the US armed forces. Figures were given on the changing balance of power and the resulting turn toward offensive strategy. Commitment to a relentless drive for victory was linked with concern to maintain a clear vision of the ultimate purposes of the war. Half the speech centred on issues around the meaning of freedom, and the nature and achievement of an adequate, durable peace. 'I have been told', he said, 'that this is no time to speak of a better America after the war. I am told it is a grave error on my part. I dissent.' He returned to his Four Freedoms concept for the framing of his vision and concerns; focusing especially on freedom from want and from fear, and on conditions for these freedoms to prevail.

On returning from Casablanca, Roosevelt's report again reflected (in part) his fine tuning to inner frames of reference and to personal and more general meanings, together: 'Ask *them* what they are fighting for' he said of US servicemen, 'and each . . . will say: "I am fighting for my country." *Ask them what they really mean by that* and you will get what, on the surface, may seem to be a wide variety of answers'; answers expressing an individualized but common theme of fighting for freedom. With wider inference, deepening into prescience, he continued:

> Today the personal freedom of every American and his family depends . . . upon the freedom of his neighbors in other lands. *For today the whole world is one neighborhood.* That is why this war . . . has spread to every continent and most of the islands of the sea. . . . And unless the peace that follows recognizes [this] . . . and does justice to the *whole* human race, the germs of another World War will remain a constant threat to mankind. (Zevin, 1946: 355–356, italics added)

Nearly a year later, Roosevelt and Churchill journeyed to Teheran for a summit conference with Stalin.[14] In his radio address at home (December 24, 1943) following this meeting, the President pointed out that the US armed forces now numbered over *10 million* persons and, in another six months, 5 million would be serving overseas. He warned plainly against expecting a quick end to the war. In heart-rending ways, things would get worse before

---

14 En route to Teheran, from prior meetings in Cairo, and in apparently unplanned response to personal interest, Roosevelt gave instructions for his plane to fly low over Jerusalem and other centres of biblical and historical importance in the region, meanwhile identifying numerous features with delight (Hatch, 1948: 259–260).

they improved: 'The war', he said openly, 'is now reaching the stage where we shall have to look forward to large casualty lists – dead, wounded and missing. War entails just that. There is no easy road to victory. And the end is not yet in sight.' At the same time, he reiterated his profound concern for the quality and realism of provisions for the peace that eventually would be won; and pledged to do the utmost in his power toward the creation of effective conditions and structures for this peace.[15] Finally, after its long preparation, and with effects in keeping with Roosevelt's words, the Allied counter-invasion of Western Europe began, on 'D-Day' June 6, 1944. Fierce opposition was met with increasingly overwhelming force, in a vast campaign inevitably of shocking human cost. Armies building up to millions poured into Europe from the west, and were driving forward from the east.

In his own sphere, Carl Rogers also was very significantly occupied with the war, by 1944. His article 'Psychological adjustments of discharged service personnel', published at year's end (Rogers, 1944b), must have been prepared or finalized as the churning, tidal movement of armies in combat swept back through France and the Low Countries, and as the casualties mounted and more individuals finished their time in service. Rogers reported that already over one and a half million men had been discharged since the Pearl Harbor attack, and that great numbers sought some form of counselling assistance in the context of their transition back into the civilian world. The personal difficulties given special and vivid attention by Rogers included the frequent deep anger and pent-up hostilities of returning veterans; disturbances to self-esteem which a diagnostic approach to helping quite often exacerbated; a frequent loss of purpose in the more amorphous civilian context; a wide range of distressing problems in marriage and family relations; and the hardships of learning to live with physical handicaps. The article ends with a clear, practical statement of suggested helping principles.

That autumn (1944), with the war at its peak, and almost automatic renomination for the presidency, Roosevelt took the opportunity to speak out on issues vital to his overall mission, for example in presenting his Economic Bill of Rights concept (October 28, 1944 – see Zevin, 1946).[16] His final campaign speech, a week later, although tuned to the election context, again reached forward in wider vision:

---

15 In reference to the German people, he emphasized: 'We wish them to have a normal chance to develop, in peace, as useful and respectable members of the European family.' For this, an essential condition is 'to rid them once and for all of Nazism and Prussian militarism and the fantastic and disastrous notion that they constitute the "Master Race"' (see, e.g., Zevin, 1946: 383). Eight months after this speech, the first major conference pointing toward a new world organization concerned with conditions and structures for peace took place at Dumbarton Oaks. The work of this conference contributed directly to the eventual United Nations Charter.

16 These were 'economic' in the broadest sense: including the rights of social security as previously defined, specified rights to farmers and businessmen and the right (by implication) to fair wages for work, *and also* the right of employment and an adequate income, the 'right of every family to a decent home', 'the right of adequate medical care' and 'the right to a good education'. In spirited defence of his far-seeing vision, he argued that the 'impossible' had already been achieved, repeatedly since 1933, and that a just society demanded fulfilment of these rights. The statement was another expression of his ultimate concerns, which did not centre on the war.

> And around us we see an unfinished world – a world of awakened peoples struggling to set themselves on the path of civilization – people struggling everywhere to achieve a higher cultural and material standard of living.
>
> *I say we must wage the coming battle . . . for civilization on a scale worthy of the way we have unitedly waged the battles against tyranny and reaction . . .* we must wage it in association with the United Nations. (Zevin, 1946: 437–438, italics added)

Days later, the president was elected once more to the position he had now held for nearly twelve years.[17] Although he tried not to show it, age and the burdens of office by now had caught up with him. His campaign activity had been a heavy added drain, not the literally invigorating stimulus of the past. There was little let-up following the election, as he prepared for a crucial further summit conference with Churchill and Stalin, laboured with others on planning and negotiation over the projected permanent United Nations organization, and coped with his other roles in the context of the war – with Allied armies pressing on the borders of Germany itself and an escalating network of military power and offensives forcing the war against Japan.

Perkins reports that her first clear awareness that Roosevelt was seriously ill occurred in an encounter on the eve of his inauguration. She wrote: 'As I sat down beside him [to settle her own resignation, after three terms of Cabinet service] I had a sense of his enormous fatigue. He had the pallor, the deep grey color of a man who had been long ill. He looked like an invalid' (Perkins, 1947: 315). Nevertheless, he stood in apparent strength the next day to take the oath of office and deliver his short inaugural address, with his characteristic hopefulness reflected in the statement that 'the *trend* of civilization itself is forever upward' (Zevin, 1946: 438–439, italics added). Two days later, he sailed for the Yalta conference, in the faraway Crimea.

The first nights at sea were an ordeal for Franklin, although the total journey reduced his fatigue (Hatch, 1948: 278). The last part was by air and road and, in seaside Yalta, it was early spring. Experts disagree on the outcomes of the Crimea conference, partly according to the later time and angle from which it is viewed. While gruelling and exhausting for the President, the situation was climactic in its challenge. The official report of the conference (cited in Hatch, 1948: 303–307), a document in which Roosevelt's hand is clearly seen, was initially and widely greeted with enthusiasm, giving heart and hope even to most critical observers (Divine, 1967: 268).[18] On arriving home, the President gave his own account in characteristic style on the substance and

17 Also, in the coinciding elections 'voters split their tickets everywhere to retire senators and congressmen with isolationist records no matter what their party' (Hatch, 1948: 277).

18 Main foci of the Yalta meetings included (i) developing plans for the zoned post-war occupation and other provisions in regard to Germany, (ii) the working out of a wide spectrum of principles and arrangements (some not honoured by Stalin) in respect to Poland and other parts of Eastern Europe and the Balkan region, (iii) the hard-bought agreement for Russia to enter the War against Japan after Germany's defeat, and (iv) work on a spectrum of important issues regarding the United Nations. In respect to point (iii), the formidable prospect of ground invasion of Japan remained very real, with costs in lives estimated *to exceed the total US losses in the war to that stage.*

implications of the Yalta meetings (Zevin, 1946: 440–453). This was the last major address he actually presented. That March (1945), much of the activity at home centred on planning for the San Francisco conference on the United Nations, as agreed at Yalta but with much hard negotiation and debate still required to hammer out specifics of the charter.

Finally, Roosevelt went to rest in Warm Springs, preparing for the culminating meetings on the UN, in daily touch with developments at home and abroad (including the accelerating collapse of Germany), and then finalizing his Jefferson Day speech.[19] On March 12, sitting reading dispatches, Franklin suddenly complained of a 'terrific headache'. Within moments he was unconscious and death followed shortly through massive cerebral haemorrhage (Hatch, 1948: 298; Divine, 1967: 277). The nation was in shock, people wept in the streets, and many abroad felt his death as a personal blow and loss. A young congressman spoke for many: 'He was the only person I ever knew – anywhere – who was never afraid. God, how he could take it for us all' (Burns, 1956: 438).[20]

In his first inaugural address Roosevelt had asserted that 'the only thing we have to fear is fear itself'; and the ending of his last fully planned speech includes the echoing words, 'the only limit to our realization of tomorrow will be our doubts of today' (Zevin, 1946: 456). While referring to the war, his emphasis was on the aim and conditions for enduring peace: 'More than an end to war, we want an end to the beginnings of all wars – yes, an end to this brutal, inhuman and thoroughly impractical method of settling the differences between governments' (ibid.: 455). Of striking relevance in the present context, the words he would have spoken also included:

> Today we are faced with the pre-eminent fact that if civilization is to survive, we must *cultivate the science of human relationships* – the ability of all peoples, of all kinds, to live together and work together in the same world, at peace. (ibid.: 455–456, italics added)

The San Francisco meetings on the United Nations were held on schedule, with the nation still mourning its former President. Hitler's death and Germany's final capitulation occurred, as critical features and details of the UN Charter were being hammered out. The latter process continued intensively for two long months of debate, crisis, compromise and development, and the completed, agreed-upon Charter of the United Nations was born. In remarkable vindication of the late President's labour and vision, the US Senate ratified American membership with only three of ninety-six senators opposed. Via the fateful use of the atomic bomb (not assumed by Roosevelt in the negotiations with Russia at Yalta) the war with Japan ended much more quickly than expected. By early September, the world was formally at

19 Initially drafted for him by Archibald MacLeish.

20 In the simpler grieving words of a young soldier in France, 'It's like somebody dying in your own family.' A woman in New York, asked if she had heard the broadcast news, replied 'For what do I need a radio – It's on everybody's face' (from examples cited in Bonner, 1963: 306).

peace again, facing the enormous task of rehabilitation of many shattered nations, and millions of individuals deeply scarred by the horrors now behind them but still living within.

Carl Rogers (as mentioned) deferred taking up his new post at Chicago until the summer of 1945, in order to continue his intensive contribution to the development of counselling resources for returning veterans. Besides the emotional legacies of combat itself, a core issue in the difficult decompression process faced by these veterans would have been the transition from a highly organized, structurally authoritarian military system to a fluidly undefined (relatively nondirective) peacetime democracy. Most simply, the change was from a situation where there was nearly always someone to tell the individual what to do to a position where decisions were mostly up to the person him/herself. Whether the veteran had become directly dependent on external authority, or had accumulated feelings of revolt against authority, the central emphases of the new therapy were ideally suited to assist in the transition. An expression of the broad philosophy, from that time, reads as follows:

> One of the aims of this book is to challenge the counselor to think about the social implications of his counseling procedure and to point out the effectiveness of a democratically oriented client-centered approach as compared with the more authoritarian orientation of traditional counseling. (Rogers and Wallen, 1946: 24)

It is not feasible to continue this discussion of the broader milieu after the war, by which time client-centred therapy had become an established school. So far as the wartime period and its termination is concerned, conditions at home of particular relevance for the development of client-centred therapy may be summed up as follows:

◇ *There remained a close fit between Roosevelt's outlook together with special needs of the time, and Rogers' values and what his new counselling had to offer.* Most of the (ten) features already discriminated as providing a strongly conducive setting for the philosophy and form of Rogers' viewpoint and practice, remained salient. Rogers identified strongly with the liberal democratic tradition and ideals of his country and, in the context of the war, saw his work as directly harmonizing with and even helping to preserve the practices and freedoms associated with genuine democracy in this tradition. He accepted the war as a tragic reality that had to be gone through, and would have been supportive of most of Roosevelt's war- and peace-related goals. He advanced his counselling as an aid to morale (especially when used with servicemen whose anxieties and fears could also infect others) and as valuable to men stressed by combat but capable of going on. The therapy was seen as offering critical assistance both to persons affected as 'psychic casualties' and to those facing 'normal' problems of readjustment to civilian life.

◇ *The leadership qualities of statesman and psychologist had much in common.* Frances Perkins describes Roosevelt's qualitative influence in the war in terms that are strikingly in keeping with Rogers' then-evolving views of leadership (see Gordon, 1955) and his own way of being a leader in the Chicago Counseling Center. Perkins writes:

> To sum up Roosevelt's role in the War, I would say that he was the catalytic agent through whose efforts chaotic forces were brought to a point where they could be harnessed creatively. He was a creative and energizing agent rather than a careful, direct-line administrator. He trusted people to whom he gave a job, to do it. If they couldn't or wouldn't or didn't, he appointed someone else or gave part of it to someone else. (Perkins, 1947: 308)

Contrary to what did happen, it is in theory entirely possible that authoritarian political leadership might have surfaced in the extremity of total war, that human rights at home would have been greatly curtailed and abused – in fact, the only serious black mark seems to have been the enforced removal and virtual internship of Japanese-Americans from the West Coast region (see Bonner, 1963: 304-305). Also, priorities in the social welfare and human service spheres might have declined very sharply. These possible, but not actual, effects would have stifled the client-centred innovation.

◇ *The war was a time of social dislocation and new awareness of personal-emotional needs*. Personal costs of the war included separation of families and huge changes in the interpersonal worlds of a vast number of people, due both to military service and the labour demands of war-production industries. Among the multiple effects were frequent short courtships and long, formative separations. Many children were virtually fatherless from birth, or during an influential period in early childhood, and in a position of attenuated relationship with their working mothers. A decline in the numbers of students and male teachers in senior high-school and college/university settings brought associated changes in train (see Nash, 1971: 335–336). The roles of women in the working world, the economy, and in public life expanded greatly – although attitude change did not keep pace with practice. Important changes *toward* equality of opportunity and status for black citizens and other ethnic minorities occurred in military and employment contexts. Such changes increased the demand for and acceptance of counselling assistance in more versatile, practical and 'person-centred' forms than traditional psychotherapy.[21]

◇ *For many persons, the transition from war to peace involved stresses as great or greater than the war itself, and, seeking personal-emotional help was more accepted.* As earlier implied, the new therapy was to become unrivalled in its responsiveness and availability (through the United Service Organizations and other contexts) to discharged servicemen and women not under psychiatric care or intensive medical treatment. Further, the culture as a whole was undergoing major transition in the emerging post-war world, of which heightened personal psychological interest and awareness was an aspect. Emotional suffering, lack of a sense of meaning or direction, loneliness

---

21 A particular change noted was that families tended to become looser, more democratic units, 'in which each member contributed to the making of decisions' (Nash, 1971: 331). Expectations were altering and changes already taking place in the family were accelerated by the war. Nash, not a psychologist but a historian, points out that psychological counselling as well as legal aid and other selected human services expanded responsively during the war period.

and felt deficiency in relationships with others, were all less acceptable, less taken-for-granted than before. And in some ways these problems were growing as rootedness in extended family and close community systems declined. Thus, more people experienced both the need and possibility of change in themselves. The more actively they themselves sought relief and change, the more suited the new therapy was to their needs.[22]

◇ *Aid to veterans under post-war legislation included special support for those interested in undertaking university studies, often in the human sciences.* In their own search for meaning, including more informed understanding of human and societal behaviour, many were drawn to the psychological and social science sphere. Of these, more than a few were individuals for whom a philosophy centred on the person and on the issues emphasized by Rogers was particularly attractive in respect to values, their own needs and/or a desire to help others. Thus, the surge of educational and professional interest among veterans contributed to the momentum of the post-war development of client-centred therapy. By the time the conservative swing in social and political thought took place (during the Eisenhower presidency, for example), the Rogerian school was strongly established and recognized, and powered by its own visibility and achievement to continue its course amid the more conservative currents then visible in psychology and other human science fields.

A whole book could be devoted to the topics explored in these last two chapters, and the new mapping is illustrative, not exhaustive. Collapsed into one theme, my view is that the larger social, political and economic milieu, especially during Roosevelt's presidency during the 1930s and war years, was enormously important for the incubation and the early flourishing development and impact of the Rogerian client-centred innovation. Moreover, even in the same period of history but under conditions prevailing elsewhere in the world, it is difficult to imagine the same fertilization occurring. If one thinks of Europe, Britain at the time, other countries, there is no other plausible context for an equivalent school of thought and practice to arise *and* rapidly assume such ascendancy.

If there is one general aim to this chapter it is to entice the reader to share in the venture of connecting particular innovations to the larger tapestry of circumstance and influence under which they form and flourish. To do this is to leave well-beaten tracks of method and find a problem-centred working pathway across disciplines and domains of interest. To me, this enterprise has been deeply absorbing, rich in new learning, strong in challenge as in its demands. To inquire without *set* boundaries is very much in keeping with the client-centred innovation; a system on whose specific, unfolding content it is now high time to focus.

---

22 It is surely significant that the two non-English-speaking countries in which client-centred therapy had greatest impact in the fifties and sixties were Japan and Germany, where the cultural systems had been most authoritarian, and where counterbalancing new belief systems and views of *human* nature were desperately needed.

PART II

THE NEW VISION UNFOLDING

4

Contours of the School Phase of Client-Centred Therapy

> The development of the Counseling Center – its staff, its therapeutic principles, its research, its administrative procedures – was a most exciting process. I believe I learned more and contributed more during the twelve years at the Center (1945–1957) than at any other period. I learned to set the staff free, to make all of us jointly responsible for the work of, the welfare of, and the future of the Counseling Center. It was a period in which our basic views about the helping relationship came to fruition.
>
> Carl Rogers, 1967a

As the world awoke from the real-life nightmare of the war, and nations and individuals turned to confront the difficult challenges of healing and peace, very significant transitions for people were occurring everywhere. Besides changes visibly resulting from war and the outbreak of peace, other developments were connected to this wider flow in more complex ways. One such was Carl Rogers' move, planned the year before, to the University of Chicago. The transition in this instance involved shifting to a related setting, with continuity of direction but vital new dimensions of challenge and opportunity. The most immediate new feature was the provision for Rogers to proceed at once to establish his own counselling centre; a centre whose mission, combining service, training and research, would also involve radical experimentation in leadership and organization.

Rogers' counselling centre: embodiment and base for innovation

Almost a year before he actually moved to Chicago, Rogers first put pen to paper to record his views for University officials regarding the proposed centre. Expressing himself firmly, the centre already present in his mind's eye, he wrote:

> It is the purpose of the student counseling organization to deal with the student as a total individual. There is no attempt to treat the individual as a bundle of separate parts – educational problems, vocational problems, social problems, etc. There is a clear recognition that difficulties in adjustment are difficulties in adjustment of the whole individual.
>
> It is not the purpose of the counselor to assume responsibility for the life of the student. . . . Neither is it the purpose of the counselor to control the student's environment. . . . Rather the counselor provides a situation in which the student may work out clearly and independently the adjustment to his college experiences and to later life which is realistic for him and which satisfies his own desire for increasing maturity. (Rogers, 1967a: 363–364)

The author went on to emphasize, in conclusion, that the counselling organization's success would not lie in the elaborateness of its record-keeping or formal elements of its structure. Rather, success would hinge on 'the feeling of the student that he has achieved a satisfying plan of action for himself' (ibid.: 364). As the new centre actually evolved, through the second half of the 1940s, formally as a laboratory wing of the Psychology Department but partly funded from the Dean of Students' Office, its mission included service to the general community as well as to students. This both enriched the education and training function and made it possible for research to be based on a wider clientele than students alone would have provided.

Besides developing the new counselling centre in ways attractive to venturesome younger faculty, and that were a magnet to graduate student colleagues, Rogers was active on other fronts. These included leadership in professional affairs (notably as President of the American Psychological Association in 1946/47), and activities following on from his contribution to counselling programs for veterans. Increasingly, his sustained and eloquent writing was reaching distant audiences and, during the middle and late forties, his vigorous band of associates began to make significant contributions in their own right. For example, important books were written in this period by other members of the Counseling Center group, including Axline (1947), Snyder (1947a) and Porter (1950). Other colleagues contributed chapters to Rogers' new work *Client-Centered Therapy* (1951), then and for a long time the most complete and mature exposition of his approach. Concurrently, the flow of doctoral studies and other research and expository reports mounted strongly.

By 1951, the momentum of the new school had reached a very high level, and the decade of the fifties may be considered the heyday of client-centred therapy as a distinct, cohesive, rapidly evolving and outstandingly productive school of thought, practice and research. During this period the system ceased to belong only to its place of origin but became international in influence, outlook and membership. At least five years subtracted from the beginning of the fifties, and no more than five years added to the end, embraces what may be appropriately regarded, in my estimation, as the School Phase of Rogerian psychotherapy in its country of origin. Elsewhere, Rogers' work was not influential so soon, and a 'School Phase' may be less apparent locally, or not follow the same time frame.[1]

During its phase as a unified school, client-centred therapy flourished through the quality, timeliness and clarity of its innovations, the resourcefulness and energy of its founder and linked band of other exponents, and the unforced consistency of direction. Carl Rogers remained the natural leader, most luminary advocate and pivotal integrating influence in the movement he had started. Most visible new developments originated with the group centred at the University of Chicago and, after Rogers moved to the University of Wisconsin in 1957, evolution occurred in both settings. There was in this overall period a quality of strongly experienced identification with a value stance, a distinct although evolving theoretical viewpoint, and (most of all in the Chicago group) a mode of helping practice of a sharply defined and highly consistent nature.

Adherents of the client-centred school who had worked or trained with Rogers or with his previous close associates and students, generally experienced a strong personal and professional sense of belongingness with others in this circle. Rogers' own immensely communicative and articulate writing, published in many contexts, and the generally searching, original and often eloquent presentations of other 'Rogerians', also attracted substantial interest in a growing circle of readers beyond the field of professional counselling or the boundaries of active membership of the school.

The idea of fixed doctrine or ideology, or of disciples literally following in the footsteps of the master, was out of keeping with Rogers' philosophy and value system. The labels 'non-directive', 'client-centred', 'group-centred' and, in later years, 'person-centred', are associated with principles and modes of practice designed to release inner forces or tendencies toward integrative healing, growthful development, and enhancement of autonomy and creativity. Given these emphases and the increasing geographic dispersal of original members of the client-centred group, and the development and influence of their student associates in turn, it was inevitable that client-centred therapy would tend to diversify rather than to remain a highly cohesive school. As an approach *under one name* its influence has waned in the 'post-school' period. As a discernible but many-sided movement, with over a half century of substantial history, it embraces a still-widening circle.[2]

---

1 The publication year of *Counseling and Psychotherapy* (1942) seems to me the earliest date at which it could be said that a new school was visibly in the making around Rogers' work. This development became quite clear in the later war years, certainly by the time of Rogers' move to Chicago. Two decades later, with Rogers by then in California in a new phase of his career, and dispersed former students pursuing their own courses, the school (as further noted) was loosening and starting to diversify. Where a School Phase can be distinguished elsewhere – in Germany, say – its emergence probably occurred in the 1950s or later. In some regions (South America, even in Britain) Rogers' work did not have a visibly large impact or generate a substantial local movement until after the unified phase in the United States had ended.

2 Except in specific reference to psychotherapy, the term 'client-centred' has now been largely supplanted by the more inclusive term 'person-centred' – this itself a 'post-school' development slow to find favour with some wings of the movement.

This circle overlaps and influences other-named areas in the helping field, in many contexts. These include counselling and clinical psychology, humanistic psychology, psychiatry and social work, the field of educational guidance and education itself, pastoral psychology and family counselling, aspects of nursing and medical practice, small-group work and the encounter and support group movements, organizational and community development in their human relations aspects, conflict resolution and peace studies, and concepts and methods of inquiry in the behavioural sciences!

The client-centred school evolving: ten landmark features

A number of important sub-phases and milestone developments, in which Rogers' work stands out but is strongly complemented by other exponents and contributors to client-centred therapy, may be distinguished during the School Phase. The following synopsis of this course of development is both a self-contained summary within its time frame and a prelude to the remainder of this volume.

Refinement of nondirective-reflective psychotherapy

In a searching early examination of nondirective therapy and its precursors, Raskin (1948) described Rogers' special contribution in very cogent terms. The practice-relevant achievements included, first, his introduction into therapy of systematic use of the recognition of feeling response. Second, by this means, 'he gave to the Rankian "client-as-central figure" philosophy a definite technique, which Rank, Taft and Allen had pronounced impossible' (Raskin, 1948: 104). Third, 'he gave a new, more exact and deeper meaning to the concept of "acceptance" of the client'. Fourth, the therapist centred on the client's frame of reference with the singular and delimited purpose 'of providing deep understanding and acceptance of the attitudes consciously held at this moment by the client as he explores step by step into the dangerous areas he has been denying to consciousness' (Rogers cited by Raskin, 1948: 104–105. Also in Rogers, 1949a: 86).[3]

The emphasis on refining and 'purifying' the meaning and method of non-directive-reflective therapy remained the central issue in client-centred therapy practice into the early 1950s. More concretely, the focus was on accompanying the client with continuous, accepting recognition of his/her feelings and personal meanings, by means of reflective restatement and clarification of these feelings and signified meanings. Snyder's *Casebook of Non-Directive Counseling* (1947a) is a further classic record of this emphasis, consisting primarily of annotated interview transcripts from the work of five therapists.

---

3 This passage appears never to have reached print, as had been expected, in Rogers' 1946 (or 1947) articles in the *American Psychologist*.

Research studies, particularly those of Snyder (1945) and Seeman (1949), also reflect this focus of interest and provide direct evidence that the frequency of non-directive responses by Rogerian therapists rose through the 1940s, while lead-taking, directive and 'semi-directive' statements diminished correspondingly.

In *Client-Centered Therapy* (1951) Rogers gives his most full-bodied portrayal of the rationale and process of reflective therapy, in which the counsellor's responses are targeted consistently on the internal frame of reference and experiencing of the client. In addition, however, his account reveals an incipient but very important shift in emphasis. While the way the therapist proceeded (at the level of his verbal, responsive behaviour) remained central, Rogers also emphasized strongly that this behaviour needed to be supported and accompanied by a genuinely client-centred attitude; more specifically, by a view of persons, a value-system, sensitivity and expressive style that corresponded with the overt behaviour. How the therapist experienced him/herself and felt toward the client, and the relationship of these to overt behaviour, were discussed directly as growing-edge issues among client-centred therapists. In a 1952 article, Raskin advanced further in the same direction:

> Very recently, many therapists with a client-centered orientation have been groping for a formulation of counselor attitudes which will go beyond the possession of a genuine client-centered attitude. There is an attempt here to see the counselor as a whole person, in the therapeutic relationship. (Raskin, 1952: 240)

Other ideas and formulations cited in the same article indicate even more sharply that some client-centred writers had begun to focus strongly on the therapist's experience and personal functioning in the helping relationship. In retrospect, it is clear that a new way of viewing the importance of the therapist's frame of reference and expressiveness in therapy was emerging. Nondirective-reflective psychotherapy had reached its peak and very significant modifications were in the wind.

Research begins: the study of pattern in the interview process

The essential issue providing the main starting point of substantial research effort by client-centred investigators was: what is the operational substance of therapy itself, in terms of the content and structure of events in the sequence of client–therapist meetings? Is it *a* phenomenon in the sense that there are consistent patterns that form meaningful regularities, in the behaviour of the interview participants and sequential unfolding of the process? The most representative set of studies in this first, descriptive-inductive phase of interview-process analysis was published in 1949, as an entire issue of the *Journal of Consulting Psychology* (vol. 13, no. 3).

This composite report, of the 'Parallel Studies Project', opens with a uniquely informal and lively 'non-objective introduction' by Carl Rogers. He reveals the underlying story of the research in some of its most human dimensions, including the sheer frustrations of getting fully recorded and transcribed cases with relatively primitive equipment, and the suspense and excitement around results. Ways in which the 'interlocking' component studies actually unfolded, and some of the connecting questions they answered and raised, are pictured. Two broad outcomes were the strengthened conviction that 'it can be done – therapy can profitably be investigated by scientific means' (Rogers, 1949b: 152); and, a shift in outlook from reliance on a particular view of truth toward an allegiance to processes 'by which truth may gradually be approximated' (153).

The mentioned journal issue was itself a co-operative project. Raskin (1949b) introduces the specific data source and general strategy of the overall project, and its experimentally crude but ground-breaking studies. A classic study of process, reported by Seeman (1949), focuses on the analysis of counsellor technique (now 85 per cent 'non-directive' in form) and also of client content categories, such as problem descriptions and insight statements, and client feeling categories including positive and negative attitude expressions toward the self, the counsellor, and other persons and situations. The work by Sheerer (1949) examines clients' expressions of self-acceptance and respect, and of acceptance of others, and found that these expressions increased during the course of therapy, and that they were intercorrelated. Stock's related study focuses on feelings toward the self and others (1949). Haigh (1949) and Hoffman (1949) report on defensiveness and maturity of behaviour, respectively, from client statements over the course of therapy. One study examines pre–post outcome data – foreshadowing the next main focus and phase of client-centred research (Carr, 1949). The main substance and implications of the work are finally drawn into a composite whole, by Raskin (1949a).[4]

The development of self-theory

As the above-mentioned investigation of the content and patterning of events in therapy interviews proceeded, a related current of development was flowing and gathering force. To explain and adequately connect the events of therapy, a view of human personality was needed. The events themselves were highly suggestive in regard to fundamental aspects of personality. The temptation was great, and literal theory-building began. The first major fruit of this work, presented as a general theory of personality, forms the last chapter of *Client-Centered Therapy* (Rogers, 1951). The core of this theory is articulated in nineteen interlocking propositions, the first group of which focuses on posited basic properties of the human organism. Important examples are that this organism reacts as an organized whole to its perceptual field, apprehended as 'reality'; and that as a whole it has one basic motivational tendency, to actualize, maintain and enhance itself.

---

4 Interested readers will find a much fuller account of the Parallel Studies in Chapter 12.

Further theoretical propositions deal centrally with the origins, properties and functions of the self. Proposition 9, for example, indicates that the self is a portion of the individual's total perceptual field which becomes discriminated as 'me', 'I', 'myself', and in development is differentiated to an increasing degree from the environment of 'non-self'. Immediately following principles are concerned with ways in which the self-structure is formed and the processes by which it then affects, and is affected by, future experience and behaviour. A core proposition is that, in adults, 'most of the ways of behaving which are adopted by the organism are those which are consistent with the concept of self' (Rogers, 1951: 507). This in turn leads to more differentiated principles of relationship between the self-concept and behaviour.

The development of self-theory had begun with Raimy's (1943) dissertation and was visibly evolving by the time of Rogers' address in 1947, as retiring President of the American Psychological Association, on the topic 'Some observations on the organization of personality'. The idea that the individual's perception of self and environment might literally be the key to understanding behaviour was the radical nucleus of what was gelling in Rogers' thought. Soon, it was possible to say, more specifically, that 'the client's concept of self is now believed to be the most central factor in his adjustment and perhaps the best measure of his progress in therapy' (Raskin, 1948: 105).[5]

The mentioned articles (1949) by Elizabeth Sheerer and by Dorothy Stock, focus directly on self-attitudes and feelings; and Hogan's dissertation (1952) as well as Haigh's report (1949) effectively drew on the developing self-theory. Rogers' nineteen-proposition statement was a further order of development and established his school of therapy as a new source of an articulated, psychological perspective on human personality.[6] Further research focusing on the self-concept, in the 1950s and 1960s, notably by John Butler and collaborators, further illuminated the nature and functional significance of the self-concept, self-ideal and related constructs and variables (see Butler and Haigh, 1954; Butler, 1968). Rogers' most systematic statement of his overall theory (1959a), in the mammoth series *Psychology: A Study of a Science*, also pivots on principles relating to the self and self-change. The next chapter of this book pictures the theoretical base of the client-centred system in full.

---

5 Raskin's 1948 article, as a whole, is of interest still. It includes a closely documented exploration of the approaches of prominent precursors of the new nondirective therapy; with attention to Freud's practice learnings and a focus on the work of Otto Rank, Jessie Taft and Frederick Allen (also see my Chapters 8 and 16). Raskin was perhaps the first to stress the importance of nondirective *attitudes*, as distinct from technique.

6 The standing and visibility of Rogers' work took another spurt, with his article in the *Scientific American* (1952a). 'Psychotherapy' is in the title but the substance is mainly an accessible story-sketch of the foundation phase of therapy research, and the emergence of focus on the self.

Special applications: therapy with children and in groups

Rogers had in his first book (1939) discussed various approaches to therapy with children, with whom so much of his early clinical experience was gained. Written during the incubation of his own distinctive approach, the author's account of expressive therapies with children is of the greatest warmth, and bears clearest relation to later developments. He includes illustrations from clinic records at the time, especially records of therapeutic free play sessions forming an adjunct to work with the child's school and/or family. Aspects highlighted by Rogers include the expression and release of pent-up feelings toward family members, teachers and others, thus reducing hostility and resentment, and bringing in train other changes in actual life relationships. Another identified effect is the relief from guilt, especially around strong, 'bad' feelings.

Development of nondirective play therapy followed quickly on the establishment of the Counseling Center in Chicago; and by 1947, one of Rogers' students and colleagues, Virginia Axline, had published her book *Play Therapy: The Inner Dynamics of Childhood*, destined to be a classic in its field. Axline described her work 'as a presentation of the implications of the non-directive process for play therapy and for education' (Axline, 1947, preface). This presentation is a vividly practical manual, knit together by the consistent philosophy and technique, the author's intrinsic commitment and open-eyed caring for children, and her expository powers. Besides focusing on the principles and practice of therapy in special playroom settings, she illustrates applications of the same principles in school classroom contexts (already, in 1947!), and provides extensive session excerpts from both individual and group play therapy.

The next important work is a long chapter on client-centred play therapy by Elaine Dorfman (1951). Extensions in practice, further developments in theory, and the beginnings of systematic research in play therapy are reflected in Dorfman's more tightly written account. Moustakas' early work (1953), contributions by Ellinwood in the mid-fifties and later, and Axline's remarkable case-study of her therapy with 'Dibs' (1964), were among other important contributions during the School Phase. Chapter 8 of the present volume includes expanded study and illustration of the client-centred contribution to child therapy through this period and beyond. My introduction, next, to client-centred group therapy is followed up in depth, in Chapter 9.

'Group-centred' (more accurately, group member-centred) therapy came into distinct view with publication of Hobbs' (1951) forty-page chapter on this topic, in *Client-Centered Therapy*. Following experience with special groups, ranging from young children to war combat veterans, university students composed the main clientele in the therapy groups Hobbs centres on. He proceeds at once to express a theme that comes up in various ways throughout his careful statement. In the group context, 'this multiplication of the number of participants means more than the extension of individual therapy to several persons at once; it provides a qualitatively different experience with unique therapeutic potentialities' (Hobbs, 1951: 278). While the author clearly demonstrates differences from the vantage point of group members – such, for example, as the opportunity to become co-therapists for one another – he does not point to distinctive, added dimensions in the way the therapist works. Little attention was devoted to this latter issue until the development of encounter therapy in the sixties.

Hobbs was able to draw on one directly relevant published research report and three other connected studies that appeared as a composite report the following year (Gorlow, Hoch and Telschow, 1952). These investigators' principal data consisted of the complete transcripts of fifty-seven fully recorded therapy sessions, taken from three different, long-running groups! In spite of the strong beginning reflected in Hobbs' work, group therapy in the client-centred mode did not receive the same attention and visibility as individual therapy, until encounter groups entered the picture and helped to usher in the post-school era (see Chapter 9).

In the mid-1960s, encounter therapy, and the sensitivity training/encounter group movement came strongly into view as a major new focus of Rogers' own work and the work of others sharing his orientation. A study at the transition point, formally focusing on group therapy (Berzon, Pious and Farson, 1963), was indicative of the fine line between group therapy and 'basic encounter' (Rogers, 1967e). Theoretical writing and research on the intensive group process beyond formal therapy emerged as the School Phase of this system was yielding to less closely linked and more varied development.

The focus on therapy outcome: does it work?

By the early 1950s therapy research data were being collected, in the University of Chicago Counseling Center, in multi-purpose 'blocks' for grant-supported programs of investigation, as well as for use in more independent studies. The first major, multi-study project to be formally designed as a whole, was devoted primarily to the investigation of therapy outcome. By now it was clear that client-centred therapy was a consistently patterned phenomenon in terms of the interview behaviour of the participants. Systematic knowledge was accumulating in regard to the 'interior' characteristics of therapy but its specific 'exterior' consequences were relatively uncharted. It was possible and timely to seek to remedy this limitation.

The first major fruit of the new focus was the now-classic volume *Psychotherapy and Personality Change*, edited by Rogers and Dymond (1954). A team of investigators reported varied studies based on a common data pool, of changes in personal functioning with and without an intervening therapy experience. Some clients served as their own controls, being tested at the beginning and end of a two-month interval before therapy began, as well as at the end of therapy and six to twelve months later. A partially matched control sample of 'normal' volunteers not in therapy was tested at the same intervals as the sample of therapy clients.

Component projects in this ground-breaking program include studies of self-concept change, personality change based on Thematic Apperception Test (TAT) data and theory, change in social attitudes, and change in emotional maturity, the latter using information from friends of each client as well as from the clients themselves. In overall trend the findings are positive regarding therapy outcome, while also leading to more differentiated questions. Two case studies, each drawing in depth both on interview content and research data, are illuminating examples, respectively, of success and of failure in individual cases. In his concluding overview Rogers' own summation is that 'the research sets forth for the first time objective evidence that one defined approach to psychotherapy produces certain measurable and significant changes in the individual coming for help and that certain other changes which have also been hypothesized failed to occur in significant degree' (Rogers and Dymond, 1954: 433). Chapter 12 in this volume returns to the topic of research on client-centred therapy outcomes, for much closer examination.

Emergent new concepts: unconditional positive regard and congruence

In 1954, an important *theoretical* PhD thesis in psychology (then a rarity) was completed by a student of Rogers. The study (Standal, 1954) postulated a basic 'need for positive regard' in human beings; and developed a careful schema of connecting explanatory ideas and constructs. A further core concept was that of 'unconditional positive regard'. Simply stated, this refers to a felt attitude of respect and caring for another person with no 'strings' attached; a non-judgemental 'prizing' of the other as a whole person. Related earlier concepts, not interwoven in close-knit theory, were acceptance and warmth. Unconditional positive regard of the counsellor toward his/her client was advanced as a basic ingredient of the therapeutic relationship, a concept which was rapidly incorporated into the thinking and language of other client-centred workers. It became a nuclear component, as will be seen, in the evolving theory of change; and later found its way into the language, if not the practice, of most people formally training in the personal helping field. Standal did not publish his dissertation but his sponsor, Carl Rogers, at once adopted the concept and term, and his writing became the main vehicle of its dissemination.[7]

About the time that Standal was completing his thesis, another major new concept in therapy had begun to germinate, under the name 'congruence'. Used initially in reference to consistency between the perceived actual self, and the ideal or wanted self, the term began to take on another meaning as a core quality of counsellor presence in the therapy relationship. During the mid-fifties the quest to refine the idea and stress the importance of therapists being themselves, not contrived in their response but expressive, genuine persons in their therapeutic mode and context, culminated in the deepened new meaning and usage of the concept of congruence (Rogers, 1956, 1957a). Referring

7 The first direct published mention I know of, by Rogers, of 'unconditional positive regard' is in his 1956 article 'Client-centered therapy: a current view', probably written in 1955. One can see in this work that his pivotal 'conditions' formulation (1957a) is almost within grasp.

now to consistency within the person in the sense that (i) his/her underlying experience, (ii) conscious perceptions, and (iii) outward behaviour, all matched or were of one piece, the congruency of the therapist in the therapy interaction was also postulated as a fundamental therapeutic ingredient. It was not assumed that well-functioning therapists would always be congruent in their everyday life relationships. More plausibly, there would be episodes of avoidant guardedness or reactive-protective response now seen as counter-productive in a therapy relationship.

From a practical standpoint, the emphasis was on therapists *not being incongruent* with their clients. Lack of congruence would be associated, for example, with unclear or mixed messages from the therapist, less accurate discrimination of the client's feelings, and reduced trust, self-disclosure and self-exploration on the client's part. From its first clear articulation, personal congruence was seen as being of basic significance in interpersonal communication and facilitation generally, not only in therapy (Rogers, 1957c).

The conditions and 'equation' of therapy

As early as 1946, Rogers presented a major paper clearly embodying the idea of an 'equation of therapy', without using that term. In this substantial but somewhat neglected article, he set forth a set of six 'conditions' of therapist attitude and behaviour which, he argued, led predictably to a pattern of described qualities of therapy process and outcome. The listed conditions, in effect, called on therapists to view their clients as basically responsible for themselves and motivated by their own drive for (self-actualizing) development and change; to create a warm, accepting, safely non-judgemental atmosphere; where necessary, to set limits on behaviour but not on attitudes and feelings; to respond with 'deep understanding of the emotionalized attitudes expressed . . . [especially, by means of] sensitive reflection and clarification of the client's attitudes'; and not to engage in actions such as probing, blaming, interpreting, reassuring or persuading (Rogers, 1946). The author went on to say that 'if these conditions are met' then it is generally the case that changes of the kinds he outlined, both in client process in therapy and in behaviour beyond therapy, will occur (416). This early statement foreshadowed to a remarkable degree one of the most outstanding milestones in Rogers' own writing, the client-centred school and, quite possibly, the history of psychotherapy.

Ten years after his 1946 article (and without reference to it) Rogers formulated his now-classical statement of the 'necessary and sufficient conditions of therapeutic personality change' (Rogers, 1957a). The intervening decade of theoretical development and research had set the stage for a full-fledged explanatory focus on the issue of what generated and sustained a healing or constructive change process in therapy. In his breakthrough statement Rogers proposed that if a few specified, primary conditions exist in the client–therapist relationship, an orderly, definable process will be set in motion, leading to a predictable pattern of outcomes. These conditions, elaborated in my next chapter, include the qualities of therapist congruence, unconditional positive regard and empathy, a communicative process through which these qualities become visible to *and are perceived by* the client, and also the client attribute of anxiety or vulnerability.

The author made it clear that his hypotheses referred to psychotherapy generally not just client-centred therapy. Controversy, even furore, as well as intense interest, occurred widely in relevant professional circles. A whole new phase of research opened up, beginning with dissertation studies by Halkides (1958) and the present writer (Barrett-Lennard, 1959), aimed at testing and refining the new conception. Implications for practice, in a wide range of helping situations, were articulated. The conception has remained highly influential. Much more will be said about this theory, its research investigation and elements of refinement, in the course of this volume.

Level of client process in the helping context

In 1956, the American Psychological Association honoured Rogers and, indirectly, the client-centred school, with one of its first Distinguished Scientific Contribution awards. Presentation of the award involved an invited address to the APA the following year, at which Rogers chose to launch his newly formulated 'process conception of psychotherapy' (Rogers, 1958c). This and the more fully worked out statements that soon followed it comprise another main development (Rogers, 1959b, 1961b; Walker, Rablen and Rogers, 1960). Essentially, the process conception is a systematic description of individual differences in personal functioning observed in a relatively constant relationship environment. The broad constancy is that the individual is psychologically 'received', in terms of the mentioned conditions of therapy as offered by the therapist.

Rogers' definition of the process continuum, and his careful account of the spectrum of distinguishable levels or stages of functioning, grew in large part from his own process of sustained, reflective 'immersion' in interview recordings from different clients and stages in therapy. The overall direction of change he discriminated was from a fixed, closed, self-perpetuating mode of functioning to a state of fluid, open but integrated changingness; briefly, from a condition of stasis to one of process. This basic direction was reflected in distinct component aspects of functioning, seven such 'strands' being initially distinguished. The strands concerned with manner or 'level' of experiencing, with the role and nature of personal constructs, with the individual's way of expressing and dealing with problems, and with his/her manner of relating in therapy, became foci of research in their own right (Rogers, Gendlin, Kiesler and Truax, 1967).

The process conception and directly related work by Gendlin (1961a), Tomlinson and Hart (1962) and others, provided the major foundation for study of in-therapy process during Rogers' Wisconsin years. The whole approach and substance of this work is quite different from the early interview process research by Snyder (1945) and in the Parallel Studies Project (Raskin, 1949b). This shift reflects the rapid evolution of knowledge and investigative methods rather than any basic change in scientific interest or in the underlying metasystem of values and view of human nature. The process conception as articulated by Rogers, while influential in its time, has not retained the visibility, or generated nearly the research activity that his therapy conditions theory has done. A major component aspect, the experiencing scale, developed and refined by Gendlin and colleagues, remains directly important. However, the conception was an influential part of a movement in thought toward viewing the person in process ways rather than as an entity or end-product. I will return to the concept, its application in research (Chapter 13), and its legacies.

Client-centred therapy with schizophrenic persons

Soon after Rogers moved to Wisconsin, he was joined by Eugene Gendlin, then a recent student-associate and graduate from Chicago, whose original work was already beginning to make its mark in the client-centred school. Gendlin and Rogers, joined by others, undertook the development of a massive study of psychotherapy with hospitalized schizophrenic patients. Most client-centred workers had little prior experience with psychotic individuals, and the opportunity for intensive, carefully researched application of his therapy with schizophrenic clients was one of the attractions to Rogers in his decision to move to Wisconsin. His academic teaching affiliation with the Department of Psychiatry and association with the Wisconsin Psychiatric Institute also gave opportunity for involvement in psychiatric training, residency and research programs, and for pushing out the boundaries of his own experience and knowing.

Within two or three years, important articles from this added context of practice, theory and research with schizophrenic clients, were being published. Memorable among these, in terms of sensitivity and impact on the reader, is a paper by John M. Shlien, another leading exponent of the client-centred viewpoint and member at the time of the Chicago group. Shlien's article concludes with a richly documented case-study of psychotherapy with a deeply disturbed hospitalized client (1961). Articles by Rogers (1961c) and by Gendlin (1963), at about the same time, also included direct and sensitive portrayals of the human condition of the schizophrenic person.

The 'schizophrenia' project ran throughout the period of Rogers' Wisconsin years and beyond, finally receiving full publication in a major, multi-authored volume from the University of Wisconsin Press (Rogers et al., 1967), nine years after concentrated planning for the study had begun. The results overall suggest that psychotherapy in the client-centred mode was crucially helpful with some at least of the 'chronic' or long-term schizophrenic patients. However, gaps in the projected data, and the complexity in pattern of specific results, work against generalizations for the total sample. The work is more of a milestone in respect to the conduct and reporting of research in its complex sphere, and in the development of strategies and instrumentation, than in terms of clear-cut findings from fully tested hypotheses.

The long duration of the project was not due solely to its complexity. The research team suffered vicissitudes and crises around delegated management, individual ambitions and physical dispersal of team members. Remarkably, the working integration necessary to complete most phases of perhaps the most ambitious single therapy research project undertaken by the client-centred school was achieved. The massive report, subtitled 'A study of psychotherapy with schizophrenics' (Rogers et al., 1967), reached circulation after the school itself was beginning to diversify into what became a many-sided movement, and when the principal authors were all engaged in new enterprises in differing locations. A much fuller account of this project appears in Chapter 13.

The expanding circle of non-therapy applications

By the early 1950s, theoretical and practice principles of the client-centred system were being applied in a variety of contexts beyond the confines of counselling and therapy. In view of the educational setting in which the system was evolving and the participation of its principal exponents in formal teaching and supervision, it is not surprising that education was an early and continuing context for extension of client-centred principles. As usual, Rogers' own first statements in this area aroused considerable controversy, particularly his presentation in a conference on 'Classroom approaches to influencing human behaviour' at Harvard University (Rogers, 1952b, 1961a: 273–278). Besides trenchant criticism of prevailing educational practice, Rogers has offered proposals and documented innovations, in contexts from elementary education to graduate school. His principal writings concerning education, up to the mid-1960s, were drawn together in a volume entitled *Freedom to Learn* (Rogers, 1969a).

Group leadership and administration, especially in face-to-face organizations, was another early developing focus of application. Major contributions in this field were made initially by Thomas Gordon (1951, 1955). The influence of Gordon's and Rogers' work, and that of others from the client-centred school, is to be found in literature and practice within the fields of education administration and management, to some extent in organizational studies, and also in community development.

The area of family life and relationships has understandably been another focus of interest and contribution by client-centred workers, for example via application of principles of interpersonal communication and facilitation both in 'normal' families and those in difficulty. In a 1953 paper Rogers discussed the nature and effects of actual openness and honesty and its lack in family relationships, especially in the ability of family members to listen and to know each others' feelings, and in its bearing on acceptance and helpful caring among family members (Rogers, 1953/1961). Writings by van der Veen and collaborators (van der Veen et al., 1964; Novak and van der Veen, 1970) and Gordon (1970a and 1970b) are among the important contributions of client-centred workers in the area of family relations and change. Gordon's program of 'Parent Effectiveness Training' has since had international impact on a large scale. All of these aspects receive fuller attention in later chapters.

The wider sphere of understanding and alleviating conflict between groups and among larger social and national systems has been of significant concern to client-centred workers, and increasingly reflected in tangible initiatives in practice and concept. Rogers launched his direct contributions in this area with a conference paper given in 1951, later 'twinned' with a presentation by the distinguished industrial psychologist, F.J. Roethlisberger, for publication under the joint title 'Barriers and gateways to communication' (Rogers and Roethlisberger, 1952). Twelve years later, Rogers returned to a similar focus and theme in another main conference paper, then published in the first volume and issue of the *Journal of Applied Behavioral Science* (Rogers, 1965a). The diversified post-school period of the client/person-centred movement has spawned further major lines of work and development in small and large face-to-face groups of varied purpose, as later described.

In the broad area of the social uses of psychological/behavioural science knowledge Rogers and other client-centred writers have spoken eloquently and urgently of the dilemmas, dangers, and enormously consequential choices involved. Rogers' presentations include the notable sequence of debates with B.F. Skinner, concerned broadly with the control of human behaviour (Rogers and Skinner, 1956; Rogers and Skinner, 1962/1989), and other papers presented from the late fifties on (Rogers, 1958b, 1961d and 1969b). The present writer has contributed to the discrimination of issues in this area (Barrett-Lennard, 1965).

This chapter has advanced an overview of the main foci and developments in the client-centred domain, from the early 1940s to the mid-1960s. It remains to fill out the picture so far sketched, and to trace the still-wider course and substance of later development. A natural starting point for this larger endeavour is to examine more closely the fundamental theoretical ideas that define and undergird this whole approach.

5

Human Nature, Personality and Change

Theoretical Foundations of the Client-Centred System

> A theory provides a basis for an active approach to life, not merely a comfortable armchair from which to contemplate its vicissitudes with detached complaisance. . . . Men can play active roles in the shaping of events. How they can be free to do this and still themselves be construed as lawful beings is a basic issue in any psychological theory. . . . The truths the theories attempt to fix are successive approximations to the larger scheme of things which slowly they help to unfold. Thus a theory is a tentative expression of what man has seen as a regular pattern in the surging events of life.
>
> George Kelly, 1955

This chapter aims to provide a concise view of the orientation of the client-centred system: its main constructs, propositional theory, and assumptive principles. Thought articulated in the 1950s and 1960s, which can be said to represent client-centred theory in 'mid-life' or developed form, will be the main focus. Later theoretical innovations are considered in subsequent chapters. While I have worked carefully to document the origin and sources of particular features, their precise selection, framing, and synthesis are my own. In these ways the statement does not duplicate any existing literature, and modestly extends it. My starting point is at the level of key contextual ideas and principles.

General orientation to human nature and knowing

Client-centred theorists have portrayed a view of human nature clearly belonging in the 'third force' cluster of viewpoints, as distinguished by Maslow (1962) from behaviouristic and psychoanalytic perspectives. The differences include such basic issues as the ways human activity is conceived to be 'powered', the processes by which significant *change* in attitude or conduct occur, and the nature and role of conscious experience in human functioning (Barrett-Lennard, 1965; Rogers, 1964b).

Client-centred thinking stresses that human beings act on and respond to reality as they personally experience and perceive it to be; and that a person's total phenomenal field includes as a core component their sense of who they are, or their image of themselves. An individual's perceptual field is influenced by a variety of factors: his or her expectancies and needs, the behaviour of others and non-personal events. Whatever goes into the mix from which the person's view of reality emerges it is this view by which he or she acts. This emphasis has led to the system being described as phenomenological in character (see Shlien, 1963). Another generic designation is that the viewpoint is broadly an existential one (Braaten, 1961a). It particularly emphasizes the importance of first-hand experiential knowledge as against simply knowing about something or possessing an intellectual awareness of the end-products of the learning and discovery of others.

The potential of humans for personal freedom, for taking responsibility for their felt experience, for having the courage to look openly within and beyond themselves, and for proceeding purposefully, are stressed. Also emphasized are both the separateness of individuals and their deep connection with others, and the synergy of searching contemplation and committed engagement; in a wondrous and hazardous world (Braaten, 1961a; Gendlin, 1966; Rogers, 1964a; Rogers and Skinner, 1962/1989). Such a pattern does not flourish and become manifest *inevitably*, since less of our repertoire is 'hard-wired' than in other species, but is a potential or latent tendency of the human person.[1]

While stressing, with argument and passion, the importance of personal psychological freedom, self-determination and individuality, client-centred writers have not eschewed the principle of determinism applied to human experience and conduct. In fact, the application of this principle to the experiential realm was very strongly furthered by the determined, highly resourceful efforts of Rogers and others to bring psychotherapy into empirical, scientific daylight. In his 1955 article 'Persons or science: a philosophical question' Rogers first publicly shared the two-sided commitment and tension he felt between (i) his deep involvement in and respect for human subjective experience, including the experience of choice and freedom, and (ii) his search for verified scientific knowledge with its underpinning of deterministic assumption and objectivist methodology. Both the sides (i) and (ii) are forcefully presented and the author proceeds via a searching inner debate to a partial integration. This is developed somewhat further in subsequent papers although a measure of paradox explicitly remains. The experience of freedom, in Rogers' later words, 'exists not as a contradiction to the picture of the psychological universe as a sequence of cause and effect, but as a complement to such a universe'. The free person moves voluntarily 'to

---

1 In the course of a symposium in the early 1960s, Rogers spoke directly of the phenomenological–existential movement in psychology and related fields, leaving no doubt as to his own stand: 'Man has long felt himself to be but a puppet in life – molded by economic forces, by unconscious forces, by environmental forces . . . [and] enslaved by persons, by institutions and by theories of psychological science. But he is firmly setting forth a new declaration of independence. He is discarding the alibis of *un*freedom. He is *choosing* himself, endeavoring, in a most difficult and often tragic world to become himself – not a puppet, not a slave, not a machine, but his own unique individual self' (Rogers, 1964c: 130).

play his significant part in a world whose determined events move through him and through his spontaneous choice and will' (Rogers, 1964a: 39).

Rogers' full, evocative but paradoxical statement invites further working out of the issues. Both experienced freedom and the principle of lawful causation are each too compelling to dismiss, and the view of human nature explicated by Rogers and colleagues has further potential in searching for resolution. For example, when persons are seen as inherently active, directional, curious and self-generating it follows that their built-in freedom is of a different order than if they are viewed as basically moulded, patterned and 'determined' by their environmental history. In a debate from the same era, on the control of human behaviour, I accepted that if humans are viewed as essentially reactive agents conditioned by external forces, then the notion of personal freedom has little meaning and can seem merely a comforting fantasy:

> But if we take the contrary view that man is *inherently* active . . . [and] motivated essentially to develop his potentialities and exercise his capacities, then concepts of inner freedom and choice can be deeply meaningful.[2] If this second description is accurate, and providing the tendencies are not blocked or distorted, one would expect man to *feel* free and responsible. He would *be* free in the sense that the essential initiative for what he does and strives to become arises from an inherent tendency to maintain, express and actualize his experiencing being. (Barrett-Lennard, 1965: 30)

In the discussion so far, several very basic general characteristics of the human species, underlying the more specific constructs of client-centred theory, are implied:

First, a person is an experiencing (feeling, thinking, inquiring, willing, self-aware) being with a highly differentiated consciousness linked closely to his/her history of communication and relationships with other persons. Human consciousness is the apex of a vastly complex intra-personal system, and the primary seat of individual identity. While much of this total system normally is largely self-regulating, consciousness is its highest integrating and controlling centre or subsystem. *For humans, to be alive means to be conscious*, if not at the moment then potentially or at other moments. Having desired experiences and achieving certain qualities of consciousness are ultimate values in humans.

Second, reality is variously perceived and construed by different individuals and different groups. Each person or group acts according to their present

---

2 A person's freedom is also a function of the process level or quality of their functioning. A major effect of successful therapy, from the client-centred standpoint, is that of achieving a new level of inner freedom (e.g., Barrett-Lennard, 1965; Rogers, 1963b and 1963c). Rogers, Gendlin and others have emphasized that the defensively organized, 'structure-bound', 'low-process' person is relatively unfree, compared with the fully functioning, highly self-actualizing or 'high-process' person. Expanded awareness, discrimination and experiential knowledge work to increase an individual's autonomy, mastery and freedom. The difference is such that the whole person is now (in altered language) a higher-order, integrative and responsive open system.

view of the nature and relevant features of this reality. Persons are better understood from their inner pictures than from some impartial or external mapping of the terrain they face.

Third, persons are inherently active rather than merely reactive. The individual's mind is not a *tabula rasa*, passively acquiring its content and anchor points by sensory stimulation and associative mental processes. Nor is he or she simply controlled by complex patterns of reward and punishment. To the contrary, persons are active, curious, purposive and directional in their inherent nature, prone to organizing and reflecting on their primary experience, expanding their capacities, and actively changing their worlds according to their own goals. Typically, individuals devote great energy, directly, to their own development.

A fourth point is that a person grows into being. Life implies and depends on growth and developmental processes which themselves evolve. Human beings do not act primarily to restore internal equilibrium or homeostatic balance. While they may be said to have survival-type needs, a primary focus on such motivation is held to be invalid. An underlying growth principle is central in formulations and discussions relating to human motivation, learning and change, by client-centred writers.

Fifth, for a living thing to grow certain basic supporting conditions and nutrients are necessary. Given the nourishing conditions, the human organism will develop according to its own nature as a species and individual. Even a plant takes 'initiative' in spreading its roots and leaves to expose itself to the life- and growth-giving elements it requires. Higher animals have vastly greater versatility in acting to sustain and, often, to partially create conditions necessary for their growth and well-being. Humans have unique potential for knowledge (and also for confusion or self-deception) in regard to their own nature, and for actively pursuing positive self-realization.

The human organism

More specific, basic properties of the human organism viewed as a whole, are also distinguishable in the client-centred literature. Some of these follow directly from broad principles mentioned above, and others are a further conceptual step.

◇ Rogers held to a unified concept of motivation from the time his serious theorizing began. As initially formulated, *the human species 'has one basic tendency and striving – to actualize, maintain, and enhance the experiencing organism'* (Rogers 1951: 487). The 'actualizing tendency', as further refined, is seen in behaviour which promotes and preserves the life of the organism as well as being manifest in the organism's life-long disposition to develop and transcend its previous limits. Hunger for food, water and oxygen, for example, works equally in the service of preservation and of growth. In careful summing up, the actualizing tendency 'involves development toward the differentiation of organs and functions, expansion in

terms of growth, expansion of effectiveness through the use of tools, expansion and enhancement through reproduction. It is development toward autonomy and away from heteronomy, or control by external forces' (Rogers, 1959a: 196).

Rogers' (1963a) article 'The actualizing tendency in relation to 'motives' and to consciousness' is the most systematic and complete expression of his thought on this topic.[3] A central idea is that an inherent and active directional tendency is present generally in complex organic life forms, implicit even in the DNA molecule. It takes only a tolerant environment and essential nutrients for each organism to hasten on its developmental path, pushed by imperatives of its species, guided by its individual code, drawn by its own unique experience and, in the case of humans, moving also by the intentionality of evolving consciousness and meaning.[4]

- ◇ *The organism functions as an organized whole, responding to its own, moving perceptual field.* The perceptual field is its reality, and includes the immediate, fresh incoming data of experience as well as the map of reality charted and built up over time by the organism (see Rogers, 1951, 1959a). This thought is in accord with viewing the organism as a purposeful open system, in particularly active interchange with its environment, although this language is not used by Rogers. Pentony (1970) has suggested that the concept of 'team' does more justice than 'system' to the proactive intentionality of humans, individually and in interdependent combinations ranging from families to large organizations.
- ◇ Through its behaviour, *the human organism interacts with perceived 'outer' and 'inner' reality in the service of the actualizing tendency.* This tendency may be thought of as a directional energy subsystem, organized to promote life-preserving, developmental and self-enhancing processes. Motivational constructs in the form of a scheme of specific needs have been viewed as unnecessary and even heuristically unsound by Rogers and other client-centred thinkers, a position shared incidentally by behaviourist schools (Rogers, 1959a, 1963a; Skinner, 1953: 143–154).
- ◇ In infancy, and *through healthy child- and adulthood, human beings engage in an organismic valuing process.* Experiences tending to maintain or enhance the organism are valued positively, and the converse, negatively (Rogers, 1959a, 1963b, 1964b). Under certain conditions, mentioned shortly under discussion of the *self*, the organism develops strong

---

3 Rogers' later writing includes the differentiation of an even broader principle, the concept of a 'formative tendency' existing throughout nature (Rogers, 1978, 1980b). In support of these principles, the author presents evidence and cites other scholars of varied interest – for example, White: 'Even when its primary needs are met and its homeostatic chores are done, an organism is alive, active, and up to something' (1959: 315, cited in Rogers, 1963a: 5).

4 A very different approach to the concept of self-actualization, from within the client-centred movement, is advanced in another classic paper of the same period, by Butler and Rice (1963). Under the title 'Adience, self-actualization and drive theory', the authors carefully examine drive reduction theory and related laboratory research and adduce the concept of 'adient motivation' – also referred to as stimulus hunger – as a motivational principle consistent with experimental findings and the self-actualization hypothesis.

inhibitory tendencies and 'defensive' patterns that block the flow of some classes of experiential data, impair and restrict the organismic valuing process, and imply a lowering of integration.

◇ *Differentiation is an important effect of the actualizing tendency*, and a portion of the young organism's experience becomes differentiated and symbolized in an 'awareness of being', of having its own separate life and pattern. Broadly, this awareness may be termed self-experience, and this 'becomes elaborated, through interaction with the environment, particularly the environment composed of significant others, into a *concept of self*' (Rogers, 1959a: 223). The self-concept is a pivotal region of the organism's perceptual field, and a major influence in guiding behaviour.

◇ *The organism is always in motion*. Central to this motion is the stream of felt processes, embodying or leading to symbolic meanings, to which the term *experiencing* is given. In an important mode of experiencing, particularly articulated by Gendlin (1961a, 1964, 1969), the conscious organism engages in direct reference to inner felt meanings and concretely or bodily sensed qualities, the latter a primary substrate of experience. In effect, the conscious self 'listens' to and interacts with the organism's underlying body life. Specifically, this interaction includes finding words and other symbols for organically felt experience beneath the surface of articulate consciousness. As this occurs, shifts on both levels take place. Such flow within the organism sustains and enhances its wholeness and integration.

The self

In client-centred parlance, the term 'self' is used in more than one context but, most often, in reference to the person's concept of self. The self-concept emerged as a primary construct, not right at the start but during the first decade of the new client-centred school. It was first highlighted by Rogers in his featured address as retiring president of the American Psychological Association (Rogers, 1947).[5] With the appearance of *Client-Centered Therapy* (Rogers, 1951), 'self-theory' – so named by Hall and Lindzey (1957) in their popular text *Theories of Personality* – came of age. Although Rogers disclaims early interest in the self as a concept (Rogers 1959a: 200) its ancestry, in a form approximating the concepts of actual and ideal self, is clearly apparent in a test for children developed at the start of his career (Rogers, 1931b).

---

5 Rogers' 1947 paper presents an extensive range of therapy excerpts and client statements, cumulatively suggesting and pointing to the individual's self-picture as a primary factor in understanding behaviour and change. Surprisingly, Raimy's (1943) doctoral dissertation, 'The self-concept as a factor in counseling and personality organisation', is not mentioned here. As an early student of Rogers, at Ohio State University, Raimy's original work undoubtedly had a bearing on the direction of thought in the new therapy – as noted by Raskin (1948), among others.

The best account of the evolution of the concept of self to a pivotal position in his own thought, is to be found in Rogers' most systematic general statement of theory (Rogers, 1959a). There, he emphasizes the gestalt or configurational (I would say, 'system') nature of the self-concept, in which change in one element could alter the balance – and in therapy often did – of the whole. He also stresses that the organism applies a criterion of consistency in organizing experience as part of the self, and acknowledges the supportive influence of Lecky's work (1945) on this point. As interest in self-actualization and the idea of the fully functioning person evolved (Rogers, 1961a: 163–196), paralleled by development of the process conception (Rogers, 1958c, 1961b), the self-concept was seen as varying across a wide spectrum of function. It could be a governing determinant of behaviour or a reflexive consequence of it. Following is an outline of the heart of self-theory in its most systematic form, drawing on Rogers' major formulation of theory (1959a) and other fifties sources.

1 The theory postulates that as the individual's awareness of self emerges, even before it evolves into an organized self-concept, a need for the *positive regard of others* becomes apparent in experience and behaviour (Rogers, 1959a; Standal, 1954). This need is potent and pervasive in the young individual's social behaviour and it can override the organismic valuing process or full expression of the actualizing tendency.
2 As the individual continues to develop, a need for *self-regard* evolves. Personal behaviours originally associated with regardful and rejecting responses from others now have similar force in satisfying or frustrating the individual's need for self-regard. In effect, the person 'experiences positive regard or loss of positive regard independently of transactions with any social other. He becomes in a sense his own significant social other' (Rogers, 1959a: 224).
3 Thus, self-behaviours or attitudes that significant others originally defined as 'good' or 'bad' may come to arouse positive or negative *self*-regard. When any expression of self is avoided or sought solely because of its effect on self-regard the person is said to have acquired a *condition of worth* – a concept which became a centrepiece of self-theory after its development by Standal (1954).
4 An effect of conditions of worth is that the individual is no longer freely open to experience. Perception becomes selective in that experience consistent with a person's conditions of worth is accurately represented in that person's awareness while experiential data contrary to these conditions tend to be denied or distorted in awareness.
5 Denial to awareness implies that certain behaviours and/or inner states of the person are not recognized as *self*-experiences, and in this sense not owned by the individual and not organized into his or her self-picture. The resulting *incongruence* between self and experience, involves a state of 'vulnerability' and a degree of dysfunction. However, its effect is also to minimize conscious inner conflict and anxiety.
6 In the vulnerable person, some behaviours are in keeping with the self-concept and are accurately perceived and actualizing to the self. Other,

contrary, behaviours can only satisfy and actualize features of the individual's experiential being that are not admissible to the self-structure. The inadmissible (thus, 'not-self') features do not affect conscious self-regard, or have minimal effect (Rogers, 1959a: 227).

7 However, in the process described, there is 'subceived' threat and the reaction is in the nature of psychological defence. This 'defence' allows the individual to maintain an acceptable self-concept, while the implicit conditions of worth remain out of view and unaffected. There are also costs to maintaining an inaccurate view, including the aspect of vulnerability already mentioned, a tightness or rigidity of perception, and the potential for intense arousal or over-reactivity, in some areas (ibid.: 222–228).

The theoretical problem that remains is that of how self-defence breaks down and how forward change ensues. The 'costs' just referred to are a crucial factor in the potential for such change. Individuals can run into experiences which present them with such intense or starkly obvious evidence of contradiction between their self-picture and their actual behaviour that the defence/denial process fails and acute inner conflict and anxiety occurs. Perhaps also there can be cumulative effects from gradual development in aspects of self not constrained by defensive organization which finally trigger awareness of anomalies in the self; anomalies which result from the conditions of worth.[6]

Dimensions of therapy and personal facilitation

Conscious inner conflict or anxiety does not alone undo conditions of worth and lead to integrated and healthy functioning of the self. For assimilation into the self-structure of a previously threatening desire, attitude or behaviour tendency to occur, its subjective meaning and impact on self-regard has to change. It is posited that the change process hinges on the communicated unconditional positive regard of an empathically understanding significant other (see Rogers, 1959a: 230).

It is held that the individual must actually and substantially experience these mentioned qualities in the significant other's response for her/his own conditions of worth and self-regard to change. Assuming this happens, the customarily threatening experiences are openly perceived, explored and integratively accepted as expressions of the individual's acknowledged self. Further, the person is now relatively less vulnerable, more congruent, the balance shifts to more positive regard for self and others, and the individual's functioning is more often or fully reflective of an organismic valuing process.

In the client-centred view of therapy, and healing/helping relationships more generally, this process and cycle repeated many times, around the 'same'

---

6 In his major theoretical statement, Rogers (1959a: 228–390) carefully examines the 'process of breakdown and disorganisation' involved in the collapse of defence systems.

and different conditions of worth and conflict areas, is the nucleus of therapy. The specific nutrient or enabling conditions over which the therapist-facilitator has at least partial control, and which are conceived as crucial features in the therapy relation, were already gaining wide attention by the mid-sixties (Barrett-Lennard, 1962a, 1965; Butler, 1958; Gendlin, 1962; Rogers 1957a, 1959a, 1962, 1965d; Shlien, 1961).

In Rogers' original formulation of the conditions of therapeutic personality change (Rogers, 1957a), six components altogether are distinguished. The first of these, that 'two persons [here called client and therapist] are in psychological contact', is implied in the later ones and is not singled out in most subsequent research and writing. The second condition refers to what the client brings to therapy, and simply specifies that s/he 'is in a state of incongruence, being vulnerable or anxious' (ibid.: 96).

As earlier mentioned, vulnerability implies conditions of worth, such that the individual is prone to being threatened. When actual threat occurs, by persons effectively breaking the rules of their own conditions of worth with actions that they cannot avoid discriminating as their own self-behaviour, the active inner tension state of anxiety exists. Some degree of vulnerability and anxiety seems bound to apply to anyone voluntarily in therapy and, perhaps, to most people. For this reason and others, including the difficulties of operational definition, this condition has not been a major focus in subsequent research.

The further and mainly emphasized components focus on the therapist and his/her response in relation to the client. First, unlike the client, the helper needs to be 'congruent or integrated in the [therapy] relationship'. Rogers makes it clear that he does not mean that the therapist needs to be a paragon of self-actualizing virtue exhibiting this quality of integration and wholeness in every area of life, or even continuously in therapy (1957a: 96–97). I will return shortly to further discussion of this concept.

Two further conditions refer directly to qualities of relational response. In a word, Rogers hypothesized that the therapist needs to experience unconditional positive regard (or 'prizing') for the client, and an empathic understanding tuned to the client's own internal frame of reference and feelings. Although necessary it is not sufficient that these qualities exist within the therapist's response. Distinguished as a further condition, the client in some measure must actually register the therapist's unconditional positive regard, and perceive the therapist's empathic understanding. As implied, it was boldly proposed that these features were both all necessary and collectively sufficient conditions for therapeutic personality change to occur. Notable, for example, was the omission of any requirement in regard to therapist technique, or any necessary property of the client beyond the broad requirement of being 'vulnerable or anxious'.

As soon as Rogers' conditions of therapy formulation were circulated, two investigators began to plan doctoral studies designed to test the main features of the theory. Halkides, whose unpublished study (1958) is reported in outline by other writers (Barrett-Lennard, 1962a; Rogers, 1958a, 1965d), effectively focused on the conditions of therapist response, but not on the crucial final condition of the client's perception of this response. Her method was to use observer-judges who rated therapist congruence, unconditional positive regard, and empathy, from segments of recorded therapy interviews. The same essential method was adopted by Truax and others, in extensive later work (Truax, 1961; Truax and Carkhuff, 1967; Rogers et al., 1967: Appendix B).

The other foundation study in this area was conducted by the present writer. It employed a distinctly different approach and method, one which also opened the way to a stream of later research. A starting point was the logical presumption that it is what the client him/herself experiences that has direct effect. It follows from this that the relationship *as experienced by the client* will be most crucially related to outcome of therapy. Moreover, although it is not supposed that a client's conscious perceptions would reflect the totality of his/her underlying experience of the therapist, it is held that the client's own report, given under suitable conditions, would be the most direct and reliable evidence we could get of his/her actual experience (Barrett-Lennard, 1962a: 2).

Clients' perceptions were conceived as resulting, in turn, from the interaction of their own characteristics with the ways their therapists 'actually' responded. 'In the hypothetical case of two clients with identical characteristics, the differential response of the therapists would be wholly responsible for the different perceptions of clients and, hence, for differences in therapy outcome' (Barrett-Lennard, 1962a: 3). Thus the therapist's response remained as a main contributor to the client's experience relevant to the therapeutic conditions variables. In keeping with this rationale, the therapy conditions/relationship data were gathered directly from clients and therapists using a questionnaire instrument developed for this purpose, called the *Relationship Inventory* (Barrett-Lennard, 1962a, 1976, 1978 and 1986a; Gurman, 1977).

The conditions variables themselves, viewed broadly as basic dimensions (not all-or-nothing conditions) of a helping relationship, were freshly formulated in the course of the writer's research. These formulations were a further refinement of theory, and underlie the extensive work by other investigators using the Relationship Inventory (e.g., Barrett-Lennard, 1978, 1986a; Gurman, 1977; Rogers et al., 1967). A further delineation of the four main variables is briefly as follows:

1 *Empathic understanding* was conceived, first of all, to be an active process of '*desiring* to know the full present and changing awareness of another person' and '*reaching out* to receive his communication and meaning'.[7] Reception then entailed an inner processing of the other's expressions (both words and other signals) into *experienced* meaning that matches the client's awareness in ways immediately important to him, or her. The empathic process culminated in 'an experiencing of the consciousness "behind"

7 A far cry from the early image – never accurate – of the passively listening non-directive therapist, engaging in wooden reflection.

another's outward communication, but with continuous *awareness that this consciousness is originating and proceeding in the other*' (Barrett-Lennard, 1962a, 1981 – italics added).

Freshly expressed, empathy in this perspective is a form of inquiry and knowing, a caring but disciplined opening of self to the living feelings and meanings of the other. It is the other's distinct and separate consciousness that is reached and bridged, from the self of the therapist-partner, in moments of deep empathy. Even at points of strongest resonation, the empathizing partner retains background awareness that the feelings and flow of consciousness so immediately vivid are originating in and belong to the separate other person. At any moment, this awareness can rise to focal consciousness.[8]

2 The interactive quality of *unconditional positive regard*, theoretically pivotal in undoing conditions of worth, is conceptually and operationally difficult to handle as a single variable. The writer separated the concept into the two component aspects or dimensions of 'level of regard' and 'unconditionality of regard'. The concern for clear operational definition in the measurement context is especially visible in this case. A's level of regard for B is conceived as the net balance of all the various qualities and strengths of A's personal feelings and attitudes (positive, negative and indifferent) experienced toward and in relation to B. Positive feelings include respect, caring, appreciation, affection, and others. Negative feelings include dislike, disapproval, expressed indifference, impatience, contempt, etc. In a precise formulation, level of regard was defined as the 'composite "loading" of all the distinguishable feeling reactions of one person toward another, positive and negative, on a single, abstract dimension' of which the lower extreme 'presents maximum predominance and intensity of negative-type feeling, not merely a lack of positive feeling' (Barrett-Lennard, 1962a: 4; Gurman, 1977).

3 The aspect of *unconditionality* implies that A's attitude or feeling toward B does not depend on what B happens to be revealing or showing about him/herself. More precisely, A's attitude does not vary contingently, that is, according to the particular self-revelations, feeling reactions or other expressions of B. Conversely, conditionality implies that A's regard for B does vary according to the light that B shows him/herself in, or to differing qualities that s/he spontaneously expresses (Barrett-Lennard, 1978, 1986a). B's own awareness or acceptance of self-attributes is prone to be selective in any event, in accordance with her/his conditions of worth. To the extent that

---

8 This writer's research and reflection has lead to further developments in empathy theory, advanced later in this volume (Chapter 13). One pivotal idea is that empathic interaction is a multi-step process occurring in a distinct sequence of phases. Following the crucial inner resonation phase is the step of communicative expression of this aroused awareness of the other's felt experiencing. A complete cycle requires the further phase of the other becoming aware that the listener is indeed with him (her), in immediate experiential understanding (Barrett-Lennard, 1976, 1981, 1993a).

A responds conditionally, in keeping with B's own 'self-conditionality', this would tend simply to reinforce the status quo in B's functioning. Alternatively, if A responds in a strongly conditional fashion along *new* lines, s/he may lay the seeds for new conditions of worth in B (Barrett-Lennard, 1978).

4 The reader may recall that *congruence* refers theoretically to wholeness, integration, inner consistency. More exactly, it implies consistency between the three levels of (a) a person's primary experience, (b) their symbolized awareness, and (c) their outward behaviour and communication. The concept is theoretically centred on consistency between the first two of these levels, this being considered the main determining condition for congruence between awareness and communication. Thus, congruence first of all is an intrapersonal process state and quality of functioning. In his classical paper, Rogers did not speak of congruence needing to be communicated, as he specified in reference to empathy and unconditional positive regard (Rogers, 1957a). However, his discussion and formulation in terms of 'genuineness' implies a necessary communicative aspect in this variable too. In my own work, congruence is treated in the same way as empathy, regard and unconditionality, with the central issue being the client's perception of the therapist's genuineness, transparency, honesty with her/himself and the client, and other congruence-related qualities.

An enormous range and quantity of research, starting with mentioned work by the writer (Barrett-Lennard, 1959, 1962a) and by Halkides (1958), has been spawned by the conditions of therapy and interpersonal facilitation conception, stemming initially from Rogers' 1957 classic and his related writing (Rogers, 1959a, 1962). In terms of results, there is substantial consistency in numerous studies in the finding that empathy, congruence and level and unconditionality of regard, particularly *when measured from client perceptions of therapist response*, are significantly related to indices of client change over the course of therapy (Gurman, 1977). Chapter 13 of this volume looks in some depth at this area of research and its current status. Among other studies, was the monumental Wisconsin investigation of psychotherapy with schizophrenic clients (Rogers et al., 1967), with its focus on levels of the therapist conditions studied in relation to movement in client functioning within the therapy relationship. The further developments in theory that underlie this research, form my next focus.

Experiencing and the personal process continuum

Rogers' 'process conception' amounted to a new way of thinking about variation in level of personal functioning, a way that blended with powerful new description and thought regarding the nature of experiencing articulated by Gendlin. As such, it represented another evolutionary advance in client-centred thought. The new conception took form following development of the conditions of therapy theory just outlined, and basically extended the equation of therapy on the outcome side. Implied now was the formulation that if conditions X, Y and Z are present, then *in-therapy change in client process will ensue*, as well as before-to-after shifts in the client's outlook and functioning (Rogers, 1961b; cf. Rogers, 1959b).

The process conception is a systematic framework, anchored in close description and examples, making it possible to plot the client's level of functioning from behaviour at any stage in therapy. For this behaviour to have consistent meaning as a client quality, it is necessary to assume that it is occurring under relatively constant conditions. Rogers proposed that this constancy resided in the client being psychologically received, in the sense that the therapy conditions were satisfied (Rogers, 1959b and 1961a, ch. 7). In practice, for reliable comparison from one occasion to another with the same client, or from one client to another, the consistency of the conditions would be the critical factor.

A central idea of the process conception was that significant change in therapy was not a movement from one kind of fixed but faulty structure to another kind of set but adequate structure, not a change from one constantly repeating pattern to a different one. Rather, the essential direction was from a relatively fixed, closed, self-perpetuating quality to an open, flowing, self-transcending quality; from fixity and re-cycling motion to a formative changingness; briefly, from a condition of stasis to one of process (Rogers, 1959b and 1961b).

The process model of functioning reflects the influence of Gendlin's early work on experiencing (Gendlin, 1958; Gendlin and Zimring, 1955), this in turn drawing from Rogers' thought and encouragement (Gendlin et al., 1968: 223; Rogers, 1959b: 106). While the continuum was at first described as a single multi-faceted dimension (Rogers, 1958a),[9] a number of component 'strands' or layers were soon identified (Rogers, 1959b). Strands brought into focus were (i) the way the individual deals with feelings and feeling life; (ii) the manner of experiencing, especially, in terms of immediacy and the interplay between articulate awareness and preconceptual experiencing; (iii) the degree of congruence between experience and awareness; (iv) whether/how much personal constructs work as fixed templates versus flexible hypotheses; (v) the 'relationship to problems', particularly the extent of direct ownership of problems as against a general sense of difficulties lying outside one's cause or control; (vi) the way the person refers to and communicates self and experience (closely related to other elements mentioned); and (vii) manner of relating to others, especially in terms of desire and ability to be in contact through expression of immediately felt experience and meaning (Rogers, 1959b, 1961b and 1961a: 125–159; Rogers et al., 1967: 109–131 and 589–611).

Rogers chose to distinguish seven levels or stages, for the continuum as a whole and for any component strand. He also saw the strands as being much more separate and distinct at the lower end of the continuum than in the

9 And measured as a single continuum in the first research which stemmed from it, by Walker, Rablen and Rogers (1960).

integratively functioning 'process' person at the other extreme. The following passages provide a succinct account of the two extremes, and further illuminate the dimension as a whole:

> At one end of this tentative scale or continuum we find the individual living his life in terms of rigid personal constructs. . . . He has little or no recognition of the ebb and flow of feeling life within him. . . . His communication, even in a receptive and acceptant climate, tends to be almost entirely about externals and almost never about self. The form tends to be: 'The situation is . . .', 'They are . . .', 'They say . . .' [or, possibly] 'My characteristics are . . .', but he would almost never say 'I feel . . .', 'I believe . . .', . . . He does not recognize himself as having problems. He does not perceive himself as a responsible agent in his world. He exhibits no desire to change and shows many signs of wishing to keep himself and his environment as unchanged and stereotyped as possible. (Rogers, 1959b: 96–97)

> At the other end of this continuum we find the individual living *in* his feelings, knowingly, and with a basic trust in and acceptance of his feelings as a guide for living. His experiencing is immediate, rich and changing. . . . The ways in which he construes his experience are continually changing in the light of further experiencing. He communicates himself freely as a feeling, changing person. He lives responsibly and comfortably in a fluid relationship to others and to his environment. He is aware of himself, but not as an object. Rather it is a reflexive awareness, a subjective living in himself in motion. (ibid.: 97)

Not surprisingly, one finds in Rogers' other writings, shortly before and in the period following his differentiated account of the stasis–process continuum, very clear reflections of the same basic vein of thought. One example is his paper 'A therapist's view of the good life' (Rogers, 1957b), which, although echoing principal features of his still-earlier work on the fully-functioning person, uses language much more attuned to a 'process' way of thinking.[10] Another 1957 article subtitled 'A therapist's view of personal goals' speaks of personal change and functioning in terms that bridge earlier expression of his thought and the forming nexus of the process conception (in Rogers, 1961a).

In taking up a related theme several years later, in a major paper on values and the process of valuing, Rogers' discussion under such headings as 'Restoring contact with experience' and 'Valuing in the mature person' closely builds on features of the earlier creative work on process and experiencing (Rogers, 1964b). Similarly, his later-described 'emerging person' (Rogers, 1977a: 255–282), pictured as the vanguard and hope of our species, is portrayed as living in basic accord with the upper levels of the continuum discriminated two decades earlier.

Translated into measurement-oriented form, the process conception evolved as the primary vehicle for the study of client process in therapy, in the Wisconsin program of research on psychotherapy with schizophrenic patients (Rogers et al., 1967). Up to four scales, representing differing component

10 Rogers' (1963b) paper on 'The concept of the fully functioning person', only published in 1963, was written and circulated privately ten years earlier.

strands, were used in tracing and analysing client process levels and movement in therapy. Central among these was the 'Scale for rating of experiencing' (Gendlin et al., 1967; Kiesler, Mathieu and Klein, 1967; Rogers et al., 1967, Appendix C1). This continued in use, due in part to its connection with another milestone development of the client-centred system: Gendlin's theory of personality change (Gendlin, 1964/1970).

Gendlin's theory of change

Gendlin's theory rejects views of personality that pivot on description of mental contents and apparatus, *states* of mind, constant behavioural patterns, and motivational entities such as drives or needs. It argues that theories of repression (designed, one might say, to explain repeating behaviours of low functionality) are not compatible with regarding the person as a process and with comprehending change in process qualities. The idea of an unconscious as a depository of repressed events is not a credible one in this viewpoint. It would be seriously inaccurate to speak of experience being driven underground out of awareness, where it resides, ready in some circumstances to burst forth again, full-blown.[11] One can, on the other hand, speak meaningfully of an experiential process being stopped or at a standstill, or left incomplete or, in original language, as 'structure-bound' (Gendlin, 1964/1970; Gendlin and Zimring, 1955).

Theories of personality – often grounded in observations from psychotherapy – acknowledge that change can happen but generally do better at explaining constancy of personality. However, Gendlin notes, observers have mostly agreed that change which does occur involves some intense emotional-feeling process. Reference to a client/patient as 'merely intellectualizing', as against being 'really engaged' on an emotional-experiential level, is indicative of the stress on feelings or felt process. Similarly, it is observed that people mostly seek out a *relationship*, as with a therapist, through which to gain relief and change. Gendlin's approach is compatible with these observations and the thoroughgoing emphasis on process makes it amenable to explaining change.

A primary construct in the theory is that of 'direct referent', later called the 'felt sense'. This 'inwardly felt datum' is in some sense present all the time but not articulated, may not even be discriminated, until attended to or 'focused on'. Yet we dip in and out of it constantly, in a process that is fundamental to human experiencing. Expressed broadly, Gendlin points to an implicit, preconceptual level of inner life process, seen as the primary substrate of experience. This includes unarticulated bodily felt processes, 'gut reactions' for which words have not formed, images without clear shape, unlabelled *sensed* emotion and energies, and implicit connections not yet born in symbols. Ordinarily, to know of and begin to engage with this organic inner

11 Even the Rogerian concept of 'denial to awareness' is seen as fitting a repression paradigm, not helpful in explaining change and at odds with Gendlin's process-centred perspective.

sense or direct referent 'only' requires attending to it. A special or full way of attending leads to the process that Gendlin identifies here as focusing, and which ever since that time has comprised the core of his theory of change.

In the initial 'direct reference' phase of focusing a person attends to a definitely felt but non-verbal inner referent sense. This is a form of active, inner listening and communication, with a quality of excitement as the person increasingly recognizes and articulates the form of this felt inner referent. When or as this happens, the unfolding process merges into the next phase of 'referent movement'; a perceptible 'give' or shift in what is concretely felt. An exclamation, or sudden light and mobility in the person's expression, may signal this motion, often then followed by many words, pointing to core elements and details of what the person is now symbolizing from felt experience. Like the slight turning of a chandelier, a small underlying shift may reveal a myriad of new facets of light or personal meaning (my metaphor). As focusing is sustained and the unfolding process continues, a third phase of 'wide application' tends to ensue, in which a variety of implications and applications to differing situations comes to mind. What at first seemed unitary now has many sides or faces. As either a further phase, or as an outcome of focusing, an additional step of 'content mutation' is described, in which the person reframes the connection and content that initially excited him or her. The focusing process can freshly begin with some new unclear felt referent, and lead to further integrative movement. (Gendlin, 1964/1970, 1969; Gendlin et al., 1968).[12]

The idea of a spiral-like cycle, recurring with differing content, is implicit in Gendlin's account of the motion of sustained focusing. Together, the ingredient elements of focusing are seen as the essential core of therapeutic change processes; and the resulting transformation of experiencing becomes the central outcome of therapy. The nature of this transformation is essentially in keeping with the stasis-to-process continuum already outlined. While some people can engage in focusing much more readily than others (Gendlin et al., 1968), the qualities of interpersonal response that facilitate this process include versatile expression of the conditions of therapy principles already outlined, especially finely tuned empathic listening in an active, expressive mode. A further implied condition is an active willingness to guide the other person into the focusing mode (Gendlin, 1969).[13]

The account just given is a bare outline of Gendlin's theory, centred on his view of the core process mechanism of change as he originally presented it.

12 Gendlin and collaborators describe the four-phase sequence somewhat variably in the main 1960s papers advancing this conception (Gendlin, 1964/1970, 1969; Gendlin et al., 1968). The writer has worked to integrate the essential, strongly overlapping features in these accounts. The differentiation and language in Gendlin's later, more popular work (Gendlin, 1978, 1981), is somewhat different still, and was not directly drawn on here.

13 Whether such guidance is a truly responsive process, and its implementation in full accord with the therapy conditions viewpoint, or whether it has an impositional hue or tends to neglect other principles, is a matter of some debate within client-centred circles. Debated issues in the more pluralistic 'post-school' phase of the approach come up in later chapters.

There is much elaboration, and some further territory, in his total statement (Gendlin, 1964/1970). Two large pages of fine print, for example, are devoted to spelling out what he does *not* mean by direct reference. It does not mean re-experiencing or being caught up in some strong emotion or feeling; it is not a familiar inner conversation or argument, nor an effort to explain away something, nor a process of self-engineering and control (ibid.: 149–151). Rather, it entails an attitude of receptivity and a special kind of active inner listening and dialogue, a literal inquiry into and through what is felt or sensed but not yet discovered in articulate or formed consciousness.

Gendlin writes at length about qualitative features and modes of experiencing, especially in their occurrence and progression (or failure to progress) within a help-intended relationship (ibid.: 152–162). He suggests that verbalized experiences are the rendered symbolization of experienc*ing* processes. The symbol is a shorthand substitute for the original experience, static like a photograph until further interaction with the primary stuff of experiencing yields fresh or modified images. Where experience is stopped or stuck or 'structure bound' in a particular region, interaction has ceased and the residual symbols repeat on their own. Gendlin further proposes that environmental and interpersonal interaction, inner body life and feeling, cognitive functions and self-reflection, are all facets of a single larger process (159–160). He does not name this process but his evocative discussion suggests a *systemic* way of thinking, where unities can exist on many levels, and influence is interactive and reciprocal. I will return in later chapters to facets of this thought, and to some mention of pertinent research.

This chapter, taken as a whole, has focused on theoretical perspectives and their development within and at the end of the School Phase of the client-centred system. Newer frontiers of systematic thought are taken up in parts of this volume still to come, including the chapters which follow next, as Part III. These are concerned broadly with 'principles in practice', both in the laboratory of therapy itself and in a spectrum of other enabling contexts. I do not use the phrase 'application of principles', since the directly relevant theory has arisen largely from intensive practice observation and linked reflection rather than being the determinant of practice. Once articulated, theory may help *interactively* in further refinement of practice. However, if the emergent theory comes to be used as total guide and criterion for practice, neither level is facilitating evolution of the other. In the present case, a leavening third component – empirical research – has advanced in active relation with the other two. Contributions of this research axis have been touched on already, and are examined in close view in the chapters that follow after the next group.

PART III

PRINCIPLES IN PRACTICE

6

The Helping Interview

> Any [therapy] technique concerned with the other without the self, with behaviour to the exclusion of experience, with the relationship to the exclusion of the persons in relation, with the individuals to the exclusion of their relationship, and most of all, with an object-to-be-changed rather than a person-to-be-accepted, simply perpetuates the disease it purports to cure.
>
> R.D. Laing, 1967

This chapter and the next are devoted to the original focus and practice core of the client/person-centred system: the process of one-to-one therapy. In view of the over half-century life span of client-centred therapy, and the many significant contributors to its evolution and practice forms, it is no mean challenge to characterize succinctly the principles in action. Classic sources such as *Client-Centered Therapy* (Rogers, 1951) are landmarks from what I have called the School Phase of this approach. To base a view of the therapy on main early sources would be to rely on formative history alone. While veins from this history continue to pulse in present work, there have been several decades of subsequent transfusion, fresh application and unfolding.[1] To draw only on recent work and statements, however, would fall seriously short in another way. Presenting the end product, without any tracing of origins and development, could suggest a finished and static position rather than a current working view.

---

1 Significant sources from the seventies onward, in book form and by exponents other than Rogers, began with Wexler and Rice's *Innovations in Client-Centered Therapy* (1974) and include Gendlin's (1978) extended delineation of focusing, and the multi-faceted volume edited by Levant and Shlien (1984). Later additions include the major collection focusing on psychotherapy across various 'wings' in the client-centred movement, edited by Lietaer, Rombauts and Van Balen (1990), and the fine teaching manual *Person-Centred Counselling in Action*, by Mearns and Thorne (1988).

My resulting choice is to advance a fresh distillation that draws on literature from varying periods, and which also builds on this foundation, especially in the next chapter. Taking the two chapters together, readers who identify strongly with the client/person-centred orientation, and whose interests include therapy practice, will no doubt find the territory familiar but in some ways newly lit. For this group, I would like my statement to help in keeping track of 'our' identity as an approach, expressed in current language and with forward-reaching elements. For the serious newcomer or general explorer, it is hoped that the account will be illuminating through familiarity in idea of some elements, the freshness of others, and the overall synthesis.[2]

An axiomatic hypothesis of this system is that a helping relationship does not literally produce change but works by releasing or nourishing inbuilt recuperative and actualizing tendencies. It is held that personal healing or growth cannot literally be induced and directed. Attempts to instil a new pattern may alter behaviour but cannot produce wellness, since *wellness is a fruition of being not a rendered shape or adjustment* (Barrett-Lennard, 1985a: 287). Growth is development that flows from the nature of an organism in a favourable environment. The client–therapist relationship is one such environment.

Client-centred therapy (unlike an earlier stereotype) is very far from being a passive, merely *re*active process on the therapist's part. To the contrary, by his or her quality of attentiveness and highly active listening, of literal direct interest that conveys its own invitation, by a readiness at any moment to expressively communicate what is being heard, wondered, imagined or construed, by an unusual synergy of stillness and motion; through all of these and other features of presence and response, the therapist radiates a kind of total, unjudging receptivity and openness to contact on an experiential level.

This special quality of engagement with the other literally absorbs the helping person. He/she is not simply carrying out a task, not just performing a function, not merely following a laid down path. Yet, the process engaged in has a direction and is, at best, a highly skilled form of resourcefulness which inheres in the person creatively expressing it. Such skill cannot be acquired solely by imitative learning, by training in technique, by simple reinforcement, or by cultivation of a closely established repertoire and role. While any of these elements may play a part, more fundamentally helper development and growth in skilfulness partakes of the nature of therapy itself.[3]

---

2 Some concepts and elements from the client-centred approach have influenced thought and practice in the personal helping field over a broad front, finding their way into many other systems of therapy and human relations. There also has been some flow in the opposite direction, especially from alternative systems in the humanistic stream. Contributors who have worked to blend client-centred practice principles with those of another humanistic approach (Gestalt, for example) include Cochrane and Holloway (1974) and O'Hara (1984).

3 By the phrase 'partakes of the nature of therapy' I mean to imply that the conditions conceived as crucial for therapeutic change are vital also for helper development. Psychotherapy and growth-training processes have different starting points and total content, but hinge on similar enabling principles. This and related issues are closely explored in Chapter 15.

These features are in keeping with the interview process having a character, which includes distinctive, flexibly patterned qualities of form. The major aspects of process-form are framed, described and illustrated here with the previously outlined concepts and theoretical principles in mind (see last chapter), although the same structure is not slavishly followed. The features separately distinguished are, in action, interwoven aspects of a larger whole. The letters T (or Th) and C (or Cl), in the passages which follow, refer to the therapist and the client, respectively.

Sharing initiative and responsibility in the interview

Generally, the adult client has chosen to seek assistance around troubling problems in living. Initiative in regard to the problem and topical content of the communication lies largely with the client. On the other hand, the nature of the relationship between the therapy partners and, particularly, the salient qualities of interaction in the interview, are more in T's hands. This is not to imply any rule against T expressing owned feelings and meanings of his or her own, or against asking open questions about content or inviting C to explore a particular issue. Nor is C without significant influence on the nature or qualities of the helping relationship, especially as he or she perceives them.

The distinctive qualities and balance of initiative of client and therapist reflect their differing objectives, expectancies and resources, within an engagement in which one is seeking help and the other seeking to provide it through an enabling process. C, for example, knows best where s/he is hurting, troubled, or wanting to move beyond some present quality of functioning and consciousness. T has working personal-professional knowledge of ways of being and responding that are potentially helpful in C's distressed struggle or 'stuckness'. Applying this knowledge desirably involves a *living* of the therapy conditions, in the helping relationship.

The therapist's range of overt initiative expands further with withdrawn or deeply troubled persons, as described, for example, by Gendlin (1961b, 1962, 1963 and 1966), Rogers (1961c and 1967f), and also Prouty (1990, 1994), in their work with schizophrenic clients. Children and younger adolescents naturally call forth a somewhat differing repertoire, too. The initiatives may embody more active offering of contact and relationship; more explicit indications of the attentive-receptive presence and personhood of the therapist; and increased sharing of suggestions as to process that may further the helping engagement. T's initiatives and self-expression, while open and clear in direction, retain a non-impositional quality. If a client tries to *insist* that the therapist partner respond in a particular way this tends to be acknowledged both in terms of T's sense of the feeling thrust in C's demand and in reaction to the demand itself. The responding communication may directly include an empathic message and also a simple, owned refusal or other expression of non-compliance that has little if any loading of moral judgement.

The therapist's equalitarian outlook and practice, including the expectation of the client other taking the lead in problem-discrimination and topic choice, is not invariably welcomed by clients. Finally reaching out for help in a fee-paying professional service context clearly can itself be a very big plunge. Factors such as the client's attitude toward authority, previous experience with helping professionals, or a generally active or passive stance, may lead C to expect specific appraisal or advice, and more 'direction' in the helping interview than s/he encounters.

If C perceives a lack of sincere interest in T's response, or a puzzling unwillingness to apply professional initiative and expertise in expected ways, the interview process may bog down. A primary challenge, for T, is to remain receptive and sensitive in the face of C's immediate frustration or perplexity, in effect, to be just as perceptive to this experienced problem as to issues outside their alliance. Meeting this challenge entails responding not out of desire to get past the problem but, first, from concern to understand exactly how the situation feels and appears to C. T may then responsively assist C in relating her/his goals and personal style to the approach and person of the therapist – coming into further view through their dialogue. At the least, C would experience being taken very seriously around his/her felt concern and perplexity of thought.

A person enters therapy, at least in part, out of concern to make sense of their experience. It is manifestly in accord with this need to want to make sense of therapy itself. The client's effort to do so may be affirming to their hope that the process will be personally valuable, with this therapist. Or, it may lead to contrary evaluation. Such evaluation, even when it leads to a decision not to go on, need not be viewed as defensive and self-avoidant or, necessarily, a failure on T's part. Usually, therapy clients arrive on their own initiative, and leave therapy by choice. Considered 'early' departure is potentially an expression of independence or self-agency – generally a positive value as far as T is concerned. It is also distinctly possible that open exploration of the issues will lead both to an increased feeling of empowerment and sense of partnership on C's part. The prospects of the therapy enterprise would then have been enhanced.

Experiential responding and immediacy

The participants' attention and responding in the client-centred interview focuses broadly on felt experience. Personal experience is usually imbued simultaneously with feeling and with meaning: feelings helping to inform meaning and meanings contributing to what is felt. Experiential or 'self'-exploration does not centre on experience that is already well sorted out and distilled. Finding further connection and meaning in unclear but pressingly felt experience is a basic kind of discovery particularly associated with therapeutic inquiry. In the helping interview, extensive description or cataloguing of events normally is absent, in favour of a growing emphasis on present feelings and felt meaning, and on the contexts from which these are arising.

Gendlin (1968) has used the term 'experiential response' to refer in a generic way to what T does. This implies a response to experienced feeling and meaning: not an occupation with feelings reported or pointed at but without immediate life, nor with observation or analysis from which emotion is washed out, but an engagement with the other at the presently active point of their search and expression and current of feeling. As expressed by Gendlin: 'A therapeutic response always aims at the client's own directly felt sense of what he [she] is talking about' and 'aims to carry the client's experiencing further' (1968: 'rules' 4, 5 and 6). The following excerpt, from a second interview, is a glimpse in action of some of the features mentioned and to follow. (Extended excerpts from this interview appear, with independent discussion, in Butler, 1974.)

Cl: You know what I was thinking yesterday? I was thinking and, if I'm not happy with S— , why in the world did I go back to him? [Phrases omitted]. I feel that I don't have to feel so guilty that I didn't love him. I feel like I've cared about him. But maybe it's this, maybe some people you can care about only so much and other people you can care more; and I know I *can* care about somebody much more than I care about him. Or else maybe I'm kidding myself, I don't know.

Th: But that's the way you feel. Like he, somehow – you can't care for him with *all the caring* you've got in you.

Cl: That's it! And that's what I want to do – as much as I can; and then to feel that somebody cares about me as much as *they* can.

Th: Give yourself and be given to.

Cl: *That's right. That's exactly what I want.* Really, I don't know if I can get it. If I find out I can get it – then I'll probably get so I *want* to live. . . .

The experiential mode also has the quality of immediacy. The client partner in the helping interview tends increasingly to communicate felt meanings that surface in words and non-verbal expressions *as she/he goes along*. Effectively, T is doing this too – as in the illustration just given, where the therapist's response was intuitive and spontaneous. Such communication cannot be rehearsed, or even premeditated in its specifics; and in many ways is just the opposite of planned reporting or calculating intervention. The familiar and well-travelled pathways of C's construed world of meaning are allowed to recede as he or she gains security and mobility in the new environment of the therapy-helping relationship. (These much-trodden pathways may have had needed effects. However, they are not directly conducive to new personal discovery and change, and their suspension occurs partly through the experience of safety in the helping relationship.)

The quality of immediacy is implicit in Rogers' accounts of the therapy process, especially since the time of his process–stasis formulations. Heightened immediacy of experiencing and communication is an expected effect of therapy. In the deeply accepting and responsive safety of the therapy relationship C tends to function at his/her own upper limit of immediacy, and to expand this limit. All aspects of therapist response discussed here can be rather deliberate in expression or, more spontaneous and transparently indicative of the immediate flow of feeling and thought that T is tapping into in her/himself. Without empathy and genuine warmth such expressiveness could foster anxiety in an already vulnerable, uneasy client partner. In context, it helps open the way to more immediacy and spontaneity on the client's part.

Rogers gives a vivid picture of therapist immediacy and congruence in the 'epilogue' of his article mentioned above. 'So what then is the process of counseling and therapy', he asks rhetorically. He then offers an account 'from the inside', in effect, from what it is like subjectively for the therapist listening within as well as to the other, and aware of the inner – and unconcealed – presence of his/her own surfacing feelings. I will quote later in this chapter, and at some length, from this portrayal (Rogers, 1961b: 42).

Active listening and empathy

Active, concentrated empathic listening is a hallmark of the client-centred interviewer's response, and one that has been pivotal ever since the term 'client-centred' first came into vogue (Rogers, 1946; Rogers and Wallen, 1946; Rogers and Farson, 1957). The interviewer tries, in Rogers' words, 'to hear the sounds and sense the shape of the other person's inner world'. He asks himself, 'Can I resonate to what he is saying, can I let it echo back and forth in me, so deeply that I sense the meanings he is afraid of yet would like to communicate, as well as those meanings he knows?' (Rogers, 1969a: 223). For C, the impact of such understanding may be so powerful that it is 'as though something that had stopped inside him has begun to move and live again, that some part of his loneliness in a world of imperfect communication and knowing has dissolved, or that some vital connection he had been unable to bring into focus has become suddenly and vividly clear to him' (Barrett-Lennard, 1963). The processes of deeply attentive, sensitive listening and resonation and of expressive, empathic responding may be said to comprise the manifest 'work' of the therapist-interviewer (Rogers, 1966a). Gendlin adds as a further aspect of this work, critically linked to listening, the feature of helping the other to 'focus' (Gendlin, 1981: 118–135).

Since words are not the only important signals in communication, T's 'antennae' are at best receptive to a whole range of cues, in the helping interview. Of course, effective understanding can diminish if T's excitement over picking up indirect messages replaces attention to what C is expressing from his/her focal consciousness. In another place, I spoke of these issues as follows:

> Listening beyond the other's words means hearing the literal content of those words but, *in addition*, responding to the other's manner of expression, gestures, and to the other nuances interwoven in the total communication. With such broad and deep listening, we may pick up diverse or conflicting messages, as though from different voices in the other person. If, when we hear the more submerged voice, we neglect the other's spoken words, our listening will have become selective in another way and, to that extent, insensitive. Sometimes, what we hear or sense may go beyond

> what we feel the other person could bear to have acknowledged. It is as though our sensitivity has made us an intruder in their private world. However, if we truly have heard the other, and are not ill at ease from the impact, then usually it is safe and helpful to let them know what we are aware of – especially if we then continue to listen sensitively. (Barrett-Lennard, 1988: 418)

What T 'hears', while triggered by and pointed towards C's experience is, of course, a process going on within T and influenced in some measure both by his or her own characteristics and by the particular context at the time. The interviewer, at best, always indicates or implies in some way that it is his or her own refracted personal consciousness of the other's experience – and not literally the experience of the client – which is conveyed in T's reflectively expressed understanding. Typically, the helper does not convey total assurance in knowing how it feels to be the other person, even at a given moment. To the contrary, T responds to the other in terms of his/her 'best understanding of his meaning at the moment, with the attitude that this understanding is continuously open to correction and change' (Barrett-Lennard, 1963: 224).

These mentioned elements tend to be more explicit in beginning interviews than later in therapy, as suggested by their visibility in the first interview excerpt now presented, and to become more subtle or economical in expression as therapy advances. The following segment begins only about fifteen minutes after the client and therapist had first met:

Th: . . . I guess you mean you want a much more positive feeling, somehow, about being on top of your life, of being able to cope and manage? A sort of expectation that you will, instead of fear (*Cl*: Right), perhaps you won't.

Cl: It's a little bit wider than that though. You used the word 'to be on top of things'. And I would like to feel that I don't *have* to be on top of things – that I can just be, you know, kind of equal to them. [Cl's voice breaks and tears begin to come.] Right now I feel I have to be on top of them which I don't think is exactly the way everybody, you know, that it's a realistic expectation.

Th: Somehow that touches a feeling that's close to home for you.

Cl: Yes, right [blows nose]. [Pause]

Th: 'On top' is *not* the right word – ehr – you, that suggests pushing yourself and having to be better, maybe other things – I'm not sure. [Gently] I guess I don't want to push you with a question – it's your immediate feeling that I'm –

Cl: Well, you did hit home there, but I don't know exactly how – how that works. [Pause]. I mean I would like to feel I don't have to be in control of things in order to survive. It's what I mean about – you can't expect always to be on top of things, and I don't think that one should need that feeling in order to survive. Some people manage quite well without having to feel in complete control, all the time of what's happening. . . . So, is that realistic or? (*Th*: [At once, softly] I don't know.) Do most people feel they have to be on top? I don't know – whether you know either.

Th: I don't really know. But I'm trying to sense your feeling. I'm not sure how close I am, but it's – and I would like you to correct me – but . . . you would like to be able to take things more as they come, somehow. Does the expression 'rolling with the punches' – are you familiar with that?

Cl: Yes – Yes, I would like to have that capacity (*Th*: Yes).

Th: I guess my sense is that something kind of hurts you about the way – some way – that you push yourself or feel that you have to try to be.

Cl: Right. I always feel like – ahm, like if I just [voice quivers and breaks] just forget to try, everything would sort of collapse and I'm just tired of always trying [takes another cigarette, lighting it with the previous one]. I ran out of matches – [After a brief interlude, the client is again speaking from within her feeling, expressed with strong example.]

Cl: . . .When I'm in a plane I'm convinced when we finally land that it was just me holding it up there. Not really but emotionally, when I'm up there, if I'm not just thinking about it staying all the time [voice breaks again] I'm convinced we're going to crash. I am just bringing that up symbolically – I think that holds for just about everything.

Th: I don't know, I just have the image that it must be so *exhausting* for you to carry that load, to carry that weight! (Th leans back, involuntarily miming the strained holding or pressing up of a heavy weight.)

In keeping with this illustration and prior discussion, the message that T's communicated understandings are an expression of him/herself as well as of C is openly conveyed to the client in any of various ways that fits the language and styles of both participants, and the stage of their relationship. Much less is taken for granted in the therapy encounter than in most life relationships, and precise or full understanding by T usually is not assumed in advance of verifying signs by C, even if it has often occurred before. As the client–therapist relationship evolves, some features of communication change, as later discussed. However, one way or another the message is repeated and sustained that it is vitally important to T to know whether his/her impression is accurate, partially right, or off target. To the extent that this understanding is faulty, T *wants* to be put right by C, or to listen and try again until clearly in touch with C's experiencing.

By way of further example, an incident occurs between the same client–therapist pair, three interviews after the above excerpt. By now, it is clear that the client can let T know in easy direct fashion that, although he has grasped the gist of her message, his response understates the *strength* of her feeling – that it is 'a little bit limp'. As the episode begins, she is speaking in particular of her relationship with her husband.

Cl: It's like there's a war going on and I expect – every time he comes home I expect him to tell me that he wants a divorce [client's voice breaks, and she speaks through tears] and that he's fallen in love with somebody else. It's an expectation that I have, and it happened also with my first husband, and it happened a few times when I got interested in dating some boys. . . . [Client is no longer crying, as she describes earlier relationships; until suddenly she touches some deeper sense of herself, which briefly stops her words. The therapist, struggling a little, responds to her current experience.]

Th: I'm wanting to really – to be sure I'm understanding how you are feeling – (*Cl*: Am I mumbling – I was just wondering if –) No, I can hear you quite clearly. I can hear your words quite clearly. Is it expressing more than you mean to say that . . . when you let your feelings come to the surface, you are always afraid that your husband won't want you any more? When he's been away and comes home that somehow he won't want *you* – (*Cl*: That's right) and that there will be someone else in his life (*Cl*: That's right. That's right.) And – [T pauses, looking at C to respond or continue.]

Cl: That's not said too strongly. It's even a little bit limp [laughing slightly].
Th: [T now speaking more firmly, quickly] You – okay: it's an awful, wounding kind of fear that he'll *abandon* you –
Cl: Yes [reflectively]. The word to be abandoned – uhm, or that he's been laughing at me all this time and that he just doesn't care. In my worst times I'm confident that he's just been pretending all this time.

The way that the quality of T's listening is expressed, and also checked out, in these excerpts takes the familiar 'reflective' form. I think of reflections as *potential* channels for the flow of empathy (Barrett-Lennard, 1993a: 8). The reflective form has another special asset: not only may it convey (empathic) understanding but it serves as a very effective check for both therapy partners on whether T's impression is indeed accurate. In the example just given, the therapist's words did not at first communicate a resonating awareness of the *force* of her feeling. T's 'mirror' showed C this element of mismatch, and facilitated correction.

It will be evident that the terms 'reflection' and 'mirror' are not applied in a narrowly literal sense but serve as useful, simplifying metaphors for processes that are subtle and many-sided in full portrayal. I will borrow my own words from another place both to suggest more of this richness and lead up to the next focus here. My language is personal, the meaning more general:

> Our attention as client-centred helpers is centred on trying to understand what the other is experiencing, what their world is like to them, . . . how it must be in their shoes, seeing with their eyes, feeling with their senses, concepts, attitudes, presumptions, bearing the weight of their past and the circumstances of their present. My genuine experience and response is in large part my wanting (not demanding) to know the other, my sensing of their world and their immediate feelings or meaning, the dawning of shared knowing between us, the excitement I feel when the other's awareness is actually unfolding or shifting in some way before me. It is this whole spectrum arising from my focus and absorption with the other person that is truly and largely the substance of my experience as therapist, in company with my client. (Barrett-Lennard, 1993b: 103)

Beyond the explicit: empathic inference, intuition and imagery

Through absorbed empathic listening and experiential responding one may go significantly beyond the client's directly expressed messages. It may surprise some readers to know how long ago, and with what firmness, Rogers expressed himself on this point. It is not the case, he wrote,

> that the client-centered therapist responds only to the obvious in the phenomenal world of the client. If that were so, it is doubtful that any movement would ensue in therapy. Indeed, there would be no therapy. Instead, the client-centered therapist aims to dip from the pool of implicit meanings just at the edge of the client's awareness. (Rogers, 1966a: 190)

In the same passage, Rogers likens this aspect and quality in the client-centred therapy interview with the aspect of skilled analytic interpretation as characterized by Fenichel, in particular, who stresses that 'effective interpretations can be given only at one specific point, namely, where the patient's immediate interest is momentarily centered' and some new awareness 'is striving to break through' (Fenichel, 1945, cited in Rogers, 1966a: 190). Gendlin also speaks in similar terms:

> The client-centered response at its best formulates something which is not yet fully formulated or conceptualized. . . . It formulates the meaning which the client has not yet symbolized explicitly but which he does now feel and which is implied in what he says. Sometimes it formulates the felt whole which the client has been trying to get at by various different verbalizations. (Gendlin, 1961a)

Many years ago, I thought it useful to make a distinction between the recognition aspect of empathic response and a more inferential aspect (Barrett-Lennard, 1959: 6–7; 1962a: 3). Experiential recognition may occur quickly, especially in response to very immediate, direct communication of feeling. At other moments, T's inner picture and consciousness of C's experience is building up, as cues are added or C gets closer her/himself to an immediate core of feeling and meaning. The two aspects work together because the end result, in full-bodied empathy, is still an experiential recognition. On another level, apt, responsive use of imagery and metaphor have come to seem of vital importance, to me and to others in client-centered circles (including Butler, 1974; Rice, 1974: and Bebout, 1974). Such images – tending to just happen in my experience on some intuitive 'right-hemisphere' basis – often work as 'carriers of empathy' (Barrett-Lennard, 1993a) and perhaps of other relevant qualities. They may go far beyond the client's explicit communication but are not interpretive responses.[4]

By and large, the more that T departs from C's explicit messages and transparent implications, the more felt risk there is that his/her understanding and images will be distractingly off-target within the client's frame of reference. For example, it may turn out that T has moved outside 'the edge of the client's awareness', or has failed to connect with any new awareness 'striving to break through', or is hindering rather than aiding discovery of a 'felt whole' or other experiential shift. In practice, however, providing the therapist always returns to listen and check with sensitive care against the client's experience and perspective then owned, responsive sharing of the

---

4 Butler (1974: 197) sums up the central task of the client-centred therapist as being 'to encourage and facilitate the expressive embodiment of feeling' by the client, through representations that include 'well-rendered *images of client feelings*' (italics added). Butler illustrates at some length from the same interview what my first short excerpt in this chapter is drawn from. At the time of my selection, directly from the whole interview transcript, I was not aware of coincidence with Butler's usage. Afterwards, I felt that readers might find interest in seeing the interview portions in the two distinct contexts of Butler's analysis (1974: 183–188) and my own illustration.

intuitive and 'poetic' elements of T's experience with C may further the relationship and movement in therapy.[5]

The excerpts which follow catch in flavour and partial substance the primary elements mentioned under this heading. The first extract is from an interview early in the client's therapy experience. The therapist's modest use of metaphor seems to contribute to a qualitative shift in the client's experiencing and communication. The client had been speaking of very troubling, extreme feelings of jealousy, but describing and analysing her experience rather than seeming to feel it immediately.

Cl: Well, the reaction is always – always out of balance with the cause, you know, with whatever set it off. There doesn't seem to be any wish. . .
Th: A little thing, it's like pulling a trigger (*Cl*: Right), can set off a very big bang in you.
Cl: Right. And in my past – this is what also worries me right now – is that with —, and with another very important person, the only way I could handle these feelings when they got out of bounds was to consciously go out of my way to stop having them, and to terminate (*Th*: Terminate?) the whole relationship [client's voice breaks – pause].
Th: You mean your feeling was so overpowering and unbearable that somehow you had to get right out of the relationship – to go on.
Cl: [Speaking softly through tears] Right.
Th: [Gently] I guess that brings back a *lot* of feeling right now.

Following this interchange, the client turned at once from past contexts to the loaded present: a minefield of intensely felt experience and events in relation to her spouse. Later in the session her feeling softened. The sequence is a familiar one in therapy. Distress carried from the past, when it is rather fully expressed and received, often works as a gateway to grappling with related current issues; issues that are even *more* tender and difficult because of their immediacy in the client's life.

Sometimes, a therapist image seems to connect with experiential information that hasn't been expressed at all, as well as capturing a clearly implied theme. The following example is taken from the middle part of a later interview with the same client. Troubling experiences and fears around failure or falling short had been prominent in the session. The excerpt opens with the last phrases in a longish statement about what the client expects of herself.

Cl: . . . I still feel that I'm over-extending myself . . . [words omitted]. But I don't see how I could be satisfied with less, I don't see it.
Th: You feel you're constantly expecting too much but on the other hand, when you look at it, you don't see how [C starts to speak, T continues] you could possibly settle for less, and be happy – and be satisfied.

---

5 Rice (1974) speaks in related language as well as idea, in her paper 'The evocative function of the therapist'. In his case-study report, 'A silent young man', Rogers (in Rogers et al., 1967: 401-416) directly illustrates his use of 'empathic guessing', and shares his thought about circumstances under which this might be helpful; and not hindering even when the acknowledged guessing is off-target. See also Gendlin's related thought (1968: 'rules' 4 and 5; and 1974: 216–226).

Cl: So it's like being greedy: I don't see how one could cut life more than that and still feel that one has lived – is really living. . .
Th: I, ehr, I guess another way of putting it that I wanted to express – and was hearing you say earlier when you described the episode of trying to get the drier fixed, and all that got caught up in and around that –
Cl: [Chuckling laugh] Yes, like a comedy.
Th: Looking back it can become a comedy, and you laugh even now. I guess a way of putting that is that you feel a great – [pauses briefly] . . . I have an image of you standing there, and you are being *fired at by 'shoulds'*. Your house *should* be clean and tidy before that electrician or drier man comes in, because you were just too damned embarrassed to have such a [client breaks in] . . .
Cl: Yes, I wish I could say to hell with it – why should I have to explain to him. I have been sick for the last two years, that's why the house is a mess. But I couldn't – I wouldn't either lower myself to excuse myself with him, or have him come in and look at me living there. . . . Anyway, I interrupted, I'm sorry –
Th: That's all right – *I* don't feel that. I just wanted to share the impression that – implied in what you were saying, as I was hearing it – there were a hell of a lot of ways that you feel you *should* be somehow.
Cl: And you've been hearing more than that, because you just heard my story which is called 'Snipers' – the story I wrote [explaining to Th].
Th: [Softly] Is that right!?
Cl: [Clicking her finger] How's that for hearing!

At the end of this last excerpt, the client is clearly feeling partnership in the interaction with T, and enjoyment of him being tuned to her experience to the point of using a metaphor so much in accord with her thought set and theme in the story she had just been writing. This was the first mention of the story but whether or not a subtle cue from C subconsciously triggered T's metaphor, or whether her short story somehow fitted and reflected feelings she had then described, is less important than the expressive quality and feeling in the interaction at this stage. Although both partners are 'working', in C's case around issues in her own living, they also seem present with each other, the atmosphere is not heavy and the engagement process – simultaneously with self and other – is rewarding. One of its ingredients is an evident warmth.

Warmth and caring, without conditions

In the nature of the situation, C is in a position of acknowledged or implied need as a person. This 'neediness' largely provides occasion for the association with T, and is behind the unusually direct and persistent focus on self-related experience and behaviour. Taking as given that C both wishes and fears to expose the sensitively charged territory of her/his feeling life, then T's own identity, purposes and resources as a helper contribute crucially to the way the client can proceed. These features, and the responsibility each feels in their relationship, contribute to the further focal aspects of the helping interview.

One such major aspect is the evocation of real feelings of warmth, interest and caring on T's part toward C as a person. In the client-centred interview, personal detachment or distance mitigates *against* the helping process. Feelings of compassion, warmth, respect or admiration, interest or liking and other positive feelings toward C as a person usually arise in T and are allowed to show. This means that the therapist's feelings are not hidden; I do not mean to imply that they are flaunted. Their natural expression occurs in the context of other emphases, including T's persistent concern to really hear and be in knowing touch with the other in their experiencing, itself an important manifestation of caring.[6] Striking illustration of how distinctly positive feelings toward C may surface and be shared, within the larger whole of the helping interview, occurs with 'Gloria' (published ten years after the event itself, in Rogers and Wood, 1974). Besides the obvious expressions later in the interview, a few words by T just after they begin – following a simple greeting and acknowledgement of the situation – at once suggests a perceptive and caring responsiveness that undoubtedly helped to set the tone of what followed:

Cl: Well, right now I'm nervous but I feel more comfortable the way you are talking in a low voice, and I don't feel like you'll be so harsh on me. But . . .
Th: I hear the tremor in your voice, so –

Warmth and caring, and active interest and openness to being deeply in touch with the other's inner world and experience of life and self, tend to imply a non-judgemental, no-strings-attached attitude. However, across a range of clients, or many interviews of therapy, T is not likely to be equally receptive and accepting of all feelings and attitudes. It is even less likely that T will react the same way to all client behaviours, although this need not imply up-and-down acceptance of the self or identity of the other. A discrimination between (past) behavioural acts and the (present) inner person or self needs eventually to be made by C as well as by T, especially in reference to behaviours linked to deep inner conflict and self-rejection. My own view is further expressed elsewhere, as follows:

> To be unconditionally responsive to the experiencing person does not mean accepting all their behaviour and certainly does not imply condoning everything they do. It is not the other's actions but their self or personhood that I, as client-centered therapist, prize. I do not wish to critically judge or evaluate the experiencing self of the other, especially in interaction that has a personal helping goal. This is not to say that I don't warm more to some component self-systems, 'voices' or motivations within the other person than to others, but if I am not to reinforce attempted inner domination of one self and feeling system over another

---

6 My emphasis here and in other passages is on the overt experiencing and real relationship of the therapy partners. But, in the final reading of my text for this book, it struck me that the notion of unconscious 'transference' in the client–therapist relationship – so dear to the thought of psychodynamic therapists – should at least be acknowledged. Rogers devoted a chapter of *Client-centred Therapy* (1951) to 'questions raised by other viewpoints', including transference, and the concept has not simply been ignored by Rogerians. A notable, later case in point is the searching and evocative examination by Shlien in his 'countertheory of transference' (1987), and the series of responding papers also published in the 1987 volume of the *Person-Centred Review*. My own contribution to the topic appears within an article in another journal (Barrett-Lennard, 1985b).

> but, instead, am to help open and free inner channels and dialogue, I need to be receptive and regardful of all the constituent 'selves' and their feelings. (Barrett-Lennard, 1993b)

The core of unconditionality is its evenhandedness in regard to the competing selves, and options for self, that C struggles with. An unconditional attitude gives no support for any expectation that C will be likeable or acceptable to T if s/he is one way (or displays one aspect of self) and disliked or rejected if another way (or if another side of self is shown). If T did respond differentially in this way it could hinder and would not help C's search for the truth about him/herself and, thus, for greater wholeness. It is also less difficult, or more possible, to find this truth and authenticity if the therapist companion embodies it.

Congruence, openness, transparency

The typically positive ambience of T's response to C has been discussed. To use another term, there is at best a 'prizing' quality in T's felt attitude toward C (see Butler, 1968). In practice, however, there are times when a helper will experience negative feelings toward the immediate self of the other, and if these feelings become strong they are almost certain to be communicated in some way. In these circumstances, client-centred workers have increasingly favoured acknowledging such feelings, if not at once to the client then with another enabling-consulting partner. Through disclosure and exploration with a helpful consultant, there probably would be change in T's feeling toward the client. Such change may make it easier (and perhaps more constructive) for T directly to share and express his/her feeling to C (Rogers, 1966a).

This issue ties in directly with the emphasized aspect of therapist congruence in the helping encounter. Broadly, T is fully *present*, with his/her internal and external engagement in flowing unity. This unity does not imply continuous total attention and high empathy, or unwavering acceptance and warmth. It does involve an unusual and special quality of openness, an expressive 'in-touchness' with felt experience and meaning, and of being there with the other in such a way that all sides of one's activity are aspects of one unhidden whole. A contrary state would be that of presenting a contrived, cultivated but non-integrated, role or part of oneself.

At best, T either is fully and deeply attentive, is non-judgementally listening to and beyond the words and gestures of the other, and is communicatively regardful and empathic, or he/she is transparently not responding in one or more of these ways. This transparency, although at the time and of its nature not done with calculation of effect, implies an openness to experience – to experiencing of the other, of self in response to the other and, at some moments, more of self than the other. When T's attention turns (albeit briefly) away from the client, this shows to both partners and does not obscure the main path, which might now continue with deeper attention and connection (Barrett-Lennard, 1985a: 290).

In earlier discussion of immediacy, effectively an aspect of congruence, I foreshadowed quoting a paper in which Rogers (1961b) includes a vivid description of what it is like subjectively for a therapist moving into a depth of engagement with the client other. Rogers' portrayal not only depicts a therapist congruently open to his/her experience, but helps to draw together other threads in my account here of the helping interview. The form is inner dialogue by the therapist:

> Here is this other person, my client. I'm a little afraid of him, afraid of the depths in him as I am a little afraid of the depths of myself. Yet as he speaks, I begin to feel a respect for him, to feel my kinship to him. I sense how frightening his world is for him, how tightly he tries to hold it in place. I would like to sense his feelings, and I would like him to know that I understand his feelings. . . . I would like my feelings in this relationship with him to be as clear and transparent as possible, so that they are a discernible reality for him. . . . I would like to go with him on the fearful journey into himself, into the buried fear, and hate, and love which he has never been able to let flow in him. I recognize that this is a very human and unpredictable journey for me, as well as for him, and that I may, without even knowing my fear, shrink away within myself, from some of the feelings he discovers. . . . I realize that at times his own fears may make him perceive me as uncaring, as rejecting, as an intruder, as one who does not understand. I want to fully accept these feelings in him, and yet I hope also that my own real feelings will show through so clearly that in time he cannot fail to perceive them. (Rogers, 1961b: 42)

Rogers quietly adds another significant sentence, 'I do not need to be uneasy as to whether my own feelings are "therapeutic".' What he means is that if he can be openly himself, albeit in helping mode – an important qualification which he omits mentioning here – the relationship is very likely to be releasing and healing for the client (1961b: 42). It is not held that *any* authentic expression of the self, by a 'helping' partner, would be freeing and enabling to the distressed or suffering other. Rather, it is the view of this approach that no expression that is unauthentic or incongruent can be substantially therapeutic. This feature is the final one in this survey of the helping interview components, to be merged now in brief restatement.

Conclusion

In the therapeutic relationship in client-centred mode, the helper is responding from the reality of his/her human presence and engagement with the other. Desirably, this reality includes a ground of actual regard and interest on the helper's part for the experiencing self of the other person, a respect for them and sense of kinship with them in their struggles, even in their ways of protecting themselves, and a feeling of partnership and literally shared responsibility in the therapy enterprise. There are at best many moments of substantial or even high empathy, flowing from the helper's deeply attentive listening to the other from within a resonating but also distinct other self, this in turn growing out of an absorbed wish to be in touch, to understand, and to build a bridge of personal knowing. All of these elements are in keeping with another, namely, to approach the client person with a receptivity that largely excludes approving–disapproving judgement of them, that conveys no requirement that they be one way or another in themselves, to satisfy the helper, that offers scope for a deeper aim and possibility – the fuller discovery and unfolding of their own selfhood.

Finally, all this said about the helping interview, that is, about what is held to be important at any and all times in the client–therapist relationship, there is another whole complementary level or angle of view from which the process needs to be considered. As therapy proceeds, and assuming client and therapist stay the course from their first meeting to a fruitful later conclusion, there are major developmental shifts in the helping alliance, in the client's concerns and process, and in the communication between the partners, shifts that flow from a journey of relationship, discovery and healing that grows on itself. This further level is the focus of the next chapter.

7

The Course of Therapy

> Whether by chance, by insightful understanding, by scientific knowledge, by artistry in human relationships, or by a combination of all of these elements, we have learned how to initiate a describable process which appears to have a core of sequential, orderly events . . . similar from one client to another.
>
> Carl Rogers, 1953

The therapy conditions model, now entering a fifth decade of influence, is concerned with the agency of change not with its unfolding course. The model's elegant economy and focus on qualities of therapist response considered of primary importance in the helping interview generally, that is, at any stage in therapy, has had one unfortunate side-effect which this chapter seeks to redress. The model has tended to divert attention from a complementary focus on the course or pathway of therapy, where the feature of interest is the change and progression in process from start to conclusion.

Therapy as a natural progression

Nothing stood in the way of pursuing the broad interest of this chapter during the emergence of non-directive client-centred therapy. As already mentioned, in his founding book on the new therapy Rogers suggested that the approach involved a sequence of twelve typical steps. He took care to acknowledge that these 'steps' are not all discontinuous events but shade into each other, and that their stated order is an approximation. His central point was that there is foundation for 'the hypothesis that skilfully conducted treatment interviews are not a hodgepodge of discrete elements, but that taken as a whole they represent a complete chain in which one element tends to follow another'

---

1 The history of this chapter may interest some readers. Its first formulation (*c.* 1981/82) was part of my original work, in Canada, toward this book. The draft lay in my files until unveiled at the Third International Forum on the Person-Centred Approach, San Diego, 8/1987. I further revised it for presentation at the International Conference on Client-Centred and Experiential Psychotherapy, Leuven, Belgium, 9/1988, and for publication in the substantial volume that grew out of this conference (Lietaer, Rombauts and Van Balen, 1990). This present chapter is a further revision, effectively returning the material to its original context in this long-planned volume.

(1942a: 47). A fresh summary of Rogers' original account of this chain is given in my prior publication on the topic of this chapter (Barrett-Lennard, 1990).[1] Later in the book I will come back to related early work, in discussing the first phase of empirical study of client-centred therapy, a phase which centred on analysing interview content to discern both constancies and shifts in pattern as therapy advanced.

What follows here is a new explorer's map of the general route of client-centred therapy. The therapy enterprise is broadly a means to the end of healing and growthful change, each step reflecting and building on gains already made. Thus the path or course of events *is* the enterprise, in basic part; and to map this path is to throw further light on the phenomenon and nature of therapy.

In seeking to freshly characterize the course of client-centred therapy, issues at once spring to view regarding its fundamental nature. Is it an educative process, centred on personal-emotional learning? Is it a form of healing, of recovery from psychic damage? Is it a matter of discovery and development of undeveloped potentials? Does it centre on emotional and interpersonal growth? Is it a means of transformation from being a passive or reactive recipient of influence to being an active agent in one's world? Is the therapy an approach to redress from the alienating effects of much of contemporary life? With individually varying emphasis, it is surely all of these, and more.

Can such a broad spectrum of purpose in its manifold expressions be pursued through the 'same' overall process, or reach fruition through the same kind of journey? This at first sight seems improbable. Yet it is the *process* that largely defines client-centred therapy, or therapy of any distinctive orientation. And consistency of process, or means, implies a coherence of ends or outcome; a complex singularity to the nature of help in a given approach. Client-centred therapy in particular is a many-sided living whole in which a certain diversity arises naturally from the uniqueness of each client and each emergent relationship between therapy partners. However, the diversity may seem greater than it is, as a result of mixing process or effects that belong to different stages in the journey.

Thus the process of therapy has more than one principal face, as well as many features within each one. A major, now familiar aspect or face is the quality of the therapist–client relationship, especially as seen through the lens of the therapy conditions model. Looking at the whole phenomenon in its developmental dimension yields another principal face. Immediate distress may ease fairly quickly in therapy but pattern change takes more time and literal work, work that hinges on the therapy alliance. A healing and growthful engagement – unique in kind to most clients – does not spring full-blown into being. Working steps in therapy occur within this evolving relationship and contribute to it. Client issues change as progress is made, and these and other features combine to trace a pathway which constitutes the journey or course of therapy; a dimension as fundamental as the general level of the relationship conditions.

The phases of therapy

Following is a contemporary view of the basic 'pathway' of client/person-centred therapy. It encompasses five main, qualitative phases, each distinct in principle but shading into the next in practice. As described, each phase is like a crest or hilltop from which the view is clearer and the location more discernible than on the slopes and in the valleys between. The phases, together, span the whole therapy route I see, although in practice this may be cut short and end almost anywhere along the way.

A. Beginning: *the entry phase*

This description of the way therapy unfolds assumes that the client is present voluntarily, even if pushed by inner desperation and pain, or if approaching therapy tentatively as a possible recourse; and that client and therapist are meeting together in these capacities for the first time. Assuming they are not already in close relationship, whether they are acquainted from other contexts, or meeting as strangers, has no consistent significance.[2] More important is whether the client has effectively made an informed choice of therapist and approach *or* has come with little or no knowledge of the particular therapist (T) or of the process and philosophy of helping with which T is identified.

Where the client is making an informed choice, the entry phase generally includes the period from the client's (C's) first approach to the therapist as helper, through whatever preliminaries are involved before the first therapy meeting, to the end of that meeting. What happens, among other effects, tends to confirm C's choice and add more specific experiential meaning to it. Where the choice is not an informed one, the preliminaries to the first therapy contact generally involve greater information exchange, and the first meetings tend to have a more visibly exploratory character with regard to the therapy medium and enterprise. The entry phase, in this case, may easily take more than one therapy interview session – and it might not come to fruition at all.

Several elements help to signify and mark that the beginning phase is accomplished – but without implying that therapy will necessarily continue through its whole potential course, or that a highly productive outcome is certain. The proposed signs of advancement through this starting phase, straightforward in essence, are as follows:

◇ *Present by choice.* C has indicated that s/he is there, meeting with T as a counsellor, by her/his own decision – or, at the least, by agreement with

2 There is no proscription in client-centred therapy against C and T knowing each other beforehand, or being in contact on other levels (of a less self-intimate nature than therapy) during the period of therapy. Indeed, since no transference is being cultivated, such contact may further the anchorage between in-therapy experience and outside life experience and behaviour. From one significant vantage-point, the aim of therapy is to become unnecessary. For this literally to happen fresh shoots of healing or growthful change need to be exposed and tested in outside life contexts, and then refined further in the nutrient laboratory of therapy, in alternating progression.

any external advice to take this step. This may only become quite clear when arrangements are being made for a further interview or series of meetings.

- ◇ *Owning to personal difficulty.* C has taken steps to account for his or her presence, owning to difficulty or distress with self, with relationships, or the disturbing impact of particular life events. There is a message in some form that 'All is not well with me (I'm troubled, dissatisfied, confused, or hurting), and that's why I'm here.'
- ◇ *Feelings are an issue.* C has directly expressed feeling or, at minimum, acknowledged that feelings exist and need be reckoned with, for example, by facing and clarifying them, gaining relief from some torment, or changing the balance of inner feeling life.
- ◇ *Beyond rehearsed content.* At least part of the time, C has departed (as it were) from a prepared text. Communication is not limited to reporting experiences, or reciting rehearsed content. There are discernible moments in which C is speaking from what is coming now in his/her feelings or thoughts.
- ◇ *Monologue to duologue.* There is a perceptible shift in C's awareness of T, which T of course plays a part in. It is a qualitative shift, perhaps from thinking/feeling aloud to an awareness of engagement with the other person, *or*, from addressing a figure made up from variously based expectations, to communicating with a person now felt and coming into view as a distinctive other presence.
- ◇ *Awareness of being heard.* There are indications that the client has begun to feel heard by the therapist and to anticipate further personal understanding.
- ◇ *Being here matters.* What is happening in *this* forming relationship has begun to matter to both participants. Neither C nor T could walk away from their association without significant after-thought or feeling; and in balance both wish to go further.[3]

A great deal *can* happen in the first interview in (client-centred) therapy. Usually, it seems, few sessions are as critical, although later on eventfulness may be differently experienced and measured. The following excerpts from the first interview with a woman client in her early or mid-thirties, and whose choice was relatively informed, are thought to illustrate most elements and features so far mentioned. The dialogue begins with the first client statement, following an invitation by the therapist to say what brought her to therapy or to share how she is feeling; in effect, to begin wherever she wishes. She knew that the session was being both observed and recorded.

---

3 Another element that seems often, but not always, to signal that the therapy engagement has actually started is that C's step is a little lighter when s/he leaves the session than when it began; that whatever kind of load C has been carrying and has finally sought help with, is not quite so heavy. The exact sources and forms of this difference are many, but it seems to have some fairly consistent physiological counterparts, often including visibly deeper and more even breathing and reduced muscle tension, and less noticeable adjustments in circulation.

Cl 1: I've been thinking about where to start. There's no really logical place. I guess I'll go from the general to the specific. I've been in therapy a few times and I find each time it helps me but as soon as anything out of the ordinary happens I go back to stage one. So that I find that even though I've gotten some partial help to cope with a specific situation that there hasn't been any – enough change, I find, in my vision or whatever, that makes me feel safe enough for the future, I guess. I always –

Th 2: [Interrupting] But you came into this situation, *this* therapy – this prospective therapy experience – with a background of having been in therapy before . . .

Cl 2: [Quickly breaking in] Does that invalidate it in any way?

Th 3: No, I'm just responding to – making sure I'm catching your meaning – and what I'm hearing is that you have tried therapy; you haven't given up on it or you wouldn't be here, *but it hasn't been of any long-range help so far*.

Cl 3: Right! [Pauses, thinking]. Specifically what happened this summer, or last year, when things started to get uncomfortable, was that I was in a dancing class and I suffered some damage to my knees . . . [details omitted]. One of the doctors seems to think there may be some permanent damage and that my life might possibly be narrowed down, that my activities might be narrowed down, for keeps. That threw me into a pretty severe depression which brought on a lot of other things kind of tied to it. [T begins to respond, C interrupts and, after a few short exchanges, they return to the same theme.]

Cl 7: And I guess I was just a little bit weakened to handle them, I was – wasn't – I was.

Th 8: Demoralized?

Cl 8: Right! I was pretty demoralized. And all of a sudden it just flashed on me how – I think even though this time I'm by now maybe feeling that I could control them again and just push them into a closet, I never know when they'll come out again under different circumstances. I just don't feel safe any more, I just feel very – er – that I'm just not really handling them [C agitated, moist-eyed, continues speaking], that I'm just repressing them which doesn't help so far [C's voice breaks a little] because they are still very active. And I'm conscious – all of a sudden I started seeing patterns that I haven't seen before. I always saw every situation apart, and I was sort of wondering how much I did to get myself into these things, how much of it was [pause] was perhaps self-destructive. [C pauses, her eyes moist.]

Th 9: Hmm. Sounds, as I'm hearing what you are saying, it's . . . you're feeling rather upset as you try and express how it is for you, now, and how it has been recently. And, especially this aspect of feeling that you begin to see a pattern where you may have been – I'm not quite sure what you mean by self-destructive – but somehow *bringing injury on yourself* [said both with emphasis and a question mark].

[After brief further discussion/clarification of the client's meaning she turns to another side of the same issue.]

Cl 12: [More firmly] When I get to the point that I'm functioning well I *add* things. I add too much, and hmm . . . until everything just topples from the load of it.

Th 13: Until you just can't cope with it all.

Cl 13: Right; and I find I've been doing this a lot. After my daughter was born, I was just barely coping with having her and studying, and as soon as I was just barely able to fit her and my husband and my studies together I started dancing again, and that really got me very rushed, got my husband very rushed because he had to give me rides back and forth, gave me much less time with my daughter. It was like I just – I insisted on it very much, and even after I hurt my leg I went on back dancing two or three times. So, you know, with hindsight, I'm wondering if . . . [pauses].

Th 14: If part of your way of being is to push yourself all the time beyond your own limits, somehow?

Cl 14: So then I have a good excuse to fail. I don't know; this is just seeing with hindsight . . .

[Client adds a bit more context and history, and then returns to the theme of her efforts to understand and explain.]

Cl 17: . . . I guess I'd always been *trying* to explain why I got myself in hot water before. And every time I had a different explanation. And I was wondering if I couldn't find one that would fit everything; if it seems to be a habitual pattern . . . I was [C clearing her nose] wondering if it had to do with, with that particular – [C stops].

Th 18: By the way, I'm – Oh, there is some Kleenex [pushes it over to client]. It sounds as though you – ehr – you know, you *really* wish you could understand; that you were on top of whatever the hell it is that's going on underneath in you, somehow, that's behind the things, that's driving you or propelling you in the ways that you go.

[Passage omitted until T asks a question, inviting C to focus on the change she is seeking.]

Th 24: I guess I find myself sort of wondering, wanting to get more of a feeling for *how* you would like to change or *what* you would like to change, what ways you would like to be different than you are?

Cl 24: [Pause] I suppose self-assurance springs to mind, but that can mean anything. [Slight pause] Yes, I suppose that would cover it. . . .

The interview continued with deepening expression by the client of how tightly and painfully she was 'holding everything up' in her life. This part of the dialogue (immediately following *Cl* 24) appears in Chapter 6, under the heading 'Active listening and empathy'. Toward the end of this further sequence the client, who had been chain smoking, mentioned that she had run out of matches. This problem, which T could not help with directly, created opportunity for an episode which undoubtedly brought the client and therapist more distinctly into view to each other, and also provided the lightest moments in the interview.

The episode began with T returning to the client's predicament and mentioning that if they looked outside the door of the interview room shortly, he believed there would be a box of matches there. Only momentarily puzzled, C tuned to the tacit message to the unseen observers. Sure enough the matches were there! T was glad C knew *how* they had appeared, saying that he did not want her to think he was any kind of magician, either in reference to the matches or to therapy. The spontaneous 'lesson' was fun; C was alive in her awareness and evident feeling of contact with T. There was increase in her confidence and spontaneity in the therapy situation, linked to a rise in the immediacy of her communication. At the end of the session she planned a series of appointments, envisaged as continuing for a number of months – seven months, in the event.

It became quite clear, within this interview, that the client felt she was in trouble in her own functioning; that this had led to a choice to seek help through therapy; that she experienced distressing feelings, which she wanted to change or gain relief from; that although she started out by describing difficulties and reporting on her experience she soon began to pick up on the therapist's responses to her and go into what she was feeling as she spoke; and that the therapist came into view to her as another person closely listening, seeking to understand and actively responding to her – mostly in serious vein but, at one point, almost in playful mode. An engagement of consequence to the participants had begun which they both wished to continue. Thus, each of the suggested criteria for the Entry Phase was met in the course of this interview. As well, the sessions that immediately followed were broadly consistent with the next phase to be described.

B. Forging a personal-working alliance and the passage from woundedness to hope

Two main streams flowing through the course of therapy can be distinguished. Each feeds and furthers the other, but is distinct. *One stream is the development of the client–therapist relationship*, encompassing each one's evolving perception of the other and the view each has of the kind and quality of their partnership in the enterprise they are engaged in. The other stream (to come back to), centres on client issues and process, as these unfold and change over the course of therapy. Since the client is in some way struggling or stuck in his/her own process, in a situation of troubling adversity, and has enlisted T's help to gain relief and work through and out of this affliction, the client-centred helping association is a form of alliance. And as the relationship between C and T is employed as a means, and the enterprise is both person-focused and demanding, the term 'personal-working alliance' seems usefully appropriate.

In this phase the helping relationship comes strongly into being, although not yet to optimal fruition. As this is happening, the therapist comes to be experienced as a resourceful ally in a rather unique sense. (If this does not occur, therapy is likely to be aborted.) In client-centred therapy the client leads the alliance in terms of content issues, and contributes (if not as senior partner) to determining process. C may wish that T would 'take over' more, but this wish recedes as the alliance grows stronger. In fact, initiatives expanded beyond T's usual repertoire may naturally occur; for example, if C truly seems lost, frozen, in an abyss of confusion or despair, or in the grip of extreme anxiety or other emotion seeming to have a life of its own. Even without such extremity, Gendlin (1978) and other exponents of focusing may become active during this phase in working to directly help clients engage and dialogue with their own inner felt sense.

In effect, this is the make-or-break phase of therapy from the standpoint of therapists. The therapist ally needs to come into view for the client in his/her own distinctive likeness as helper-person; and the client likewise needs to become not just a string of feelings and perceptions responded to one by one but an increasingly known whole configured person to the therapist. The alliance evolves unevenly, as any significant relationship does, but in overall pattern toward deeper engagement and eventfulness, and greater commitment to what has become a sharply real and consequential enterprise. Alternatively, such development never really takes off, or it begins to and then falters and ceases, or is aborted by circumstance. C may never move into a full-fledged therapeutic mode of self-inquiry and discourse with T, perhaps resting instead with modest gain in terms of the immediate felt situation that prompted entry to therapy. In the latter case, therapy would stop without the alliance aspect or stream developing to fruition. One might refer to this as a Phase B termination.

The reader might wonder about my use of the term 'forging'. To speak of forging the personal-working alliance could evoke imagery of hammering something softened by heat into shape, which seems scarcely in keeping with a humanistic person-centred approach! However, if figurative usage is granted, and given that people can be drawn from within to undertake strenuous and difficult tasks requiring an unusual kind of team effort – one-to-one therapy in this instance – the term begins to seem more fitting. As with any complex collaborative or team effort, instant fruition is not possible. Hard-working practice experience, including some trial and error, is inherent.[4]

Part of the unusual demand of therapy is that clients cannot for long coast through a well-practised repertoire, without the process grinding to a halt or becoming visibly pointless. Add further the feature of a therapist-partner who usually is a stranger and whose way of responding is unfamiliar in its total pattern. Then, it is indeed the case that the alliance is not simply present or given but something produced through strenuous application in a mode of searching dialogue; at once with self and with other. However, in a fruitful alliance so forged, the engagement becomes self-propelling for both partners. As 'person-centred' implies, the therapist as person is present too, in such a way that experience or expertise do not diminish the challenge or lessen the rewarding elements for the helper partner in a personal helping alliance.

The second stream in Phase B flows from the general nature or thrust of issues likely to be paramount for the client at this still early stage in therapy. My approach to identifying and framing the central or underlying client issue cuts across a wide range of individual expressions. It starts from the idea of a shift or passage from X to Y, *from* something that is part of what propels nearly anyone to enter personal therapy *to* something that encourages and makes them want to keep going with the enterprise of therapy. As I pondered on this, what stood out to me is that the 'X' in this transition is some quality of woundedness, and the 'Y' amounts to an increase or awakening of hope.

Reflected in this distinction is the idea that nearly all of us are wounded at times, in a psycho-social sense, and that we carry old wounds that may, under relevant conditions of stress, flare up again. Clients typically begin personal therapy with past wounds that have flared up again and which may have been augmented by present/recent wounding. These varied wounds tend to have in common painfully diminished self-esteem or sense of worth, feelings of apprehension or anxiety, a degree of depression or a more existential kind of despair and loss of meaning, and some fresh hurt or disturbing life difficulty in which anger and pain are often fused. Such woundedness from long-term and immediate causes, leaves the person without confidence that 'good' can

---

4 Surgery epitomizes a sharply contrasting form of helping association, in that one highly skilled person operates on another person who is completely passive *during this treatment*. Psychotherapy cannot work without the highly active involvement of each collaborating partner.

come of his or her efforts, leading to a view of things as through a darkened and narrowing lens – in short, a loss of hope. Persons choosing to enter therapy have not lost all hope, and the fact of taking this plunge itself typically brings some increment.

The client's woundedness may be said to arise from some form of psychic or psycho-social assault. Experientially, it is something which happens *to* the individual, even if later it is seen to have been brought on or played into by self. Hope on the other hand arises within the person and is energizing and activating. In a wounded state the individual naturally retreats, or hits out reactively. The hopeful person reaches from within, initiates, takes action. In passing from woundedness to hope the person typically shifts from suffering passivity or reactiveness to a wide-awake, more purposeful and active mode. Such movement may not be large in Phase B but the direction is discernible.

In navigating the passage through Phase B, the client's exploration begins to loosen areas of pain, anger, sorrow or other woundedness, and the helping partnership that meets this test significantly evolves in the process. One outcome is that C ventures, dares now, to actually believe and feel that there is a way ahead that is better than the track behind. Therapy has begun to ease the burden C has been carrying, it is giving safety to communication and search from the heart and the edge of awareness, and there is promise of further respite, discovery, even new vision. There is, it seems, a route to change in a journey that has actually started. Hope has reawakened.

Of course, this transition does not occur for every client, and its completion is a matter of impression and judgement, not of literal and marked discontinuity in the therapy process. Its duration may have been only two or three eventful meetings, or a three-month saga of hardworking therapy sessions. With very deeply disturbed clients, it may take longer still but happen none the less, as implied for example in the case of 'The silent young man' in the Wisconsin psychotherapy research project (Rogers, 1967f: 401–416). Moving to Phase C is like rounding a wide, rising curve, distinct at the end to the alerted driver, both in rear-view and in terms of the new vista and discernibly changing landscape ahead. It is as though the travellers feel, if they pause to think of it, 'Now we are really on the way, and able to count on each other. Change *is* possible, although it's hard going – so let's get on!' 'Getting on' is not a matter of either changing gears or of going on just as before, but of finding and creating the way through newly central issues in the alliance and in the client's quest.

C. *Trust development, and the quest for self: 'Who am I?' 'How do I want to be?'*

The two streams (i) of relationship development and (ii) of client issues and process, continue their flow, on further levels, through Phase C. The recovery or awakening of hope in the client is as individual in specific quality as the client is distinct as a person from others. However, in one form or another, this awakening leads into a new intensity or scope of self-exploration, a more literal questing search for the heart of the individual's identity or for a reconciliation of elements in conflict within the self. By 'self' I do not mean to refer solely to the person's inner or intra-psychic being but also to the self as manifest and related to others in the world. It is this world which helped to fashion such aspects as the owned accepted-me, the me-I-fear, the wanted-me and the not-me, and in relation to which change has its primary eventual meaning.

In order for C to deeply open the self to view and review, especially in its generally hidden and most problematic aspects, therapy must be a safe haven and unusual in the authenticity and measure of therapist empathy and other crucial relationship qualities. Put in other terms, in order for C to searchingly disclose unshared thoughts, feelings and actions of the self *and* to work openly at inner dialogue with very indistinct but pressing elements of his or her being – in effect, to search, feel and inquire into the very soul of self – a rare quality of experienced safety and positive trust of T is necessary. This trust, implicitly building in Phase B, is, in its fuller development and significance, advanced as the central feature of the therapeutic relationship and alliance in Phase C.

In original application of the process conception and scales, the assumption was made that clients in therapy were in the relatively constant situation of being 'psychologically received' (Rogers, 1961b: 130–131). Trust in the sense used here, has related, even stronger meaning. The client is not only 'received' but actively companioned in the risky enterprise of open-ended self-exploration in its fullest sense. Requisite conditions for the needed strong trust in the therapist-companion include repeated experience of being deeply heard, of C having literally felt T resonating and almost knowing at critical moments 'what it is like to be me'. It is not necessary or realistic that C experience this quality of empathy continuously, or during every pregnancy and birthing of fresh awareness. The important element is that genuine close personal understanding has happened and led to confidence by C that it will recur, especially when his/her feelings flow into little-explored inner territory.

Such trust also depends on C having experienced T's caring interest coupled with absence of personal evaluative judgement. Most crucial are contexts where C censures him or herself, that is, in sensitively difficult areas where other people in C's life, and finally C him/herself, have tended to be chronically evaluative. Usually crucial to the quality of trust is C's experience of T as open and revealing of her/his own personhood, not necessarily via informational communication but through a way of responding that expresses what is immediately present in T's experiencing, with transparent ownership of this experience. Clients themselves may stress the importance to them of this openness or transparency, especially near the close of therapy.

For the therapist to share, even with simple and straightforward brevity, from his or her own life, involves an element of risk-taking. At minimum there is likely to be some felt risk of distracting the client or of seeming to invite a shift in content focus from C to T, or perhaps (for the novice therapist) of being 'unprofessional' by behaving in a fashion out of keeping with providing a specialized therapeutic service to the client. The positive thesis here is that personal realness and transparency works to *disarm* and evoke trust in the other – legitimately so since it is showing what is actually present. (To mimic transparency would be such a contradictory process that cues of a kind to deter trust seem very likely.) This trust in turn melts away motivation in C to keep up his or her accustomed guard.

Thus, a high level of trust reduces concern to portray a socially acceptable self and allows self-known secrets which burden the client to come into open view. Beyond this, such founded trust helps inner walls to become permeable or gradually transparent. The continued exploration provides additional confirmation that T is there unafraid and unjudging beside C, sharing in awareness of that which is gradually emerging or sometimes erupting into C's felt view. In alternate metaphor, C's trust of T permits them to approach and hear together the first whispers and growing voice of newly released inner dialogue and communication, amplified in volume, clarity and movement by the act of sharing.

Clients very often are struggling with severe and deeply stressful crises in their lives, have not necessarily played a foremost part in precipitating their crises, and might be average or above the norm in respect to basic personality integration, or to level of functioning on the process continuum or Gendlin's experiencing scale. However, those who elect and choose to continue in client-centred therapy, in effect hold themselves responsible in significant degree for the pain and needs that bring them to therapy, and have implicitly opted for *self*-change, within the broad meaning of 'self' earlier discussed. It would follow that they tend to hold 'internal locus of control' attitudes, implying assumed agency and responsibility in their lives. In practice, it may seem to them that their self-influence is at present blocked or impaired, and that a broad purpose of therapy is to restore and develop effective self-propulsion. Effectively, they seek to attain a self or 'me' at one with itself, which reaches out resourcefully and without censure from its own core, that senses where it is going and knows how to proceed with the journey, and which feels alive and part of lives beyond itself. Persons on the other hand whose orientation is strongly external, whose pervasive feeling and stance is that the causes of both trials and joys lie outside them*selves*, are less likely to make an active choice of client-centred therapy, or to follow through in the course outlined here.

A major sub-issue or theme in Phase C is the client's feeling and exploration of responsibility in his/her life, for example: 'How *am I* making things go wrong?' A more positive, self-affirming counterpart is also likely to arise: 'I'm better [or stronger, more resourceful, more 'with it'] than I thought'; 'Although disappointed, feeling I let myself [or others] down, I *now* see how/why I did it, and feel wiser for the future'; or, 'I don't *want* to play that kind of game [specified], or model myself after that person. It's not me.' There is increasing ownership of the self or 'I' as the agent of experience as well as where it is happening, and more sense of the ability to make active choices and to discover, learn and change. The latter can lead to the theme: 'What do I most want to change about myself – in ways that I feel, how I react to other people, or the load from my past that I carry around?' or, 'What are my goals for myself, for the ways I want to develop and grow?' In the nature of client-centred therapy, the last questions are almost certain to become prominent in some form, and especially so when the client is working directly at sorting out and further establishing his or her personal identity.[5]

Rogers' process conception grew out of experience in therapy and some of its main elements tend to be apparent in Phase C, as features or issues in the client's exploration and modes of self-expression. Shifts in process level in the environment of therapy occur, although perhaps not over such a wide span as initially implied (Rogers, 1959b). Rogers originally suggested that 'many people who seek psychological help are at approximately the point of stage three', on the seven-stage continuum distinguished. He continued: 'They may stay at roughly this point, for a considerable time, describing non-present feelings and exploring the self as an object, before being ready to move on to the next stage' (Rogers, 1961b: 136–137).[6] When such movement does occur, and in terms of about stage 4 in Rogers' portrayal, feelings tend at first to be reported in an objectified way from the past ('It felt'), in the client's life in general ('My feeling has always been . . .'), as desirable possibilities ('It would mean a lot to me if . . .'), and in other 'pointing at' or arm's length ways. Then, in stage 5, 'we find many feelings freely expressed in the moment of their occurrence', and previously denied feelings really begin to 'bubble through' into awareness (Rogers, 1959b: 99). Hesitantly at first, but increasingly through stages 4 and 5, clients *ascribe meaning* to and from their own experience. This reflects awareness that the constructs they use, especially in discriminations regarding self and others, are not absolute givens but invented lenses that can be modified, replaced, experimented with. Inner discrepancies and incongruence, and sometimes a recognition of self as a complex plurality or system rather than an indivisible monad, are significantly and increasingly in view in process stages 4 and 5.[7]

In its operational formulation by Gendlin and collaborators the (manner of) experiencing scale is depicted as concerned broadly with 'the degree to which the client manifests inward reference in his verbalizations'. The core

---

5 Many more specific themes in the overall quest portrayed could be discerned and illustrated. One example is: 'When/how far can I trust my feelings and intuition as a guide to what I do?' Another imagined/real illustration of what a client might actually say is: 'I wish, I *want* to *listen* to my feelings and what I'm sensing, and kind of keep in step on the outside with the me that is inside! I want to keep the inside channel open when I'm occupied with other people and tasks. I feel better and do better, when this is happening.'

6 What Rogers posits here appears to be consistent with Phase B or, at least, with a main variant of this phase. How long and difficult a process it is to develop a strong personal/working alliance seems to depend a good deal on the client's process level on entering therapy and on the therapist's versatility in engaging in the helping mode with persons of varying initial capacity to experientially express, question and explore their own selfhood.

7 Somewhat fresh language is used here, slightly advancing but largely in keeping with Rogers' earlier thought. The aspect of 'manner of relating', as explicated and rendered in operational form by Gendlin (1967), has to do with the therapeutic relationship as itself an experiential theatre for self-change. Stage 4 in Gendlin's formulation is headed 'Parallel and together: the relationship as a context of therapy', and his differentiated account under this heading both complements and is consistent with the view advanced here, as a description of a well-established, personal-working therapeutic alliance. Stage 5 in Gendlin's portrayal builds on stage 4 to include use of 'the relationship as specific therapy', and overlaps with Phase D in the present conception.

feature of stage 4 is that the client describes him/herself, or at minimum tries to communicate directly what he/she is like. However, although aware of personal feelings and qualities, the client at this level is not strenuously exploring self. But assuming therapy progresses, a major corner is about to be turned. At stage 5, 'The client is now using his feelings in a struggle to explore himself' and at this point is seen as 'clearly engaged in a process of self-exploration in order to achieve self-understanding' – with all the effort and unevenness that 'struggle' implies (Gendlin et al., 1967).

Phase C of the course of therapy thus encompasses elements and qualities particularly associated with in-therapy client functioning at stages 4 and 5 in the process conception and experiencing scale. As seen from a matrix of convergent viewing planes, the client's advance through this phase is made possible by the deepening quality of trust in the relationship, in the meaning described. The association is a recursive one: the trust is 'earned' and evolves as the client ventures a cautious step or unexpected leap, is companioned in helping mode, strives again and is confirmed once more in T's response. Within the client, not only are rigid, unchosen older moorings left behind, but any *fixed* anchorages are used in diminishing degree by an increasingly buoyant and mobile, becoming self.

Assuming therapy runs the full course outlined here, Phase C is expected to be the longest in working duration; and in such cases probably the phase in which greatest personal change occurs. A proportion of clients would proceed from Phase C directly to termination, or to a termination phase that included foreshortened elements from Phase D. There is no clear-cut boundary between Phases C and D, but a qualitative transition, most evident after its occurrence, in the working process of the relationship between C and T and in the ways in which C is proceeding in his or her quest. These two streams now tend more than in earlier stages to move and flow together almost as one.

D. *Synchronous engagement; and the becoming self in action*

In Phase D, feelings and thoughts arising within the client tend to be recognized as forming within the context of the relationship with the therapist and often as having reference to it. The therapy discourse is synchronous on several levels. First, there is an in-phase quality to what is happening from moment to moment in the inner experiencing of the client and its outward expression to T, as responsive partner and contributor to this experience. (In familiar, older terminology, the client is being congruent.) Second, there is generally close coincidence between what each partner is experiencing and meaning in their expression and what they are taken to be feeling and meaning by the other. Simpler expressions of this more 'sympatico' mutual awareness are that either partner at times accurately finishes the other's words, or 'reads' non-verbal signs without distortion of the other's feeling or thought. (These aspects of strongly synchronous interaction are substantially founded on the development of trust in Phase C.)

The in-phase quality applies in a further pair of ways, the first related to congruence. At this stage, much of the client's communication is an encoded surfacing of the flow of feeling and experiential meaning *as the latter is occurring*. (In older terms, this implies immediacy.) Very little is said that is planned ahead. While self-exploration may still, at moments, involve struggle, the quality of this struggle itself tends to be communicated as it occurs; and there is a relatively small and diminishing gap between what is immediately beneath the surface of expression and that which is put into words or conveyed in an explicit non-verbal way. The twin to this feature of the process is the interlock and interplay between the client's undifferentiated felt sense and the symbolizing meaning-giving level of consciousness. The client now generally can find verbal form and expression for immediately present features of this organic inner sense and substratum of experience.

Whether portrayed through the language and vision of focusing (e.g., Gendlin, 1969, 1981) or under the heading of self-empathy (Barrett-Lennard, 1997a), a condition of easy interchange or 'dialogue' between the symbolizing, form-giving self, and the person's underlying, organically present self, is assumed fundamental to wholeness and *well*-ness of functioning. In Phase D, this capacity is both clearly manifest and further developed in the context of the helping relationship mode in its more advanced, synchronous expression. Discernible instances of such inner dialogue generally have occurred before this point but have not been such a prominent or major feature. It seems that spontaneous engagement in this dialogical process hinges on other process qualities, especially the strong development of trust described in Phase C.

As well as moving to the process qualities so far described, clients now experience or notice new levels of personal change. Often, they are conscious that their *values have been shifting* and that at minimum there are clarifications and alterations in balance among involvements that are important to them. Their personal priorities, what they most cherish, aspects of the ways they wish to live, have all moved somewhat and are in sharper focus. *One's body*, visible and internal, *tends to become a more integral aspect of self*, in this phase; and clients may have a new sense of their own whole presence, of the space they occupy when in motion or still, of their mass and momentum and of their life energy radiating and receiving from the energy of others.

In Phase D the client is likely also to explore, reflect on or notice *change in his or her time sense*, and of living in time. If such change is only noticed and mentioned after it happens, this may not come up until the next, concluding phase. It may be, for example, that C is now very conscious of being able in a new way to live in the moment, to be interactively in touch, as with the therapist, at the instant things are happening. In addition, C often has a stronger, more differentiated sense of his or her own identity not only in the moment but as a life. There is a new reality to living through and in one's whole life span, to *being* one's life as well as being more nearly one's whole present-becoming self in each step and moment of time.

The use of metaphor and the sharing of literal subjective images, by the client as well as therapist, generally is more prominent and more telling in its expressive-communicative power in Phase D than in other phases. Feelings may be portrayed using space-time metaphor, or as geometric forms, or as though they could be touched and had physical texture, or as being like solid objects or living organisms, and in other ways associated with corporeality. In seeming paradox, such language can help to intensify and give more accurately fitting and communicative expression to highly personal, felt meaning than more literal and less muscular formulation can achieve.

Effectively, there is in Phase D more poetry both in the therapy interaction and in the way the client tends to construe and express felt experience. Partly because most of us live in a 'left-brain' world, stressing rationality, analytical thought and measured description, in the course of achieving greater wholeness in therapy the more artistic/poetic/intuitive-expressive side comes forward.[8] 'Man', Rogers has argued, 'is wiser than his intellect', and the spontaneous use of metaphor and subjective images is reflective of this wisdom. As an assimilated part of the person's way of being, it can add to personal effectiveness in real-world contexts. Client-centred therapy sustained at Phase D tends to liberate the creative artist within the client, if not literally then in the sense of being a contributing architect of self and a more creative builder in relationships with others.

The becoming self in action looks backward largely to enhance or deepen experience in the present, and to see more clearly ahead. Memory of what has gone before is open, not barred, and very strong feelings may come to the fore through this memory. However, memories do not of themselves (any longer) produce agonies of despair or mourning, intense fears or high exultation. As earlier implied, the person experiences, senses, his or her identity in the whole process of becoming, even in the trajectory glimpsed ahead as well as in the 'now-being' of the self.

Intensive, personal therapy, in keeping with other potently formative experiences, has some of the elements and qualities of birthing. In the case of client-centred therapy, this does not imply regression to redo an earlier stage of development but does connote emergent shifts in awareness and ways of processing experience, broadly in the direction of a more self-transcending and becoming way of being. As such change occurs it is highly likely that at some stage in Phase D, and in ways consistent with other mentioned aspects of in-therapy process and wider movement, clients will explore the 'fit' or lack of it between the becoming self they now experience and the larger context of their life activity and priorities.

Usually, the importance of existing close relationships is affirmed, with a sense of furthered discovery of what is actual and desired in these relationships. As well, where it has been deeply at issue, a desired–feared separation is by now largely drained of internal conflict (and is a matter in and of itself rather than a symbol of something broader), and clients in open dialogue with self can now weigh and choose their course on an organismic basis. They may

8 High trust, as this term is used here, tends to be a prerequisite for the client to relax the guardedness of 'left-brain control' and to experiment with expressive metaphor and intuitive imagery. Such expressiveness can seem to leave the self unprotected – even at the risk of ridicule – in a world commonly experienced as demanding a literal practicality, objective description, logical and rationalistic forms of reasoning, and consistent, predictable behaviour.

take steps to develop new associations; and are both more open to the perceptions of others, and less concerned about their image in public contexts or casual encounters. Major decisions are not necessarily made in the vocational sphere, but active reappraisal typically occurs, the client feels less imprisoned where this has been an issue, and the increased vitality and assurance of the becoming self is evident in his/her working life as in other spheres.

Transition from Phase D to the concluding Phase E often is influenced by practical considerations that, indirectly or in part, are a consequence of therapy. These potentially include financial and time/energy/priority considerations on the part of the client, relocation or extended absence by client or therapist, and the existence of fresh or altered situations and relationships in the client's life which are now effective growth contexts.

More *intrinsic termination conditions* evolving in Phase D tend to include the following:

1 The crises or other conditions precipitating the client's entry to therapy have receded or taken on different meaning to a person whose formerly constricted energies are in flow again, and whose resources are more integrated and in harmony.
2 The client has learned or rediscovered how to travel and move inwardly, knows vividly how it is to be out of touch and recover connection, and is applying the fruits of his or her therapy journey to outside life contexts. The relationship with the therapist is now enjoyable rather than essential to sustain altered qualities of experiencing and questing.
3 When a client has for some time been working in therapy in ways inclusive of Phase D level qualities, the therapist may begin to anticipate termination. In the open flow of the relationship, indications of the shifting balance in T's expectancy are experienced by C and, in practice, form part of the data by which the client judges when the time is ripe to conclude therapy.
4 A more tentatively advanced condition is that the client becomes ready for a time of psychic relaxation or 'letting be', rather than continuing so directly to question, explore and work at his/her own functioning and identity.
5 The client typically is less vulnerable and much less strained and anxious. This change diminishes one of the posited main conditions of therapy (Rogers, 1957a). It also allows for a greater sway of conserving or homeostatic processes, seen as existing side by side with the growth and actualizing tendencies.

In these outlined circumstances, it is likely that C will come to the topic of termination and explore experienced issues and meanings around this in accord with the same kind of in-phase, inward/outward and forward-moving process as other felt issues. Such exploration would herald the transition to Phase E.

E. *Termination process: ending and entry*

The explicit termination phase in client-centred therapy, if following on from phasic mode D (or, C)[9] typically is brief in terms of interview duration. It might directly occupy only a single meeting, usually, after being foreshadowed in a previous session. Where the total course of therapy is lengthy, or where the time of ending is governed by external circumstances known in advance, the termination phase may directly include several meetings.

The ending of client-centred therapy, while it may be uncomplicated in the actual event, contains elements of paradox. It occurs at the point where C and T know each other best as persons, probably value their relationship the most, feel their association merging or capable of merging into a literal friendship relationship and, aside from any anxiety around their separation, when they are generally most relaxed with one another. Precisely the same features would make it most difficult for C to continue to 'buy' T's time or for them to proceed on the basis of an underlying or explicit contract for service.

The last-mentioned aspects contribute in a mixed positive–negative sense to the possibility and meaning of termination of ongoing contact between co-workers, fellow travellers and would-be friends. There is no proscription in client-centred therapy against actual friendship or collegial associations continuing after therapy but, often, various features of the personal and life situations of C and T mitigate against such an association. Thus the ending of a deeply meaningful human association is naturally and often one important issue; an issue revolving around ways that the therapy partners feel with each other and toward the other, the ways they can communicate self to self, and their pool of experience together. Each is managing a very real separation which in some ways is a prototype of other life partings.

The process of leaving therapy and, usually, any active association with one another, naturally includes some sharing of its import and meaning to the participants. Particular, appreciated events and qualities together, and outcomes beyond their relationship, are likely to be singled out. Typically there is reference to current outside projects or forward-reaching plans in the client's life, ones that may sharpen further in their mention, and which express the refreshed or re-awakened becoming self. As the phase continues, images of birthing (as mentioned also in Phase D), of literal unfolding or metamorphosis, quite often occur to the client or therapist. In any case, termination of the journey and course of therapy finally impresses itself as a beginning more than an ending, an entry not necessarily to a new life context, but to a quality or way of being in life. Elements of this 'way' include an openness to feelings as they are happening, a quality of in-touchness and fluency in speaking from differing levels of one's experiencing, a more continuous, regardful and

---

9 If termination occurs before mode D is evident, but after a period of Phase C interaction and process, the termination phase is likely to resemble the pattern described here. If it occurs at a still earlier point, before fruition of therapy, the ending naturally would differ.

resonant engagement with others, and a quality less of effortful striving and more of spontaneous purpose.

There may be moments of sadness in the parting of client and therapist, but termination when the time is ripe, especially following mode D, is such an affirming step that there is little or no continuing sense of loss. While there *is* any sharp sense of loss or distinct lack of closure, or while the client is more occupied with departure issues than entry ones, the termination phase is not yet complete and, desirably, one or more further meetings would precede literal parting. As with any significant human association, to a degree the relationship lives on within the participants; but the memories bring no sorrow or regret, in the case of optimal termination. Further, in client-centred therapy, the door is rarely closed permanently. Unless changes in location would make any further contact impractical, the therapist is potentially available in the case of future emergency. And even without such emergency, if C's and T's paths should later cross, each would welcome this contact and easily move to sharing communication.

Concluding implications

I am now conscious that as the thought presented here evolved, through periodic work over a number of years, plotting the pathway as such became less an end in itself and more another useful vehicle in the search to work out and communicate the process nature of client-centred therapy. For me as author many threads have come together, in this search, and I shall be pleased if the result is also evocative for the reader. Clearly this chapter, unlike most others before it, is not a closely documented distillation calling step by step on an array of sources. It flows, rather, from a fertilizing immersion in the approach over a long period, influenced in both visible and subtle ways by the work of many others but none the less my own envisioning beyond their responsibility.

It would be contrary to my own meaning to interpret the 'phases' deciphered here as uniform steps or exact markers. They flow from an attempt to catch the essence of a distinct, unusual quality of association and quest, one which in its specifics is as individual as are the participants in the enterprise. Given the requisite resources and commitment, this enterprise and process builds on itself until it becomes evident that another phase, or level, has been reached. No main level can be entirely skipped, for each is a vital part of the foundation for the next. Thus, also, no phase mode in full expression can simply be switched into at will, or as an instant product of specific technique, for its emergence is a growth process and not just a matter of where or how attention is centred.

Therapy of course can come to an end, in practice does end, almost anywhere along the broad continuum. Moreover, the journey is not always as distinctly unidirectional as my picture might suggest. In or out of therapy, we are subject to mood swings, biochemical rhythms, ups and downs in relationships and achievement, uneven life stresses. Clients can move ahead strongly in therapy and then seem to slip back, with the process being more like an earlier phase. Oscillating motion, or spiral-like return to familiar issues tackled on a somewhat different level, complicate identification of where the travellers are on their journey. Nevertheless if therapy is to come to strong fruition, the journey is a progressive one and its underlying direction generally in accord with the sequence discussed. Beyond this, client issues or therapist emphases may work to favour processes in one phase more than in another, especially as between phasic modes C and D.

In introducing this perspective, the issue of therapy as recovery and healing, as re-education or growth, or self and interpersonal learning, or social reconnection, etc., was acknowledged. More than difference in language is implied by these alternative and complementary designations. They connote axes and levels of change which appear in differing balance in the phases distinguished. Literal healing and recovery processes are most obvious in Phases B and C. Growthful change to new levels of functioning are discernible earlier but most evident in Phase D. Clients may largely heal and recover, with important elements of growth, without going on to Phase D. Development of a person's values and life-style would occur more strongly through Phase D process than in other phases. The 'person of tomorrow', in Rogers' eloquent description (Rogers, 1977a: 262–274), would soon be at home in Phase C interaction and be likely to move on to Phase D. The person identified as schizophrenic may struggle in therapy (as earlier implied) for a long time before reaching a Phase C process. Coming to that stage would represent a great deal of healing movement.

Therapists of a most distinctly client-centred approach, especially if trained in the heyday of self-theory, or for whom Rogers' own work remains a central model and influence, would tend to set much store by Phase C process, work hard and patiently in facilitating its fruition with clients, and not judge that therapy was faltering if phasic mode D did not appear in any full-fledged way. Therapists particularly influenced by Rogers' later process thinking and, especially, by Gendlin and others of more 'experiential' persuasion, may have greatest interest and confidence in therapy that clearly moved to the Phase D level of process. For therapists of either emphasis, working with clients in Phase D probably helps most in the *therapist's growth*.

This chapter and the last have focused mainly on individual therapy with adults, the original context of development of the approach and a central core throughout its history. Other areas of client-centred helping practice – child therapy, work with couples and families, and group therapy and encounter – have drawn on the same principles, even when adding to them, as seen in the next two chapters. Interest in the sequential unfolding of process becomes prominent again, when the spotlight is on group therapy and encounter.

8

The Helping Process with Children and Families

> In his difficulty the patient comes, or in the case of a child, is brought, to the therapist with whom he has no previous relationship. But the fact of coming to a therapist, with all the feelings crystallized by that act, brings this new person into his life in a way unlike that of any other human relationship.
>
> Frederick Allen, 1942/1947

In this chapter, close but stressed relationships are in view, and the helping process is not only individual but also a therapy of relationships. This emphasis becomes explicit in couple and family therapy, is apparent in 'filial therapy', and is an implied feature in play therapy with children. Historically, child therapy using a play medium was the first of these areas to emerge as a distinctive application with its own specifics of setting, process and concept.

Child play therapy

Client-centred play therapy very clearly has its roots in the work of pioneers in the field associated with Otto Rank. Rank himself did not conduct therapy with children,[1] but associates who broke new ground on this level include Jessie Taft (1933) and Frederick Allen (1942/1947). Taft used and may have originated the actual term 'relationship therapy'. Part of her purpose was to distinguish the approach she espoused 'from psychoanalysis or any process in which either the analytic or the intellectual aspect is stressed, or the immediacy of the experience denied or confused with history' (Taft, 1933: xvi). Educated at the University of Chicago, where she had studied with Dewey, Mead, Angyal and others, Taft's scholarship and quest carried her through the arduous process of translating Rank's best-known writings into English. The fruits of this enterprise appear in relief in the single-volume edition of *Will Therapy* and *Truth and Reality* (Rank, 1936/1945).

Taft begins her searching introduction to Rank's work by singling out an emergent quality of outlook potentially at the heart of his contribution:

---

1 See Virginia Robinson's Introduction (p. ix) to the Dover edition of *The Dynamics of Therapy in a Controlled Relationship* (Taft, 1933; republished 1962, 1973).

> If one were to pick out the particular attitude which finally led Rank to a new comprehension of the therapeutic task on which he had worked in association with Freud for so many years, one might well select his complete *respect* for the personality of the neurotic patient, combined with absence of medical presupposition, *which freed him from the tendency to regard the neurosis as illness*, with an external cause and cure to be discovered. (In Rank, 1936/1945: xi, italics added)

Taft's whole introduction remains a fascinating account of the large and innovative divergence of Rank's thought from that of Freud, an innovation that lent inspiration to Rogers in his forming direction.[2] This inspiration was furthered by Jessie Taft's own separate contribution (see Rogers, 1939: 340–347). The book she authored (1933), centring on the presentation of two child therapy cases, begins with her classic essay on 'The time limit in therapy'. The quotation which heads my first chapter in this book is from that essay. Continuing in the same passage, Taft observes incisively that 'no one wants another to *apply* any process to the inmost self', a self which is 'defended against every encroachment, even the most benevolent' (1933: 3; italics added).

For Taft, the therapist's function is an enabling one wholly dependent on motivation from within the person. 'No one', she wrote, 'is going to experience change, call it growth or progress if you have the courage, because I think it would be good for society, good for his family and friends or even good for himself.' As a therapist, facing a person in need, 'one must accept one's final limitation and the right of the other, perhaps his necessity, to refuse help or to take help on his own terms not as others might choose' (ibid.: 4). In these and other passages a non-directive, person-centred attitude is eloquently, even powerfully, conveyed.

Boundedness in time is one of the realities of therapy. This is not only an issue for clients, child or adult, but a matter on which therapeutic approaches divide. Taft searches into the issue, with both philosophical and practical bent, seeing limits of time as anchoring therapy to everyday reality but not necessarily leaving the person hostage to qualitative boundaries in their experiencing. Personal attitudes toward time and its limits are, she believes, of fundamental significance:

> Time represents more vividly than any other category the necessity of accepting limitation as well as the inability to do so, and symbolizes therefore the whole problem of living. The reaction of each individual to limited or unlimited time betrays his deepest and most fundamental life pattern, his relation to the growth process itself, to beginnings and endings, to being born and to dying. (ibid.: 12)

For therapists, accepting limitations in and of time brings a certain transcendence of these limits. Every interchange and moment matters, the pregnancy of therapy is immediate, steps happen now:

---

2 In a paper that came recently to my attention, Robert Kramer (1995) searches deeply into Rank's work, and points to the remarkable convergences in basic idea and stance between the two men (as further brought out in my Chapter 16, pp. 354–358). The interested reader would be hard put to find a more searching and luminous exploration of its topic in one article.

> In the single interview, if that is all I allow myself to count upon, if I am willing to take that one hour in and for itself, there is no time to hide behind material, no time to explore the past or future. . . . I can no longer escape my responsibility, not for the client but for myself and my role in the situation. Here is just one hour to be lived through as it goes, one hour of present immediate relationship, however limited, with another human being who has brought himself to the point of asking for help.[3] (ibid.: 11)

Near the end of her essay, Taft also makes a strong plea for *self*-development of the therapist. As if anticipating Rogers, she wrote 'I do not mean that knowledge is not necessary, that technical skill is not necessary; they are, but they are of no value without the person' (21). The child-centredness of Taft's orientation and practice is vividly apparent in the first case she presents. In her own words, the sessions were conducted

> as far as I was humanly able, in terms of the child as she actually was at the moment, and my recognition of her immediate will, feeling and meaning. Everything centered in her, was oriented with regard to her . . . even when my response was a prohibition it was also a seeing of her, never a denial of the nature of her impulse or her right to have it. (28)

Although sound recording was not yet practicable, her session-by-session process notes break new ground in detail and specificity. The therapist often and easily asked questions but rarely seemed to probe. Some of her responses were in the nature of reflection and clarification of feeling. Not surprisingly, more space is given to words, feelings and actions of the child client than of the therapist, and the complete range and balance of her part in the sessions probably is not captured.

In his book *Psychotherapy with Children*, published later than Taft's work but written from experience overlapping in time and place, Frederick Allen sets forth an approach in which self-definition and self-worth are central issues, and immediate here-and-now experience in the therapeutic relationship is seen as the primary vehicle for change (1942/1947: ch. 3). 'The therapist', he writes, 'begins where the patient is and seeks to help him draw on his own resources toward a more creative acceptance and use of the self he has' (1947: 47). Moreover, convergent with Rogers' thought, the approach presented is founded on the belief that 'people have within themselves, irrespective of what has gone before, capacities which can be utilized creatively to effect harmonious relations with the realities of their living' (ibid.: 49).

The focus on immediate experience and reality in therapy is a repeating theme, expressed in ways only later in vogue; for example, to foster the other's growth 'the therapist must maintain his own realness and not be drawn back into the dark recesses of the past to the exclusion of the here and

3 As more fully discussed in Chapter 12, Taft's thought, and particularly her views on time, were highly valued and influential in the work (on time-limited therapy with adults) of another key contributor in the client-centred domain – John M. Shlien.

now' (51). Another author is quoted with particular approval: 'The spontaneity of the person, that which he can do and actually does *on his own* and in his own way, without external prompting or coercion, is what interests us above all else' (Adolf Meyer, cited in Allen, ibid.: 51–52). In related thought, Allen sees the healthy individual as 'free to live in each new present and to borrow from previous presents the stuff that gives continuity to life' (54).

The idea of conjoint family therapy had not yet come into view but the parent's needs and parent–child relationship were addressed directly by the regular practice of a second therapist holding concurrent sessions with the parent who accompanied the child. The illustrations from therapy sessions and cases are rich and varied, and Allen's work still stands as a valuable and engaging resource in the area of child therapy of person-centred inclination.

The overtly client-centred literature on child therapy opened with the publication of Virginia Axline's *Play Therapy*, in 1947. The book is a manual on her approach and practice, advancing principles and studded with process illustration, but lacking any mention of the work of other innovators besides Rogers. Although Taft's experience and viewpoint are not acknowledged, historical circumstance and other congruencies leave no doubt that they influenced Axline's approach; probably directly, certainly through Rogers.

Play is seen by Axline (as by Taft and Allen) as a young child's natural medium of self-expression, and thus a primary vehicle for personal communication. The playroom resources included puppets, a doll family, finger paints and clay, a sand box and basins, nursing bottles and running water, toy animals, cars, soldiers and weapons, costumes and cutting out materials, and other items with expressive potential. Calling on these resources, with inventive mix of words and action, the young child plays out and communicates feelings. In context with the companion-therapist's distinctive and highly perceptive response, there is movement from expression to discovery to growth.

Eight principles of nondirective play therapy are discriminated, and illustrated from near-verbatim play session dialogue notes and Axline's eloquent commentary. Half of these posited basic features are directly concerned with interpersonal qualities of therapist response. Foremost is the aspect of establishing rapport, of developing a friendly, warm relationship with the child, as soon as possible. It is not suggested that the therapist-helper should press for a close affectional tie with her child client, or depend on a warm response from the child. Implied, rather, is an attitude of welcoming, of wanting to be in the company of this child-person in the play sessions, of actively caring to know children in their own worlds of experience. It is a non-judgemental, accepting receptivity toward the child as an individual with his/her own distinct consciousness and identity. At best, this quality of the helper's presence connects seamlessly with the other features.

Among these is the principle that 'the therapist accepts the child exactly as he is'. It is suggested that this quality calls for special vigilance since typically the young client is brought by a parent desiring to produce change and in this context the child 'is a very sensitive being . . . apt to catch the most veiled rejection of himself on the part of the therapist' (Axline, 1947: 87). Axline distinguishes between acceptance and approval, seeing praise as the other side of the same evaluation coin as disapproval and rejection (as in the later concept of unconditionality). Her illustrations point both to the difficulty of maintaining this attitude and the rewards of doing so.

Closely linked to acceptance is the further principle of establishing a permissive ambience such that the child will feel free 'to express his feelings completely'. Beyond the therapist's initial structuring, which may draw attention to limits as well as possibilities, Axline stresses the importance of leaving most initiatives to the child, and of being ready to wait and follow the direction of these initiatives. In no way, she stresses, should the child be crowded, or subjected to any probing inquiry. Her emphasis on therapist neutrality and self-restraint is in keeping with Rogers' stance, prior to his later vision of the therapist's personal engagement and congruence being a factor of vital importance in therapy. Therapist positive regard and unconditionality are implicit in the principles mentioned.

Another crucial, familiar aspect is that of recognizing the child-person's expressed feelings and reflecting these feelings back, 'such . . . that the child gains insight into his behavior' (1947: 99). The term 'insight', with its now old-fashioned ring, is used broadly in reference to growth in awareness and understanding. In line with adult therapy, this accurate recognition and effective reflection becomes the pivotal therapeutic task of the child's helper. Implied are several effects, for the child: (i) awareness of the therapist's closeness in understanding, (ii) increasingly clear and integrated perception of self, and (iii) confirmation that being self-expressive is safe and fruitful.

The second group of principles in Axline's portrayal are concerned centrally with issues of control and responsibility. The child has the capability, she avers, and 'the responsibility to make choices and to institute changes' (108). To allow and support exercise of these potentials, the therapist avoids direction or any attempt 'to hurry the therapy along', thus following rather than leading the child. However, there is one area in which the therapist clearly sets conditions for the relation with her young client, explored in a chapter headed 'The value of limitations' (130–138).

Axline argues that certain practicalities of the therapy situation provide part of the 'reality anchorage' important for the child's learning and development. The therapist establishes boundaries by means of 'structuring' information given at the start of therapy and, in more specific and convincing ways, as pertinent situations arise. There are limits on the duration of play sessions, the need to avoid behaviour that would endanger the child him/herself, a proscription against physically attacking the therapist and also against wilful destruction of the play materials or environment. As called for, the therapist gives clear messages that she will not accept such *behaviours*, and may act to prevent them. At the same time she continues to appreciate and acknowledge the child's *feelings* (cf. Taft, in the passage quoted above, p. 125, 'even when my response was a prohibition . . .').

Axline's portrayal gives only brief attention to the parents of children in play therapy. Although parent figures are seen as responsible in significant part for the child's difficulties, Axline firmly asserts that 'it is not necessary for the adult to be helped in order to insure successful play therapy results' (68). She observes that as a child changes s/he sees a different world, and this new vision produces changes in the way significant others respond. This and other observations are picked up and developed in the next general presentation of client-centred play therapy, by Elaine Dorfman (1951).[4]

In Dorfman's language, a child's 'stimulus value' to others may change significantly through engagement in therapy. 'Once he is differently perceived he is differently reacted to, and this different treatment may lead him to change further.' In this way, the child in therapy can trigger a cycle of change. And even where a parent is so unavailable or fixed in attitude that the child's behaviour change has minimal impact, it appeared that play therapy (without linked parent therapy) at least gave child clients more resources to see and deal with the reality of their lives (ibid.: 239). By and large, issues related to parental involvement are more differentiated in Dorfman's work, less black and white than they appear in Axline's perspective.

In her discussion of the child therapist's role, Dorfman cites a case from Axline. Three eight-year-old boys were in a play therapy group together. One of them, Herby, suddenly asked the therapist about her work. Ronny wanted to know what Herby meant, and Owen joined in. The first child explained:

> 'I mean I wouldn't know how to do what she does. She doesn't seem to do anything. Only all of a sudden I'm free. Inside me I'm free.' (He flings his arms around.) 'I'm Herb and Frankenstein and Tojo and a devil.' (He laughs and pounds his chest.) 'I'm a great giant and a hero. I'm wonderful and I'm terrible. I'm a dope and I'm so smart. I'm two, four, six, eight, ten people. . . .' [The therapist responds: 'You're all kinds of people rolled into one.' Ronny reacts sharply; and the therapist reflects more fully. Herby, still exultant, breaks in:] 'I'm good and I'm bad and still I'm Herby. . . . I can be anything I want to be.' (1951: 242)

Of course, children were not always as articulate and exuberant as Herby, in this passage. Some children were still or silent for long periods and overt interaction was minimal. Or, the child was active but not in directly self-disclosing and exploratory ways. It seemed that in these instances as well, the therapy hours were important and eventful episodes from the child's point of view, usually with effects visible to others.

In his first book, *Children in Play Therapy*, Clark Moustakas (1953) draws particularly on the client-centred school and the preceding work of Taft and Allen. Although his sensitive and imaginative perspective does not lend itself to labelling, the basic philosophy and working practice he portrayed are strongly in the client-centred tradition. His second book focusing directly on play therapy (Moustakas, 1959/1970) complements Axline's and Dorfman's work. He, too, provides rich illustration from therapy process records with a

---

4 In 1948, Axline moved to New York. Her destination was Teachers College, Columbia University, where she completed her doctorate in 1950, and joined the regular faculty. Thus, by the time *Client-Centered Therapy* (1951) was in active preparation Axline was involved on another path. Dorfman, still a graduate student but on the way to her doctorate in Chicago, was invited to speak for the special area of play therapy in Rogers' book.

broad range of children – disturbed, 'normal', creative, and handicapped. In discussing major issues in child therapy, the matter of limits again comes to the fore, with refinement in keeping with an emphasis (now) on therapist congruence:

> When I set a limit in psychotherapy it is an aspect of my being, an expression of who I am at a particular moment in time. It is my limit, a boundary for me. When the child accepts the limit a bond is formed between us. The limit is . . . held in a relationship, not an isolated expression of the individual personalities of therapist or child. The child confirms me and together we accept a structure through which our relationship can develop. (1959/1970: 15)

Within the Chicago group itself, following the heyday of Axline's original work and Dorfman's contribution, child therapy became a less prominent focus of development. It did not disappear but continued through the whole remaining life of the Counseling Center, being co-ordinated in the later years by Charlotte Ellinwood. By the late fifties, it was apparent to Ellinwood that child clients often were withdrawn prematurely from therapy if there was no concurrent ongoing contact with a parent (1959). She noted that parents were being left on the sidelines unless they actively sought personal help for themselves. Then, the paradox became evident to her

> that we were devoting all of our attention to the children and overlooking the basic fact that it was the *parents* who were feeling concerned and had brought their concern to us. We were actually ignoring the persons who had come to the Center seeking help and were turning our attention entirely to the persons they had come about. (ibid.: 4)

Yet, trials at the opposite pole of insisting that parents enter therapy for themselves did not produce substantial therapeutic experiences. The whole dilemma around therapy for parents was examined also in light of current theory (Ellinwood, 1959; cf. Rogers, 1957a, 1958c and 1959a).

From Ellinwood's account it is apparent that a good many of the parents who brought their children for therapy truly saw the difficulties as centred in the child and external to their own functioning. Others felt the opposite, even to the point of seeking direct help solely for themselves, triggered by the disturbing interaction with their child. Parents of the former kind seemed to be functioning near the 'stasis' or low extreme on Rogers' process continuum (Chapter 5, pp. 82–85). This functioning and their linked attitudes toward what 'getting help' meant, stood in contrast to therapists' expectation of clients, and loaded the situation against realizing the therapeutic conditions. Ellinwood felt, however, that it should be possible to work with parents literally from wherever they actually were in attitude and needs (1959: 25 ff.). In a later report (Ellinwood, 1989), she notes that one practice that developed was to allow for a child in therapy to invite a parent or sibling to accompany them in particular sessions. Then, as will be mentioned further, conjoint therapy as a significant option came into view.

By the mid-1960s, Axline's second book *Dibs: In Search of Self* (1964) had made its eventful appearance. Although her presentation includes extensive dialogue, the work is not a transcript but a story; an absorbing multi-dimensional account of a child's inner/outer journey through intensive therapy with the author. Axline speaks through the words and actions of Dibs, those of other important people in his life, and through her own interaction, reflections and feelings with him. It is a gently powerful, evocative story. The process depicted accords with principles Axline had earlier advanced, but is freer in regard to the forms of response and depth of involvement by the therapist. To my sense, the account is closer to Rogers' view of the helping relationship after therapist congruence and other therapeutic conditions were freshly differentiated in the late fifties.

Axline had limited but crucial contact with Dibs' parents. Their communication at the start was vital in establishing necessary agreements regarding her work with the child. It seems clear that this work would not have been able to proceed had there been any requirement for the mother, or parents, to participate directly (Axline, 1964: 18–23). However, at later times during therapy Dibs' mother twice initiated a highly eventful and consequential interview session with the therapist (ibid.: chs 8 and 17); and there is dramatic indication of change in her own attitude and the family relationships.

Just as *Dibs* was published a new emphasis and approach to parent participation came into view, with Bernard Guerney's first article on 'filial therapy'. Several years earlier Rogers' daughter, Natalie, had published an account of home play therapy sessions with her own daughter (Fuchs, 1957). This case and others involving parents in therapeutic play sessions with their own children was soon afterward mentioned also by Moustakas (1959/1970: Chapter 8). The idea of developmental 'training', using behavioural learning concepts, was strongly gaining ground by the sixties. Guerney blended principles from approaches often considered incompatible.

Filial therapy

'Filial therapy', so named by Guerney (1964), centres on ways of preparing and involving parents in the conduct of therapeutic play sessions with their own child. The goals of training are based on principles derived from Axline's work and later conditions theory, while the training method is learning theory based. Filial therapy evolved as a treatment approach in response to children in rather serious difficulty within their families, if not in other contexts as well. Central assumptions are that parent–child relationships have been influential in causing or maintaining the child's difficulties, and that if parents can learn to respond empathically and in accord with other helping conditions they will become a healing resource to their child.

In a word, Guerney and colleagues propose that the necessary unlearning and new learning best takes place in the context of parent–child interaction, where the difficulties either arose or are painfully manifest. They observe that the parent's morale and motivation are heightened by the experience of developing resources to be of direct help themselves, in contrast to being powerless in the face of stubbornly self-perpetuating patterns. As a parent experiments with new ways of being with her child, and experiences altered consequences, it seems that changes soon follow in the whole relationship. Favourable long-term prospects are maximized when the parent successfully consolidates the new ways of 'seeing', feeling and responding in relation to her child.

For parents, the filial therapy method as originally reported (B.G. Guerney, 1964; Guerney et al., 1970; L.F. Guerney, 1976) involves an experiential learning sequence which includes, at each stage, regular parent group meetings with a therapist. The sequence starts with parent discussion/training sessions designed to promote a working understanding of the principles involved in client-centred play therapy. Demonstration play sessions are introduced, with continued parent–therapist process discussion. Each parent then brings her/his own child for play sessions observed by, and discussed with, the rest of the group. After at least ten, perhaps twenty, learning/training meetings, parents move to play therapy periods at home, while continuing with their own therapist-led parent group for a period of several months or longer.

Aims of training focus first on parents developing and applying their capacity for empathic attunement. This means learning to make 'every effort to understand how the child is viewing himself and his world . . . and what his feelings of the moment are' (Guerney et al., 1970: 378). A linked goal is to help parents learn (better) how to *communicate* their understanding, by such means as reflecting the feelings the child shows and by clarifying implicit meanings. A further main aspect is to help the parent move to a new or deeper quality of acceptance of the child in his/her own world of experience. But there is also the adult's reality and boundaries to take account of. Thus, a complementary aim is to help the parent to target and effectively manage essential limits on physically destructive behaviour, without rejection of the child's *feelings*. (A usually effective sanction in the parent–child play sessions was simply to terminate the session immediately on appearance of such behaviour.) Aside from a few boundary limits, parents are specifically encouraged to leave the topical direction and content of play sessions entirely up to the child. Thus the broad mission is to help parents to develop a 'therapeutic' repertoire.

Guerney et al.'s 1970 report includes a case illustration. The mother in focus is evidently well-educated and articulate. She is pictured as having been 'rigid and controlling in all phases of her life', and very demanding of appreciation from her son. Initially she was most reluctant to participate in a parent *group*, and felt sharply critical of other members. She mistrusted reflecting her son's feelings and giving him the lead. However, she expressed and worked at her reactions, her attitudes changed, and she became responsive and skilled in this context. She came to value the group experience and be something of a leader in it. The boy's 'play' sessions with his mother included much expression and working through of anger, over some forty occasions. By the fifty-fifth session the picture had greatly changed, and organized parent–child play therapy sessions ended after sixty-six meetings.

Around this ending the boy staged 'pretend temper tantrums', accepting his mother's reflective summing up that 'Big Fred is laughing at Baby Fred' (1970: 382–385).

The Guerneys' report having made every effort at the start of each parent group to explain and account to participants for the process goals chosen in advance. They view the parent training process as having both didactic and experiential components, and as being at once leader-guided and highly responsive to parent issues and feelings. Over time their work developed to include modified programs of a preventive nature, with extension to the level of relations with adolescent children (L.F. Guerney, 1976). An excerpt from a therapist-led parent training group suggests a process conducted largely, although not entirely, in familiar client-centred mode. The most distinctive feature lies in group leader contributions from his/her own frame of reference, described as didactic interventions (ibid.: 75–77). Such 'teaching' input is viewed as one of three or four basic aspects of the training program. The examples given can alternatively be seen as ways in which the leader-therapists are congruently sharing and acting on their own view, although with less *personal* ownership and immediacy than in highly congruent expressions. It is interesting that the congruence–genuineness condition is not emphasized. Possibly, *training* for congruence or transparency is seen to be contradictory, or, as an inappropriate training objective given that parents are consciously breaking set and responding in new, initially unspontaneous ways.

In more recent years, the term Relationship Enhancement (RE) has been used in connection with filial therapy and its derivatives (B.G. Guerney, 1984). Filial RE therapy, also called Child RE family therapy (Guerney and Guerney, 1989), has continued along closely similar lines, and with the same essential rationale, since its inception. One of the later adaptations, a form of marital and couple therapy, is touched on later in this chapter.

All in all, the Guerneys' work, steadily pursued over three decades, is the most determined and integrative blending developed of client-centred principles with methods imported from social learning theory. Whether filial therapy can be wholly true to both of these sources remains in some debate (see Ellinwood and Raskin, 1993: 271). The evidence of research (see pp. 311–312) and informal accounts provides an enviable pattern of support for the practical efficacy of the approach. Its advocates have remained explicitly committed to its origins in client-centred therapy yet firm in seeing change as flowing also from knowledge of how to modify contingencies and implement experiences to bring this about. To its architects, filial therapy and its underpinnings are one effective whole. Its beneficiaries must also have found the varied elements of the approach congruent in their experience.

Marital counselling and couple therapy

Client-centred therapy has had very wide impact in the field of marital counselling, although this is a matter of spin-off more than direct focus by Rogers and the majority of other leading exponents. As an approach, it is highly responsive to the context actually encountered: for example, two partners desiring and coming for help in joint meetings; one or both partners preferring individual sessions; or only one willing to take the plunge, but bringing their partner and relationship issues internally.

At first, Rogers (1945a) advised against meeting with couples together, in view of the difficulty of maintaining a truly unjudging nondirective attitude with protagonists holding very divergent perceptions. In practice it was observed (Rogers and Wallen, 1946, ch. 8) that one partner usually takes the initiative in seeking assistance, as tends to be the case still. However, if this person finds real help around issues arising in the marriage then enhancement or clarification of the spousal relationship is likely. It is advised that even 'when both partners come in together to consult the counsellor, it is usually best to listen to the preliminary statement of the problem and then to make arrangements to see each individual separately' (ibid.: 110). If circumstances dictate that the parties be seen together, there was some evidence to support the view 'that by being a nonjudgmental individual, and by reflecting the attitudes expressed, no matter how contradictory, counselling of two people at the same time may make progress. By helping each to clarify his own attitudes . . . a means of adjustment may be discovered' (111). This cautious and limited statement appears to be Rogers' first reference to dyadic marital counselling, seen as an uphill process of counselling two individuals at once.

Marital or couple counselling receives no mention in Rogers' next book (1951). Even in *On Becoming a Person* (1961a) he writes as it were all round the topic (see chs 16, 17 and 18) but without addressing it directly. In fact, *Rogers himself never wrote a book or major paper focused directly on marital or couple therapy*. He developed an interest in the field of conflict resolution at a fairly early stage, an interest that remained a thread in his work until the end of his life (Rogers and Roethlisberger, 1952; Rogers, 1965a; Rogers and Ryback, 1984; Rogers, 1986a). Although increasingly concerned about conflict between groups, cultures and nations, in practice his focus was on the facilitation of communication, awareness and understanding between persons.

Already by the late fifties and the sixties, practitioners gravitating to the field of marital counselling and making their own choice of sources, often drew on or embraced the client-centred approach. Rogers' philosophy of persons, the practical and 'learnable' nature of his counselling, the rather straightforward theoretical base, and the eloquence and clarity (the 'reader-centredness') of Rogers' writing, all contributed to its strong appeal and usefulness. It was generally taken for granted that difficulties in marriage grew out of the personalities, especially problems of personal adjustment, of the two participants. Indicative are the succinct opening words of one research author: 'Marriage counseling [she wrote] has emerged within the last twenty years as a specialized branch of personality counseling' (Luckey, 1960: 3).

A decade later, Rogers published three books outside the field of therapeutic counselling, each one for a broader potential readership than the last

(Rogers, 1969a, 1970 and 1972a). The culminating work in this triumvirate is titled *Becoming Partners: Marriage and its Alternatives*. Of the publisher's view of this book, Rogers wrote in a letter to this author: 'They seem to think it will sell very well.' Of his own perspective, he said 'I don't regard it as one of my best books by any means but it does contain fascinating taped material with couples of various sorts, and a chapter on communes with taped material from members of communes' (Rogers, 1972d).[5] The taped interviews were not counselling sessions, but information-gathering ones. Rogers includes generous excerpts from dialogue, assigning first names to the other participants and identifying himself simply as 'me'. The way he proceeds is clearly effective in releasing and bringing out the experience of those interviewed. Indications are that the process tended to sharpen self-perceptions and further communication in the case of couples. In a word, the experience was evidently therapeutic although not intended or understood as therapy.[6]

Developments in Australia illustrate Rogers' early impact in the marriage counselling sphere. By the late fifties, Rogerian thought and practice was widely in view and becoming influential in counselling circles in Australia, including in particular the nascent fields of school counselling and marriage guidance. In the sixties the latter became a major field of practice, with federal funding available for direct subsidy of this practice. Counsellor education had not been much developed in universities, and the selection and training of front-line counselling staff usually took place within local marriage guidance agencies. For federal assistance, both training and service in these agencies had to meet certain guidelines collaboratively developed with a senior psychologist (L.V. Harvey) at the federal level, whose own orientation was client-centred. The 'lay' trainee counsellors had varying backgrounds of tertiary education and of occupational and life experience. Those deemed potentially qualified were selected, finally, on the basis of personal qualities, particularly:

> sincere regard for others, tolerance and ability to accept people with values different from one's own, a healthy regard for the self, a warmth and sensitivity in dealing with others, and a capacity for empathy. . . . The aim is to select a person capable of creating a relationship with his client *so that the necessary and sufficient conditions for successful counselling as described by Rogers are developed.* (Harvey, 1964: 349, italics added)

---

5 The same exchange of letters contains another element of interest. I had mentioned the feeling of being 'carried protestingly into "middle-age"' and spoke of noticed effects of getting older. In response Rogers wrote, 'I was particularly touched with the feelings you have about getting older. I have the same feelings only much more so. At age 70 I don't have the energy I used to have nor do I do as good work. However, I do continue to produce things. My book on encounter groups has gone well.' He then mentioned his forthcoming book *Becoming Partners*, and made the comments I have quoted.

6 I make this point because Rogers uses direct questions far more than he did in formal therapy interviews. The fact that the purpose was inquiry rather than therapy seems to have made for a freer process. The questions are context-sensitive and reflective of empathy as well as concern to gain a clear, shareable picture.

As for the nature of the learning programs for the selected trainees, Harvey pointed out that the central objective was to develop skills in one method of counselling, and that 'the non-directive client-centred approach of the Rogers' school is the technique most widely used' (ibid.: 349). Another pertinent source from that time is the journal *Marriage and Family* (published by the [Australian] National Marriage Guidance Council). Papers concerned with counselling and training in early volumes (mid-1960s) are predominantly client-centred in perspective. This period also saw inauguration of the 'Armidale workshops' by the present author. These drew participants from mental health disciplines and centres across the country and New Zealand, including many involved in the marriage counselling sphere. The members took part in intensive residential 'workshops in therapeutic counselling', with client-centred underpinning and process (Barrett-Lennard, 1967). Rogers himself led one of these workshops, on a visit reported informally (Barrett-Lennard, 1987a).

Returning to developments in North America, an experimental approach called 'conjugal therapy', an outgrowth of filial therapy, has been applied with volunteer partners experiencing stresses in their marriage (Ely, Guerney and Stover, 1973). In the first phase, there is demonstration and practice in adopting the roles of 'speaker' and 'listener' around predetermined themes. As listener, the partner's task is to take in what the other is expressing, seeking to understand deeply the speaker-partner's perception and feeling, aiding in its further clarification rather than muddying issues or stirring troubled waters. This sounds a tall order in a strained relationship, but (i) the listener knows that shortly there will be a chance to speak up from his/her own feelings, and (ii) a guide is present mainly to assist *the listener*. The requirement to listen closely and reflect reasonably accurately before the next turn at speaking gives working form to a personal 'experiment' Rogers had proposed much earlier. He suggested that the next time his listener/reader began to slip into an argument with someone close to them they take a deep breath and try following the rule that 'Each person can speak up for himself only after he has first restated the ideas and feelings of the previous speaker accurately and to that speaker's satisfaction.' He warned that 'you will discover it is one of the most difficult things you have ever tried to do' (Rogers and Roethlisberger, 1952: 48).

In the reported account of conjugal therapy, a leader-guide was always present, with the intention of helping the participants to master the process with each other over a spectrum of real issues in their lives, however sensitive or charged. Related 'homework' periods were also used regularly. In one concrete illustration of process from a main session the wife involved had recently had an abortion, under pressure from her husband, and the couple interact in speaker–listener mode around this intensely felt life issue (Ely, Guerney and Stover, 1973). A later report by another author (Snyder, 1989), under the main title 'The relationship enhancement model of couple therapy', complements the earlier description. Gaps are filled in and additional steps described. Direct attention is given to the skill of effective self-expression, in addition to that of empathic listening. Acquiring facility in switching from listening to speaking from one's own feelings, and back again, is a distinct component feature of the overt learning described.

There are other quite separate developments in client-centred marital/ couple therapy. Bozarth and Shanks (1989) report therapy with couples, interspersed with more inclusive family sessions. In adapting the Rogerian conditions model, their work gives strong emphasis to the actualizing principle (motivating individual change) and the formative tendency (seen as accounting for system change). A couple or family system is conceived of as an organic whole with 'the inherent capacity to move in a growth-oriented direction' (ibid.: 282), and the therapist works as a catalyst for the inherent growth direction of this whole as well as that of individual members – as illustrated in a particular case (286–292). In related vein, Esser and Schneider (1990) distinguish between psychotherapy with couples and *partnership therapy* focusing on the relationship. The former mode, oriented to the personal growth or healing of each partner, has predominated historically. The second, with its direct focus on interactive processes and experiencing, and the difficulties and functioning of the twosome itself, is more recent. These modes are presented as complementary, neither supplanting the other.

Auckenthaler (1980) is cited as suggesting that the goal of the individual-centred approach is 'to change the client's relationship with themselves toward more self-empathy, self-esteem and congruence' (in Esser and Schneider, 1990: 831). The relationship-centred mode aims to bring about 'highly empathic communication between the partners'. In broader expression, 'the goal of our approach to client-centred therapy of the relationship is to foster open communication between partners and to guarantee the transfer of this style of communication to real life' (ibid.: 832). The same authors argue that the foundation for partner relationship therapy can be found in Rogers' own writing, for example, in his 'theory of interpersonal relationship' (Rogers, 1959a: 235–240) and his German-language book *Partnerschule* (1975). However, Rogers' conception pivots on the effects of incongruence and congruence on communication in a relationship, thus reducing problems with the partner entity to individual personality factors. He does not imply that a twosome has emergent existence as 'one organism' (Esser and Schneider, 1990: 830) or even as a living system.[7]

Interesting discussion and advocacy of co-therapy, involving a male and female therapist working together with each couple is also advanced by Esser and Schneider. They point out that client support, and challenge, may be enlarged with both sexes represented on the helping side, that two acute listeners hear more than one alone, and that separate and parallel one-to-one therapy sessions can readily occur. As well, the two therapists have a mutual support system at difficult times, and can share the demands of the therapeutic enterprise all the way along. For these writer-practitioners in particular, therapeutic advantages result from their being in a close couple relationship

---

7 Nor do these authors speak of the couple as a system, or call on directly related thinking – although the idea seems near to their thought. With this further step, theoretical *extension* would come into view, and be available for refinement.

with each other, this relationship acknowledged to their client couples (Esser and Schneider, 1990: 838–841).

A further European report is by Rombauts and Devriendt (1990). Their observations are based largely on feedback, in response to a detailed questionnaire, from client-centred practitioners working with couples in conjoint sessions. The problems and attitudes of these client couples were very varied. They differed in commitment and hope around resolving their relationship problems but were consistent in experiencing dissatisfaction and pain. The authors were struck by the responsive flexibility of the therapists: for example, by 'their facility to change from couple sessions to individual ones, and often [to] combine both' (860). Intensive empathic listening and responding centrally occupied the counsellors, but this empathy had a differing focus in the joint sessions – where 'there is not only the individual experience of the two persons but there is also their interaction, their relation on which the empathic attention of the therapist is mainly focused' (853–854).[8]

The reporting therapists were oriented to being personally present and open with their clients, not through any focus on partner experiences of their own but by the quality and expressiveness of their absorption in the process of the client couple. In practice, in conjoint sessions, improvement in communication was a primary goal. Therapists worked directly to facilitate this communication, but also were conscious that their close attention to feelings, and their active listening and acknowledgement of what they heard, was a model that clients probably would draw from in their response to each other. Procedural initiatives, such as suggesting exercises outside the couple's usual pattern, also fell within the therapists' repertoire. The authors conclude that the general approach conveyed in these therapist accounts was a distinctively 'person-centred' style of couple-partner therapy (1990: 861–862).

Family relationship therapy

Family therapy in the client-centred tradition also attends very closely to the feelings and frame of reference of each participating family member, and the emphasized therapy conditions remain highly relevant. There usually are one or more parent *and* child participants, but family members may not all be present from the start, or to the end of the meetings. There is no pressure from the therapist for every member of the nuclear family to take part. In natural response to changing awareness and concerns, sessions may become more inclusive, or less so, as they go on. Meetings might also include a grandparent, an in-law, or others closely involved with the primary family.

Historically, Rogers' professional involvement with families in difficulty preceded the emergence of his own therapeutic orientation, and could be said

---

8 Rombauts and Devriendt do not explain how this distinctive focusing of empathy works. The process has been articulated in my own writing, starting in 1981 – see Barrett-Lennard, 1993a.

to have helped to give rise to it (see Rogers, 1939: ch. 7). His autobiography includes a vivid early instance of his hard-working but fruitless attempt to assist the mother of a problem child, using the interpretive approach he had been trained in. It was only when he literally gave up on what he was attempting, expecting the contacts to end, that the client asked about help *for herself*. They both changed direction, he gave her the lead and listened, and she 'began to pour out her despair about her marriage, her troubled relationship with her husband, her sense of failure and confusion. . . . Real therapy began then and ultimately it was highly successful – for her and for her son' (Rogers, 1967a: 359).

Notwithstanding Rogers' exposure from the start of his professional career to crises in families, around child behaviour problems or debilitating conflict, his direction did not lead on naturally to the idea of conjoint personal therapy. Like most others in the personal helping field, he was steeped in a psychology of the individual and his origins as therapist and helper (which he did not totally break away from) were in the psychodynamic tradition. He saw the maladjustments and suffering his therapy would help to overcome as being rooted in intrapsychic conflict and disorders of the self.[9] Certainly, external circumstances could exacerbate and confront the individual with his or her need for help, but it was to this internal need that client-centred therapy was addressed. It was taken for granted that through healing and growth on this inner level the person naturally would function differently with others. S/he would bring different resources and attitudes to difficult family relationships such that they became more open and healthy.

Rogers' experience-based belief in individual therapy as a route to significant change in family relationships is spelled out most directly in a paper focusing on this topic (Rogers, 1961a: ch. 16).[10] He drew out several aspects of client change with important effect in family relations. First, he noted that clients are more freely expressive of their feelings, negative as well as positive. There is less accumulation and bottling up of feelings, thus diminishing strain or conflict. A related effect is that communication becomes more open and honest. In Rogers' language, 'the client discovers, often to his great surprise, that a relationship can be lived on the basis of the real feelings, rather than on the basis of a defensive pretence' (ibid.: 318).

Beyond these aspects, clients 'learn something about how to initiate and maintain real two-way communication'. For example, the client finds that now 'he can really listen to, and understand, another member of his family. He can let himself see how life appears to this other person' (323–324). Finally, there is often more opportunity for other persons in the family to be themselves, since 'our clients tend in the direction of permitting each member of the family to have his [her] own feelings and to be a separate person' (325).

---

9 I lately discovered an observation along the same lines, by Rice. She notes that Rogers' views of threat and defence 'suggest a conflict model similar to that of Freud' (Rice, 1974: 293).

10 Although not published until 1961, this paper was prepared for a talk in Chicago in April, 1953 (to the International Society for General Semantics) and thereafter circulated privately. As was typical of Rogers, having reached closure, he did not later revise the paper appreciably.

Altogether the points made are strikingly simple in expression and illustration, and of their nature based mainly on the reports of the therapy clients and not the other family members affected.

In the first visible account of conjoint family therapy practice in client-centred mode, Raskin and van der Veen (1970) describe the flexible introduction of family therapy meetings, responsive to the choice and concerns of family members in contact with the therapist. As therapy unfolds, the participating family group may change in its composition. The authors illustrate with a case in which the two parents first consult jointly with the therapist, followed by meetings in which one or both of their children participate as well, therapy sessions with one child alone, and then meetings with the parents again. Both client and therapist initiatives are involved in varying pattern, in these shifts in composition and focus. Reported therapist interventions are very much in an empathic-reflective, non-confrontational but also self-expressively 'immediate' mode.[11]

Rogers himself, to my knowledge, gave no account anywhere of conjoint family therapy. He did at one stage actively bring out relevant personal experience of a colleague. The context was a therapy-like family meeting process with evidently growthful impact for members, relationships and the family as a whole (Rogers, undated, Tape #7; Rogers, 1977a: 34–37). In the taped presentation the colleague explains how the process worked in her blended family, following remarriage. The sessions were held at home, at prearranged times, with priority over all other activities, and an open agenda allowing for sharing and discussion of any matter important to any member. Topics ranged from practical difficulties and problem-solving in everyday living together, and particular hassles in relationships, to anxieties around inclusion and commitment to the new family. Since one or both parents had professional interests in the helping field, and were highly motivated to enhance the connection and wholeness of their blended family, they may have been calling on unusual resources in the process achieved. It seems that they suggested the meetings, not unlike actual family therapy where the ball is set rolling by particular members proposing outside help. Where the helper is client-centred, as the parent-initiators clearly were in this instance, the process continues in ways that help the family call up and build on resources latent within it. Such a stance differs from more interventionist approaches popular in the family therapy field.[12]

Levant (1978, 1982) considers the client-centred approach a natural fit with family therapy, because its 'theory addresses the processes of enhancing close interpersonal relationships' (1982: 74). The approach thus takes into account

---

11 In the late 1960s, long after Rogers had left Chicago, some staff remaining in the Counseling Center there had begun to experiment with family sessions 'as an adjunct to individual therapy or, in some instances, as the only form of therapy' (Ellinwood, 1989: 258). This work ceased in that setting in 1971, when the Center as developed in the University closed down.

12 Guerney, for one, speaks with passion of the contrast between Rogerian attitudes, as reflected for example in his own structured program, and the directive and prescriptive orientation he sees as widespread in the family therapy field (Guerney, 1984: 269–270).

the social context of behaviour and *can* encompass 'both intrapsychic and family systems dynamics' (1978: 37). Levant's experience includes work in a short-term private psychiatric hospital. He observed that placement of one family member in that setting usually intensified guilt feelings in other members, and resistant sensitivity to therapy. Members he found were most receptive to 'an approach which does not force an agenda on them, but instead demonstrates understanding and respect for their situation and allows them some control over the process of therapy, particularly in regard to the timing with which delicate issues are surfaced' (1982: 74). By proceeding in client-centred mode, even families initially hostile to therapy became engaged in the process.

Clearly, diverse approaches to a theoretical understanding of family experience and process are possible. To the client/person-centred theorist, the image that members have of their family, their *family concept* (by analogy with self-concept), has been a crucial aspect and construct (Levant, 1978: 38–39; 1984: 253–254). The construct, however, can be used in at least two ways. One meaning refers to the specific view held by any one person of 'my family'. Another meaning is the more general idea or understanding of the family identity that members share – their intersubjective view of 'our family'. Van der Veen, the originator and primary investigator of this concept, worked with a definition of the first kind (see van der Veen et al., 1964), although also interested in the family as a totality. He wrote, with Raskin:

> The family concept consists essentially of the feelings, attitudes, and expectations each of us has regarding his or her family. . . . [This] is assumed to have several characteristics: it influences behavior; it can be referred to and talked about by the individual; and it can change as a result of new experience and understanding. These characteristics are evident in family therapy, where the family changes as a result of talking about, sharing, and changing various aspects of the family concepts of the members. (Raskin and van der Veen, 1970: 389)

Unfortunately Raskin and/or van der Veen did not follow up their 1967/1970 paper, specifically in the context of family therapy. The research using van der Veen's Family Concept Assessment method is mentioned later (pp. 308–310), as is work based on this author's conception of family relationship systems (Barrett-Lennard, 1984). Several papers mentioned earlier (by Bozarth and Shanks, Ellinwood, and Snyder) appeared in a valuable, special issue of the *Person-Centered Review* (1989, 4, No. 3). It also contains a fresh summary by the Guerneys (1989), and contributions by Anderson (1989) and Warner (1989).[13]

---

13 Papers by O'Leary and by Cain complete the main contributions. O'Leary (1989) also discusses the Rogerian conditions, and draws attention to their importance for healing work by systemically oriented therapists. Cain (1989: 249) argues that 'Rogers never moved from an individual to a group or systems perspective in his thinking', and that although needed expansions in perspective have begun they are proceeding under some difficulty. I agree with Cain on his point about Rogers' own perspective, but am freshly impressed by the unconfining inspiration that so many *others* who practise with couples and families have none the less found in his work.

For Anderson, psychotherapy is a process of 'lending coherence and meaning to our lives by the telling and hearing of stories in social contexts' (1989: 295). The therapist's empathy entails unusually careful attention to narrative, with the implicit criterion that a personal story is *heard* when its meaning for the teller is neither imposed nor extracted but is 'come upon' in the dialogue of therapy. Further, an empathic response can be elicited by a collective We experience (296–301) as well as by an individual one. In conjoint therapy, the therapist shifts between individual 'frames' ('I/you feel . . .') to collective ('We') frames, and back again. A We reference can of course be a matter of individual perception or a consensual one. As therapy progresses members share in clarifying their family process and identity. At the least, they find that their collective has a communicable nature and meaning. As Anderson puts it: 'The meanings of stories empathically framed by the therapist, and often by family members, are found, followed, elaborated, or discarded. Some are finally judged as effective and meaningful by mutual accord.' And, in the process of therapy, 'children and parents are learning how to dialogue, how to keep talking in the face of problems, how to listen to, expand upon, and respond to each other's stories, and how to hone in on individual and collective experience' (302–303).

Warner (1989) searches into the indirect communication processes occurring in families in serious internal difficulty. A good many behaviours, she finds, are 'strategic'. Their purpose is not to communicate a feeling or view but to have an impact on other members or the family system. The intention of having this impact is not conveyed, as this could undermine the effect. Indeed, the strategic 'intention' may not be in the intender's discriminate consciousness. The therapist who beams all of his/her empathic radar to sense and bring to clearer view true individual feelings and meanings can therefore be threatening exposure and impotence, producing an escalation of anxiety. Such response, in other words, can be on a collision course with the 'requirement' for covert action, which may spring from an anxious need to protect others as well as self. The more effective therapist notices the sequences of expression and response, senses the needs behind disguised intentions, and sees where the impact is self-affirming. Therapists open to such awareness, while reaching from a base of client-centred sensitivity and values, have in Warner's view excellent assets for family work.

Another colleague active in the same sphere over a span of years, is Ned Gaylin (1989, 1990). Gaylin, too, examines Rogers' therapy conditions in the special case of their application to conjoint family therapy. He points out that the family therapist is not only in contact with individuals but also with '*the subtle ecology of the family context* through the complex interactions played out directly in the therapy hour' (Gaylin, 1989: 266, italics added). He observes, for example, that 'transposing the concept of congruence to the milieu of the family extends its richness: The incongruence of each family member, as well as the incongruence of the system as a whole, requires attention' (1989: 267). One level of familial incongruence is that of discrepancy between a member's family concept and what s/he actually experiences in the family. Gaylin is less precise about the meaning of incongruence on a whole system level, sometimes seeming to equate this with generalized distress in the family. A clear instance of systemic incongruence is the case where a particular member is consensually mis-identified as the source of a family's difficulties (the 'scapegoat') (Gaylin, 1989: 268; 1990: 819).

High-level presence of another condition may have mixed effects, as 'when the therapist expresses feelings of unconditional positive regard to individuals who claim to have lost any positive regard for each other, and where feelings of caring and prizing have been replaced by those of judgement and condemnation' (1989: 272). Such response might help a recipient member to feel and regain more sense of personal worth, might even provide a model for emulation, but can also draw reactions of frustration where members initially look to the therapist as arbiter, perhaps from an attitude that 'validation of their position requires the invalidation of another's' (272). Expressed empathy can also have (positive) effect on more than one level: each family member is an involved observer of a distinctly empathic response by the therapist to another member, perhaps really seeing that member's feeling for the first time. Interestingly (to me), the possibility is also mentioned of 'an empathic understanding of the entire system', one that can help family members to see their interactive whole in a way denied to them from inside their stressed family (274; Barrett-Lennard, 1993a).

In overall perspective, Gaylin depicts family-centred therapy as a 'progressive integration' of (i) central tenets of client-centred thought and (ii) a view of the family as an emergent organic whole. This whole, born of persons 'in intimate context', expresses the formative tendency (Rogers, 1978) as much if not more than individuals do (Gaylin, 1990: 815–816; cf. Bozarth and Shanks, 1989). It is through family experience, influenced by the implicit concepts and values of older members, that children largely formulate their idea of self (Gaylin, 1990: 817). Conjoint therapy invokes family concepts and processes directly, without neglect of self, in Gaylin's and others' visions expressing a client/family-centred approach. Therapy with families is not only a temporary helping relationship but an activity in a region of experience at the centre of each person's lifeworld.

Current trends and overview

Therapy with child clients in clinic playroom settings has been an important area of practice by client-centred therapists, with influence spreading beyond the original context. Judging by the dearth of more recent literature, however, child-centred clinical play therapy practice has declined. Exceptions to the trend include the work of Herbert Goetze and collaborators, in Germany. (There is, for example, an edited text by Goetze [1981] on person-centred play therapy.) Perhaps the interests of most relevant practitioners have simply not been drawn to work with young children but, instead, toward older, more verbally communicative and voluntary clients. In this case, play therapy might just be in dormancy, 'waiting' for a revitalization via a new Axline or Ellinwood, or a change in demand for services. There are two other likely contributing reasons, however, for the evident diminution in use of the vehicle of play therapy as such.

The first of these probable reasons is the mushrooming and strong development of family therapies, in their various forms. Family therapy had not begun in the forties, and did not really take off until the sixties. Now, it is quite often the therapy of choice when older children are seen to be in serious behavioural, emotional or developmental difficulties, or when there is a major family transition or a crisis in parent–child relationships. However, the extent to which family therapy actually includes children of playroom age, such as those that Axline worked with, is unclear.

Ellinwood (1989) cites Zilbach (1986) as finding that young children are often excluded from family therapy sessions. Even in client-centred family therapy small children may miss out. And if they are directly included, they may not receive the depth of therapist awareness, respect and openness enjoyed by older children and adults. Levant and Haffey (1981) argue for integration of young-child and family therapy, with full commitment to each member in their individuality and also in their existent 'we-ness' (my term) in relations lived two by two and as a family whole. This may naturally call for differing formats: the therapist meeting with the child alone, with total attention to their experiencing and the language of play; with the parent couple, around their adult relational and parent–child concerns; and with the whole family, in motion together – each context important in its own right and helping to inform the others (1981: 140).

Another likely reason for diminution of classical play therapy is the rise of behavioural methods, especially, in this case, the development of filial therapy and its derivatives. This approach of course works to bring about growth in resourcefulness of parents to the point of becoming helpers rather than (unwitting) contributors to their child's difficulties. Boukydis' interesting work with infants and parents is another quite distinctive expression of the same broad aim. The capacity for deeply responsive contact with a baby person *in his/her distinctive consciousness* is not something parents fall into automatically. 'Interactional play therapy', as outlined, is a vehicle to help parents in developing perceptive awareness and interaction with their preverbal baby child (Boukydis, 1990). These and related approaches evidently provide a viable alternative to therapist-conducted child therapy, for many parents and children. Another wider shift, in the culture as well as in the helping professions, also has bearing on the use of separate child therapy.

There are many indications of a gradually growing awareness that multiple interacting and interwoven influences typically are at work in human experience and behaviour, as in the ecology of life more broadly. Personal-emotional crises are less often seen, now, as simply expressive of individual inadequacy, maladjustment, neurosis, and the like. Thus, tackling personal problems solely at an individual, intrapsychic level is less likely to be viewed as a sufficient or always effective approach. This movement toward a more contextual perspective may have gone further in reference to understanding and aiding young children than it has in the case of adults.[14]

The later contributions discussed in this chapter have shown that a systemic view is gradually being incorporated into client-centred thought and practice in the family sphere. It is premature to call this a vigorously flourishing development. It is, however, building more decisively than generally realized, and seems certain to evolve into a true extension of theory and practice in the client/person-centred movement. As will be seen in the next chapter, there are many parallel issues in the domain of group therapy and encounter.

14 Education, community health care, and remedial therapy services shade into each other with very young children, and where any of these systems is both of high quality and highly accessible, a growthful context that can also be healing is open to children.

9

Group Encounter and Therapy

> In significant respects, group therapy is like individual therapy. It is also distinctly different. The similarities arise from a common purpose and from a shared conception of the nature of human personality and how it changes. . . . In group therapy [the] multiplication of the number of participants means more than the extension of individual therapy to several persons at once; it provides a qualitatively different experience with unique therapeutic potentialities.
>
> N. Hobbs, 1951

> Those who may have thought of the encounter group as a fad or phenomenon affecting only a few people temporarily would do well to reconsider. In the troubled future that lies ahead of us, the trend toward the intensive group experience is related to deep and significant issues having to do with change. These changes may occur in persons, in institutions, in our urban and cultural alienation, in our philosophies, our values, our image of man himself.
>
> Carl Rogers, 1970

The quotations above touch on a number of the issues of this chapter, and reflect the evolving role of intensive groups in the client-centred/person-centred movement. Group *therapy* was a relatively early development. However, the approach was into its second quarter-century before intensive groups came to centre stage in the sixties, in work by Rogers, this author, and a range of other exponents. The new emphasis was on encounter groups rather than formal therapy, and fed into the more pluralistic era that followed the therapy-centred School Phase. Interest spread to include support and self-development groups working without any specialist leader. However, the early focus on group therapy with troubled clients seeking help remains rich in implication.

Client-centred group psychotherapy – from Hobbs to Beck

In the first years, client-centred therapy focused on one-to-one counselling almost exclusively. There is no account of group work in *Counseling and Psychotherapy* (Rogers, 1942a), and visible writing on adult therapy in the 1940s is silent on this topic. Incipiently, interest in small-group contexts was building even then (Blocksma and Porter, 1947; Rogers, 1970: 3–4), and became serious by the start of the fifties. Fruits of this interest came into prominent view through chapters in *Client-Centered Therapy* contributed by Nicholas Hobbs (1951) and Thomas Gordon (1951). Gordon's work, concerned with group leadership generally, is taken up in the next chapter.

Hobbs, in Client-Centered Therapy

Hobbs titled his contribution 'Group-centered psychotherapy'. The name is somewhat misleading, since the therapy remained highly individual-centred in its focus. The main principles were in common with individual therapy, and crucial features of process were largely an extension of elements emphasized in single-client counselling. Augmentation, rather than a different kind of effect, is suggested in numerous passages, for example: 'It is one thing to be understood and accepted by a therapist, it is a considerably more potent experience to be understood and accepted by several people who are also honestly sharing their feelings in a joint search for a more satisfying way of life' (Hobbs, 1951: 287).

Groups, Hobbs observed, were more evocative of self-in-relation issues and feelings than individual therapy, and especially conducive to personal growth, for many people. Sharing of feeling by one member helped to trigger another's expressive exploration. The group fostered changes in self-awareness via an environment of significant others, 'a context not unlike that which initially created the need to distort the perception of the self, and of the self in relation to others' (ibid.: 291). There was immediate social opportunity to express and try out emerging perceptions and new behaviours. The realism and potential of the group situation was enhanced by the fact that a participant could be a giver of help at the same time as receiving help.

None the less, features in common between individual and group therapy overshadowed their differences. Therapist aims and interventions were of the same kind in the two contexts. In each case, 'what the therapist attempts to do is to reconstruct the perceptual field of the individual at the moment of expression, and to communicate this understanding with skill and sensitivity'. The term 'reconstruct' refers here to a response 'such as clarification of feeling, reflection of feeling, restatement of content, simple acceptance, [or] structuring' (ibid.: 289). Both in Hobbs' main account and the excerpts from group sessions, the focus is clearly on self-processes, including the relating self. Learning from the dynamics of group interaction, or differentiating subtleties of interactive process, were not priority issues. Feelings and understanding toward self and other are highlighted.

Relational experience in the group did tend to be identified as having significant residual effects. Fuller awareness and increased valuing of connection with others was of major import, at least in some cases. One young woman wrote as follows of how much, through the group, she had come to want such connection in her life:

> For me, this is a big change in attitude because I have always fought against building up such affectional ties . . . and, actually, refused to admit their necessity for a satisfying and rich life. The risk always seemed too great. . . .
>
> The group therapy meetings planted the idea and then convinced me that the atmosphere of acceptance, warmth, real sympathy and responsiveness which existed during them is a vital part of everyone's life and that any risk involved is worth it. (Hobbs, 1951: 290)

Diaries kept by each member after each meeting helped to throw light on the course and impact of the group experience. In the words of one participant: 'I felt that after the initial awkwardness, the group gained a certain identity and solidarity within itself. . . . I feel a warmth and sincerity in the group that I have never felt in another group. . . . The most outstanding reaction I had was my feeling of identity and sympathy for Kay.' In her notes after the fourth meeting the same person speaks of newly discriminated feelings, triggered by other members' sharing: 'It was quite a revelation to me. I feel very relieved after this session.' Many of her diary notes mention the freeing effects of her fellow feeling for other members, as they shared their experience and struggle: 'I felt a close sympathy with Anne and her inability to talk' (session 7); 'At first I couldn't express this in the group, but I find it much easier since Laura feels the same way' (session 8); 'Kay's talking about roles struck a responsive chord' (session 11). Later, she speaks of feeling as she did 'because Mary finally opened up', and also that Betty spoke for her in saying that 'her old established values are getting mixed up' (session 12) (1951: 297–299).

These diary excerpts do not single out the therapist-leader's part in the life and character of the group. The therapist's skill, in Hobbs' view, was tested in bringing out the therapeutic potential of the group membership. Members could and often did become effective resources to one another, aided by the therapist's example. The opportunity of the group lay in significant part in the constant occasion for close member-to-member attention and responsiveness. Hobbs speaks directly of members assisting each other therapeutically, illustrating this feature in a long passage headed 'Group members as therapists' (1951: 309–312). To support opportunity for this, the therapist may often wait a little for others in the group to respond to sharing disclosures, although involved, inwardly responding, and ready to express this response. In Hobbs' apt expression: 'The therapist is not a passive member of the group; he must be in there pitching. If he withdraws too much, discord mounts, and exploration of feeling becomes more precarious for members of the group' (306–307). Research was already confirming a familiar and effective emphasis on therapist expressions of simple acceptance, restatement of content, and clarification of feeling (see pp. 252–254).

Sometimes, group member diary records gave direct clues as to helpful ingredients and effects of the therapist's response. For example:

> I can remember a statement that seems to have helped me most. The group leader's clarification that I do not feel my values to be as important as those of others seems to have been something I have thought about for a long while in almost those exact

> words. . . . Recognition of this by someone else gave me a great feeling of relief. Now I do not feel called upon to hide it. (Hobbs, 1951: 309)

Another group member reported that process/response qualities in the group were somehow permeating through to the level of inner dialogue or ways of relating to self. For example, when experiencing tensions outside the group:

> I find myself kind of verbalizing the feeling as I do in [group] counseling, reflecting back to myself my own feelings; in other words, I was a kind of counselor to myself, and I worked through some of my own problems that way. . . .
>
> I'm beginning to feel that maybe it's not just the particular insights, but the process that underlies the insight that is so valuable. . . . You feel permissive about your own feelings, you can reflect them, and that makes you sort of an independent individual. (Hobbs, 1951: 316 – from Peres, 1947)

Although dated in some respects, many features in Hobbs' account retain a contemporary ring. Some of the crucial ideas he advanced, for example regarding the group as a therapeutic agent, would have been promising ones to elaborate and build on in subsequent work. Unfortunately, Hobbs' own writing on group psychotherapy did not continue, although his learnings from this context no doubt fed into his contributions in the Peace Corps and other spheres (Hobbs, 1963 and 1966). It was ten years before Rogers published his next book, *On Becoming a Person* (1961a), and that collection gives no direct attention to group therapy or other intensive groups. However, a turning point in Rogers' involvements was soon to appear, coming to a head with his move out of full-time academia and into the free-standing Western Behavioral Sciences Institute in California, in January 1964. Intensive group work rose to became one of his primary interests, as spelled out in a further main section of this chapter. Another main initiative in the small group sphere began back in Chicago about the same time.

The path of group development: Beck's delineation

Group therapy re-emerged as an active practice and research focus in the University of Chicago Counseling Center, spearheaded by Ariadne Beck. A core series of twelve groups were each conducted over fifteen to twenty sessions, and studied in depth. Participants included clients from individual therapy, students in therapy training, and parents of children in play therapy. Each small group had a main official leader, and a second therapist trainee leader without prior experience in groups. These and many other features of the leadership and course of the groups are carefully described in an early report (Beck and Keil, 1967). In her first widely available publication, Beck carries the account considerably further (1974). The leadership approach was born in individual therapy and adapted to the group context. Leaders saw the client members as active agents, responsible for their experience and behaviour in the group, this attitude encouraging a general sense of 'ownership' of the group and of self-experience and personal agendas within it. Communication on a here-and-now experiential level was a leader priority. Precisely expressed, a crucial mode of response was 'one that focuses sharply on the client's statements as expressions of what he [she] is experiencing, with the result that pressure is put on the client to seek a closer identity between what he says and what he experiences' (Beck, 1974: 428). Leadership contributions by members (cf. Hobbs) formed another directly encouraged expression of responsibility (427–428).

Enhancement of self-understanding and empathy among members was viewed as basic to group and personal development. Thus, therapists tended to be highly responsive both to self-expressions and to more group-oriented and interpersonal expressions. They placed a high premium on being personally accepting and to development by 'the group' of its own particular agenda. As Beck puts it, when 'responded to in this way groups seem to have a clear sense of what they want to work on' (428). She acknowledges that evaluative reactions occur between members but notes the tendency, as a group evolves, 'to push the limits of conditionality back, so that each individual becomes willing and able to accept more in others than he did at first' (429).

The core of Beck's interest is the evolutionary process of groups, articulated through a sequence of developmental phases. The group itself, she stresses, is a phenomenon both to the observer and participant members. As she expresses it:

> A group has an existence in its own right in the sense that there are processes and properties that can describe it; in the sense that it has a history, and in the sense that its members not only have a commitment to participation in it but have a conception of it as a unit that is somehow separate from their perceptions of each member. (Beck, 1974: 423–424)

Beck and colleagues speak of *phases in the development of group structure*, the term 'structure' referring to the underlying pattern of the group's process (not to structures that a group begins with, such as its composition, the presence and style of formal leadership, and its time framework and setting – all aspects distinct from its process [Barrett-Lennard, 1975]). Nine phases are distinguished, based on the systematic observation of groups similar in composition, formal leadership (client-centred), time frame and setting (Beck, 1974: 422, 427 and 436).[1] Each phase has several principal aspects: the group's focus or main issues at that point, its characteristic process, and the way leadership is working. Leadership comes in several distinctive, regularly observed forms.

In the **entry phase**, the central issue is to establish a collectivity, an experienced 'We' emergent from the initially unconnected 'I's'. In the process,

1 The author is careful to point out that although her schema spans the full course of development for the groups studied, it is not necessarily exhaustive. Additional phases would be likely, she suggests, in groups running for a much longer time, or of indefinite duration.

the membership becomes a working group, with goals and some implicit rules or norms of group functioning. Typically, there is a round of introductions, therapist communications that help to set the style for the group, a growing sense of involvement, and the beginning of personally meaningful sharing and self-disclosure. This all gives rise to a feeling of commonality and linkage; 'group members seem to be saying "Although we are separate and different we have a common bond in experiences that are very similar".' An implicit contract 'to work together in this group' emerges (Beck, 1974: 437–438). In a later paper (Dugo and Beck, 1984), it is suggested that fruition of Phase 1 depends on each member forming at least one pair bond with another member, as well as the whole-group bond developing.

The designated or 'task' leader is expected by members to be influential in the group, to be skilled and a person to look up to. Whether active, passive, or of other style, he/she plays a visibly crucial part in initial interaction in the group. In therapy groups, this leader 'is the basic supportive person to all members'. A different 'emotional' leader (using language from Bales, 1958) also can be discerned from Phase 1 onward. This person helps to integrate the members and designated leader, and functions as a kind of energizer/manager of the group's emotional life. 'He [she] tends to be the person in the group who is most ready to make use of what it offers. . . . He is usually turned-on by the group process almost immediately . . . [and] tends to have a high level of interaction in phase 1.' The emotional leader quickly develops an especially warm, strong relationship with the official or task leader, and becomes something of a model of the change process early in the group's life (Beck, 1974: 438; Dugo and Beck, 1984: 29 and 38).

The **second phase** brings more substantial and explicit *development of group identity*. The group is not only a personal collectivity but some main properties of this 'We' are now forged. Members have communicated, explored, and struggled over the key issue of the purpose of the group, its style of communication, the question of norms or code of conduct (my term), and the matter of leadership and roles. Competitiveness comes to the fore and may be palpable, and Beck notes that in all of the groups she observed scapegoating was visible in this phase. (Indeed this dynamic appeared inherent in the development of strong in-group feeling.) The scapegoat person is initially experienced as holding the group back, and as antagonistic to purposes and meaning dear to others. Resolution tends to flow from someone helping to illuminate anxieties in the group, casting the 'threat' in a different light, and reframing implicit norms in a way that accommodates diversity and acceptance of the 'scapegoat' as belonging (Beck, 1974: 439–442; Dugo and Beck, 1984: 31–33). This resolution can herald the next phase.

Phase 3 is characterized by *co-operation* (although the transition to this quality is not achieved by all groups) and interest in other members, and greater reflectiveness. There is an emphasis on sharing and exploration; members are personally forthcoming in new degree, and look for others to be open and 'known'. Greater cohesion develops, and the group is now working on personal growth and on enhancing the conditions for this to happen. The emotional leader, particularly, is seen as going through a growth spurt, and s/he tends to provide a significant, even dramatic model for others (Beck, 1974: 442–444). There is a natural evolution into **Phase 4**, focusing on *emergence of intimacy* in the group. Group issues may centre on the expression of closeness and tenderness, and perhaps on the experiencing and expression of sexuality in members' outside lives (and sometimes as a dimension of attraction and felt relationship in the group). Individuals and qualities within the group may be compared with relationships outside the group. There tends to be more playfulness and humour than before, in the context of members feeling closer, safer and more relaxed with each other. The designated leader is more accepted as a person and participant in the group, and there is open valuing of the emotional leader's qualities and contribution (444–446).

In spiral-like motion, following the experience of new closeness and safety, feelings of vulnerability recur, heralding **Phase 5**. Members feel connection and warmth toward each other, but does this mean (anyone may ask her/himself) 'that I really matter to them?'; does it mean 'that they will use or take advantage of me, of my caring?'; 'will they accept my demands and need?'; or (using Beck's words) 'will my needs be met in return for what I give?' Resolution of this vulnerability involves the *exploration of mutuality*, of relationships based on equal and reciprocal responsibility, coupled with movement toward more self-dependence and autonomy as a group. The designated leader remains a resource but is not looked to as director, expert or guru. All this is likely to be too much for someone in the group, a person feeling unsafe and mistrustful in such a climate of freedom and equality, who possibly has experienced abandonment, and who can no longer call on the familiar lifeline of a clear-cut leader. Beck speaks of this person emerging as the 'defiant member' in Phase 5. In some groups this person leaves, in others they become accepted in their deviance, with different expectancy and understandings than apply to other members (446–448).

Phase 6 amounts to a direct carrying forward and bringing to further fruition of positive developments from the two previous levels. One discernible shift lies in the potential for leadership among members now being openly asserted. The role of the emotional leader further evolves into more of a co-ordinating and support function to others, including the designated leader. Members contribute in a variety of functional ways as needs arise, and there is a climate of *self-direction, bonding and autonomy* in the group. **Phase 7** then brings more intensive, sustained support to *self-confrontation* and exploration on the part of members. The group in this phase is most literally therapeutic in its function, in a climate of mutual reliance and interdependence. Beck notes that deeper understanding and openness toward the formerly scapegoated person is often evident, and this person may experience very significant change themselves.

Phase 8 is both a culmination of all that has gone before and a preparation for the ending stage in the life of the group. A likely main focus is on relationships outside the group, and the potential for deeper, fuller communication and closer bonds with others. Members are working at transferring their expanded awareness and learning into their ongoing lives, especially each one's life of relationships. The achieved quality of interdependence is a foundation from which members can move toward independence from the group, without feeling cut off and bereft.

The concluding **Phase 9**, in Beck's schema, is usually a time of deep feeling, but not of emotional complication if all previous phases have reached consummation. The central motif of the termination phase is of course the separation process, and ending of the group's ongoing life. (I say 'ongoing' because each person carries with them memories, including an inner representation of the group which may continue to be alive, active and a source of reference in their consciousness. Sometimes there are actual group reunions, and quite often contact is sustained between pairs or subgroups.) Saying good-bye tends to involve finishing what is unfinished in personal communication, and sharing the broader sense and feelings members have around their intensely lived experience together. Beck does not use the term feedback, but her account is consistent with the idea of context-sensitive feedback being part of the completion process within the group.

Termination was not a problem for those groups that achieved 'functionality' in evolving through the full course outlined. Other groups had considerable difficulty around ending. 'Incomplete and unsuccessful development of group structure' (455–458) could arise in a number of ways. It might happen, for example, through non-resolution of the scapegoat conflict, through the designated leader responding to pressing needs of individuals without concurrent awareness of the developmental state and needs of the group, or perhaps where inter-leader or leader–member attraction had some major dimension (sexual, for instance) that was not acknowledged.

In another paper, concerned with the **system-forming process** in groups, Beck (1981) casts her theoretical net more broadly still. The process through which a 'group's living structure' emerges is formulated via several broad propositions.[2] In effect, the author stands further back from the phenomenon, repositioning herself to give a wider conceptual base for her nine-phase model. That model assumes something that is now made explicit, namely, that there is a discernible order through which the living structure of a small group evolves in the process of becoming functional for its members. A second step is to specify what this order is, in keeping with the phasic sequence already portrayed. A third proposition delineates conditions which lead to completion of the full course of development depicted; and another proposition turns attention to the outcomes expected to result from successful traverse of this course. The group as a whole, and individual members, should become more self-aware and effective. Effectiveness is also seen in the group's capacity to work on tasks in line with its purposes and, finally, in

---

2 Beck first discriminates six kinds of 'influence' that enter into the process of a group. Some of these are contextual structures, as I use the term. They include the broad environment and immediate setting for the group; the purpose for which it comes together as seen in progressively elaborated goals; the nature of the work to be done or the content of the group's task; the personalities and skills of members; the qualitative aspects of group life, particularly including the styles of leadership and member participation; and the group's living structure and developmental pattern – this last the aspect of focal interest (Beck, 1981: 318–319).

the ability of members to achieve comfortable termination of the group (Beck, 1981: 323).

A fifth proposition articulates the dialectical interplay between group and personal development. During movements in personal integration the group's living structure evolves. In the course of group differentiation, an aspect of the individual person's own structure is likely to unfold; the two faces of the process ideally working in synchrony. Communication about group issues is a personal exchange of viewpoints and feelings, which is both integrative for the group and individuating for each person. 'This natural and essential process creates the vehicle by which each group member defines himself and emerges more clearly to the group and to himself' (ibid.: 324). At the same time, the array of distinctive and thus differing viewpoints 'hangs in the air' (my term) as a challenge to group feeling and wholeness until experienced as expressing a wider commonality and quality of We, this latter a further step in group integration.

Two further propositions are concerned with the naturally occurring leadership functions in the group, particularly including the modalities of task, emotional, scapegoat and defiant leader behaviour. Groups can be said to engage in 'boundarying', and each type of leader attends to boundaries in distinctive ways. Each type also has particular group maintenance and other functions (326–329). The functions set forth add a close texture of meaning to the author's general view that each mode is an inherent component of the group's development, notwithstanding the frustration to members that some phases of scapegoat and defiant leader expression bring.

It will be clear to the reader that I see Beck's work as a primary expression of thought in its sphere, emanating from a client-centred background and stance. The systematic quality of the thought involved in her contribution may have worked to temporarily limit its full potential impact on practice. I hope this presentation will help add further to its growing accessibility, and also leave the reader 'beckoned' by original sources. In Chapter 14 I will return to the research side of this contribution. In the meantime, some common threads in idea may be discerned in work that follows.

Experiential learning/encounter groups: nature and process

Client-centred work with intensive groups, whether defined as group therapy or as experiential learning or encounter, differs mainly in the composition and setting of the groups, but little in the style of leadership or basic nature of the process. In effect, person-centred 'encounter' groups extend the philosophy and principles applied in group therapy to a wider population and purpose. I say 'in effect' because most principal innovators, including Rogers himself, did not literally build from a base of experience in *group* psychotherapy. They made a direct transition to the encounter group from a foundation in one-to-one therapy, augmented by experience in facilitative teaching and/or administrative leadership. In practice, therefore, the fertilization of ideas has been two-way between the encounter and group therapy contexts, and the best work on a theoretical plane has application to the process and leadership of intensive groups generally.

My own work with intensive groups flowed from a background with Rogers and others in the University of Chicago Counseling Center (a hothouse of interaction in varied small groups), from counselling and therapy experience in varied contexts, and from my teaching in student-centred vein. Another impetus was the paucity of opportunity to work with like-minded others in my immediate academic setting. As a result, in 1962, I conceived the idea of initiating a residential 'workshop in therapeutic counselling' which hopefully would bring together interested colleagues from mental health-related disciplines across Australia. The setting was a provincial university in a remote centre to which participants would have to come from distant points, and where they could readily be in residence together, largely undistracted by outside commitments.

The first workshop came to fruition the next year, starting a series in that place, and sparking related developments elsewhere. We announced the main goal of the early workshops as being 'to assist those taking part to further develop their capacities to engage in psychologically helpful relationships with other persons'. It was promised that participants 'would not be confronted with a pre-arranged syllabus or program of topics, and every effort would be made to ensure that the specific content of the workshop experience grows out of the thinking and concerns of the persons choosing to engage in it'. To help make good this promise, there would be 'regular intensive discussion meetings in small groups' (Barrett-Lennard, 1967: 4). These 'discussion' meetings, as they developed in practice and as the terminology evolved, clearly belonged as a ground-breaking expression of the basic encounter process. Data for evaluation and research were regularly gathered from members before, during and after the workshops, as later discussed in substance (pp. 294–298).

Rogers on encounter groups

Rogers' own movement toward a recentring of his practice activity visibly began during his last year in Wisconsin and became full-fledged after he settled in California (from January 1964).[3] In his first major article in the

---

3 The first Armidale workshop, planned and announced in 1962, was held in May 1963. I wrote to Rogers soon afterward. His reply, from Wisconsin, reflects his own fascination and excitement with this (for him, too) newly discovered medium:

> I can't tell you how deeply moved I was by your letter of July 5. . . . The thing which was so exciting was that we had just completed a Workshop with 26 people and you might have been writing about the workshop here. . . . The Madison group was made up of mostly psychologists, some psychiatrists and educators, all of whom knew a good deal about therapy. Your workshop was composed of people from another culture. . . . Yet, with the establishment of a few simple conditions, which are close to but not identical with the conditions we have described for establishing a therapeutic relationship, these . . . groups all went through an experience that must have been so parallel as to be almost identical. (Rogers, 1963e)

small group field, Rogers (1967e) described the course of development of what he called the 'basic encounter' process. The fifteen overlapping elements distinguished are reminiscent of his early account of steps in individual therapy (1942a: 30–45). Although his formulation and Beck's developed separately, suggestive comparisons are possible. Rogers' first set of steps depict an initial awkwardness and 'milling around' in the group as members try to get their bearings, an ambivalent 'resistance' to personal disclosure and exploration, references to past feelings rather than those emerging now, and then some expression of present negative or critical feelings. These steps, all part of a broader process of engagement, roughly equate with Beck's Phases 1 and 2. (Beck's is the more studied and conceptually differentiated view and Rogers does not, for example, speak of varied emergent leadership roles.)

As the process develops, in Rogers' account, the atmosphere becomes much more positive, members draw closer together, have begun to trust each other, and venture into meaningful personal exploration. There is a growing expression of immediate interpersonal feelings culminating in the visible 'development of a healing capacity in the group'. These steps broadly resemble Beck's Phases 3 (co-operation) and 4 (emergence of intimacy). In typical style, Rogers draws on excerpts from group sessions to provide illustration of the stages; and this is true in particular of his next focus on 'self-acceptance and the beginning of change'. But the maturing group, as he depicts it, is not all sweetness and light. He speaks of 'the cracking of facades' as members demand straight talk from someone else seen as avoiding the reality of their feelings. One way and another, present feelings come to be more freely shared and the quality of immediacy rises. The process at this point resembles elements in Beck's Phases 5 (her mutuality theme, growing out of vulnerability and conflict) and 6 (realization of autonomy as a group of peers).

Implicit in these further steps is crucial further development of trust, within the group. As this happens, members increasingly go 'beyond the organized, practised styles and contents of communication and relationship to the level of deeply sensitive, protected or unexplored areas of self-perception and response to others' (Barrett-Lennard, 1967: 9–10). Also, as safety and trust evolve, spontaneity grows, there is less internal 'editing', and members' expressions tend to follow and express the flow of their experiencing. As the process goes on, there is increasing feedback and moments of sharp confrontation. There are one-to-one helping contacts outside the group sessions, a quality of direct 'basic encounter' is seen between persons in the group, felt closeness and warmth between members is expressed, and behaviour changes often become visible. The building process of basic encounter and change (Rogers, 1970: 24–37) has significant threads in common with Beck's Phase 7 (member interdependence and self-confrontation). Rogers does not speak directly to issues around ending of the group, and there is little overlap in his account with the eighth and ninth phases that Beck discriminates.

The book *Carl Rogers on Encounter Groups* (1970) was completed at the high point of the author's active involvement and belief in the healing power of the small group. The work is eminently readable, has been widely available, and is indicative of Rogers' views within its domain to the end of his life. Under his chapter heading 'Can I be a facilitative person in the group?' the author gives an intriguing self-view of his way of functioning as group leader/member; a mode very different from the nondirective stereotype, and embracing a wider repertoire than his style in individual therapy at any stage.

Rogers refers to an aspect of his function in a group as 'climate setting'. He would, for example, begin by sharing his feeling of keen anticipation of an experience *co-created by all of its members*. His sense of not knowing exactly how those present would do this, and of being deeply interested in how *this* group and experience would unfold, was conveyed. He would go on to listen with intense absorption to each member's expressed experiencing, with broad effect on the climate of the group.[4] The aspects of responding empathically, and with acceptance both of individuals and of their joint direction, worked to reinforce his climate setting, and accord with emphases in individual therapy. Other features – operating on his feelings, at times expressing his own problems, confronting others, and giving feedback – all developed much further in the group context. Rogers speaks also of modes he had tried out or fallen into at some point, but desired to avoid: agenda planning, 'exercises', interpretive or process comments, and the like. He mentions becoming more spontaneous in his movement and contact, speaks of the 'wisdom' and healing potential of groups, and shares many illustrations. His listing of a repertoire of observed group leader behaviours which he believed *non*-facilitative remains valuable.

Vivid illustration of Rogers' approach in practice was first widely seen in the documentary film *Journey into Self* (Rogers, McGaw and Farson, 1968), based on a weekend intensive.[5] Later films and articles tended to focus on groups with common problems or groups of members from the same organization, the latter a special case of what I term life-connected groups. Already, in his 1970 book (135–157), Rogers was advancing potential and exploratory applications over a wide range. Project use of encounter groups in educational systems had started, and is discussed in my next chapter. Beginning in 1968 and continuing still, the longest-running person-centred workshop series is the 'La Jolla Program'. This program has made pivotal use of encounter type groups, later blending these with much larger experiential community meetings. The groups have personal development objectives but

4 He wanted the group to become safe for the reality of each person, that is, safe for increasingly open expression of personal issues and reactions. I agree that this safety and example leaves the situation open for individualized content. At the same time, it exerts a powerful influence on what participants will choose to do – a paradox which Rogers does not acknowledge.

5 The fullest written description of this group that I have seen is Coulson's highly communicative account, with quotes from the transcript of the group (Coulson, 1970). Published in *The Counseling Psychologist*, this article goes on to speak broadly of the encounter group process and its potential effects. Critiques and exchange with other authors follow the main article.

are also designed for the training of facilitators. By the early eighties, Wood noted that 'upwards of 5,000 persons have participated in the training program and thousands more in the weekend experiences' – the latter organized to provide hands-on learning for the trainee facilitators (Wood, 1982: 251).

Encounter type groups with membership chosen to represent communities separated by strong prejudice, communication failures or destructive conflict, were also conducted by Rogers, to explore and illustrate potentials of his approach. Two well-known examples were filmed. The first, *Because That's My Way* (Rogers and Rose, 1971), documents the process with a group composed of drug-involved black and white members. The second, *The Steel Shutter* (McGaw, Rogers and Rice, 1973), depicts a group composed of Catholic and Protestant members from Northern Ireland – persons of course who were willing to participate. In the sixteen hours of group interaction fascinating shifts in attitude and feeling occurred, and it seemed that long-standing suspicion and hatreds reinforced by personal experiences did indeed lift and change. Later, Rogers (1977a: 132) reported that the group had further private meetings after returning to Belfast, and that members showed the film and discussed their group experience in church meetings in their own communities.

The mid-seventies probably represent the high point of interest and belief in encounter groups as the pre-eminent vehicle for interpersonal growth and social healing. This is not to suggest that such groups are now seen as unimportant. Rather, they have become more taken for granted, but in the context of varied and discriminating usage. In a significant paper from the period of highest interest, Bebout focused on the meaning of encounter itself, and worked to spell out its basic nature. He began by proposing that 'an encounter between humans is first of all psychological touching . . . [or] a meeting of emotions and minds' (1974: 372). Such a meeting implies a mutual experience of contact, of feeling the other in their own experience and being felt by them. Contact dissolves interpersonal distance and at minimum suspends the condition of alienation, where this has been present. It is thus also a precondition for intimacy.

Bebout further proposes that most people have the potential to (sometimes) go beyond contact to a further, deeper level of being experientially together. He takes an illustration from Rogers, of a man sharing in the group his intense grief 'which he is experiencing fully for the first time' for the loss of his child. Another member, tears in his eyes, responds 'I've never before felt a real physical hurt in me from the pain of another' (Rogers, 1970: 33). This 'basic encounter' was, for Bebout, an instance of *experiential communality*. Defining characteristics of the phenomenon are that the feelings involved are being 'lived' simultaneously, there is a high degree of equivalence in experiential content, and these contents are not just simple sensations but gestalts in which feeling and meaning are joined. One consequence of experiential communality happening is a kind of self-transcendence, an experience of being one with a larger human whole. Buber also gives instances of a person vividly feeling from deep within the self and then, in the next or same larger moment, intensely feeling as though from inside the immediate experiencing of another. This one powerful intersection of experience can '[make] the other present to him for all time' (Buber, 1947, cited in Bebout, 1974,: 381).[6]

Is experiential communality distinct from empathy? Bebout argues in the affirmative, pointing out that an empathic response is typically portrayed as one-way, A toward B, with an unequal strength of feeling in the empathizing partner and in the other person. (Perhaps, however, these features are not inherent in empathy but tend to apply in the special case of a therapist responding to a client.) Bebout closely explores differing views of empathy, more to open and clarify ideas than to close them. Experiential communality is the pivotal feature of his original thought, adding distinctively to other accounts of the encounter process. These accounts all help to give rise, in my own thought, to a more inclusive perspective.

This author's perspective

Intensive groups comprise a complex, many-sided phenomenon that tends to be viewed selectively and through varied conceptual lenses. The descriptions so far given are not so much alternative views as complementary ones, when seen within a wider frame. Even groups with client/person-centred facilitators vary in specifics of leadership aim and style, in their setting and context, in respect of composition, size and duration, and in associated features of process and outcome. Experiential groups resemble a pregnancy, 'in which the general character of the growth process and species nature of the offspring are known while its particular characteristics are only evident after birth has taken place', and, in some respects, only much later (Barrett-Lennard, 1975: 59).

Any comprehensive view of the in-group process involves a variety of levels. The developmental course or life-cycle of the group is one such level. Another level is to describe normatively the qualities of interchange and experience that characterize an effective group. One's perspective might especially emphasize intrapersonal or self processes, or, be centred on the interpersonal-relational subsystem level, or, be primarily concerned with the group as whole unit and system. On whatever level it is viewed, the process flows significantly from the composition of the group and prior experience of its members, its formal leadership, and its time structure and setting – broadly, from its make-up and framing. It is this process, conditioned by all the factors which give rise to it, that most directly leads to the outcomes of the group. I will enlarge on this wider-angle view, starting with selected ways of viewing the 'group' process itself.

---

6 Another pertinent example flows from David Bakan's notion of the basic duality of 'agency' and 'communion' in human life (Bakan, 1966; see Bebout, 1974: 382–383).

A *normative view: the experiential group in effective motion*

This way of looking at the process describes properties that characterize a low-structure experiential group that has got off the ground and is in effective working motion. I have offered such a distillation in two or three places (Barrett-Lennard, 1973, 1974 and 1975: 63–64), not with a prescriptive attitude but simply to identify further the phenomenon called an experiential learning-encounter group. Indirectly, my account also reflects elements in Gendlin and Beebe's (1968) lively presentation of ground rules for groups. In concise formulation, the process of the group has the following features:

- Members attend particularly to their own and each other's feelings and meanings, their outlooks and styles, and their experienced worlds (Barrett-Lennard, 1975: 63). They also tend to notice qualities of interchange between other members and in the group whole. In a word, *member consciousness is tuned to the inner self, the person of the other, the interplay between selves, and the wider working and motion of the group.*
- The flow of experience and interchange does not advance along a premeditated path but, rather, *follows what is found or discovered to be present*, and which tends to change as it is expressed. Attending to what is immediately present, and following its course, may become totally absorbing.
- *The process has an inquiring, searching, exploratory quality.* There is sanction for members to be venturesome and experimental around self-expression and ways of being in contact, and also of being catalysts or enablers for others.[7]
- *Members tend to 'own' their experience*, to take primary responsibility for what they feel and think, and to expect others to do likewise. Typically, participants want to expand the domain of agency in their own lives, to enlarge their range and sense of choice, to develop a more active, outreaching stance. As a group evolves, members become more aware of their *inter*dependence, and value this quality.
- *Part of the group ethos is not to play roles or games*, not to take shelter beneath a façade, not to pretend that the group has no directional structure at all. In a well-functioning group, there is a quality of down-to-earth honesty, directness, realism; a concern to see clearly and respond openly to what is going on inwardly, relationally, and in the process of the group.
- *Members 'work' at their communication* much more than in most social situations. They generally listen attentively to one another, check out what

---

7 Many things can happen at once, over the spectrum of individuals in the group: one person's self-expressive searching may bring to another an evocative new glimpse of his/her own make-up. It may prompt a third person to say (and thus check) what they understand the first to mean. It may convey to a fourth something vividly recognized within his/her own self but never before directly known in another. It may trigger an illuminating feedback message from a fifth person; and give to a sixth a compelling example of a *process* to try later in their own search (Barrett-Lennard, 1974: 74 [paraphrased]).

they hear or notice, and try again to express their own felt meaning when others fail to understand. They are drawn to being personally present, perceptive and knowing in their contact.[8]

◇ *Participants tend not to sit in judgement of each other, especially of the other's actual experience or inner self.* When critical feelings and messages do spontaneously arise, others present usually are sensitive to the feelings of both 'accuser' and 'accused'. The protagonists feel this supportive understanding, see how others continue to own their personal reactions, and may further discover both their own triggers and ways that such conflict can be resolved.
◇ As noted earlier, *personal feedback communication is an important part of the process of the group.* Members are likely to share and explore their pictures of each other in ways that are personally important to the givers and receivers of this feedback. These pictures evolve and change as *persons come increasingly into view to one another*. Acknowledged contrast with an earlier impression is quite often part of the sharing.
◇ *Peaks in the intensity of feeling and involvement in the group usually follow some spontaneous catalytic action by one or more members*, action that sparks off a release of energy, a feeling of some block or barrier being dissolved, and a deepening of experiential-communicative interplay (Barrett-Lennard, 1975: 63). Such peaks become part of the group's history and are a factor in the heightening of trust.
◇ *For the leader of the group, facilitation is an engagement of self over much the same territory as other members.* Like others, the leader has his/her own consciousness and concerns, for example, to assist and not impede qualities of the kind mentioned here. S/he tends to be attentive to all members, wanting to keep track and know them in their actual experiencing. As a group proceeds, and participants come to know and rely on each other, initiative and responsibility is increasingly shared. The facilitator is then seen and accepted on terms closer to those applying to other members – each one with her/his own quality of presence, purpose and contribution.

Experienced person-centred facilitators may be inclined to add something to this list, or vary its arrangement and detail, but it is thought unlikely that any whole feature would be subtracted. My next perspective is a more original one. It involves viewing the process of the group as a mosaic of interacting relational subsystems, and starts with an elucidation of the theoretically available systems. Although relational units are in focus, concern for the experience and learning of each member remains pivotal.

---

8 Avoiding generalities or indirect messages can feel strange or risky until the fruits of being personal, direct and specific are experienced. Communicating to be openly in touch rather than to maintain a 'safe' distance and separation reverses usual social intercourse. It is hardly surprising if considerable trial and error and uneasiness occurs in a group, on the way to unforced immediacy and directness of expression. At moments, immediate anxiety about how others will respond to the sharing of a particular experience is uppermost. Acknowledging this anxiety may itself be a significant disclosure that works to free the person to go further.

The process as relational subsystems in unfolding action

This view considers the 'interactional topography' of the group, focusing on the interpersonal process-structure (cf. Beck). Its aim is to illuminate the whole spectrum of interflowing channels of relational experience and potential learning, doing justice to their variety and richness. Since my approach here involves abstract analysis, it may help to start with a picture drawn more vividly:

> Each of us in a group is actor and audience to ourselves and one another, in an evolving drama which increasingly expresses several interwoven realities including: The me as I am (now); the active becoming me; the envisioned or could-be-me's which I . . . try out in my further becoming; the You as you are to yourself and as you transformingly become for me . . . ; the you-and-me's that become we's in moving relatedness; the we's that link and part in differing combination with other singles and we's; the me that is still one and sometimes separate and apart from all of you; the us's and thems that find commonality in opposition; and the group 'I' that comes into being occasionally in a communion of unreserved fellowship, shared identity or deep common feeling, and then dissolves again as conscious individuality re-emerges. (Barrett-Lennard, 1979b: 843)

Each element in this picture has a counterpart in the formal analysis, starting with the most basic interpersonal unit, the two-person system or *dyad*. As a small group of *n* members develops, each person becomes variably involved with every other member, that is, in n–1 relationships. In the group altogether there are n(n–1)/2 pair combinations, 45 of them if n=10. Besides the pairings they engage in, each person is a participant-observer of all the other dyads in interaction. Among these n–1 other members (leaving out the involved observer) there are 36 possible pairs [(n–1)(n–2)/2] in a 10-person group. Already, there is a great variety of interpersonal avenues for a member to engage in, directly and by observation. Modest changes in group size make a big difference to this range and complexity. For instance, 14 persons would generate literally twice as many pairs as 10 persons do.

At any moment when one member (P_1) speaks directly to another (P_2), a third member (P_3) may actively respond not just to one or other but in a way that involves both prior participants and relates to their interplay. Effectively, a *triadic* interchange is now happening. Since a group member might respond to any other active pair (from the pool of 36 in a 10-person group) great variety and choice is possible. Viewing the group as a whole, there are n(n–1)(n–2)/2×3 *possible* triad combinations of non-identical membership; 120 such, among 10 persons. It is quite improbable that all of the possible triad interchanges would occur in a group, or that a given member would discriminate a direct involvement with every other pair.[9] However, the extent to which such three-way interchanges and systems do arise is one significant measure of group differences. Being affected by and reacting to what is happening *between others*

9 In another three-person configuration, the member would react *from within* an immediate We dyad *to* a single communicating other. This could be expected to happen in a few (at least) of the many possible combinations in the group of this further kind of triad.

occurs all the time in families, friendship groups, and work settings. Exploring one's own and other people's ways of responding to such patterns of interchange and feeling, especially between others with whom one is also involved in one-to-one relation, is an avenue of distinct experience and learning that can be as important as any other, in an intensive group (1979b: 845).

A triadic interchange is sometimes followed by a fourth person (P_4) responding at once to all three. One way this can happen is by P_4 placing his/her reaction to the first pair alongside P_3's expressed response (for example, 'What's going on between you [P_1 and P_2] hits me quite differently from the way you [P_3] are seeing it', or, 'I agree with you [P_3], to me you two [P_1 and P_2] seem to speak the same language'). A *foursome* interaction may arise in other ways, for instance, by a couple moving from a dyadic interaction into jointly comparing their process with that of another twosome (for example, 'How come you [P_3 and P_4] disagreed without getting angry, whereas we [P_1 and P_2] got all worked up and defensive?'). In a 10-person group there are many such possible double-pair combinations, and even more *possible* sets of three that a fourth member might enter into (84, in fact, for any *one* person). I like to call 4-person interactions and relational systems 'quadrals' (845–846). Their potentially visible occurrence in encounter type groups probably varies widely, and is not often discriminated unless in groups literally composed of couples. I believe nearly all of us experience quadral forms in our families or other everyday life contexts, and that being able to manage and enjoy our engagement in such relationship systems is a personal resource that an experiential group can advance and bring to clearer view.

Larger possible interactional-learning subsystems in an experiential group can be worked out in the same way, although they less often stand out as figure in the total process matrix of the group. An important dynamic that may emerge and then recede again, and which is prominent in some groups, involves the emergence, interaction and transformation of factions. *Factioning* can arise through a subgroup experiencing significant commonality that sets them apart from some or all 'others' in the group. These others, partly in reaction, may then feel their shared identity in contrast to the first subgroup. The identifying distinctions may involve some visible attribute and/or features of background, attitude, style or purpose, as perceived. In the nature of the group, the 'factioning' itself is likely to come under intense scrutiny as to its foundations and varied meanings, and may survive only a short time or continue to arise in evolving form. A distinct possibility is that members will come to see that their individual self-images and esteem are bound up with particular reference groups or persons with whom they identify. In sum, factioning in an experiential group can be a vehicle to further awareness of one's own make-up, especially in respect to ways of augmenting self-regard (847).[10]

---

10 In exploring the personal meaning of factional conflict in a process group, individuals sometimes discover that basic elements of both 'sides' are represented in their own direct feelings although one position/side is more personally acceptable to them than the other. The underlying impetus for factions may be linked to the 'defiant leader' dynamic that Beck distinguishes.

Another distinctive dynamic, with counterpart in other life contexts, involves each individual's interaction and felt relationship with 'the group'.[11] At moments, perhaps of anxiety or intense self-absorption, everyone else can appear to the worried, struggling person as having one collective judgement, intention or feeling toward them. A tendency to cast the others as an undifferentiated collective may for the moment call forth a relatively uniform response from them. In any case, the individual–group ('myself–them' or 'me–all of you') relationship is something for each member to work out and deal with in his/her own way. Nearly all of us have experiences, often painful ones, of not belonging, and of feeling the need to earn acceptance or manoeuvre to gain it. We do not yearn for one soulmate only but also to be part and partner in larger wholes and yet ourselves within them. An intensive group is likely to call these issues to the fore, so that their working becomes clearer to the person and changed by being in the open. Considering the process of the group literally as a whole introduces a further perspective.

The process of the group whole

Beyond the interpersonal focus, the group may be viewed *as a total phenomenon and system (or 'team') in motion.* I am impressed that the group-as-a-whole is a phenomenal reality often referred to by its members as well as being an entity to the outside observer. A picture of this whole might be derived through cumulating its components, for example, by noting patterns member by member and inferring what is typical, or by trying to get a composite picture of interactive and subsystem processes. A distinct alternative is to think of the group literally as a unit, a dynamic whole with its own kind of inherent properties, not simply ones extrapolated from an individual or subsystem level.

Even during confrontation and conflict, members are jointly sustaining a context in which such processes are implicitly taken as part of the life and meaning of the group. This whole has the character of a purposive self-aware system or 'team', especially as Pentony (1970) develops this term. An experiential group is generically related to other kinds of team system but quite distinct in its particularities. Typically, it has only a short history and life span, comes into being not to fulfil an external function but to meet learning-developmental needs of its members, develops continuously rather than stabilizing, centres on process with little concern for structure, and tends to become close-knit and highly valued without trying to preserve its short life beyond an arbitrary limit. An unusual species indeed!

What other group-level features of process, what qualities not of parts but of the whole, vary and help to differentiate one group from another? Three

---

11 An approach developed out of this relational system perspective on the group process can also be applied productively to the analysis and portrayal of family relationships, as mentioned later and advanced in my prior writing (Barrett-Lennard, 1984).

such dimensions, each with offshoots of meaning, seem to me to warrant singling out.

The first main feature is the level of *cohesion* of a group, the extent to which it is strongly bonded, unified and close-knit, of which the quality of 'we' feeling among members is one expression. Within experiential groups, cohesion probably develops most strongly in full-time residential workshops since contact is relatively continuous and within a shared total environment.

> In these circumstances, the participants may literally become a band of explorers for whom each scene is new, directly experienced by themselves but no others, who see themselves in and through each other and see the other through . . . their own discoveries. . . . The members' engagement and activity *together* tends to stand out as 'figure' in intense relief, while the rest of the world may become, for the time, a shadowy 'ground'.
>
> To the distant observer, the group has become a strange body, self-absorbed and preoccupied, moving and breathing almost as one, locked together in a pattern of activity unlike that of 'normal' human interchange. (Barrett-Lennard, 1975: 73)

The fact that the group is atypical helps to account for its special potentialities. Cohesion in a 'stranger' group starts almost from zero, and may become stronger than in life-connected groups, where the ongoing relationships influence group qualities. How quickly cohesion develops, as well as the peak it reaches, naturally differs from one group to another. Mention of pace of development brings to view a further main aspect.

Groups differ in their vigour, flow and energy, in their general pace and in their tendency to bursts of motion. *Tempo* seems an appropriate general term for these elements of overt energy and motion, and comprises the second group-level quality. The movement of a group may be lively and rapid, or more deliberate and gradual most of the time, or it may be quiet but intermittently very active, perhaps moving in staccato bursts with quiescence between. Sometimes, the motion has a distinctly cyclical or wavelike quality. In a generally fast-paced group there is little stillness and less 'waiting', a halting or uncertain quality is largely absent, and few silences occur besides those filled with inner activity. A group that is less active may nevertheless be unfolding and developing continuously, with occasional metamorphic shifts. No simple relationship between tempo and productivity is expected. A factor likely to interact with tempo is that of intensity.

The third aspect, *group intensity* has to do with depth of emotional involvement and level of communication. The extent to which interaction is directly personal, immediate, self-disclosing, and openly expressive of perceptions of others, all contribute to a group's overall intensity. Wilkinson (1972), among others, has worked on the delineation and measurement of 'interpersonal intensity' in learning groups. He believes that the predisposition of members to be personally trusting of others is a key to the intensity likely to be achieved. (Other factors such as the 'mix' of members and the continuity and setting of the group experience seem to me important as well.) A group could be quite cohesive and active yet not engaged on a level connoting high intensity.[12] As with the other factors, intensity not only varies widely from group to group but, also, within and across a single group's sessions. Tension and conflict in a group may produce higher intensity, productive or otherwise. Within a session, intensity is mostly lower at the start and rises in varying speed and pattern. Whether the highest intensity periods are the most memorable or valued probably depends both on the developmental stage and composition of the group.

This overall delineation of the in-group process in terms of its normative properties, relational subsystems and qualities of the group whole, is not exhaustive. A *developmental perspective* is a vital addition, as previously discussed and, altogether, six complementary levels of view were discriminated in my earlier account (Barrett-Lennard, 1975: 61–74). However it is conceived, the process must mediate change effects of the group experience. I say 'mediate', not 'produce', because the latter suggests too much in implying that the process literally brings something into being. All this leads into the further major issue of how to think about experience-based developmental change generally, with intensive groups as a special case.

Developmental change and outcomes of group experience

To be unchanging or in a condition of 'stasis' is out of keeping with the natural order of human life. Growth or maturation, learning, progression through the life-cycle, all imply movement. Adaptation to a changing environment is an adjustive change. Having a high level of consciousness, in evolutionary terms, runs counter to simply recycling or playing out a fixed program. Change, however, need not occur in an even flow, and may seldom do so in complex systems. Shifts in qualities of consciousness, in self-awareness or in perception of others, perhaps in sense of direction, may occur or climax in a short time, more like a switching or realignment process than a little-by-little advance. Sometimes a person struggles or is off-balance for a time, before such a shift. Familiar ways of seeing and coping are not sufficient. Then, rather suddenly, things fall into place again, an opening appears, meaning replaces bafflement, a whole underlying feeling or sense of connection comes to the fore, and confident decision may supplant painful doubt.

Shifts in consciousness and outward repertoire (through whatever kind of episode) presumably accord with what the person is somehow ready or primed for by prior life events and development. The new experience and development, in turn, 'primes' or readies the person to respond differently to later events that stand out from the more repetitive flow of everyday life. Thus experiential learning contexts *such as* short duration intensive groups are not significant only through immediately evident results. Doors to new

12 One result of Wilkinson's (1972) interesting study was that groups tended to find their own optimum intensity level. This intensity (in the range 'low' to 'high') was found to be linked to member personal attitudes, especially their levels of 'basic trust'. When facilitated toward intensities discrepant from their preferred mode, less growth was found in cases where intensity and predisposition matched.

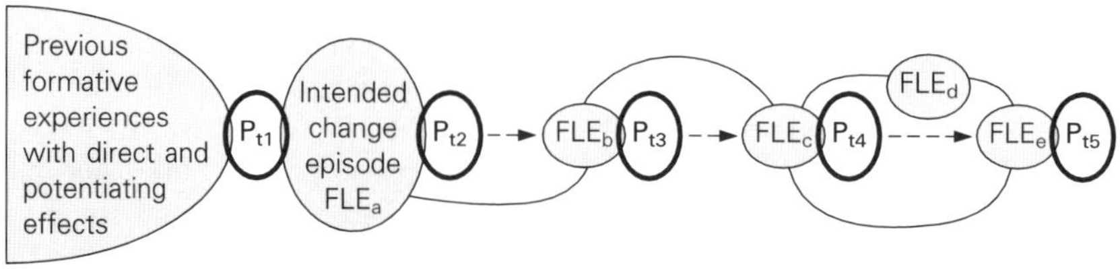

FIGURE 1 *Schematic outline of formative episodes and change, over time*

possibilities can be opened without all the thresholds being crossed at the time. Whether or when a particular 'crossing' happens depends also on what comes later. A person's choice to enter the group grows in part out of prior significant experiences, in much the same way that the group is then a contributing cause of later steps.

A conventional model of change looking essentially at pre- to post-group differences and whether these are sustained, would not arise from the thinking advanced here and cannot do justice to a truly developmental view of change. While perhaps still too simple, the following schema is a first approximation to a more adequate model. Figure 1 represents influential life events, and change, along a time dimension running from left to right. P_{t1}, P_{t2} , etc., in the figure, stand for a 'Person at time 1', 'Person at time 2', and so forth. FLE stands for 'formative life episode' or any very personally eventful experience. An 'intended change episode' such as an intensive group, is one kind or grouping of eventful and potentially formative episodes. The FLE experiences not only have direct or immediate impact on the person but tend also to potentiate or trigger further FLEs (as suggested by the curved connecting lines). Some distinct episodes have their *main* significance in laying the ground for a later choice and event of great importance in the person's life. An instance of this kind is represented in the figure by FLE_d leading on to FLE_e – both of these events arising from FLE_c.[13]

Consonant with this way of thinking about change, and with previous discussion of process, potential outcomes of intensive group experience spread in varying balance over a broad spectrum of levels:

◇ *Interpersonal level.* Enhanced sensitivity or empathy (seen in shifts in attention and quality of listening) and increased expressiveness and openness with others, are likely immediate outcomes. Enrichment of personal communication in life relationships is a potential delayed development. After a group experience of high impact there may be an initial period of confusion in outside relationships of long-established pattern. Change in attention and responsiveness to the feeling life of self and other is a likely

13 Available research flowing from this model, highlighting the range and interrelation of Formative Life Event categories, is outlined later (p. 306) and presented more fully in a separate report (Barrett-Lennard, 1996a).

effect, which may decline somewhat yet contribute to the person's values and choices at later points. When members have experienced a rare vibrancy or aliveness, attunement and expressiveness in their group, and have seen its genesis, they are likely to seek further such experience, through subsequent workshops or other channels.

- *Intrapersonal change level.* As in formal therapy, if not of such central priority, shifts in self-awareness and increased congruence of self-systems are important likely effects, both immediate and over the longer term. Such change implies greater openness to experience, and the effect tends to build on itself, enhancing subsequent learning from later involving and eventful experiences. Arising from the quality of listening *and* feedback in the group, and from experiencing oneself in new expressive/responsive action, adjustive changes in self-concept may occur. More basic still is the possible change in personal *process* toward increasing discovery of self through experience and less governing of meaning by a fixed image of self.
- *Process awareness and skill level.* Change in awareness of how experiential learning happens, especially in regard to elements that facilitate (or impede) growth in the person, in relationships, in 'we–they' interactions, and in group cohesion and identity, occurs in varying balance. Its extent depends partly on the facilitator's range of attention and response, on members' background interests, and on whether the group has an overt educational/training function. In a training context, participants may be more persistent (initially, more self-conscious) in 'practising' help-intended ways of responding.
- *Valued action level.* One potential outcome, especially for members directly concerned with helping and human services, is that they will afterwards want to create, or prepare themselves to provide, opportunities for others similar to their own experience in and through the group. This may happen soon, or be delayed as the outcomes build through further experiences. Action values furthered through the group experience may find application in differing helping/human relations fields. One kind of expression is a fresh emphasis within a familiar context (teaching, for example), another is a commitment to further self-development.
- *Social (system) change level.* Change in organizational, community, or other large-system contexts grows partly from personal and small-system development, including changes already mentioned. Where significant numbers of people from the same larger system have taken part in intensive experiential learning groups, some effect on their common system can be expected. The prior values of that system, the extent to which group-experienced individuals represent its various levels and subsystems, the flow of informal communication within the overall system, and the general mobility of system members, all would bear on large-system effects. The special case where such effects are intended from the start, and go into the design and setting up of the groups, is considered in the next chapter.

A study of formative life episodes, and other evidence of effects of person-centred intensive groups, will be revisited in later discussion of research. Here, the view is advanced that participants are primed for the group through their previous life episodes. I have implied also that the make-up of a group, its leadership, and where and for how long it is held, all have important bearing on the process and (via this process) on its outcomes. It remains to draw these contextual influences together, in systematic overview.

The influential 'givens' of group composition, context and time frame

Features of group composition (characteristics, mix and number of members and leaders), the setting and the time frame typically are all established when an experiential group begins. Because these structural conditions are 'givens' within a particular group, they may be taken for granted by participants, who naturally focus on what they can achieve in the situation that exists. When groups are looked at from the outside, or are being planned, it is evident that these features are discretionary and can be varied, plausibly with great bearing on what will ensue.

Member composition. The salient aspects of composition include, first, who the members are within themselves and in their lives, in respect to values or goals, self/other attitudes, outside life activities and relationships, and the combination of all of these. Is it an advantage for members to have much in common or to be quite diverse in make-up, style, or background? What are the process implications of presence or absence of significant outside relationships, for example, in the cases of groups of couples, or of associates from the same organization, versus groups composed of persons who are all strangers at the start, without commitment to one another beyond the life of the group? The big impact of group *size* on interactive process and relationships has been highlighted. The gender composition and age mix of the group would interact with other factors of composition in influencing process, as would the educational/vocational, ethnic and personal belief system characteristics and mix of the participants.

Formal leadership. Experiential groups differ in respect to whether/how many official leader-facilitators are present, as well as in their specific attributes and contribution. In *Journey into Self* (Rogers, McGaw and Farson, 1968), there were two male leaders, differing in generation, 'eminence', and specifics of style. The norm probably is one leader, in person-centred encounter-type groups. Cases where there is no pre-arranged leader present in the group are an important subspecies to which the next section of this chapter is devoted.

The designated leader(s) may have had a major role in initiating and planning the group, including advance communication with prospective members and a direct part in their selection. In this case, when the group starts, members all experience some connection with the leader-organizer, and may naturally expect continuation of his/her direct initiative. In other groups, the leader may be part of a larger team, not in contact with the members beforehand, and with only a small role in the advance planning. Specifics of leader personal style, their attunement to self versus interpersonal versus group-level processes, their inclination to meld into the group or to maintain a distinct role, all vary significantly even among person-centred facilitators. The general standing and perceived expertise of the leader falls on a wide spectrum (from Carl Rogers to a new graduate, say) undoubtedly with effects on member attitude and the in-group process.

Time structure and setting. Whether a group is meeting in an office or a classroom type setting, or in a retreat centre, especially in interaction with big differences in its life span and in member separation from their outside lives, necessarily affects the process. In the retreat type setting members usually are in residence together and involved with each other between sessions, in a full-time workshop situation. There is much greater continuity than in the case of periodic meetings held in a non-specific environment, cohesion and intensity can build up quickly, momentum is sustained, and experimentation can more easily occur. These things said, experience in discontinuous groups is more interwoven with everyday life, there can be more immediacy of life application and 'practice' of new behaviours, and outside experiences may continue to feed back into the group. Group events occupy time, and this time may be limited to 12–14 in-session hours, over a truncated weekend, extend to 30–40 hours spread over 2–3 months (say), or encompass perhaps 60 hours in a two-week residential workshop. The same development and scope of process is unlikely to occur under such different time frames.

In overview, I see the experiential group process as a 'multilevel complex of happenings that grows out of what the group participants (including the leader) are like and what they are up to . . ., where they are with each other to begin with and in their outside lives, how many are present, how much time they have together and how it is arranged' and other aspects of composition and context (Barrett-Lennard, 1975: 82). Thus each group is unique, and the picture drawn here is about a species of intensive group. Each person entering such a group has a distinctive history, including previous eventful and formative life episodes. The group experience is potentially another nodal episode likely to be unique in some of its qualities and consequences but whose outcomes cannot be understood in isolation. The effects flow in indirect but crucial part from prior life experiences, and they potentiate others still to come. The same is true, in more variable degree, of the groups next considered.

Engendering self-helping groups: facilitation *in absentia*

Experiential groups may form and work without a professional facilitator-leader, especially in the very extensive self-help/support group movement (Jacobs and Goodman, 1989). Usually, however, such groups are part of a larger program and have recourse to process guidelines developed for their use. These guidelines in many instances have roots in Rogerian philosophy and practice. Groups that are not leader-directed seem a natural further expression of the highly democratic *zeitgeist* of the client-centred approach.

Self-directed groups à la *Berzon, Solomon and Farson*

Betty Berzon, Lawrence Solomon and colleagues at the Western Behavioral Sciences Institute, began their experimental use and study of 'self-directed' therapeutic groups in the early sixties. First, two groups in their program met weekly for eighteen weeks. They 'were observed through a one-way vision mirror by an "on call" therapist who could be summoned into the group upon unanimous agreement of its members' (Berzon and Solomon, 1966: 491). Few summonses occurred, no one seemed to be hurt by the experience, and some found it helpful. Generally, however, the groups were uneventful, especially for members without prior related group or therapy experience.

In the next phase, twelve groups were conducted, six with an experienced professional leader, six without (and no observer/leader on call). Members in half the groups of each kind had previous experience in individual or group therapy, the other half not. This last factor seemed to be more crucial than professional leadership for development of a productive process (ibid.: 492). In a third phase, the groups were composed of 'inexperienced' vocational rehabilitation clients, and the self-directed (SD) groups were provided with programmed stimulus materials on paper. Again, groups did nearly as well in the SD condition as with a leader. However, they appeared to be over-structured, in a sense 'over-led', and at times frustrated by the programming. Two basic changes were applied in further groups. Audiotapes were used in place of booklets, and continuity was enhanced by use of meetings twice daily for two weeks.

This time, the participants began each session by listening to a guideline tape which ran for about ten minutes. The guidelines reflected stated goals linked to particular kinds of talking and/or listening behaviour. For example, the goal 'to experience more fully in awareness one's own feelings' was said to entail talking about the publicly visible self, then private aspects of self, and on to private *feelings*; these steps to reach the criterion stage of speaking 'with direct expression of here-and-now feelings' (494). Each session had its own process agenda, for instance a 'listening lab' utilized the now familiar form of triad groups of listener, speaker and observer, these roles rotating in each threesome. There were guidelines for good listening, and members appraised and gave feedback to each other. Although an exercise and theme were presented for nearly every session, and attention was drawn to goals and criterion behaviours, structuring became more generic and flexible over the group's life (494-496).

The ground-breaking volume *New Perspectives on Encounter Groups*, edited by Solomon and Berzon (1972), includes a chapter updating their 1966 report. An additional set of groups was conducted, with the sessions reduced to twelve, each one distinctive in purpose and process focus. In session 5, for example, the tape presentation focused on the aspect of giving and receiving feedback in the group. Facilitative and non-facilitative feedback were distinguished, and the former practised in a go-around exercise.[14] In session 10, members were asked to note down a secret on a slip of paper, all slips then being pooled, shuffled and redistributed randomly. Each member read aloud the note they received, and expressed how they thought it would feel to have that secret. Others no doubt joined in, probably including the originator of the secret (Berzon et al., 1972: 216–217).

In a low structure encounter group, members struggle together to find their path, are searching and taking initiative all the way along, vary in what they are attending to at a given time, and make discoveries through what doesn't work, as well as through what is fruitful. Starting each session with exposure to a 'lesson plan', even when lessons grow out of prior experience in other groups, must be a quite different experience from the much more open-ended process whose phasic development Beck delineated so carefully. Yet, the general *intent* of the structuring was to ensure that similar processes did occur. Were the experienced planners aware of any contradiction, or is there greater implicit structuring than is usually recognized by the person-centred group facilitator? This was still early days in the small group movement, with much to be learned and worked into organized thought. Because the medium was relatively unknown, there was also greater concern over the potential for harmful outcomes. And it was still quite daring to suppose that ordinary people might effectively learn to do for themselves what highly qualified specialists could contribute. A closely planned version of the process seemed to offer greater safety and assurance of result. Further, it might be argued that a specialist leader, both through what he/she does and distinctively refrains from doing, may influence and 'guide' the process as much as taped instructions would.[15]

Richard Farson reports another distinct approach to assisting self-directed groups; one making use of live example via the medium of television. In seeking to encourage the diffusion of such groups through a community a main challenge was to draw people 'away from the familiar discussion group format' and move them 'toward interpersonal exploration and involvement' (1972: 226). Issues to solve included studio-taping the regular sessions of an actual basic encounter group, and then broadcasting these one session at a time, as the group went on. This was done through a local TV station in the San Diego area and under sponsorship of a major university extension program. Application to take part in the studio encounter group was invited from a broad interest population. The selected group of seven people plus

14 The authors note that in each set of SD groups, the giving and receiving of feedback stood out as a highly valued activity, judging from process ratings and self-reports (1972: 222).

15 A further phase in the same audiotape-guided group program placed more emphasis on experiential emotional-personal learning, and modified exercises were used in the (now) ten sessions. Participants were freer 'since they were able in many instances to modify the instructions to fit their needs of the moment or ignore them altogether'. As one member said, 'We discovered that we could turn off the tape recorder, that "The Voice" was not inviolable. Once we did that, we felt we could do it any time and we were freer to hear what "the voice" had to say' (Berzon et al., 1972: 221–222). Using the structure as a *resource* is more compatible with Rogerian values.

leader, six without prior acquaintance with intensive groups or each other, participated in weekly one-hour sessions over a three-month period. A half-hour condensation of the previous session, with brief commentary by the leader, was broadcast between the meetings (ibid.: 226–228).

Twelve community groups were organized (others occurred spontaneously), with members sorted out largely by location, each group with a volunteer convener. Meeting each Sunday, members watched the broadcast and then proceeded with their otherwise self-guided session. Everyone was asked to keep a 'research diary', for mailing to the project office between sessions. After the broadcast series ended, each group came in to the institute (WBSI) for a low-structure follow-up group interview with professional staff. Of the twelve groups, ten exceeded their original time frame, and seven continued to meet for nine months or longer. Cohesion, attachment and valuing developed strongly:

> The overwhelming majority of group members felt that their group was considerably better than the televised group on the basis of freedom to expose true feelings, the ability to talk honestly and directly to others, cooperative efforts to understand and help each other, and the development of an atmosphere which made it easy for people to explore and show feelings. (Farson, 1972: 231)

All in all the feasibility of the approach was considered to have been well demonstrated, and Farson argued strongly for a shift in the mental health field toward more utilization of designed 'mass' procedures to complement and make better use of the limited expert resources. One of those who already had begun to take up the same challenge, and went on to fashion and implement a major contribution to the support group phenomenon in the United States, was Gerald Goodman.[16]

Goodman's program: 'Talk tools' and the absent guide

Goodman's first book centres on the use of non-professional companion-therapists in one-to-one relationships (1972). The 'therapists' were college students chosen for their existing qualities and resources by an original, fairly elaborate selection process. Most crucial was a procedure called Group Assessment of Interpersonal Traits, or GAIT. Small groups of applicants were brought together and, after explanation and warm up, rotated through experiences of disclosing and responding around real personal issues. Assessment data consisted of participant and staff ratings of reflective listening skills and other pertinent qualities (openness, warmth, accepting attitude) based on actual observation through the session (Goodman, 1970: 356–361; 1972: 29–42). After the selected helpers began to work with their boy clients, they took

16 Berzon, Solomon and Reisel (1972: 216) give footnote thanks to G. Goodman as the source of their 'secret-pooling' exercise, mentioned earlier above.

part in weekly support groups lead by staff who were also available for one-to-one meetings.

Recordings of the GAIT helper-selection groups formed part of the data that Goodman and his student colleagues later studied in depth, in a search to discern the basic architecture of help-intended communication (1984: 271–272). The practical goal was to create, test and refine a set of audiotapes that would facilitate communication and interpersonal learning in varied group contexts, particularly including the mushrooming field of mutual support groups. Preparatory exploration generated a large array of forms of helper response. These were finally reduced to six families of language behaviour: Questions, Advisements, Interpretations, Reflections, Disclosures and Silences (273).[17]

Goodman's program was built around the six language modes, and a number of operational types within each mode articulated as 'talk tools'. Criteria guiding the form of the program specified use both of audio cassette and print media; a scheme designed to run without a facilitator but to be compatible with having 'a professional in attendance'; and a style that would encourage active engagement, self-dependence and discovery by members. There was to be a focus on one basic communication dimension at a time, with a blending of experiential and cognitive input modes; *and candid, open communication of the agenda and concerns of the taped presenter*. The approach would intentionally draw language and 'tools' from several helping orientations (psychodynamic, cognitive, and other), as well as hinging on client-centred process concepts.

The resulting package, known as SASHAtapes, tested and refined over a number of years and through many diverse groups, has been extensively disseminated. Each two-hour tape, with 30–40 minutes' actual listening time, typically includes 'short lectures, exercises, examples, group discussions, and individualized practice assignments. Metacommunications guide the session to be sure participants are gentle and considerate of each other's feelings.' Periods at the start and end of sessions allowed for discussion of any unsettled feelings or other 'unfinished business' (Goodman, 1984: 275). Besides the taped facilitation, group members take turns as leader, drawing on a printed leader's manual. Leadership learning is seen as a vital component of interpersonal skill-building, and the rotation feature is considered 'a strong equalizer of group power . . . and responsibility for maintaining group process and achieving group goals' (284).

Among the six language modes, *questions* (although used often) have not been well studied in helping relationships. Gathering information is only one of their significant functions. Another is to convey or tell something indirectly. In this indirect category, advisory ('Wouldn't it be best to . . . [action specified]?', 'Don't you think you should . . .?'), interpretive ('Wouldn't that mean . . . [specified implication]?') and disclosing 'questions' are distinguished.

---

17 The origins and rationale for this system of broad language/response modes, in 'help-intended communication', was first carefully spelled out by Goodman and Dooley (1976).

Literal questions also come in different forms, one being a truly open-ended query, implying distinct interest or reliance on the other person's view. Or, the question may be a closed ('Are you . . . [thus and so]?', or, 'Do you feel . . .?'), or it may offer a choice of answers (266–267). In like vein, the author breaks down *advisement* 'into suggestions, demonstrations, explanations, and commands'. Each form contains a message telling, proposing or illustrating what the other person should do. Similarly for the other verbal communication modes, including the meanings and mastery of silences.

Goodman went on to devote a whole book, designed for wide readership, to the topic of elaborating and illustrating the six 'talk tools' in their helpful and unhelpful forms (Goodman and Esterly, 1988). The book focuses on communication in close relationships generally. SASHAtapes were created for the small-group context, with exercises built on this assumption, but the ingredient processes are mostly not group-specific. Goodman's approach is original in its highly differentiated focus on channels of personal communicative behaviour, and varied qualities within these channels, viewed both in help-intended interaction and in personal relationships more widely.

The SASHAtapes themselves can be viewed as a powerful guiding and leadership modality. Furthermore, the narrator tends to be experienced almost as a personal presence in the group. In Goodman's words:

> Participants rated [the] audio cassettes as 'very' to 'extremely' warm, kind, understanding, and empathic! The tape script language [however] never had the narrator pretending to be in the room with the group. . . . Metacommunications about the narration were common, and predictions about highly probable aspects of group process . . . were offered to gain credibility. Such procedures for confronting mechanical aspects of the program may paradoxically allow a stronger sense of the narrator's presence. (1984: 284)

The author goes on to note that the major context of the program is to 'guide groups of strangers with *common concerns* into becoming fully functioning, self-help, mutual support groups'. Relevant populations include incest survivors, recent widows, bereaved parents, family carers of Alzheimer's disease victims, people coping with infertility, women divorced in mid-life, parents who were physically abused as children, persons coping with breast cancer, and a host of other groups facing a similar life difficulty or crisis. The name Common Concern Program was chosen as the umbrella term for the wide public application of the approach. Materials include the basic set of master tapes plus the coordinator-leader manual, and supplementary 'Specializing Tapes' for particular categories of groups, including incest survivors and the other examples given above.[18]

Although Goodman's program was meant to be compatible with professionals being on call or occasionally attending, he hoped that mostly this would prove unnecessary. In practice, the recruitment and screening of

---

18 Sales (and loans within California) suggest that by the mid-nineties, more than 1,000 groups had used SASHAtapes and accompanying materials (Goodman, April, 1996).

participants, and initial launching of groups, depended on direct involvement of suitable professional resource persons. As he put it 'Common Concern needs a pro to help establish the group and then take their "golden presence" out of the picture' (Goodman, April 1996). How often they *do* leave the picture is unclear, and might be more the exception than the rule. The Rogerian origins and thrust of the program are not publicly emphasized or very obvious to the casual observer. This appears to have been a tactical decision by Goodman who is at pains privately to stress the close, primary grounding in client-centred philosophy and practice (ibid.).[19] Similarly with other large scale contributions, such as Thomas Gordon's later programs, rooted in or fertilized by Rogers' work but advancing without public emphasis on the connection.

Directions – in conclusion

This long chapter on small-group innovations and thought easily could be extended, with mention of additional contributions. Some of this further work will come into view in later chapters centred on research. Overall, it is apparent that at first client-centred therapists relied on the same repertoire of response and contribution in group therapy as in the one-to-one therapy mode, and saw the two alternatives having broadly the same function. From the start, however, they were witness to a total process that manifestly was not the same as the working of the client–therapist dyad by itself. Effectively, observation and thought moved ahead of practice, even in Hobbs' early accounts.

The theoretical base of client-centred group therapy at the University of Chicago was transformed through Beck's study and portrayal of the developmental sequence in groups. In similar time frame, Rogers himself and others, independently, were active in the practice and advocacy of intensive experiential learning/self-development groups in non-clinical settings. Rogers referred to the heart of the process as 'basic encounter', but the styles, thinking and values of Rogerian facilitators were distinctive, not typical, within the burgeoning encounter group movement. Their emphasis lay on the attitudes of facilitators, the group as an avenue for expression of personal actualizing/growth forces, and other features of the underlying philosophy of an approach for which the term *person*-centred was now coming into use, over its increasing breadth of application. Advances in formal theory having distinctive reference to groups were not a priority among exponents working around Rogers himself. Thus the reliance on my own thought in advancing a conceptual framework in the second main section of this chapter.

Over time, I have come to see more and more ways in which groups are a different phenomenon from one-to-one helping relationships. The same

19 More recently, Goodman has been interested in the study and utilization of 'very small groups' – trios and quartets – as mutual support agents in varied natural settings (ibid.).

attitudes and values can underlie work in both contexts, and there clearly is overlap in aim and process elements. However, a wide-angle but systematic approach to viewing the process – illustrated by Beck's work, and my own – reveals major features that simply do not apply to client–therapist dyads. The experience is quite different both for client/members and therapist/facilitators, and there is potential for a different range of learning. Seen in this light, the old question of whether individual or group therapy is more effective has little meaning: effective for whom, when, and in what ways?

In this chapter the focus has been on small groups as a medium for healing and, beyond this, for self-development and interpersonal growth. It seems timely in the next chapter to devote concentrated examination to positive goals of human development, visions of the mature or fully-functioning person, and the nature of healthy or well-functioning relationships. This examination leads on in turn to areas of application beyond therapy, group or individual: a region that includes education, parenting, community, and peace processes.

10

Wellness, Education, and Parenting

> When I have been able to transform a group – and here I mean all the members of a group, myself included – into a community of learners, then the excitement has been almost beyond belief. To free curiosity; to permit individuals to go charging off in new directions dictated by their own interests; to unleash the sense of inquiry; to open everything to questioning and exploration; to recognize that everything is in a process of change – here is an experience I can never forget.
>
> Carl Rogers, 1983

Each major school of psychotherapy has at some stage become interested in wider applications of its unique perspective on personal formation and healing. One likely extension is to describe normal human development or advance a concept of maturity, wellness or optimal functioning. Given the setting in which client-centred therapy in particular evolved, and the teaching responsibility of its principal exponents, it is also natural that education soon became a focus for extended application of its principles. That some 'Rogerians' would adapt and build on principles from therapy, applied to the context of parenting, is understandable too. The present chapter searches into each of these topics, on both conceptual and practical planes.

Rogers' most complete statement of theory (1959a) includes a closely interwoven formulation of principles in these areas, and some others. His total portrayal unfolds from a pivotal initial focus on the way change in therapy occurs. The first step outward from this conceptual core is a theory of personality; a theory which gives central attention to the development of self; and which is expanded to portray both disintegration and breakdown, and 'reintegration', processes (221–233). A closely linked account is then given of theoretically optimal personal development and functioning and, beyond this, of the processes of deteriorating and of improving relationships (234–240). The various 'theories of application' that follow all draw on this groundwork of thought and theory.

Any application of client-centred principles would include concern to promote and/or preserve both personal wellness and fruitful processes between people, however defined exactly. The well-functioning person would tend to interact in ways conducive to the positive development and functioning of others. Thus, before discussing particular areas of application, it seems pertinent to speak generally to the question, 'Application with what intent; in keeping with what concept or goals of positive human development and functioning?' A working answer can help to inform all applications, although each also has its more particular aims.

Well-functioning persons and relationships

Human maturity; positive mental health; the fully functioning person

The small volume *Current Concepts of Positive Mental Health* (Jahoda, 1958) remains a surprisingly current, forward-reaching resource. The author begins by 'clearing the air', as she puts it. She deftly points to the weaknesses of trying to define positive mental health or wellness by the absence of something – lack of disease or disorder, say – or via notions of 'normality', or in terms of *states* of well-being such as happiness or satisfaction (Jahoda, 1958: 10–21). Six criteria of a more viable nature than these are closely considered. All of the six overlap in substance with Rogerian client-centred concepts. There are clear lines of accord, for example, with Rogers' vision of the 'fully functioning person', and with my own portrayal of the mature person (Barrett-Lennard, 1962b).

One of the six criterion approaches in Jahoda's distinction focuses on *self-attitudes* and self-organization. A principal aspect of this focus, 'accessibility of the self to consciousness', is the positive counterpart of Rogers' 'denial to awareness' and accords with the idea of 'openness to experience' (Rogers, 1963b: 18–20). The aspect of self-acceptance also has a direct counterpart in client-centred thought. Approaches to defining mental health that stress 'growth, development and self-actualization' find clear example in Rogers' thinking. Within this criterion, emphasis is on the quality of 'a rich, differentiated life, [and] involvement in various pursuits not restricted to what must be done for sheer survival' (Jahoda, 1958: 34), a feature resonating particularly with Rogers' later vision of 'the person of tomorrow' (1972c; 1980a: 348–352). *Autonomy* is the pivotal element in another positive concept which Rogers also highlights, for example, in discussing the direction of the actualizing tendency, and the valuing process in the mature person (Rogers, 1964b).

The further criterion concept of *integration*, also singled out by Jahoda, has long been of particular interest to another client-centred theorist-investigator, Julius Seeman (1959, 1983, 1984: 145–150). Seeman discriminated organismic integration as a core construct in the study of effective functioning; 'organismic' to suggest the breadth of the concept, and 'integration' to imply a transactional blending of all the main subsystems of the person (from physiological to cognitive levels) in a congruent and adaptive whole (Seeman, 1984: 146).[1] *Perceiving reality without need-distortion* follows as a separately

---

1 Seeman's long interest in optimal personal development and functioning has led on to advancement of a 'model of positive health' concerned with wellness of the whole person-organism (Seeman, 1989a: 1099–1109). His pioneering analysis distinguishes five subsystem levels, in interaction: biochemical, physiological, perceptual, cognitive, and interpersonal-ecological. (I recently rediscovered a slightly related discussion paper: probably the first, close theoretical application of systems thinking associated with the client-centred school [Powers et al., 1957].)

identified criterion concept. More exactly, 'mentally healthy perception means a process of viewing the world so that one is able to take in matters one wishes were different without distorting them to fit these wishes' (Jahoda, 1958: 51). Perceiving the felt experience of others with accuracy and sensitivity (empathy) is distinguished as a major particular case and test of this wider quality. Remaining elements are subsumed under the heading of *environmental mastery*, with content ranging from the capacity for loving, close relationships to adaptive resourcefulness and efficiency in problem-solving (ibid.: 53–64).

Rogers originally distinguished three attributes of the fully functioning person (1957b, 1963b). Already mentioned is the first, *openness to experience*. Maximum openness implies that every stimulus to receptor systems in the organism, whether from an external source or arising internally, 'would be freely relayed through the nervous system', thus both interacting with other stimulus information and being available to awareness. No denial or distortion of information is imposed by underlying conditions of worth, and the person is optimally informed in regard to internal and impinging external events (see also Seeman, 1984: 133). The second, linked quality is that the fully functioning person would be *living in an existential fashion*. By this, Rogers (1961a: 188–189) means to imply fluid motion, unpredictability, and an ongoing quality of becoming and transcendence (see also Braaten, 1961a: 14–15). Particularly emphasized is the aspect of self being emergent from experience rather than the opposite of this, where experience is filtered and transmuted to fit a preconceived self-structure.

'Unpredictability' in terms of specific behaviour, although stressed by Rogers, is not at odds with consistency on another level. The mature person is not programmed to respond in set ways. 'His constancy lies in the *way* he functions, in the basic patterns of his life process, not in the specific forms of what he does' (Barrett-Lennard, 1962b: 101). A distinct inner direction results, but not in the form of 'directive' control by a part (the conscious self, for example) *over* the whole. Instead, the direction emerges from free interplay and combined action of all processes and levels activated in the individual's whole being. Effectively, such a person's conduct 'is regulated by integrative organismic control' (ibid.: 101–102; cf. Seeman, 1984: 146).

Rogers (1963b: 20) adds as his third feature an idea related to the last point. The fully functioning person, he states, 'would find his *organism a trustworthy means of arriving at the most satisfying behavior in each existential situation*'. In alternate language, the notion of a spontaneously occurring process of scanning all the data in a given situation, and arriving at a personally fitting and satisfying response, is central. This process would apply across very diverse contexts, those mentioned by Rogers ranging from a father's expressive response to frustrating behaviour by his daughter, to Einstein's clear sense of direction long before he had mapped out the solution to his relativity theory (21). Sometimes, as in this paper, Rogers does seem to neglect the importance of carried-over learning, even of an experience-based personal or 'organismic' nature; learning which he implies in other contexts is a crucial resource to draw and build upon. It appears to me that a particular asset of the well-functioning person is that of being informed and knowing from past experience, as well as being very open to the present. Functionally, such a person has guideposts which adjust in response to meanings of the present without cancelling or ignoring those from the past. In fuller expression:

> He [she] approaches each new situation *equipped but not committed* by his past experience. His own being has the quality of a continuously evolving pattern, a process that has direction but no end points, a state of becoming. He accepts this evolving, changing nature of being and does not seek stability in the sense of fixed personal values, immutable purposes, ultimate understanding or completed development. (Barrett-Lennard, 1962b: 101)

Rogers' account of the fully functioning person *within his larger theoretical statement* was formulated several years after his separate article on this topic (1963b) although published earlier (Rogers, 1959a).[2] It briefly outlines the process of *optimal* development, giving central place to the importance of unconditional positive regard and empathy in primary relationships. Resulting preservation of a free inner flow of experience remains a central idea, and other features are freshly differentiated. For example, in the well-functioning person experience is symbolized in undistorted fashion, and the self is a working structure congruent with experience thus far and responsive to change with new experience. Additionally, the person experiences self as the locus or agent of evaluation, is not hobbled with conditions of worth, and meets new situations with creative adaptation to their uniqueness. He/she engages in organismic valuing and tends to live with others in harmony engendered by reciprocal positive regard. The picture given is also substantially congruent with the top levels of functioning envisaged in the personal process continuum (pp. 82–85).

In overall summary, *the potentials realized in well or optimally functioning persons*, viewed from a person-centred perspective, can be reframed as follows:

- ◇ The person's organization and view of self has a quality of differentiated complexity yet of working as one piece, not an assemblage of parts but a multi-faceted organismic whole. This whole has a persistently distinctive configuration yet remains in continuous development.[3]
- ◇ His/her sensory and other experiential processes are accessible to conscious discrimination, and not habitually concealed from others. Broadly expressed, the person is open to experience, freely processes and balances

---

2 Rogers dates the writing of his paper on the fully functioning person as being 'about 1952 or 1953' (1961a: 183). This means that it was also formulated well before his more readily understood article, 'A therapist's view of the good life' (1957b and 1961a: 184–196). The two papers have distinctive nuances but much similarity in main ideas and scope.

3 In practice, this well-functioning self, free of chronic division and conflict, is not always in close harmony. Response to vivid new experience or crisis can challenge and unsettle previous unity, and growth may involve self-transcending shifts to a more encompassing singularity.

experiential data, and operates on the basis of all the information that registers internally.[4]

- ◇ He/she is not weighted by conditions of worth and is not judgemental in stance toward self, although at ease in appraising self-capacities and goals. Basically, the person has an accepting and regardful or valuing attitude toward self. This is a primary, spontaneous self-esteem, not a reactive need to regard self as superior.
- ◇ The person trusts and depends on his or her own capacities to organize and interpret the data of experience. Part of the significant experiential data is the response of others and information they convey, linked and transformed within the person in the process of coming to their own understanding and action.
- ◇ The individual's stance is active, not passive. S/he assumes self-agency and responsibility in life, although open to awareness of external conditions and their impact. Initiative comes naturally to the person.
- ◇ As an expression of the active stance and other qualities, the person is curious, exploratory, and developing on cognitive and action levels. S/he reaches out and engages in a process of continuing discovery or refinement of knowing – about self, others, the natural world, and the world of ideas.
- ◇ As also implied, the person is adaptable, original and creative.[5] These qualities apply distinctively over a wide range of life stages and natural endowment.

Well-functioning relationships; health in interpersonal life

The features considered thus far apply essentially to individuals; to be sure, with fairly direct implication in some instances for qualities of interaction and relationship. The idea of well-functioning relationships and 'healthy' interaction warrants attention in its own right. Rogers' theoretical view of the process of 'deteriorating relationships' pivots on processes set in train by personal incongruence (Rogers, 1959a: 236–238). The opposite conditions and process are conceived to occur in an improving relationship. Assume, for example, that X (a parent) is highly congruent within her/his relationship to Y (a child), meaning that X's primary experience, symbolization of experience, and communicative expression of this experience all match and harmonize. Y's experience of this openness and clarity of communication will trigger, or at least not inhibit, a responding transparency. This transparent expression could easily lead on to an empathic response from X, and also foster warmth in the interaction. In the context of such feeling and interplay, X's regard for

---

4 The qualities mentioned so far are subsumed under the concept that the person's whole range of knowing is informed by an openness to experience. The self-knowing component is said to be reflexive in quality, not a result of an acute noticing of self as object (cf. Rogers, 1959b: 97).

5 Among client-centred authors, Gaylin (1974) has singled out and examined creativeness, especially the process of 'creative synthesis', as a primary element in psychological well-being.

Y would tend to be non-judgemental or unconditional. Effectively, the conditions of therapy would be present in the immediate communication, with constructive consequences for the participants and their further relationship (239–240).

This thought is further distilled by Rogers in the form of a hypothesized 'tentative law of interpersonal relationships'. In a word, when two people are in contact,

> the greater the communicated *congruence* of *experience, awareness*, and behavior on the part of one individual, the more the ensuing relationship will involve a tendency toward reciprocal communication with . . . mutually accurate understanding . . ., improved *psychological adjustment* and functioning in both parties, and mutual satisfaction in the relationship. (1959a: 240)

Although Rogers' view opens out to include interactive and feedback processes, the basic causative element he sees in relationship quality is an expressed person quality – congruence. Two questions need asking: Is congruence literally an individual characteristic, that is, an attribute of personality? And, are relationships made up of characteristics of the participants, in additive combination, or are they distinct emergent entities with their own life and qualities? Rogers gives varying balance to two determinants of congruence: (i) the individual's self-structure, and (ii) the context of the other person's perceived attitude or response. If one thinks of the self as a system, in interaction with varied other self and relationship systems, context weighs heavily in the way self is expressed (Barrett-Lennard, 1993c). People no doubt differ in their potentials to respond empathically, but their use of this potential depends on the particular relationship and even the immediate context. The same things may be said of congruence. When viewed and treated in its interpersonal dimension the results are as meaningful as those from empathy, to judge from research discussed in later chapters.

The question of whether relationships have a distinctive nature of their own is rhetorical, in my perspective. An established relationship exists as an emergent expression and form of human life, with its own presence and derived awareness. I have worked to give more exact expression to this view in another place:

> Each participant in an active relationship may be considered to have two interwoven streams of consciousness. One of these, the 'I stream', reflects their individuality and distinctive positions in the relationship. The other, 'we stream', is an expression of their joint being and runs through the experience of all participants. The voice of this 'we/us' consciousness speaks *through* each member but not from them singly. The referent and source of this voice is not *a* self but a twosome – or larger emergent whole – with its own presence, a presence which exists in intricate relation to the I/me selves of each member. (Barrett-Lennard, 1993a: 12)

Stemming from the sources mentioned, and extrapolating from other person-centred writing, it is possible to outline several qualities of a *well*-functioning relationship. Some of the elements parallel qualities of the high-functioning person, others have no direct counterpart.

- ◇ There is an openness to communication in the relationship, a free flow of information, and an expressiveness and general clarity of meaning in communicative interchanges.
- ◇ A climate or attitude of trust tends to pervade the relationship. The participants are not in fear and guarded; their individual identity is not at issue and they behave in ways expressive of mutual acceptance and felt safety.
- ◇ The participants provide openings and make way for each other, less as a matter of deference or polite consideration, more as an expression of mutual interest and positive expectation of one another, and of a sense of their 'we' as having resources additional to the 'I' or 'you'.
- ◇ Self-trust on the part of members fosters interdependence in the relationship rather than promoting a 'self-contained' stance. Each one finds meaning in their own experience, looks for it in what the other expresses, and draws on both jointly and separately discovered meanings.
- ◇ In other language, the relationship is a living, open, adaptive system, self-regulating and growthful in quality, aware of itself through the consciousness of participants, and in dynamic motion through feedback both from within and from persons and systems outside itself.
- ◇ The substantial presence of well-functioning personal relationships within the same larger community, organization or other encompassing system, interactively contributes to and benefits from the health of that larger system.

The last-listed feature in this group is not so much a quality of positive relationships as an effect of their prevalence. The qualitative bearing that small and larger systems of relation have on each other underlies this effect. The issues involved are most directly followed up in the later discussion of community (Chapter 11). Student-centred teaching, next in focus, generally involves direct face-to-face relations. As will be seen, the quality of the teacher–student relationship appears also to be connected in rather complex ways with systems on other levels.

Student-centred teaching and education: principles and process

Already, in *Client-Centered Therapy*, Rogers devoted an entire chapter to the topic of 'student-centred teaching' (1951: 384–429). Arthur Combs, later a pioneer in humanistic education, had studied with Rogers at Ohio State and co-authored a book (Snygg and Combs, 1949) whose original view of education is cited by Rogers (1951: 386). A quotation from Robert Hutchins, President of the University of Chicago through the Roosevelt era and on to 1951, further helps to set the stage for Rogers' own statement:

> The foundation of democracy is universal suffrage. Universal suffrage makes every man a ruler. If every man is a ruler, every man needs the education that rulers ought

> to have. . . . The main purpose of a democratic educational system is the education of rulers. (Hutchins [1949], cited in Rogers, 1951: 387)[6]

Rogers offers several hypothesized general principles, among them the following:

> We cannot teach another person directly; we can only facilitate his learning.
>
> The structure and organization of self appears to become more rigid under threat; to relax its boundaries when completely free from threat. . . .
>
> The educational situation which most effectively promotes significant learning is one in which (1) threat to the self of the learner is reduced to a minimum, and (2) differentiated perception of the field of experience is facilitated. (Rogers, 1951: 389–391)

In keeping with these principles, the importance of establishing a climate of acceptance in the classroom is highlighted. This entails an active and respecting permission for students to find and follow their own track, thus also fostering an intrinsic quality of motivation.[7] With the teacher declining to take the usual level of initiative, students often thrashed around before finding their way, as Rogers' illustrations indicate. Student-centred learning begins, as Rogers pointed out, 'around the purposes of the students'. However, discovering these purposes is no simple matter with a group of students who are not used to pursuing self-identified objectives in a classroom context. Thus, a principal 'aim of the instructor is continually to assist in eliciting the contradictory and vaguely formulated individual purposes which gradually combine into a group purpose' (1951: 398).

The course leader remains a crucial influence on the process in the group, and as a source of information about available resources pertinent to achieving joint and individual purposes. Extreme possibilities are that the process will turn into 'pure group therapy' (ibid.: 399), or that it will turn in the direction of fostering *de*pendence as an instructor tries to meet the content of particular demands while missing the point as to the students' inner concern. The positive potential is the emergence of an exceptionally active search process propelled largely from within and resulting in highly meaningful, integrative learning. Rogers spells out a working repertoire of steps and

---

6 Rogers also particularly acknowledges Nathaniel Cantor's innovative contribution in *The Dynamics of Learning* (1946). He mentions their shared background of interest in Rankian thought, and cites some of Cantor's propositions, including the following:

> the teacher will keep at the center of the teaching process the importance of the student's problems and feelings . . .
>
> most important of all, the teacher will realize that *constructive effort must come from the positive or active forces within the student* (Cantor, 1946 [83–84], cited in Rogers, 1951: 385).

7 For Rogers, being 'permissive' does not imply a *laissez-faire* quality but a respecting positive belief in the learner's ability to utilize freedom constructively. In his richly evocative book, Neville (1989) draws on mythology to illuminate ralated values in education. 'Eros' and 'Psyche' qualities stand out in Rogers' vision. Down played, but also crucial, is a balancing conjunction with 'Senex' values relating to wisdom, rationality and careful inquiry (1989: 260–293).

ways of responding as instructor/leader in student-centred learning, and documents the process with recordings of classroom interaction (401–408).

The thorny issue of formal evaluation was also confronted, from this early point onward. Rogers singles out self-evaluation procedures as intrinsically most consistent and most valuable, even if not sufficient in terms of institutional and societal requirements. A concluding focus, recurring throughout his later writing on education, was to characterize the prevailing attitude as being 'You can't trust the student' – hence the elaborate organization of curricula and courses, reliance on extrinsic rewards and motivation, and the plethora of tests and examinations. The student-centred approach, in contrast, is based on the opposite attitude 'You can trust the student' – you can trust him/her to learn and grow, in an atmosphere for growth, to pursue concretely meaningful and connected purposes, utilize pertinent resources, and appraise his/her own progress.

Rogers was quick to follow up his opening critique of conventional education and embark on vigorous advancement of his alternative vision. His remarks the next year at a conference at Harvard on 'classroom approaches to influencing human behavior' were candid and provocative, directly challenging the concept of 'teaching' and the purposes of course grades, credits and degrees (Rogers, 1952a).[8] Research on student-centred teaching and descriptive reports by others began to appear.[9] Rogers' own publications on the topic accelerated, from the point of his 1959 article 'Significant learning: in therapy and in education', to include the pertinent chapters in *On Becoming a Person*, his well-known article from the Wisconsin era, 'Learning to be free' (1963c), and his probing and provocative statement on leaving Wisconsin, on the topic of graduate education in psychology. Subtitled 'A passionate statement', the last-mentioned paper was offered and turned down for publication in the *American Psychologist*, but received very wide private circulation following a letter by Rogers in that journal. It is a powerful statement which eventually appeared in his book *Freedom to Learn* (Rogers, 1969a). Before this book appeared, a cluster of papers embracing education and teaching in schools, had flowed from Rogers' pen (1966b, 1967b, 1967c, 1967d).

Freedom to Learn (original edition), which drew together most of Rogers' separate papers within its broad sphere, remains in this writer's view his most innovative and valuable single contribution relating to education and teaching. New material prepared for the book includes a closely illustrated account of 'My way of facilitating a class'. The author documents a recent graduate teaching experience with students working in a generally innovative context. The particular course centred on the role of values in education and human development, and course meetings were to include two weekend encounter groups. Interestingly, Rogers' planning involved a good deal of

---

8 Rogers (1961a: 273–275) claims that he did not plan his remarks to be provocative, but clearly he was not displeased by this effect and the impact on his audience!

9 Including studies by Bills (1952) and McKeachie (1954), and Tenenbaum's report in *On Becoming a Person* (Rogers, 1961a: 299–313).

structure clearly conveyed to everyone at the start, via a written statement covering general aims, a reading list, the workshops, course requirements, and the like. This differed from his approach at an earlier stage, when he 'probably would have given the group even more freedom, presenting them with the opportunity (and task) of constructing the whole course'. He explains further:

> I have learned that this arouses a great deal of anxiety, and a great deal of frustration and anger directed toward me. ('We came to learn from you!' 'You're *paid* to be our teacher!' 'We can't plan the course. We don't know the field.') . . . Consequently, whether out of cowardice or wisdom, I have come to provide enough limits and requirements, which can be *perceived* as structure, so that students can comfortably start to work. (Rogers, 1969a: 73)

The 'requirements' included a written assignment on a self-chosen topic, a record of readings each person had done and reacted to and, at the end, each student had to set down the criteria and give the results of a self-appraisal for grade purposes – then open to discussion with the instructor. While the approach remained strongly student-centred, perhaps the participant students were not quite as free to do whatever they wished in pursuit of their goals as Rogers implies (ibid.: 73). Besides the multi-level learning that took place at the time, the whole experience in this and similar instances seems to have been memorable to participants to the point of being a source of inner reference for a long time afterward (see also Tenenbaum's account in Rogers, 1961a: 299–313).

Freedom to Learn opens with descriptions based on material from other teachers working uniquely in very different contexts: a sixth grade class of formidably diverse composition, and an introductory course in psychology in a fairly conventional academic setting (1969a: 11–55). The conduct of the psychology course was markedly different from Rogers' described handling of his own course, and its rationale employed different language. The similarity lies in the quality of developmental aims, directions of opportunity and value, and implicitly in what the instructor sought *not* to reinforce. In the second edition of his book (*Freedom to Learn for the 80's*) the spectrum of reports is extended and all are presented with commentary by Rogers (1983: 43–115). This and other changes make for a rather different book, the author's last, produced in his own eighties.

Another pertinent development designed for a broad audience, but somehow not mentioned by Rogers in his books on education, is Thomas Gordon's Teacher Effectiveness Training (TET) program. This began as an outgrowth of his influential Parent Effectiveness Training (mentioned further), and has been conveyed both through a live training program and a volume for teachers and the general reader (Gordon and Burch, 1974). The book conveys a powerful message more by illumination than direct argument. The first three chapters present the contextual issues and thrust of the authors' approach, with masterful clarity. The dilemma teachers face, between controlling behaviour and facilitating learning, is well acknowledged. The need to control easily leads a teacher to respond in aversive ways that the authors portray as 'communication roadblocks'. In contrast to these are 'communication facilitators', ranging from passive listening through simple acknowledgement to *active listening*. Such listening is extensively illustrated in a diversity of school teaching and problem contexts. Ways of coping with problems and conflict and of enriching the classroom environment lead on to a primary focus on the 'no-lose' method of solving conflict – spelled out shortly, in discussion of Gordon's approach to parenting.[10]

The principles of any approach to teaching and education can be viewed through a variety of lenses. One such lens focuses on two broad components. On the one side, are the aims of the teaching/learning enterprise, implied or stated. The means to realization of these aims comprise the other main component, which includes factors from curriculum to school climate to teacher–student relationship – all intended to further a process and direction in accord with the goals. Since the aims and means have not been inclusively articulated in most person-centred writing, my attempt to do so here breaks modest new ground. Each basic *aim* (A1–A6) I distinguish is a connected aspect of the larger whole of integrated self-appropriated learning.

A1 First in mention is the development of functional or working knowledge, a 'knowledge of' rather than simply 'knowing about', an organically connected enlargement of the knower's consciousness in which the new elements and related prior learnings have merged in an advancing constellation of meaning and resourcefulness. The new knowledge is not just memorized or added on. It embodies *growth* in awareness and capacity such that the learner's subsequent perceptions and behaviour related to this knowing are necessarily different.

A2 Also implied is inquiry and learning that is purposeful on the learner's part, inwardly meaningful, an expression of their own quest, values and intentions. In keeping with its purposive nature, the effects of the learning are directly satisfying and enhancing to the self. In conceptual terms, the process is a direct expression of the individual's actualizing tendency.

A3 Another facet is learning that has the effect of reawakening or nourishing the individual's curiosity, his/her desire to know and to discover or gain new capacity in doing. If the person already is 'turned on' to learning, this quality is in no way extinguished and may be further heightened. If they have been dependent on external prodding and extrinsic incentives, such tendency recedes or drops away.

A4 The learning is releasing and enlivening; it does not inhibit but tends to facilitate the development of the learner as a well-functioning person on his/her own path. It thus also fosters originality and brings out the creative potential of the individual.

A5 There is an aspect of new or strengthened learning about how to learn.

10 I still believe that, although contrary to Gordon and Burch's aims, there is 'a little risk that teachers might selectively learn *techniques* of active listening in the service of control' (Barrett-Lennard, 1979a: 216). Being alert to this risk in a training context, should minimize its occurrence.

This 'meta-learning' enhances the person's capacity and disposition to solve problems. It involves increased awareness of fruitful processes of inquiry and a more active stance toward knowing. This combination increases resourcefulness in gaining knowledge.

A6 There is furtherance of experienced *self*-responsibility for learning and for assessing gains. External evaluations in whatever form become feedback to the learner who experiences him/herself as the final arbiter, especially for practical decision purposes, of his/her own resources and limits, personal priorities, and further possibilities.[11]

The means conducive to achieving these outlined aims and consequences can be arranged in two subclusters. One cluster centres on qualities of the teacher–student relationship broadly corresponding to the relational conditions of therapy. These are conceived as being at the heart of any interpersonal context intended to foster positive developmental or actualizing processes. The *relationship* elements (R1–R6, below) are framed here in specific reference to a teaching/learning context.

R1 One crucial feature, familiar from other contexts, is the degree of congruence or realness of the teacher in relation to the student. This is the extent to which the teaching person presents and shares her engaged self openly, without pretence or façade. It is also the degree to which she is visibly present as a whole person, absorbed in what she is expressing, responding to and calling forth from self and others.

R2 A related element has to do with responsive awareness of the experiencing self of the other. It pivots on the level of the teacher's experienced and communicated understanding of the student, who is simultaneously expressing self, ideas and external information in the learning situation. It involves the degree to which the teacher is able to sense feelings and attitudes *and* also see the subject matter issue and problem-solving process from the student's point of view. Tuning in to the student's system of meanings stands side by side with the teacher expressing her own.

R3 Another linked aspect is the extent to which the teacher/facilitator actually experiences and shows positive feeling for the student as a person. This pivots on the degree of her respect and interest, the attitude of care she brings to the relationship, the general warmth of her response, and whether there are moments of literal enjoyment of the other.

R4 A twin element to the last-mentioned one is the extent to which the person in the role of teacher is basically accepting and non-judgemental toward the student as a person. This is also the degree to which the

11 A serious outside appraisal of the person's work or skills, or their knowledge in some respect, is taken seriously. The learner is advancing in capacity to receive and *use* such appraisal, in context with the larger pool of available indicators and issues important to him/her.

student is appreciated as a separate individual on his/her own inner track and course of development.

R5 Also implied is the extent to which the teacher is able to perceive the student's own drive for development and extension of self as a trustworthy, primary motivation for learning. If the student is outwardly passive at first, this condition involves the teaching person being able to sense below the surface to a likely need in the other to be alive again in their curiosity and desire for meaning and expanded knowing.

R6 Another factor is the extent of the teacher's 'availability', the degree to which she is ready to share informational and other knowledge, including meanings of her own, in the presence of the other's desire for this. A highly available teacher contributes from that which she knows or believes, as this is seen as desired and helpful to others in achieving that which they wish to know.

Complementing these qualities of attitude and resourcefulness on the teacher's part, content is approached in ways that accord with the relational attitudes and support the learning goals. At least four aspects of *content approach* (C1–C4) can be distinguished:

C1 One aspect pivots on whether the topical content, and how it is approached, is a good match with actual student interests and aims. Fulfilment of this condition implies contact with problems and issues that are alive and real to the learner, perceived as relevant to his/her own direction or goals, and that arouse and expand a region of meaning in the person's experience.

C2 Another feature concerns provision of resources. The student-centred teacher works at 'providing all kinds of relevant raw material for use by the students, together with clearly indicated channels by which the student can avail himself of these resources' (Rogers, 1963c). Potentially included are resources to be found in a library, in a laboratory, in places where the processes studied are applied and practised, in resource people in and outside the learning group.

C3 The approach intends to minimize threat and increase personally targeted and self-appraising activity, thus to enhance purposeful and integrated learning. Two of the potential methods are the use of learning 'contracts' and of self-evaluation procedures. One or more such procedures, entailing a sharing of responsibility and contribution by teacher and student, are typically involved in student-centred learning.

C4 There is use, where possible, of varied interactive-learning contexts, including small 'facilitator-learning' groups or teams (Rogers, 1969a) as well as whole-class seminar-discussion meetings and/or lecture talks. The small groups would vary in their specific goals and level of interaction, depending on member learning styles and preferences (Wilkinson, 1972).

This outline has focused on the enabling conditions for student learning.

There is potentially another, different level of aim and effect. This further level is not about singular applications of the approach but its broad scale introduction in settings with previously different traditions and philosophy. The challenge in this case is to find a way of developmentally influencing the whole climate and qualitative direction of an educational system. Two action experimental projects of this nature stand out in terms both of visibility *and* mixed results. These projects were not only concerned to bring about a different approach to education and school relations generally but, more specifically, to experiment with the use of encounter type groups as the main vehicle for personal-attitudinal learning and change. In retrospect, there was a tendency to confuse the medium (groups) with the message (a philosophy of education and human relations).

The first experiment (the 'Immaculate Heart' project – Rogers, 1974b) took place in a parochial educational system in Los Angeles, where encounter groups were introduced and used extensively with staff, with students, and with varied combinations of membership. The total community of this system included a range of schools, a tertiary college, officials engaged in governance and administration, the teaching staff, students at the various levels and (to a degree) parents. The project grew out of Rogers' published presentation of a 'plan for self-directed change in an educational system' (Rogers, 1967d). His first progress report comprises the epilogue of *Freedom to Learn* (1969a: 327–342). Already, it was evident that the road to such innovation was a rocky one, and some difficult 'learnings' by the project team are acknowledged. One such learning led to an overall change of emphasis: 'We have come to recognize that we are not simply studying the impact of encounter groups in an educational system. . . . [Rather] *we are studying the impact of a dedicated group of individuals who . . . are interested in facilitating communication between persons, upon an educational system*' (1969a: 340). This interest came to be expressed in a diversity of helpful individual and group contacts. Rogers concedes that the use of intensive groups as an exclusive medium, or as a 'technique', is not viable.[12]

William Coulson, a leading team member on the same project, provides an alternative close account of it under the heading 'the effect of encounter groups on systems' (see Coulson, 1972: 99–166). The massive encounter group program conducted during the first six months of the project initially had releasing and valued effects for many individuals who took part. Some others were disturbed by the experience, from the beginning. On an institutional level, however, the group program had disastrous effects, in Coulson's observation. The existing structure of the system did not evolve but fractured; and the encounter group medium as employed came to be repudiated by the majority, including many initially eager advocates. For some two years after the intensive group aspect was phased out, selected members of the resource

12 It was also observed, for example, that the encounter group process was most uphill with those most senior in the hierarchy of the school system. In Rogers' (1969a: 339) blunt interpretation, 'the more prestige and status and intellectual expertise the person has to defend, the more difficult it is for him to come to a real basic encounter with other persons'.

team continued as facilitators in a variety of enabling contexts. As for the educational system, there were fundamental changes in its composition, even in its identity, and eventually a welcoming back of the modified system into the Catholic diocese of Los Angeles. The overall course of change and reintegration was not literally produced by the outside team associated with Rogers, but much of it was facilitated or helped along by them (see Coulson, 1972: 112–154).

'Project Transition', an even more ambitious system change program also largely designed around the use of small groups, followed closely behind the project just described. The setting was very different: the inner-city school system in Louisville, Kentucky. Rogers served as a consultant, but the primary initiative was taken by the newly appointed superintendent both with backing from the school board and the aid of federal funding. The need for change was critical, the symptoms including exceptionally high student dropout rates, acute delinquency problems, high teacher turnover, and low and falling educational achievement. Unlike the Immaculate Heart case, the project began by involving the board and everyone in top leadership positions in experiential learning and training groups together with close exposure to the associated philosophy. Within six months, some 1,600 teaching and other staff were or had been engaged in similar experiences (Rogers, 1983: 228). Thus, a large number of people employed at all levels within the system soon had direct knowledge of what they were getting into, and the group committed to change evidently was more coherent and representative than in the other project. As well, it seems that a single team of outside facilitators was not employed and initiatives and resources came largely from people appointed within the system.

Although optimistic, as always, Rogers did predict at an early stage that 'as change is brought about, an increasing degree of turbulence and criticism will occur in the whole educational system' (Rogers, 1970: 147). This perhaps was an understatement although it seems that extremely fruitful results did occur quite widely in staff–student relations, and in student attitudes and learning. In Rogers' view, the revolutionary changes could have been sustained if external events had not intervened to undermine and destroy the hard won gains. Opposition to the new direction reached critical mass as a result of amalgamation of the inner-city system with the far more conservative, white-dominated suburban system, a move that flowed from court decisions on racial integration in the schools. Rogers' fullest overall report of the project appears in his revision of *Freedom to Learn* (1983: 227–233), and interesting further material appears in the special issue of *Education* centred on his work (see Foster and Back, 1974).

Large-system change probably calls for principles additional to those employed in the projects discussed. One might, for example, ask the question 'What qualities of an institution and its larger context form a necessary base of supporting conditions for the successful *broad* application of self-directing, student-centred learning?' Where the focus is on those who would initiate the innovation, an additional question might be 'What awareness and resources additional to expertise in the interior process of facilitating student-centred learning are conducive to the transformative introduction of this approach in a whole educational system?' I have raised these questions only to leave them for the moment (see pp. 339–340). This section has been principally concerned with the evolution and process principles of student-centred teaching and learning, with how this works in practice, and with problems and issues of system-wide application. My next focus draws on a common set of ideas, with clear links to the conceptions of well-functioning persons and relationships earlier advanced. Perhaps even more is at stake in this next area than in the case of formal education, in regard to quality of human development and well-being.

Child-, family- and person-centred parenting

Concerns and ideas about parenting and parent–child relations often are implied but seldom build into a main focus, in the person-centred literature. A highly visible exception to this usual pattern is the work of Thomas Gordon on 'parent effectiveness training'. Some contributions already mentioned, especially in speaking of child and family therapy, are also pertinent to consider here. Rogers' prolific writing does not include work explicitly centring in this area, but his multi-sided interest in the helping relationship and its portrayal feeds strongly into the thinking of those who have highlighted and focused in the sphere of parent–child relations.

Many factors plausibly are involved in the total process of parenting, beyond the direct qualitative relation between parent and child. These factors broadly include the parent's comprehension of and capacity to negotiate the multi-layered environment within which the parent–child or family unit has its living space and support systems. Parents are called on to be providers, protectors, mediators, models, teachers. Their ability to keep track of their child's ever-changing abilities, awareness and needs is important both for their relationship and other parenting tasks. They contribute to the quality and extent of the child's connection with significant others and the wider community, and with their natural and constructed environments. How parents relate to the young child's constant process of exploration and discovery, the example they provide on many levels, how they assist in the child's discrimination of meaning and connection in his world, are just some of the broader strands in their total contribution to their child's unfolding.

Focusing on the parent–child relationship takes in a hugely important dimension of parenting but one nevertheless which needs to be seen in the context of a wider total process in which other main strands are important in their own right and in interaction with relationship quality. Put another way, the parent–child connection is not solely an interpersonal relationship, does not *only* pivot on qualities of direct interaction and communication. Further, relationship itself clearly can be viewed in different ways. The client-centred way traditionally centres on qualities such as empathy and acceptance, in one person's response to another. Another way is to think of the qualities of the dyad system (say) as a whole, as in my earlier outline of well-functioning relationships.

Gordon has introduced his thinking by outlining the 'theory of healthy relationships' undergirding his approach to parent effectiveness training (1970a). His theory lists a number of defining ways in which participants in a healthy relationship respond to the other partner. In the parent–child instance, it is the parent's response that is in focus, since the parent is taken to be in the more powerful position, and to have main responsibility for initiating change (1970a: 412). *Acceptance* is a primary dimension of relationship, subsumes other qualities, and has several crucial aspects. In a healthy relationship, the parent feels and demonstrates substantial and wide-ranging acceptance of the child. Gordon does not believe it possible to be unconditionally accepting, especially at the level of behaviours, but means to refer to a generally prevailing attitude and response. He singles out active listening (cf. Rogers and Farson, 1957) as a primary means of showing acceptance, especially through a process of reflective acknowledgement. Other means include the expression of caring feelings, the open sharing of self-experiences, and spontaneous physical contact. Most instances of ordering and commanding, warning or threatening, criticizing or ridiculing, analysing, asking probing questions, and many instances of praising and of sympathizing, are deemed non-accepting (Gordon, 1970a: 414–415).

In a relationship seen as becoming healthy, the parent would be working to extend the depth or range of his/her acceptance, would seek to be more aware of non-accepting reactions, and would communicate negative and non-accepting feelings more openly and honestly, especially in the owned form of I-messages ('I don't like . . .'; 'I feel put out (or upset) by . . .'; 'I am tired and don't want . . .', etc.). Stressed as pivotal is the further attitude of refusing to use power to settle conflicts. Nearly always, there seems to be a winner and a loser when conflict between the needs/desires of the parent and the child is 'resolved' through the exercise of power. The child loser, especially where this is a pattern, is likely to feel humiliated, angry and/or rebellious, be more prone to blame or boss others, to act out aggressively or become submissive or over-obedient, or to react in other ways that the observer would feel are diminishing to the child's positive development and well-being. Equally, in the interests of a healthy relationship, the parent needs to refuse to give in to control by the child, that is, to a pattern of the child person imposing his/her solution such that the parent's needs in effect are over-ruled (1970a: 419–422).

Gordon's further pragmatic focus is the criterion requirement of conflicts being resolved by a 'no-lose' approach. The parent would in effect decide: 'I must commit myself to use a "no-lose" method to resolve all the inevitable conflicts in my relationship with the other' (423; italics omitted). In this approach, parent and child join in a mutual search for a solution that will be acceptable to both of them. Its counterpart is in wide use in society, to avoid or resolve conflict, for example in contractual arrangements, joint personal decision-making, and out-of-court settlements; all situations where the parties have similar power and/or freedom of decision. The idea of using the approach in situations of inequality of power is more novel. Learning the skills and building the attitude to apply this principle consistently is seen by Gordon as a particular and crucial challenge to parents and to his program.

In his book *P.E.T. Parent Effectiveness Training*, Gordon (1970b) opens out the ideas and practices presented in much more detail and for a wider audience. Rich with illustration, and based on years of development and experience with PET, the book itself is virtually a teaching/training manual. Its intention, though, is not to instruct narrowly but more to illuminate, demonstrate and raise practical consciousness of what typically does happen and what (alternatively) can happen between parents and children. The author draws attention to consequences of usual attitudes and styles of communication but not in a judgemental, labelling mode. He states his own position, however, spells out aims and convictions, and promises a full clear account: 'In this book, as in our P.E.T. program, parents will be given *everything we know*, not just bits and pieces. A complete model of effective parent–child relationships will be described . . .' (ibid.: 6).

Three of the chapters revolve around listening, others focus on intentions and ways of talking, and seven chapters bear on issues of power, conflict and its resolution in parent–child relationships. Early mention is made of 'passive listening', mostly through silence and brief signals of encouragement (for example, 'Mm hmm', 'What happened?', 'I hear you', 'Tell me all about it'). Even such simple responses and the attention they signal can convey strong encouragement to the child wanting to talk and share. 'Active listening', where the parent actually restates and checks out the content or essence of what has been heard, is viewed as a uniquely powerful feedback process that allows understanding and knowing of the other to be self-corrective. By signalling caring, acceptance and respect, as well as understanding, the process can be deeply affirming and enhancing for the child. The preconditions for such listening (wanting to hear, know, understand, etc.), its specific process and its likely effects are portrayed with care, and illustrated in detail in a chapter titled 'Putting your active listening skill to work' (1970b: 62–94). The process need not depend on developed verbal skills; the use of 'active listening to help infants' is the main focus of one chapter (99–102).

Parent-to-child messages often are highly evaluative in their implication or direct statement about the child. In his book, Gordon reviews the high-frequency kinds of 'non-accepting' response and spells out the generally more constructive alternative of parents conveying directly what they are experiencing. It makes a large, often vitally helpful difference in relational communication when a person speaks not just about the other but from inside their own self; an experiencing self acknowledged within their statement ('I feel . . .'; 'I wish . . .'; 'I hope . . .'; 'I'm upset about . . .'; etc.). It is then clear *where they are inwardly coming from*, as against merely showing *what they are pointing to* or attributing to the other ('You are . . .'; 'You deserve . . .'; 'Your behavior is . . .').

Gordon gives extensive practical attention to parent–child conflict, and its varied effects and kinds of resolution. Episodes of conflictual interaction and/ or power struggle typically start early in the parent–child relation,[13] and intensify during adolescence. When both parent and child have contributed to the resolution of such an episode, and each feels that at least some of their needs are met, their bond is not diminished and is often enhanced. The process has been a very different kind of 'lesson' and developmental step than in the more usual case where one participant is overruled or overpowered by the other, and experiences a defeat from their assertion of self. Gordon acknowledges and discusses the real concerns, nevertheless, that parents may initially have as they seek to practise the 'no-lose' approach so vividly portrayed in principle (1970b: 216–235). To some, it seems at first like an expression of weakness, to others a cumbersome, impractical method of decision-making, or a failure to properly pass on the fruits of their own life experience and learning. As in the case of any shift in pattern, a working through process is involved, and each person arrives at their own consistency and style of implementation.

To aid learning and mastery, Gordon suggests that distinct steps are involved in the joint resolution process: identifying what the conflict actually is; together generating possible solutions; deciding on the best or most acceptable solution; going over or working out how to implement it; and following up to appraise how it turned out (1970b: 237–242). Many particular issues can arise, some of which (such as going back on an agreement) can bring further conflict problems to resolve. Conflict between children, and parent disagreements around the no-lose approach, are among the other practical topics explored. The author finally sums up by offering 'a credo for my relationship with my child'. This excerpt is from the reformulated version in his separate article:

> whenever I am feeling nonaccepting of you because my own needs are not being met, I will tell you as openly and honestly as I can. . . . I also will encourage you to do the same with me and will try to listen to your feelings and perhaps change my behavior. However, when we discover that a conflict-of-needs continues to exist in our relationship, let us both commit ourselves to try to resolve that conflict without the use of either my power or yours. . . . (Gordon, 1970a: 424)

Close attention was given in Chapter 8 to the filial therapy method of Bernard Guerney and his collaborators. In best-known form, this alternative approach to child therapy works through directly altering the relationship between parent and child. Since it is designed to help parents learn and develop new ways of responding to their children, and taps into a common body of thought about the ingredients of a helping relationship, there are

---

13 The reader may recall my earlier mention of Boukydis' (1990) interesting work with *infants* and parents (p. 143, above). The 'consultation services' that he describes seek to facilitate parent awareness and growth in relation to their pre-verbal child. Parents may feel 'at sea' or impotent in trying to tune in to the consciousness of their baby, and slip into a pattern of anxious or conflictual interaction. Process strategies and modes to facilitate perceptive attention and experiencing in response to an infant child are outlined (1990: 806–809). The emphasized processes are all broadly in the service of enhancing the parent–infant person relationship.

some similarities with Gordon's work. The extension of the approach to a 'parenting skills training program' (Guerney and Guerney, 1989), particularly invites comparison. The 'skills' include especially empathic responding (cf. active listening), and the setting and managing of limits (1989: 352). The authors propose that, to manage well 'in the real world', parents need to learn 'how to balance the exercise of acceptance of the child with the enculturation of prosocial and adaptive behaviors' (353). The child's social learning, in this view, is crucially affected by the parents' ability to see ahead and contribute directly to reinforcing outcomes.

As in Gordon's case, resources include a skills training manual on parenting, 'used in the program to teach parents to use empathy in daily child rearing with the goal of considering the child's point of view in every decision'. The manual is designed for parents of varied reading fluency and background. Clearly not advocates of controlling *attitudes*, the Guerneys believe that effective parenting requires a repertoire of responses 'that progresses from a fully unchallenged [and empathic] acceptance of the child's viewpoint to a full assertion of adult authority when it is unrealistic for the child's wishes, feelings and so on to control the outcome' (1989: 353). It might be said that they work to empower parents with the awareness and skills to exercise wisely a special power-of-responsibility. Their belief is that 'reinforcement cannot be avoided, that it is at work in the real world all the time, in every situation'. Flowing from this belief, a principal aim is to help parents understand and 'harness the power of this phenomenon' to achieve desirable competencies and maturity in their children (354–355).

The intentional use of judicious reinforcement to achieve objectives not necessarily within the awareness of the child puts the Guerneys on a different wave-length from Gordon. Their approach to minimization of parent–child conflict does not hinge on the same no-lose stance and approach to conflict resolution. Limit-setting (cf. Axline, 1947; Dorfman, 1951) may be necessary and can be constructive in the Guerneys' view. In Gordon's distinction between non-coercive influence and power-based control measures, any unilateral setting and enforcement of limits is seen as falling in the coercive category: 'Control methods don't really influence children to *choose* particular ways of behaving, they merely coerce or compel them to do so' (Gordon, 1988: 64).[14] On an issue of more convergence with the Guerneys, Gordon accepts reported use of cognitive structuring as helping 'children [to] inter-

---

14 Gordon makes the case against parental use of power without resorting to argument from the most extreme abuses of this power. Many children are literally at risk of life and limb, as well as of psychological damage, from a parent, as Bakan (1971) and Farson (1974a: 46–48), among others, have documented. Farson's brush is a wide and radical one. He paints a vivid picture of discriminatory, inherently oppressive and largely self-defeating characteristics of child 'care' involved in many social institutions and contexts – family, educational, political, legal, and other. Called *Birthrights*, his book (1974a) includes a philosophy of the 'rights' of younger persons which, if implemented, would require a fundamental redesign of the social order. Although the work certainly has a political dimension, the author suggests no easy solutions, and disavows confidence in social reform undertaken solely in the interests of a single group.

nalize the consequences of their behavior and develop conscience or inner control' (74). This and direct expressions of enjoyment, liking, interest, appreciation and other personally felt response are I-messages to Gordon and positive reinforcements to Guerney et al.

Gordon's later book, *Teaching Children Self-Discipline* (1989), reiterates earlier themes but with a studied focus of deep concern over effects of punitive disciplinary measures, and also of extremely *laissez-faire* attitudes, by parents and other carers. The author's own commitment is to an approach that builds internal guidance systems; systems viewed as both adaptive and altruistic. As for the 'rewards-and-punishment' approach, Gordon finds that frequent use of praise and other reward has little more efficacy than punishments in promoting integrated inner values and self-direction. Praise is a message of positive evaluation of another person, or of their behaviour or achievement. It is a 'you-message', pointed toward the other (1989: 34–77). Whether positive or negative this is distinct in kind from 'I-messages', which imply ownership by the speaker, and which refer directly to an inner experience not an externalized judgement. Gordon's book in its first part is broadly concerned with 'understanding discipline'. The remainder, Part 2, proceeds under the general heading 'alternatives to disciplining children'. Non-controlling ways to facilitate changes in behaviour, the now familiar no-lose approach to conflict resolution, the role of acceptance in *children* solving problems themselves, and the various ways active listening contributes to self-direction and responsibility are all key topics.

To sum up person-centred principles applied to parenting by enumerating points may be repetitive, even presumptuous. Being a resourceful parent is surely even more complex and multi-layered than being a resourceful therapist. Years of study and training are required for the latter function. Parenting in most cases is learned on the job, with a widely varied start from one's own child-to-parent relations, and possibly from older–younger sibling relationships or other observed happenings. Small wonder that Gordon's program has filled an experienced need – for over a million parents (Gordon, 1989: 103). Good parenting means being aware on many levels: aware of attitudes and actions that hinder the active presence and blossoming of another human personality as well as processes that advance such growth. Clearly the person who is fortunate in the fullness of his/her own development, perhaps whose qualities approach those envisioned in the early part of this chapter, and who is in a well-functioning partner relationship, has a better chance to be an effective parent than persons for whom these things are not true.

Parents have many functions, as earlier suggested, ones that start from a powerful and unique kind of bonding. Desirably, this is not a bond that binds the other. Rather, it is one through which nurture is given out of awareness and with love, according to the other's need, one that embodies deeply attentive perception but which also holds back enough for the child to come forth by choice and to have his or her own experience. It is a bond that supports the child's need to become a separate person, and which recognizes that assertion of independence may be a necessary step toward a mature interdependence. Parents, for their part, need a community and culture of belonging and participation that they can count on. Perhaps above all else, and at all stages in their unfolding, children need parents who are open and responsively honest with them, whom they can relate to with confidence in their own perceptions, and from whom they experience interest, respect, and a caring which they clearly trigger but do not have to earn.

Concluding note

True to the general course of client-centred thought, this chapter has not centred on analysis of deficiency, or on what is widely wrong in education and family life. Much has been written on these topics, and little will happen unless educators, parents and others perceive need themselves for growth and change. Such changing consciousness feeds into and links with systemic cultural evolution. My focus here has been on views of *well*-being and of positive or desired process in the spheres examined. The client/person-centred approach has, for a long time and in various ways, sought to illuminate the optimum outcome of therapy, the nature of personal health or wellness, and what the conducive or life-enhancing potential conditions are, in various areas of living and learning.

Working to discern and release positive potentialities has been perceived in this approach as more interesting and useful than fixing one's eye on what is wrong and trying to counter the defect. On another level, it seems persuasive to regard lives as *lived* not only one-by-one but, as well, two-by-two and in many larger wholes. Relationships usually have been seen as something happening *between* individuals, who remain the governing anchorage points. By taking the further step of viewing relationship systems as emergent dynamic wholes in their own right, it has proven entirely feasible to envision the basic nature of wellness or health on this level too. Generally, the portrayal offered over the region of this chapter, is both a fresh integration and a view – with features open to testing – to build on further.

The next chapter continues this review of applications beyond psychotherapy *per se*. It seems timely to acknowledge, or remind readers, that the person-centred approach is not simply an extended system of helping practice and its conceptual underpinnings, not only a distinctive view of persons and their relations, but an even broader outlook. It includes an implicit ethic, a value system, one based on deep engagement with people confronting ultimate issues in their lives, one that aspires to being informed by a continued search for clearer vision and deeper knowing, and one that has a considerable history of testing its basic hypotheses. In the end, this and other approaches are defined in significant part by the human potentialities they discriminate and give priority to. An ethic involving value choices is perhaps more evident still in the applications considered next.

11

Leadership, Large Groups, Community, Conflict Resolution

> The image which often appeared to me as these pages were written was that of an ocean liner propelled by an outboard motor, requiring not only more drive but also reconstruction while continuing to sail the high seas. Social scientists . . . participate in this reconstruction. And we are all aboard.
>
> . . . without diffuse, affective relationships, individuals cannot maintain their identity, emotional stability, and rationality. . . . In turn, these relationships need to be built into more encompassing cohesive units such as the village or community. . .
>
> . . . the active solution . . . [entails] need for a synthesis of knowledge, for a synthesis of emotions and values, and for a holistic view of the use of power. . . . On the personal level, this requires a kind of holistic education and active experience which has often been discussed but rarely implemented.
>
> Amitai Etzioni, 1972

This chapter is a continuation of the last, through most of the remaining terrain of significant application of person-centred principles. The further contexts entail distinct extensions to thought and practice which, nevertheless, are very recognizably part of the same movement as those already considered. In scale, the phenomena involved range from group face-to-face interactions to large communities and ethnic/national systems. Situations are encompassed where those taking part represent others as well as themselves. Enabling processes remain central but the purposes of such enablement extend beyond the immediate learning and development of participants. Particular attention will be given to the contexts of person-centred leadership and administration, large groups and community, and conflict resolution in personal, social and international dimensions.

Group- and person-centred leadership and administration

Thomas Gordon's work came to encompass his widely known interests in parenting and in education. This is not where his distinctive contribution began. His prior focus and main writing in the 1950s dealt with what he called group-centred, in contrast to 'leader-centred', leadership and administration;

an interest that he later returned to (Gordon, 1977/1980). At the time of his original report in this area (1951), the process-oriented, interactive learning programs of the National Training Laboratory had begun on an experimental basis at Bethel, Maine; and Gordon himself participated as early as 1949 in a 'group development lab'. The Tavistock Institute in England was also beginning to open up new approaches in such areas as leadership and organizational behaviour. Gordon, then working directly with Rogers, acknowledged in his chapter report (1951) that these innovations had also encouraged his interest and thought. One fruit of this thought was to advance a series of general propositions regarding the 'adjustive capacity' and behaviour of groups.

Groups, he proposed, involve 'a system of inner dynamic forces . . . [in] continuous change and reorganization'. Effectively, it is in the basic nature of groups to be at risk of instability or disequilibrium. 'Adjustive behaviour' is that which acts to reduce such disequilibrium, this effect flowing most strongly from the active contribution of all group members utilizing their best resources (Gordon, 1951: 324–325). Further, 'A group has within itself the adjustive capacities necessary to acquire a greater degree of internal harmony and productivity. . . . Provided certain conditions are met, the group will move in the direction of greater utilization of these capacities' (327). This proposition parallels Rogers' stress on growth forces within individuals, and the requisite conditions are reminiscent of the therapy conditions hypothesis in early form. The working of leadership in the group is crucial, as will be seen.

Groups have varied potentials, negative as well as positive. It is not uncommon for members to use up a lot of energy in 'resistive' or counteractive behaviour. Allport (1945) is cited as pointing out that 'a person ceases to be reactive and contrary in respect to a desirable course of conduct only when he himself has had a hand in declaring that course of conduct to be desirable' (Gordon, 1951: 329). Group-centred process hinges on a view of leadership as a property of the total group, in other words, as 'a set of functions' needing to be carried out by the group members (332). In practice, there is usually *a* perceived or formal leader, especially in groups that are part of a larger organization or community. Gordon points out that genuinely distributed leadership cannot be accomplished by fiat and that one condition for this to happen is that the assigned/perceived leader be committed and resourceful in facilitating its growthful emergence. He also suggests that 'the group-centred leader sees the group or organization as existing for the individuals who compose it' (337); a view very open to challenge since many groups have vitally important service responsibilities to others. However, in these cases, the same leadership qualities can be brought to bear as apply in the case of groups that do literally exist for their members (Barrett-Lennard, 1979a: 207).

Leaders who prize and foster active member participation, free and open communication, a generally non-threatening psychological climate, and literal sharing of initiative and responsibility, are group-centred in outlook in Gordon's language. Such leaders are highly attentive to and generally understanding of other members, tend to convey empathy, warmth and acceptance on a personal level, and contribute a vital linking function in the group. The last feature entails effort to see and acknowledge the connection between each person's response and the ideas already in view. Such a leader is not simply staking out another kind of exclusive territory (as *the* facilitator, for instance) but ready to draw back or engage differently as the process functions are gradually taken over and developed by other group members. Likely outcomes of the group-centred process are (i) that members relate to each other with a quality of understanding and acceptance, (ii) energy is not being used up in reactive response to authority, (iii) members are jointly monitoring their individual and collective effort, and are internally motivated toward corrective action as necessary, and (iv) participation becomes less ego-centred and more altruistic in concern for the well-being and productivity of the group (Gordon, 1951: 368–381). In everyday terms, one effect is that morale has greatly increased.

Gordons' work on group-centred leadership soon expanded into a book (1955). A self-contained statement of the vision of human nature and social values underlying his approach brings out the point of its particular salience in a democratic society struggling to maintain its ideals. The origins and specific nature and processes of group-centred leadership are explored in more relaxed detail than in the compact previous statement, and a very fully documented case study of a leadership training workshop is included. The workshop was time-limited (three weeks) and intensive, with the designated leaders perhaps being more in the position of 'trainers', in the human relations training sense, than that of leader-administrators in an ongoing organization. Complementing this study is another, focusing on leadership process in an actual manufacturing organization. The reporter (not Gordon), initially head of personnel in his firm, describes a two-stage innovation in management. In the first phase, lasting four years, he 'engineered' opportunity for a voice and influence in the organization by the actual production workers. This was achieved in spite of the attitudes of senior supervisors and department heads, whose needs were not addressed, who found their roles undercut, and who became cynical and counteractive in respect to the methods used.

In retrospect, the personnel officer/reporter felt he had been quite manipulative and neglectful of his senior colleagues and their responsibilities. This and related new awareness precipitated a second phase of innovation, approaching the group-centred mode Gordon describes. Now in the position of Plant Superintendent in charge of production, the executive worked to establish a genuinely enabling and affirming climate of relations, one that respected what people had to offer as individuals and in their positions, that fostered open communication, minimized 'distance' and engendered a spirit of collaboration between 'administration' and 'workers', etc. The positive outcomes, including development of group cohesion and morale, the growth of individuals, and changes in decision-making and productivity, were supported by independent investigation (Gordon, 1955: 348–353). Residual difficulties and constraints, no doubt stemming in part from the wider organizational culture, are also acknowledged.

Gordon eventually returned to focus once again in this area of work by adding the leadership sphere to his programs of 'effectiveness training'. His book, *Leader Effectiveness Training* (1977/1980) is expressive of the same philosophy and basic approach as its predecessors in the series. The adaptation to group management involves another domain of literature, fresh illustrations and added distinctions. The stress on building a management team and other features of person-centredness accord with familiar values. The author's Maslovian view of human motivation, his depiction of the basic process of communication, the delineation of 'roadblocks to communication', and the priority given to active listening and empathy, and to I-messages, are consistent with his presentations around teaching and parenting (Chapter 10). He speaks directly of the leader as teacher (1977/1980: 89–91) and certainly implies that the good leader is always learning. Chapters titled 'How to make your management team effective', and 'The periodic planning conference: a new approach to performance evaluation' are usefully specific to the management context. The author's discussion of the nature and importance of 'no-lose' approaches is now familiar in basic theme. This book evidently has been a popular and persuasive how-to-do-it manual that speaks also to pivotal underlying issues and values.

Rogers' own approach to administrative leadership has been touched on in several places in this volume, and is implied in passages comparing features of his style and outlook with Roosevelt's (Chapter 3). His autobiography (1967a: 364, 370–371) and a later book (1977a: 90–104) are both pertinent sources. In current expression, he sought to empower the members of any group in which he was the assigned or perceived leader. Effective empowerment is not just a matter of removing constraints – especially where strong team functioning is vital – but a process of active developmental facilitation. In a case where his leadership 'failed' (with a research group at the University of Wisconsin: 1967a: 370–371), Rogers' giving-away of responsibility to other team members was not accompanied by persistent hard-working facilitative involvement.[1] Another level that seems vitally important to optimal leadership of a group or organization is that the leaders (or all participants) are tuned not only to individuals, not merely to tasks, but also to the working of the larger system of which they are jointly a part.

Sensitivity to feelings and personal perspectives, coupled with attunement to group and organizational forces and cultures, can work in powerful synergy. Another contributor whose thought reaches integratively over this range is William R. Rogers (no relation to Carl). He too sees client-centred theory as being in transition from a highly individualistic approach in Rogers' classical work to one that is giving 'increased attention to the structural or organizational patterns that are critical in enabling full human development'. A central implication is that '*efforts to help individuals in a therapeutic mode*

---

1 This was Rogers' own later view. I have direct experience of a related crisis; one that a commitment to this approach, in classical form, does not equip a person to handle well (see p. 363). The repercussions of my own experience left me wiser but ready for divorce from an institution which *had been* a professional home base and deeply important community to me.

would always remain limited and merely remedial if the oppressive social and institutional realities surrounding life remained untouched' (W.R. Rogers, 1984: 321). Principles of person-centred administration responsive to this challenge envision leadership facilitation in its widest sense.

Rogers discriminates ten such principles, the first, 'facilitating clarity of a shared vision'. The author elaborates: 'Without a sense of common purpose, the strivings of individuals often languish in isolation and lost momentum, or get entangled in competition, frustration, and defeat' (ibid.: 322). Helping participants become deeply *engaged*, together, in pooling meanings and clarifying wider goals of their enterprise is no mean task, especially when each person's function and responsibility is viewed as distinct – as applies in higher education. The need for close consultation and involvement with anyone particularly affected by a group consensus or decision is highlighted by Rogers. Related principles emphasize 'openness of procedures', and 'inclusion of broad constituencies' in planning significant developments (327–329). It is also stressed that educational administrators need to be highly accessible to others, resourcefully empathic listeners, and perceptive in regard to hidden agendas. Further principles build on these, and contribute to a conclusion that two levels of meaning are implicit in a person-centred approach:

> On *one level* . . . are those structured elements that ensure attention to personal needs throughout an institution by allowing a 'coming together' within a gathered community where shared goals and operating procedures are clear. On the *second level* are the immediate and individual interactions with people in the . . . exchanges of daily life . . . [for] within these small exchanges, multiplied a hundred times, the style of person-centered administration is ultimately established. (ibid.: 335)

'Administration' implies an enterprise or task beyond and *in addition* to satisfying the needs of those who work on this task. In this way it differs from the application next in focus, the large-group learning workshop. When the pre-planning phase is over, everyone has assembled, and the workshop has started (in a favourable environment and with housekeeping needs well taken care of), there is little to 'administer'. This is especially true where the approach is person-centred. Nevertheless, there is a counterpart to most of the features emphasized by William Rogers, in this distinctly different context.

Large-group learning and the search for community

Work with large, low-structure groups has been a prominent feature in some of the most visible person-centred programs since the mid-seventies. They emerged a full decade after small groups became a primary vehicle for personal learning and development (Chapter 9). The large groups also emphasize experiential learning, most uniquely around the formation of community. One outcome is a serious and growing interest in the nature of community among some of those involved, including this writer. Thus, what follows leads on in turn to presentation of a person-centred perspective on the working and significance of community in human life. The initial focus on large groups begins with the issue of how such interest started, in an approach centred on personal helping.

Beginning: the group encounter process on a larger scale?

Precisely why Carl Rogers began to focus on settings much larger than the previous encounter groups remains a little unclear. One clue appears in his 1970 book on groups. He is speaking of a combined meeting of all members in a La Jolla Program workshop on group learning and facilitation. 'I vividly recall [he writes] one such meeting at which I was privileged to be present. The whole community of over ninety persons became a live and deep encounter group' (1970: 153). There was a background to the occurrence Rogers described, suggested as a pre-condition for it: '*once participants have had an encounter group experience* it is possible for the close and intimate climate of such a group to permeate even a much larger community' (153, italics added). Later, the idea of such a pre-condition faded. Participants could enter a large experiential group directly, without building up to it through the small group process (Rogers, 1977b). Then, meetings of the whole came to take responsibility for deciding what kinds of other, smaller groups were desired and how to form them (McIlduff and Coghlan, 1989; Thorne, 1988).

In 1974, Carl and Natalie Rogers, John K. Wood, and others, launched a new series of workshops under the main title 'A person-centred approach' – one of the first uses of this term. The expected experiential learning was conceived as extending beyond its perimeters in small groups or therapy to embrace social issues and community formation, although the process was not conceived at the start as involving new principles. The main series of these workshops ran, annually, for about ten years, and gave rise to related large-group experiences in many places. At least in the first years, participation in small groups tended to alternate with total 'community' meetings. The group-of-the-whole typically consisted of 100 to 200 persons, in the PCA workshops convened on a residential basis over about two weeks.[2]

Rogers published a vivid account (1977b) of the 1975 workshop, in which I also took part. His account describes how the initial nucleus of three worked to select the final staff of ten, how the ten together prepared the announcement of the workshop, the use of a sliding fee system that left each member with final responsibility for his/her exact, precommitted fee, and how arriving members

---

2 Related, low-structure interactive groups of still larger size (500–800 persons) and running for only two days of afternoon and evening meetings, have been reported (Bowen, Miller, Rogers and Wood, 1980). This report is based on three such groups or '*ciclos*', held in Brazil, in the late seventies. Their order of magnitude, brevity, and the lack of collateral avenues of contact so significant in residential workshops, imply that these macro events are as distinct from the large groups in focus here, as these groups are distinct from the small encounter group.

were received in ways that drew everyone from the start toward shared responsibility in the collective happening. Of the sixteen-day, 136-member workshop itself,

> Rogers writes as an acutely attentive and deeply involved participant-observer, broadly charting the course of events and turning points, especially in the big meetings, and bearing witness as a seasoned explorer in an unfamiliar ocean to the difficult, hazardous, exhilarating voyage of discovery of a new *human* habitat – not a place, but a way. (Barrett-Lennard, 1979a: 217)

But what was this way? On what levels was it distinct from accustomed processes, and what were continuities with these prior forms? Rogers' account focuses on immediate process and impact and reflects familiar values, albeit in more 'political' language than he had used in earlier writing. However, he does not draw back to generalize conceptually about the new features.[3] In an early report, 'Shadows of surrender', John Wood (1977) searches to discriminate both the basic continuum and emergent new quality. He notes the discovery, in one-to-one therapy, of the power of non-judgemental empathic listening and of the client-centred helper 'surrendering' or giving up 'the security of being regarded as the all-knowing expert following a clear cut plan', of turning away from a focus on destructive potentialities to a fascination and confidence in integrative growth forces within the person, of moving from central reliance on rational thought in order to give full and equal place to feeling and intuition, and of surrendering an external view in order to open contact from centre to centre of client and helper.

In group encounter, Wood continues, more is given up in terms of role position by the helper, and more added by way of personal participation. There remains, however, direct connection between all the participants, and a certain linearity and logical order to the process. In the very large group, a complete network of connections is not feasible, and the same sort of order no longer applies. Facilitation by official helpers is largely surrendered, and rarely is one participant's response to another person or issue complete; rather, a series of persons may combine in what amounts to a single releasing or clarifying expression. Even so, the energy and awareness of the many can at best be articulated by relatively few, and it is necessary to 'surrender dependence on manageable conversations and begin to trust in intuitive faculties to digest the meaning of more holistic expressions' (Wood, 1977: 14).[4] Attending to one's own experiencing while also tuning to a larger consciousness in the group is a subtle shift, Wood implies, but may occur if

---

3 A striking observation by Rogers follows a cited letter from a particular member: 'Her letter . . . confirms me [he writes] in my conviction that *lasting* revolutions are brought about not by propaganda or massed demonstrations but by changed people' (Rogers, 1977a: 181).

4 It struck me on final reading of this passage that the complexity of process Wood speaks of has some resemblance to the working of the human brain. A great number and complex networks of cortical cells, with a huge multiplicity of connections, are in simultaneous activity during thought or any experience. Out of all this ramifying activity a single consciousness emerges.

expectations suited to another context are set aside. The big experiential group, then, is not to be confused with other settings. It is starting to be seen not as a small group on a larger scale but another phenomenon with its own emergent properties and potentials.[5]

The large group event in its own right: process, potentials, issues

In a later article, Wood (1984) takes a fresh tack in exploring the positive potentials of large groups. First, he restates the underlying aim and theme of the PCA workshops as being to explore the question 'What could a client-centred approach teach us about community?' (1984: 300). His focal interest is in the process of the large group *when and if it reaches a 'creative' or well-functioning state*. When it is in this state, he writes:

> The members are intense, both autonomous and cooperative, sensitive to the subtle flow of consciousness and affect in each other *and* to the patterns created moment-by-moment in the group. The process is not bound by its own previous organization. It changes to accommodate every voice, both sensible and delinquent, will not compromise, and settles only for intelligent actions that are just, growth-promoting, and healing to the individual and to the community. The individual's awareness of the group's patterns . . . gives the group a self-consciousness. (Wood, 1984: 304)

A particular group is chosen by Wood to illustrate his vision of what one might term a fully functioning large group. Examples are given of the way the group made choices and arrived at effective although quite often unstated consensus. The balancing of individual initiative and autonomy, on the one hand, with a highly attentive and receptive 'humility' evoked in the process of the group, is another significant focus of illustration. It is proposed that a special state of consciousness or 'trance' may develop, in which usual critical faculties are relaxed and new insights or powers emerge (1984: 312–315). Wood's treatment of this last-mentioned aspect, especially around the concept of trance, introduces intriguing ideas that invite further development than was possible in this article. An account of my own of one of the original workshops complements Wood's and Rogers' presentations (Barrett-Lennard, 1994).[6]

My report begins from an interest in what the largely self-chosen members expect, and in how these expectations arise or are created. The circulated

---

5 The term 'starting to be seen' is used advisedly. Another article, by Bozarth (1981), also flowed from considerable experience in large groups, including the 'community group' meetings and process that evolved in the La Jolla Program, and PCA large group workshops. In this case, Bozarth is more interested in continuities than basic or systematic differences between large groups and the small encounter group. His series of propositions regarding community groups applies in substance to the intensive small group as well (1981: 108–111 and 130).

6 My paper originated in a conference presentation in 1977, and was circulated privately for a number of years before further revision and eventual publication. Some of its content first appeared within an article that helped to open the path to this book (Barrett-Lennard, 1979a: 219).

announcement of the workshop would have had a bearing on the choice to take part and the expectancies members arrived with. Here are some pertinent sentences from the circular:

- ◇ The aim will be to build a workshop around an approach . . . which recognizes that the potential to learn and the power to act lie *within* the person. . . .
- ◇ The workshop will provide a place where people who *believe in the worth and dignity of the individual and in each person's capacity for self-direction* can come together and create a community. (Rogers, 1977b: 151–152; italics added, in last sentence)

These passages stress broad but vitally important beliefs and attitudes that the envisioned members would share and find support for. In effect, features of the projected ethos of the workshop community are spelled out, and persons choosing to take part would do so partly on the basis of the appeal of this ethos. Further examples are:

- ◇ The workshop values what *each person* has to offer.
- ◇ We welcome every way of releasing the inner strength of the person.
- ◇ We trust the workshop will demonstrate the psychological climate which we know can evoke self-understanding and self-directed behavior.
- ◇ It is hoped that the experience will not only lead to inner personal growth but to an increased understanding of one's responsibility in the world, and how one can act on that sense of responsibility. (ibid.: 152)

Altogether, the announcement brochure builds to a potent message for those attuned to hear and respond to it. The last-noted expression of purpose would hold special appeal for persons having altruistic/social concerns interwoven with their motivation for self-development and learning. Topic areas suggested in the brochure include 'the politics of the person-centered approach; the facilitation of problem-solving change in society and its institutions; the new roles of women and men; ways of living, working and relating with people who are different; . . . the development of a broader person-centered theory and philosophy . . .'. One envisaged outcome was the development of support systems 'which will give us vitality, energy, and renewal as we take our learnings into the "back-home" situation' (ibid.: 152).[7]

Although the expected ethos and potentials were so strongly portrayed, the individuality of their realization could not be pre-formed. The participant members when they arrived were largely unknown to each other and had patchy knowledge at best of processes that would bring their desired individual–community experience into being. The particular chemistry of their combination could not be known beforehand. They had been advised in advance that 'the initial steps [only] will be planned by the staff, but the total

7 In contrast to those drawn to take part in the workshop, many would not have been attracted: persons more committed to 'time-table' structure, directive leadership and informational or 'skills' teaching, and those holding a quite different view of human nature and change. Even those who did take part often found an inner press for levels of structure at seeming odds with the philosophy that had attracted them (Barrett-Lennard, 1994).

design and format will be a mutual product, created to meet the needs of the participants, including the facilitators' (152–153). In a word, soon after it began the whole enterprise would become a co-operative effort. We, the dauntingly big group-of-the-whole, even before experiencing ourselves as a 'we', would be attempting jointly to find our way. Out of this effort a sense not only of other persons but of the larger collective would gradually form. It was like being plunged into darkness on unknown terrain where somehow banding and moving together was the key to survival. Further discerning and achieving our aim was no simple matter:

> It was novel – strange to me and I think to most others – to be a member of such a large group in which a major, self-conscious purpose was that of our development as a community, and the learnings that could evolve from this. . . . A founded sense and quality of community usually emerges or grows in a quite different way in natural-life settings, almost as a by-product of gradually working out and learning to manage the multi-sided process of interdependent living. Although many, perhaps most of us, were used to the counterpart of this new situation in growth-oriented, small groups, the community experience was not principally *intended* for personal growth – or was it? . . . And, . . . where did our wantings and 'supposed-to-be's' come from? Not merely from the brochure announcement, which had helped to pick us all out and ensure likenesses that were far less apparent in the sharply-felt present than were the uneven chasms of difference and apartness – chasms evidently of our like-minded making! (Barrett-Lennard, 1994: 71)

The 'community' group was a paradox, not in name only but in experienced quality. Perceived opportunity collided with sharply felt impotence; risk and evident safety tailed each other in unpredictable pattern; intense participation vied with the role of spectator; excitement and despair alternated; times of surging and unfolding movement and of almost complete standstill or stuckness would succeed each other; there were 'highs' of deeply felt inclusion in a rare larger whole, and 'lows' of intensely felt disconnection and isolation; a creative solution to an impasse could be offered, warmly received and then completely dropped. Small groups, and even individual therapy, can be experienced as contradictory but then the paradox is transcended as a larger unity of meaning comes into view. Perhaps the big group is so complex, and so uneven in respect to participation, that paradox and ambiguity for much of its life is inevitable.[8] My own story resumes with comment on the diversity of the group:

> Each of us had come to the workshop from our own distinct context of involvement and concern. The workshop was like an overlapping island of experience in each person's differing ocean. . . . I arrived . . . having just completed a fresh proposal for research in the intensive group sphere. For the first week, I felt that the part of me

8 The qualities of paradox and extreme ambiguity must have been *more* intense, and remained unresolved for many members, in the macro group *ciclos* mentioned earlier. Besides those who felt the experience was extremely valuable to them, 'many, it seems, were just disappointed and angry at the chaos and unproductivity, calling it anarchy. They gained little or nothing, they believe' (quotation from a Brazilian psychologist by Bowen et al., 1980: 329).

> interested in studying aspects of this new-overlapping phenomenon was utterly rejected. . . . Experiencing, relating personally, learning on a gut level, were fine and certainly *part* of what I wanted. However, at that stage in the fluid, capricious culture of the workshop, analytical/reflective *thinking* in the big group was a no-no and *research(!)* was anathema. Something very important, I felt, very powerful but extremely complex was taking place and there would be no way of really tracing its pattern afterward. But why was I angry, why affronted . . .? I think there were a number of reasons, but one central issue occurred to me later. . . .
>
> The later awareness has to do with the inside/outside distinction. When people are struggling and under stress, as was especially true in the early days of the workshop, I think they/we cannot shift readily from an empathic-subjective-experiential-inside plane to a self-observing, more objective or analytical outside plane. Some of us are not fluent in making such shifts back and forth, at the best of times. Perhaps I was suspended or stuck somewhere, between an inside and an outside position . . ., not entering fully, not clearly inside and committed to the common struggle.[9] As time went by . . . I discovered that there were after all quite a number of others curious about the process. (1994: 71–72)

A number of us formed an interest group, and a questionnaire was co-operatively devised. Limited research data were gathered at the end of the workshop, with interesting results mentioned later (Chapter 14). Although there was plenty of time for inner reflection, drawing back during the ongoing process of the big group to form a careful 'outside view' of its dynamic working was, as implied, counter to the group culture. Given that over 100 people were in the group, on average, members were listening, reflecting or waiting more than 99 per cent of the time. (Had each person taken equal air time, it would have totalled about one minute in each big group session!) As I pondered over the group's composition and circumstance, and my experiencing within it, a personally compelling perspective came sharply into focus:

> [We] listened and waited with expectancy and implicit invitation in keeping with our general values and stance as humanistic or person-centered helpers. If someone, or several, then spoke personally, with immediacy and also some struggle, a quickened, unifying interest and energy coursed through the group. Almost as one person, we would lock into a helping-encounter mode of response. Given such invitation and human overture, how could a group such as ours respond otherwise? Only, I suggest, by seeing on additional levels what it was doing, and being conscious of valued alternatives, ones which would then feed into our invitational stance and the spectrum of overtures. More particularly, also, by . . . recognizing that selectively *listening for and expressing personal here-and-now experience can itself constitute a powerful directional influence.* (1994: 78, italics added)

I was changed by this group, and the searching further activity that it evoked, on more than a personal level. Whether the large group fully reached

---

9 This at least was how some others perceived me for a time. Another element of paradox in the big group is that, although confronted early with variability in expressions, the listening majority look for a commonality they can value. Perhaps members in most new groups at first seek to discern and even fasten upon a direction they can safely follow. It took a long time and much heartache, for this large group to find and begin to show a genuine liberality such, for example, that atypical styles, perspectives and interests could work as assets in the group.

the creative state Wood speaks of is not clear to me, but that it provided a fertile pool of experience for many of us who took part is not in question in my mind. That participants were powerfully influenced both by features they recognized and some which they did not discriminate, is also not in doubt to me. If members had had contact in the big group *only*, it is likely that far less beneficial outcomes would have resulted, judging from research results to be mentioned later. These conclusions also have pertinence for a further long-running series of workshops, held in Europe since the mid-seventies. Sponsored by the Center for Cross-cultural Communication (CCC), these annual workshops have typically been in the same size range as the PCA groups were.

The earliest CCC workshop events emphasized experiential intercultural and self-learning in encounter type groups (Devonshire and Auw, 1973; Kristal-Anderson, 1975). By the late seventies, membership in the European series had grown to the size dimension of 100 to 200-plus persons. Meetings-of-the-whole evolved to become the primary context of engagement of the workshop communities (Coghlan and McIlduff, 1991; McIlduff and Coghlan, 1989; MacMillan and Lago, 1993). These authors all imply that the large group has an exceptionally arousing quality, perhaps like a powerful psycho-gravitational field or, at some moments, 'black hole' (my metaphors). They agree that it is often stressful, ambiguous, highly energizing *and* exhausting, and with other elements of paradox mentioned earlier. One paper suggests viewing the large group as a 'forum for negotiating meaning' through which participants may come to experience themselves as 'co-creators of the culture of the group community' (MacMillan and Lago, 1993: 37).

Group members are not the only ones finding their way. In one instance, the facilitators chose not to identify themselves until several days into the process, hoping that the members would be empowered more quickly. The effect was to accentuate the ambiguity, reduce the 'realism' of the situation and, while the invisibility of facilitators lasted, attenuate their contributions in the group (see MacMillan and Lago, 1993: 44–45). Another practical issue is the effect of a mix of old-timers from previous workshops and newcomers uninitiated into the process. To the naive group the situation can seem contrived and false if/when some of the old hands use in-group jargon, or even well-rehearsed lines, when purporting to express something thought and felt in the moment (examples in McIlduff and Coghlan, 1989: 84). A broader issue that was raised concerns the individualistic ethos of the person-centred approach, even in the large group CCC context. The authors argue for a stronger sense or assumption of communal responsibility, and for committed exploration at the interface of social and personal dimensions of life (95–97).

No doubt others have written of their related large-group experiences in the non-English literature beyond my scope to report. There is also a fine statement by Brian Thorne, based on large-group workshops held in Britain since 1975, under sponsorship through the first decade by the (UK) Facilitator Development Institute. Large groups in that context had ranged from 30 to 80 persons, averaging 50 or so. In view of the geometric rise in complexity as numbers increase, even among 50 persons the process is of a fundamentally different order than, say, in a group of 12 (Barrett-Lennard, 1979a). The FDI workshops tended to emphasize facilitator development in that they particularly attracted professionals and students in the personal helping field. Extensive planning and preparation preceded each workshop, relating to venue, commitment of staff, joint formulation of an announcement,[10] all the correspondence with prospective members, and the coming together and personal preparation of facilitator-staff before the main membership arrived. If the broad aim of all this careful preparation is to further the development of facilitative persons, various subgoals and issues of process arise:

> How can people be 'trained' to develop an unconditional regard for each other? How can they be encouraged to be more honest and authentic . . .? How can they be enabled to understand another individual from that person's own frame of reference and then communicate their understanding with clarity and sensitivity? In short, how can a large group become an effective context for individuals to learn how to be more accepting, congruent and empathic? (Thorne, 1988: 190)

The broad answer given to these questions is to provide for and work to set in motion a process which is itself facilitative in very much the same terms, emphasizing personal growth and process learning through each person's active engagement of self in the workshop laboratory. This 'laboratory', in Thorne's account, crucially includes meetings-of-the-whole complemented by other experiential contexts in accord with the person-centred goals of the workshop. At a particular time, a member may find a one-to-one meeting best fulfils their need. Or, small groups may be most helpful for growth. Sometimes, or in some ways, the big group will be most potently valuable. Evaluation study of the workshops has been a fairly regular procedure, using congruent approaches such as analysis of the content of participant journal logs kept at the time (ibid.: 191).

Drawing on Wood's vision of the creative state of large groups, Thorne points out that what happens in the chaotic early stages of a large group can 'be seen as attempts by individuals to discover if they can be autonomous without being rejected or ostracized by the community' (ibid.: 195). This testing leads on, if the creative state is achieved, to a synergy of autonomy and co-operativeness. Thorne suggests that the next phase of development in the big group is a search for mutuality, involving close or intimate reciprocal sharing. At best, members experience themselves as *both givers and receivers*; contributors to the well-being of others and beneficiaries of the others' response in kind. Such mutuality seems to be a key to shifts in the group toward deeper attentiveness yet with less dependence on receptivity to every contribution. There are multi-level consequences to the workshop experience adding to the picture already given. First, to use Thorne's words: 'It is as if the large group both confirms and illuminates the uniqueness of individuals,

---

10 As concrete illustration, the main part of the announcement brochure for the 1986 summer workshop appears as an appendix to Thorne's report (1988: 206–207).

while establishing beyond any shadow of doubt their inter-connectedness' (201). More specifically, a convergence of both healing and training effects is eloquently conveyed (203-204). Lastly, an element of social/societal healing is suggested (205).

Thorne's suggestion of social healing, and his thinking about co-operative autonomy, are bridges to themes in Natiello's (1990) illuminating exploration of the process and effects of 'collaborative power'. Her inquiry taps into experience in large groups, building also on thought from a number of sources in and outside the person-centred movement. She contrasts collaborative power with exercise of 'power over' others, singling out such qualities as openness, respectful responsiveness, sense of personal empowerment, and naturally alternating exercise of initiative by participants. 'Personal power' is seen as 'the ability to act effectively under one's own volition rather than under external control' (1990: 274). When power is strongly identified with position (in a hierarchy, say, or a caste system) personal and collaborative power tend to be undercut. Also, it seems that collaborative potency is in keeping with a dynamic autonomy of personal presence and engagement but not with an autonomy of separateness. More even than societal healing, cultural transformation would be entailed in a true shift in power relations and processes in society. Natiello acknowledges that such a 'paradigm' shift could not be brought about by any one group or movement but believes that it could evolve from the mutual awareness and voices of many groups sharing and holding to similar value systems (283–285).

Natiello's work is one of various examples of the potentiating effects of experience in large-group workshops, in contributing to fresh lines of thought and interest in former participants. The deeply involving quality and complexity of the process can be an evocative challenge leading on to continued inquiry and development of meaning. This was certainly an outcome for me, of the earlier-described PCA workshop. Specifically, it helped to crystallize my interest in community and the formulations next advanced.

Toward a theory of community

Community stems from the Latin *communis*, implying a quality of connection or 'community of relations and feelings'. The term then came to be used concretely, in reference to '*a body* of fellows, or fellow-townsmen', and emerged in English with this meaning.[11] Both classes of meaning have survived: community as fellowship connected by relations and feelings (or by the experience or sense of community) and community as a body of persons. One could scarcely experience community without such a body, whether or not the members are in each other's immediate presence. The existence of an organized body by itself gives no assurance that experienced connection and

11 See 'community' in the *Oxford English Dictionary*, compact edition, 1971 (micrographic reproduction of multi-volume original), p. 486, or, 'C' volume, p. 702.

belonging will occur. By the same token, when this crucial sense does arise it needs to be coupled with other practical benefits for a community to be viable. In a word, the idea of community seems to rest on two components: (i) the experience of relationship and belonging within a larger group, and (ii) a working organization of this body that serves varied member needs and communal tasks (Barrett-Lennard, 1994). In practice, real world communities usually include the following basic features:

- Members have a language in common, often with elements distinctive to the community. They have opportunity for contact and usage of this language among themselves. Proximity is usually a vital factor in this opportunity although it may be crucially aided, or sometimes largely replaced, by contact at a distance.
- The community members have further important similarities: in basic outlook, in particular beliefs, in interest, and/or in life-style. This convergence feeds into their sense of identity, and influences choices and learning, especially by newer members.
- Related to the last feature, normative practices amounting to a code of conduct tend to evolve within a community. The community's code has varied roots, usually including the impress of a larger encompassing system or tradition.
- There is an interdependence of members, involving division of labour and responsibilities in fulfilling needs and carrying out communal tasks. By this and other means the community attains relative self-sufficiency, at least in those areas of activity and need that are of shared importance to members.
- Last but not least, there is a *sense of community* on the part of members, pivoting on the experience of relationship and belonging.

Although having these broad features in common, each formed living community is also distinct. The ethos tends to be subtle, complex and highly individual. Coming to an in-depth awareness and understanding of a community, one that does justice to its individuality while also permitting meaningful comparison with other communities, is a demanding challenge. Many studies of intact settlement communities have been done; and fascinating accounts by Margaret Mead, Ruth Benedict, Ralph Linton, Robert Redfield and various others are widely known. Classically, the method of investigation has quite often involved living for a time in the community under study and even adopting some of the ways of its members. It appears, however, that for the most part investigators have not consciously entered into a highly *empathic* person-to-person association with community members in order to become deeply knowing in regard to their inner worlds, their own experience of self, relationships, environment and life purpose. An empathy-based approach can unfold into a living picture of member perspectives on the nature and meaning of life and their own place in the scheme of things. Such a process is basic to establishing the core of communal identity from a person-centred frame of reference.

Robert Redfield was one of those who was particularly sensitive to this under-emphasized aspect and process. In *The Little Community* he writes:

> The investigator has to see the meaning, understand the valuation, and feel the feeling connected with each object or act in the mind of the native. Only after he has seen it from the native's point of view may the investigator change his viewpoint and look at that object or act – together with the meaning it has for the native – as an object of scientific interest now to be described from the outside and related . . . to other things . . . according to the demands of a more detached and abstract understanding. (Redfield, 1960: 81)

Redfield speaks further of the 'necessity to take the inside view mediately, on the way to systematic understanding', and proposes that the 'tension between the inside view and the outside view, this obligation to manage correctly the relationship between them, is the central problem in studies of culture or of personality' (ibid.: 82). He refers to an investigator of the Zuni Indian culture who assumed the inside view so perfectly that he became a member of the community he set out to study and ceased to be a source of critical understanding to outsiders. A contrary danger, if each observation springs from and is positioned in an external framework, is that the living tissue of experience and meaning in its whole cloth pattern is never seen. In connection with coming to understand the ethos and world view of community members, Redfield writes:

> The outsider waits. He listens to hear if one or many of the natives have themselves conceived an order in the whole. It is *their* order, *their* categories, *their* emphasis upon this part rather than that which the student listens for. Every world view is made of the stuff of philosophy . . . and it is the native philosopher's ordering of the stuff to which we, the outside investigators, listen. (ibid.: 88)

'Outside' and 'inside' views work in close and powerful partnership, in Redfield's perspective. The inside mode is crucial and central to the process of coming to know the ethos or outlook on life of a community. This especially includes values, life meaning, the desired or good life, and ways of growing into this life. Ethos is distinct conceptually but interwoven with the personality or selfhood of community members. Entry to either realm and their intricate linkages depends on profound human engagement such that the investigator 'walks', perceives and feels as from within. Scientific use of subjectively absorbed, participant-observer information depends also on being able to leave the information source, draw back from the internal frame of reference of the personal-communal other, and carefully apply an outside view, extended by and anchored to the inside information (Barrett-Lennard, 1994: 66–67).

This direction of thought, coupled with reflection on the large group experiences, have led on to the formulation of a series of propositions regarding community. Although not necessarily comprehensive, they draw together and frame a number of core ideas about the understanding, formation and working of community. Because the distillation is careful and already tight, and little has been written in this area by other scholars sharing the same underlying perspective, what follows next is taken entirely and mostly word for word from my mentioned article (1994: 79–82).

The main ideas are condensed into just seven complementary propositions, some with two parts, each one helping to lay the ground for those which follow. Since I think it vital to say something about how a community can be understood, this seems a logical starting point. Subsequent propositions also speak to the issue indirectly.

1 An 'inside view', derived from empathic contact with a cross-section of members absorbed in expressive engagement in their world, and in moments of portrayal and reflection on this engagement, is essential to understanding the nature and identity of a community. The products of this inside view make possible an informed, also necessary 'outside view' by the participant-observer/investigator.

Emphasis on the internal frame of reference in understanding behaviour, the development of thought around experiencing processes, and the whole perceptual-phenomenological cast of client-centred thinking, are in accord with the thrust of this stated proposition. Further, any systematic frame of reference by the investigator is an outside view so far as the data-contributing person is concerned. The testing of hypothesized patterns is external; even the categories from inductive analysis are co-determined by the investigator in response to replies from varying internal frames of reference. Any comparison of one community with another entails an outside view. In an important paper, Rogers (1964c) distinguished three ways of knowing: subjective, empathic and objective modes. The first proposition implies interwoven use of all three.

2a A community forms and evolves as a collective of persons, aware of one another and interconnected in multiple ways. These ways include networks of association among individuals and subgroups, which have reciprocally valued elements for members.

2b The more – in quality and extent – that potential linkages evolve such that community members are 'significant others' in each other's lives, the stronger and more fully formed the community tends to be.

Proposition 2a is axiomatic and definitional. Community is not an instant phenomenon nor simply a result of structures. It grows into being, crucially through the working and interplay of its member subsystems, individual and interpersonal. The more specific idea of proposition 2b can be viewed as a hypothesis potentially open to testing. Twin elements, the first descriptive and the second more hypothesis–like, also apply in the next proposition. Again, the perspective is developmental:

3a Qualitative development of community tends to build upon itself; as in the case where communal life fosters growth processes among its members and flourishes and evolves through effects of this growth.

3b When communities satisfy growth or actualization needs of their own members, beyond a period of initial development, they tend to behave in constructively responsive ways in relation to other communities, organizations and individuals.

The interdependence of growth processes at different levels is at the heart of 3a. The wording 'beyond a period of initial development', in 3b, allows for the likely possibility that during a community's early formation, members' hunger for the connection it offers, or the working out of ways to meet their needs together, may leave them inward-looking with reference to their own group. As their community forms and gathers momentum members become able to give attention to other groups in ways that grow out of the life quality of their own community. Proposition 4 advances a more generic conception of community encompassing three distinct elements. The first parallels a principle familiar in its application to individuals. The other two are core aspects of the relation between a community whole and the member persons.

4 Formed communities tend to maintain if not also to enhance themselves; to have a distinctive identity interwoven with the values and self-definition of members; and to satisfy human needs for affiliated belonging and presence with others.

Proposition 5 builds on 4, and compresses and furthers meanings for which the ground has been laid here and in prior writing (Barrett-Lennard, 1993c). It incorporates a normative stance woven into a view of community as a living system.

5 A well-functioning community is an open system in interface with other systems (especially living systems, and usually including other communities), organically responsive to new external data and to fresh information and initiatives from within, and thus in evolving motion. This motion applies to the scope, subtlety and wisdom of communal or collective consciousness, and is assisted by an ethic which is at once egalitarian and responsive to the varied special resources of its members.

A now-familiar element of client-centred theory is that the well-functioning human organism is open to experience and tends to engage in an organismic valuing process, broadly in the service of the actualizing tendency (Chapter 5). Consistent with this process quality, experiences tending to maintain and enhance the organism are valued positively, and the converse, negatively. So also with communities, as already implied (proposition 4). Clearly, communities can also be poorly functioning and destructive, and the next proposition acknowledges this dynamic and seeks to portray its essence.

6 A poorly functioning or severely threatened community may withdraw and isolate itself, or engage in power-manipulation or open conflict, in relation to other human collectives. Internally, members are not openly present with one another, and tend to be caught in a personally and communally self-limiting pattern of association. The self-maintaining tendency is expressed not in growth but in a fixed repeating pattern. Extremely faulty attributions may occur in regard to outsiders – individual or collective. The 'community' can become a prison to its members and/or a violent antagonist to its neighbours.

The last formal proposition in this working set carries the idea of community as a living entity to its most direct expression:

7 *A community is an emergent whole with a life of its own which normally it seeks to maintain. In effect, it is an emergent life form, and should not lightly be conceived, aborted, subverted or destroyed.*

In this perspective, communities (and organizations that have community properties), even when they are unhealthy and suffering, even when destructive to other communities, are living human systems. A functioning community, while it lacks a *genetic* code, has other properties by which we identify life forms of a high order. The communal life system is intimately associated and connected with the lives of its members, present and former.

Communicide (Barrett-Lennard, 1994) has been endemic in human 'civilizations', occurring most obviously through colonization, conquest and persecution of minorities, less obviously through interventions motivated by self-interest but justified as 'improving' those affected. Forces that radically alter life environments, that enforce movement or induce scattering of peoples, or that undercut working systems of meaning, relation and livelihood, all pose life-threatening risk to communities. Given that community systems have emergent life beyond the separate lives of constituent members, actions or policies that break down and extinguish the life of a functioning community may in principle be compared in seriousness with the taking of individual human life.

A strong sense and quality of community in the lives of most people would not only mean a great enrichment of individual life but may radically alter the prospects for a genuinely advancing civilization. As implied in proposition 5 above, a well-functioning community tends *not* to spend energy on conflictual or coercive relations with other communities, and generally would not invite such relations. Positively expressed, a natural potential of such communities is to engage and relate to others of their kind. Local communities that reach out to others across large-system political and geographic boundaries help to bridge and build better relations between these encompassing systems. All in all, helping to create, preserve and restore well-functioning community is seen as a challenge and calling at the highest level. It might appear to some that this is a radical shift within or even away from a person-centred approach. To me it is a totally compatible and most urgently required extension, albeit one that opens new challenges within this movement. Steps in related direction are implicit in the next focus of this chapter.

Conflict resolution and peace processes

In several papers spaced out over time Rogers formulated views related to conflict resolution, culminating in his consuming interest in peace processes in the last years of his life. His visible expression of pertinent views started in a conference on communication, about the time *Client-Centered Therapy* came into circulation. The distinguished industrial psychologist, F.J. Roethlisberger, was a fellow panellist, and the contributions of the two men appeared together under the joint title 'Barriers and gateways to communication' (Rogers and Roethlisberger, 1952). Rogers suggests a close linkage between quality of intrapersonal and external communication, with free inner communication serving as the doorway to effective communication with others. (This 'door' is two-way; the external communication affecting inner flow – 1952: 46.) The all-too-familiar tendency to evaluate, to judge and approve or disapprove, is identified as a principal perpetuating factor in misunderstanding and conflict. Because the exploration of conflict between large groups usually occurs through representatives speaking not just for themselves but for their constituencies, any resolution is uphill, uncertain, and slow-moving. Yet perhaps this obstacle can be overcome, and Rogers speaks of possible steps that are almost a prophecy of what he began to do himself, over a quarter of a century later.

> Let us suppose [he wrote] that a therapeutically oriented international group went to the Russian leaders and said, 'We want to achieve a genuine understanding of your views and, even more important, of your attitudes and feelings toward the United States. We will summarize and resummarize these views and feelings if necessary, until you agree that our description represents the situation as it seems to you.' . . . Then suppose they did the same thing with the leaders in our own country. If they then gave the widest possible distribution to these two views, with the feelings clearly described but not expressed in name-calling, might not the effect be very great? (Rogers and Roethlisberger, 1952: 49)[12]

The author goes on, in deft, vigorous language, to point out that 'we can understand the feelings of a person who hates us much more readily when his attitudes are accurately described to us by a neutral third party than we can when he is shaking his fist at us' (ibid.: 49). A dozen years later, Rogers spoke in related vein, in an address that later helped to launch the *Journal of Applied Behavioral Science* (1965a). By this time, his thinking had further differentiated, and his focus was explicitly on tension situations and their resolution. He first proposed that in a wide spectrum of conflicts the

---

12 It is remarkable to me to find this particular expression by Rogers originating so early. It is as though his directly expressed concern and proposal, beyond his existing field and recognized competence, was then put on hold for nearly thirty years! By then he had extensive experience in facilitating groups both small and large, and had no time to delay longer if he were to pursue peace issues directly. As will be seen, his approach on this new/old level was almost continuous with his thinking so long before.

protagonists *on both sides* typically hold beliefs to the effect that 'I am right and you are wrong', and 'I am good and you are bad.' Granted these attitudes vary in expression, an extended formulation with considerable generality is offered:

> I am correct and accurate and sound in my view of the situation, my perception of its elements, my interpretation of its meaning. My view is the right and true one. You are unfortunately mistaken and inaccurate in your view of the situation and in your analysis of what it means. Your view is false and wrong, yet you stubbornly hold to it.
>
> I am honest and straightforward and fundamentally good in my approach to our relationship and its problems. Unfortunately, you are none of these things. You are essentially bad and evil and untrustworthy in your approach to the whole situation. My motives are good. Yours are not. (1965a: 8)

Rogers' view of personal-emotional disorder is basically a conflict model, and his theme has its counterpart in psychotherapy. The client in therapy typically 'feels that there is within him this decent and reasonable self which is at war with vague, bad, false, wrong forces underneath the surface which he cannot understand. Therapy is an attempt to help the individual reconcile these opposing forces' (ibid.: 9). In the case of serious disputes between individuals 'there is no doubt at all but that I am right and you are wrong. I am on the side of the angels, and you belong to the forces of darkness' (13). This attitude undermines communication and, in particular, leads to inability to hear the other. Perceptions are distorted to fit the preconceived views, and the whole relationship becomes permeated with self-confirming suspicion and mistrust. As in his 1952 article, Rogers points out that this cycle may gradually be broken by a skilled therapist-mediator, one who listens empathically to each disputant, accepting and restating their meanings until fresh awareness develops, threat recedes and each begins to recognize the other's reality. Implied in this account of the loosening of fixed attitudes, and coming of fresh awareness, is the idea that interactive conflict reflects inner dividedness. However, it is not an idea that Rogers brings out and works on, as an ingredient cause of conflict.

Turning for a moment to Gordon (1977/1980), considerable attention is devoted by that author to applying his 'no-lose' approach to conflict resolution in organizational/work settings. In this case, it is conflict between leader and staff member, or manager-supervisor and a subordinate. The resolution process is portrayed as a special case of problem-solving in which distinct steps are discriminated: identifying the problem, generating potential solutions, evaluating these alternatives and making a clear choice, implementing this decision, and evaluating the solution afterwards. While active (empathic) listening on the leader's part is viewed as the central process ingredient, keeping track of the steps and acknowledging genuine concerns are stressed. The main example given (ibid.: 179–188) is a dialogue between a leader-manager, who manifests unusual listening and expressive ability, and a supervisor not in conflict with the manager so much as with a subordinate he wishes to fire – a situation that creates the need to resolve differences in philosophy with the manager. Gordon's interest is in leader training and development, and he does not depict use of an outside consultant to facilitate crisis-resolution.

Managing tensions between groups – union and management, for example – is the next level considered by Rogers (1965a: 15–20). Where the protagonist groups are speaking for themselves, not as representatives, the dynamics of conflict are seen as essentially the same as between individuals. Facilitating resolution is not thought to differ in principle, merely in complexity, as between the one-on-one and group-to-group instances. Rogers' paper was written in the first flush of his love affair with groups. His warm account implies that the small group releases an inner hunger for connection and fosters communicative openness and authentic mutual presence of participants. The conditions for and process of this development in the small group would also be fundamental, Rogers believed, in working with parties in conflict (19–20).

International tensions provided the concluding focus of this mid-sixties presentation by Rogers (19–23), and he cites simulation experiments conducted at his then home base, the Western Behavioral Sciences Institute. Several laboratory 'mini-nations' were organized, with varied defence and other resources, and differing political-economic systems. All too readily, there was a build-up of distrust and tension between these nation groups. One 'chief of state' was then secretly instructed to utilize the strategy of 'graduated reciprocation in tension reduction' (GRIT – Osgood, 1962). In initially modest steps that could be verified, and that were announced to the world in advance, this nation reduced its posture of threat and made overtures for new areas of exchange and co-operation. Its leaders had first to struggle through a period of anxiety and alarmed counter-pressure from *allies*. In due course, protagonist 'nations' found themselves in an atmosphere that strongly called for response in kind, and the GRIT process began to work. Rogers does not argue that the process studied was directly applicable to a live international context, but that it held great promise for further research and learnings that would in fact be applicable, in the context of the Cold War at its dangerous height.

To carry further research and other avenues of peace assistance strongly forward, Rogers proposed that a high level interdisciplinary task force be formed, entrusted with substantial responsibility and resources. Task force members' complementary expertise would come together around tension processes and conflict resolution. They would be on call to the State Department, Peace Corps, aid agencies, programs concerned with race relations, and a spectrum of other major program groups. They would have ample support for basic and action research, pilot demonstrations, the development of articulating theory and, of course, for intensive consultation and educative programs. It was a great dream but not one that took hold or materialized in recognizable form. Rogers had many other irons in the fire, and it was not for another 16–18 years that he gathered his resources and concerns into a primary focus on peace-related work.

There were many implicit steps toward the peace focus, most in one way or another involving Rogers' work with groups, large and small.[13] A staging point is his chapter article 'Resolving intercultural tensions: a beginning' (Rogers, 1977c). In his luminous writing style, Rogers carries the reader through diverse examples of people separated by deep chasms of social division and conflict but who learn to listen, communicate and feel for each other in person-centred groups. He cites a number of examples, most already in view (Rogers and Rose, 1971; McGaw, Rogers and Rice, 1973; Kristal-Anderson, 1975), a few that are new to this report. Rogers' commitment to the approach presented is very strong; his message of 'quiet revolution' is simply framed, with persuasive illustration.

Rogers' next report in sequence, titled 'A psychologist looks at nuclear war' appeared in 1982. The author (writing early in the Reagan years) speaks with passion about the trivialization of nuclear war in arenas as far removed as foreign and defence policy, and video games. He cites evidence of hopelessness about the future, any future, among particular groups of young people studied by his grand-daughter (1982: 11). Osgood's GRIT concept remained very much in Rogers' mind, and he cites as illustration an earlier initiative by President Kennedy, resulting in a reciprocating sequence of moves by the US and USSR prior to Kennedy's death. The Russians are said to have labelled the process 'the policy of mutual example' (12–13). The author moved to other examples, from first-hand experience, where high levels of tension were defused by joint participation in experiential groups. The evidence of changes in attitude by those who participated is compelling; how far this change spread to others in the referent communities is unclear (13–16). The process by which Sadat and Begin came to an unlikely meeting of minds is given close attention by Rogers in this article but, more particularly, in his next publication in sequence (Rogers and Ryback, 1984).[14]

This later report, in the pages of *The Counseling Psychologist*, includes a detailed account of the Camp David meetings in 1978, with Sadat and Begin as protagonists and President Carter as 'facilitator' (Rogers and Ryback, 1984). It is presented as a compelling example of what remains *possible* in the face of extreme, war-hardened division. Drawing on reports by Dayan (1981) and Carter (1982), Rogers discriminates a number of distinct features and steps in the meeting saga, which he believed crucial to its success. The sessions were held in a retreat setting, with relative informality, no set

---

13 Overlapping summaries of this strong group process 'connection' are to be found in Rogers, 1977c and 1982, and in Rogers and Ryback, 1984.

14 Rogers' 1982 paper concludes with an impassioned plea for the US to change its stance and 'embark on a serious, vigorous program of communication with the USSR and the Russian people'. Rather than waste billions on nuclear weapons we should, he urged, 'put some of that money and energy to work in pursuing, developing, expanding the communicative process that leads toward peaceful reconciliation'. He felt that the responsibility for changing direction was in everyone's hands: his 'personal share of this responsibility' led him to speak out forcefully (1982: 20). Rogers did more than speak on paper and at home. Within *the last months* of his long life he travelled to Moscow and Tbilisi, for a strenuous round of activities later described.

agendas, and no ongoing media coverage. The principals were able to speak personally and with feeling, with authority and without continuous consultation with constituents or advisors. Carter sometimes sought to persuade but generally took a much more neutral stance than either of the others, seeking to ensure clear communication and to mediate as necessary. The meetings ran for almost two weeks with mostly sustained momentum and increasing intensity. I say 'mostly' because by the morning of the eleventh day it seemed that the exercise had failed, and Sadat was packed and ready to go. This still seemed true even as the last day began, and Rogers draws attention to an incident in which Begin became deeply moved in company with Carter, about his grandchildren. This appeared to be a turning point, residual blockages dissolved, and an agreement on crucial issues was reached. The leaders were experiencing deep feeling at the public signing, and the result was a watershed.

Rogers carefully points out that, successful though the conference was in the end, the process could have been much more substantially facilitative. His central point, supported by Dayan's account, was the absence of any deeply empathic response to inner feeling-concerns, a lack of indwelling response to the spirit and yearnings of each participant. He believes that a facilitator of his own kind would have set the stage for much more direct, face to face contact between the contenders, and he also repeats his call for a specialized high-level committee such as he advocated earlier. Now nearing his mid-eighties, and clearly with time running short for his own involvement, Rogers began preparing for a peace workshop organized for November 1985. Held in Rust, Austria, with government figures from Central American countries, writers and academics participating, this controversial event became known in his own writing and circles as the Rust Workshop.

The workshop project was a joint venture, 'co-directed' by Carl Rogers and Rodrigo Carazo, former president of Costa Rica. The facilitator team, headed by Rogers, was from the Center for Studies of the Person. The main financial sponsor, an Austrian bank, had arranged the comfortable residential retreat setting for the conference. Rogers' report (1986a) of the project was written soon afterward and published only months later. It forms an up-beat narrative record of how the event unfolded. The fifty-strong membership plus staff met sometimes as a whole forum but largely in four pre-arranged groups, each with a cross-section of the total membership. Through almost the first half of the workshop, the meetings were largely presentations of the views and positions of members, with little person-to-person dialogue. Two evening meetings centred on informational question and answer sessions with Rogers and with Carazo, and may have supported the tendency for a presentation style in other settings. By the later part of the second day, 'temperatures' were rising, impatience was in the air, and talk and argument went on far into the night. On the third day, angry and bitter feeling was palpable but it surfaced in the context of a broadly increasing confidence in the workshop process. Rogers noted that people were engaged, listening, and responding to one another. That night a traditional social event (Austrian Heurigen) strongly furthered the loosening and connecting process. During the next and final day continuity was disrupted by an afternoon press conference at another site, requested and organized by the sponsoring bank.

A press conference would naturally tend to draw participants back into their public roles and the taking of positions. A shared position in this case was that the workshop had been unique and valuable. Reading between the lines, it appears that diverging agendas were also surfacing again. In his mention of the warmly positive exchanges and feedback that were expressed more privately that evening, Rogers (1986a: 39) notes that this may not have been the whole picture: 'I feel [he writes] that insufficient effort was made to draw out any possible negative feelings' (also in Kirschenbaum and Henderson, 1989a: 471). He goes on to acknowledge 'mistakes and disappointments', including the disappointment of having no participants from US Government circles (some had signed up and then withdrawn). There were deficiencies in advance planning and co-ordination between the co-sponsors, in Costa Rica and California; and problems of limited informal availability of CSP staff during the workshop, as a result of the separate staff support meetings (1986a: 40–41).[15] Notwithstanding such difficulties, Rogers saw the workshop as deeply productive, and he enumerates a series of reasons for its success (41–44). His account gives no hint of any shortcoming in concept.

Several other reports from staff contributors to the Rust Workshop complement the picture drawn by Rogers (Swenson, 1987; Bowen, 1987; Solomon, 1987; and Wood, 1994). I will return to Wood's critique in a later passage. Solomon's account extends factual information about the participants, their groupings and expectations, and some of the critical events, appraisals, and limitations of the workshop. He couples his 'cautious optimism' regarding outcomes with suggestions for differences in approach and (especially) in preparation. He notes that there appeared to be 'general disappointment with the conference among the Latins', evidently the group accounting for most participants with roles in government, and those seeing least connection between 'the political and the personal' (Solomon, 1987: 346).

Maria Bowen contrasts the Rust event with other PCA workshops. For example, it had a strong thematic focus – achieving peace in Central America – and concerns centred on societal issues and conflict, not the achievement of personal insights and growth. There were few I-messages but much expression of viewpoint in the search for solution to real-world issues of profound concern. Further, most participants were invited and did not come at personal expense or with high motivation to experience and work with Carl Rogers (many scarcely knew of him in advance). There was a great sense of urgency to achieve outcomes perceived as tangible and capable of impact beyond the group (Bowen, 1987: 349–354). It was an experience with new challenges for the facilitators as much as for any others. Another staff member, Doug Land,

---

15 After each of the three afternoon small-group sessions, the facilitator staff also took time to complete a questionnaire for a modest research study, exceptional in being conducted at all, and later reported by Solomon (1990). This study is further cited in my Chapter 14.

'quipped that the facilitators had to die in order for the workshop to survive' since their special sensitivity and repertoire often seemed irrelevant (358). This growing awareness, and their ability to hold back, may itself have been a positive force in the workshop.

Swenson (1987: 320) stresses that a high level of tolerance for ambiguity and 'non-linear' process was crucial in the Rust context. Her examination of ambiguity and divergence between the personal encounter-oriented and more 'political' perspectives remains of interest. It struck her that these two language/mindset cultures view productive or 'real' dialogue quite differently. Each has experience of 'forward-moving' processes resulting from their preferred modes of dialogue. The former group tend to be 'processors' (who 'value taking time to create consensus and to hear subtle meanings hovering below the surfaces'), and the latter 'decision-makers' (who 'must act fast, with authority and conviction, in order to get the most accomplished in a world urgently demanding solutions'). The decision-makers rely more on marked-out implementing structures, but the wish to make a difference (and to be seen as doing so) applies equally to the processors. Swenson works to see validity and complementarity in both styles, stressing the need in practice for respected and unusually resourceful integrators to bring out the creative potential of a mix between them (325–326).

Within three months of the Rust meetings Rogers was overseas again, accompanied by Ruth Sanford, on a long and hard-working visit in South Africa, constituting 'one of the most significant experiences of my life' (Rogers, 1986c). This was a follow-up to their first trip there, in the early eighties, described by Sanford (1984). Her succinct report of that visit presents the verbal interchange in a thirteen-person group session conducted by Carl and herself, on stage before an involved audience of 600 persons. The transcript from this racially mixed group speaks quite powerfully for itself in respect of issues on both personal and societal levels. Direct experience-based communication took place, and became increasingly immediate and responsive. For participants the experience on the face of it was important and, in all probability, memorable. In raising the question 'was the group effective?' Sanford notes movement in qualities of interaction, mentions later feedback, and hints at attitude shifts (1984: 12–14). Beyond this, she does not closely examine or speculate on wider implications, perhaps because she felt these would be a matter of surmise, or because of a belief that greater self-congruence and altered person-perception are the keys to societal as well as personal change.[16]

---

16 Rogers was also prevailed on to give demonstration therapy interviews, which he drew on for two later reports on the interview process. The one with 'Jan' (which he was pleased with) is a useful illustration of his way of working as a therapist late in his life (Rogers, 1986/1993). In the other interview, the client was a psychologist employed within 'the system'. After some delay, Rogers wrote this case up under the heading 'The dilemmas of a South African white' (1986b). He acknowledged his own dilemmas, and moments of failure, and the interview illustrates how even the most resourceful of therapists can at crucial moments 'lose' a complex client. To his credit, Rogers did not bury the incident but exposed and used it to learn and teach from.

One of the tangible outcomes was the encouragement Rogers found for his further visit with Sanford to South Africa. By this time, in the New Year of 1986, the socio-political climate was *more* volatile, and even within the person-centred movement views were mixed as to whether the perspective brought to bear by Rogers and Sanford was at all adequate to the realities of the crisis involved. Some suggested that a focus on personal communication and empowerment, as though the individual were self-contained and free standing, was counter-productive, tending to draw attention away from the perilous, entrenched problems of a systemic and structural nature (see Holdstock, 1990). In the event, judging from his detailed journal record (Rogers, 1986c), a dialogue just before his death (Hill-Hain and Rogers, 1988), and another brief paper (Rogers and Sanford, 1987), it is evident that Rogers' own awareness of what constituent groups in South Africa were experiencing and enduring greatly expanded during this second visit. However, this sharply increased awareness still left his personalized perspective on the *solution* to societal cleavage and conflict largely intact (Rogers, 1986b and 1986c).

Rogers worked principally with groups of moderate size, whose members then paired off to serve as facilitators in a larger workshop context, where his own role was as a presenter. Given his open and receptive style and non-impositional approach, and the experience and resourcefulness of those with whom he and Sanford did work intensively, it seems unlikely that over-simplifying elements in their outlook would have negated the positive features. (And, their stated optimism as to the *possible* outcome in South Africa seems justified by later events.) More might have been published from Rogers' own pen regarding this episode, except for the proximity of another major trip, and the sudden ending of his own life soon afterward.

Only six months after returning from Africa, Rogers and Sanford were in Moscow. Again they engaged, mostly via interview demonstration and in question-and-answer mode, with large groups (up to 900 persons), and worked intensively with smaller ones (Rogers, 1987). Their activity centred in Moscow itself and in Tbilisi, Georgia. The meetings were primarily with psychologists, therapists, educators and students. Papers by Rogers had been sent on ahead and indications were that most participants had reading knowledge of his work – unlike the situation at the Rust Workshop. There was no explicit focus on international relations although it seems that some relevant spin-off occurred on this level. From Rogers' account, explosive frustration and angry conflict among participants, with almost total lack of listening, marked the first day or more of meetings in the low-structure smaller groups (1987: 286–287). Perhaps partly for this reason, and the 'small' group size (40–50 persons), speaker–listener–observer triads were adopted as a major and successful format (289–291). The climate evolved, and Rogers reports on the outpouring of positive feeling and valuing at the end. The large public meetings evidently were marked by intense interest and attention. One of Rogers' strongest impressions was of the basic similarity between concerns, fears and hopes of the Soviet professionals he worked with, and their American counterparts. His report was to be his last freshly written article. One is struck by the enthusiasm and fluency, even sparkling quality, of his writing. He is reporting another adventure, new in context and specifics, familiar and affirming in many salient qualities.[17]

Rogers was projecting additional peacemaking initiatives at the time of his death, including a further visit to South Africa. Thus, at an advanced age, he was investing quite remarkable energy in an area he had long thought about and recently made his *dominant* active concern. It emerged too late to account for any large proportion of his later publications, and most of the handful of substantive articles by collaborating associates have been mentioned here.[18] Late in 1984 the Carl Rogers Institute for Peace had been founded at CSP, spearheaded by Gay Swenson. She continued to devote great commitment and energy to this enterprise for a number of years after Rogers' death, until insufficient funds were coming in. Why did this work not gather and retain more momentum? Answers might be offered on more than one level, but perhaps the central issue lies in the nature of Rogers' approach to the phenomena that concerned him so deeply. The fact that he did not make the transition to incorporate a systemic perspective has been touched on before. Large groups are driven by forces extending beyond the personal motivations and feelings of individuals, that is, external to the sphere in which Rogerians have been most at home. The perspective Rogers brought to bear spanned a relevant but limited part only of the multi-level domain involved. It is also possible that in feeling his way in this new terrain, the form and 'message' of his work tended to hold sway over its spirit. At least one collaborator has expressed this strongly.

Speaking from the position of a participant-insider, and carefully looking back on the Rust Workshop in particular, Wood (1994) takes issue not so much with principles of the person-centred approach but with deficiency in their application by Rogers and the facilitator team, including himself. The workshop, in his analysis, was over-structured, 'over-facilitated', and over-inclined to emphasize an ideology. As he puts it:

> When the organizers apply, instead of participate in, the person-centred approach . . . with an attitude, conscious or not, of having pre-determined answers for the group, of wanting to 'give them an experience of the approach', or wanting to 'model values to them', the group is undoubtedly hindered in achieving its self-governing and innovative potential. (1994: 102)

The distinctly differing expectations of participants who responded to organizers in Central America and those who came on the basis of

17 The *style* of Rogers' writing remains unmistakable, reminding me of his letters from much earlier (part-holiday) trips to the Caribbean and overseas. I put together a sample of these, numbered 34 to 40 within a larger selection 'Writing person to person: letters from Carl', for a memorial publication after his death (Barrett-Lennard, 1987b).

18 In its five years of publication, the *Person-Centered Review* carried only two papers flowing directly from this work, one of these (Rogers, 1986b) being centred on an interview case analysis. One issue of the *Journal of Humanistic Psychology* (vol. 27, no. 3), from which several of the cited articles are drawn, is substantially devoted to this work.

information directly from CSP, posed a difficulty but was not the basic problem. The critical weaknesses, in Wood's view, resulted from not using the wisdom and strength of the approach. He also suggests (but then leaves the point) that 'the basic assumptions of the person-centered approach to the resolution of conflicts for this event were too simplistic' (97).

Granted both conceptual and procedural limitations to Rogers' peace-making efforts, much can be learned from them, as I hope this outline suggests. Discerning the lessons of shortcomings and the promise of positive elements, are vital to any related further initiatives. I admire Rogers for his effort to contribute on this level, out of his concern for the suffering and well-being *of persons*, and his consciousness of possibly even greater dangers ahead. He acted, late in life, seeking to make best use of the formidable skills and resources of knowing that he possessed, and I believe some good came from his effort. He, like most of us in the same field, might easily have done less, and it is not clear that he could have done more. He was literally drawn along by the momentum of his own achievement and reputation, in psychotherapy, group work and education, even when travelling in zones where the overall fabric of society was stretched to its tearing point, as in South Africa. He liked to extend the domain of his work but his own direct effort was at times secondary. Others who saw in his thought or practice special meaning and value for their own sphere often had much more to do with this extension than Rogers himself. My conclusion provides further illustration.

In conclusion: other applications

The total account given of applications beyond psychotherapy completes the areas that are most visible, at least when viewed from within the social sciences. It is not possible to do justice here to all additional contexts in which Rogers' work has had impact. These include (among others) liberal religious reflection and pastoral counselling, and medicine and health care. Theories of human nature have implications in the realm of values and the meaning of life. It may be only a small further step to discern moral and even spiritual dimensions.[19] Many have taken this step, in relation to Rogers' work, notably including Thorne (1991) among colleagues within the person-centred movement. The

19 During my final checking of this chapter I have just seen Prilleltensky's striking contribution in the *American Psychologist*, on the implicit value-stances and associated implications of different basic perspectives in psychology. Four such emerged from his examination of 'the moral dimensions of psychological discourse and practice' (1997: 517). Two tables, the first identifying a series of 'questions for assessing the moral implications of psychological approaches', distil much of the author's thought. The implied value characteristics of 'traditional', 'empowering', 'postmodern', and 'emancipatory communitarian' approaches are summarized in Table 2. Surprisingly, Rogers receives no mention. However, the person-centred stance can be related, at different stages of its evolution, to all four of the emphases Prilleltensky distinguishes.

relevant independent contributors include Seward Hiltner (1958) and Robert Fuller (1984). Both men had backgrounds at the University of Chicago, the former in overlapping time with Rogers. Hiltner, a major figure in the pastoral counselling sphere, believed that a drawing out and freeing of the inner person for truly open contact with their own experiencing was a pre-condition for spiritual awareness. For Hiltner, the actualizing tendency of Rogers, and the potential for an organismic valuing process, was a near-perfect fit to his own concept of a life tendency toward the development and deepening of consciousness. Self-knowledge, a lived sense of connection transcending self, and an evolving spiritual awareness, went hand in hand. Both pastor and counsellor worked not to shape and inculcate but to assist in a kind of birthing. 'Does this mean', he wrote, 'that pastoral guiding is nondirective and client-centered? In the sense of the purpose for which these terms were coined by Carl Rogers, the answer is YES' (Hiltner, 1958 [p. 154] as cited in Fuller, 1984: 355). The spark of the divine that inhered in being a person could, in the presence of ingredients for growth, become a flame.

Fuller points out that Hiltner was committed to a 'process theology'. This is taken to imply that God is viewed not as a distinct and separate personal presence but, rather, as 'an immanent spiritual energy that propels an evolving universe toward the realization of its inner potentials or possibilities . . . [and] is active within each and every moment of experience as that directional force . . .' (Fuller, 1984: 355). No doubt this is less than Hiltner's full meaning but it is sufficient to suggest not only a basic compatibility with Rogers' thought but the possibility of a common origin. After all, Rogers' career choice preceding his move into clinical psychology had been to train for a reforming role in the ministry and Church, following very relevant family history and experiences during his college years. Indications are that basic tenets of his early beliefs or meaning system were revised and transmuted over the subsequent course of his experience and reflection, not simply discarded in a radical discontinuity of thought.

Fuller also cites Clebsch and Jaekle (1975) and numerous other sources in the literature to document not only the great influence of Rogers' work in the pastoral counselling field but his considerable impact on contemporary liberal religious reflection, not confined for that matter to Protestant circles. His public conversation-debates with two luminary theologians, Martin Buber and Paul Tillich, were of wide and continuing interest (republished in Kirschenbaum and Henderson, 1989b: 41–78). Perhaps less widely known are his own statements of basic observation and belief as shared in *A Way of Being* (Rogers, 1980a). He mentions, for example, experiences in altered states of consciousness that defy ordinary explanation and contribute to his sense of having underestimated the importance of a 'mystical, spiritual dimension' in human life. He summed up in more accustomed language. In freeing others to be their deeper selves, he wrote:

> We are tapping into a tendency which permeates all of organic life – a tendency to become all the complexity of which the organism is capable. And on an even larger scale, I believe we are tuning into a potent creative tendency which has formed our

universe, from the smallest snowflake to the largest galaxy. . . . And perhaps we are touching the cutting edge of our ability to transcend ourselves, to create new and more spiritual directions in human evolution. (ibid.: 134)

Of course, other voices in the Church have been critical of Rogers and of the humanistic movement more generally, perceiving his work (for example) as contributing to a secular, ungodly society lacking the values of any ultimate moral authority or framework of meaning. Fuller believes that such a view quite misses the mark, observing that Rogers' 'career has been devoted less to the secularization of theology than to what might be called the spiritualization of psychology' (1984: 365). This inference is backed up with salient further quotations from Rogers, woven into the author's careful scholarly discussion (365–369). In now leaving this all-too-brief examination my hope is that the interested reader's appetite will be whetted to turn to original sources.

Medical thought and practice includes an increasingly vigorous 'holistic' wing that emphasizes the working of the bodymind whole, and the close-knit interrelation and recursive influence of the many levels of activity and subsystems within this whole. Such change is accompanied by a broader emphasis on relationship and communication in medical practice, and a shift in attitude toward patient-consumers taking increasing responsibility for their own health care. Authoritarian styles are 'out'; even the idea of benevolent authority does not sit well. The patient–doctor encounter is more often a genuine 'consultation', in which the physician is expert advisor and resource person and the 'patient' a vital informant desiring to comprehend what is wrong and directly contribute to treatment decisions. These and related shifts have a variety of causes but their stronger expressions have links with Rogerian thought and contributions, and some innovations reflect direct influence.

Barnard (1984) has explored a range of pertinent issues entailed in a broadly client/person-centred approach to medical practice. Sensitivity to the *personal* significance of illness, to the patient's own explanatory model and agendas, and to potential cultural influence, are among the elements stressed in such an approach. Drawing on Katon and Kleinman (1981), 'negotiation' is advanced as basic to person-centred physician–patient interaction. The key factors in this genuine negotiation are identified as an attitude of partnership, responsive empathy, and a congruent way of viewing the healing process (Barnard, 1984: 348–350). The importance of empathy is highlighted: 'Indeed, we regard empathy as so crucial to the negotiation model that it is unlikely that the elicitation of the patient's model and subsequent negotiation is possible without [such] an affective bond between doctor and patient' (cited from Katon and Kleinman, 1981: 266). Further, the underlying role of the physician is 'to assist the patient to reclaim or renew his or her own strengths and tendencies toward growth' (Barnard, 1984: 350). By implication, *healing* is not just an instrumented change but a potential or tendency within the person, a tendency which physician and patient ideally work together to enable.

In their later report, Pfeiffer and Ripke (1990) effectively pick up where Barnard ends. They discuss the therapeutic triad of congruence, caring and empathy as distinctively applied in medical practice. In this context, the doctor is needing to make some diagnostic judgements, there is substantial collaborative exchange of information, and this unfolds into negotiating a total view of the problem, and forming a treatment response. Particularly interesting, is these authors' careful extended account, attuned both to the experiencing of the two persons involved and imbued with a specific practicality. A main aspect is that of information exchange and progressive convergence on a diagnosis that both partners actively accept. Also, steps in a person-centred process of physical examination are sensitively portrayed; and the course of joint planning of therapy/treatment is brought into further focus. Where hospitalization is entailed, the involvement of a broad spectrum of staff, in a highly structured institution, makes provision of a person-centred environment a more difficult challenge than within the doctor–patient dyad. However, nurses make up a major part of this environment, and the person-centred approach has been a contributing influence in their field. A notable illustration of this follows.

In 1980, the School of Nursing, Medical College of Ohio, began a master's program founded on a holistic person-centred health care approach. A broad aim of the program was to prepare nurses for leadership roles in nursing practice, education and administration, thus with much wider reach than the immediate practice of its graduates. As for the officially stated orientation of the program, it was designed 'to enhance the provision of nursing care to clients which is person-centred, family focused, holistic and self-care oriented' (Chickadonz et al., undated). Helping the client/patient become a more active and resourceful agent in their own health care meant responding not only with technical expertise but to the whole person, in respecting and facilitative mode (Chickadonz, Whitmire, Lindstrom and Utz, 1986: 203–205). Qualities in this approach to nursing were reflected also in teaching/supervisory relations in the program, with faculty and students working in an atmosphere of partnership. Far from being 'soft' on critical thinking and knowledge acquisition, the spelled-out requirements of competency span an impressive spectrum of levels, and point to an expectation of high professional and scholarly accomplishment (Chickadonz et al., undated). Experience over the early years of this innovative program, including the problems encountered and their resolution, have been reported in detail (Chickadonz et al., 1986). This account has a further implication.

Chickadonz wrote her report, with colleagues, from the position of Dean of the Nursing School, and a person-centred style of leadership is clearly implied. It brings this chapter full circle in that the approach is distinctly in the same genre as Gordon's picturing of group-centred leadership, three decades earlier. There is a research connection, too, around data from student evaluations (Chickadonz et al., 1986, Table 1). In this and earlier chapters, the nature and contributions of empirical research emanating from the client/person-centred innovation have been noted only in broad brush strokes. Medical settings have provided the context for some of the more ambitious studies. More important than the setting, however, are the linked issues of stage in time, purpose and method of the research, as the next three chapters reflect. These chapters are entirely devoted to the story and evolving substance of the research enterprise within and generated by this approach, and now spanning more than half a century

PART IV

RESEARCH

12

The Search for Order and Effects

> Basically the reason for the predictability of the [client-centred] therapeutic process lies in the discovery – and I use that word intentionally – that within the client reside constructive forces whose strength and uniformity have been either entirely unrecognized or grossly underestimated. It is the clearcut and disciplined reliance by the therapist upon those forces within the client, which seems to account for the orderliness of the therapeutic process, and its consistency from one client to the next.
>
> Carl Rogers, 1946

> I am tempted to say of what follows in this book, 'It isn't a good research in psychotherapy; it's just the best that there is.'
>
> Carl Rogers, 1954 in Rogers and Dymond, 1954

Empirical research on the process of psychotherapy began as a field with the work of Carl Rogers and fellow-investigators, in the 1940s. Their principal initial data were verbatim transcripts from sound recordings; recordings not only of entire therapy interviews but of the sequence of interviews for whole cases. The best-known example of such a transcript is the eight-interview case of 'Herbert Bryan', published in full in *Counseling and Psychotherapy* (Rogers, 1942a). A further book in the forties was devoted entirely to therapy interview records and linked commentary (Snyder, 1947a). It would be difficult to overestimate the demystifying impact of opening up the specific, step-by-step details of the whole client–therapist discourse to scientific and public scrutiny.[1] This was the setting for the first stage of a long and many-sided course of systematic inquiry. Viewed in retrospect, this research can be seen to form a

1 With the technology of the time, achieving an audible recording of the complete series of hour-long interviews, as in the case of Bryan, was itself remarkable. By 1947, Raskin (1949b) notes, there was a pool of about twenty fully recorded cases that could be drawn on for research.

natural and understandable sequence. The phases of this saga provide a useful map with which to keep one's bearings in examining particular work in the total investigative terrain. For this reason the sequential map itself is my opening focus, and the remaining sections in this chapter and most of the next, are arranged in keeping with it.

The course of research on client-centred therapy

My earlier bird's eye view of main developments as they emerged in the new client-centred school (Chapter 4) has already introduced issues and areas of work to build on here. The new therapy was distinguished above all else by the therapist's complete concentration on literally following the client's feelings and meanings, and giving step-by-step feedback on his/her understanding via reflective and clarifying statements. Certainly, this accords with the way it was described and illustrated by Rogers. What could be more natural than to begin serious research by placing the client–therapist discourse under a microscope for thorough and detailed examination of its pattern. Whole cases, the entire discourse for different client–therapist combinations, would be studied. A system for identifying and coding all of the interview data would be generated inductively, in the early phases of the research, and rigorously applied to the full available sample. The main categories and consistency of therapist verbal response, the changes (if any) of client and therapist communication over the course of therapy, and targeted features such as kinds of client self-reference, would all be amenable to examination.

Once the interview therapy process itself was shown to be a consistent phenomenon with its own order or lawfulness, what might sensibly come to the fore as a further focus of research concern? The therapy enterprise had in principle one main aim and justification, that of being personally helpful, of making a beneficial difference to personal functioning and life quality of clients. But was it really effective? Did clients in fact generally improve and change, and if so, did shifts during therapy hold up, or lead to continued growth? If such changes, on the basis of data separate from the interior process of therapy itself, were objectively measured and demonstrated, the therapy would be confirmed as a powerful human and social resource.

Assuming that efficacy was confirmed, perhaps not for every client but in varying degree for many clients, the question of exactly how the observed outcomes came about, or of what the crucial change-producing ingredients were, would be extremely pertinent. In other words, the cause–effect equation in therapeutic change would become an urgent one to illuminate and test. In fact, this was the next focus of theoretical refinement and empirical study in client-centred therapy research, and is my starting point in the next chapter. Beyond this focus, new ways of viewing client process within therapy could be expected to surface, and possibly permit a tracking of progress.

Therapy is not only a vehicle for change, not just of interest in terms of its function as a means to an end. It is a context of profound personal engagement and distinctive experiencing. It is itself both a laboratory and a theatre of life. As in other laboratories, the crucial variables can be targeted and approached in more than one way. One salient way is to take the functioning and response of therapists as the 'independent' or causative variable, and to study the impact of components of this variable – for example, therapist empathy – on client change. This accords with the conditions of therapy, cause–effect focus mentioned above. A second distinct strategy, with differing aim, turns the first position around. It takes the attitude and response of a particular group of therapists as approximately constant, and looks at the ways clients differ in their functioning in this given relationship environment. Research in accord with this interest is only likely after the nature of the therapeutic environment is clearly envisioned and can be assessed. In fact, conceptually framed study of client process levels within therapy followed closely on the first studies to test Rogers' conditions of therapy theory. This research, too, is taken up in the next chapter.

From this point on, therapy research broadly in the client-centred domain could be expected to focus more sharply than in the ground-breaking exploratory phases. One kind of thrust would target particular process elements to illuminate their role, even their nature, in more differentiated ways than was earlier possible. Another broad mode would study development of the therapy in its application to special populations (initially, schizophrenic patients) and particular contexts of distress and need – for example, in close relationships, where problems are personal but not individual. Studies would also tend to become more diverse and 'ecumenical', with relevance for somewhat different approaches and theoretical systems. And research, plausibly, would tend to follow the expansion of practice to areas beyond therapy, such as education, parenting, and self-help. Actual developments in the latter range of inquiry are examined in Chapter 14. For now, let us 're-search', and discover anew, the course and fruits of the crucial first phase of client-centred therapy research, where this realm of investigation all began.

Discerning the pattern of the discourse of therapy

William Snyder's 1945 journal report on the process of 'non-directive psychotherapy' summarizes one of the very first doctoral studies to be completed (in 1943) under Rogers' supervision. It is based on a detailed content analysis of forty-eight interviews from six different cases, five considered successful and one unsuccessful. The categories of counsellor statement include a cluster around therapist lead-taking. Among them are 'structuring' comments by the therapist (about aims, arrangements and limits in therapy), which occurred most often at the start and tapered off to a low level. 'Nondirective leads', some 6 per cent of responses in the first decile of therapy, fell off more gradually. Altogether, lead-taking evidently accounted for 15–20 per cent of therapist responses early in therapy, and perhaps 5 per cent in the last decile (Snyder, 1945: Table 1 and Figure 1).

'Nondirective response-to-feeling' expressions were in fact the dominant modality. In particular, simple acceptance ('Yes', 'I see', 'M-hm', etc.) and clarification/recognition of feeling responses accounted jointly for nearly two-thirds of all therapist statements through nine of the ten deciles of therapy (ibid.: Figure 1). Interpretations, coded by Snyder as 'semidirective', also constituted a distinct category, justified by modest direct frequency *and* by an appreciable count of client responses classed as 'rejecting an interpretation' (Figure 2). 'Directive' categories of therapist response included 'persuasion, disapproval and criticism' and 'approval and encouragement', which peaked at 5 per cent and 10 per cent respectively in the last decile of counselling. Clearly the new therapy was *not* wholly nondirective although weighted in that direction. As Snyder put it, initially in 1943:

> A fair amount of structuring of the situation, approval and encouragement, and non-directive leading is used. The asking of direct questions, counsellor's proposing client activity, persuasion by the counsellor, and disapproval and criticism by the counsellor, while present, are kept in very limited amounts. Interpretations and the giving of information are also rather limited. (1945: 214)

The verbal interview data from clients were also sorted into a range of content categories, including 'minor' ones (such as greetings and other friendly exchanges, and appointment-setting conversation). Each statement was also classified in terms of whether feeling was expressed and, when expressed, whether its thrust was positive, negative or ambivalent, and whether toward the self, the counsellor or situation, or other persons. Content categories of much the highest frequency were problem expressions, and communication of understanding or insight. Over the course of therapy, problem statements did diminish and expressions of understanding did generally increase (1945: Figure 2). Discussion of plans, decisions and the like, also increased from a very low starting point up to one client statement in ten. Feeling expression was found to be frequently involved in all of these categories of response. Feelings were predominantly negative in valence in the early sessions, and became generally more positive as therapy proceeded.

Snyder also sought to discover regularities in linkage between classes of therapist behaviour and of the following client response. He found that client expression of problems was especially likely to follow a non-directive lead, less likely to follow a clarification of feeling response. Expressions of understanding and insight usually arose following simple acceptance responses. Client requests for information often came in the wake of structuring efforts, counsellor questions or more directive interventions. Such regularities of sequence do not, of course, guarantee direct causal linkage.[2] Based on various data cues, Snyder speculates that *clarification of feelings produces an experience of acceptance* 'which assures the client that he is in a free and permissive situation' and that, within this climate of acceptance, 'non-directive leads . . . bring out statements of the problem by the client'. Then, as the client begins

---

2 In a later report, the investigator himself acknowledges that a weakness in his approach to the study of sequel relationships 'is the fact that a client's statement is a sequel to more than the immediately preceding counselor statement' (Snyder, 1947b: 347).

to gain 'insight into . . . his problems, the counselor would seem to shift from an attempt to clarify the feelings to a use of simple acceptance'. This 'seems to result in deeper insight and eventually in constructive planning' (ibid.: 211–212).

Snyder's study stood on its own, with some precedence for certain features but breaking much new ground. It helped to pave the way for the more ambitious *group* of investigations identified as the *Parallel Studies Project* – already flagged in Chapter 4. This work and its main reporting in 1949, as a complete issue of a major journal, constitute the high point of the opening phase of research. A main component study, by Seeman, is a careful replication and extension of Snyder's work, on the new sample of ten client cases (Raskin, 1949b). Seeman used the same main content categories as Snyder, adding subcategories. Unlike the earlier study, four judges were used in the interview content analysis, who engaged first in considerable training preparation to establish high reliability of coding (Seeman, 1949: 157–159).

The non-directive response-to-feeling categories as a group were distinctly more predominant than in the earlier study – now 85 per cent of all responses in contrast to some 63 per cent before, by Seeman's calculation (1949: 159). Frequency profiles across the categories were not the same as in the first study, and the balance of therapist statements no longer changed over time in any even trend. As in Snyder's case, clients spoke of problems very often (about half the time) at the start of therapy, and this frequency declined progressively. Expressions of understanding or insight, and reference to outcomes or planning, rose very steeply, especially in the last part of therapy (ibid.: 161). As before, client expression of negative attitudes and feelings diminished over therapy. Interestingly, clients moved from being like each other in balance of positive and negative expressions, at the start, to being increasingly diverse and distinct as therapy proceeded (164). Furthermore, over the course of therapy positive attitudes became more often expressed in the present tense, whereas expression of negative attitudes not only diminished but more often were located in the past. The increase in positive references to self, and diminishing negative feelings toward self *and* others, presumably reflected rising self-esteem (ibid.: Table 10).

Overall, in terms of the way therapists were responding, the therapy discourse followed a substantially regular and predictable pattern. Clients, on the other hand, while somewhat consistent in overall pattern of verbal response, became more distinct as therapy proceeded. Whether there was 'one main current or process of therapy which clients attain in different degree', thus accounting for individuality in process, or whether they took essentially different paths to personal reorganization, was not entirely clear from the data – and is an issue still. Seeman favoured the former alternative as the main explanation (1949: 166). That clients behaved more distinctively as therapy advanced is not surprising in light of later thinking about the nature of well or optimal functioning (see my Chapter 10). By the end of the project, Seeman was keenly aware that the client categories fitted a concept of therapy as a means to identify and solve problems. They were not attuned to therapy seen as a vehicle for reorientation of the self (167). His sense of this more relevant possibility illustrates the self-transcending nature of the research.[3]

Sheerer (1949), in her 'parallel study' to Seeman's, tested a hypothesis of positive correlation between *self*-acceptance and acceptance of *others*. Her operational definition of these variables remains an interesting feature. Twenty attributes and signs of self-acceptance are distinguished, and acceptance of others is similarly differentiated (1949: 170–171). A rating scale, anchored point by point, was developed for each acceptance variable; and applied to all fifty-nine interview protocols. Ratings spanned the full range on each measure (1949: Table 1). The correlation (r = .51) between the fifty-nine pairs of means was highly significant. When alternatively plotted for each decile of therapy, the variables clearly followed a similar, upward-inclining curve. The author's main conclusion is simple: 'the individual's evaluation of others – the degree of acceptance and respect he feels for them – is significantly related to his attitude toward himself' (175).

Stock (1949) examined feelings toward the self and various categories of others; rating these feelings in steps from strongly positive to strongly negative. She, too, averaged the obtained ratings for each interview. Generally her finding was of modest positive association between rated self-attitude and feeling toward others. A study by Haigh (1949) focused on 'defensive behaviour'. Conceptually his work was rooted in the theory of defence then recently developed, and published later, by Richard Hogan (1952). Defence in this view pivots on perceptual distortion such that the individual avoids contradiction between the meaning of fresh experience and prior conceptions. Haigh searched through all the interview protocols to locate statements embodying contradictions which the individual dealt with by avoidance, denial or other perceptual distortion. Such defence was expected to diminish over therapy, and a modest decline did occur. However, in at least two of the ten cases the overall trend was reversed; and in one case no contradiction data were discerned. The sample clearly was not homogeneous, one subgroup having markedly diminishing instances of defence, and another moderately increasing instances (Haigh, 1949: 184–186). It seemed that some clients either did not 'progress', or new conflicts surfaced. It was also possible that the method did not discern some important kinds of defensive-avoidant response. In all, more questions were raised than answered.

---

3 Raimy's research (1943, 1948) on 'self-reference in counselling interviews' had finally been published, and Rogers' own articulation of his 'self-theory' of personality, in *Client-Centered Therapy*, would at least have been incubating by 1949. Raimy's contribution was both theoretical and empirical. For the latter, he used complete session data (median = seven interviews) for fourteen clients in successful and unsuccessful subgroups. All self-referential statements were classified by judges. His main categories were positive self-reference (PSR), negative self-reference (NSR), and ambivalent SR (where PSR *and* NSR both applied). At the start of therapy, clients generally expressed self-disapproving and ambivalent attitudes, the latter at first increasing. By the end of therapy 'the *successful* cases showed a vast predominance of self-approval; the *unsuccessful* cases showed a predominance of self-disapproval and ambivalence' (1948: 161).

In counterpoint to Haigh, Hoffman (1949) centred on maturity of behaviour (past, present or planned) as reflected in client statements. All pertinent self-behaviour references were sorted into one of three categories of 'maturity'. Least mature were behaviours implying relative absence of control over self or environment and/or little sense of responsibility; most mature were those considered to reflect substantial 'self-direction, maturity, and responsibility' (ibid.: 192). The rated maturity levels increased, from the first to final third of therapy (chance prob. = .07). The clients were then sorted into the five 'more successful' and five 'less successful' cases, based on data reported by Raskin (1949a: 213, Table 5). Both groups started at similar level, the less successful group remaining on that level. The more successful group rose in marked and significant degree, in rated maturity (Hoffman, 1949: 194).

The final contribution to the journal issue is Raskin's (1949a) unifying overview of the evidence. The interview mean scores for five measures – positiveness of self-attitude (Stock), self-acceptance (Sheerer), insight (Seeman), maturity of behaviour (Hoffman), and defensiveness (Haigh) – are tabulated, graphed (1949a: Table 2 and Figure 1), and correlated across the sample of interviews (Table 3). The analysis brings out both the interrelated overall movement through therapy and the distinctive patterning for individual clients. For the sample of ten the self-attitude and self-acceptance measures were very strongly correlated, and there was a much weaker inverse link between positive measures and defensiveness. Raskin's total account builds to an emphasis on achievements of the project and mention of questions left open.

The parallel studies research was extremely labour-intensive, uncomplicated in design, and painstaking in execution. The investigators must have become intimately acquainted with their data, both in raw form and at each step in its hands-on analysis. The cases ran for only six interviews, on average, this brevity helping to make the intensive analysis of all interviews possible. The brevity also would have placed limits on client change. Therapists followed a distinctive, disciplined and highly predictable pattern of verbal response. It seems clear that the clients' interview discourse followed a more individual path, especially for those considered to have profited most from the therapy. No body of developed theory guided the research. Its method centred on systematic naturalistic observation and (fittingly) contributed to theory generation, not its testing.[4]

A more theory-based doctoral study conducted in 1957–1958, on 'movement from non-self to self' in client-centred therapy, is effectively a sequel to

4 Looking back, it is interesting to note that the terminology investigators used often reflects prior mind sets that the approach was working to transcend. Haigh speaks freely of 'defensive' behaviour, and sometimes of 'defensiveness', as discriminated largely from an external frame of reference. Hoffman (1949: 192) approaches maturity in terms of whether 'the individual is behaving with little or no control over himself or his environment', or whether he 'is exercising some control', or, behaving with substantial 'self-direction' and 'responsibility'. Language and attitudes were (and are) framed by a larger context than the innovations in focus.

the parallel studies research, and connects with the next focus on outcome.[5] The 'private inner self' was distinguished from the 'interpersonal self', leaving other client statements as 'nonself' (Braaten, 1961b). Each expression unit was also identified as to the time it referred to: phases in the person's past lifetime, the immediate or non-immediate present, and the perceived future. 'Here-and-now' communications typified the immediate present; and a client's 'non-immediate' present was located outside the therapy hour or immediate process. Braaten studied fifty-six interviews, from fourteen clients. The therapy was much longer than in the early research; up to sixty-four interviews. The interviews were taken two each from the first and the last quarter of the series, for each client.

Three distinct indices of change from non-interview data were used as criterion outcome measures. In a word, these indices (detailed in the next section of this chapter) were (i) pre- to post-therapy change in congruence between the selfpicture and ideal self (Butler and Haigh, 1954), (ii) pre- to post-shift in adjustment ratings, from TAT data, and (iii) a success index from therapist ratings. Correlation analysis showed that therapists tended to see their clients as successful when they increasingly dealt with self issues (private *plus* interpersonal) as against non-self matters, expressed themselves with immediacy of feeling, or explored self in relationship to the therapist – a subcategory of the interpersonal self (Braaten, 1961b: 22).[6] TAT adjustment change also tied in with increase in immediacy and relatively greater focus on the private self. Increase in self–ideal correlation was modestly related to greater emphasis on self issues. All in all, results were in fair accord with a hypothesis that increasing attention to the self-in-action contributed to progress in therapy.

The measures of change that Braaten used played a significant role during the shift in research emphasis from tracking the inner course of therapy to seriously addressing the question of outcome, using evidence external to the interview process. The interview-centred research had given support and refinement to the view that the therapy process was *a* phenomenon with its own order. As a known entity, this process could be meaningfully viewed and studied as a potential agent of personal change. The focus on outcome came to a head in the early 1950s, assisted also by the further development of self-theory, and building to a whole new area of research.

---

5 Vargas' (1954) study is an even closer sequel to the 'parallel studies', as well as interlocking with the phase of work that followed these. He, too, investigated change from non-self to self-description in interviews. Beyond this, he looked at the extent of re-cycling of self-perceptions as against 'change from description of familiar aspects of self to description of previously unknown aspects of self (increase in emergents)' (1954: 147). A striking result was that increase in proportion of emergents was highly correlated with counsellor ratings of integration and overall outcome.

6 Gendlin, Jenney and Shlien's (1960) study (conducted in the mid-1950s) had also implied that the extent of client use of the therapeutic relationship *as a source of new experience* influenced counsellor-rated success of therapy.

The study of the changing self: effects of adult therapy

Already, in the forties, projective tests had been used in a handful of studies of client-centred therapy outcome. Most of these (Carr, 1949; Jonietz, 1950; Muench, 1947; and Reader, 1948) employed the Rorschach, administered pre- and post-therapy. Muench had found very significant positive changes on adjustment indicators. Carr worked to replicate and extend this work, using a somewhat different scoring system and qualitative global evaluation, but found only a slight non-significant upward trend (1949: 202). Reader's further study used modified indicators and a much larger sample, and found modest but significant pre- to post-therapy change (see Carr, 1949: 205; Haimowitz and Haimowitz, 1952). Given the complexity of Rorschach analysis, the less than clear-cut results, and the move to more theory-guided research, different measures were chosen and developed in subsequent work. The major classical example of this outcome research is reported in the volume *Psychotherapy and Personality Change* (Rogers and Dymond, 1954).[7]

Spotlight on outcome – a 'volume' of studies

One innovative feature of this overall project was in its serious attempt to introduce experimental controls where this is practically and ethically difficult.[8] Three approaches to control were used. One approach was to test and retest, in the same way as clients, a group who were not in therapy. This control sample was intended to match clients, one-for-one, by sex, age, student/non-student status, and socioeconomic level. However, attrition of initial participants led to the modified goal of achieving equivalence by groups. The key aspect of motivation for change was targeted in a separate feature of the control design. About half of the clients were asked to wait two months to begin therapy, and tested before and after this wait period, thus serving as their own controls. The third feature was the familiar one of testing both at the end of 'treatment' and after a significant follow-up interval – six to twelve months, in this case (Grummon, 1954: 38–48).

The experimental sample consisted in total of twenty-nine clients, eighteen men and eleven women, 21 to 40 years old (1954: Table 1). Their (twelve) therapists varied widely in experience but did not include novice trainees. Most incoming clients were invited to take part in the research, while the

---

7 Before this outcome project, but after the Parallel Studies, Seeman and Raskin (1953) published their searching and comprehensive examination of client-centred therapy research to that stage (*c*. 1951). Their report, including a forward-reaching exploration of paths and priorities for further empirical study, escaped my attention while actually writing this chapter.

8 Wherever research 'subjects' are recruited from persons in need and seeking help, investigators who themselves are helpers face a potential collision of priorities: They/we *want* to ease the individual's burden and assist to our best ability and knowledge, in accord with their need. But we thirst also to test our 'knowledge', to know more ourselves and advance the sum of knowledge. Client-centred investigators are very accustomed to wrestling with such conflict and, where reconciliation eludes us, acting on individual client interests.

sample built up. About half of them agreed, undeterred by the plan for repeated testing, regular recording of interviews, and a possible two-month delay (ibid.: 41–43). Six interviews was set as the minimum time in therapy to confirm inclusion in the final experimental group. Losses from the potential sample mainly resulted from early attrition or (less often) failure to take part in post-therapy testing. Each stage of testing required two sessions of about three hours (50–51), and complete data required three or four such stages – up to 24 hours in total! Some of the participating clients must have spent as much time in testing as in therapy consultations!

The actual test and rating data, and derived criterion measures, also broke new ground, especially in the area of self-concept measurement. Systematic pictures both of the perceived actual self and of the ideal or most wanted self were obtained from each participant at each testing. One hundred brief, self-descriptive statements initially culled from therapy protocols, and refined for clarity and distinctiveness, had been made up on separate cards. Each subject sorted the cards into a pre-set normal distribution, with just one or two cards at the extremes of 'most like me' and 'most unlike me'.[9] In the case of the 'ideal sort' the instruction was 'Now sort these cards to describe your ideal person – the person you would most like within yourself to be' (Butler and Haigh, 1954: 57). The sorting task and method (known as Q-technique) amounted to a modified ranking of statements, with many ties allowed for, especially in self-aspects that the respondent felt less strongly about. The process of repeatedly selecting out items from pairs and larger groups, for higher or lower ranking, ensured multiple comparisons.[10]

Butler and Haigh (1954: 58) took it that discrepancy between the self-concept and wanted/ideal self implies self-dissatisfaction, this is an important motivating factor in seeking help. In the increasingly open exploration of therapy, the balance shifts toward self being discovered through experience and away from the self concept being so much the arbiter and determinant of experience. In becoming more experientially rooted, concepts of self and ideal self acquire more common ground. In a word, 'Q-sort' pictures of these two

---

9 I well remember administering this Q-sort to research clients, with use of a large board marked in columns of varied height. The board was set up sloping slightly back from vertical, and had shallow horizontal shelves across the columns, on which to mount the cards so that they all remained visible next to each other. As more cards were placed on the board repositioning would become necessary, to maintain the right subjective order from 'most like me' to 'least like me' *and* maintain the number pre-set for each column. Of course, I tried the procedure out for myself. If the reader can picture a person arranging and facing such an array of highly personal statements about his/her self, it becomes understandable that the task was deeply engaging and contained real elements of self-confrontation. Plausibly, in these and other 'data-gathering' contexts clients often experienced issues that fed back into their therapy. I would go further: for a proportion of clients, I believe the testing was a potent adjunct to their interview therapy.

10 Butler and Haigh briefly note (1954: 57) that their method was tested first in unpublished research, notably including the dissertation study by Margaret Hartley (1951). William Stephenson, then at Chicago, had recently published his book (1953) centred on Q-technique. His much later, short account (Stephenson, 1980) is a digestible and refreshing illustration of his thinking and method (an account which I first saw as a reviewer, when it was submitted for publication).

concepts should tend to converge through therapy. In the methodology used, this would be shown by increase in correlation between the pairs of sorts. Although the self-concept might be expected to shift most, where the self-ideal was heavily based on introjected values it would tend to be revised as well (ibid.: 59).

In the total experimental sample (N=25, for these data), at each test point, there was wide variation between clients in self–ideal correlation. The mean correlations, however, rose distinctly (from .01 to .34), remaining significant at follow-up (.31). Although starting from such different positions (–.47 to +.59), nearly all clients (22/25) increased in their self–ideal correlation pre- to post-therapy. The picture was completely different for the control subjects who had completed the testing. Their self–ideal correlations were much higher to start with (range –.01 to .86; mean .58), and almost identical at follow-up. For the fifteen clients who additionally served as their own controls, the mean self–ideal correlation was .01, both at pre-wait and pre-therapy testing (1954: 69). The passage of time and motivation for therapy did *not* produce change. (One might speculate that both within client and control samples there was wide variation in the amount of dissonance within the self that participants were able to confront, acknowledge and live with.)

Another investigator (Dymond, 1954a) used the self-concept data quite differently. She favoured a constant standard in measuring 'adjustment' levels. The self–ideal correlation as an index rests on a vision of a desirable way to be, set by the individual client. Dymond devised and substituted a single criterion. Through a two-stage process, expert judges selected 37 of the 100 statements deemed indicative of positive adjustment *when identified as 'like me'*, and 37 others having positive significance when 'unlike me'. In scoring a self-sort, items placed in the big central pile were ignored, and the remainder collapsed into two broad groups, 'like me' and 'unlike me'. The theoretical scoring range was 74, in case of a perfect match with Dymond's criterion arrangement, to zero (no matching placements) (1954a: 78–79).[11] Her results were straightforward. Q adjustment mean level did not change during the wait period; for the whole client group it increased significantly from pre- to post-therapy, and pre- to follow-up; and there was virtually no movement in the control group (80). Before therapy, clients scored significantly lower than controls; after therapy and at follow-up, the difference was insignificant.

A still further study used the self-concept data, but with addition of a third sorting to describe 'the ordinary person' – the way the respondent feels people

---

11 Illustrative items that score when placed on the 'unlike me' side are: 'I put on a false front'; 'I often feel humiliated'; 'I feel helpless'; 'I shrink from facing a crisis or difficulty'; 'I am afraid of sex'; and 'I feel insecure within myself'. Items which score when positioned as 'like me' include: 'I am responsible for my troubles'; 'I usually like people'; 'My hardest battles are with myself'; 'I can usually make up my mind and stick to it'; and, 'I understand myself' (ibid., Table 1). Rudikoff suggests an alternative method of scoring, one in which all of the 74 items would carry weight wherever positioned. Each item placed opposite to the criterion arrangement would not merely fail to score but would count negatively (1954: 93, footnote 4).

generally are. It was reasoned that big discrepancies between a person's view of self, the ordinary person and self-ideal would imply 'psychological discomfort and pain' (Rudikoff, 1954: 86). The investigator confined her attention to the eight wait group clients with full data at all test points. (Before therapy, their three constructs were in fact sharply divergent.) It was predicted, and found, that the self-concept shifted more during therapy itself than over the waiting period, and more than either of the other constructs did. Rudikoff also expected and found a significant narrowing of the gap between self and ideal *and* between self and ordinary person, over the actual therapy period (88–90). Use of Dymond's Q adjustment scale gave similar results. Interestingly, the perceived ordinary person also increased in adjustment, in this sample. Some items moved in step, for example, *both* self and ordinary person came to be seen as more self-understanding and more responsible (94–95). As for Q adjustment scores from *ideal* self data, the mean change was small, but directions of shift in item positioning suggested 'that the desire toward perfection was lessened' over therapy (96).

The self-concept/Q-sort focus had, of course, particular connection with self theory. Four other distinct kinds of data (the TAT, social attitude and emotional maturity scales, and counsellor ratings), originating largely in other theoretical perspectives, generated further outcome measures.[12] Two investigators made quite different analyses of the TAT data, one (Dymond, 1954b) using an uncomplicated eclectic approach, and the other a complex rating scheme based on psychoanalytic theory (Grummon and John, 1954). Both usages were adapted for this research. Dymond asked her raters to pay attention to 'the ability of the hero to solve his own problems versus dependence on others or on magical forces to do this'; to consider the aspect of 'well-developed fantasy and well-structured stories versus inability to form a story . . .'; and to discern 'the degree of comfort versus disturbance of the heroes, and the appropriateness of these states to the situational context'. These and other indicators yielded a single adjustment measure from each TAT protocol, on a scale ranging from 'severe disturbance bordering on psychotic' to 'well-integrated . . . socially effective' functioning (1954b: 110–111).

Grummon and John's (1954) more elaborate scheme involved numerous primary rating scales concerned with relationships, attitudes and dynamic personality variables (such as defence mode and energy level). Each aspect was seen as providing a distinctive window to the person's underlying level of psychosexual development. Two global indices were used, one an overall diagnostic rating, the other a rating of life-adjustment (1954: 123–127). Main findings were that the direction of change for clients was positive (chance prob. < 5 per cent), on a majority of the scales. Control subjects showed limited or no positive changes (132–133).[13] For clients, movement also

12 The reader desiring a fuller picture of this interesting work than I can give here should still find the ground-breaking Rogers and Dymond (1954) volume in a good research library.

13 In this study, as in Dymond's, TAT protocols were coded so that raters were left blind as to whether any given protocol was from a client or control, or from before or after therapy.

occurred on the diagnostic impression scale. Given the 'foreign' theoretical perspective involved, it is interesting that the evidence of positive outcome is about as strong as in Dymond's data.

Dymond found that her mean TAT adjustment rating increased significantly, staying at this level through follow-up (1954b: 114). Nevertheless, a good many clients did not change on the rather coarse seven-point scale, and a subsequent controlled comparison and re-rating of tied protocols was done. With original ratings amended by addition of a plus or minus sign, 20/25 of the client subjects, and 4/10 controls changed in a positive direction, pre- to post-therapy (111 and 115). Better than chance association between rated TAT adjustment and self–ideal correlation, was also discerned (115–117). Grummon and John (1954: 142) did not find an association between their scales and other measures of therapeutic change, except where TAT data were the common source of such indices. (It is beginning to seem as if different types of data may catch different aspects of change.)

Seeman (1954) focused on end-of-therapy counsellor ratings (on nine-point scales). These included dual estimations (i) of the client's functioning at the start of therapy, viewed retrospectively, and (ii) of how he/she functioned at the conclusion; the difference being an index of movement. Personal integration and life adjustment were among the applicable scales. As well, the counsellor estimated *client* satisfaction with the outcome of therapy and, finally, rated the overall success of therapy (1954: Table 1). The correlations of success rating with the other indices were .89 (integration), .74 (life adjustment) and .73 (client satisfaction). These results, and the movement scores, were all strongly significant (ibid.: 102). Women clients received higher success ratings (mean 6.7/9) than men (mean 5.0); and longer cases (20+ interviews) were more consistently rated as successful than shorter ones (ibid.: 105). That therapists have a great deal of data on which to base such judgements can scarcely be a matter of question. The problem lies in using this information objectively, in view of a nexus between client gain and implied therapist effectiveness, and scope for variation in what is being assessed under the broad language of the scales. None the less, the success ratings gave one vital measure of outcome.

Gordon and Cartwright (1954) carried the study of outcome to another level, effectively opening out the notion of acceptance into that of being democratic in outlook. The negative extreme included authoritarian attitudes, intolerance of difference, ethnocentrism, and desire to reform and direct the lives of others. Pertinent measures were borrowed, adapted, and combined into a total self–other (S–O) scale on which high scores represent an intolerant antidemocratic orientation and *low scores are positive* (1954: 171–174). Clients and controls started out with similar mean scores, and the slight change for clients overall did not distinguish them from the controls. However, when sorted into success and failure groups, on the basis of a composite criterion, mean scores dropped (positively) for successful clients and rose for unsuccessful ones (chance probability .10: Table 8). Further analyses suggested that clients whose therapy is most productive move away from a pattern of answers implying either totally democratic attitudes or distinctly antidemocratic ones. Perhaps there is an inflexibility and denial of experience in both extremes of self-depiction (194–195).

Tougas singled out the ethnocentrism component (see E-Scale of Adorno et al., 1950) already reported as predictive of improvement versus unimprovement in Sullivanian therapy (Barron, 1950; Tougas, 1954: 200–201). Using a two-way division of the Chicago client group, from success ratings, Tougas replicated Barron's result. In both studies, improved clients clustered in the lower scoring range, and those considered unimproved mostly scored above the mean on ethnocentrism.[14] Further analysis involving a three-way breakdown of clients suggested that the most propitious E-score is close to the Chicago mean of 45, *not* in the lowest part of the range (1954: 205–207). Very low scorers appear to be highly idiosyncratic in perception, socially isolated and with impaired ability in relating. It seems they rely heavily on introjected guidelines, and their anxieties pivot around their view of self. *High* scorers tend to 'project' good–bad qualities onto others and their anxieties consciously revolve around externals. It seems understandable that persons in either group would have difficulty in psychotherapy (209–212).

Rogers' direct contribution to the outcome research

The remaining study of sample outcomes is reported by Rogers himself (1954a). His perspective here is fairly traditional: becoming more mature means behaving less defensively, in more socialized ways, and with more acceptance of others and of internal reality. An instrument familiar from Rogers' past, the Willoughby (1931) Emotional Maturity (E-M) Scale, was chosen.[15] The 69 (judge-validated) items each carried a maturity value ranging from 1 (for example, 'Subject characteristically appeals for help in the solution of his problems') to 9 ('S welcomes legitimate opportunities for sexual expression; is not ashamed, fearful, or preoccupied with the topic'). At each test point, the Scale was to be answered both by the client *and* by two nominated observer-friends. Friend data did not yield any significant increase in mean scores over the period of therapy, or therapy plus follow-up. Other data gave a more differentiated picture. Counsellor success rating correlated strongly ($r = .70$) with movement in observer E-M scores, such movement being positive only for higher success clients (1954a: 228). E-M scores from *client* returns, all in one sample, did increase significantly. Rogers inferred that self-estimated increases for 'unsuccessful' clients were driven by defensive processes, unlike the case with clients appraised as successful (232). This

---

14 Tougas (1954: 201) used E-Scale scores from each client's first test point, literally to predict success. He also mentions (1954: 197, 203) Pearl's (1950) finding that high-scoring hospitalized clients (E-Scale mean 74.4) had showed little improvement in therapy.

15 Rogers cites Willoughby's (1931) definition as 'fitting well' with the behaviour changes he considered important: 'Emotional maturity is freedom from narcissism and ambivalence; in other terminology it is release from egocentrism, the achievement of socialized impulses, of insight.' It also implies 'emotional acceptance of the reality principle' (in Rogers, 1954a: 216). The thought here clearly predates, for example, Rogers' concept of the fully-functioning person.

inference places the problem under another heading, *but no longer satisfies as an explanation.* (Contributors to the Rogers and Dymond volume use the inherited language of 'defence' unselfconsciously and often.)

Rogers' other direct contributions are highly original, and extensive. In the form of two separate studies of individual cases, they occupy a full third of the volume. One client was considered distinctly successful (Rogers, 1954b) and the other is designated a 'failure case' although including productive elements (Rogers, 1954c). The reports are daunting to read all the way through but this scarcely accounts for their limited visibility within Rogers' work. More salient is the fact that they are single case empirical research studies, drawing on a great quantity of data and conducted before such work came into vogue. Extensive illustration from the transcribed interviews is included but in a role secondary to data external to the therapy process. (In one case, interview excerpts only come into view after fifty pages of other information, analysis and interpretive discussion!) Rogers was finding his way in terms of method and his pioneering is impressive, not a literal model for future work but with features of enduring interest.

I will centre on the case of 'Mrs Oak', who was the first client in the research block to finish therapy and all of the testing. Indeed, additional data were collected, including an extra Q-sort after therapy (for the way the client *remembered herself*, pre-therapy) and also sorts by the therapist picturing the way he thought the client would perceive herself, her self-ideal, and the ordinary person. As the therapist, Rogers said of Mrs Oak, 'not one client in fifty has taught me so much' (1954b: 265). His ratings given post-therapy on Seeman's scales are highly positive: on client integration, a 3-point shift; on life-adjustment, 4 points; on client satisfaction, a rating of 9; on the outcome of therapy, success at the 8/9 level (266). After an eventful debriefing interview at the end of her follow-up testing, this client sought and received (eight) additional therapy sessions; and most of the test battery was repeated (its fourth administration) as a second and final follow-up

Mrs Oak's four sets of TAT stories suggest marked change over the total course of her therapy (1954b: 267–273). The other primary data source, the Q-sort, was used in all twenty-six times, mostly by the client to describe herself, her ideal, and the ordinary person (at several points) *and* her remembered self. Each sort was correlated with all others, and the big resulting matrix and its shifting pattern over time, are presented in closely studied view (278–287). Results accord with those cited earlier for the more improved group of clients, including marked change in self-perception over therapy, and big increase in self–ideal correlation (from .21 up to .79). Pictures given at the follow-up points, of the self as remembered, were less favourable than the client's earlier-stated view of self, a change attributed to reduced defensiveness after therapy. Expressed exactly, Rogers' view was that 'sortings for the remembered selves approximate a picture of self prior to therapy which includes material which was not at that time in awareness or, if in awareness, was not communicable' (281). (This inventive addition of the remembered self to the data spectrum apparently was never followed up in further reasearch.)

Another original twist was to have an external judge study each TAT record and its analysis, one set at a time and without any other information, and then to sort the Q cards 'to give a picture of the client as she diagnostically was at the time of that TAT' (1954b: 288). The procedure supposes that the judge (R. E. Farson) would have something of an X-ray picture, including elements invisible to the client ('denied to awareness'). Reliabilities of this 'diagnostic sort' were very modest, probably because judges faced a complex discrimination, with items worded literally for *self*-description (288–289). Despite this, correlation of diagnostic sorts with pertinent client sorts yielded interesting results. The 'diagnostic self' changed greatly from pre-therapy to final follow-up ($r = -.33$). Its relation to the client's own ideal for herself also changed from negative before therapy to substantially positive at follow-up (290: Table 6). Overall, the external sorts suggested even more positive change than implied by client perceptions (295).

Therapist Q-sorts convey Rogers' sense of how the client saw herself after seven interviews, and at the end of therapy. His prediction was off target at the first point ($r = .14$), more accurate at the second ($r = .57$). His second sort also anticipated the client's follow-up self-perceptions ($r = .63$, and $r = .66$). Interestingly, the client's self-sorts correlated most strongly with the diagnostic sort made not at the same time but next in sequence, as though her self-picture leapfrogged the visible present to signal the way she was becoming (300). Maturity scores from Willoughby's E-M Scale rose markedly from pre- to post-therapy, with further gains at follow-up. Item answers imply that the client became 'less defensive and better organized . . . less dependent, less inclined to blame others, . . . less ambivalent and conflicted'. Positive changes included 'more acceptance of her capacities and limitations, more basically democratic behaviour, and less conflict and inhibition in the sexual area' (304). The S–O Attitude Scale also revealed marked shifts toward more democratic attitudes and diminished ethnocentrism. Rogers notes that issues tapped by this scale were not discussed in therapy, suggesting that changes in the client's value system were generalizing well beyond the immediate scope of her therapy.

Probabilities were not formally tested in this single case study, leaving a distinct possibility that some shifts were idiosyncratic or adventitious. Rogers counters this limitation by laying out eleven hypotheses, all supported, and arguing that a coincident pattern of expected results would not plausibly occur by chance (308–310). The logic is not flawless: the variables are not all independent and some circularity of argument is discernible. However, the study gives prima facie evidence for a very rich spectrum of possibilities which, overall, do not seem peculiar to the client. This spectrum is enriched by the ensuing, close qualitative examination of process and change illustrated generously from the 48-interview course of the therapy. One overall impression (not caught in Rogers' comments) from rereading this transcript material is that communicating her experience in words remained a struggle for this client, with continued trial and error through most of her therapy. The therapist, on the other hand, is highly skilled and always resourceful in this realm. At the end of therapy, especially in the last three or four reported excerpts, there is a new fluency in the client's expressions. It is as though she has reclaimed part of her human inheritance: a confident capacity to embody and communicate her felt experience and meaning in spoken language.

Rogers himself cautions, finally, against easy generalization, noting that 'the . . . statement which can be made is that these changes did occur in one client and, consequently, *may* occur in other individuals undergoing client-centred therapy', and that 'the effective agent of change appears to be the therapeutic interviews' (1954b: 344–345). Writing his report in or about 1952 (preceding Gendlin's earliest work), he advances the proposition 'that "experiencing" – the complete *awareness* of the *total* organismic response to a situation – is concomitant with, or basic to, the process of therapy' (345). By way of firmest conclusion, a long summary list is given of outcome effects for the particular client. The last is most encompassing: 'In every type of measurement obtained there is change . . . in the direction of a more realistic, more comfortable, more confident, more unified, less defensive adjustment' (346–347). This study is perhaps Rogers' most ambitious personal report of research. It is an illuminating view not only through what is revealed by the singularly close-up study, but of the author's talents and style as an investigator.[16]

The 'change project' – a sequel on measurement

An ambitious further program of research on therapy outcome, referred to as the 'change project', followed not long after the 1954 report. New data were gathered from a large sample representing the client population of the University of Chicago Counseling Center in the late fifties (Cartwright, Kirtner and Fiske, 1963: 169). In some ways the planning of this study was meticulous, although there was no control group, and follow-up data were gathered but little used. Ninety-three therapy clients participated. Instruments from previous research, the Minnesota Multiphasic Personality Inventory (MMPI) and a sentence-completion test, and (most important) a brand new set of fourteen 'behavioural adequacy' (BA) rating scales, were used. The BA scales were rated from three perspectives: those of the person in therapy, the client's therapist, and a diagnostician who had studied the client's TAT protocol. Thus, 3 × 14, or 42, change measures were generated by use of these scales. The remaining sources yielded another 42 measures (1963: Table 3). Change scores were literally the net movement from pre-therapy to post-therapy.

---

16 I hope the sketch of this unique study does carry my feeling of it being a neglected resource, and that some readers will be drawn either to go to the original or to its companion piece 'The case of Mr Bebb' – a therapy 'failure'. In the fifties, it was characteristic of Rogers to acknowledge lack of success. Later, it seemed more difficult for him to confront equivocal outcomes, as in the case of some of his initiatives in education, in the large group sphere, and in peace workshops. Innovation inevitably involves trial and error, not success every time. Rogers' 'failures' were rarely trivial, and I believe their lessons remain valuable for others of us open to them.

The BA scales spanned aspects of self functioning, relationships with others, and other emotional-behavioural tendencies suggested by previous research (1963: 166 and Table 3). Five anchor positions were formulated for each scale. As illustration, one scale was concerned with 'contentedness in relationships with others'. At the bottom level:

> The person feels extremely uncomfortable with others, feels that relationships with others are strained, never flow easily and relaxedly, are devastating to a sense of contentment. . . . Being around others, . . . dealing and communicating with them . . . are a continuing and very great strain upon him. . . . 'I feel awful around people'. 'I just feel completely nervous in social gatherings.' . . . 'People are so difficult to get along with, just impossible.'

At the other end of the scale – 'In general, his experience of interaction is of a smooth interpersonal flow – an experience of comfort and satisfaction. . . . The person is calm around others . . . [and] dissatisfactions are transient experiences. . .' (166). Since these are excerpts only, from just two anchor points on one scale, the proportions of the instrument made it formidable to read through and answer the first time!

Research interest centred on measurement issues, not on further demonstration of the efficacy of the therapy. The sample size and a big 84 × 84 correlation matrix invited factor analysis, from which five orthogonal factors were discriminated. First was a factor arising from the client's view of his/her own functioning, which amounted to favourable change in self-concept (1963: 170–171). (This had high loadings on several of the MMPI scales, on selected BA scales from client ratings, and on the Q adjustment score.) The total domain of client self-perception and appraisal was not represented in this factor, only those aspects that tended to move closely in step with each other and (after rotation) not in step with other factors. A second change factor rested entirely on the BA scale ratings made by diagnosticians. This factor arose from the singular evidence of TAT protocols interpreted by the same judges. A third factor clustered BA scales as rated by the therapists for their own clients. The fourth factor picked up much of the change variance in other MMPI scales, and the fifth factor loaded only on length of therapy.

The results underlined the influence of 'method factors' in research on outcome, as expected by the investigators. No account, however, was taken of the method of factor-analysis as an influence on the resulting picture. This method sorts out variables that hang together, in a linear correlational sense, in separated clusters. It works on a kind of metric we–they principle, sorting correlational bedfellows that can be set apart from other groups. (Scales that persistently align with more than one camp may lose a place altogether.) Viewed after the event, it is hardly surprising that clients, therapists, and external judge-diagnosticians – each group in a quite different experiential position – would generate distinctive views of change. The fact that measures from the same distinct sources or data types did not line up completely is interesting. For example, standard MMPI scales loaded on two different factors; and only about half of the change measures from client self-estimations loaded substantially on a common factor. The project overall was a large, ambitious and sophisticated investment, but with modest pay-off. The authors' absorption with measurement issues and questions is total, and they draw no explicit conclusions regarding the therapy's impact. A companion report on the project (Fiske, Cartwright and Kirtner, 1964) is similarly both impressive and bounded.

This further report focuses on *prediction* of change. It grew in part from Kirtner's earlier dissertation research (see Kirtner and Cartwright, 1958). In that study, five differing configurations were found in client initial behaviour in therapy. Named V, W, X, Y, and Z, they fell on an implied spectrum. Clients classed as Type V assumed responsibility for their difficulties and focused from the start on self-feelings and behaviours they wanted to change. In contrast, Type Z saw their difficulties as almost entirely external, tended to focus on these externals, and experienced little self-responsibility or agency in regard to life problems (1958: 329–330). Success cases (therapist rated) in the sample studied were mainly V and W types, while failures fell mostly in the Y and Z categories (ibid.: Table 1). The Fiske et al. report draws on the previous data, augmented by an additional layer of BA scale measures and further test results. The factors obtained before were further purified (each factor now created from a maximum of three original scales) and the data treated to obtain both pre-therapy scores and change scores *for each factor*. The pre-therapy scores, and certain added indices, were used predictively (Fiske et al., 1964: 420).

With scattered exceptions, the various 'predictive' indices failed to predict the change measures (1964: Tables 1 and 2). The authors reluctantly conclude that 'the overall pattern of our results is distinctly unpromising' (423) and, at the very end, reach briefly beyond their previous orbit. 'Where else', they ask, 'should one look for predictors? The belief structures or expectancies of the client regarding therapy? The specific dyadic relationships between each therapist and his client? Untapped dimensions of therapist behaviour?' (425). In reconsidering this ambitious work, and its disappearance from view, I am led to speculation, too. Had a study of similar data span and sample grown out of a search to test a theoretical vision of ways that personality changes in therapy, I think the impetus to further work probably would have been much greater. If measurement issues still had come into strong relief, this would have been incidental to a larger search. It happens that another study began in the same setting and time frame as the change project, also concerned with effects of therapy but otherwise with very different interest.

Researching the effects of time limits

The further project, by Shlien and collaborators, focused on therapy of pre-arranged duration. Philosophically, the work was inspired by Jessie Taft's writing. For Taft, a time frame encloses all human activity but does not govern it qualitatively, as notably the case in therapy (pp. 124–125 above). When a person learns to live and work in freedom within the boundary of a therapy hour 'he has in his grasp the secret of all hours' (Taft, 1933 : 17). The study had another underlying concern: the issue of best utilization of scarce resources. The initially brief Rogerian therapy had been growing steadily longer. Perhaps, with a limit on number of interviews, the productivity of each one would be enhanced. By reducing reliance on other hours, *this* hour might be more intensely approached and energetically used. The study relied primarily on a modified (eighty-item) self (S) and ideal (I) Q-sort, to measure change. There were two groups of clients, each limited to twenty interviews, one set in client-centred therapy, and the other working with Adlerian therapists. Test data were gathered pre-therapy, after seven interviews, at the end of therapy, and at a follow-up point. Comparable data were available for Counseling Center clients who were not time-limited (mean of thirty-seven interviews). By the first journal report of the research (Shlien, Mosak and Dreikers, 1962), it was clear that self–ideal correlations rose at least as much – and more quickly – in both experimental groups as they did in the unlimited group, and that increases were sustained in all three groups.[17]

In a later report (Shlien, 1965), comparison was also made with a 'high success' component of the unlimited sample, who stayed in therapy longer than average, scored 6 or above on the 1 to 9 scale of therapist-rated success, and were judged 'improved' from their TATs. Their S–I change only marginally exceeded that of time-limited participants, and took more than twice as long. To infer, however, that time-limited therapy is 'twice as efficient as unlimited therapy' (1965: 121) seems inconsistent with another part of the author's own reasoning. The S–I correlation presumably reflects the individual's ease and satisfaction with self, versus conflictual unhappiness and pain. Shlien's evidence suggests that clients become more quickly satisfied with their functioning when therapy is time-limited. He is at pains to point out, however, that the similar S–I correlations for clients in the two different therapies constitute a broad convergence abstracted from varying individual arrays of data. Change may not be qualitatively the same in client-centred and Adlerian therapy – or, by the same token, in the time-limited and unlimited groups. In fact, an interesting case is made for expecting change criteria at differing levels of abstraction to yield different results (1965: 123–125). Thus, the similar S–I correlations under the two time arrangements might well have masked significant differences in change features viewed in their specifics. At the least abstract level, each client's change would be idiosyncratic. Shlien's perspective also can further inform the meaning of Cartwright et al.'s results, where the clustering and separation of measures probably grew, in part, from similarity and difference in level of abstraction.

Neither Shlien nor Cartwright was closely involved in the major project, by Rogers, Gendlin and colleagues (1967), on the process of psychotherapy with schizophrenic clients, planned in Wisconsin while their own studies were still being completed. Effectiveness of the therapy was an issue in this research, but not its primary focus. By that time, new formulations by Rogers had led to a recentring of research interest on the conditions of therapy and on

---

17 The same and additional results, and a wider exploration of issues, appear in Shlien's longer individual report the same year (1962).

qualities of client process within therapy. These further phases in the overall advance of client-centred research are reserved for the next chapter. In the meantime, two other spheres of investigation, each distinct yet having much in common with the research already in view, call for attention.

Research in group and child therapy

Client-centred group and child therapy evolved in the same time frame, both adapted from adult individual therapy. Another conjunction is that play therapy was conducted in groups as well as one-to-one. Research in these areas began in the late forties, and continued through the School Phase. By the mid-sixties, client-centred child therapy research had largely run its course, in settings where Rogers had been influential. Group process research was receding from the clinical arena and beginning around experiential learning/self-development groups. Thus the School Phase is distinctive in both of these areas, and a convenient time frame for this section. (Later work is considered in Chapter 14.) Relative to the child therapy area, research in group therapy was more sustained, and invites greater attention.

Group therapy studies in the School Phase

The research has a clear starting point: a study reported in summary by Hobbs and Pascal (1946) in the first volume of the *American Psychologist*. It compared three group approaches – 'authoritarian', eclectic, and nondirective – via classification of client and counsellor verbal behaviour in the groups. On the heels of this study came another, by Peres (1947), closely modelled in method and category content on the early studies of interview process in individual therapy. The group consisted of graduate students interested in counselling, whose gains were inferred from self-estimation reports after therapy. Some members reported substantial, continuing gain from the group experience; others said they gained little. Transcript analysis revealed a differing balance of verbal behaviours in high versus low benefit subgroups of clients (see Hobbs, 1951: 304). Peres' exploratory study helped to pave the way for the far more ambitious project considered next.

In this team research, reported in book form by Gorlow, Hoch and Telschow (1952), each collaborating investigator carried a main component of the project through to its final writing-up. The group participants, again graduate students but from varied fields at Columbia University, New York, were recruited via campus announcement inviting application. Those applying were first seen in an intake interview to check that they actually desired help over a serious personal difficulty or stress (1952: 21–24). Application largely on the basis of curiosity, or of uncertainty over their educational/vocational path, did not suffice. The seventeen women and men finally selected were placed in three *small* groups, each group led by one of the investigators (ibid.: 24). The leaders viewed themselves as distinctly nondirective, and are warmly cited by Hobbs. The groups ran for about ten weeks, meeting twice-weekly, and generating fifty-seven audio-recorded group sessions in all.

The raw data for the study consisted of some *1,200 pages* of transcript, plus test protocols. The tests, a Rorschach, sentence completion instrument, and a self-rating checklist, were used to validate judgements by the group leader-investigators of initial adjustment and of positive change. The latter was simply a two-way breakdown into those for whom clear gain, or else 'little profit', was discerned. The transcripts were unitized by theme rather than by single utterances, a theme being an episode (undefined in duration) started by a member but involving others reacting to the person or issue. When anyone else took off on a new tack, or became the central focus, this signalled a fresh theme. Three broad kinds of communication were distinguished: 'A member could act as "client", as "therapist", or as "participator in general intellectualization"' (1952: 28). Both client and therapist roles were manifest in a large variety of ways, roughly a score of possible categories being discriminated for each role. Intellectual discussion also embraced a variety of categories: 'comparing experiences', 'proposing [a] course of group action', asking and answering informational questions, etc.[18]

Hoch studied the transcribed sessions of the groups, using the familiar approach of content analysis (Gorlow, Hoch and Telshow, 1952: 37–62). The frequencies of entries in the various category groupings were ranked for the data from each group. The correlations of these rankings for pairs of groups were all in the .80s, providing one evidence of commonality. Similarity of trends over time was another kind of evidence. Among these trends, expressions of negative emotion were low at the start (in contrast to individual therapy), tended to peak in the middle stages (when members would have felt more secure in the groups), and then tapered off in the last two quintiles. In all, the expectation that the groups would share a similar configuration was supported (ibid.: 39–49). The data also implied more inter-member variation within groups than overall variation between groups. As between the 'most-profited' and 'least-profited' subgroups in the overall sample, process comparisons failed to reveal clear-cut differences.

Gorlow's method in studying *the therapist behaviour of members* (ibid.: 63–87) was interesting. The relevant group member responses had been coded in similar fashion to those of official therapists. Categories ranked as most therapeutic, included 'clarification of feeling', 'restatement of content', and 'simple acceptance', whereas 'evaluation' and 'disapproval, criticism' fell at the low, non-therapeutic end of the spectrum. Behaviours of the former kind increased significantly over the lives of the groups; and use of the more negative categories significantly diminished. It seems that members became better therapists during the course of the group experience. But did this pattern apply, alike, to the more and less profited members? Gorlow found

18 The categories were placed in rank order within each group, in terms of their judged therapeutic quality or relevance. Careful attention was given to the aspect of reliability of classification and ranking (1952: 28–32).

that the 'profited' group had a clearly greater preponderance of responses in the positive (therapeutic) categories. Also, when frequencies in the three top-of-the-list categories noted above were charted over time, the contrast was strikingly in favour of profited members (ibid.: 78–79). In all, there was evidence of change over time toward more facilitative member interaction. This direction of change particularly applied to the high gain subgroup of members.[19]

The final component study (ibid.: 88–105) focused on therapist leadership in the groups. The content analysis of leader verbal behaviour confirmed a rigorously nondirective, non-initiating approach in all three cases, each leader responding more than three-quarters of the time with 'simple acceptance', 'restatement of content', or 'clarification of feeling (general)'. About one further response in ten was a more specific type of clarification, for example, of negative (or positive) feeling toward self. Only about 3 per cent of leader responses centred on clarifying *interpersonal* messages or group-wide feelings (ibid.: 89, Table 29). In looking at the amount of client verbal expression 'released' by different therapist responses, *pauses* were included as a distinct response type. Longer client expressions tended to follow pauses than followed active response modes; a result to 'give pause'. But by criteria of *productive* client expression, both clarifications and restatements of content had more positive sequels than pauses did (100–101; and Table 3).

Telschow commented that 'the decidedly restricted range of therapist behaviour' made for less clear-cut results than might accrue from close comparison of more than one therapeutic approach (90–91). As if in response, Ends and Page (1957 and 1959) undertook research which, in its first phase, compared the efficacy of three forms of group psychotherapy with hospitalized alcoholics. Self-concept and other data were gathered from clients in Rogerian and in analytic group therapies, and in a learning theory-based group approach (Mowrer, 1953). From all their results the investigators concluded, unequivocally, that 'the Rogerian group-centered approach possessed the widest applicability and greatest effectiveness' (Ends and Page, 1959: 2). The next research phase replicated some aspects of the first study, within a scope both narrower and deeper. Attention was devoted solely to the group-centred approach, extended from fifteen to thirty contact hours, a control sample provided 'tough' comparison, and the use of Q-sort data in hypotheses-testing is perhaps the most versatile in the classical research literature.[20]

The basic hospital program was active and advanced for its time. It included a considerable array of informational communication, opportunities for individual counselling, and discussion/exploration sessions in groups

19 It seems to me more than possible that the investigators based their estimates of member gain or 'profit' on observed features of behaviour very like those later found to distinguish the high and low gain subgroups. Tempering such likely circularity is the fact that some checks were made on the estimates of gain, using test data (Gorlow, Hoch and Telschow, 1952: 34–36).

20 The 100-item Butler and Haigh instrument, after needed slight amendment, was used throughout. It is reproduced in full in the Ends and Page monograph (1959: 30–31).

(1959: 1–2). The AA approach was emphasized but was not exclusive. The range of activities must have occupied residents for a considerable part of each day. All residents, including the controls, were in intensive treatment from the hospital's standpoint, with group therapy being an add-on. Bed patients, and others with psychotic symptoms or low general aptitude, were excluded from the research. In each batch of people who qualified, half were randomly selected to serve as controls, and the other half *placed* in a therapy group – with quite varied initial motivation. MMPI as well as Q-sort data were gathered from all research participants before and after the six-week treatment period. The *therapy* clients completed additional self and ideal self sorts ten hours and twenty hours into their group experience. The therapy and control samples each totalled twenty-eight persons (ibid.: 3–5).

In addition to the standard self and ideal sorts, a 'criterion sort' was developed by merging the data from five clinician judges who arranged the cards to represent 'the healthiest possible self-concept' (ibid.: 4). For each person, five Q-sorts were available – the pre- and post-self, the pre- and post-ideal, and the criterion sort – these yielding ten pairs for intercorrelation. Eight movement indices were drawn from the resulting correlations: for example, the mean r between post-therapy self and criterion *minus* the corresponding pre-therapy mean; and, the shift in relation of self (tapped before and after therapy) to the post-therapy ideal (ibid.: 7, Table 3: indices 1 and 6). Significant positive movement occurred in seven of the eight indices, in a configuration seen as building to 'a picture of healthy, well-integrated therapeutic growth' (7). The control group showed significantly less movement, shifting modestly in a pattern not implying an integrated 'reorganization process' (8). Movement on several MMPI scales occurred in both groups, peaking for the therapy sample on the paranoia (Pa) scale, and suggesting a 'reduction in suspiciousness, oversensitivity, and feelings of persecution' linked to the group therapy experience (12).

The second issue investigated was whether doubling the number of therapy hours resulted in significantly greater movement. Looking at tabulated results, gains in the earlier 15-session group were more like the new control sample than like the 30-session therapy group (Table 6). All mean *differences* between the 15s and 30s (significant on four indices) favoured the 30s sample. Viewed qualitatively, self–ideal convergence in the 30s group flowed from changes in the self-concept and, in the 15s, was greatly influenced by shifts in portrayal of the ideal self. Further, no significant MMPI changes had occurred in the 15s group (Table 7). Overall, the evidence suggested that therapy had ended prematurely for the 15s, at a point (in self-process and group development) of a readiness for change rather than actual achievement of integrative healing. The final component of the research supported this inference indirectly.

The Ends and Page report deals at length with Q-sort changes tracked across the four test points (18–28). Clinical and research information interweave in depicting the dynamic course of participant experience over treatment. Residents entered the groups at a point of crisis, anxious and needful of reassuring acceptance and belief that they were improving. Their first reaction is summarized as a 'flight into health', lasting approximately two weeks (ten sessions, in the 30s groups). This was followed by 'regression and the initiation of the reintegrative phase in the second two weeks; and the . . . reintegration and consolidation of gain in the final two weeks' (28). The flight into health phenomenon was observed also in the control group, whose 'recovery' involved forming another externally anchored structure working much like the one it replaced (29). As for the 30s group, it seems possible, even likely, that features of the regime within which the group therapy was applied served to augment its impact and effectiveness.[21] In interesting relation to Shlien's work, the authors speak of the advantage of time limits in helping to produce 'maximum gain for the patient' (29). A set time frame is often a feature of group work, and was applied also in the intriguing study, by Berzon, Pious and Farson (1963).

Berzon et al. examined the 'therapeutic event in group psychotherapy', from written responses by members of two client-centred groups. At the end of each meeting, each member described the event that 'contributed most to you personally'. Respondents were asked to note which group members were involved in the incident, what was said, and what behaviours occurred (1963: 205). Over the life of the groups some 280 satisfactory event-reports were garnered, grouped in the three clusters of cognitive elements, affective-feeling processes, or overt behavioural expressions. 'Cognitive' events included recognition of an important similarity to others (C1), gaining new/expanded awareness of one's own emotional pattern (C2), 'witnessing honesty, courage, openness, or . . . emotionality in others' (C3), or, seeing self as seen by others (C4). The affective area embraced felt experiences of caring/understanding by other members (A1), experiencing such response toward others (A2), or distinct feelings of warmth and closeness in the *group* (A3). 'Expressing self congruently, articulately, or assertively in the group' (B1), and directly ventilating experienced emotion (B2) were identified as behavioural categories (206–207).

At least two of three judges agreed on the classification of nearly every described event, and more than half of these valued events fell into categories C1 or C2. Adding C3 and C4, two-thirds of the events were accounted for. Only about one event in five was counted in the affective domain (A1, A2 and A3). The cognitive categories pivot on fresh awareness important to the respondent, an implied priority in the group context. Notwithstanding the affective image of intensive groups, interpersonal feeling events came a distant second in discriminated importance. Even with the 'behavioural' categories – involving felt experience (B1) and feeling expression (B2) – added to the overtly affective cluster, only one event in three was accounted for. The authors conclude their report with advocacy of the *group* therapy context as having unique growth potentialities, including 'the opportunity to witness

21 Other features of the full-time regime in the hospital (often on an involuntary basis) pressed hard on the participants, perhaps making for high arousal and energy, and little 'coasting', but also for appreciation of the accepting, enabling climate and approach of the group therapy.

honest expression of emotionality . . . [and] recognize similarity to others, to give help and support . . ., to see oneself as others see one, and . . . to discover, express, or accept oneself in intimate relation to others' (212).

Charles Truax's study (1961) of group psychotherapy was completed before the report by Berzon et al., but depends on later theory development and linked methodology. Readers interested in the saga and substance of small-group research will find the story continued in Chapter 14 (pp. 292–307), starting with Truax's study and including principal work from the mid-sixties into the nineties. It remains in this chapter to consider research on play therapy within the same School Phase time frame.

Child therapy research

Axline's important contribution did not include systematic research, and there are few studies to examine. One difficulty lay in the realm of data-collection. Sound recordings alone were not an adequate record of the events of play therapy. To augment such recording with synchronized observations by a non-participant observer was logistically formidable. This of course was the era of content analysis of audio-recorded and transcribed interviews. In her important chapter, Dorfman (1951) was able to cite two very modest studies of process, and one or two concerned with outcome. In the first, Landisberg and Snyder (1946) evidently used written records of the play sessions involved. Four children composed the sample, and Snyder's original framework with adults was adapted for the child data. Of therapist responses, 75 per cent fell broadly into the non-directive categories, and 5 per cent were classed as interpretations. As for client categories, Dorfman notes (267–268) that physical activity in the last three-fifths of therapy showed marked increase over the initial phases. During this active period, about 70 per cent of the child client responses were deemed expressions of feeling, verbal or non-verbal. Recorded expressions of negative feeling, and of feeling directed outward, tended to increase not diminish.

Finke (1947), developed a schema of feeling-expression categories coming out of play therapy process records; again, based on therapist notes, and relying heavily on verbal expressions (Dorfman, 1951: 269). The clients were six children each seen over a series of eight to fourteen contacts. Categories included 'story units' (child stories declined in the latter half of therapy), 'aggressive statements' (again, declining in the later part of therapy), and both positive and negative references to self, and to family members and situations. Unlike the case with adults, most categories showed no clear pattern of increase or decrease. Another study investigated nondirective play therapy with retarded readers (Bills, 1950). Eight children were chosen from a third grade class of 'slow learners'. The reading age of each child selected was discrepant from his/her measured IQ (mean 123, on the Stanford-Binet). The audio-recorded play therapy contacts were both individual and group. Children served as their own controls, in a three-phase design: a six-week waiting period, a similar period in treatment, and a six-week follow-up interval. Tested reading gain was very significantly greater in the treatment period, or that of treatment plus follow-up, than during the wait-control time (cited by Dorfman, 1951: 271–272).

Dorfman discussed additional work, of less interest or adequacy, and suggested future directions – to little avail, as subsequent research continued to centre on adult therapy. One exception was the important investigation by Seeman, Barry and Ellinwood reported first in 1957 and, in more formal mode, in 1963. The investigators were centrally interested in comparing the in-session behaviour of well-functioning children with that of poorly functioning children. Effectively, the study foreshadowed later 'process' research (next chapter) in working to identify *in-therapy* behaviours indicative of outcome or change. Tests were administered from which to single out high and low adjustment children from the second and third graders in a large city school. Eight of those from the low adjustment end, and four at the top of the range, were brought for individual play therapy. Observers of each of ten sessions for each child made systematic ratings, especially, on aspects of therapist–child interaction and of 'expressivity' of the child.

As between the two groups of children, the 'lows' spent more time in direct interaction with the therapist, more often or strenuously resisted limit setting, and attempted to structure the therapist's activity more, than the 'highs' did. The lows also were rated as significantly more impulsive, less expressive, as manifesting much more hostility, and more fear, and as appearing more dependent. Put another way, from these data, 'the child of high integration relates to the adult in a relaxed and expressive way'. He/she 'does not display a need to structure or control the adult's behaviour in the way characteristic of the low adjustment child', and tends to accept limits in a matter of fact way. For this group, interaction with the therapist was noted 48 per cent of the time, and for the others, 72 per cent. Finally, the ways that the children organized themes in their play differed. For the group of highs, there was only one episode in forty sessions classed as 'over-organized and perseverative'; 30 per cent of the low groups' responses were of this kind (1963: 15–16). Clearly, change could be examined meaningfully from behaviour within the therapy sessions. Regrettably, however, no study ensued that drew and built directly on these findings. Indeed, play therapy in the same tradition appears not to have been further investigated. I will later return to an approach centred on the parent–child relationship.

Issues in conclusion: a 'debate'

In writing this chapter I asked myself the question 'Why go back so far and fully?' 'What value, what lessons for us now, are to be found in this early research?' The writing, for me, has brought more connected knowledge of work long in my sights, a fresh experiencing of some of the excitement of the chase, and ideas about further investigation. The process has been to locate, and remap, the trail of a ground-breaking path of inquiry. However such an odyssey is not the same experience for others as for its author. Thus my attempt, now, to step aside from my route so far and into a position closer to the reader's. The issues I see – sharper looking backward than with the chapter not yet written – can be formulated as critical propositions and questions, and responded to one by one. This is not just a *playing* of the devil's advocate. The main points arose from moments of inner questioning of what I found myself doing; questions answered provisionally, but also set aside to revisit in this conclusion.

- ◇ *Client-centred therapy itself has changed since the late forties and fifties. Why focus on past studies of a therapy which has continued to evolve, and is no longer the same phenomenon that these studies examine?* Yes, I agree that the therapy approach itself has not stood still. Probably it never has. Snyder's results, and those of Seeman a few years later, imply that movement toward a more literally client-centred approach was taking place in the 1940s. In the fifties, the therapy became typically much longer term, no doubt with qualitative development. Since the School Phase ended there has been increasing diversity, and different practice 'wings' have come strongly into view (Lietaer, 1990). How great the overall change is, and the particular ways main variations actually differ in practice, are not simple to determine. To clearly see and understand this variation, thus also to choose our way wisely, we may need to emulate aspects of the early research – devoted as it was to illuminating the actual content, pattern and effects of the therapy. Bringing its substance again into sharp view prompts such questions as 'Why not be *more* active now in open, discovery-oriented process research?', and 'Can we not again achieve the same vital synergy between out practice, theory and research?'
- ◇ *Our theory has evolved significantly since this early research. We have come to look at the process of therapy rather differently, and to ask different questions.* I grant that this is true. Indeed, my next chapter examines research prompted by the subsequent development of theory. The early work, especially the initial process research, was relatively theory-free, and remains interesting partly for this reason. Particularly, it helped to show us *how* we practised, and with what effects. Research is not only about testing theory. More basically, it is about *letting things show clearly*, so that we see better what is happening and how. The early studies seem to have done pretty well on this level, in relatively uncomplicated and straightforward ways.
- ◇ *Research methodology has also evolved, and there are now more promising paths to systematic inquiry. Is what was done then a model for current work?* My short answer is 'Yes' and 'No', and I will return later to issues implied in it. The studies were largely forms of naturalistic investigation, with little focus on hypothesis-testing. The investigator 'listened' more laterally than in strongly deductive research, looking for the pattern rather than testing only for pre-selected associations. Most of the statistical analyses were not highly involved and were carried out by hand, such that investigators remained very much in touch with the data and results, at each step. Quantified material is now computer-processed,

using pre-packaged statistical programs, with loss as well as gain. Content analysis approaches retain a vital role (as will be later illustrated), and phenomenological inquiry and other evolving qualititative methods, together with techniques such as forms of pattern tracking and analysis, can help to empower current investigation in keeping with the spirit of earlier work.

◇ *What about the research informed by conditions theory, Rogers' process formulations, and later developments? One chapter is reserved for all of this work, in the context of individual therapy. Should studies in the first two decades receive similar emphasis?* My own research falls in subsequent phases, and I have not skipped lightly over this question in reaching an affirmative answer. To begin with, client-centred therapy research was uniquely active, continuous and connected from the early forties through the early sixties (Rogers' Ohio State, Chicago, and Wisconsin years). Because there had been no such systematic empirical study of the therapy process before, the work was literally breaking untravelled ground, and bringing a new field of research inquiry into being. Its story has a special interest and, with the sources now out of general view, its telling has even more cogency.

In a word, given adequate retelling, I think the narrative can hardly fail to have aspects of relevance for the thinking we bring to bear in research now, how we focus it, for choices or details of method, and (vitally) for our energy and motivation for the enterprise. What I turn to next are different developmental phases in the continuation of this story through to the present. Although each phase is distinctive, all are interrelated in a living tapestry that remains in the weaving.

13

Conditions and Process in Personal Change

> When the phenomena under consideration are not well described . . . the person who insists on starting out with precise experiments lacks the required imagination to observe, to look around and see . . . what seems to be going on. Experiments which precede rather than succeed observation amount to being precise about vagueness and suggest a disproportionate concern for the opinions of other scientists.
>
> Butler, Rice and Wagstaff, 1962

> I have come to realize that all science is based on recognition . . . of a dimly sensed gestalt, a hidden reality. This gestalt or pattern appears to give meaning to disconnected phenomena. . . . I regard this sensing of a pattern of relationships as perhaps the heart of all true science.
>
> Carl Rogers, 1965c

It struck me at the end of the last chapter that, if written as a separate article, I could simply have called it 'The birth of psychotherapy research'. The metaphor of 'birthing' is nearly as apt for the stages that followed next in sequence. Rogers' last few years in Chicago were the high point of his scholarly achievement. They marked the filling out of his theoretical system and concepts, the encouragement of innovation by associates and students, and new phases of research inquiry. Direct involvement in research receded from his path after Rogers moved to California – apart from final reporting of the major Wisconsin program (Rogers, Gendlin, Kiesler and Truax, 1967). Studies of psychotherapy with roots deep in his work cumulate to a great river of development which I will trace through principal tributaries. Two such main tributaries – concerned with the therapy relationship and with client process – have distinct headwaters that invite attention first.

Cause and consequence in psychotherapy: spotlight on the therapy relationship

The early research (pre-1957)

Research on the client–therapist relationship began well before Rogers' 1957 therapy conditions formulation, and investigated desired as well as actual patterns of therapist response to their clients. Four dissertation studies – by

Fiedler (in 1949/1950b), Quinn (1950), Heine (1950/1953) and Bown (1954) – are pertinent. Fiedler's is best known due to its prompt, rather full publication (1950a, 1950b). He first assembled a set of 119 statements, to be sorted in normal (Q-sort) array by exponents of psychoanalytic, nondirective and eclectic viewpoints, to portray the *ideal therapist-to-client relationship*. Unexpectedly, his experienced therapists were more in agreement with each other, regardless of orientation, than with their associated therapists-in-training (Fiedler, 1950a: Table 2). The aspects of communicative understanding by the therapist, of tolerance and acceptance, and of an active stance by both participants, were highlighted features of the ideal. Fiedler wondered about his results. Did they, perhaps, reflect limitations of the Q-sort, or idiosyncrasies of the group involved? And what would be the view of lay individuals? A more systematic replication study seemed called for.

This time the instrument was indeed systematic: a new 75-statement Q-sort with three planned areas, each area represented by 25 items, each item reflecting one of five levels in its area. The area groupings were communication and understanding, preferred emotional distance/closeness, and the implied relative status of the client (inferior/equal/ superior) and therapist. Seven therapists and three lay persons completed the sorts. Correlations remained strong, and the data from experts were merged in a *composite ideal sort*, published in full (1950a: 243–244). Quality of communication and personal understanding stood out at the positive pole, and attitudes of equality also were emphasized.

Fiedler then took a differing direction in a further study, this time of actual relationships as seen in early interviews with psychoanalytic, nondirective and Adlerian therapists – half of them recognized experts, half non-expert. Each session was rated by four observer-judges, using the 75-item Q-sort. Q-sort pictures of actual sessions with expert therapists were closer to the composite ideal previously obtained than the pictures for non-experts were (Fiedler, 1950b: 440; 1953: 300). Further, the three most expert therapists were seen by (most) judges as having more in common with each other than with non-experts from the same school. This much-cited feature flowed from a big disparity between experts and non-experts coupled with *moderate* commonality among the various experts (mean r of .54, derived from Fiedler, 1950b: Table 4). Some items did differentiate along school lines. Most consistency across schools occurred in the sphere of communication and understanding (442) and, in Fiedler's view of his findings, this was the crucial unifying factor in therapist effectiveness.

Quinn's study used the same 75-item Q-sort and sample, with differing aim. He was interested in whether therapist expressions alone could index the quality of the therapy relationship, and distinguish experts from non-experts. Four judges first rated each therapist expression (with client speech removed) on Quinn's 'security in communication' scale. This intriguing device asked judges to listen to a therapist expression, sense the thought-feeling quality behind it, and rate the degree to which this would 'impede or aid his [therapist's] grasp upon the patient's thoughts and feelings'. In addition, therapist 'receptivity', 'sensitivity', and 'givingness' were each rated (1950:

Appendix). The judge's second main task was to answer Fiedler's Q-sort, for the actual relationship in each whole session protocol.

Quinn found that his new communication scale clearly distinguished the three most expert therapists from the group of non-experts. He followed this up by correlating each whole session Q-sort (N = 10) with Fiedler's criterion ideal relationship. This gave an index of session quality which correlated strongly with estimates of quality from Quinn's communication scale data (1950: Table 4). The best evidence on whether therapist expressions alone could substitute for whole interview protocols was not conclusive (Tables 5 and 6). It did appear that, for *most* of the therapists/interviews involved, therapist speech sufficed to convey the attitudinal qualities spanned by Fiedler's Q-sort.

Heine asked clients of therapists from the same three approaches (eight clients each) to describe the changes they experienced (on one Q-sort) and what they attributed these changes to (using another sort). The latter contained 60 items descriptive of technique (interpretation, free association, reflection, questioning, etc.), and 60 items concerned with 'therapeutic atmosphere' (communication elements, warmth, trust, etc.). Regardless of therapist orientation, similar changes were reported by clients. Differences entered the picture when respondents were accounting for these changes. For the psychoanalytic clients, features of technique were emphasized; the nondirective group stressed qualities of atmosphere. However, most items did not discriminate, and these were examined for areas of agreement. One main area was 'assisting the patient by asking questions which have the effect of clarifying feelings or attitudes', and a second was 'expressing for the client straight-forwardly feelings which the client approaches hesitantly and hazily'. Advice, and emphasis on past history, were agreed by clients as unfavourable. On the atmosphere side 'agreement centres about feelings of trust, of being understood, and of independence in reaching solutions to problems' (Heine, 1953: 20).

The last and most 'contemporary' study in this series was conducted by Bown (1954), who called on six clients and their counsellors to picture their relationship, after two, five, ten and twenty interviews of therapy. A new 121-item Q-sort was used, with content emphasizing the relation between client and therapist as persons; an emphasis advanced through Bown's contribution (see Rogers, 1951: 160–171).[1] Before and after the twenty interviews, the partners also gave their view of the *ideal* therapy relationship. For therapists

---

1 The personal emphasis remains striking, in Bown's unpublished sort. Illustrative items include the following: 2. The client feels like a guilty child – the counselor 'catches' him being dishonest with himself; 12. The client wants from the counselor the kind of personal relationship he has never had but always wanted; 22. The client holds himself apart, is afraid of any closer relationship with the counselor; 34. The counselor is able to see the client as the client sees himself; 40. The counselor has a kind of love for the client; 45. The counselor is intellectual and analytical without much real feeling for the client; 67. The client feels a certain amount of contempt for the counselor; 86. The client feels a certain added respect for himself in his relationship with the counselor; 109. The client likes the counselor just as he is; 116. The client is baffled by his feelings toward the counselor. As can be seen, not only do items point to the counsellor's perceived response but many refer directly to the client's own feelings-in-relation.

(all client-centred), agreement as to the ideal relationship was reflected in mean correlations before and after therapy of .71 and .73 (Bown, 1954, derived from Tables 2 and 17). The clients, too, saw the desired relationship in moderately similar terms, as reflected in a mean correlation of .6 in their pre-therapy sorts (derived from Table 2). There was greater diversity in the way the actual relationships were perceived (ibid.: 54, 57, 60 and 63). Over the course of therapy, actual and ideal drew closer in the more successful cases, not so in those rated less successful (101-108). In higher success cases, client–therapist partners also had more convergent views of their relationship than in other cases (109).

Rogers' conditions of therapy formulation: the original studies

Bown's hypotheses grew creatively from prior work and reflection on the process of therapy but were not anchored in developed theory. It was two years after completion of his study before Rogers' conditions of therapy theory came into view (1957a; privately circulated in 1956). Two doctoral students, Halkides and this writer, at once began to plan dissertation studies based on this theory. Halkides' study (1958) remained unpublished, although briefly reported by others.[2] She devised scales for judge-rating of unconditional positive regard, empathy, therapist congruence and, also, similarity in 'affective intensity' of client and therapist expressions (her own addition). Two interviews from each of twenty cases provided the recorded segments for rating.[3] Significant associations were found between her criterion of success and the relationship conditions proposed by Rogers. On the variable of affective intensity matching her results were ambiguous. Although seldom acknowledged, this study opened the way to a plethora of subsequent work employing judges' ratings on scales in the same domain, devised by Truax and others (Truax and Carkhuff, 1967; Rogers, Gendlin, Kiesler and Truax, 1967: Appendix B).

Barrett-Lennard's doctoral research (1959) was the study in which the Relationship Inventory (RI or BLRI) was first developed. Although similar in aim, the investigation was unlike that of Halkides in its specific understanding of theory and consequent approach to measurement. This work, as extended and published in 1962, has served as resource and trigger for a lasting flow of further studies, and thus invites careful summary. Rogers' theory implied that the relational attitudes and response of the therapist, and the ways these were *perceived* by the client, were fundamental to movement in therapy. This led to a twin focus, (i) on the therapist's inner engagement and response, and (ii) on the client's experience of his/her therapist in their relationship. Since the theory pivots on *experience* in relation, the interperceptions of the dyad members were tapped, in preference to interposing outside judges (Barrett-

---

2 For example, by Barrett-Lennard (1962a), and Rogers (1958a, 1965d).

3 I was one of her judges and spent a good many hours listening to the brief interview segments, usually with the other judges. After training practice together, Halkides would play an excerpt and each of us would silently record our rating for the variable then in focus.

Lennard, 1962a: 2–3). The challenge was to utilize the information participants possessed, within a systematic framework of measurement. To this end, parallel forms of the new inventory were planned for the therapist and client, respectively, to answer.

The variables for measurement needed tighter definition than Rogers (1957a) had offered, as outlined earlier (pp. 80–82). A distinct subset of items was generated and tested for each variable: level of regard, empathic understanding, unconditionality, congruence, and willingness to be known (WK) (Barrett-Lennard, 1962a: 3–7). Within the transactional therapy relation the primary focus was on measures from the client's perception of the therapist. To safely regard the participant's impressions as growing substantially out of their experience together, several interview hours of contact were deemed necessary. On the other hand, it seemed important that the data-gathering not be left too late, since the *eventual* quality of the relationship might be a resultant by-product of therapy as much as its cause. It was decided to tap the relationship after the fifth interview, as the main test point. On average, therapy ran for 33 interviews, in the total study sample of 42 client–therapist dyads (1962a: 8).

The underlying hypothesis of the study was that each of the relationship qualities, especially as they seem to the client, is a contributing factor in the facilitation of change. What therapists experienced and did in response to their clients was crucial but always filtered through the clients' reading of their response. The fact that relationship quality was tapped relatively early in therapy, thus having credence as predictor and potential agent of change, did not eliminate the theoretical possibility of clients having governing influence both on relationship and outcome. As a further control strategy, the sample was composed of relatively expert and non-expert (novice) therapists, each subsample working with an equivalent group of clients. The fact that the data both on relationship *and* on client change were to be supplied by both participants, also gave leverage in teasing out the meaning of correlational linkage (ibid.: 10).

Close attention is given in the 1962 report to the detailed structure, scoring and measurement characteristics of the original RI. Suffice it to say that client and therapist scores were similarly distributed overall, and split-half reliabilities were high in both cases (1962a: Tables 1, 2 and 3). Change data included therapist judgements made at the start and end of therapy, which were used to divide the sample conservatively into a 'more changed' group (with rating evidence all positive) and a 'less changed' cluster (evidence less positive or mixed). Relationship scores were significantly higher for the first group on four scales (excluding WK) when assessed from the client RI data. Further, the client RI scores predicted therapist estimations of change as well or better than the scores did from the therapist-answered RI.

A composite score from three distinct but substantially correlated self-inventory measures – the Q adjustment scale (Dymond, 1954a), Taylor's (1953) Manifest Anxiety Scale, and the MMPI Depression scale – provided a second index of change. This, however, suffered in the sample as a whole from a marked ceiling effect; the initially high scorers had little room to increase their scores, and there was a strong negative correlation between pre-therapy position and change. To overcome this effect in otherwise unbiased fashion a simple median split by *initial* scores was used, the lower scoring half only being retained for hypothesis testing. Tau correlations between relationship and change in the truncated sample reached significance on all RI scale measures from client data. From therapist RI data all associations were positive, too, but at low significance levels.[4]

The more and less expert therapists were distinct in several ways: in level of experience, in their selection for continuance of this experience in the Counseling Center, and in age – the experts averaging seven years older. Their clients were matched and alike by groups in ways that included ratio of males to females (plus similarity in same-sex/opposite-sex pairings with therapists), age characteristics, educational level, and pre-therapy Q-adjustment and Taylor Anxiety scores (Barrett-Lennard, 1962a: 21). In accord with prediction, *RI scores from the clients with expert therapists* (N = 12) *were higher than those with non-experts* (N = 15) on all scales (except WK), at chance probability levels of .05 to .10. Differences from therapist RI data were all in the same direction, and similar in degree for empathy and unconditionality (ibid.: Tables 16 and 17). Also as expected, *a bigger proportion of clients with the expert therapists group fell in the 'more changed' category* (ibid.: 22).

With the sample already divided, a further change criterion for only part of the total sample would not work. However, it had been found that length of therapy could be used as an indicator of change (Cartwright et al., 1961; Standal and van der Veen, 1957). Since the client groups were equated in various ways, any large differences in duration of therapy could scarcely be a result of the longer-running cases taking more time to make the same gain. In fact, records revealed that the cases with expert therapists ran on average for twice as long as the other group, a strongly significant difference.[5]

This study's direct evidence of a relationship–change connection is perhaps strongest for more troubled clients (since two quite different, pre-selected criteria of change were employed) than for a broader grouping represented by the whole initial sample (for which therapist appraisals were the pivotal criterion). The fact that therapist evaluations of change were best predicted by client-provided relationship information strengthens the meaning of this association, however. Also, it was clear in the data that therapist expertise was jointly linked to relationship quality *and* change, implying that therapists were having an interrelated impact on both levels.

In a much later review of research pertinent to the conditions-outcome hypothesis, Watson affirmed the appropriateness of measurement in this

---

4 RI data were also gathered at later points, especially, at the end of therapy. Had the relationship as it developed been a consequence of change, increasing strength of association with change would be expected. No such increase was found, using the pivotal *client* RI data.

5 Results from secondary hypotheses were consonant with the picture outlined. For example, comparison of the pairs of RI scores yielded an interesting result: as between the two client-matched subgroups, expert therapists and clients converged much more in perception of the therapist's level of empathy than did non-experts and their clients (Barrett-Lennard, 1962a: 26).

study but considered that no research had satisfactorily tested Rogers' theory since all had relied on correlational method. He claims that all studies '[failed] to address the issue of the hypothesized conditions as causal factors' (1984: 35) and, again, that 'none addressed the issue of causality' (37). It is a pity to over-state this limitation, since much of Watson's step-by-step critique is incisive, and the issues are vitally important ones. As noted, care was taken in this study in choosing when to tap the relationship quality, in order to give leverage on its potential agency in change. The issue of causality was explicitly addressed at the levels of theory, design and appraisal of results. The use of matched groups of clients with therapists of differing expertise was undertaken precisely to offset some limitations of correlational analysis. While not proving beyond doubt a direct causal link, the design and pattern of results 'make it plausible to infer that the factors of perceived relationship were involved in the generation of the associated change' (Barrett-Lennard, 1962a: 31). There was much still to learn about precisely *how* they are involved.

Therapy conditions with schizophrenic clients: the Wisconsin project

The first of the further studies to utilize the relationship measures was planned (in 1958, soon after Rogers' move to Wisconsin) after the main results, above, were evident if not yet reported formally. The project, involving schizophrenic clients, was another fresh advance in planned design. The (hospitalized) subjects were to be selected in matched pairs, none with opportunity for *individual psychotherapy* except in the research context. By random choice, one member of each pair would receive therapy, and the other serve as a control. There would be parallel testing and appraisal of all participants. Diagnostically, hospital clients were to be equally divided between those resident less than eight months (the 'more acute' group) and those already in hospital for longer (the 'more chronic' group). A range of both change and process measures was envisaged. The RI, now with four 18-item scales, was to be administered to clients and therapists, after the fifth interview, and at later points. The matched control patients would answer in reference to 'the person who has meant most to you in your trouble' (Rogers, Gendlin, Kiesler and Truax, 1967: 32).

The bold overall plan (ibid.: 23–38) proved impossible to implement fully. Finding pairs of patient subjects matched on the several criteria was inordinately difficult (44), more than a few failed to complete particular test instruments or refused the needed recording of their interviews (46–47), and there were unexpected discharges and hospital transfers. Some initial subjects were replaced, others could not be.[6] As a result of gaps in the data for persons

---

6 Carl Rogers' own client, 'James Brown' (also called 'Mr Vac'), provides an instance of the missing data problem. This client, whose case was chosen for illustration and appraisal of the therapy process (Rogers et al., 1967: chs 17 and 18), and who evidently made great gains over the period of his therapy, refused with new-found assertiveness to take the final test battery and was, thus, excluded from the sample for outcome data analysis (ibid.: 415).

included, the actual sample used varies across differing components of the analysis and reporting of results.

For the *small* sample (N = 8 clients) from whom RI data were successfully gathered both early in therapy and at termination, early–late correlations showed a high level of stability (ibid.: 169), commensurate with reliabilities attained with less distressed clients or from therapist RI data (Barrett-Lennard, 1962a; Gurman, 1977). Interscale correlations were fairly high early in therapy (mean rho = .60), much lower at termination (mean rho = .23), suggesting more differentiated perception at the later point. Clients tended to see their therapists less positively than in my original study. Conversely, therapists were inclined to describe their own response more positively (Rogers et al., 1967: 170; Barrett-Lennard, 1962a: 10–11, 14). It is hard to know how representative the figures are. Did therapists really experience a higher level of therapeutic self-engagement than therapists with relatively well-functioning clients?! Judging from all the descriptive information, they were working with persons with whom forming a relationship of understanding, trust and healing was truly a *most* uphill process (Rogers et al., 1967: chs 4, 16, 17 and 18).[7]

Most research growing out of Rogers' conditions theory has used the RI in some form, or versions of the (Truax) rating scales which the schizophrenia project brought into view (ibid.: Appendix B; Truax and Carkhuff, 1967: 43–72). Best-known of these scales, for rating therapist-to-client response, is the measure of 'accurate empathy'.[8] Nine levels of such empathy were initially distinguished, from no apparent awareness 'of even the most conspicuous of the client's feelings' through a middle stage of targeting on feelings and conveying an 'awareness of the problem of understanding another person's inner world', to the top level of 'unerring response' 'to the client's full range of feelings in their exact intensity' (Rogers et al., 1967: Appendix B1).

Truax used the term 'nonpossessive warmth' as a synonym for unconditional positive regard, distinguishing five levels of this quality. The lowest rating level was assigned if 'the therapist is actively offering advice or giving clear negative regard' (ibid.: 570). At the mid-point, 'the therapist indicates a positive caring . . . but it is a *semipossessive* caring', with elements of conditionality. At the top stage 'there is a deep respect for the patient's worth as a person', a prizing 'uncontaminated by evaluations of his thoughts or

---

7 The *negative* correlations between client and therapist RI scores also fit the notion of relationship formation being a struggle. Where outcome was most favourable, client and therapist RI scores were more in step, especially on Level of Regard (Rogers et al., 1967: 178).

8 Developed in 1961, the Accurate Empathy scale evidently was meant to go beyond Rogers' formulation. Truax and Carkhuff (1967: 43) inferred 'that "empathy" is not so related to client improvement as "accurate empathy", which contains elements of the psychoanalytic view of moment-to-moment diagnostic accuracy'. In his separate book published the same year, Carkhuff (1967: 27) again notes a convergence of source ideas, but does not use 'accurate' in naming the scale. He both draws from and is strenuously critical of psychoanalysis, client-centred therapy, and other main approaches – each presented in stereotypic view (chs 4–8).

behaviors' (570–577). The third variable in the rating triumvirate, often called 'genuineness' but based on the congruence condition, posed special difficulty. Again, five rating steps were distinguished. If the therapist is seen as presenting a façade, or there is judged to be 'very considerable discrepancy between what he says and what he experiences', the lowest rating applies. At the mid-point, 'the therapist is implicitly either defensive or professional, although there is no explicit evidence'. At the top level 'the therapist is being freely and deeply himself in the relationship', and his 'verbalizations match his inner experience' (Truax and Carkhuff, 1967: 68–72). The rater is in a difficult position: it seems that the person's underlying experience has to be inferred from the same behaviour that is then compared for match or mismatch with this experience.

More than 300 four-minute segments, one from each chosen interview with fourteen therapy patients, were methodically rated, one scale at a time, by student judges. Interviews 2–15, roughly the first half of therapy, were regularly sampled. Reliability of ratings was modest but adequate for empathy (AE) and congruence (CONG), although most CONG ratings were at scale points 3 and 5. For unconditional positive regard (UPR), initial reliabilities were so low that the data for this scale were screened, retaining for further analysis only the 40 per cent of segments yielding consistent ratings (Rogers et al., 1967: 145; 149–150).[9] Client experiencing level was also rated from interview samples, as detailed later.

Correlations between the three conditions scales were minimal. Even when all ratings for the same case were combined into a single mean, and the mean figures ranked, the rho correlation between AE and CONG was low and non-significant. Significant associations with UPR were found, using 'consistent' data only (ibid.: 159–166). In overall summation, the authors conclude that rated AE appeared to be a sound measure but the CONG and UPR ratings 'raised serious interpretive problems', and that it was 'impossible to have confidence' in them (166–167). Nevertheless, their usage continued: first, by assessing them against RI measures. Mean AE ratings on nearby interviews were substantially correlated (in the small sample) with initial client RI measures except for 'U'. At termination, AE correlated most strongly with RI Congruence. There was no discernible correlational link between rated CONG and any of the RI measures; and the truncated UPR data yielded equivocal results (173–175).

For therapist RI returns, those who reported more positive response tended to be seen by judges as 'offering' *lower* levels of AE. This and other results, although not resolved as to meaning, left the authors inclined to discount *therapist* judgements as a useful index of relationship. The positive correlation of AE with RI readings from the crucial perspective of clients, was seen as

9 This surprising procedure assumes that on segments where it turned out that the judges produced concordant ratings the measure had an integrity of meaning that was lacking where the ratings were discrepant. Later studies reported better reliability (Mitchell et al., 1977: Table 1). They left other serious questions about the methodology, stability and actual meaning of the three measures taken as reflecting core therapeutic/helping 'skills' (ibid.: 491–494).

validation evidence. It did not validate AE specifically as a measure of empathy, but as a more global index of the 'conditions quality of the therapist', especially, 'his communicated therapeutic commitment as well as the genuineness of this involvement' (184). In hindsight, these and related conclusions appear overdrawn (see also Mitchell et al., 1977). However, they resulted from evidence available at the time, coupled with the integral of the rating scales in the design of the project and in special interests represented within it.

Following evaluation of the conditions measures, the Wisconsin report devotes central attention to client process level and movement during therapy, and to how these levels connect with the therapist conditions. The revisioned exploration of client process within therapy is the second main region of client-centred research taken up in this chapter.

Tracking client process levels over therapy: the pioneering work

You may recall that Rogers' process conception envisions a continuum ranging from a pattern of self-repeating fixity at the 'stasis' extreme to a flowing, self-transcending (open system) quality at the 'process' extreme. At the stasis end, it is as though the person is applying fixed templates to every situation and experience, and trying to hold all interaction at a distance from his/her vulnerable and guarded, but little recognized, inner subjective being (Rogers, 1958c, 1959b, 1961a: 125–159). The first pertinent study, by Walker, Rablen and Rogers (1960), began before Rogers' new formulation was in print.

Walker et al. used six fully transcribed cases from Counseling Center files, taking from each case four samples, two from early interviews and two near the end. Each of the twenty-four samples, typed on a separate sheet, was coded and anonymous as to stage in therapy. Two judges trained together, learning to rate levels on the seven-stage scale of process taken as a whole, and achieving inter-judge correlations in the .8–.85 range. Independently, Rogers ranked the six cases as to progress and success of therapy, calling on a range of data (Walker et al., 1960: 82). Process movement scores for each case were obtained by subtracting early levels from the later ones. The rank order of these movement scores correlated highly (rho = .89) with Rogers' outcome ranking. When clients were grouped by outcome, early to late *change* in mean process rating for the three substantially improved clients (2.3, 2.0, and 1.5) distinctly exceeded the equivalent figures for the three showing minimal improvement (1.2, .3, and –.6) (ibid.: 83).

Tomlinson and Hart (1962) took a fresh sample of ten cases from Counseling Center records. Two judges rated process levels from second interview and next to last interview samples. Inter-judge reliability was modest in this case (r = .65). As before, late interviews were generally rated above the corresponding early ones (chance probability < .05). A tendency for the more successful half of the cases to increase more than the less successful half was overshadowed by their *starting* as well as ending at higher process levels

(1962: Tables 1 and 2). In all, this study contributed some support for validity of the process scale, but also implied that refinements were called for. In fact, the main Wisconsin research did not apply the continuum as one dimension but drew out four primary component scales for separate operational definition and rating (Rogers et al., 1967: Appendix C).

Best known of the four component measures is the scale for 'rating of experiencing'. An external story or narrative of events, without self reference or mention that it is the person's own experience of these events that is being reported, earns a rating at the bottom of this scale. If the speaker directly indicates that it is his/her story, but at most only refers to emotion embedded within this story, stage 2 is represented. Skipping a stage, at level 4 the person does 'communicate what it is like to *be* him', with expression of owned feelings. These feelings, however, are not being used to gain new information or in a struggle to explore the self, which would imply stage 5. At stages 6 and 7 immediate feelings are content in their own right. The person can both hold an inward felt reference and explore its meanings and (at stage 7) move readily from one felt reference to another. The free-flowing nature of inner signals results in an immediacy and clarity of self-presentation (Gendlin, Tomlinson, Mathieu, and Klein, 1967).

A second scale focuses on the way personal constructs work in the individual's mental/emotional life. At one extreme, no guiding inner constructs are reported (stage 1), or constructs are extremely rigid and treated as facts (stage 2). At stage 4, there is an assumptive quality to constructs, and they are seen as 'mine' and sometimes needing refinement. At higher stages, constructs are looser, not solid givens. At stages 6 and 7 the person easily uses emergent meanings and amends prior ones. Experience is the main source and testing ground for construed meaning (Rogers et al., 1967: 317–318, 593–597).

A scale devised by van der Veen and Tomlinson (1967) indexes the way individuals talk about problems; from no such talk to freely expressing problems and engaging in resolution. A rating at stage 1 of this Problems Expression Scale (PES) applies where no problems are mentioned. If there is some mention of problems but not of involvement, stage 2 applies. For a rating at mid-scale, the person speaks of his/her own reaction but not of this reaction being part of the problem. At the upper levels, s/he expresses self-understandings around the problem (stage 6), or speaks of its actual resolution and how this feels (1967: 600–601).

The last scale pivots on 'manner of relating' (Gendlin, 1967). Refusal of relationship, or keeping the I-self closed off from overt contact, falls at the lower extreme. At the next stage the individual provides no sign that personal sharing is the issue or meaning of contact that occurs. In the middle stages, the client is actively using the therapy relationship as a *context* for self-inquiry. At higher levels, relationship events and feelings become intrinsic to the therapeutic process. The therapy association is more than a theatre for rehearsal, it is part of the play itself, with implication for the person's relational life outside therapy.

An initial study found the four scales strongly correlated in the data used, at levels approaching their reliabilities (cited in Rogers et al., 1967: 129).

These results, which could have reflected peculiarities of the sample, insufficient cues in the small rating units, *or* major overlap and redundancy, evidently were not further checked. For the experiencing scale, most ratings were confined to the two lowest scale points, and stages 6 and 7 were not represented at all in the 617 rated segments from interviews with hospitalized clients (ibid.: 151–152). The evidence used seems an insufficient basis for selecting out the experiencing scale mostly for use on its own, incorporating the other scales only when searching for process-outcome links in one later chapter.[10]

A close search was made for expected shifts in experiencing level (Rogers et al., 1967: 191–197). When a broad sampling of interview segments was used, from each third of the span of therapy, estimates of the 'peak' level of experiencing increased in the final third of therapy (194–197). Various analyses to check the primary hypothesis that level of therapy conditions was linked to process *movement* failed to yield positive results. Some conditions measures (AE and RI congruence) predicted level but not increase in rated experiencing. However, this predictive pattern changed *on removing effects of 'extraneous' client differences*, especially 'initial verbal IQ, . . . initial TAT mental health ratings, and initial level of depressive symptomatology (Wittenborn scales)'. It was found statistically that if clients did not differ in these ways, AE (mean of ratings from interviews 2–15) would *not* predict total EXP level (mean from all excerpts for the client). 'On the other hand, none of these factors influenced the obtained relationship of Pt-RI-C [patient RI congruence] and EXP_{TOT}' (ibid.: 289, and Table 11.15). A clear-cut picture was distinctly lacking.

Kiesler, Mathieu and Klein's major contribution to the Wisconsin report ends with a probing summing-up (Rogers et al., 1967: 295–311). Their 'critical re-evaluation' of the design and conceptual base of the study is a heartening attempt to come to terms with the complexity of their data, and contribute to thought more broadly. The authors imply that the model of one-way causal relation between conditions, process movement and outcome may not suffice to take account of the interactive processes evidently at work. Their observations have a discernible thrust *toward* a systemic rather than linear way of thinking. They do not offer any formal revision of the theory with which the study began, but their confrontation of issues enriches the cumbersome and many-handed report. Overall, the greatest positive energy of the research was devoted to giving fresh operational form to the significant

10 This chapter study, by Tomlinson (Rogers et al., 1967: 315–335), drew on a range of outcome data to arrive at a consensual classification of twelve out of fourteen therapy clients, as either 'more successful' (MS) or 'less successful' (LS) (Table 13.1, p. 321). Data for the process ratings were two four-minute segments from an early, a middle and a late interview in each case – 72 segments in all. Inter-scale correlations ranged from .57 to .85. Outcome was found significantly linked to change in process ratings, for three individual scales and the mean of all four. Process levels rose in the MS group and fell for the LS group. *The Personal Construct scale was most representative of the four scales, in terms of correlation with the other three* (ibid.: 325). Cited reliabilities are high.

theoretical extensions entailed, and to testing the theory in a context of ultimate challenge to any psychotherapy. Great energy was devoted to applying and adapting the practice with schizophrenic clients. Perhaps too many things were being attempted at once, and actual theoretical revisions were an unlikely addition.

Van der Veen (1967) describes an interesting study, supplementary to the main Wisconsin project, and involving its own, distinctively composed sample. The work grew out of incidental observation. Therapists would sometimes go into the wards, to establish contact with nominated research patients who declined to come for office therapy interviews. They would mingle with patients in their usual milieu, who came to feel a familiarity and reassurance leading on to acceptance of private interviews. Patients not involved in the primary research also seemed glad for this informal contact with the therapists. Out of this experience a project was born to test an unconventional way of initiating therapy. (Gendlin's [1961b] clinical paper on the project, usefully complements van der Veen's scientific report, in focus here.)

The eight participating therapists recorded interviews with at least twenty-four patients. Most patients experienced contact with more than one therapist. Three met at least twice with *each one* of five therapists in common, making fifteen combinations and a resource pool of thirty interviews. Three four-minute segments from each interview were rated on EXP and PES and two of the conditions scales (AE and CONG). Variance analysis revealed predicted main effects, both by patient ($N = 3$) and by therapist ($N = 5$), with patients making the larger difference on process ratings, and therapists (as expected) having more influence on conditions ratings. Both CONG and AE were moderately but significantly correlated with the two process scales, with the possibility that client process influenced therapist empathy and congruence, as well as vice versa.

The Wisconsin project started during the cohesive School Phase and ended in the more pluralist era that has followed. It was the last big research project founded on innovations in application and inquiry in which Rogers himself was a central player. He drew the formal results together in valiant, unifying summary (Rogers et al., 1967: 73–93), but my own estimation is less positive, especially on the issue of literal, clear findings. There were large but uneven developments in instrumentation and detailed method, with ramifying influence in subsequent work. Clinical data leaves little doubt that the therapy was of crucial benefit for particular patients, although sample-wide outcomes are modest (80–81, 320–322).[11] Work in the post-Wisconsin era is now as long in

---

11 The Rogerian condition that client and therapist are in psychological contact, while not formally considered in the Wisconsin research, is ignored at peril in working with severely schizophrenic clients. Restoring contact functions is a primary goal of Prouty's 'pre-therapy', in his visible contemporary work with persons in a regressed schizophrenic state (1990). This literally reflective/mirroring approach and its rationale is most closely described in his recent book (1994). Reported data consist mainly of case studies with generous illustrative transcripts (1994; and journal reports referenced therein). A group of independent contributions appear under the heading 'Severe disturbances' in the volume of conference papers edited by Hutterer et al. (1996).

years as the whole preceding period of client-centred development, and more variable in scope.

Research on individual therapy *after* the School Phase

Psychotherapy research began to mushroom in the 1960s, and there is too much potentially relevant work to avoid being selective. In pondering an approach to this selection, a number of issues and criteria occurred to me. In the end, what follows is best described as a feasible, *care*ful but individual sampling.

The fascinations of quantitative analysis and a more cognitive emphasis

Among the client-centred group, Butler continued in the Chicago situation through the sixties, moving then to Ontario.[12] Besides his committed interest in psychotherapy he had a special bent and fascination with quantitative methodology (Butler, Rice and Wagstaff, 1962, 1963) and published a series of original papers on factor-analytic method (for example, Butler, 1964, 1969; Butler and Hook, 1966). His research papers include work following up his 1954 study with Haigh. This includes added analysis of data from the 'own-control' group who waited two months for their therapy to begin. Comparing only the clients' pictures of actual self, at different points, he found more change over the first two months of therapy than in the two-month waiting period (Butler, 1966: 54–56). He also found it possible to discern 'success' and 'failure' factors in post-therapy self-concept data (57). In comparable aspects, the results from later work – with a larger sample and more built-in controls – were supportive of earlier findings (58–59).[13]

The collection *Innovations in client-centered therapy* (Wexler and Rice, 1974), encompasses work evolving in the sixties to early seventies, mostly by contributors linked at crucial stages with the flowering of the approach at the University of Chicago. Several articles have a distinctly cognitive emphasis, often drawing on information processing concepts (Anderson, 1974; Rice, 1974; Wexler, 1974; Zimring, 1974). Gendlin (1974) describes the development of his work around listening and the use of focusing, identified as 'experiential psychotherapy'. Butler (1974) advances his concept of the 'iconic mode' in psychotherapy, not so much a variation in practice as a fresh way of describing

---

12 To the University of Waterloo, where I was located; and in the same area as his close former associate, Laura Rice (at York University).

13 Another paper by Butler (1968) is an accessible summary of the results of his analyses of self concept and self-ideal data from a number of samples. He includes a broad-brush account of the content of factors from both self and self-ideal descriptions; and finally changes pace with the broad inference 'that increase in self-ideal congruence implies a change from a self-limiting to a self-actualizing life style' (ibid.: 17).

the therapy process. The accounts have a specificity such as to invite further research. One such study came into view (Wexler and Butler, 1976) after Butler's untimely death late in 1975.

The limiting effects of being inexpressive, and the release of self-expressiveness in therapy, had long been of interest to Butler. Wexler and he (1976: 262) suggest that most psychotherapies 'are heavily dependent on the client's adopting an active stance toward exploring self and inner experience – a stance that is usually reflected in the energy of the client's voice and the vividness of his/her words'. Cited research supports the view that expressiveness has a role in outcome quality. Could the therapist, just by responsive example, lift a clients level of expressiveness, thus assisting change? Wexler and Butler chose for their study a person who had functioned with low expressiveness over seven interviews. The intervention, in interview 8, was for the therapist to remain within the client's frame of reference but also to work at being highly expressive, using imagery, metaphor and figurative language 'rich in nuance and associations'. In seeking to capture the client's current experience the therapist would make 'an explicit stylistic attempt to do it in as vivid and evocative a manner as possible'; and thus to evoke an enriched range of inner experience in the client (262).

Interviews 7, 8, 9, and 20 with this client, provided the data for analysis. All client and therapist responses (> 500) were separated, effectively shuffled, and rated for expressiveness (see Wexler, 1975). The ratings, for both partners, indeed rose very markedly in material from session 8. It remained on a higher level in sessions 9 and 20, relative to 7. After session 8, the therapist was no more expressive than the client, suggesting that the change was self-reinforcing (Wexler and Butler, 1976: 263–365). The authors were affirmed in their view that intended stylistic change on the therapist's part could be helpful. More radical conceptual and practice changes were evolved by Butler's former colleague, Laura Rice.

Modelling and enabling the processing of experience: research by Rice and colleagues

Rice's mentioned chapter article (1974) is threshold to a stream of later related work, and a bridge back to her prior thought. She suggests that maladaptive emotional-behavioural reactions reflect faulty 'schemes' or ways of processing information from experience. In 'this formulation the problem of change in psychotherapy is the problem of changing inadequate and distorting schemes' (Rice, 1974: 296). Therapeutic enabling is interpreted as assisting the client in transforming dysfunctional schemes so that they work to process all of experience. 'Evocative reflection' is used to facilitate vivid recapture of the whole force and dimension of an intense experience that was originally misprocessed. When the experience has come back full-bodied but newly construed, schemes have altered, and the capacity for inner tracking is enhanced. The more Rice zeroes in on the actual working process of therapy, not its explanation, the more recognizably client-centred her portrayal is. Ten years later, in her book with Greenberg (1984), interest in the micro-processes of therapy had taken more exact and detailed form.

This later work advances an investigative approach involving 'intense scrutiny' of certain recurring episodes in therapy, to discern 'moments of change' and the signposts heralding such moments (Rice and Greenberg, 1984: 13). The method is referred to broadly as task analysis. 'Referring inward' is one example of such a task. In the interview situation, a marker is a consistent sign that a particular affective task, with potential for change, is available to be engaged in (Rice and Saperia, 1984: 29). The marker of immediate interest is a 'problematic reaction point' (PRP), amounting to a clear signal of perplexity and conflict about one's own reaction in an identified context. In response to this marker, a process of evocative unfolding (hinging on evocative reflection) is advocated. A focus on particularities and meanings of the problematic reaction experience is sustained until resolution in terms of felt relief and understanding is reached (33–35).

In an initial study, volunteer student clients came to two interview sessions with a PRP experience already self-chosen. Systematic evocative unfolding (SEU) was used in one session and, in the other, a 'nonspecific client-centred' approach. In each case, the student clients rated 'how productive the interview had been in leading to new perspectives'; and also answered a form of the BLRI. Their ratings favoured the evocative unfolding interviews on productivity but not on quality of relationship. It seemed that the use of SEU improved outcome in an otherwise comparable relationship environment (ibid.: 36–37). However, the context was a therapy *analogue* structured to centre on PRPs, and singling out the issue of achieving new perspectives. Rice and Saperia progressively refined their performance model of client process, for example by testing their initial formulation (based on an idealized client) against close analysis of the process in actual interviews. More interesting to this reader than the model itself was the back and forth progression of theoretical reflection and data-examination used to refine it. Also interesting is a lengthy interview illustration, examined through the new conceptual lens (47–51).

In further empirical work, a spectrum of task-relevant 'molar codes' was derived from interview content analysis, arranged in clusters concerned with recognizing *or* describing the stimulus situation, *or* focusing on internal reactions, *or* examining higher order value constructs, etc. (52–53). In addition, two kinds of process descriptors were coded, centring on *voice quality* (later detailed), and on mode of perceptual processing (54–55; Toukmanian, 1986). Some coded behaviours implied inner attention and tracking, other kinds a more external stance, and expected association with different voice qualities was found. A predicted association between molar code patterns and levels of perceptual processing was also upheld (Rice and Saperia, 1984: 55–57). These results fed into a fuller 'client operations model' portraying the stages involved in resolving PRPs. The first steps entail vivid experiential 'reconstruction' of the original stimulus scene. With combined external (situational) and internal (self) attention, the person sees him/herself as an actor in the original situation, involved in construing events in a particular way. The described process leads on to exploratory generalization to related situations and, further, to consideration of broader personal meaning systems and options for self (58–61).

Wiseman and Rice (1989) later employed actual therapy clients whose agendas were known to include PRPs. The counsellors, broadly client-centred, had direct training in PRP resolution. Sessions with five moderately depressed and anxious women provided the process data. EXP ratings were made on client responses in the course of PRP unfolding and resolution. Both client and therapist vocal quality (VQ) were also classified; and actual therapist activity monitored (ibid.: 282). Sophisticated loglinear and related analyses were used in mapping effects of one step on another. Therapist vocal quality (especially 'irregular voice') was demonstrated as influencing both subsequent client VQ and client peak experiencing level. EXP levels increased more when therapist interventions corresponded to the model-specified step of the PRP task (283–284). Thus the results were internally coherent, although not studied in relation to outcome change.[14]

The Rice–Greenberg book (1984) is not primarily a volume of research reports but of expository analyses of therapeutic process in which the steps are closely described and illustrated. An intention was to lay the ground for future research within and beyond the client-centered domain (1984: 290–300), and some of the close accounts of therapeutic practice (for example, by Mathieu-Coughlan and Klein) would lend themselves to research follow-up. The radical shifts in conceptual approach are such that Rogerian client-centred therapy is mostly not a distinct focus. These characteristics apply even more to a later integrated guide to training and practice (Greenberg, Rice and Elliot, 1993). The same authors, in company with others, had in the meantime contributed to a major resource handbook for psychotherapy *process* research (Greenberg and Pinsof, 1986).

Four contributions to the handbook are most clearly rooted in client-centred work, one of them (Beck et al., 1986) taken up in my next chapter. Another is a detailed, developmental account of the work on voice quality (see early report by Butler, Rice and Wagstaff, 1962: 91–94). 'One of the most basic beliefs of client-centered therapists', the reader is reminded, 'is that it is the manner in which the client engages in the process of exploration, rather than the focus on some particular content, that is decisive for therapeutic change' (Rice and Kerr, 1986: 74). Studying vocal *quality* is a logical extreme of this principle. How might one begin to do this? One starting point was the

---

14 Academic institutions have distinctive value and reward systems; and psychology departments, in particular, are noted for 'tough-minded' emphasis on clearly describable behaviours and sophisticated data-analysis. Such contextual factors are not without effect, and the original work by Rice and collaborators is seen as a case in point. Their innovations, in research and practice conjointly, reflect a thrust towards precise operational description, the framing of these operations in models, and the (seductive) further step of describing intervention pathways applicable in particular circumstances. The relationship conditions stressed by Rogers tend to take a back seat while the chase is on in such differently framed directions.

observation that an inward-turning 'groping along new paths' tended to generate new experience, and that such inner tracking seemed reflected in a voice quality that became identified as focused. A contrasting mode of *outwardly* attentive expression, usually with a deliberate reporting quality, was called 'externalizing' (76–78). A quality identified as emotional was signalled by abrupt shifts in pace or emphasis of speech, feeling 'overflow', and other disruptions in speech flow. The remaining mode entailed a withheld or limited vocal energy, illustrated in a tailing off into 'breathy silence' (77–78).

To distinguish the categories, several vocal elements were employed, including accentuation, evenness of pace, energy, and disruption/nondisruption of speech. Each category had a distinctive signature of elements. Judges achieved adequate reliability in classifying speech units (81–82); and this reliability improved with training (Rice and Wagstaff, 1967: 559). Focused voice has tended to characterize higher success groups (560–562), or be predictive of therapy outcome (Rice and Kerr, 1986: 82). Frequency comparisons for the (therapy-negative) externalizing voice have also been in expected directions. Emotional voice has been too infrequent for meaningful comparison (82–83).

Therapist vocal qualities (TVQ) later became a complementary focus growing out of a view, influenced by Rogers' conditions theory, of *how* therapists were enabling to clients. The multiple categories first distinguished were drawn into two groupings, called 'expressive' and 'distorted'. A trend toward positive association between the composite expressive voice and assessed success was found. The distorted grouping predicted inversely, but only with a wide spread of therapists (ibid.: 89–91). Refinement was called for. After two revisions, by Kerr and Rice, seven categories emerged, freshly defined (91–95). Of these, three ('softened', 'irregular', and 'natural') were 'hypothesized to accompany good therapy'. The first, for example, is said to be a relationship component: 'the therapist communicating to the client that the situation is safe, that the therapist can be trusted, and that the client is prized' (96). Rice and Kerr report preliminary findings in which the 'irregular' category (but not 'softened' or 'natural'), was found positively predictive of ratings of therapist empathy, helpfulness, and the like. The category called 'restricted' was, as expected, quite strongly predictive in a negative direction (97–98).

In their summing up, Rice and Kerr do not advocate use of TVQ analysis, or for that matter client VQ, on its own but as a complement to other measures directly concerned with content or relationship qualities. The question might be asked: Interesting as it is, has all this work on voice quality itself actually moved thought and/or practice forward? The issue is complex. The work has demonstrated that a distinctive level of analysis that filters out content yet has subtle connection with it can be applied to therapy interactions previously viewed in terms of felt process, message communication, or relationship quality. The path of study has more than one level of possible value; not only that of a direct contribution but also one of encouraging other productive inquiry in the same setting and helping to seed future development. There seems little doubt of such effects.

Experiencing levels and focusing, in psychotherapy

Following up a main thread in the Wisconsin research, Klein, Mathieu-Coughlan and Kiesler (1986) trace the history of the experiencing construct (carefully giving joint credit to Rogers and Gendlin), encapsulate the dimension and its seven stages, and outline the range of usage and research. They note that careful application produces high reliabilities, even in interview contexts besides therapy (1986: 35–37, and Table 2–6), and mention that rated EXP level tends to be higher with larger units of information. However, the authors are silent on the point that rated experiencing *level* does not have the same meaning in diverse contexts, especially outside the relative constancy of a therapy environment.

The close exploration of research bearing on validity of the scale (ibid.: 42 ff.) exposes a complexity of evidence. One grouping of results implies that EXP relates more to styles of cognitive processing than to open feeling expression (42). Clearly, too, higher experiencing level need not imply more healthy functioning; in fact, levels may tend to increase under conditions of distress and help-seeking. Overall, the span of research evidence reveals little or no regularity of pattern between initial EXP level and personality functioning or disturbance (44–46). Since the scale was conceived as a measure not of adjustment but of personal process within a highly receptive interpersonal context, one would hardly expect otherwise than this result. On the matter of 'teaching' higher levels of experiencing, it seems that change occurs over the short term and when the coaching is specific (46–47). Evidence since the Wisconsin study does not show linkage between judge-rated accurate empathy and EXP levels. Nor has any clear-cut pattern of association been found between EXP (or EXP shifts) and therapy outcome. Broadly, the evidence is most consistent with viewing the scale as 'a reflection of a mode of productive functioning rather than a stable personality trait', in accord with the original process conception (53).

A new development is the *Therapist* Experiencing Scale, designed 'to assess the degree to which the therapist (or speaker) is engaged in the patient's (or another speaker's) experiencing' (54). At the lowest levels, the therapist (T) refers to external events but not directly to the experiencing client person (C), and is handling information from C in a detached or intellectual mode. In the mid-range, T is empathically involved, speaks as 'I' to 'you', and is 'an active sharing partner in the interchange' (58). At the upper levels, T focuses on C's immediately sensed feelings, or on C's linking of inner referents and meaning. T is involved, almost co-experiencing, in fluent interplay and affirmation of C's moving awareness, with high immediacy. The process appears akin to what I have called 'synchronous engagement' (Chapter 7). Klein et al. describe application of the therapist EXP scale but empirical studies were not yet available.

Focusing, in Gendlin's best-known accounts (1978 and 1981), can be practised by individuals on their own, who have suitable capacity or training. Iberg's encapsulation of the process 'as a distinct form of introspection' (Iberg, 1990: 174) is similarly flexible as to context. However, guidelines for a do-it-yourself situation may not be optimal for therapy, the total process is not the same, and the issues for research are different. Therapy alone includes at least three distinct cases for research. One case is the study of 'focusing' movements emerging unguided in a client-centered interview (Iberg, 1990). In another case, clients are 'taught' focusing steps outside the main therapy relation, and the influence of this coaching on their therapy is then studied (Leijssen, 1996). A third case would study the process and effects of explicit focusing-oriented therapist initiatives during the course of therapy (Clark, 1990).[15]

Iberg (1990) undertook a searching examination of the sequential process in focusing, as reframed in broader phases. Uniquely, these are studied as natural emergents within a client-centred interview process. Interview excerpts attest to the therapist's concentration on empathic following (ibid.: 185–188); and Iberg's study of data from a single interview is an inquiry into method as much as result. A birthing metaphor provides the names for three basic movements. In the initial *pregnant* phase the client conveys his/her problem, feeling the way, and moving implicitly toward the next, *parturient* phase. Effectively, the person 'comes into labour', with increased self-searching/listening effort and pain. Finally there is the '*nascent*' or actual birth phase, with relief and new/wider connections and meaning (174–175). Iberg sorted client speech into utterance units – forty-four such during the interview – and developed a multi-item rating scheme to assess each one. Rating items include 'Reporting a pertinent sequence of events' (pregnant), 'Certain words or analogies favored because of their special fit with feelings' (parturient), and 'Statement of perspective that was not there before . . .' (nascent) (ibid.: Table 2). Each utterance was scored on all three phase types. Sequential graphs showed that pregnancy scores predominated initially, parturiency oscillated in low profile but with one pronounced spike, and nascency scores rose in the second quarter, and held this higher level (184).

Iberg's study contained another primary feature. Drawing on Levy's split brain research, he distinguished two sets of cognitive functions, each characterizing one hemisphere (Table 1). The left brain (L-mode) functions, including linguistic processing, deductive thought, and naming tasks, were seen as especially pertinent to activity in the pregnancy phase. R-mode functions – visualization, matching and the like – plausibly would become a resource in the parturient phase. It was thought that the nascent phase would entail a balance of both kinds. A rating-based index for each set of cognitive functions was also tracked over the course of utterances. Positive linkage was indeed found between pregnancy and L-mode levels, and between parturiency and the R-mode index. However, high-nascency utterances were less balanced in R- and L-mode activity than low-nascency ones (191–192). Searching into this unexpected result, and looking at scores *in sequence*, Iberg observed more

15 Extra-therapy experimental study of particular processes entailed in focusing can take many directions as richly illustrated, for example, in a report by Zimring (1990a). The ingredient elements and effects on cognitive performance of the first phase of focusing ('clearing a space') are placed under a microscope. The reader is taken through the logic and results of an extensive series of studies, and the author comes at the end to a fascinating discussion of implications.

frequent switches back and forth between the two modes of cognitive functioning, in the nascent phase. Rather than working conjointly, it is as though each mode is a readily available resource, used in depth in turn-taking pattern (192–194). The results beckon follow-up research, with diverse therapy dyads.

Leijssen (1996) wanted to know the effects of specific training in focusing. Several long-term clients, deemed to be 'stagnating' in their therapy, spent four 'teaching' interview sessions with another therapist, then returned to their original therapists. Research data included transcribed interviews and questionnaire returns for the training sessions and for the interviews immediately before and after training. All clients increased in rated EXP over the training period. After training, however, they largely reverted to former levels of EXP, and no retained new skill or ability was evident. Continued 'process-guidance' from the therapist was needed if EXP levels were to be heightened (1996: Summary). This salutary result was complemented by others. When clients answered the question 'What did you experience as the most helpful event during focusing training sessions?' they did not point toward the goal of these sessions. One client with a history of incest explained: 'What was most helpful to me was the experience of being treated respectfully by a man. It was the first time in my life that I felt that I could trust a man.' Another, still mourning the death of her child, wrote: 'The most helpful was the moment the therapist expressed that she as a mother could understand that the pain of losing your child doesn't stop after five years' (Summary). In a word, it was the training-therapists' attitudinal and empathic responses that clients largely singled out.

In a separate (large-sample) phase of Leijssen's research, soft 'focusing invitations' blended with the largely client-centred emphasis of therapy. Client experiencing of the therapist as very authentic, or as giving words 'to something that the client hardly dared to feel or express', stood out among helpful moments. It was also observed that clients whose EXP levels stayed comparatively low were as successful in life adjustment terms as those on a higher level. And some of the most resourceful focusers, regularly high on EXP, were unable to finish therapy successfully. Leijssen moved to the view that 'focusing is one of many possible helpful micro-processes that sometimes can come in during therapy, not "the" process as was claimed by experiential therapists' (Summary). Her work, and Iberg's, are substantial focusing studies with strong client-centred connection. A wider spectrum awaits the reader interested in focusing beyond this context.[16]

The Relationship Inventory: later development and application

The BLRI and its trajectory also feature in the Greenberg–Pinsof volume (Barrett-Lennard, 1986a). The 64-item revision of the original Client and

16 Clark's (1990) clinically and conceptually substantial doctoral study would be among those justifying attention in a broader-based account of focusing research.

Therapist forms, available since the mid-sixties, is the version most widely used. A full account of the revision process was published (Barrett-Lennard, 1978), shortly after Gurman's extensive and still useful review (1977). The revision entailed amending the definition of two scale variables, refining the formulation and sampling of items (using item-analysis data, and with both therapy and life relationships in mind), and balancing positively and negatively worded items (Barrett-Lennard, 1978: 3–4). Elements of the original willingness-to-be-known scale became part of the re-examined variable of congruence, and the concept and scale of unconditionality was further refined (6–11). Conditional *self*-regard implies that the person feels worthy (or acceptable to him/herself) if one way, and unworthy (or unacceptable) if another way. Conditional regard has reference to the inner person not simply to outward actions. Reactions evoked by behaviours but not *experienced* as (selective) censure or magnified regard for the self or 'me' are deemed neutral on this variable (6–8).[17] The subtle distinctions of meaning, and commitment to a balance of positive and negative wordings, make for some residual awkwardness in certain 'U' items.[18]

The original Client RI became Form OS-64 (**O**thers' response to **S**elf, 64 items).[19] The therapist RI evolved into Form MO-64 (**M**y response to the **O**ther, 64 items). The latter follows the OS form, item by item, with limited rephrasing to avoid unnatural forms of expression in the first person. Inter-scale correlations vary considerably, according to the sample, but self-agreement (reliability) of each scale measure has much greater stability. Gurman's review (1977: 510–511, Table 1) provides an extensive compilation of reliability data, both internal and test–retest. Most coefficients are in the range .75–.95, and no scale has a test–retest reliability mean across samples of less than .80.

In brief, the evidence is that the basic forms of the RI yield adequately scaled, repeatable measures, thus with the psychometric *potential* to yield valid indices. Besides the original content validation procedure (Barrett-Lennard, 1962a: 6–7), during the revision three colleague judges were called on to provide specific feedback before finalizing the items (Barrett-Lennard, 1978: 14). Other steps, including flexible use of multi-sample item-analysis data, contributed to item selection and formulation (ibid.: Appendix A). Well founded hypothesis-testing studies are a major source of predictive/construct validation evidence. From his survey of studies, Gurman considered there was '*substantial, if not overwhelming, evidence in support of the hypothesized*

---

17 This distinction allows for the case of particular behaviours being liked or disliked, without meaning that part of the self is accepted and another part rejected. In practice, dislike/rejection of a recurring behaviour is usually perceived as rejection of an aspect of self.

18 The rationale for equal presence of positive and negative wordings in the RI pivots on offsetting the effects of any respondent tendency to be a 'yea-sayer' or a 'nay-sayer'. It is also compatible with every answer carrying weight, either positive or negative, in the scoring.

19 Initially there were two revision variants: Form OS-M-64 and OS-F-64, for Male and Female others, respectively. These were later combined into Form OS-64, allowing for a dyad partner of either sex. Small adjustments in item wording accompanied this merger.

relationship between patient-perceived therapeutic conditions and outcome in individual psychotherapy' (1977: 523). This pattern of results implies a coherence of theory and measurement supportive of both.

In one refinement of theory, distinct phases of empathy are distinguished. There is the listener's emergent recognition of the other person's experiencing (empathic resonation – Phase 1), the communicative expression of this awareness that may follow (expressed empathy – Phase 2), and the actual awareness by the recipient person of being so understood (received empathy – Phase 3) (Barrett-Lennard, 1981, 1993a). Although this model describes a sequence, it is one where each step provides the *potential,* not necessity, for the next one. Phase 3 of *received* empathy – logically most directly linked to outcome – cannot occur in the absence of empathy at Phase 1 (1993a: 5–7).[20] No single empathy measure taps all of these phases. The MO/therapist RI relates to Phase 1 of the cycle, and the OS/Client forms provide data pertinent to Phase 3 . Effectively, each of the RI-measured conditions variables 'starts' with an inner response, embraces overt communication, and finally depends on perception by the client/other (Barrett-Lennard, 1986a: 447–448).

In their classic study, Kurtz and Grummon (1972) gathered data for a number of empathy and outcome measures. Client RI empathy (Phase 3) proved significantly and much more strongly related to outcome than any other of the six empathy measures used. Communicated empathy, judged from interview recordings (Truax/Carkhuff scale), thus relevant to Phase 2 empathy, was positively but weakly associated with outcome. Therapist RI E scores (and the other empathy measures) were non-predictive in this sample. Viewed as a test of predictive validity, one RI measure (client data) is strongly supported, the other (therapist data) not. (This author's original study did lend support to both – Barrett-Lennard, 1962a: Tables 9, 12 and 14). Since Kurtz and Grummon used a truncated RI form, with empathy items only, the instrument would have been highly transparent to therapists, in a professionally sensitive area. Actual *experience* in the particular relationship may not have been the sole determinant of response to all items. Relatively small 'error variance' in the E scores from therapist data could dilute and mask a modest underlying association – 'modest' because the link between Phase 1 empathy and outcome is necessarily mediated through other phases, and thus is indirect.

The data pertinent to validation of the RI have accumulated from diverse contexts.[21] Wampler and Powell (1982), for example, compared mean scores from several studies tapping couple relationships independently identified as distressed or non-distressed. The RI scores (item means for each scale) were consistently much higher for the assorted non-distressed groups than for the groups, including those seeking counselling, classed as distressed (1982: 143).

20 Phase 3 is sometimes called 'perceived empathy'. Although perception by the recipient person is quite crucial, 'received' implies that something is passed as well as taken, and fits the phasic conception much better. Something 'perceived' can at the extreme be entirely attributed, and does not have the clear connotation of being a link in a larger chain.

21 And an organized summary appears in the author's cited 1986a report (458–462).

In a different plane, the factor-analytic evidence, based on item intercorrelation data, in Gurman's view supported the theoretically based dimensionality of the instrument (1977: 513). This is not to imply that all factor-analyses would yield consistent results. Lietaer's important work with Dutch-language forms of the RI is a case in point. He initially extended the item sample, and his factor-analytic procedures tended to separate the subgroups of positively worded items from the negatively worded. For two of the original scales this resulted in a pair of factors: Positive *and* negative regard; and 'transparency' *and* 'incongruity'. The factor of 'directivity' was the only distinctly different construct to emerge from Lietaer's analyses, *and loaded mainly on items that he added* (Lietaer, 1976; Barrett-Lennard, 1986a: 461).

Lietaer applied the modified RI to compare relationships in psychoanalytic (p-a) and client-centred (c-c) therapy, in substantial clinical samples. Client RIs reflected a view of the p-a therapists as distinctly more directive and the c-c therapists as generally more transparent. In other ways, differences appeared minimal in client data, more evident in therapist returns (Lietaer, 1979: 150ff.). Leaving aside 'directivity', the corresponding scores of client and therapist partners correlated at low but positive levels (mean r = .26, on seven scales) in the c-c sample, but at near-zero levels in the p-a group (mean r = .06) (ibid.: Table 7). Given other research results, the associations are about what one would expect in the case of the c-c group, and suggest that p-a therapists had difficulty identifying their personal response to clients, or, were simply less communicative on this level. Such inference ties in with clients tending to see them as less transparent. The evidence also accords with a broader impression that MO form measures in the client–therapist setting are of inconsistent validity. Gathering sound RI data *from therapists* is probably even more sensitive, more dependent on confidence between researcher and 'subject', and the care and integrity of steps involved, than gathering the corresponding data from clients.

Despite broad application of the Relationship Inventory in psychotherapy research no study seems to have followed up the idea of obtaining baseline measures of client-experienced interpersonal life quality outside therapy (Barrett-Lennard, 1986a: 463). RI (revised) Form OS-S-40 taps the respondent's experience of significant others over a broad spectrum of ongoing life relationships.[22] These are selected from the spheres of family relations, of friendships, and of work–life relations. *If the therapy conditions are the critically important factors in enabling change, they must be present in some unique concentration or level in the client–therapist relationship, as compared with other current relationships in the client's life.* It may not be the absolute level of received empathy (say) that is crucial for therapy, but whether it is present in unique degree for that person. Related is the question of whether, over the course of a productive therapy experience, relations with

22 The item sample was cut to 10 per scale to make the task manageable when describing multiple relationships. On the back of this development, a more economical 40-item version of the regular OS and MO forms was devised; and OS-40 is coming into use as of this writing.

significant others become experienced as generally more positive. And if life relations do improve, has the 'gap' narrowed between the therapy and other relationships, and does this narrowing (if found) have any causative relation to voluntary termination of therapy?

The issues mentioned suggest another frontier of possible research. Here the focus is on *client* empathy, viewed as a vital aspect of functioning and significant axis of potential change. The way clients relate to their own experience and their openness to and connection with the inner experience of other persons, both fall in the domain of empathy. A systematic account of these twin aspects, under the headings of self-empathy and interpersonal empathy, has now been advanced (Barrett-Lennard, 1997a).[23] Various research possibilities are open. For example, does empathic attunement become a more significant priority and source of meaning to clients, through therapy? And, does the individual's empathic sensitivity as experienced by significant others, increase over therapy? On the second issue, clients might be asked to nominate individuals whom *they* feel they understand relatively well. These 'understood' persons would then be called on to describe the client's response to them in empathy-relevant ways, both before and after therapy, to test for change. As an added feature, if the client's own view of his/her understanding of these persons was also obtained, client empathy seen from the external and 'inside' vantage points should be more congruent afterwards than before (presuming therapy had been effective in helping the client become more open to experience). Work to test such hypotheses may now tempt investigators.

Therapy content analysis renewed

Interview response patterns came under the spotlight again, in the eighties, with work by Brodley and others. 'Demonstration' and published interviews by Carl Rogers comprised a main part of the data. Bozarth (1990) implies that Rogers held to the same working approach in therapy from the mid–late forties to his death some four decades later. Although his later style seemed more expressive, he consistently placed high trust in his clients, focused on understanding their worlds, and responded largely in 'empathic following' mode (see later-mentioned work by Brodley). From a study involving 'six notable CC/PC therapists' Bozarth extrapolated more broadly, in characteristic style: 'The essence of CC/PC therapy is the therapist's dedication to going with the client's direction, at the client's pace, and with the client's unique way of being' (1990: 63).

Brodley (1992) cites results that she and Brody obtained from close analysis of Rogers' responses over a range of client interviews. His predominant

23 The volume containing this paper (Bohart and Greenberg, 1997) includes substantial new work on empathy from a span of resourceful contributors, including both editors. I only lately came across Bohart's interesting earlier (1991) exploration and comparison of both psychoanalytic and self-psychology treatments of empathy with the client-centred process view. Some features that Bohart points to could be tracked and further illuminated through targeted interview analysis.

empathic response mode 'tracked' the signified experience and meanings of clients wherever these led. An implicit, highly consistent feature is that *clients were treated as the active source of the experience they expressed* (1992: 22). Brodley uses the term 'actions of personality' to refer to feelings, intentions and volitions, evaluations, and other categories of human experiential action to which nearly all of Rogers' responses referred. Empathic awareness entails a contact of recognition with another self in *whom the recognized experience is happening*. Communication of empathic contact not only conveys an understanding of experience but also the recognition of its live immediacy within the other 'self as agent'.[24]

Extending this work, Brodley (1994) presents analyses of Rogers' total spectrum of responses found in thirty-four interviews conducted over a 46-year time span. 'Empathic following' (EF) responses, and responses variously indicative of the therapist's own frame of reference, were distinguished. Questions, the use of metaphor and the like, as well as reflections, often were discerned as expressions of empathic following activity which, altogether, accounted for over 86 per cent of all articulate verbal responses. The other largest category, 'therapist comment', accounted for 10 per cent of responses overall. Less than 4 per cent fell in the remaining categories of 'therapist leading/probing questions' and 'therapist agreements'. When the interview sample was divided into three groups – three sessions (1, 5 and 7) with 'Mr Bryan' (Rogers, 1942a: Part IV), seventeen interviews from 1944–1964, and fourteen interviews from 1977–1986 – interesting differences emerged. With Bryan, only 46 per cent of responses fell in the EF category, 30 per cent were comments and explanations from the therapist's perspective, and 24 per cent were leading questions or agreements (Brodley, 1994: 42). Evidently, Rogers' practice had not yet caught up with his ideas of non-directive total attention to the client's world of experience and meaning.

By contrast, in the 1944–1964 sample over 95 per cent of responses fell in the EF category and nearly all the remainder were classed as comments. This period runs through the School Phase, to the point where Rogers' serious involvement in groups began. The third sample, of fourteen 'demonstration' clients, leapfrogs to the last decade of Rogers' life. EF responses have dropped back to 84 per cent, therapist comments account for another 14 per cent, and 2 per cent are classed as leading/probing questions (ibid.: 42).[25]

24 In his paper examining Rogers' process with clients, Zimring (1990b) distinguishes between (i) responding to the (troubling) topical content that the client brings to therapy and (ii) acknowledging the immediate experience s/he is having in the process of introducing and working on her/his problems. Interview illustration brings out distinct possibilities and choices therapists make in respect to the levels or 'frame' of the experience they respond to, even within a broadly empathic mode. Zimring notes that 'methods of responding give rise to knowledge' (ibid.: 446), and discusses kinds of knowledge that flow from the engagement and response of Rogers and other client-centred workers. The paper is a searching 'study' although not formal research.

25 Merry's (1996) related descriptive study, based on ten demonstration interviews by Rogers, also entailed coding modes of empathic following. The remaining categories – direct questions, self-references, 'offering observations' – accounted in all for 7–21% of responses.

Brodley notes Rogers' later acknowledgement of sharing from his immediate experience (first publicly evident in his interview with 'Gloria'), and his view that his own *presence* seemed to be healing when deeply absorbed with his client. Implied is an expansion of his therapeutic mode of being, with empathy still the central motif (43–45).[26]

Lietaer and colleagues conducted a different kind of content-analysis study, focusing on client and therapist views of helpful and 'hindering' elements in therapy. The therapist-practitioners were members of the Flemish Society for Client-Centred Therapy, trained broadly in the Rogerian tradition as augmented by focusing and other experiential methods. Written data were gathered a number of times over the course of therapy, from forty-one clients and their therapists, yielding a total sample of 325 interview reports. Answers to the question 'Did things happen in this session that you feel were really helpful?' are the centrepiece of the report by Lietaer and Neirinck (1986). Over thirty categories emerged from content analysis of the answers, grouped in three sectors: relational climate, specific therapist interventions, and client process.

Climate features – including the familiar therapy conditions – were singled out as especially helpful over twice as often by clients as by their therapists. 'Specific therapist interventions' were mentioned in similar frequency by clients, *and much more often than climate attributes by their therapists* (444–446). Especially noted were interventions to stimulate self-exploration, assist full or deeper experiencing, or provide here-and-now feedback, sometimes in 'confronting' mode (Table 3). The 'client process' sector accounted for over half of all helpful features mentioned by either partner. Aspects ranged from 'having the opportunity to talk' to 'living through and experiencing more fully', and, achieving fresh insight (445). The insight categories stood out in frequency, especially in the client data (Table 3). The question eliciting these data 'Did things happen . . .?' may have invited mention of events more than of qualities. For some, it evoked recall of what was helpful in the therapist's response or the process engaged in (sectors 1 and 2). For others, it triggered a focus on valued happenings and outcomes of the session (sector 3).

The answers to the complementary 'hindering' question were also interesting. The request: was carefully direct 'Did things happen in this session that you feel were not helpful at all (or perhaps even the opposite)?' This time, a differing set of categories was needed for the client and the therapist data. The context was long-term therapy, generally experienced positively. The negative elements/episodes were 'missed opportunities', even

26 Lietaer (1995) also published a case study analysis of a Rogers' interview with a hurt and angry young black client, 'Dione' (interview date *c.* 1973.) His study of the therapist's verbal response employs a category system interesting in its similarities and contrast with the categories used by Brodley. Much the most frequent response mode (61%) is the familiar reflection of feeling (1995: Table 5.1 [8 + 9a + 9b]). The second largest (10.4%: Table 5.1 [13a]), under the broader heading of self-disclosure, is 'task-related process comment about own responses or C's process' (English wording from Lietaer). Interpretation, feedback, and confrontation around discrepancies or avoidance, in all accounted for 14.6% of Rogers' responses (Table 5.1: [10 + 11 + 12]).

painful setbacks, but not rupturing crises (Lietaer, 1992: 150). Both partners tended to feel responsible themselves for the session deficiencies they noted (Table 6.3 and 6.5, cluster B). Where clients did blame the therapist, it was that they had been over-guiding, too interpretive or intrusively active, less often that they seemed remote or inactive (Tables 6.3 and 6.5, cluster A). Therapists were sometimes conscious of pushing their own view on the client excessively but were as likely to feel they had been too passive or uninvolved (Table 6.6 – implied). More often, some failure of empathy was a significant concern. Client failure to tap into their inner experiential life was also a therapist-voiced problem (Table 6.6).

Lietaer's category systems are recent portraits of the range of experienced helping and hindering processes, and thus a primary product of the research (1992: 140). They certainly imply that the therapy itself has shifted substantially from the phenomenon revealed by the early process research. The study method throws an illuminating spotlight on participant-valued and unwanted happenings of therapy. The detailed results suggest to me some 'struggle for balance' on the part of therapists generally committed to the Rogerian conditions but also having the self-expectation of actively leading clients into deeper levels of experiencing. Results from additional data gathered at the same time appear in Dutch-language publications cited by Lietaer (136). Another European study complements this one in its approach.

Tscheulin (1990) was interested in 'experience-activating' therapist intervention, based on the idea of client and therapist complementarity. Conditions theory provides an example of this notion, namely, the requirements of therapist congruence and client incongruence (implied in anxiety/vulnerability). Clients who are attentive to their inner self and functioning, and prone to conflict anxiety, are distinguished from 'action-centred' clients with hungers expressed in external activity. The latter are seen as 'spontaneously less capable of self-reflection' and more likely (say) to develop hysterical conversion symptoms or delinquent patterns (ibid.: 328). It was proposed that confrontations would be productive with the second kind of person, *un*productive with the former. (Other therapy conditions were vital to the context of such 'confrontations'.) As a test of this perspective, extreme groups of student clients were selected from a larger population, one group very centred on self and the other strongly action-centred. Half of each group was exposed to a confronting therapist approach, half to a non-confronting style. Thus, half received the theoretically wrong emphasis and half the one expected to be right for them. The favourably and unfavourably matched groups differed in the expected direction, a result replicated in a further study (330–331).

Interviews from the therapy portrayed were content-analysed for group differences and to discern what actually seemed to trigger therapist confrontations. Preceding such response, therapists were being exposed to distinctly contradictory or self-avoidant client behaviours, which seldom occurred before non-confronting responses (332). The mentioned characteristics of action-centred people suggest to me that they would not knowingly choose a highly nondirective form of psychotherapy, and possibly tended to be 'failure cases' in earlier practice and research (see Chapter 12). Another broadly related study, using content-analysis methods to discern and track process features, is reported by Dierick and Lietaer (1990). The context in this case is group therapy, in which feedback confrontation and other interventions occur member to member, as well as in leader–member interaction. This study is discussed in my next chapter.

In conclusion – other strands and visions of research

Mention here of European studies skims a much larger domain. An accessible English language review sources the full range of 'research on experiential psychotherapies', published between 1978 and 1992 (Greenberg, Elliot and Lietaer, 1994). This work includes reference to comparative outcome studies of client-centred versus behavioural or psychodynamic treatments, undertaken by proponents of the latter approaches (e.g., Tables 12-2 and 12-3). As one main example, Meyer, Stuhr, Wirth and Ruester (1988) compared client-centred and dynamic therapies (and non-treated controls), using short term and very long term (twelve-year) follow-up testing and evaluation, with a starting sample of eighty-five. About 80 per cent of the original therapy cases provided test data at all points. Clients in both therapy groups clearly improved pre- to post-therapy on the measures of extraversion and depression, with sustained or increased improvement at twelve years (1988: Tables 2 and 3). From the results of this and other research, Greenberg et al. (1994: 517) carefully conclude that 'there is evidence for the comparability of the effects of experiential therapy with those of cognitive-behavioral and dynamic treatments'. A later report from a major US study provides grounds to extend this conclusion (Blatt, Quinlan, Zuroff and Pilkonis, 1996).

The National Institute of Mental Health Collaborative Research Program on treatment of depression included manual-specified interpersonal therapy (IPT) and cognitive-behaviour therapy (CBT). IPT may owe more to Sullivan than directly to Rogers but has kinship with the client-centred approach. Exhaustive analyses of the many-sided outcome data showed that clients improved under both therapy regimes – and with medication and clinical management. The IPT approach worked somewhat better than CBT with more severely depressed patients (Elkin et al., 1989). Blatt and colleagues studied the client-experienced therapy relationship, in each treatment mode. This was assessed from the BLRI answered after the second of twelve or more therapy sessions. Outcome differences were 'generally not predicted' by type of treatment but *were* linked to quality of the therapist-to-patient relation (Blatt et al., 1996: 169). Thus, the conclusion that it seems 'more productive to explore dimensions of the interpersonal relationship established between patient and therapist . . . that affect therapeutic change than to continue to look for differences among different types of therapeutic intervention' (170).

Reinhard Tausch and collaborators, in Germany, have also been pivotal contributors to research. Rudolph, Langer and Tausch (1980), for example, followed up a series of earlier reports with a compilation of results from a large sample of clients and their '80 person-centered psychotherapists'. For the total group 'changes . . . were only moderately greater than the changes of the control group' (ibid.: 32). Change varied widely and was found linked to level of the therapy conditions (modified BLRI) and, in particular, whether all three, two, or only one, of the relationship conditions was present to a 'high extent'. Empathy alone, for example, did not suffice for a favourable outcome. In broad conclusion, 'the probable changes of clients can be predicted . . . after the 4th contact by statements of their perceptions of the facilitator and their feelings during the talk' (33). Evidence from varied sources contributed to Tausch's growing conviction of need for a more 'ecumenical' approach to therapy. He forcefully advocated *responsive* introduction of other validated therapeutic options, in context with a basic client-centred relationship and communication process (Tausch, 1990). In another place, he reached outside client-centred theory to illuminate the cognitive dimension in empathy (Tausch, 1988); finding, for example, that Rogers attended and responded more often to cognitive elements than to affective-emotional ones, in his classic interview with 'Gloria'.[27]

The research reviewed in this chapter mostly employed fairly standard research methodology, with emphasis on measurement, control samples where possible, statistical probability estimation, and the like. Distinctly qualitative methodology has been a component of some studies but rarely the main or whole thrust. A recent exception and good example of qualitative work is the dissertation study by Sharon Myers (1995). Myers worked to illuminate further the basic *nature* and meaning of empathy occurring within a helping relationship, using intensive phenomenological investigation. Her study is as carefully crafted in its own mode as a well-thought experimental project. Five articulate recent clients were called on, each of whom had worked in turn with two therapists (A and B). Therapist A conducted semi-structured, in-depth interviews centring on the relationships with B, and B interviewed clients about experiences with A. (These interviews, transcribed, were then coded independently for all empathy-related themes.) Additional data included therapist narratives of relationships with each client, BLRIs from all participants, client written supplements to their interviews, and client-completed Q-sorts – individually *composed from their own prior data.* Data integration evolved around broad questions, framed at the start. Conclusions build a picture of the experience of empathic connection, its individuality, course of development, and pervasive impact.

A fine resource on qualitative methods forms a large part of a recent textbook on counselling research, by John McLeod (1994). Chapters titled 'Listening to stories about therapy: from qualitative research to human science', and 'Systematic inquiry into individual cases', suggest the orbit of

---

27 Tausch's results indirectly also lend some support to Pentony's theoretical analysis of the way empathic reflections work (1994). He argues that therapy is centrally a process by which change occurs in the meaning to clients of events in their lives (55). Reflections help to transform primary experience into broader meaning, centred in the client, and often are like mini-hypotheses for further testing. Pentony's searching total exploration appears most fully in his 1981 book.

interest. Foci include the concept of 'grounded theory' – grounded, that is, in the lived experience of participating informants – and research that this thought has triggered (1994: 93–96). A very pertinent example is the work of David Rennie (1990, 1994). The emphasis is on descriptive/theoretical discovery, the theory derived in stages from an immersion in the stories of informants describing and reflecting on particular experience. Rennie adapted Kagan's Interpersonal Process Recall method, the recalled process being the client's immediately preceding, recorded therapy interview, to which investigator and client listened in a relaxed inquiry session of two hours or longer. Clients could speak at any point about their recall of their engagement, their inward process, and its significance or meaning to them. In Rennie's 1994 report, the sample consists of fourteen clients seeing eleven different therapists.

All of the recall inquiry sessions and referent interviews were transcribed, and found to contain in sum over 1,000 discriminated 'meaning units'. These were sorted into the categories and clusters delineated in the earlier report (Rennie, 1990: 157–159; McLeod, 1994: 95). Rennie's searching discussion of his results is itself an original and illuminating discourse, not possible to distil in a few lines. To take one aspect, it was clear that the in-therapy consciousness of clients formed a much larger pool than their overt expressions. Evidently, 'the information processing capacities of people are so vast that a dialogue with the self can be carried on while the individual is engaged in a dialogue with another person' (1990: 162).

McLeod discusses other modalities of qualitative research, and suggests a range of criteria for evaluating the validity of studies (1994: 97–101). A decade earlier, he had collaborated with David Mearns in suggesting the characteristics of 'a person-centred approach to research' (Mearns and McLeod, 1984). These are not distinctive methods so much as a bringing of client-centred values into the research arena. The persons from whom information is sought are approached respectfully, as equals, in a spirit of partnership. They are seen as co-participants or collaborating informants, and sensitivity to their frames of reference is not only a matter of respect but has bearing on the integrity of the information provided, and a proper understanding of it. The researcher is authentically searching, and is open, not guarded, in style and approach to co-participants.

Person-centred investigators are most at home with research informed by a fusion of practical and theoretical interest. The methodology may have a qualitative leaning or rely on measurement and statistical inference, according to the stage and goals of the inquiry. Knowledge-seeking and 'knowledge' itself are human enterprises which flourish when motivated by curiosity, concern for human well-being, and attitudes not of seeking final truths but progressive enlargement of understanding. The immediate story of this search, beyond the domain of one-to-one therapy, is carried forward in my next chapter.

14

Investigation Beyond One-to-One Therapy

> The investigator has to see the meaning, understand the valuation, and feel the feeling connected with each object or act in the mind of the native. Only after he has seen it from the native's point of view may the investigator change his viewpoint and look at that object or act – together with the meaning and the value it has for the native – as an object of scientific interest now to be described from the outside and related . . . to other things . . . according to the demands of a more detached and abstract understanding.
>
> Robert Redfield, 1960

Research by client-centred and allied investigators is by no means confined to individual psychotherapy. Studies have ranged over a much broader domain: the small-group sphere (itself a broad region), couple and family process and counselling, teacher–student relations, friendships and various other categories of relationship and, by way of slender beginning, community and peace processes. This research has been conducted in a great variety of settings by independent investigators mostly not building on each other's work. Its reporting has been incomplete, with interesting results quite often not finding their way beyond dissertation reports and other unpublished sources. This chapter aspires to sample across the full range, giving significant attention to unpublished work. The scope of ideas, method and result, and richness of further possibility, may tempt the reader to join the search in a particular area, or to refine plans already in the making.

Small groups for healing and growth

Small-group research in particular has advanced through initiatives dispersed in location and kind. Unlike the earlier work described (pp. 252–257), concepts and method no longer borrow heavily on individual therapy research. Within the decade from the mid-sixties to mid-seventies, data were being actively gathered by a number of investigators of Rogerian background: Beck, Bebout, Barrett-Lennard, Braaten, Clark, and Solomon and Berzon, among others. Rogers himself collected follow-up evaluation data in the 1960s. One of his first doctoral students in Wisconsin, Charles Truax, chose to study group *therapy*, before group experiences outside clinical settings became the focal interest.

Truax's PhD study; Rogers' encounter survey; & the Solomon/Berzon research

The groups entailed in Truax's study (1961), were conducted with main concern for *self* recovery and without explicit focus on interpersonal healing. As in the main Wisconsin project, the subjects were psychiatric hospital patients, and the groups were a context for personal psychotherapy. The study explored associations between (i) measures of therapeutic conditions, rated from the therapist's response, and also from the response of group members, and (ii) levels of client self-exploration rated from Rogers' process scale and other indices. In Truax's closely argued view, therapeutic change is a direct function and result of *intra*personal exploration (his preferred term), this exploration a function of the level of the therapy conditions. He believed that before-to-after personality measures were more speculative and value-laden, when it came to assessing therapy benefit, than evidence of the level of process clients engaged in within therapy.

Each of three patient groups was studied over a span of forty-two sessions. The brief sample drawn from each session gave a 'peephole' view of personal exploration process in the group, from whomever was visibly active at the time. Thus each of the 42 × 3 segments allowed a set of ratings, these segments forming the sample for statistical analyses. The various conditions rated went beyond Rogers' triad (Truax, 1961: Table 1), and the process scale was supplemented by an insight/seeing new relations measure. Associations between therapist accurate empathy and genuineness/congruence (on the one hand), and the process and insight scales, reached significance (with N = 126) (ibid.: Table 2). Some conditions rated from *member response* also co-varied with the indices of self-exploration (Tables 3, 4 and 6). Were the links causal ones or did the measures have some basis or element in common? The data accord with either possibility. Truax's work and conclusions (1961: Summary) fed into his contributions in the main Wisconsin project but did not lead on to further group therapy research.

Rogers' own follow-up evaluation data from encounter groups involved a large combined sample (481 persons: 82 per cent of those contacted) who reported three to six months after their intensive group participation. Of these, two persons said the experience had been damaging, 'moderate numbers' experienced minimal or no sustained personal-behavioural change, and the great majority reported distinctly positive outcomes (1970: 126). Actual questions and more detailed results are given for a particular, large workshop, one in which the whole membership was witness to the *facilitators'* ongoing small group (127–128). Most felt in retrospect that these observed sessions, as well as their own groups, had been valuable. One question asked respondents whether they now behaved differently with various categories of significant other, and most checked one or more categories. Co-workers, for example, were mentioned by over half the sample. Eloquent excerpts from the free-answer part of the questionnaire are quoted but no content analysis is mentioned; and Rogers lets the selected information speak largely for itself.[1]

Solomon and Berzon's work with self-led groups (see pp. 170–171) also generated empirical data, especially in 'Study 3' of their series (1970: 318 ff.). Professionally directed (PD) and self-directed (SD) eighteen-session groups were initially conducted, using both in-session and before-to-after tests. Evidence of positive change in either kind of group was modest, and the conditions levels as measured actually declined from early to late in the life of SD groups (ibid.: 321 ff.). Observer ratings of therapeutic climate, made session by session, showed overall rise only in the PD groups (324). Members did report less discrepancy between 'The way I felt inside' and 'How I must have seemed to others' in both group conditions. It seemed that the SD groups suffered from an overly cognitive/insufficiently experiential emphasis, and changes were made.

In the second phase, goals were spelled out more clearly, and stimulus tapes and exercises also reflected them (p. 170, above). Self-rated readiness to share and reveal self, in best friend and other relationships, showed increase in this sample (1970: 336–337). The index of discrepancy between inside feelings and outside appearance again yielded positive results. Therapeutic climate ratings increased *within each* of the two weeks of group sessions. Generally it appeared that the changes made for this phase improved outcomes; although the label 'self-directed' seems a misnomer. Indeed, the acronym PEER, standing for Planned Experiences in Effectively Relating (!), was adopted for subsequent phases (344–346; Berzon, Solomon and Reisel, 1972). Practice innovation and evaluation research worked in fruitful synergy, in this mid-sixties context.

Research features of the Australian workshops in therapeutic counselling

The experiential group workshops held in Armidale, Australia (see p. 154) included process and outcome data-gathering from the start. Outcome evaluation data were obtained after a delay of six to seven months rather than when members were fresh from a 'high' of releasing connection within self and with others. About 90 per cent of the members (sixty-two persons) from Workshops 1 and 2 provided these data. Free answer questions, presented first, asked what changes (if any), attributed to the workshop experience, were discerned in each of three areas: personal functioning, process as a counsellor, and group leader/member behaviour. A single content analysis system for all mentioned effects was developed. Two-thirds or more of respondents spoke of

---

1 Rogers also outlines a dissertation study of process movement in an encounter group, later published by its author (Meador, 1971). The group studied was filmed for the documentary *Journey into Self* (Rogers, McGaw and Farson, 1968). For each member, two brief excerpts from each of the five sessions were chosen and reordered on a random basis (Meador, 1971: 72). Trained judges made a single rating on each segment. Process level for each individual changed significantly over the course of sessions, and the group mean process level increased significantly (ibid.: 73).

increased ability to be open and accepting in relationships, and/or of more regard for self, of some new self-awareness affecting behaviour, of counselling seen 'more as an I–Thou relationship than as a role', or of greater appreciation for 'the basic rights and worth of . . . clients' (Barrett-Lennard, Kwasnik and Wilkinson, 1973/1974: 39). Relational and self change, and shifts in attitude in a helping role, were on this evidence commonly experienced.

Further items, in alternative-answer form, asked directly about growthful effects, and called on respondents to estimate any change in confidence or (separately) effectiveness as helpers. Possible change in sensitivity to the experience and feelings of others, or to a more expressive, open style in work-related groups, were also targeted (Barrett-Lennard, 1974/1975). Most answers clustered in the strongly or moderately positive options (ibid.: Tables 1–3). The 1964 group members were additionally asked whether 'other persons who know you well [have] noticed and commented that you have changed in your outlook and response to people since the workshop'. More than might be expected (44 per cent) from other data indicated that they had *not* received such feedback, suggesting that significant others saw more limited effects than the participants did. Observations by self and by others flow from different data pools and person-views, and different investments in judgement. Thus, it would be over-simple to validate one against the other, and each has the potential to refine the meaning of data from the other source.[2]

Some results from this work have never been reported. As example, an early version of the 64-item 'My response to the Other' (MO) form of the RI was answered just before and just after Workshop 1, in reference to the 'last client' to enter a therapy/helping relationship with the respondent. The second time, the directions were to answer for the same relationship 'as you [now] perceive it was before the workshop began . . .'. It was thought that participants would afterwards admit further data into their awareness and/or set different personal standards for themselves, and the RI measures were examined for decrease or increase. Congruence scores diminished for 26 of the 32 members, increasing for 6 only, a result with chance probability of < 1 per cent (Sign Test – Siegel, 1956: 68–75). Virtually the same proportion also diminished on the Unconditionality scale and, in one of the two groups, empathy scores mostly fell, as well (Barrett-Lennard, data-analysis records, 1963 workshop). The workshop experience evidently had marked, immediate impact on the members' perceptions of their past helping behaviour. It seems that participants recognized limitations that they had not been able to acknowledge before.

---

2 Non-participant others might well bring a more sceptical view to bear, not expecting change effects of any depth. And actual change can be difficult to discern: some inwardly sensed shifts only become visible through later new experiences (above, pp. 165–167; and Barrett-Lennard, 1996a). Other evidence of shift in self-perception was found in data from an 80-item Self-Concept Inventory (descended from the Butler and Haigh Q-sort – pp. 305–308), answered pre, post and six months later by Workshop 2 members. In this sample, self-descriptions shifted over the eleven days of the workshop at least as much as in the six months following (Barrett-Lennard, 1967: 7).

The same results were not found, however, in Workshop 2, where RI score increases and decreases almost balanced out. Closer study showed that in Workshop 1, the strong effect had resulted largely from 'Group X' (one of the two experiential working groups), leaving a trend only, in 'Group Y'. In Workshop 2, results for the group with the same leader/facilitator as Group X tended in the same direction. For example, on the C scale, scores decreased for 8/11 respondents (chance prob. = .11). These and further data suggest that leadership *and* member composition were jointly contributing to the variability across workshops and groups.

The RI was used in another way in Workshop 3 (in 1965). Intending members were each asked in advance to nominate a current client and/or other person in close contact. These 'observers' were called on before the workshop, and again a few weeks later, to complete the OS RI on the member's response to them, and mail their returns directly to the investigator. Workshop members also answered this form of the RI *for the way they expected their observer(s) to perceive them* (Barrett-Lennard, 1967: 6–7). They did this after arrival at the workshop, and a few weeks later. The complete before and after returns from 23 member–observer pairs revealed that responding members anticipated their observers' perceptions of them more accurately following the workshop than beforehand.[3] Members' predictive scores mostly shifted more than the observers' scores did, suggesting that the change was in fact mainly in member awareness rather than altered observer perception.[4]

In the follow-up questionnaire for Workshop 1, a semantic opposites item had also been included. As example, the scale ranged over seven points from extremely harmonious (or 'quite' or 'a little'), through 'neither/both equally', to a little, quite or extremely conflicting. Respondents checked the point 'that best describes your perception now of the most typical atmosphere and process in your workshop group' (Barrett-Lennard, 1972b: Appendix B). Results imply that the two groups, broadly of one kind, had also been quite

---

3 The *difference* in RI scale score from the pairs of observer and member returns pre- and post-workshop were looked at in terms of direction of change and (secondarily) by average magnitude. As predicted, the differences typically diminished – as shown here for the first time:

PreW to PostW	Regard	Empathy	Unconditionality	Congruence
Reduced difference cases	16	16	15	16
Increased difference cases	5	7	7	7
Unchanged difference cases	2	0	1	0
Probability (Sign Test)	< .02	< .05	.07	< .05
PreW mean difference	15.4	21.4	22.2	19.5
PostW mean difference	10.1	15.1	17.1	13.9

4 On the C and R scales, for example, the mean shift in member prediction scores was 8.7 and 8.5 while for observers it was 4.0 and 4.2. As for the direction of these shifts, member estimates of the way their relational partners would see them tended to rise. This was most striking for Congruence (16 >, 4 < [3=] preW levels), and on this scale observer scores also tended to increase (Barrett-Lennard, RI data-analysis file, 1965 workshop).

distinct, and each was consistently remembered after the interval of six months. Twelve of fifteen respondents from Group Y converged in tagging their group as 'quite' harmonious. (No one from Group X checked this part of the scale.) Ys also remembered their group as gentle and accepting, caring, warm, 'quite' revealing, and predominantly genuine and understanding. Every X respondent remembered *their* group as 'quite' or 'extremely' turbulent, whereas Ys had the impression of calmness. Xs agreed that their group had been tense, and implied that it was intense. Ys characterized their group as comforting; for Xs it had been upsetting, or a mix of both. Xs, in some contrast to Ys, also felt the experience had been 'fast', 'varied', and 'active'. For both groups (and especially for Xs) the process had been 'searching', and the sessions 'valuable' (with modal ratings either of 'extremely' [Xs] or 'quite' [Ys)]) (1972b: Table 5).[5]

Data gathered *during the on-going process of the workshops* included rating sheets answered at the end of each (two-hour) session. The multiple-choice items first used gave a kind of 'barometric reading' on a few key aspects of each session: how productive it was felt to be, experienced level of involvement, extent of mutual understanding and contact, sense of discovery (if present), and felt responsibility for what took place. The obtained 'readings' varied over time and (less sharply) between members. On the question 'Was this a productive session for you?', with answer choices of 'no' (0), 'only slightly' (1), moderately (2), and 'very much so' (3), mean scores for the item rose to 2.6, in the seventeen-person Group X. To the question 'Did you feel really involved in what went on?', ratings peaked initially at session 6 (mean 2.75/3), everyone felt high involvement in session 14 (mean 2.9/3), and the remaining three sessions were rated similarly. As for inter-member understanding, however, the mean for session 14 was only 1.5/3, and ratings peaked in (the last) session 17 (mean 2.7/3). Ratings on whether members had 'a sense of discovering new meanings during the session' began at a low level, rose to 2.2 toward the end of week 1 (sessions 6 and 7), and peaked in session 14 – evidently an episode combining frustration and fruitfulness. The simple check-sheet was providing a useful view; and it was augmented in Workshop 2 by a semantics opposite list (like the one used at follow-up, in Workshop 1) on which members could quickly check the 'climate' of the session.

For Workshop 3, a rather different session-by-session rating instrument was devised. Twenty distinct questions were each answered on a five-point

---

5 Workshop 1, in 1963, was the first of its kind in Australia. The thoughtful and adventurous participants travelled far, arriving with high hopes but varied expectations. The ratings at follow-up are consistent with observation at the time. In Group X, the clash of differing views and styles was particularly marked, and members struggled with determination to come forth and be known in their own distinctive presences. Their intense, searching engagement seemed to lead to powerful individual experiences and to strong group feeling and bonding. Group Y, by common consensus, engaged in quieter, gentler, less confronting interaction, but with outcomes almost equally valued. Word got around after Workshop 1, and motivations the next time were not quite the same. Some members were looking for the kind of experience they had heard about, some had been actively *encouraged* to come. The three group leaders in 1964 had all been in Group X the year before.

scale from 'no, not at all' to 'definitely yes'. Six items were concerned with influencing/controlling processes or pressures (perhaps coercive) that might be experienced in a group. Three questions related to possible stress or anxiety, self-experienced or observed.[6] Provision to rate growth in positive feeling toward any other group member(s) was balanced by inquiring as to more negative feeling. Remaining items, positively expressed, included a 'personal outcome' cluster around perceived value for the self, gain in self-awareness, and gain in theoretical understanding. Two 'self-within-the-group' items asked about a sense of being able to share more of oneself, and about feeling oneself as 'making a difference' in the group. Possible change toward more genuine and more sensitive interaction, and an item about the value of the session for other members, were included (1972b: Appendix A).

Mean ratings on each item were tracked session-by-session over the course of the workshop. Again, profiles differed enough between the two groups to suggest that each was evolving distinctively. Some pairs of rating items were strongly associated, and four meaningful clusters were identified from the inter-item correlations. One cluster, a 'personal gain' (P) dimension, included most items in the personal outcome *and* self-within-the-group categories mentioned above. Another, 'group gain' (G) dimension, included the items next-mentioned, above. Three items concerned with observed pressure or stress on others formed a co-varying group, as did two concerned with feeling oneself under personal pressure or strain (ibid.: 3–6). The sum of P plus G seemed the single best index of group session quality and effect. In Group B, session 2 was perceived as highly productive, with a P+G score not exceeded until late in the first week, and in the ending session in week 2. By contrast, Group A built up more gradually, peaking in the middle of week 1. Both groups fluctuated widely in week 2, Group B declining more sharply and reaching former levels only in the last two meetings. Group A dropped off, rose strongly, and then plunged to its lowest level in one evidently conflictual meeting. Experienced productivity lifted rapidly again, to a high point in the last session.

The results demonstrate that fairly simple forms of rating questionnaire can throw into relief differences between groups and contribute to understanding the nature and effects of the process. The research, with basically simple intent to further appraise what happened and its effects (as in the Berzon/Solomon work), was one stimulus for me in moving to a more systemic viewpoint (Chapter 9). In its current form, the session process instrument includes added 'feedback' items: 'Did anyone directly share *their* impression or picture of you in some way that was helpful . . .? Which person[s]?'; and 'Did you (successfully) convey to anyone else in the group something of your *own* true *picture* or impressions of them? Which person[s]?'. Another item

---

6 The original item sample was a collaborative effort, by myself and Prof. Pat Pentony, reflecting aspects that at least one of us felt it important to call attention to. It grew out of our experience to that point, and a healthy respect for the potency of intensive groups. Two non-discriminating items were dropped at an early stage in study of the data, leaving the twenty reported.

reads 'Did you find yourself actively responding to what you saw going on *between other persons* in the group? Who were they?' (Barrett-Lennard, 1996b).[7] Different ways of studying process include an interesting approach adopted by Clark and colleagues.

Members as therapists: the study of relations between group members

Clark believed that the two-person interactions in an intensive group were most responsible for personal change (Clark and Culbert, 1965; Clark, Culbert and Bobele, 1969). One approach would be simply to assess how each person experienced the response of separate others in the group. But the investigators went beyond this, implying that it was especially propitious for change when *both* members of a dyad experienced relatively high conditions levels from each other. It was predicted that individual movement would occur according to the number of 'mutually therapeutic relationships' (MTRs) that the person engaged in. Ratings on the Problem Expression (process) Scale (p. 271) were made from speech samples early and late in the life of the group, yielding a movement index for each person. For the conditions data, each participant completed a BLRI on each other member. The RI scores that person generated were ranked, and an MTR existed if a given other member fell in the upper half of these ranks *and if* that other member's scores also placed the first person in the upper half position. A significant association between process shift and number of MTRs resulted (Clark and Culbert, 1965: 191–192). A replication of the study in groups of somewhat different make-up, leadership and duration, yielded a trend that only weakly supported the initial finding (Clark et al., 1969: 68). While the MTR concept remains interesting, a current perspective (pp. 158–169) would not lead one to expect the relation studied to be so robust as to hold up under conditions varying substantially in other ways.

Mente and collaborators conducted twenty long-running, closely studied therapy groups, through the 1970s. Client empathic understanding, both in its effects and development, became a focus of their interest. A nine-point judge rating scale was used to index each client's empathic understanding (CEU) within interaction samples from the recorded groups. For their sample overall, CEU was significantly related to change on six clinical MMPI scales and the other measures of therapy outcome used. A subsample of clients with initially low levels of CEU developed higher levels over the course of therapy (Mente and Spittler, 1980: 130–151; Giesekus and Mente, 1986: 166–167). The results are compatible (i) with viewing inter-client empathy as a therapeutic condition, in the client-centred group therapy context, and (ii) with regarding increased client empathy as an effect of the therapy, at least for clients starting at lower levels of empathic response.

Marques-Teixeira and colleagues (1996) came by a quite different route from Mente to a broadly similar conclusion regarding the pivotal importance of

---

7 Readers may request the revised Session Questionnaire (or my 1972 report).

empathy in the small-group process. Five kinds of small group were studied: an actual therapy (psychodrama) group, a group of psychotherapy trainees, a religious group, a close friends group and a team of workers. After the groups were well-established, participants answered an OS RI for the response of their *group* to them. Sophisticated data-analysis supports a conclusion that an integrated 'group effect' hinged on the presence and development of empathic communication, this in turn seeming to depend partly on the presence of a facilitator. In quite different work, Eckert and Biermann-Ratjen (1990) present results from close study of outcomes of client-centred group therapy (CCT) versus psychoanalytic psychotherapy in groups (PA). Patient gain occurred in both types of groups, with similar features (less depression and introversion, more comfortable life adjustment) *and* different effects. The differences showed when members appraised their change, where 'the point of reference for PA-patients appears to be their sense of internal and external autonomy . . .; the point of reference for CCT-patients is their ability to enter into relationships and make contact with others' (1990: 463). One might speculate from this that inter-member empathy is more relevant to the goals of CC groups than to those of PA group therapy.

Development phases and multiple leaders: Ariadne Beck's *research*

Beck's visualization of group development and process – portrayed above, pp. 148–153 – evolved from searching observation (Beck and Keil, 1967) and has increasingly generated formal research. Much of this research draws from fully transcribed sessions. This allows close tracking of phase transitions, such as the transition from her Phase 2 to Phase 3. In this case, three strands were singled out:

1 A shift from interacting with anger or tense discomfort *to* a quality of 'relatively positive feeling and mutual support',
2 Movement from a self-withholding or aggressive-defensive quality *to* 'more open, mutually exploratory behaviour',
3 'Movement from concern, apprehension, and struggle over organizational and norm development issues *to* a focus on individual members and their personal concerns' (Beck et al.: 1986: 621).

A 'Hostility/Support Scale' was devised to measure component 1 and the Experiencing Scale (pp. 271 and 279, above) was adapted for component 2. A third rating measure reflected the issues of component 3, and each scale was applied to the opening series of sessions in three groups. Graphed results for the first component showed a rather sudden, clear shift to a Phase 3 quality near the end of session 3, in two of the groups studied (ibid.: Figures 18-1, -5, and -6). There was no such shift, through session 7, in the stalled third group (Figure 18-7).

Experiencing Scale levels were examined in more than one way, including 'group-as-a-whole level', and individual member levels (ibid.: 640). Rated group level reached one high point at the phase shift already determined

(Figures 18-1, 18-6), and individual members' levels peaked in turn, after this shift (Figure 18-8). Component 3, rated episode by episode, ranged from 'mainly normative-organizational concerns' to (especially at the phase boundary) 'mainly personal exploration issues' (Figures 18-1, 18-6; cf. Figure 18-7). Supplementary speech behaviour variables such as length of statements, and the usage and kinds of 'we' statement, are also examined in detail. The authors emphasize that their work so far is exploratory, illustrative, a beginning – albeit a substantial one. Additional papers focus on Beck's four leadership modes.

The four leaders were found to be identifiable quite early in a group's life, by clinical judgement and from an end-of-session sociometric test. In the test, each member ranks others in the group in several ways: for example, in terms of how much the respondent enjoys their presence in the group, their relative influence on what happens, their similarity to the respondent, and the extent of understanding felt in relation to them.[8] The Task Leader (TL) is usually the official leader. The Emotional Leader (EL) is active, quickly responsive to TL, typically in effective contact with and liked by other members, and his/her overall sociometric ranking stands out.[9] The Scapegoat Leader (SL) may rank high in perceived influence, quite variably in other ways. It seems the Defiant Leader (DL) receives the lowest rankings, and is the most isolated person in the group – in fact, often leaving before the group terminates (Beck et al., 1983: 146–147.) The EL and SL showed high verbal participation rates in a group where these were closely studied (Beck et al., 1986: 664–668; 1989: 159). On the aspect of risk-taking/trying new things out, the EL ranked clearly highest across all phases, and the DL lowest (1989: 162).

How consistently each of Beck's four leadership roles are clearly visible in other intensive groups, and how often roles pass from one person to another in the life of a group, are interesting, open questions. The team around Beck's contribution have a great pool of data, for present and further lines of study. Standing back from present research, a 'meta-level' question arises: *What compositional factors, task leader styles, and contextual influences, help to call particular leadership roles into prominence?* Other investigators have studied issues around leadership and helpful process in complementary ways.

Studying the impact of groups: research by Bebout and by Braaten

Bebout gathered data, beginning in 1969, from a very large sample of personal development/encounter groups who met in community settings with non-professional leaders trained through the program. The groups ran for ten weekly sessions of three to four hours and over a marathon weekend. Members generally were single students in their twenties, male and female, from white middle-class families. Most of the leaders had been members of

---

8 See Beck and Peters (1981), Beck et al. (1983), Beck et al. (1989), and/or Brusa et al. (1994).

9 See Beck et al., 1983 (p. 146); Beck et al., 1989 (pp. 160–161).

prior groups. Elements from several humanistic approaches were blended with a basic client-centred thrust – Bebout's own background. The multi-level evaluation of outcomes was a main aim of this action research project. To this was added a special interest in resources and talents that made for effective leadership, and a concern to illuminate further the process of the groups. Not merely a data pool but a great lake of material, easy to get lost in and formidable to navigate, was amassed from the more than 100 groups and over 1,000 participants. Bebout and Gordon's original publication richly suggests this potential and is still the most accessible and informative report (1972: 83–90).

Test data encompassed Q-sorts for self (S) and ideal (I), an extensive Problem Check List, and response to other personality instruments, rating items and open questions. A Survey of Interpersonal Values was used, and the BLRI was answered by outside friends and by participants. Participants began with a much higher mean S–I correlation (.35) than clients did, in the original Chicago studies (pp. 240–242), and this mean rose (ibid.: 96–99). On a life events Ranks Test, some 50 per cent of respondents placed the group among the significant experiences of their lives. 'Friends' became a little more positive in their perceptions of member empathy (105). A unique Q-sort was also used, with seventy-two items, each referring to a possible quality of the *group*. These reduced to six group self-description 'dimensions', then pooled with other measures for further analysis. Several group types were distinguished, varying in expressive-exploratory quality, leadership style, aspects of climate, energy, and the like (112–117). Excerpts from free-written member reports complement and vivify the more formal analysis (106-112).

Working in Norway, Braaten (1989a) reported research from his two decades of serious practice and investigative interest in intensive groups. His focus is on outcome, especially in terms of (i) personal goal attainment (using a positive measure he developed) and (ii) reduction in symptomatology. The Symptom Check List (SCL-90R) developed by Derogatis (1977) and colleagues tapped the second aspect. Three 'client groups' and six groups of graduate students taking an experiential credit course (N = 94, in all) answered the instruments before and after about forty-two hours of weekly meetings. A control group (N = 17) provided equivalent data. Leadership was constant, in that the investigator led all working groups; and the 'clients' were all mental health professionals.[10] Significant gain above controls was predicted in both client and student groups, with greatest shift among clients. Braaten notes that, as group leader, he worked 'to build a productive group climate, high in cohesiveness and trust', and in empathy, but saw the achievement of these qualities as vitally a function of other members as well.

Braaten's own questionnaire, detailed in another report (1989b), presents a

10 Most clients were rated middle class, and educated to the level of a Masters qualification or above. The controls were recruited from a graduate 'methods' course in personality measurement (Braaten, 1989a: 188).

large number of possible self-development projects and asks the respondent to indicate the priority of each one in their life, in the range 'none at all' (0), low (1), moderate (2), considerable (3), and extreme (4). Illustrative items are: 'Stop blaming others too much'; 'Learn to value more differentness between partners'; 'Become better at giving of myself to others'; and 'Stop condemning myself when I fail' (1989b: Appendix and Table 2). A mean level of urgency of self-change projects was derived. A lowered mean, implying less urgency and some achievement in the project areas, represented positive change. SCL items were similarly rated, with reduction in that mean forming the other change index. The findings were salutary. The significant change found for mental health clients did not occur in the graduate student groups. Moreover, the change among clients stood out on the projects measure, but was a weak trend only on the symptom reduction index (1989a: 194–196 and 205). Braaten considers issues relating to his 'monoleadership' (my term), possible desire by respondents to please the leader/investigator, and the contrast in student and client results. On the last aspect, he argues that the sample groups differed in motivation for personal change, opening an issue of relevance broader than his study.

Helpful process in groups: the Leuven *studies, by* Lietaer *and* Dierick

In their distinctive line of work, Dierick and Lietaer (1990), gathered data post-session at various points, from the participants in fourteen personal development and therapy groups. The group leaders were clinical psychologists, most client-centred, and the groups made up largely of Masters students in training. Two questions asked first, whether things happened in the session(s) 'that you feel were particularly helpful *for you personally*', and second, whether there were happenings 'that you feel were particularly helpful *for other group members or for the group as a whole*'. The second question was also adapted for parallel response by the group leaders (1990: 742–743). The data from these questions were coded via a single system of categories grouped in three spheres: (i) group climate and relational structure, (ii) particular responses/interventions by members or leaders, and (iii) 'aspects of the process which the member mainly goes through himself' (744–751).

In the *climate-relational sphere*, group cohesion – including aspects of felt belonging, shared involvement, active responding and informal contact – stood out in frequency of mention as helpful. Further qualities of freedom, acceptance and 'space' in the group, of feeling understood, of personal affirmation and support, and of willingness to be vulnerably open, also received mention as helpful features. Since all of these aspects are qualities of being-together, cohesion broadly was prized (754). Unlike individual therapy, other members may respond as the therapist does and, in the *sphere of specific responses*, data from all participants were coded in one set of categories. Besides the aspect of 'empathic interventions' (only modestly emphasized), that of 'stimulating and structuring interventions' (including questions, invitations and proposed exercises) was implied in about 5 per cent of mentions (Table 1). The 'largest' response type in this sphere, called 'feedback and confrontation', accounted for over 16 per cent of therapist response entries and a lesser proportion of member responses (747).[11]

The *third sphere, of member process*, had many aspects, accounting altogether for over 60 per cent of self mentions of what was helpful. A number of categories imply that dipping deep into the well of inner experience, and being able to actually talk through and discover from these depths, was precious to the respondents.[12] The category term 'spectator therapy' is used for the experience of seeing self in others, and learning by observation of them. The aspect of trying out new behaviours and discovering their consequences is at the core of another category. The heading 'experiencing hope and progress, the capacity to help others, and relief' encapsulates a still further valued feature. The authors examine other elements in their data, and they touch on joint implications of this research and the similar study of individual therapy (Lietaer and Neirinck, 1986: see above, pp. 287–288). Their main interest, however, led on to a further group therapy study.

A large sample of group therapists completed an Intervention Style Questionnaire to describe their responses over a given set of meetings. They were called on to make a judgement of the frequency ('never' [0], 'seldom' [1], 'every now and then' [2], or 'often' [3]) with which they engaged in a given kind of action, such as 'explaining how to work in a productive way in a group'. The forty-five items were reduced by factoring to nine scales plus important residual items, falling altogether into four broad clusters. Groups with client-centred (CC) leaders accounted for 37 protocols. The remainder included psychoanalytic (PA, n = 13), Gestalt (G, n = 9), behavioural (B, n = 20), psychodrama and body work (n = 19) (Lietaer and Dierick, 1996: 565). Therapist patterns for the client-centred orientation were particularly examined, and considered in relation to the others.

Group therapists see themselves as working variously at 'facilitating the experiential process'. Results show clearly that in this realm of assisting self-exploratory process and personal-experiential communication, CC therapists view their approach as active (2 and 3 ratings); as do therapists of other orientations except for the 'inactive' PA therapist group. A similar pattern applies to the 'personal presence' cluster, encompassing varied ways in which therapists bring their own person into the process (1996: 566–67). The CC grouping gave lower emphasis than others to explicitly furthering insight, clarifying interactions and group process, or offering psychodynamic interpretations (where B and CC therapists were lowest). In a cluster of aspects headed 'executive function', CC therapist ratings implied less structuring and direction than other groups did, except for the PA contingent. This area

---

11 This category was described as follows: 'Group members or therapist give their own impression about a group member; point out certain things which they observe in him; or reveal thoughts or feelings which he evokes in them. A member is confronted with aspects of himself which he does not see, something which is difficult for him, but nevertheless helpful.' For example (in reference to another member), 'We have made it clear to him how he stops people in the group by always advancing and defending general statements' (1990: 747).

12 In briefest, eloquent expression 'A group process wakes up a lot of things' (1990: 756).

included overtly reinforcing or disagreeing, advising or requesting information, and presenting exercises and homework. It also encompassed focusing on 'process rules and evaluation', working with a selected member, and making challenging/provocative responses.

In overview, 'the client-centred group therapist appears to be minimally structuring but often stimulating the experiential process . . . he comes across as a "visible" person in the group by communicating explicitly his concern and support' and giving here-and-now feedback (ibid.: 568). Behind this generalization, lay a considerable spread of ratings. Context was one factor: in therapy groups CC therapists 'apparently direct more than in growth groups and interpret more in a cognitive way. A more "steering" approach is thus adopted for clients with more serious problems.' Also, in training and growth groups, therapists indicate much more informal contact with members. Thinking laterally from their data, Lietaer and Dierick cogently argue that 'what happens between group members themselves is the most important part of the event, and it is there that the main therapeutic processes are to be found' (569). Thus *the main task of the leader-therapist is to promote, facilitate and ensure a well-functioning group*. This means not just responding person by person but assisting in fruitful inter-member engagement. The authors go further, speaking of 'promoting therapeutic group norms' and being attentive to group phenomena such as informal leadership, coalition subsystems and scapegoating.[13] It is fine to view the group as an interpersonal laboratory but not wise to over-emphasize the here and now, for 'it is exactly this spiral movement between "here, elsewhere and past" which makes the group therapeutic process so deep' (570). In these and further respects, a mix of careful 'listening' to the data and forward-reaching vision are conjoined.

A *wider domain: glimpses of other linked research*

C.L. Cooper conducted several small-group studies from the late sixties onward, drawing on client-centred research and practice principles while also tapping into social psychological literature and the language of T-groups. An initial study (Cooper, 1969), examined two kinds of possible trainer–member influence, one pivoting on identification and resulting assimilation, and the other on inner search and integration. Group members (N = 107) and their trainers, in twelve T-groups, participated. In a word, it was found that 'when the trainer is seen as attractive participants identify with him and become more like him in attitude and behaviour; when the trainer is seen as self-congruent [RI Congruence scale], participants change toward increased congruence [self–ideal consistency]'. A subsequent study (Cooper, 1973), with differing sample, obtained observation data from work colleagues six to nine

13 My normative view of effectively functioning experiential groups is given on pp. 159–160, and Beck's work on informal leadership modes appears on pp. 150–153 and 300–301.

months after the target persons' T-group experience. Remarkably, significant association was found between member-experienced level of trainer congruence and the later, colleague-observed level of member change (184).

One sequel to the Australian workshops was a long-term follow-up study flowing from the vision of developmental change advanced in Chapter 9 (pp. 165–167). A main idea is that adult life journeys do not unfold in an even progression but typically include episodes of outstanding personal eventfulness and impact. These 'formative life episodes' (FLEs) potentiate later choices and events, including further FLEs. An intensive group experience is potentially such a formative episode that 'seeds' new possibilities. A Formative Life Episodes Questionnaire, reflecting this thought as then formulated (Barrett-Lennard, 1975), was sent out individually to former workshop members. Open-ended questions invited respondents to reflect on the previous 'dozen years or so' and record critical events (i) in their personal lives and (ii) in their occupational/professional worlds. Question 1 read, in part, 'please identify the essential nature and . . . the time and context of *directly experienced events and episodes that affected you deeply*, for example, in your outlook and values; your personal development or resources; the kind or quality of relationships you have with others; the meaning of your life to you'. Further questions asked about the kinds and quality of effects associated with each listed event or episode, and elicited information on perceived connections between events (Barrett-Lennard, 1996a: Appendix).

Data for the study were taken from thirty complete returns, with replies varying from factual tabulations to moving personal stories (ibid.: 188–189). Two assistants, not connected with the workshops, later worked in sequence on the content analysis, each contributing to the category system.[14] The thirty-six primary categories were gathered into clusters, these falling into three broad groupings. The grouping called Significant Life Happenings has clusters identified as Milestones, Life Crises, Uprooting Experiences, and Career and Job Changes. The area of Interpersonal Relationship Episodes includes thirteen categories clustered in family, friendship and colleague relationship spheres. The third grouping, of Self-Initiated Activities, is perhaps most distinctive to this sample, with categories spanning personal development (therapy, intensive groups/workshops, and cultural/artistic creations), educational/professional development, and 'social development/discovery of meaning' (ibid.: Table 1). The category of most numerous mention (23 of 30 persons) was participation in intensive groups and workshops. The fact that everyone had this experience in common makes such a result possible but by no means necessary. It was also most often cited as leading on to other growthful experiences or training (ibid.: 193). The study is exploratory, confirming promise of the approach and inviting related work.

---

14 Not quite all the given information was pertinent: 'Whether resulting from intention or happenstance, and whether over a brief or longer span of time, a reported episode had to be a distinct, externally manifest occurrence or step in the person's life, in order to be coded . . .' (Barrett-Lennard, 1996a: 189). A total of 358 episodes – averaging twelve per person – comprised the data pool.

This long account is by no means exhaustive, even in regard to reports in English. Because of space and language limitations, it is not feasible to outline additional significant research in the small-group sphere, by German, Japanese, Belgian and other investigator colleagues reporting in their own primary languages. A summary in English of research by Tausch and collaborators, across a range of areas including encounter groups, lists his primary German-language sources to that time (Tausch, 1978). My file includes an 'Interim Survey' of person-centred small-group research in Japan, with nearly thirty abstracts in English translation (Murayama and Shin, 1986).[15] Nearly all pertinent small-group studies have drawn their data from *practice contexts*. This is not the case in the area next considered.

Studies of couple/family process and therapy

Relationship-centred therapy, whether with couples or intergenerational family units, is a little-developed sphere of research by person-centred investigators. Basic study of family relations and process has received relatively more attention, and employed concepts and instruments with potential application to therapy studies. For these reasons, this survey interweaves consideration of research on family process and on couple/family relationship therapy. Study of dyadic family relations with the Relationship Inventory began soon after its first use in therapy research. In similar time frame, van der Veen and collaborators began their investigation of family concepts (analogous to self-concept study). Pertinent research on therapeutic/remedial change in parent–child relations may be said to have started with the Guerneys' distinctive work (discussed in Chapter 8). Studies by Vansteenwegen focus on couple therapy.

Thornton (1960) had twenty married student couples describe their relationship, and also complete Burgess' original Marriage-Adjustment Schedule (MAS) (Burgess and Cottrell, 1939). Each partner looked at both sides of the relationship: the other's response to them (OS RI) and their own felt response (MO RI). It was found that the more divergent these two RI pictures from the same partner were, the lower the MAS level tended to be. Discrepancy between the two views, say, of the husband's response, also correlated negatively with MAS level (Thornton, 1960: Tables 4 and 5). Intercorrelation figures suggested that the MAS and OS RI both tapped core features of relationship satisfaction in marriage.[16] Rosen studied parent–child relation-

---

15 The reports are from various publications, including the *Research Bulletin of Educational Psychology* of Kyusyu University, *The Japanese Journal of Counseling Science*, *Japanese Journal of Clinical Psychology*, and *Japanese Journal of Humanistic Psychology*.

16 Later, Wampler and Powell (1982) added further evidence and argument that the RI provides an index of marital relationship satisfaction. In separate work, Ganley gathered data with the OS RI (omitting the U scale) from a large sample of married women, and reported that '47 of the original 48 items loaded above [the criterion] of .30 on the derived factor that clearly replicated the original subscale containing these items' (1989: 112). In this light, further applications in family systems research were advocated and discussed.

ships experienced by repeating offender boys and a non-offender control sample (1961). The controls reported much higher regard from their own parents, and mostly greater congruence, but no contrast with the offenders on other RI variables.[17] Rosen speculated that 'there seems to be a total "child-mother-father" interactive effect operating' (23), and suggested that it would be pertinent to know how the *child* sees each parent responding to the other. An extension of his thought would target the child's view of his/her parents' dyad, as a unit, or discover how each member experiences their family relational whole – as done in later work by Gomes (1981).

Gomes investigated relational systems in twenty intact one- (1C) and two-child (2C) middle-class Brazilian families. Forms of the RI were specially adapted and translated for the study. These tapped three levels of relationship: each family member's perception of the one-to-one response to them of each other member; the ways *pairs* of others were experienced as responding (parents jointly, and parent–child combinations); and perception of relational quality and feeling in the family as a whole (e.g., 'We nearly always know exactly what the other means'; 'We find each other dull and uninteresting'). Close study of correlations across the various relationships suggested greater homogeneity of relationship in the 1C families, and that the whole-family We was more distinct from other relations in the larger, 2C families (1981: 63–70). Family size was linked to another kind of difference: in 2C families the children experienced mothers as responding more positively than fathers (on all RI dimensions); *not so in the 1C families* where parents were experienced more equally. Direct follow-up is lacking but further research could usefully build on Gomes' methodology and the underlying theory (Barrett-Lennard, 1984: 238–240).

Another intriguing line of work is based on van der Veen's Family Concept Test (FCT). As in the whole-family RI, the family 'We' is the referent unit, and the test calls forth the respondent's ordered image of his/her family. Initially developed in 1960–61 as an eighty-item Q-sort, the test was later adapted to alternate, inventory form (van der Veen and Olson, 1983). Sample items are 'We can usually depend on each other', and 'Success and reputation are very important to us'. Some of the statements are adapted from self-concept items: 'We [I] live largely by other people's standards and values'; 'It is important to us [me] to know how we [I] appear to others'; and 'We are [I am] a strong, competent (able) family [person]'. Some new items could be reverse adapted *to* self-depiction, others have an inherently group/family reference ('We do many things together'; 'We do not like each other's friends') (1983: Appendix B).

---

17 Hollenbeck (1965) drew on a very different sample of parent–child relationships. Fifty men and fifty women students from intact families rated their relationship with each parent (OS RI), and also completed self and self–ideal descriptions. The hypothesis of positive association between self/self–ideal congruence (an index of inner harmony) and quality of relationships was supported for the total sample, except on the U scale (1965: Tables 1 and 2). For the men, E and C scores from father relationships modestly predicted academic achievement (239).

Respondents classify the eighty FCT items into nine categories from 'least like' (or completely false, in the inventory version) through a neutral central position to most like/very true. Sorts can be done to picture an ideal family as well as a real family. A component scale is a family adjustment measure scored from forty-eight of the items according to their placement in a particular region of the like/unlike me spectrum, on the same principle as Dymond's Q Adjustment Scale (p. 242). An initial study with the FCT used a sample of ten families pre-identified as poorly functioning (PF), and ten established as well-functioning (WF) (van der Veen et al., 1964). Parents provided both real and ideal FCT sorts and other data to test marital adjustment (MAT). FCT adjustment scores were in fact significantly higher in WF than in PF families, and correlated substantially with the MAT scores. Real and ideal family sorts converged much more in the WF group (mean $r = .78$) than in the PF case (mean $r = .48$). Also in the former group, mothers and fathers held a relatively convergent view of their families (1964: 50–52). In all, the evidence supported validity of the FCT.

A subsequent study applied the FCT to two fresh sets of families described by both parents and child members (Novak and van der Veen, 1970). The 'clinic group' of (thirteen) families had at least two children, one of them 'disturbed' and the focus of clinic involvement. The control group of children from the same number of broadly similar non-clinic families were diverse in *school adjustment*. (The mean age of children in both groups was 15.) FCTs were completed both for the real family and wanted-ideal, yielding two indices: the real–ideal correlation, interpreted as family satisfaction (FS), and the family adjustment (FA) measure. Control children scored their families significantly higher than clinic children, and the *siblings* of child patients fell between these levels, nearer to the controls. Parents in clinic families had the more negative picture of their family (1970, Table 3). FA is not an 'objective' measure of family functioning but reflects a personal reality: the experienced family world of a given member. It is when members experience this world very differently from each other, as well as from the way they would like it to be, that the *family* is probably in trouble.[18]

Van der Veen and Novak then added to their data by use of the 64-item OS RI (slightly simplified) administered to the children in both groups of families, and on each parent (1971). The siblings of child patients effectively provided an added, same-family control group. RI scores on the father's response were significantly lower for disturbed children than for either sample of controls, except on the U scale where scores were very low in all groupings (Tables 2 and 3). The two parents were seen as responding co-ordinately in both control groups. In contrast, the pairs of RI scores from child patients were out of step (Table 4). FCT measures of FA and satisfaction correlated positively with RI

18 In their interesting concluding discussion, the authors critically examine the idea that problem children are 'scapegoats' for broader family–parent difficulty. Their argument is up-to-date: any such dynamic would occur in *interaction* with other influences.

measures, with one exception. For the disturbed children this strong linkage applied only in the case of fathers (Table 5), suggesting that the attitudes of male parents were a pivotal determinant of the family concepts of disturbed boys in the population sampled.

Data on 'interspousal empathy' among couples in counselling (measure adapted from the Client RI) and on marital satisfaction (six-point self-rating scale) were gathered pre- and post-counselling by Boettcher (1977). By groups, the partners became more satisfied, wives especially so, and experienced empathy increased, especially from husbands (who started from 'behind'). These two aspects of change were significantly associated (Table 3). The author suggests that the experience of greater empathy from the partner helped to bring about increased satisfaction, although he is also careful to acknowledge that other factors are likely also to have bearing on this link (106 and 109–112).

Other investigators have examined effects of 'marriage enrichment' experiences of a broadly person-centred nature, such as the Minnesota Couple Communication Program (MCCP). Wampler and Sprenkle (1980) compared three groups, one a no-treatment control. In one group, the six-week MCCP came first, followed by a similar interval of lecture-discussion sessions, and then a wait period before follow-up testing. A second group reversed the MCCP and lecture-discussion phase. Effects were studied using the RI and a behavioural measure of 'open' versus 'closed' communication style – which was a focus of the learning program (1980: 580). The first group changed to a more open style over the MCCP period, *but then reverted*. Any gain in the second group also fell away by the follow-up point. However, the experienced quality of relationship rose and held (except among controls) with significant pre- to follow-up differences on the empathy and other RI scales. Thus, change toward the more open behavioural style did not persist but enhanced relationships evidently did (581). The crucial comparisons were made only for those persons who stayed with the project for the whole thirty-three weeks, suggesting both motivation and time for relationship quality to develop.

Vansteenwegan (in Belgium) studied outcomes of couple therapy in an extended program of action research. The therapy itself, plus structured group learning sessions, drew from varied approaches, leaning toward a cognitive and skills-development emphasis (Vansteenwegen, 1990: 183–185). The research, however, focused on expected change in relational attitudes, and rested on client-centred work in the choice and measurement of relationship qualities (Vansteenwegen, 1979). About fifty couples completed the six-month treatment and testing, and a waiting list control sample was equivalently tested. Lietaer's revision of the RI, including 'Directivity', was answered by each partner both for the other's response to self and self response to the other. A short form of Shostrom's Personal Orientation Inventory (POI) was answered before and after the therapy period, and clients were asked both times to describe their current problems.

Significantly greater overall shifts in experienced relationship occurred in the treated group than in controls, especially in perception of the other's response, where differences were significant across all scales (1979: Table 1). Post-treatment, the clients scored more highly on Autonomy (POI); and their 'problem outlines' implied considerable improvement. Vansteenwegen tracked the treated couples for long-term follow-up assessments. After two years, most original clients were reached. The changes from pre-therapy to this further follow-up included reduced Directivity, and a positive direction of change on all other RI scales and the POI measures (Vansteenwegen, 1982: Table 2).

In the later follow-up, after seven years, about 60 per cent of the original sample could be retested. Relationship change over this long time span, no doubt with other significant life events intervening, did not hold to the same pattern as before; except in one interesting respect: mean 'directivity' scores remained significantly lower than at pre-therapy (Vansteenwegen: 1990: Table 1). Individual change on the two POI scales held up strongly, and other evidence suggested lasting impact. The research reasonably demonstrates useful effects of the treatment over the long haul and for a good-sized sample. It is unlikely, however, that the clients were one homogenous group, and breakdown of this sample may have added useful knowledge of differential benefits. And what was the interview and total treatment process exactly, especially as experienced by clients? Data on this level might have been linked to outcome with additionally illuminating result.[19]

Guerney and collaborators have been active in research since initiating filial therapy (pp. 130–132). The therapy has been seen as a way of empowering motivated parents as therapeutic facilitators, in place of their being caught in dysfunctional interaction that they unwittingly contribute to. In subsequent development, the same basic approach and principles are applied in various non-clinical, preventive and educational contexts, through programs of 'relationship enhancement' (Guerney, 1977, 1984). The research has been primarily of a systematic evaluational nature, across various contexts of application. A good example is the study reported by Guerney, Coufal and Vogelsong (1981).

A pool of mother and adolescent daughter pairs was recruited and randomly assigned (after informed consent) either to a no-treatment control group, or one of two treatments. These included the filial therapy derivative, called a Parent Adolescent Relationship Development (PARD) group 'which systematically teaches communication and problem/conflict resolution skills' (1981: 929). Matched against this was an approach conceived as more traditional, although in person-centred vein. It encouraged clients to select personally important topics to explore 'after building a foundation of understanding and trust'. In both types of group, the leaders 'were to attempt to provide the highest levels of genuineness, warmth, and empathy' (929).

---

19 Another investigator Verwaaijen (1990) worked hard at this further level. Her interesting study draws directly on client-centred research only through use of the RI – modified from Lietaer's forms – as an *outcome measure*. The context was an intensive home-based family therapeutic approach (also an eclectic blend), centred on behaviourally disturbed adolescent girls and their parents. The methodology developed is of more general interest than particular results.

Distinctive 'homework assignments' closely dovetailed with the primary learning experience in the case of PARD groups. In the traditional group (TG), interaction and feedback between members was much freer than in the very structured PARD alternative, where mothers and daughters were coached in skills of expression, empathic responding, mode switching, and a 'facilitator mode'.

A range of data was gathered with procedures developed by Guerney and associates to assess empathic and expressive skills (Guerney, 1977: Appendix). Change on these measures favoured the PARD groups both over the controls and TG participants (Gurney et al., 1981: Table 1). The 'general quality' of the mother–daughter relationship was also studied, using scales that tap directly into relational experience and satisfaction. An example is the Dyadic Relationship Questionnaire (DRQ), adapted from Truax's arrangement (which in turn draws on item content from the RI [Truax and Carkhuff, 1967: 74–79]). Although measures of change in this area also favoured the PARD group, the TG group shifted significantly from its own starting point, on the DRQ and two other scales (1981, Table 1). Guerney observes that effectiveness of the traditional groups 'seemed to depend a lot on the fit of group members with one another, their wit, and their articulateness', and on full attendance at meetings (1981: 937). In the PARD context, the main focus was on individual pairs and their learning, and change did not hinge on the factors contributing to outcomes of TGs.

The authors considered the results of this study to be the strongest demonstration yet of superior effectiveness of the PARD approach in achieving relationship enhancement. One asset of the study, however, was also a limitation: leader personality was controlled, but (the same) leaders had to work in distinctly different ways in the two treatment contexts. The real question remains as to whether they were equivalently effective practitioners of the two approaches.[20] Another 'strength' that was limiting, too, concerns the predominant use of the investigators' behaviourally anchored measures. Results on these measures unequivocally favoured their preferred treatment approach. Results on the less behavioural measures were not unequivocal. Guerney provides a concise summary of related research within a subsequent wider review of his work and its client-centred roots (1984). Later pertinent research would also be accessible to the interested reader.

Thomas Gordon's Parent Effectiveness Training (PET) was a focus in Chapter 10 (pp. 194–195). This has high visibility as a program of application, much less in its quiet generation of research. Cedar and Levant (1990) conducted a meta-analysis of PET outcome investigations, encompassing all (twenty-six) then accessible studies that had the necessary design features and reported information. Most of the effect sizes (before-to-after gains) 'were calculated from comparison of PET with an untreated control group' (1990:

20 One could argue that different leaders, each experienced and committed advocates of the approach they practised, would have been a better match in this context.

376). From the described analytic procedure, an average effect size of one-third of a standard deviation unit was found. This modest but significant overall result hides different levels of effect for different categories of outcome (1990, Table 1) and does not encompass delayed effects sometimes evident in follow-up data (378). The seven studies selected as *best*-designed yielded a larger mean effect: .45 SDs (378–379). Gains were more likely to show up in older, more verbal children than young ones, and in learning-disabled than delinquent children (382). It is very possible, too, that the differing quality of implementation of the PET program contributed to the variation. For an enterprise sometimes seen as lacking in tested validity, the trend of results provides balancing support.

Investigating relationships – interpersonal to large system

This section looks briefly at research on interpersonal and group relations, beyond family relationships. Much of this work, as known to the writer, has used the Relationship Inventory. The study of teacher–student relationships, albeit qualitatively uneven, has been one of the most active areas of investigation.

The relation of teacher to student

A diversity of studies has investigated teacher-to-student levels of empathy, congruence, and other facilitative conditions. The first was by Emmerling (1961). Twenty teachers were selected from a larger sample, from results on a Problems Q-Sort. Ten were identified from the item placements as 'more open' and ten as 'less open'. (An emphasis on self-related, future-oriented, or 'central' problems contributed to the 'more open' designation.) Six hundred high school pupils of these twenty teachers completed a modified OS form of the RI, on their teachers' relational response. The hypothesis that the more open teachers would receive higher scores than the less open group was supported for each RI scale. A separate 'student-centredness scale' was answered by pupils, on which the more open teachers also scored more highly. The dovetailing of evidence suggests that the relational qualities had bearing on teacher effectiveness.

Scheuer (1971) conducted a related study in which the teachers were independently rated for 'effectiveness' by their supervisors. A Teacher–Pupil Relationship Inventory (TPRI), initially adapted for this study, was answered by 169 boys in a residential treatment centre, in reference to their main teacher. An hypothesis of significant correlation between supervisor-rated effectiveness and pupil-experienced quality of relationship, was *not* upheld. Modest correlations *were* found between the TPRI measures and pupil gain on the Stanford Achievement Test (1971: 278–279). Any replication study would call for extreme care in gathering the sensitive data from distressed children, and also for use of more differentiated indices of teacher effectiveness.[21] Mantaro (1972) obtained a clear finding that measures of pupil-experienced teacher empathy, regard and congruence in a large sample of fifth- and sixth-grade children significantly predicted changes in reading comprehension and reading improvement. Results of a related investigation with college students (Griffin, 1978) suggested that the interpersonal conditions affected attitude toward reading; and that this attitude change contributed to gain in reading achievement.

Rogers' last book (1983; on education), written for an even wider audience than his earlier *Freedom to Learn* (1969a), includes a chapter titled 'Researching person-centered issues in education' largely written by David Aspy and Flora Roebuck (1983: 197–224).[22] In Aspy and Roebuck's work, versions of empathy (or 'understanding the meaning to the student of his experiencing'), congruence ('genuineness') and positive regard ('respect') are rated from audiotaped samples of classroom interaction.[23] These 'attitudinal skills' are studied in relation to a spectrum of educational outcomes and other teacher, pupil and school attributes. The interested reader will find a many-sided summary of results from the massive Aspy/Roebuck program and data pool in Rogers' accessible book (202–217). Included, too, is a brief sketch of the Tauschs' important work in Germany. Tausch's own English summary has been mentioned (1978: 1–6) and there are many primary sources (for example, Höder, Tausch and Weber, 1979).

The research mentioned here begins to illustrate the spread of work pivoting on the study of the facilitative conditions in teaching relationships, taken rather directly from Rogers' basic therapy formulation. An extended span of principles of student-centred teaching and learning is identified in Chapter 10 (pp. 187–189), in which the Rogerian conditions are preserved in basic idea but do not stand alone. This more comprehensive adaptation to teaching–learning contexts could serve as a foundation for related further investigation. Research desirably is a true process of inquiry, of getting closer to what is real or essential, not of gaining evidence to support a prior position. To search into the relation of children and their teachers in order to discover learning and developmental consequences is to enter a crucible with many ingredients and a region of highest challenge.

---

21 The original 64-item TPRI itself would have been very demanding for the younger children (down to age 9), and the pertinent version is now only 40 items, in simpler format.

22 I personally like the style of the original *Freedom to Learn* better. Rogers asked me what I thought of some of the work he considered presenting in his revised edition research chapter. I studied several reports carefully, and offered written observations, some of them critical. Uncharacteristically, he seemed not to 'hear' the opinion he requested. I could not avoid the perception that this was at least partly because he liked the results of the research in question so well.

23 With some blurring of distinction between conditions and presumed effects, the scales are said to range broadly from 'adding, encouraging, exploring responses' through a mid-point of 'minimally effective responses' to the bottom level of 'crippling responses' (1983: 201).

Friendships and interpersonal environments

Research on one-to-one friendship relations, and studies where respondents describe a span of relationships or report their experience of an interpersonal milieu, includes a range of interesting work. In the area of friendships, Duncan Cramer is the most active contemporary investigator, with particular interest in linkage between quality of close friendships and self-esteem. In his initial study (1985), the original Client RI was answered by each participant for the response of their self-selected 'best friend'. Consistent associations were found between relationship qualities (friend empathy, for example) and a measure of self-acceptance (substudy 1), or an index of self-esteem (substudy 2), *for the female participants* (1985: 167). In a larger study using the OS 64-item RI and the same measure of self-esteem the link was replicated for the female group (mean age 18) and held on most scales for the male respondents as well (mean age 19) (Cramer, 1987).[24] The added measure of advice-giving was found *positively* correlated with the facilitative variables (more strongly for men). On the face of it, receiving 'advice' from one's best friend can be experienced very positively. 'Advisements' are one of the common talk tools Goodman and Esterly distinguish, and which they depict in a wide variety of forms, some helpful, some others destructive (1988). Perhaps best-friend relationships are ones which maximize the likelihood that 'advice' will be responsive and sensitive.

Cramer extended his exploration of the self-esteem/facilitative relationship link, finding significant associations in the case of parent relationships as well (1989). Another study added a simple index of self-rated *disclosure* within each relationship, and distinguished types of friendship relation (Cramer, 1990a). (The mean age of participants, mainly women, was about 18.) Self-esteem was again linked to the relationship measures, most strongly in the 'boy–girl' relationships, not among same sex friends (ibid.: 190–191). Level of self-disclosure was also associated with experienced facilitativeness in the romantic relationships. Cramer has employed sophisticated statistical procedures in attempting to pin down the presumed causal influence of relationship quality on self-esteem. The results in one report of this 'statistically experimental' work imply that the linkage 'is predominantly determined by unconditionality of acceptance' (1990c: 190). A later study (1994) extends this picture, using relationship and self-esteem data gathered twice (with a fifteen-week interval), thus enabling statistical procedures to tease out likely causal

---

24 McLennan and Omodei (1988) discuss limitations in Cramer's original study and present a modified replication. More generic measures of personality and a composite index of personal health/adjustment (not self-esteem *per se*) were utilized. Relationship and adjustment were again more strongly correlated for women than for men. However, on controlling for effects of the personality measures *correlated with adjustment*, this link disappeared for females and reduced for males (1988: 288). Cramer in turn reanalysed the reported results, omitting 'personality' the factor of Neuroticism (on the grounds that it also reflects adjustment). Facilitativeness in the close relationships entailed then remained significantly correlated with well-being, for both sexes (Cramer, 1990b). The articles raise issues of meaning easily overlooked in quantitative analyses.

links. Among principal results, unconditionality alone and total conditions level predictively affected self-esteem (1994: 332, Table 2).[25]

The conditions response of one class of participants (treatment staff) to another class (patients) in a self-contained setting, was the focus of a study by Gross et al. (1970). The patients – near discharge after over sixty days in their ward – answered the RI in reference to the staff (for example, 'How much staff members like or dislike me is not affected by anything that I think or feel'). The U measure again was distinctive. Staff members tended to a more positive view than patients, especially on this scale; and vector analysis of patient returns showed unconditionality on a separate dimension than the other variables (ibid.: 543–544). Another study examined the perceived response of the total milieu, by the client participants in a residential rehabilitation program. They too answered an OS RI, worded even more broadly (item 1: 'People here respect me as a person'). Study of the data, by age and gender, revealed that young males (observed as least happy/most difficult) gave far lower scores than did other groups (Wargo and Meek, 1970/1971: 43, 47). The milieu was perceived as less facilitative by clients with emotional or sensory disabilities than by those with familiar physical handicaps (46–47). The authors, affirmed in their focus on the experienced milieu, advocated similar study in other settings.

Gilmour-Barrett (1973) investigated relational processes in another residential helping/treatment setting, a group of over twenty-five centres for disturbed children. Child care workers described their own response to the children collectively, in their care (RI item 1. 'I respect them as persons'). The managerial style of each centre was classified from interview data, and workers responded also to a Programs Environment Scale (see Moos, 1972). Management qualities such as high trust versus low trust were moderately associated with the way workers saw themselves responding to the children (RI total score and RI unconditionality). Other inter-level associations were examined across the sample of centres/management systems, in an original path of inquiry.

Sundaram (1977) pioneered use of an interpersonal life space form of the RI, devised after seeing the writer's draft work on a corresponding form (further mentioned). The OS instrument he used was shortened to twenty-four items, and arranged for rating of the other's response in up to twenty relationships – with individual family members, friends, teachers, and additional significant others. Participants were forty-nine young, first year tertiary college students, men and women, who took part in the necessary testing, and retesting after five months. Sundaram was interested, much as Cramer was later, in the bearing of facilitativeness of life relationships on personal well-being. He deduced

25 With different aim, Ranney (1995) called on 160 women, also largely in their late teens and twenties, to describe their 'current primary adult relationship' on the OS RI (E and C scales). Her sample included fifty-nine reporting childhood sexual abuse. Most (88%) of the relationships described were with men. Significantly lower empathy and congruence scores were found for the formerly abused group than for others. Within this group, E and/or C scores varied with age at the time of (first) abuse, and with the way authority figures had responded to disclosure of the abuse.

adjustment levels from Minnesota Counseling Inventory returns. A major hypothesis was that the general quality of relationships would correlate with *change* in adjustment from test to retest (verified: 1977, 34-39). Careful (step-wise multiple regression and path) analyses were used in an effort to establish causality, with a model of reciprocal causal interaction between relationship and adjustment being the best fit to the data (ibid.: 49–52).

Sundaram's dissertation came to my attention some time after Holland's validity study (1976) of RI Form OS-S-42. This form yields a profile of measures from experienced relationships across the person's family, friendship and vocational world. Holland's subjects were upper high school and university students. Fairly high split-half reliabilities were found for each RI scale. From a group of quite separate questions it was evident that some subjects lived in a much more connected and supportive family and friendship environment than others did, and they were sorted into three groups according to the sources and extent of support. This breakdown served as a somewhat crude criterion predictor of relationship quality. Mean RI scores were all higher for the top support group than the bottom one, providing modest validation evidence (ibid.: Table 7). It was also reasoned that vocational relationships would tend to be less nurturant than those with family and special friends, and higher mean RI scores were found for the latter areas. Despite the promising beginnings, opportunity to follow this work up was unavailable at the time.[26] Much more recently, and after revision of the instrument (now identified as Form OS-S-40), another student-run validity study was carried out. This led to further refinements in detail, and to the availability of this form for new research.

Relationships in supervision and service

Several studies of school principal–teacher relations and supervision have a distinct person-centred connection. First such, was Cline's inquiry into the 'confirming behaviour of school executives' (1970/1971). About 700 teachers completed the OS RI on their principal's response. The principals answered the same Inventory for the way they *expected* their staff generally to perceive them, and also responded to the California Psychological Inventory. From CPI results, respondents (and their schools) were grouped in quartiles. The best or most fully-functioning principals comprised Q^1, the least well-functioning (on these data) Q^4. Comparison of these two groups on the teacher RI data, revealed a significantly lower mean level for Q^4 principals on *unconditionality* (ibid.: 32), viewed by Cline as a key element in confirming behaviour. Q^4 principals' prediction of how teachers experienced them also were of lower accuracy than predictions of the Q1 group, especially on level

---

26 RI Form OS-S-42 received occasional use by other investigators, notably including Townsend (1988). She used total score *means across all relationships* – as an index of experienced facilitative environment – which correlated strongly with measures of loneliness and of interpersonal self-efficacy (ibid.: Table 4). Further results suggested that actual self-disclosure with partners was a function of overall level of facilitation as well as past self-disclosure (47 ff.).

of regard (36). Cline felt that his results overall accorded with a view of the school as a self-balancing field system, under strong influence of cultural values. More than this, some evidence seemed 'to substantiate the idea that each school faculty represents a nuclear unit with perhaps a reflected personality of its own' (30).

In a later illustration, 362 teachers in rural elementary schools completed the OS 64-item RI in relation to the school principal, and also described the organizational climate of their school on a multi-factor questionnaire instrument (Jaeger, 1989: 221–223). The author's laborious data-analysis and tabulations include interesting results (134–178). RI Regard vied with Total Score as a significant predictor of organizational factors such as intellectual climate, achievement standards, and organizational effectiveness (171–185). Jaeger broadly concludes that the relationship attitudes of principals directly relate to more positive or negative school climate, and that RI-measured qualities in the teacher–principal relation affect achievement aspirations of the school. Spence turned close attention to teacher supervision in the teaching process, drawing on a model of clinical supervision in which Rogerian conditions and the idea of growth are pivotal (1989). The supervision process is defined in terms both of helping relationship dimensions and task steps; and participant satisfaction with supervision was studied in relation to these features. For teachers, satisfaction hinged mainly on the quality of relationship response, while for supervisors it was both relationship and task achievement. Spence clearly delineates the theoretical and practice grounding of her study, and its interesting range of results.

Spain had investigated a somewhat related issue in *therapy* supervision: the impact of similarity/dissimilarity in orientation between supervisor and supervisee (1977/1978). Total scores on the OS RI, answered by interns in reference to their supervisors, comprised her quality-of-supervision index. Supervisor and intern orientations were assessed with Sundland's Therapist Orientation Questionnaire (TOQ), answered by the sample of thirty-one counselling interns and their twelve supervisors. Orientation difference on certain TOQ scales significantly predicted quality of supervision as 'high' or 'low' (RI total), although linear correlation was low (pp. 48–52, 57–59). In this and other ways, the path of inquiry promised more than it delivered in distinct conclusion. Handley also studied supervisor–supervisee similarity, but in respect of broad cognitive style rather than therapeutic orientation.

Practicum trainees and their supervisors each reported on their relationship after a semester of individual supervision, using modified OS- and MO-type RI forms (Handley, 1982). Participants also answered the Myers-Briggs Type Indicator, measuring extraversion–introversion, sensing–intuition, thinking–feeling, and judgement–perception dimensions. Analysis revealed significant correlation between *trainee* style on the sensing–intuitive dimension (scored positively toward intuition) and *supervisor* response on each RI scale (ibid.: Table 1). (Trainee–supervisor similarity on this dimension correlated significantly with Regard level viewed from either source [Table 3].) Supervisors also reported being more satisfied with intuitive trainees and regarded them as more competent (512). The twenty supervisors evidently were not all trained in one orientation. Since their values were reflected in the results, replication adding the TOQ or similar information would bring out further meaning.

There are *many* issues in supervision that research might help to illuminate. Another of these is the process and value of peer supervision. Peer interchange can be a vital element in learning through group supervision, and play an even bigger part in other types of developmental groups for trainees, as discussed in the next chapter. Byrne (1983) explored reciprocal peer supervision in a practically oriented study of therapy training. Six graduate students were taped during three individual sessions with their faculty supervisor and three with their peer partner, these sessions then content analysed. The nature and categories of supervisee talk are closely explored in Byrne's report, with 'client focus' and 'self focus' as primary categories. More teaching in the supervision from faculty, and more support from peers, were both expected and received. Scores on the OS-64 RI scales were 'in the positive range for both faculty and peer supervisors, with peers scoring higher on all dimensions' (1983: abstract). Results supported the use of peer supervision as a complement to working with experienced faculty.

Another research region with the Rogerian dimensions as a focal point is that of nurse–patient relationships and communication. It is not possible to extend this survey to include any substantive account of this work, but most such research has *singled out nurse empathy*, as experienced by patients, as the interpersonal quality of primary interest. Illustrative studies familiar to the writer include those by Forsyth (1979),[27] Johnson (1980), Madrid (1993), Soldwisch (1990), and Stetler (1977).

Large groups, community and peace processes

Although experiential process in large groups has long been a serious interest in the person-centred movement, it is a neglected area in terms of organized research. One of few examples is an exploratory study using questionnaire returns from members of the large-group workshop portrayed in Chapter 11 (pp. 206–210). As earlier mentioned, a research component was not built in, and issues had to be cleared and plans formed within the workshop itself. Participants interested in research and more systematic understanding, had first to find each other, give time to sharing ideas and perspectives, and work on the content. The most tangible product was a rough-hewn instrument, simply identified as the End-of-Workshop Process Questionnaire. I have referred to it as 'a catchment for issues and patterns suggested from an inside view' (Barrett-Lennard, 1994: 73). Most members answered the questionnaire as the workshop was breaking up, others sent their returns by post, or on

27 Forsyth wrongly interpreted RI empathy scores in the positive range (above zero in my scoring) as implying high experienced empathy (1979). A zero score results from an equal balance of empathy-positive and empathy-negative answers to the pertinent individual items. The reported mean (22.6 by regular scoring) suggests that perhaps *half* the nurses were experienced as responding with medium to high empathy, as helpers (see Barrett-Lennard, 1986a: 454–456).

reminder. Altogether about 95 of a possible 130 reached me. Data for the structured questions were adequate for analysis.

The main question listed fifteen whole-group process qualities, rated as to increase or decrease over the course of the workshop. As well, each person circled the four or five elements perceived as *most* important for the development of community. Elements that were highly rated both in importance and in positive change include 'Climate of respect/caring/trust', 'Attentive listening to others', 'Tolerance for ambiguity and conflict', and 'Sharing and surviving crises'. The aspect of sharing initiative and leadership fell in the mid-range, and 'Discovery and use of member [special] resources' was low-rated in relative importance, becoming a significant issue only when the workshop was drawing to a close (1994: 73–74). Priorities were themselves evolving; and a check sheet answered periodically during the workshop would have been clarifying. Members also ranked six contexts of engagement as to their relative importance for 'sense of membership in the community'. Most had been taking part in small encounter-type groups, and this context was ranked first by half of all respondents. Its average ranking was appreciably ahead of the magnetic but second-placed community meetings. One-to-one meetings were third-placed, not far behind (ibid.: Table 3). The three further contexts of interest groups, social events, and alone times, drew very few first ranks, although also deemed important. Interestingly, fully half of the respondents ranked 'alone times' as more important for their sense of connection than one or more of the interactive contexts (76–77).

MacMillan and Lago sought to obtain data from a large group of past participants of CCC workshops in Europe (see p. 210), although their questionnaire (1996: Appendix) only drew a response rate of about 10 per cent. They inquired about facilitative events or 'moments', asking respondents to describe 'an episode with a distinct beginning and end, that contributed to your personal learning or that added meaning to your experience in a large group' (1996: 607). In the small sample of returns, a main remembered high point was that of 'allowing oneself to be seen (congruence/transparency)'. References to understanding or empathy, and to warmth or acceptance, were also frequent. Other questions asked about experiential events linked to a high sense of engagement. A strong sense of emotional identification with experience expressed by others was stressed by some respondents (anyone is mostly silent in a big participatory group, and 'vicarious' experience must carry much of the meaning). Sometimes, a feeling 'that the outcome of things depended on me' was a high point. Generally, times of greatest engagement 'tended to be accompanied by intense emotional arousal', positive or negative (603).

Study of large person-centred groups can overlook the aspects of new cognitive-experiential understanding, or of shifts in priorities, although these are among pertinent features. The large group whole has been taken as a *setting* for self and relational experience, less as a phenomenon in itself working by principles that act back on individuals. Of course, members contribute crucially to the group/community formation, but the whole is not a sum of its parts. Complex interactive processes occur, some visible, some unseen but decipherable through interested and patient inquiry. Even the exploratory studies mentioned here begin to give suggestive results and could be stepping stones to innovative investigation in which the 'subjects' are co-participants working to further their individual learning as well as to assist in advancing knowledge. In the final context to be mentioned, participation is not primarily for personal enrichment but reflects concern with large social problems that members wish to address more effectively.

Although the area of inter-group conflict resolution and peace processes absorbed so much of Rogers' energy in his last years (see pp. 221–226), systematic data-based investigation was not encompassed. The only evident exception is a modest study from the 'Central America Challenge' workshop. Solomon (1990) used data gathered from all the small group staff, after each of three sessions (the workshop started and ended in four days). A questionnaire, answered by the two facilitators in each group, included the sentence completion items: 'As a result of this session I feel. . . .', 'What pleased me most about this session was . . .', What displeased me most . . . was . . .'; and a question about the incident perceived as most important (1990: 45). Answers to the first item became generally more positive over the sessions (Appendix, Table 1). In the second sentence 'the facilitators clearly expressed their valuing of those behaviours judged to be characteristic of small group person-centred interaction', including mutual understanding, liveliness, risk-taking, attentiveness, warmth and self-disclosure. In the third sentence, entries 'tended to reflect the facilitator's disappointment at the absence of some of those dynamics which were prized in the preceding question' (45). 'Most important' events were often self-disclosure incidents, specific confrontations or actions that helped to build trust (46).

Data from additional questions revealed a perception of rising effectiveness of sessions, and increasing confidence that objectives could be achieved (Figure 1). Rating of members on empathy and other process qualities all increased over time (Figures 2 and 3). In all, 'the quantified experiences of the facilitators show a consistently upward trend in all "person-centred" variables over the course of the workshop sessions' (48). What this orderliness means in terms of later attitudes and behaviours, far outside the workshop context, or for subsequent decision behaviour in sociopolitical contexts, is unknown. Solomon would have agreed that an extended reach of theory is crucial for understanding and enabling peace processes in international or large human-system domains.[28]

---

28 Rogers' focus was on achieving peace through communication, enhanced personal consciousness of the Other, and resulting attitude change. But who is the relevant Other? Is it the persons present, or others in their larger grouping or constituency? I think there is evidence all around that where a relationship bond *is* forged the other person can become an exception without the 'rule' being changed. A generalized shift in attitude need not occur. And, any movement toward a new receptivity has potential to threaten the person's existing reference group, or collide with interests served by the status quo. The communication and fresh consciousness Rogers worked to bring about may be crucial in kind but insufficient in scope, for change (see Chapter 16, below).

Conclusion

My picture of person-centred research, beyond the domain of one-to-one therapy, has drawn attention to its ramifying reach, aspects of accomplishment, and real limitations. Research has hardly begun in the last-mentioned areas. In prior spheres, especially the small-group area, studies may be more extensive and varied than the reader would have supposed. Relationship and family counselling is an area wide open for further empirical research, drawing on theory that now extends beyond Rogers' own formulations. Distinctive lines of basic study of family process invite and give leads to further exploration. Teacher–student relations, friendships, interpersonal environment effects, and supervisory process in varied contexts, have each drawn significant research attention while also opening up issues for extended exploration. Large-group, community and intergroup processes are so far little-studied empirically, which is out of keeping with their practice importance and accompanying development of thought. There exists both need and opportunity for serious research study in these areas, by person-centred investigators.

Studies beyond the orbit of individual therapy research easily could seem to be narrower in scope than they are. Besides the important advances that are relatively visible there is a great deal of 'dark matter', both in actual and potential senses: (i) as demonstrated here, the existing investigations far surpass the work that has been reported in visible journal publications and books; (ii) experience and learning by many practitioners who notice patterns and theorize about what they are doing, amounts to a rich depository of working knowledge only a short step away from compatible empirical study. Most of the research outlined here flows from practice contexts, and is either of a systematic naturalistic or quasi-experimental kind. Some studies have used very sophisticated statistical analyses and others, of equal interest, have relied on close observation and sifting out of patterns in ways not congruent with formal probability estimation.

It is not difficult to think of natural scientists who without elaborate quantitative analysis have *seen into* their data in profound depth, to the point of changing human understanding of our world: Darwin is but one example. Equally, it is difficult now to imagine scientific work in varied areas – the final trials of new drugs, for example – being effective without probability analysis and error estimation. Altogether, a big range of methodology is available, including the further-evolving more qualitative methods discussed in the last chapter and represented in some passages in this one. Too often, thoughtful practitioners have been intimidated by assumptions regarding 'proper' methodology or analysis, or by the reporting styles in formal research journals. I hope that my long account of the work done by person-centred investigators elicits fellow-feeling in the reader for some of the problems and issues entailed, and for particular efforts and achievement. Research possibilities and needs are all around, and the 'water' is more buoyant and interesting to swim in than may at first appear. One's desire to know, coupled with a certain discipline in acting on it, are the main prerequisites for absorbing and fruitful inquiry. In the concluding chapters I will speak in effect of other expressions of this desire, as a primary and enduring value in the movement of nearly six decades that we now call the person-centred approach.

PART V

LEVELS OF BECOMING

15

Development of Therapists and Facilitators

> I cannot exaggerate the excitement of our learnings as we clustered about the machine which enabled us to listen to ourselves, playing over and over some puzzling point at which the interview clearly went wrong, or those moments in which the client moved significantly forward. . . . We discovered that we could pinpoint the therapist response which caused . . . significant expression to become superficial and unprofitable . . . [or] which turned a client's dull and desultory talk into a focused self-exploration.
>
> But this tendency to focus on the therapist's responses had consequences which appalled me. . . . The whole approach came, in a few years, to be known as a technique . . . 'the technique of reflecting the client's feelings'. . . . I was so shocked by these complete distortions of our approach that for a number of years I said almost nothing about empathic listening, and when I did it was to stress an empathic attitude. . . .
>
> Carl Rogers, 1975

> What we have then is a combination in which the experiential exploration helps the supervisee maintain ownership of his or her own experiences and discoveries. . . . [We] create a situation in which the supervisee can grow in competence and also maintain her or his own selfhood. These tasks are . . . oriented toward the goal of professional self-development.
>
> Julius Seeman, 1989

'Training', the central topic of this chapter, has diverse meanings. In therapist training, the acquisition of skills and mastery of technique may be emphasized. Or, stress may be placed on the learning of a theoretical perspective and framework of meaning through which to arrive at a coherent understanding of each client's struggle, and how best to respond to their need. Or, the focus might be on the personal growth or even healing of the trainee (perhaps through therapy), to achieve openness to self and capacity to connect with others in the depths of their experiencing. Each emphasis refers to features that may be interwoven, and each raises issues for person-centred training that are explored in the first section of this chapter. Consideration then centres on the role and nature of fruitful supervision experience and process, in the compass of this approach. Cutting-edge issues around developing resourceful sensitivity to human *systems of engagement* are also explored. There is finally a shift of level, to look at the evolution of person-centred training programs around the world, their directions and their contemporary span.

Issues and process in the training of therapists were of vital interest to Rogers and colleagues, from the earliest development of nondirective client-centred therapy. The main text of Rogers' original book on the new therapy ends with an outline of suggested 'characteristics of a satisfactory course of training' of counsellors. Areas of foundation study are sketched, and a breadth of pertinent theoretical and practical preparation is recommended – not an unusual approach (1942a: 254–258). A written commentary to one of Rogers' students in training at the time implies an unexceptional mode of supervision. After listening to several interviews by the trainee, Rogers' feedback was directly evaluative and guiding.[1] By the time *Client-Centered Therapy* was published (1951), his stance was far more distinctive and student-centred. His supervisory approach had caught up with the orientation to persons and change entailed in the therapy itself. Training and therapy remained distinct contexts in circumstance and aim, but alike in respect to applicable principles and attitudes.

The phenomenon of 'training': concept, aims, process

In his later, long chapter on training (1951, ch. 9), Rogers is quite self-critical of the distinctly guiding, technique-oriented and evaluative approach employed in his practicum at Ohio State. Although the evidence of research is that practice became more consistently nondirective and client-experience-centred through the forties, this was not due to any growing actual push for conformity. Indeed, the opposite of this was intended. Emphasis on technique, or making 'good responses', diminished as attention to the trainee counsellor's underlying experience and attitudes increased. Rogers did not want to mould his students to be 'client-centred'. He aspired to free them to move more deeply in this direction or else find their way to an experientially

---

1 The supervisory comments were succinct. The case, Rogers said, was 'on the whole well handled', and 'rather successful, though not fully so'. He gave feedback on each session:

> The second interview shows too much of an attempt on your part to select topics, to ask directive questions, etc. . . . The third . . . is marked by a considerable amount of interpretation, and one evaluative comment which is poor. . . . The fourth interview shows real progress, but it seems to me that you miss the most important feeling expressed. . . . The fifth interview starts out horribly. Your evaluative comment turns out to be all wrong, and is so lacking in confidence in him that it may be one of the reasons he did not return. . . . In the remainder of the interview you largely retrieve your errors, and the material is well handled. (Rogers, 1943/1987)

preferred approach.[2] Through student-centred teaching and close supervisory relationships, and also through highly accessible personal therapy experiences, student growth in self-integration, empathic sensitivity and other pertinent qualities, was fostered (1951: 432–433). It seems that the meaning of being 'skilled' changed.

Training as development of skills

For a long time, skill in client-centred therapy has *not* been thought to inhere simply in mastery of a particular form of response or mode of verbal discourse. Another level is more crucially involved. In a searching, late forties paper on the role of counsellor attitudes, Rogers noted that in place of 'technique' there was reference to 'implementation', since the counsellor 'is always implementing, both in conscious and unconscious ways, the attitudes which he holds toward the client' (1949a: 85). But attitudes and operational response can (desirably should) work in synergy, as he further clarified:

> Once the student has clarified his own attitudes . . ., then a detailed consideration of the ways in which he and others operate in the therapeutic interview is highly fruitful. New light is thrown on his attitudes by observing the operations he uses in therapy, and new ways of behaving are perceived as he thinks more deeply about his attitudes. (1951: 433)

Ideally, trainee therapists would come to the point of *congruently* implementing attitudes of acceptance and warmth, and an openness and sensitivity to the client person's inner felt experience and meaning. There was/is an aspect of skill, especially, in communicating this highly perceptive awareness in ways that assist and do not impede the other's inner search and expression. Perhaps the process of deeply attending and tuning empathically to the other's actual inner experience (never mind whether it is like the listener's personal feeling or meaning) could be conceived as skilled; certainly, it is a resource that may be further developed through conducive training and experience.

There are other ways of thinking about development of skill, which make it an uncomfortable concept in person-centred counsellor training. Acquiring skill in the sense of learning to *emit* certain 'attitudes', to decode verbal expressions in order to follow with a smooth process of reflection, or systematically to apply selective attention or other 'reinforcement' to particular

---

2 I am drawn to speculate on how increased consistency and regularity in crucial aspects of therapist response, identified by Seeman (1949) and others, accompanied diminishing emphasis on forms of 'good response'. Once Rogers' work and training centre became strongly visible at the University of Chicago, it increasingly attracted students drawn to *his approach*. Also, the reflective and clarifying response mode, when authentically expressive of inner attitudes and sensitivity, tended to be self-reinforcing – it was rewarding for counsellor and client and contributed to an evolving, non-repetitive discourse on the clients's part. Integrated development of an approach concordant with the striking model that Rogers embodied was more likely.

elements in another person's communication, are *not* goals of person-centred training. It can be argued, however, that heightened attention on certain levels is involved in any consistent approach to therapeutic helping, including one that stresses empathic following. It is not plausible to think of a therapist as literally and totally open to whatever comes, like a large inert bin into which anything at all can be dropped. More realistically, a vital issue is for the therapist to be open to awareness of the ways in which s/he is responding selectively, and transparent to the client in respect to aims or values brought to their joint search. At least from the fifties onward, it has been at odds with client- or person-centred values to have an agenda that the client cannot be trusted to know, or to use therapeutic strategies with disguised intention.

These issues are all equally relevant in the supervisory relationship. The exercise of skill by the supervisor, and its development in the novice therapist/facilitator, occur within the larger framework of commitment to authentic human encounter – a true meeting of persons with individual purposes. The difference between client and therapist, or supervisor and student, is pre-eminently that of the differing aims and needs they bring to their association, the distinctive reasons for the presence of each with the other. In most cases, they could be (probably have been) in the other's position, broadly viewed. The client, too, draws on long-practised communication skills, quite often including problematic elements that are part of the reason for their association. These habitual features presumably evolved from past need and circumstance, to become part of the individual's repertoire. As 'skills' they may no longer be functional, or not in keeping with the person's desire for self. Unrehearsed communication is of such complexity in the synthesis of inner levels of affective and cognitive processing, and in trial and error articulation – all in the immediate and perhaps unnerving presence of a potentially evaluative other – that it is small wonder if the person struggles and sometimes fails to get it all together in a justice of truth and clarity. To come to such fuller truth, apprehended in the process of its expression and empathic reception, some existing communication skills may need to be unlearned and superseded by alternative patterns.

In the specific context of training, any substantial new skill development must hinge on feedback information, external and internal. A powerful source of such feedback, pioneered by Rogers and associates in the forties, was that of observing oneself in audio-recorded interviews, from a position outside the frame of immediate involvement with the client. In a paper from that time, Rogers remarks that 'probably the most significant use of our recordings is in the process of supervision' (1942b: 431). The self-observer, hearing him/herself in action, and also with other observers sharing their impressions, is being exposed to major additional information. The combination of one's inside and outside view tends to illuminate any significant discrepancy between supposed intention and visible behaviour, and to aid the trainee in working toward greater congruency. Often there are cues within the interview as to causative connections between response as therapist-helper and immediate client process. Using video-taping, the trainee literally sees him/herself in action, with accentuation of these learning possibilities – and also some risks.

A 'risk' is that concern and opportunity for refinement of *performance* will erode commitment to encounter the other with the reality of one's fallible, human helping self. An earlier cost was a caricature impression of the approach (see front of this chapter).

Some rather simple skills can be learned by copying the behaviour of someone already possessing the skill. Therapy trainees profit from contact with excellent 'models', but not in order to copy them in a sustained way, since this is unlikely to yield well-integrated growth as helper. Trying out what the mentor is perceived as doing may be a useful starting point, likely to lead on to requests for further aid by the trainee person in their quest to understand and grasp the 'way' that is appealingly modelled to them. But if the supervisor's larger aim is to facilitate the other's growth in resourcefulness on levels implied here, sooner or later emulation gives way to developmental discovery-learning flowing from inner tracking and inwardly processed feedback. Well-functioning novitiate therapists, strongly advancing in their development, may draw actively from others but are not (or are no longer) copying anyone. Their unfolding has taken its own direction, even with a self-transcending aspect – as now explored.

Training as growth; and the trainee in therapy

Clearly, in this general approach, training is more than a 'learning how'. Such learning is individualized, as one expression of an organic process of growth. The trainee is not acquiring the capacity to exude receptivity and warmth, or emit empathic responses, or *show* evident immediacy, or merely to 'portray' any quality (Mearns, 1997a). He/she is engaged in a process of becoming; becoming more sensitively aware, evolving beyond self-conscious technique or reactivity, and growing in capacity for literal absorption in following and meeting another self in *their* experiencing. It is a growth not simply of part processes and abilities but also in wholeness or integration. Implied is an increasingly free flow from level to level within the trainee person, and a developing ease and permeability in the flow of experiential engagement, person to person. As the person becomes more self-connecting, s/he is more 'sure-footed' and able safely to enter the inner world of another person who is uncertain and anxious about *their* footing.

Personal therapy is one potential path to growth, for trainee as for client. A conviction of this approach is that active discovery and movement from within is what makes a real difference in experiencing and behaviour. Viewed as learning, the new meaning is self-sought, grasped and appropriated. Depth learning can take place within personal therapy about enabling inner dialogue, the impact of particular qualities of listening, and the difference it makes when the helper is responding, self to self, from genuine engagement. An example would be to experience not only the effect of easing and relief around some painful self-judgement but the way it came about in the therapy relation. However, to make personal psychotherapy a literal requirement of training is hard to reconcile with non-impositional values of the approach, and would invite a different kind of motivation from self-sought therapy.

Moreover, trainees often come to choose a therapy experience for themselves, as their own awareness includes more acute consciousness of inner strains, or areas of aversion in connecting with others in depth (Barrett-Lennard, 1997a: 111).

A distinction, however, is possible between personal therapy entered into from a state of acutely painful inner conflict or other suffering, and therapy that is undertaken from a position of some anxiety and dissatisfaction but with the general aim of growth and learning. Although there is overlap, emotional healing may be considered the primary issue in the former case, and growth in the second. Experiences intended to facilitate personal experiential learning and growth typically are built into person-centred training programs. The contexts include trainee participation in intensive groups and in facilitative 'supervision' meetings. Lietaer is among those who speak in advocacy of a therapeutic component to training (1993: 29) and he describes a program with built in periods of group therapy, in addition to extensive group and individual supervision (1980). Some exponents carry the idea and provision for trainee therapy further. In particular, Keil (1996) has advocated what he calls 'training therapy', as distinct in concept from personal healing psychotherapy. Another distinction is also vital to the grounding of Keil's concept.

The proliferation of programs that interpret the therapy conditions as behavioural skills susceptible to direct training is seen by Keil as a paradoxical consequence of Rogers' opposition to any prescription of training methods. This, in Keil's view, has 'had the damaging result that hardly any client-centred forms of [therapy] learning have been developed'. One foundation learning is 'the fundamental experience that it is personally significant for one to sincerely venture into oneself'. Genuine client-centred learning occurs when (for example) self-experience brings out 'a basic attitude that corresponds to one of the central hypotheses of the approach' (1996: 418).[3] It is vital for 'one's own existential basic attitudes and self-transcending intuition [to] arise' since 'client-centred therapy requires . . . an intuitive presence of being, not simply the application of acquired information or skills' (423). Thus, training in this therapy needs to foster a profoundly developmental and progressively deepening quality of learning.[4]

Keil's perspective is significant not only through what he advances himself but because it helps to illuminate the whole spectrum of experiential learning modalities in becoming a therapist. In the case of intensive group experience as an avenue, the groups clearly are distinctive in membership and justification. Rather than leaving their rationale to tacit implication, Keil's thesis

---

3 Keil is not writing in his first language and when he speaks of 'imparting' a basic attitude my rendering of his meaning is to 'bring out' the qualities, such as empathic sensitivity, that he emphasizes (1996: 418). The trend of his thought is clear enough; and rich, as shown.

4 Some programs combine structured interpersonal skill training with use of intensive groups for personal growth learning. 'Skill level' is assessed with rating measures such as the Truax-Carkhuff scales, which may also be used as training aids. Cilliers' (1996) account of a facilitator (not therapist) training programme, in post-apartheid South Africa, is a recent example.

suggests that they be identified as a goal-oriented training activity and only incidentally as a general self-development or therapeutic adventure. This need not imply any shallowness of experiencing and inquiry; members can and need to bring their true inner feeling, attitudinal and interpersonal selves into the experience. But very basic principles-in-action of an approach to human relations and helping are at issue, and the particular group is justified as a vehicle for the learning–becoming process of development as a practitioner deeply informed in this approach. Keil's evocative presentation does not specify just how best to introduce and add individual training therapy to an existing spectrum of avenues (or address the issue of full-fledged personal therapy desired by a trainee). Readers who draw persuasive meaning from the overall line of thought would come to their own solutions on specifics of implementation.

Gaylin notes in similar vein that 'psychotherapy training is a laboratory for continuous discovery of the self of the therapist', this 'self' being the crucial instrument of helping (1996: 384). A positive vision of paths to such developmental self-discovery is (tantalizingly) not spelled out, although Gaylin speaks against *requirements* of personal therapy (385). Mearns has searched into these issues in positive view (1996). His point of departure is the challenge of developing resources to work with clients at 'relational depth'. To do this requires a quality of experiential 'fearlessness', pivoting conceptually on personal congruence. Mearns sees a three-stage process: becoming aware of fears, understanding their origins, and actively experimenting with 'fearless' (less fear-inhibited) relating (1996: 1–2). He advocates availability of specific training therapy noting, however, that present ethical guidelines in Britain inhibit such development (1997a). Goals such as growth in congruence and span of receptive consciousness call for a variety of personal development avenues. This variety allows for individualized learning structures, and opportunities to 'visit and revisit' self issues relevant to working in depth with clients (1996: 6).

What should therapy training build on? Selection, preparation, getting started

Trainee therapists in this approach typically have been selected as much on personal-attitudinal qualities as on formal qualification or theoretical knowledge. Where training is offered as part of an advanced professional qualification, selection encompasses academic criteria. University-based graduate programs were the context in which Rogers' experience and leadership in psychotherapy training developed. At Chicago, he cited criteria formulated for graduate clinical admission as also providing likely potential for therapy training (Rogers, 1951: 434–435). In addition to aspects of 'superior intellectual ability', breadth of cultural/educational background, and a deeply curious, inquiring and original bent, a range of attitudinal-personal qualities were identified. These included genuine, regardful interest in persons, self-insight and sense of humour, tolerance and sensitivity to complex motivation, personal integrity and well-developed ethical values.

For the would-be therapist, in particular, 'the more he has been able to achieve of empathic experiencing with other individuals the better will his preparation be' (1951: 437). It is interesting that training, in this writing of nearly half a century ago, is the context in which Rogers was most explicit about the importance of empathy, later to occupy such a central place in his theory of therapy and in research flowing from it. Interesting on another level is his suggestion that literature, and drama, 'can provide an entrance to the inner world of other persons', and that thoughtful, internalized knowledge of personality dynamics (not a diagnostic attitude) was quite relevant. An examined personal philosophy was considered valuable; and it was all to the good if a person's background included a self-chosen and helpful personal therapy experience (437–438).

Once admitted to therapy training, Rogers believed that trainees should start seeing clients 'from the earliest practicable moment' (433). This moment for graduate students at Chicago, typically began soon after a 10–12 week pre-practicum course on counselling principles and process. The course was conducted in strongly learner-centred style, with much discussion and heated comment, and special resources that included provision for tape-listening. In the practicum itself, student trainees would engage in experiential learning modalities with other participants, and then see a small number of clients in recorded sessions and with facilitative supervisory consultation.[5] (Therapy internships formed the next potential stage.) Outside the regular graduate program, intensive training programs were sometimes mounted, with client contact beginning much sooner (1951: 444–448). In one described instance, outcomes of a six-week training course were closely studied, with findings of much more commitment after training to reflective responding, and to a lower incidence of interpretive, moralizing or 'ought' responses. Data gathered a year later provided evidence of significant residual effects (452–457).[6]

In a paper presented at a major conference on training, Rogers acknowledges useful functions of cognitive preparation (1957d). However, 'experiential learning' processes, as distinct from purely intellectual learning, are explicitly singled out as being of central importance.[7] There are grounds still for his comment then that 'to facilitate an experience seems to many psychologists to be doing too little'. None the less, his view that it is experiential learning 'which is directly related to effectiveness in psychotherapy' has largely prevailed (ibid.: 79). Rogers pictured the preparatory stages of such learning much as he had done in 1951. He mentions finding that he could conduct therapy with student observers present in the same room, preferring

---

5 The basic pattern of the training sequence Rogers described in 1951 (462–477) helped to draw me from Australia (in 1954), and was maintained for a decade or more after he left Chicago.

6 Rogers (455–457) cites interesting data from Blocksma's doctoral research (unpublished). One of the tests used appears in Porter's book (1950: 40–44).

7 Concepts are pivotal in the development and communication of ideas and, although Rogers eschews purely cognitive learning, his own cognitive act of discriminating 'experiential learning' as a generic concept for crucial experience-based knowing lends enrichment and force to his perspective. Such knowing can be facilitated but not passed on directly by another (1957d: 78).

this to having them hidden from view. (In my own experience, the observers can be in *or* out of view, each option having advantage in differing circumstances.) Rogers newly suggests and explores ways that the helping engagement itself is a growth stimulus for the therapist. Developing capacity to work as a therapist with relatively well-functioning clients is by now (in 1957) seen as an issue of growing importance and challenge (88–90).

Mearns advocates screening of applicants to counsellor training on the basis, in part, of their level of personal development. If they are 'over-fearful' this may entail an externalized locus of evaluation and, by implication, a level of process functioning insufficient for propitious entry into the intensive and demanding training experience. A very fixed, protected view of self also creates the potential for anxiety by a person wanting to perform well but unable to take in and profit from challenging personal feedback (Mearns, 1997a). A current announcement of the Strathclyde Diploma in Counselling program includes the plainly stated selection issue, 'Does the applicant have a personality which is appropriate for counselling?' (Mearns et al., *c.* 1996: 15–16). Within this aspect is another hard-to-assess element, 'Would this person be able to handle appropriately his or her power in the counselling role?' Is the course 'coming at the right time in the applicant's development' is also asked. Indications of ability to meet the 'academic challenges' of the course, and of evident compatibility with the person-centred orientation of the course, are other practical considerations (16).

Selection on personality criteria is a sensitive issue, especially to those not involved in psychotherapy training. For those within this approach, personal congruency is one vital aspect with considerable history in relevant thought. Rogers' own attitude was clear: 'I believe it is the *realness* of the therapist in the relationship which is the most important element. It is when the therapist is natural and spontaneous that he is most effective. Probably this is a "trained humanness" as one of our therapists suggests, but in the moment it is the natural reaction of *this* person' (1967g: 186). Lietaer distinguishes congruence from transparent or open expression of immediate conscious experiencing (1993: 18). 'Transparency' may not show what is experienced 'all the way through' since this also depends on the person's congruent openness to their experience. The process of *self*-empathy (Barrett-Lennard, 1997a) would be a naturally occurring resource in highly congruent functioning; and congruence is seen as a foundation quality for interpersonal empathy (Lietaer, 1993: 22–23) and the ability to work at relational depth (Mearns, 1996).

Within the Strathclyde program (as illustration), self-development is highlighted 'since it is the "self" of the counsellor which is the major "tool" in advanced person-centred counselling' (Counselling Unit, 1996: 3). Emphasis is placed on development across a mapped out spectrum of aspects of self '*which affect the professional working of the person-centred counsellor*' (3–5). The primary avenue of 'personal/professional development' groups is not at odds, in its aims, with Keil's concept of training therapy. In broad statement, 'the responsibility of the PPD group members is to help each other explore, understand and even experiment with aspects of self in relation to counselling' (1996: 5). Topical workshops, and meetings of the whole course community, are among other learning/developmental avenues. The course book includes sections on 'skills training' and its aims, on the range of theoretical study and mastery, the assignment requirements, and a close account of the rationale and process of assessment – the latter pivoting on self-assessment within a well-defined structure (ibid.: 17–21).[8] Actual client counselling, accompanied by regular group and individual supervision, extends through all or much of the program. In this as in other pertinent programs, supervision in its full breadth is seen as a crucial context of learning. It is one that throws up basic issues in the approach and that has given rise to a modest literature beyond sources so far mentioned.

Learning to be a therapist-facilitator: levels of supervisor contribution

The supervisory relationship: teaching or therapy

Person-centred supervisors see trainee therapists as persons developing around an activity that engages them down to the level of their own innermost attitudes and sense of self and that poses ultimate challenge to their capacity to connect effectively with others in the full depths and range of ***their*** *experiencing.* The development called for is multi-level and integrative, with a quality of 'growth-learning'. The supervisory relationship can vitally contribute over a broad range of levels, from the most personal to the most counselling-specific and practical. Some supervisors will accept the role of regular therapist to particular advisees if requested, although this may limit the extent of their feedback and ability to serve as enabling escorts to trainees working with their own clients. By his actions in accepting some of his own students–advisees into therapy, and continuing his supervisory/teaching association with them, Rogers believed he could combine these roles.[9] Mearns (1991: 122) has mentioned accepting a therapy supervisee into individual therapy, but with explicit terms of reference distinct from his supervision 'contract' with the same person.

Hackney and Goodyear's (1984) interesting contribution to the teaching–therapy debate flowed from a recorded interview meeting with Rogers. Part of the interview was *about* his approach to supervision; another part, a supervisory session around a video-taped interview. Rogers made it clear that he

8 The text of Mearns' new book *Person-Centred Counselling Training* (1997b) became available to me as I was ending this chapter. It is the first whole book from this orientation devoted to training, and it complements my exploration. Sections focus on trainee selection, personal development, skill development, understanding the *theory*, and a reach of other topics. Neither Mearns nor I single out the area of group therapy and facilitation as an explicit focus of training. It is evident that groups are a pivotal experiential learning context in most person-centred programs, as a vehicle for personal and counselling process learning, *and* as a training ground – implicit or overt – for the participants' own subsequent work with groups (see also pp. 166–167 and 292–305).

9 As he did with me and, to my knowledge, with other trainees at the time.

still saw a very fine line between supervision and therapy, with the interaction shading in and out of being indistinguishable from therapy. He did feel free to share occasionally with a supervisee how *he* would have responded, and was ready to convey other perceptions as desired. However, didactic instruction, he implied, adds another 'voice' tending to distract the supervisee from crucial listening for the meaning of their own experience.[10]

In the supervisory interchange itself, Rogers' empathic radar was working strongly as he listened to the inner thrust of Hackney's communication about felt issues regarding his client's motivation and his own response. Succinct clarifying reflections and occasional questions were in empathic following mode (1984: 288–289). Later, he asked simply whether Hackney would *like* him to also share his personal impressions of the client and interchange; and followed his partner's 'yes' with some interesting observations. The authors consider that Rogers 'did function in a teaching role' during this portion of the supervisory meeting, and wondered how much part the setting played. This context included preview of the video-tape, and the recording of the supervision session itself for other audiences. I would want to say 'How could all this not play a part?' This said, Rogers' communication seemed very much in character, with elements true to his way in therapy and others a natural part of his repertoire in teaching and supervision.

The 'teaching' aspect included acknowledging Hackney's process with his client as well as offering another perception directly linked to events in the interview. Effectively, there was a sensitizing element, as distinct from any attempt to coach the supervisee in a particular form of responding.[11] This feature connects with Bowen's (1986) distinction between 'form-oriented' supervision, and what she called 'philosophy-of-life-oriented' supervision. She felt that an emphasis on forms of response, and concern to preserve a purity of approach, did apply to some person-centred colleagues. Her advocacy was for the alternative emphasis, with its allowance for real differences in personality and style, *and* for nurture of the supervisee's internal locus of evaluation (1986: 294).[12]

Bowen implied that varying but complementary perceptions and styles flow naturally from a living of the therapy conditions with clients, by therapists varying in their own make-up. To her this did not imply eclecticism, and certainly not any lack of rigour in examining patterns of response and consequence in the therapy engagement (295–296). She saw growth of awareness

10 Rogers' response on this issue is certainly predictable. That he was asked about teaching and goal-setting reflects in part the orientation of his interviewer and supervisee – described as a 'cognitive-behavioral approach using a family systems orientation' (1984: 283).

11 C.H. Patterson is reported to have said of the Hackney–Rogers supervision encounter: 'It seems to me that the session was not productive, or a useful experience for either of them, primarily because they were not functioning with any sense of commonality' (in Freeman, 1992: 224). Such a perception is very surprising to me. Although the two came to the session from different theoretical positions, as a result of intense listening, and attitudes of goodwill and openness, substantial communication took place. My own sense is of usefulness not the lack of it.

12 I have slipped into the past tense in speaking of Bowen's view, as one of those saddened by her death in 1994, as a creative, vital, and richly experienced young 60-year old.

and openness to self, *especially development of one's intuitive sense*, as priority features. But the growth experience is not therapy *per se*, because the referent context is always the helper's engagement with clients. This context tends to draw from trainee therapists a strong desire to help through a specific self-observed process, and to see concrete results as quickly as possible (298–299). All this can interfere with a total, absorbed focus on the experiencing and meanings of the other person.

The 'interference' may include inhibition of intuitive processes with subconscious roots, roots that imply inner processing beneath the level of rational, articulate consciousness (300–301). Demonstration interviews, co-therapy sessions, joint review of interviews, and other such searched-into activity, can all contribute to enhanced discrimination and developmental use of deeper-lying resources. Bowen hypothesizes that therapy crucially entails the sharing of 'integrative impressions [that] are the catalysts for personal reorganization' (304). Four kinds of therapist 'impression' are distinguished and illustrated. These are reflection of feelings, 'identification of underlying issues' (blending empathic, inferential and intuitive processes), the 'creation and use of metaphors', and 'use of experiments' (responsively adapted to the particular client and issue) (303–306). By implication, fruitful supervision would call this whole spectrum of response into action, in a balance and with content specific to each supervision relationship.

Typically, trainees who came to be supervised in their therapy by Rogers himself were drawn to this association by prior knowledge of his work and thought. Patterson makes the point, however, that in practice supervisor/supervisee compatibility in theoretical viewpoint or working philosophy often cannot be taken for granted, in practicum placements and internships (1983). He believes that such compatibility, or at least willingness to follow essentials of the same approach, is a necessary foundation not for any teaching but for a fruitful *supervisory* relationship. He goes further: providing students have a good grounding in the ideas and theory of his variant of the client-centred approach, they can soon be ready to see clients, that is, without the extended experiential work that most exponents advocate (ibid.: 23). Application and mastery of the 'core conditions', as assessed by ratings on the Truax-Carkhuff scales, is his reported criterion for evaluating supervisees (ibid.: 23). Given a belief (which I do not share) that the helping process is centrally defined by levels of accurate empathy and the like as assessed by these scales, and that such response qualities can be learned directly, then a lot of self-development and interpersonal learning work can seem superfluous. Yet Patterson, too, emphasizes the importance of attitudes, not 'mere' technique and skill (23).[13]

The participants are often anxious at the beginning of a supervisory experience. Shohet and Wilmot particularly stress the importance of 'a safe enough environment for supervision to take place' (1991: 87). 'Sufficient

---

13 Patterson has been prolific in his publications, which include several papers concerned with supervision. I personally find his original (1964) statement in this area, in the *Journal of Counseling Psychology*, *11*, the most satisfying of these papers.

safety' will still involve some anxiety, as the trainee therapist comes with recorded interview in hand, a sense of being on the line as a novice, and a self-focus from this apprehension that can leave their client's vital contribution to the interview process in the background. As for the supervisor, owning to any felt uneasiness or worry about being effective is more to the point than reassuring effort to make the transaction as comfortable as possible. When the supervisor has an assessment role as well as that of facilitating mentor, the way that this reality is being experienced and how it can best be managed is vital to both participants.

The working out and use of 'supervision contracts', including advance agreement as to the structure of the work together, and responsibilities that each one assumes, is advocated by Shohet and Wilmot (ibid.: 92–95). Person-centred supervisors may avoid the language of 'contract', out of concern for structures that could inhibit unfolding and discovery processes. However, any supervisory arrangement must entail understandings, with considerable room for differences in perception if these remain on a tacit level. Mearns (1991) speaks of a too-frequent 'unspoken relationship' in supervision, including unexpressed assumptions and unvoiced reactions, even aspects that are unexamined inwardly (119–121). Thus in general a strong case can be made for supervisor readiness to discuss and negotiate agreements that both participants experience as clarifying and/or freeing. In case any agreed arrangement is later found inhibiting to growth-learning goals of either one, changes by mutual agreement are not ruled out.

Further views of task and process in person-centred supervision

Self-evidently, clients do not enter therapy at the same starting line, and therapeutic change is not some uni-dimensional shift in functioning. However a broad aspect in common is that of change in quality of awareness toward a more open and inclusive consciousness, at least in respect to self and, usually, beyond this orbit. Development as a therapist/facilitator also entails such evolution of consciousness, not only in respect to self but in span of receptivity toward the experiencing of others, and in fine-tuned discrimination of different qualities of self and communicational process. Within the latter aspect is the seeing of connections that were not in view before. This enhanced discrimination is part of the trainee's informed growth in capacity to be helpful to another person mired in distress/dissatisfaction in aspects of their living and functioning.

Laura Rice sees a creative tension in the client-centred approach between viewing the therapist as engaged in an authentic human relationship, with spontaneous immediacy of encounter and, also, seeing this engagement as a process that can be learned and perfected. She feels that supervision needs to take account of both levels, in a balance that varies with the context and proclivities of the participants. Specific process has its meaning within the relationship of therapy, and the quality of relationship is found partly in the therapist's evolved awareness and range of response. More particularly: 'Although the kind of listening and responding we are talking about can be studied explicitly, and even translated into 'techniques', it can never become an empty push-button device, because it requires the therapist's whole processing capacity, the whole self. It cannot be learned perfunctorily . . .' (Rice, 1980: 146–147).

Rice also advocates that novice therapists start with some form of experiential group training program, in order to 'learn attending behavior, learn to distinguish the internal frame of reference . . ., learn to focus on a "feeling" level, and learn to express in their own words what is heard' (142). Once such basics are established, a supervisor can be crucially helpful 'in enabling the therapist to move to a more deeply empathic and evocative mode of functioning' (142). Trainee learning in how to listen with sensitive attunement to what is *most live and poignant* within the client's total expression is a pivotal aspect. For Rice, focused voice quality is a key sign of what is most immediately present in the person's inner flow, and the client may dip only briefly into this reflectively searching/sensing 'voice' in telling some larger story. That 'dip' is a moment of pregnancy; a potential opportunity for the therapist, perhaps by evocative reflection, to enable fruitful return to something that is deeply felt but unresolved (143). Especially vivid use of words or images can point to similar potential. Sometimes, the learner-listener *truly* does not understand, and discovers that communicated non-understanding, while seeking empathic connection, can be more helpful than 'surface understanding' (144). Reflections (or questions) can have an open or closed quality, and another aspect of therapist learning is to respond in such a way as to 'leave an edge open for exploration'. Helping clients to explore their *own* experience entails textures of listening and response, and awareness of steps, that become increasingly differentiated through exploration with an enabling supervisor (145).

Rice's entry to supervision issues is very much from a view of therapy itself. Seeman (1989b) moves quickly through his own distinctive view, which is highly person-centred in practice. In his broad concept, effectiveness hinges on open-system functioning and multi-level integration. Free information flow within the person, between all potentially relevant (subsystem) levels and domains – physiological, affective and cognitive – is seen as the decisive factor in functioning well (375–376). By implication, wellness (integrative functioning) and professional effectiveness (resourcefulness in counselling) are deeply interwoven. The general goal of 'experiential' counselling supervision, in Seeman's terms, is no less than the development of an effective professional self. The challenge of supervision is to assist in a growth-learning process that is truly focused on and happening within the supervisee (377 ff.). This assistance is given through facilitating and supporting the trainee person's level of integrative functioning in the counselling engagement sphere. Supervisor–trainee communication on a cognitive level, including generalized observations anchored in experience, has a natural and integrative role when it relates to the trainee's search for a framework of meaning, at once conceptual and operational.

Seeman notes that supervisor–supervisee dialogue conventionally puts the client at the centre. However, 'in experiential supervision the action takes place between the supervisor and supervisee, and the narrative about the client is only a vehicle for entry into the livingness of the supervisee' within the counselling arena (378). Generous excerpts from supervisory sessions are given in illustration. One such centres on exploration of the supervisee/counsellor's conflictual uncertainty about terminating counselling with her client. The supervisor listens to her intently, asking responsive questions and sometimes offering his (clarifying) sense of her felt dilemma. Occasionally he leads her a little, to examine aspects of her own wishes or judgement. By his attentiveness to her experience and, at moments, direct encouragement (response 17, p. 382), he supports her in acting on her judgement and true attitude, once her mind is clear on these levels. Unlike the confidence implied in this instance, the situation *can* arise where a client's well-being with a particular trainee therapist is perceived as seriously in question (example in Mearns, 1991: 125–127). For the supervisor to confront this issue may at first seem contrary to a facilitative mode with the trainee counsellor. Not to do so, however, would imply a lack of congruent openness and also suggest a disowning of responsibility beyond the trainee to the client (or client community). Not least, opportunity for a difficult but crucial learning-developmental step by the trainee may have been missed.

In a second illustration, Seeman is supervising a trainee supervisor working with her own counsellor/supervisee. Again, he (JS) listens with very close attention to what the issues are for her, with responses that acknowledge, clarify, and help to draw her out. She is feeling her way as a supervisor, tending to hold back while also wanting (as she and JS explore it) to be somewhat more active and focused, but not directive. How to achieve this is an immediate concern. JS's work with her is a model exactly in these ways, and in this reader's strong sense that the live illustration is not lost on her; she is learning *from it directly* as well as through its effects on her exploration (1989b: 386–391). Other excerpts enhance the portrayal. JS is drawing on his experience all the time, but at moments he dips from it explicitly, in mentioning what he would think and do in like circumstance. He follows these suggestions by immediately connecting with her response and aiding its unfolding. All indications are that the supervisee left the session more connected, engaged and energized; more sure of her direction, and eager for the next round in her own learning-facilitating work as supervisor (392–396).

The person in context: developing sensitivity to engagement systems

In the perspective of this book, the human person is not literally free-standing but is always situated and engaged in his or her world. Even in the ideal, 'autonomy' is relative since life is lived interactively. The well-functioning person sees more openly into self, the world 'beyond' the self, and their commingling relations. This world, experientially internalized in many of its features, particularly includes direct relations with significant others. It is these others, in classical Rogerian theory, that may trigger development of conditions of worth, which in turn provide the principal source of vulnerability to emotional and interpersonal difficulties. This theory, *taken without extension*, draws a line around the person and his/her proximate relations, leaving out of view any larger chain or surrounding constellation of influences. Beyond the level of family or special friendships, human pathways entail close involvement in face-to-face groups: in school, at work, in play, in religious/spiritual life and/or self-development contexts – to name some of the more obvious. Most such groups are part of a larger organization, institution or community system, and share its particular culture and ethos. These larger entities exist in interface with still more encompassing systems: ethnic, political and legal, commercial and economic, national or international. All human systems share with each other and other life systems the limited habitat of our planetary biosphere.[14]

Rogers devoted efforts to bringing about change in educational systems, before his eventual peace initiatives in South Africa and elsewhere. Essentially, he worked at the level of facilitating communication person to person and, through this opening to consciousness of the other, to foster attitude change. Policy and culture changes would, hopefully, flow on from shifts in attitude. His initiatives in school systems, discussed in Chapter 10 (pp. 190–191), brought into play systemic effects beyond perspectives brought to the projects. In the Louisville inner-city schools case, a large number of people at all levels of a run-down system became creatively and enthusiastically involved – it seems with highly beneficial effect on student and teacher morale, motivation and learning – by the transformative program introduced from within the system (Rogers, 1983: 228–231). Quite possibly, there was a 'critical mass' of member involvement sufficient for much of the change to have a self-propelling and enduring quality *had the educational system itself been free-standing*. However the whole system 'lived' and interacted with other systems in a larger context than itself; and eventually 'for all practical purposes, the "marvellous experiment" was dismantled'. Rogers suggests that it came to an end as a result of 'circumstances having nothing to do with educational philosophy or practice' (1983: 232). The point is misleading, given the outside community's view and values.

By Rogers' own account (ibid.: 233), a highly mistrustful and negative reaction to the kinds of change introduced was a big factor in local opposition. The innovative inner-city system predominantly included black students, with a substantial proportion of black administrators and teachers appointed. The surrounding suburban and county school system was predominantly white, and evidently much more conservative in its staffing, policies, and the constituency of parents. The changes so empowering to rank and file teachers and their students were perceived from this near-outside position as undermining authority, and putting educational and social values

---

14 In fuller expression of these ideas, I have elsewhere sketched some foundations of a 'systemic model of change' (Barrett-Lennard, 1993c), which I will return to in the next chapter. Holdstock has specifically challenged, with scholarly passion, any view of self as a separate, demarcated, (literally) autonomous entity, implying that selves form, vary and are manifest in relation. He searches toward a transcultural and interactive re-envisioning of 'self' (1993, 1990).

at serious risk. The superintendent who had such a major role in the innovations was 'hated and feared' (233). No doubt, too, there were threatening elements related to racial attitudes. While the systems were separate these intersystem stresses were manageable. Their subsequent amalgamation resulted from the impact of a powerful encompassing system – federal law and policy on school integration. Enforcement of this law proved catastrophic for the transformations in train. As part of the merged new whole, the innovative system lost the autonomy it had possessed, with policies now determined by a quite differently composed school board and administration, and a reactionary dominant community.

Dramatic or revolutionary change tends to bring strongly countervailing forces into play. In the present case, resistive turbulence *within* the original system seems to have been anticipated, since the approach took account of virtually all interests, embraced all constituencies, and proceeded in thoughtfully planned sequence. However, the reaction of lateral systems appears not to have been considered, certainly not thought through. The verdict on school integration was already well known but its impact in conjunction with more local attitudes evidently was not foreseen at all. System/intersystem dynamics may be complex but need not be indecipherable. The needed mind-set takes the working and relations of systems, as well as of individuals in their inner life, very seriously; thus developing the whole added dimension of interactive or contextual awareness.

Psychotherapy is no panacea for problems of human misery, with their multi-level sources and expressions. It is almost a truism that crucial relationships in a person's life may be stressed, impaired, even warped, by their context in larger systems of relation and influence. Many people who do turn to counselling, seek help from within a context of troubling or dysfunctional engagement systems. Thus, it seems vital to me that student trainees not be distracted from realizing their potential consciousness not only of 'individual' experience but of the experience and process of human engagements over a broad spectrum. I say 'not distracted from' in the belief that we naturally experience and identify with multi-person wholes, starting with our own family or the families of others (Barrett-Lennard, 1984). One might almost say that some of these wholes have a supra-individual consciousness; certainly, individual consciousness shifts from one significant engagement context to another; and each whole may have a 'voice' we can tune into or even empathize with (Barrett-Lennard, 1993a).[15] Further, many of us are becoming fairly used to thinking ecologically, in reference to the natural world, and it is not a big step to develop a similar way of seeing the world of human engagements.

In helping situations, responsive understanding can extend beyond empathic awareness in the range we are most familiar with. There is also the potential for other presences – personal relationships and broader engagements in the

---

15 Relationship systems have their own presence, and even an awareness through the consciousness of engaged participants, as earlier discussed (e.g., pp. 182–183).

person's world – to be perceived and felt by the attuned listener. The helper is drawing on experiential knowledge beyond the client's immediate communication, and so too is this happening in empathy in its more familiar sense. In the present case the listener is not only 'taking in' the client in their separateness and singularity but in their connectedness and engagements in their world. The latter have a reality both to and beyond the individual person. Close empathic recognition of the client's experiencing of such a reality can coexist with an evolving perception that belongs to the helper. This separate view may be informed by a ground of systems-sensitive consciousness within which multi-level, interweaving systems of engagement are seen as intrinsic avenues of life.

Such sensitivity leads naturally to being strongly receptive to client relational concerns and situations of lived *engagement*, generally. One mission of therapy is, or can be, responsively to facilitate the achievement by clients of an expanded consciousness of their connectedness, of how avenues and levels of interconnection work in their lives (and the lives of significant others), and of what they wish to conserve or work with others to change, in this crucial sphere. Relating this view to supervision, a first stage would be simply to introduce it to supervisees, through their reading and in preparatory discussion. Some may find difficulty at first in tuning to such ideas, which depart from the highly individualist model implied in most therapies. (It has been a long process for me to reach my present view.) Others would have no difficulty in concept and thus naturally bring up connecting issues. In either case, recorded interviews are likely to contain pertinent cues. My advocacy is to work mainly from these cues and issues that supervisees themselves advance. I see no implication for a basic difference in the *process* of supervision, with or without this contextual dimension. There are, however, further consequences to mention.

The perspective helps me to appreciate why many people who are in serious difficulty in the process of their lives do *not* turn to personal therapy as a resource. Practical considerations aside, is it simply that an admission of inadequacy is felt to be implied in seeking help from a counsellor, and that this is too threatening? I think the situation is mostly not this simple; that there is a more basic and potent barrier. Why *should* a person take this step if they have the idea that therapy will focus on their own personality and inner self but they are in agony over their relational or communal life systems? For a person caught and in torment in these systems, or deeply alienated by them, where would confidence in their individual capacity to transform their lives, through therapy and self-change, come from (Barrett-Lennard, 1993c: 23)? And if such a person, or one in related but lesser extremity, does come in contact with a helping professional, the helper's knowing sensitivity to them in their life context and systems would seem pivotal in order for a truly enabling process to occur.

Since individuals influence their engagement systems, and vice versa, when personal healing change does begin to occur it tends to have repercussions, small or large, throughout the relational systems in which most of the person's living happens. Presuming that interaction with these extra-therapy systems is continuous, early influence back on the client's therapy and functioning is also likely. Looked at in fine grain, an increment in self-integration, say, will tend to be reflected in some modification of process in the person's family or other significant engagement context. This process adjustment (perhaps, more open communication) might now work in an affirming way, effectively supporting the client in his/her movement. An alternative reaction would work in the opposite way (perhaps others depend on the client's neediness) and may make the client's shift very difficult to sustain or harder to follow with similar shifts. Thus, self change may build on itself in association with movement in system qualities, or may not build but bog down in the context of strongly counteractive engagement systems. When a client seems to advance and then to stop or slip back, it can be a reminder that the therapy relation is one part only of their world of influential engagement with others. Actively open listening for the voices of this engagement, echoing in the client's sharing, carries potential for a fuller contact of understanding between the therapy partners.

Since our clients always come to us from and within a matrix of life engagements, we never do work solely with individuals. Even in counselling with couples or families, the immediate system clearly is not self-contained and its contextual-interactive life in the larger community and other embracing systems is similar in principle to that of individuals. Personal discovery and knowledge has varied faces. One main face is that of seeing into, and being at home in the many engagement systems in our worlds. Being able to work in partnership with others toward maintenance or renewal of particular relational life systems is part of such personal knowing. To facilitate such development in trainee therapists, I see myself in company with other supervisors as needing to extend my own boundaries. Person-centred training programs often give attention to relationship counselling and group work, as well as individual therapy, but have yet to frontally address the issue of facilitating growth in contextual consciousness as explored here. I offer this comment, and challenge, with recognition that programs need to have their own vision and integrity, and that those of strongly person-centred thrust have broken a great deal of new ground as it is. Their development is my next focus.

Training programs on the move: evolution and span

In recent time, there has been considerable expansion of person-centred training programs in Europe generally, and in Britain in particular. The reverse trend applies in North America; scarcely a handful of extended whole programs with a distinctly client-centred core are to be found in the country of origin of this approach. Clearly there is no permanence to such programs: they emerge, tend to become active and known, often go through reorganization, possibly find common ground with developments along other lines, or shift in their emphasis. Their longevity varies widely but they are mortal. It can be instructive to examine something of the natural history of client/

person-centred programs, in their range of habitats. No full inventory so far exists, and my exploration approaches a comprehensive outline view, in terms of long-term/depth training availability.

In the later forties and fifties, there was no ambiguity about training opportunities being centred at the University of Chicago, and being highly influential from that setting. Students travelled from across North America and many other parts of the world to study and train in the Counseling Center and in a graduate program of the University itself. There also was some flow of short-term visitors, and occasional extended affiliations of persons on leave from their home institutions. The fact that the trainees were enrolled in a top university noted as a centre of intellectual ferment was literally a unique context for the support and development of a new school of psychotherapy. Graduates fanned out from that setting as second-generation 'Rogerians', often starting related courses and program emphases, innovative teaching or pertinent research and, sometimes, whole new training programs. Behaviour therapies were only just coming into view, and other newer psychotherapies – Gestalt, rational-emotive therapy, transactional analysis and others – were still to emerge or were not yet influential. As noted earlier, interest in and demand for practical counselling resources mushroomed in this period. A near-equivalent constellation of circumstance would not occur again, at least in North America.

At the zenith of his scholarly productivity and influence in clinical psychology Rogers left the setting he had founded, drawn in significant part by a vision of fresh training opportunity in psychiatry as well as psychology. His new microcosm of collegial involvement and activity at Wisconsin never equalled the rare and integrated 'centre of creativity' that had evolved around his work in Chicago. The effective impact of his unique educative approach on *immediate students and colleagues* began to wane, in what proved to be a far less conducive context for his work.[16] He no longer had a base and training centre of his own, with the level of autonomy formerly enjoyed. Also, the University and the psychology department in particular, in his new location, placed the selected graduate students in a highly competitive, win–lose situation in which the majority failed or balked at some hurdle and only a small minority emerged with their doctorate (Rogers, 1967a: 370). This meant that much stress and involuntary attrition occurred among those directly associated with Rogers, and his later 'passionate' critique (1969a: 169–187) of typical assumptions of graduate education in psychology was triggered by this experience. After moving to California, he never again mounted a full-scale, extended training program, although serving as inspiration and consultant to innovative educational groups and programs developed primarily by other exponents.

---

16 Although the immediate context caused him grief, Rogers' writing became vastly more widely known during the Wisconsin period. As Brian Thorne puts it: 'He went to Wisconsin to make an impact, and notably failed. He wrote a book [*On Becoming a Person*, 1961a] and discovered that he was suddenly influential beyond his wildest dreams', with people in all walks of life. Thorne also suggests (1992: 17) that this helped to give him the confidence to leave academia.

One of these other exponents is Rogers' daughter, Natalie, who established her Person-Centred Expressive Therapy Institute (in Santa Rosa, California) in the mid-1980s, as the base for a program of experiential workshops, training practice and study – in varied formats. Progression through a sequence of levels, over three or four years, constitutes a training stream for mental health practitioners in the field of expressive arts therapy. The principle of healing growth through *creative self-expression*, using a variety of largely self-chosen artistic-expressive modes within an ambience of person-centred facilitation, is at the heart of Natalie Rogers' work (N. Rogers, 1993; Merrill and Andersen, 1990; Merry, 1997).

Rogers' former unit in Chicago continued for over a decade after he left, finally losing priority in the departmental and university system. Phoenix-like, a new centre arose. Former members and students of the University centre brought the independent Chicago Counseling and Psychotherapy Center into being, in the early seventies. The concept included service (first), training, and even research if that proved feasible in a self-supporting context. A basic practicum in client-centred therapy was reintroduced in 1974, and the Center later developed and is conducting a full-time, year-long psychotherapy internship program. Students and interns participate in individual and group supervisory consultation, with periodic access to specialized and topical training seminars, for example in client-centred marital/family therapy. It is doubtful that any other current *internship* program in the US provides such a full-fledged focus on practice-relevant learning and supervised experience in client-centred therapy. Sustaining such a focus through a complete and substantial foundation practicum is also rare.

A program in another part of the country, that also has worked hard at providing opportunity for in-depth training in the approach, is the Center for Interpersonal Growth (CIG), a privately run institute in Sedona, Arizona (and New Mexico). The Sedona program is new in its present form but its initiators (Peggy Natiello and Curtis Graf) worked together in a previous version and location, throughout the eighties and with contributions by Rogers until his death. The present three-year program is planned to include extensive participation in residential training workshops, individualized learning and writing projects pursued in consultation with senior adjunct staff, and supervision of on-going practice work by 'alumni' in various locations (Natiello, 1997).[17]

By the mid-seventies, client-centred therapy had been overtaken as the most visible contemporary school by behaviour modification approaches – including the emerging cognitive behaviour therapy – and by some other of the proliferating new therapies. By then it was also less unified; beyond its School Phase in my earlier distinction. Rogers' own main focus and energies had moved from therapy to encounter groups and the beginnings of his

17 Significant efforts at various times have been made to establish *long-term*, national or international person-centred training programs associated with the Center for Studies of the Person. A new three-year program is being initiated as of this writing, by Ernest Meadows, *centred* not in counselling and psychotherapy but on leadership (Email <camelot@cerfnet.com>).

involvement in large-group/community workshops. He felt that the term person-centred was a better fit than 'client-centred' to the situation where participants were not therapy clients, although happy with the earlier name for its original use. (The new name also suggested more reciprocity of involvement than the term *client*-centred, and probably was more comfortable for colleagues who simultaneously drew from other newer therapies.) In the same time frame, Gendlin began to refer to his work, increasingly centred on focusing, as 'experiential' rather than client-centred, therapy. The name changes did not reduce, and may have accelerated, the attenuation of psychotherapy *explicitly* associated with Rogers' innovations, in North American clinical circles.[18]

Also in the mid-seventies, at least two centres in Canada had been making provision for a concentration on this approach within broader graduate programs. One of these programs (at Waterloo) was soon to be phased out. The other, at York University, has continued to thrive, but evolved from an explicit client-centred focus into a broader experientialist thrust, and is a vital centre both for training and research in its scope. The complex picture in Latin America invites longer exploration than is possible here, and I will touch mainly on Brazil. There, Rogers' work began to be known in limited circles as early as the late forties and fifties, and conditions gradually developed for important initiatives in the seventies. Starting in 1970 and running through the decade, a specialization program first named 'Rogerian Psychological Counselling' was established at the University of São Paulo (by Rachel Rosenberg and O.B. Santos) (Tassinari, 1995/1997). Psychoanalysis was dominant in clinical psychology, and a counselling service unit was formed as Rosenberg's vehicle for the alternative. (The unit still exists, with modified conceptual thrust, and an outreach to street children and youth.) With its two-decade training history, the private Centro de Psicologia da Pessoa, in Rio de Janeiro, is probably the longest running client/person-centred institute that has an extended program of experiential, theoretical and supervised practice training. It takes in ten to fifteen students per year, down from an earlier level of forty to fifty (Tassinari, 1995/1997). Some training programs have come and gone, and some others have changed direction but not always their label.

Rogers and colleagues from CSP visited Brazil in 1977 and conducted large-group workshops (Rogers, 1980a: 316–335). The main input did not

---

18 A contemporary development menacing or already inhibiting not only to Rogerian and related experiential-humanistic approaches but to *psycho*therapies generally, at least in North America, is the heavy regulatory hand of so-called 'managed care' provisions. Through the health insurance industry and related systems it seems that a self-healing and growth concept is being displaced by a focus on symptomatic and narrow 'recovery' targets. The pressure is on for treatment methods to be 'manual-specified', and 'empirically validated' by experimental methodology appropriate perhaps to the testing of singular effects of new drugs, or behavioural learning regimes, but quite the wrong paradigm for evaluation of complex psychotherapies. The misfit is glaring in the case of person/experiential/meaning-centred therapies with aims quite unlike the intent to cure specific disorder by standardized treatment (see Bohart, O'Hara and Leitner, 1998).

entail a therapy or training focus. It stimulated further workshops, wider interest, and more *connected* involvement by adherents to the approach, but effects on sustained, intensive training appear uncertain. By the time Rogers' work came into strong visibility, alternative newer approaches were gaining ground and the traditional psychodynamic emphasis remained well-guarded. In Argentina, Chile, Bolivia, Peru, certainly in Mexico,[19] and probably in all Latin American countries, there are established individuals, in and outside academic settings, with serious interest in the values, concepts, research and/or practice features of PCA. They typically are not in a position to implement specialist *programs* of training. Another issue is likely to have important bearing. The individualist thrust of person-centred self and change theory, even with an emphasis on personal empowerment, is not a voice of change to many people facing acute social-economic problems or very oppressive political systems, as suffered so much in Latin America.

In Japan and Germany Rogers' work began to fill a philosophical need and practical vacuum in the personal helping field, in the post-war fifties. Japanese translations of *Counseling and Psychotherapy* and *Client-Centered Therapy* were published, respectively, in 1951 and 1956 and, after Rogers' multi-workshop and lecture visit in 1961, 'the approach of CCT found wider applications in business and government offices as well as in clinical and educational settings' (Hayashi et al., 1992: 118). Client-centred therapy initially became *the* approach to professional personal helping, by adoption in the guidance and counselling field before any other formal approaches came into view, in post-war Japan. The still active Japan/Tokyo Counselling Centre was founded in the fifties by a principal translator (F. Tomoda) of Rogers' writing. Pertinent courses began in Japanese universities in Tokyo and Kyoto, in the same time frame, and then spread further.

Wide acquaintance with the approach in Japan came about through workshops, in-service training, and individual university teachers and courses, but it is not clear that specialist professional training programs, searching into the approach in depth, were able to be developed. Hayashi et al. mention general 'lack of clinical opportunities for trainees and systematic practicum and internship programs including supervision' (1992: 128–129). Limitations of professional training were not due to lack of source materials. By the mid-seventies, Rogers' then published writings had all been translated into Japanese (Rogers, 1974d: 115), and these cumulated further to twenty-three volumes (Hayashi et al., 1992: 120)! The relative decline of CCT/PCA as a distinct clinical-counselling approach in Japan is due in part to conditions already mentioned: limitations in theory and range of focus and a tide of other approaches. Hayashi and colleagues believe that these conditions are

19 The Masters' program in Human Development, at Universidad Iberoamericana, Mexico City, has been running since the mid-seventies, with person-centred emphasis. This course occupies four semesters, and opportunity for studies to the doctoral level has been reintroduced (Segrera, 1997). I am not aware of the level of opportunity, specifically, for supervised practice training in client-centred therapy. On Alberto Segrera's initiative, this university hosted (in 1982) the first of the continuing series of International Forums on the Person-Centered Approach.

not inevitable barriers; that attitudes and stresses in the human fabric of Japanese society create both need and potential for important further contribution.[20] It appears that the contemporary challenge is for the approach to become more culture-sensitive and community oriented, partly through *further evolution of its theory* and associated practice (ibid: 131–133).[21]

The needs of a post-war Germany in revulsion from recent patterns and desiring to rebuild a democratic and humane culture, also provided fertile ground for the client-centred approach. In the 1950s pertinent training and research began in Hamburg, through the work of Reinhard and Anne-Marie Tausch, and German-language accounts of the approach soon were available (Tausch and Tausch, 1956; Tausch, 1960). A growing stream of applied research extended beyond psychotherapy and into the field of school education – where application of student-centred principles was a significant factor in the revision of traditional emphases in German education. Graduates from Tausch's department at the University of Hamburg fanned out across (West) Germany, and extensive development of client-centred studies and practice evolved. One result was an association that became the strongest, most highly organized national society representing the client-centred approach, anywhere. Called *Gesellschaft für wissenschaftliche Gesprächspsychotherapie* (or GwG) this society became more influential in practical training and accreditation than the universities. Prior to German reunification – back at least to the early seventies – research, training and practice in client-centred therapy was occurring in East Germany as well, through universities in Berlin (Humbolt University), Leipzig and Jena; and the approach became broadly represented in clinical practice contexts (Frohburg, 1997).

A recent survey study found that most of thirty-seven pertinent university psychology departments across Germany include courses, or parts of courses, introducing ideas or practice features originating in client-centred therapy (76 per cent). As a frequency measure, this is a close second to the representation of behaviour therapies (84 per cent) (Frohburg and Auckenthaler, 1996). The pertinent course treatment varies widely in scope and depth, and is accompanied by commitment to client-centred research only in a few centres. Available work in universities needs to be coupled with external training projects (typically the larger part), perhaps over four years altogether, to lead on to recognition and certification by GwG. The preparation usually extends beyond a specifically client-centred focus to include attention to experiential techniques, especially focusing, and/or to accommodate selective call on behavioural approaches. The person-centred approach retains a strong presence in Germany, with moderate representation in

---

20 Indeed, Japanese students are now taking advantage of the intensive PC training opportunities in Britain and, as of this writing, Yoshihiko Morotomi is studying these training systems with a brief to translate them as appropriate to Japanese culture (Mearns, 1997c).

21 A community dimension *is* basic to the long-running human relations development network, centred in Fukuoka and extending to nearby population centres. The network pivots on Rogerian encounter-type groups, coupled also with open meetings that function as a kind of hub, permeable to the whole network and larger community (Murayama and Nakata, 1996).

academia and a large, organized body of practitioners who have a wider total repertoire than formerly.

Programs also evolved strongly in the Low Countries, from the sixties onward. These notably include the one in Leuven, Belgium, developed through formation of a university (KUL) counselling centre, established in 1964 partly on the model of the original Chicago centre. Rogers visited after this centre started, lecturing to a big, enthusiastic audience, and noting afterward that 'the greatest professional fun was talking with the young staff of the Counseling Center. It seemed like my first days in Chicago all over again' (1966c). Besides its involvement in research and broader studies, the Centrum offers a post-Master's professional therapy training program (half-time for three years). Other avenues in Belgium also provide a concentration of training in the approach. In The Netherlands, an FD Institute was formed, but the Society for Rogerian Therapy (since 1996, the 'Society for Client-Centred Therapy') has long been most important in the development and program opportunity for full therapy training. Earlier steps, notably, the Dutch-language volume by Kinget and Rogers (1959),[22] had also prepared the way.

The *Österreichische Gesellschaft* [Austrian association] *für Wissenschaftliche* [for scientific] *klientenzentrierte Psychotherapie und personorientierte Gesprächsführung*, or ÖGWG, is responsible for a major program in that country, running now for more than two decades. Trainees have a previous primary qualification in some pertinent helping field, and spend four years or more part time in the planned program, with strongly client-centred focus and extended practice supervision (ÖGWG, *c.* 1996). The enterprise is 'going strong', resource staff are in universities and varied practice settings, and there is a large body (800 plus) of graduates from the years of operation. A second long-term training program, in Vienna, also with extended history but more identification with the 'person-centred' later phases of Rogers' work, is conducted by a separate association, the *Arbeitsgemeinschaft für Personenzentrierte Psychotherapie und Gesprächsführung*, or APG. The third International Conference on Client-Centred and Experiential Psychotherapy was organized principally by these two groups, in 1994.[23]

Some further new training programs in Europe grew from initial formation of facilitator-development institutes (FDIs), in the seventies to early eighties, particularly aided by Charles Devonshire. In a related initiative, a Person-Centred Approach Institute started in Lugano, Switzerland, in 1979–1980, to initiate a learning program and with intention of seeding others. Rogers' own

---

22 This book includes a translation of Rogers' major theoretical treatise (1959a), giving Dutch-language readers early introduction to the fullest systematic expression of his thought.

23 The name itself of this conference series, 'client-centred *and* experiential', has its origins in Gendlin's usage of the term 'experiential' for an understanding he conceived both as more encompassing than prevailing client-centred thought and as identifying the essence of therapeutic change (1974). Within the person-centred movement, this work (in which focusing is pivotal) is variously seen as an extension of client-centred therapy, or an emergent departure with its own separate identity. Brodley, especially, has searched closely into the Rogerian client-centred and Gendlinean experiential stances, to illuminate distinctive and differing features (1990).

support and ideas for the development of (additional) person-centred learning programs in Europe is expressed in a circulated memo which outlined the breadth of issues and the quality of inquiry he foresaw (1979b). The FDIs typically began with sponsorship of workshops, special seminars and other short courses. Strong 'local' response and initiatives were of course also crucial in each case, especially for any subsequent evolution into a long term training program.[24]

By 1979–1980, the 'Institute for Facilitator Development – Italy Center' was offering a course in client-centred therapy, and the start of a multi-year learning program very soon followed. Centred in Rome, this has operated with continuing evolution since that time, under the principal leadership of Alberto Zucconi (with input from Rogers and direct contributions by Devonshire, in the early years). Zucconi had studied in California and was already associated with Rogers (Zucconi, 1987). In the mid-eighties the 'Italy Centre' acquired the more independent identity and name of *Istituto dell'Approccio Centrato sulla Persona* (IACP). In 1993, by further evolutionary shift, IACP became a state-recognized tertiary training institution, leading to further development and expansion of programs. A number of course groups run concurrently in the four-year psychotherapy stream, and also in a two-year Rogerian counselling program. About fifty persons a year are completing the four-year program, and there are larger numbers in most shorter courses, which include an extensive training contribution with teachers (Zucconi, 1997). Drug rehabilitation, health promotion, and community mental health, are also active program or project areas.

The training activity based in Lugano moved around, from one site to another and, as regional developments evolved, the Lugano centre had a diminishing role and eventually was phased out. The original and most strongly established, full training program in Switzerland, dating from 1979, had its main starting impetus and influence from GwG in Germany. The Swiss counterpart is *Schweizerische Gesellschaft für Gespädchspsychotherapie und personenzentrierte Beratung*, or SGGT (SPCP in French and Italian speaking regions). SGGT, nominally based in Winterthur, has about 600 members. Its full person-centred psychotherapy training program runs part-time for five years, one or two new groups beginning each year.[25] Another current program, based in the Geneva area but with strong French connection, reflects local initiatives by a collegial resource group, extended by its initial 'graduates' and further students. (The first four-year cycle ended in 1996.) This program group, *L'Association Francophone de Thérapie Centrée sur la Personne*, has maintained itself and its distinctly Rogerian emphasis, without sponsorship by any larger organization.[26]

---

24 Programs tend to come into being through devoted exponents who have found or created a footing from which to do this. However, the long-term *continuation* of these hard-won programs depends partly on the initiators/founding members wisely becoming 'dispensable'.

25 Most SGGT information given here was kindly provided by Rainer Buerki, in Zurich.

26 Information given here is from one of the founders, Françoise Ducroux-Biass (in Geneva). The program is registered in France under the national continuing education system.

Another program with a French/Swiss border location (Veigy-Fontenex), possibly does owe its origins (at least partly) to the Lugano institute. Rogers visited France itself in late April through May, 1966, having an interesting time personally but receiving an atypically mixed reception from his audiences and workshop participants. French 'intellectuals' were at the more negative pole, by his own account (Rogers, 1966c). This episode accords with the evidently limited program developments, lack of institutional support, and modest spread of the approach in main centres of France – perhaps with more diffusion lately occurring.[27]

More recently developed, long-term training programs are being conducted in the Czech Republic, in Greece (Athens),[28] Hungary (first three-year training course finished), Portugal (fourth course group in progress), and in Slovakia. There are persons seriously interested in the approach in Poland, and potential for emergence of extended training. The interest of colleagues in countries of the former USSR evidently has yet to coalesce into distinct program development. Scandinavian centres include individually very active exponents of the approach (notably Braaten, in Oslo; and Andersen [Denmark] and Draskoczy [Sweden]) but full training 'programs' have not formed there. P-C counsellor training is in development at the University of Rijeka, in Croatia (Mearns, 1997c) and new courses may soon emerge in other Balkan or Eastern European centres.

Interest has built quite strongly in South Africa, with many workshops and the approach being widely introduced to students in pertinent disciplines. If a full, specialized training program emerges there, some diffusion northward in Africa seems likely. Client-centred therapy became influential in Australia in the fifties and sixties, one distinct focus being the area of marriage counsellor training (see pp. 134–135). As elsewhere, the tide of other approaches and dominance of behavioural psychology have reduced its more visible earlier role. A generic person-centred approach is emphasized in at least one current Master's program in counselling (at La Trobe University, Melbourne), and this writer offers a foundation course in another university (Murdoch University, Perth). Pertinent developments in Britain are more substantial, as earlier flagged.

The Facilitator Development Institute in the UK was formed in 1974 and sponsored workshops and short courses in various parts of the country, for a decade. In the mid-eighties, this became 'Person-Centred Therapy (Britain)', sponsoring a part-time three-year training program, initiated by Mearns, Thorne and Lambers. Within a few more years, Mearns, and then Thorne, went on to also develop the full-time university-based programs, respectively in Glasgow (University of Strathclyde, encompassing Jordanhill) and Norwich (University of East Anglia). The free-standing three-year program continued for over a decade but is now being wound up since the principal

27 All this said, there might be a current, client-centred therapy-oriented but not especially visible full training opportunity in France proper that is missed from this account.

28 The program in Greece has been substantially assisted by representatives from other leading programs, especially Strathclyde, and offers a diploma accredited by that university.

staff are all involved in the mentioned unversity programs and additional universities and centres (presently in London, Keele, Manchester and Wigan) are providing innovative person-centred training opportunities.[29] The full-time diploma programs in counselling take a year at least. Carefully structured self-assessment procedures, as in the Strathclyde program for example, far from ensuring that candidates all pass in minimum time, quite often contribute to extension of their programs beyond one year.[30]

Conclusion

No mention has been made of programs in the two most populous nations of the world, India and China – or of numerous other countries in Africa, the Middle East, Asia and Oceania. Social conditions and traditions, political climate, and standards of living, plausibly all have bearing on whether a humanistic therapy of Western origin is likely to have significant and valued meaning, and become a feasible resource to develop locally. Socio-economic change, and tendencies to diffusion of thought systems and practices, suggest the possibility that India and China are 'sleeping giants' in terms of person-centred work conceived *as a truly evolving thought and practice system*.[31] If attempts were made to introduce this or any approach as a fully-formed, totally complete vision and helping practice system, it would scarcely deserve implantation.

Those who develop and conduct programs, wherever located, clearly have a difficult task. The approach is partly defined by its evolved concepts and body of theory, and any serious student would be expected to desire and achieve significant familiarity with this body of thought. Part of its *zeitgeist* is a valuing of active inquiry above passive learning. This implies a continuing search and self-transcending process, not only in individual perspective but in the growing body of the system of thought itself. Thus any careful syllabus needs to be implemented with the 'learning theory' of the approach in mind. And even *this* theory is not a final truth but part of a viewpoint that is being

---

29 Client-centred/person-centred extended, professional or specialist training clearly now has its main concentration in the European region. A timely new book, edited by Brian Thorne and Elke Lambers (1998), is directly concerned with the development of and contributions to the approach in Europe.

30 The extensions may be arranged to complete supervision experience or other projects, and for candidates to meet standards and commitments they expect of themselves (Counselling Unit, 1996: Appendix 3; Mearns, 1997a).

31 Rogers visited China late in 1978, in an openly inquiring mode and not on a workshop circuit. His account of the personal and group life he observed and reflected on remains interesting. Not a person to sit on the fence, one of his conclusions (1979a) was that Chinese groups and PC workshops 'represent polar opposites' in intentions and process, perhaps in kinds of needs they satisfy. Reading between the lines, he felt that China was not 'ready' for his approach but that its system would gradually change – as has been occurring. It is now two decades since his visit, PCA also is evolving, and I expect there are like-interested colleagues in China.

simultaneously acted upon and inquired into. I will attempt another distinction in the fine line we tread.

As a facilitator of trainee learning, simply repeating oneself is not very exciting, and scarcely a principle of this approach, with its valuing of openness to experience and stress on growth and actualization potentials. The learning-enabling process is more enlivening all round when the facilitator is also inquiring; facing the unfamiliar as much as what is 'known', and to a degree finding a new path every time. As a resource person with (let us say) a rich experiential and knowledge base, one always has an implicit choice between carefully bringing a developed viewpoint and practised way of working to bear, *or* bringing the resources of one's own presence and total experience, one's hopes, apprehensions and goodwill, and capacities to respond from this self to the search and concerns already in progress in the other person(s). The first mode entails applying a repertoire of existing knowledge and skills; the second is an engagement of one's resourceful and fallible self with other learning and inquiring selves. Either mode in pure form is unusual in pertinent settings, and their interweaving is likely in the teaching-facilitation process as a whole. Maintaining congruency over different kinds or levels of engagement is no mean challenge, and consequential within this approach.

Training is a primary interface between those already recognized as having expertise and those seeking it, or, in a larger sense, between presently cumulated thought and experience and that which lies ahead – carried forward and further evolved by succeeding contributors. This chapter has encompassed a broad canvas of issues, in concept and practice. One theme is that to view training mainly as achievement of skill is to risk encouraging 'portrayal' as against expression of integrated resourcefulness. Related is the idea that therapy and facilitation amount to a special use of the self; and that training, like therapy itself but over a distinctive domain, pivots on self-development. But even such development of self (including evolved communicative skills), although crucial, falls short of potentials envisaged here. Given that persons live largely in and through engagements with others, developing sensitive attunement to relational/contextual dimensions of living, and conversance with a broad spectrum of engagement systems, is a vital sphere of training development. The next, concluding chapter, although distinct in total aim, revisits this issue and suggests further extension of theory having to do with the ambient, dynamic presence of human engagements.

16

Openings in a Dynamic Continuity

> If the child is to gain real help to grow in his own way toward goals of his own choice, the therapist must create a relationship where such growth can take place.
>
> Carl Rogers, 1939

> In this atmosphere of safety, protection and acceptance, the firm boundaries of self-organization relax. . . . Underlying this entire process of functioning and of change are the forward-moving forces of life itself.
>
> Carl Rogers, 1951

> This new world will be more human and humane. It will explore and develop the richness and capacities of the human mind and spirit. . . . It will be a world that prizes the individual person. . . . It will be a more natural world, with a renewed love and respect for nature. . . . Its technology will be aimed at the enhancing, rather than the exploitation, of persons and nature.
>
> Carl Rogers, 1980

Retelling and fresh vision interweave in this book. It is time to look across the now considerable history of the person-centred approach to see further into the continuity of ideas, practice and values. It is a dynamic not a static continuity, with evolving threads running through the lifetime of the approach, brought here into fuller view. The dynamic quality is compatible also with evolutionary shifts, one of these being an unfolding theme of this book. This shift is towards viewing the experiencing person – still focal – in a much more contextual way than Rogers did in his systematic thinking. An awareness that lives are lived interactively and in relation, on many interwoven levels, poses a serious challenge and great potential opportunity. This chapter responds further to the challenge, especially with added thought about change and the span of human engagements, and a fresh way of seeing the full spectrum of our practice.[1] All of this thought can fruitfully contribute

1 In my original plan for this chapter I envisaged searching further than is possible here into what I framed as 'Persons in or above nature: The personal focus in a life-centred ecology'. Human engagements include relations with other species and the natural environment. In widest view, we live in a limited habitat for life, the slender envelope of our planet's biosphere. Humans are an experiment of nature, like the more ancestral species with whom we share this precious habitat; and the results of this experiment are not yet in.

to a re-examination of our field, our total 'clientele', and how we move forward – issues I shall end on.

Six decades in motion: a path of connection, in thematic view

The total story given in this book begins even before Carl Rogers started his first professional job, now almost seventy years ago. It is six decades since the writing of his initial book (1939), reflecting his values and style and germinating viewpoint. The book was a valuable resource to fellow-clinicians working with children and youth, and found wide use in training programs.[2] Before its recognition and usage peaked, Rogers himself had moved to the different professional stage of university professor, and to a focus on adult psychotherapy and counselling. His next book, three short years later, cites the first only twice, once near the beginning and once at the end of his main text.[3] The reader will find no mention of the early book in most of his later writing, such as the volume *On Becoming a Person* (1961a), notwithstanding major continuities with his later emphases. Of course, there were shifts too, linked to moving into such a different world of activity, and then into the discovered role of founder of a new school of psychotherapy.

Throughout the cohesive School Phase of this development, Rogers' contribution clearly remained pivotal on all fronts. But his direct influence then began to recede, first in the sphere of research and, more gradually, in terms of *new* developments in theory. His visibility did not diminish but widened, and the push into new areas of application marked his whole professional life. It was a natural progression for basic developmental innovation to be increasingly the work of other contributors. Some innovations moved far from the base Rogers had established; but advances in the compass of this book are conceived as evolutionary, not shifts to a contrary view. My immediate aim is to explore further not the literal sameness across sixty years but aspects of living continuity in which beginning qualities echo discernibly in the moving present. The six decades in this analysis begin after Rogers' consequential meeting with Otto Rank, in mid-1936, and by the time he finished writing his first book some two years later.

There appears to be no record of the content of that early meeting with Rank – already famous for his own contributions and differences with Freud. The evidence that the contact was significant starts with the fact of its occurrence in Rogers' clinic in Rochester. And, in Rogers' subsequent book, equal space and warmer attention is given to 'relationship therapy' than to the reigning analytic methods (1939: 191–210, 322–358). Rank, Taft and Allen, are each cited several times in the book, and a prominent setting for their

---

2 In places as distant as Perth, Australia; where my own copy was acquired, in mid-1951, during a pioneering basic course in clinical psychology.

3 The first citation occurs under the heading 'Environmental treatment' (1942a: 3–14), and Rogers also repeats his prior enumeration of desired personal qualifications of a therapist (254–255).

distinctive approach receives illuminating mention: 'The fact that the Philadelphia [Child Guidance] clinic has especially followed and developed one type of intensive therapy has enabled it to make very significant contributions to our knowledge of treatment' (1939: 363). Exactly the same observation could be applied to Rogers' own subsequent innovations in his Chicago Counseling Center!

In his main autobiography, Rogers remarks (in connection with Rank's visit) that although his theories didn't impress, 'I was very much impressed with his description of his therapy' (1967a: 360).[4] Elsewhere he mentions that a colleague 'who had a background of Rankian training, helped me to learn that the most effective approach was to listen for the feelings . . . whose patterns could be discerned through the client's words . . . [and] to "reflect" these feelings back to the client' (1975: 2). Kirschenbaum quotes him as speaking informally, in much stronger expression:

> I became infected with Rankian ideas and began to realize the possibilities of the individual being self-directing. This certainly fitted in with earlier ideas I had absorbed from Kilpatrick and John Dewey. I was . . . fascinated by Rankian ideas but didn't quite adopt his emphases for myself until I left Rochester. (1979: 95)

The indirect but equally compelling evidence of a crucial intersection of ideas in Rogers' and Rank's work has been brilliantly researched by Kramer (1995), to the benefit of this part of my own search.[5] Rank did not believe that humans were driven centrally by biological 'instincts', sexual or other. He saw conscious will and purposed action as a 'new primary cause' in humankind (Rank, 1936/1945: 44), and viewed creative potential not as derivative (as in Freud's concept of sublimation) but as inherent in the make-up of humans. He implied a form of growth principle, a facilitative concept of therapeutic helping, and an essential client-centredness. He spoke of working 'to bring to fruition the *autotherapeutic forces* in the neurotic',[6] and stressed in a 1935 lecture that 'real therapy has to be centered around the client, his difficulties, his needs, his activities' (Kramer, 1995: 73). For Rank, the client's consciousness and meanings, his/her awareness of present felt experiencing, and development toward more *pro*active willing, are all vital issues in therapy. Historical explanations of how patterns developed, or interpretations of why they repeat in the present, may have some educative value but are not

---

4 We do not of course know just what features of his complex and learned thinking Rank chose to share, in a rather short time, or how well this thought was communicated in English.

5 At the time of his visit with Rogers, Rank had been associated with the Pennsylvania School of Social Work for a decade, and his devoted colleague, Jessie Taft, had recently completed her long project as translator of his pivotal writing on psychotherapy. Kramer notes that Rank's book *Will Therapy*, subtitled 'An analysis of the therapeutic process in terms of relationship', finally appeared in English just a month after his meeting with Rogers (1995: 59).

6 In Rank (1936/1945: 156, italics added). Further expressed, the 'illness' of neurosis 'includes from the beginning self-creation, no less than self-destruction, and I believe that a dynamic therapy should bring these constructive forces in the individual into play' (ibid.).

therapeutic, not intrinsic to psychic healing, in Rank's potent arguing (1936/1945: chs 3–4).

The Rank–Rogers connection was touched on in my early chapters. Returning to it now in greater depth and width of perspective, helps to bring out themes discernible sixty years ago and familiar in person-centred thought today. These interwoven, enduring themes can be distilled, one by one, as follows:

1 *First is the recognition that each person lives in his/her own experiential world. It is only through 'entering' this world with the person that a depth of actual connection, with the possibility of healing engagement, occurs.* Rogers had not reached a formulation of this meaning as early as his 1942 book, but his practice implies that the idea was working in him. Nor did Rank formulate it, but his emphasis was on the conscious struggle and vicissitudes of 'will' on the part of his patients. In therapy, what was happening now in the self-experience of the client, and between the persons of client and therapist, were of primary import (Rank, 1935/1945: 26–27, 105–106). By the later forties this theme as noted was becoming explicit in Rogers' work (1947), and it is pivotal both in his theory and illustrations of practice in *Client-Centered Therapy* (1951: 65ff., and 483–485). Its expressions are legion in Rogers' later work and the writing of other exponents. Even more than the idea, it is the way it was implemented in the new nondirective, client-centred therapy that was and is notably distinctive.[7]

2 *The idea of a growth force in the individual, of an inherent thrust to develop and exercise potentialities, holds in varied formulation over the whole history of the approach.* The helper does not need to 'motivate' the client; indeed, efforts to do so tend to inhibit, not foster, the person's inner drive toward development. As noted in Chapter 1, in speaking in 1939 of the relationship approach, Rogers singled out 'the fresh viewpoint of non-interference and reliance upon the individual's own tendency toward growth' as an especially significant emphasis (1939: 200). This view, clearly drawing him, soon became a cornerstone of his own position (1942a: 29), and then evolved into the core concept of the actualizing tendency (Rogers, 1951: 487–491; 1959a: 196–197; 1963a; 1980b). Whether or not the term 'actualization' is used, the idea of a directional growth tendency which flourishes when nutrient conditions for it exist, remains deeply woven into the thought and practice of the approach.

3 *Therapy and helping conceived as a facilitating, enabling process (and not one of evaluating, explaining and putting the person on the right path) is consistent with Rank's ideas and the direction in which Rogers was moving at the time of his first book. Over the next few years, this view became a defining*

7 Concordances in thought need not imply close similarity in practice implementation. This point shines clearly in Raskin's early (1948) and still valuable, close analysis of the emergence of Rogerian nondirective therapy viewed in the context of Freudian, Rankian, and related thought.

feature of his approach. In 1939, Rogers was still occupied with literal guidance, with modes of expert intervention in acute problem situations involving children, but he was already drawing back from an equivalent mode in psychotherapy itself. This noted feature is reflected throughout his work from the forties to his last books, papers and demonstrations. The *language* of non-directivity fell into disuse, but the idea in positive form has remained strongly present. An effective therapist is in some way having considerable impact. The primary way in this case is through qualities of relational helping response that work to nourish and enable a growth/discovery process that brings the person's own inner compass to the fore. Rogers' progressive working out of the relational qualities spanned a fifteen-year period of rare fertility, from his 1942 book (87–90) to his major therapy conditions formulation (1957a). Essentially he 'rested' with this latter conception, restated in broader contexts and numerous papers, for the remaining thirty years of his life; and it remains a hugely influential legacy.

4 As already noted, *Rank's later view qualifies in many ways as 'client-centred' and once committed to his own similar direction, Rogers never deviated from it.*[8] Qualitatively, he learned and grew over time in the dimension of his presence and totality of engagement in meeting the other in their immediate feeling-thinking consciousness. An enhanced inner connection and expressiveness seemed part of his fuller-bodied engagement, and one effect in the helping encounter was to minimize any sense of the process being one-sided. The basic direction held through Rogers' own growth, and survived name changes in the approach and important shifts in external climate. This direction has facets that are hard to state, easy to sense in the process. Helper attention to self, or even consciousness of just how one is responding, almost disappears in the context of absorption with the other in their experiencing. Responsive warmth builds or peaks as the other opens inwardly and in expression, and genuine receptivity holds through widely varied contents of shared inner consciousness and meaning. I believe that most contemporary exponents, who themselves have engaged in searching depth with thought and practice in this approach, tend to manifest these qualities. For a long time, they have helped to define the meaning of client/person-centredness.

5 *The self of a person, in two main senses, has been pivotal in client- and person-centred thought. In the broader sense, the self is the inner experiencing person, both place and process of personal consciousness. The other, sharper meaning is the self of construed personal identity, encompassing the self as observed (self-concept) and as desired (self-ideal).* A third possible meaning is the self as actor, with a particular signature of outward behaviour lending itself to estimation of a mode or level of 'adjustment'. This last meaning, important in Rogers' early work, did not have much play in the approach

---

8 Rogers himself early noted that 'The philosophy of the client-centered approach and its application to work with children is persuasively presented by [Frederick] Allen' (1946: 415).

later.[9] His own earliest research (1931a) and his clinical treatment book (1939) embody a broad theme of concern with the social-behavioural self and adjustment but, by 1942, growing explicit attention to the person's self-perception and regard for self is evident (as example, 1942a: 192–194). A chapter in Rank's *Truth and Reality* is titled 'Self and Ideal', and the author in his own language and constructs reaches into territory crucial in Rogers' thought a decade and more later.[10] As client-centred therapy formed its own theory, notions of self and the self-concept became pivotal (Chapters 4 and 5), and for a time its view of personality was dubbed 'self-theory' (Hall and Lindzey, 1957: 467–502). Later, the self-*concept* became a less pivotal, explicit focus of interest, but concern for and valuing of the inner experiencing self is basic to the meaning of 'person-centred', in the terms of this approach.

6 *The approach encompasses a philosophy or vision of human nature and potentialities. It is a philosophy in which experiencing and consciousness are held as the centre of human life. The realities to which individuals respond are features primarily of the world (including self)* **as experienced**. Although not an explicit feature, the philosophy has treated the individual – in whom living experience resides – as central, and regarded groups and other engagement systems as settings rather than being at the core of life. This strongly individualist leaning flows from the historical origins and culture in which the approach developed. It has never been entirely consistent with the *accompanying emphasis on relationship as the avenue through which healing and development occurs* and through which its fruits are manifest in a life of connection and (potentially) of community. It seems that there has always been some struggle within the approach around this issue, and this tension is part of the impetus to further advances in thought.

7 *Rogers' stance and the person-centred approach generally, in all its stages, reflects values around enhancing human life qualitatively, and concerns about being in a position to make a difference and getting on with the job. One can say that activity and advance have reflected a mix of idealism and pragmatism – in varying balance.* The shifting balance can be seen within Rogers himself and between stages of development of the approach. The pragmatic quality was reflected very strongly in his 1939 book, in Rogers' career through the war years, the setting up of his centre in Chicago, the initial gaining of substantial research support, and associated steps. Even Rogers' mentioned linkage of his approach to the values of democracy (1942a: 11; Rogers and Wallen, 1946:

---

9 Rank had sharply stated his pertinent view much earlier: 'For real psychotherapy is not concerned primarily with adaptation to any kind of reality, but with the adjustment of the patient to himself, that is, with his acceptance of his own individuality or of that part of his personality which he has formerly denied' (1935/1945: 105).

10 Interestingly, Rank saw distinctly different qualities of self-ideal, implying that one mode (to use later Rogerian language) grew out of conditions of worth, and that another was congruent with self-acceptance and in harmony with the individual's positive will. In this latter form, the self-ideal works creatively, in a self-transcending way (Rank, 1935/1945: 264–267).

22–23) was not necessary to convey its nature but plausibly helped to show its relevance and enhance its appeal, in the patriotic wartime/post-war climate. The idealist commitment to helping persons to heal, unfold, and move to a path of discovery and self-realization, is more strongly evident as the vision itself of human nature and possibilities formed clearly. It is notably presented, with both clarity and passion, in *Client-Centered Therapy* (1951: Preface and ch. 2). In the more recent life of the approach – now a movement with many and varied followers – some supportive affirmations edge beyond ideals to idealization. No motive then remains to quest for deeper, more inclusive theoretical and value principles. The paradox is that multi-level, searching inquiry had played a pivotal role in the development and integrity of the approach.[11]

8 *The main path of development of the client-centred approach entailed a synergistic interplay of theoretical ideas, practice and close observational inquiry and research. Practice experience and observation helped to spawn the theory, this then being tested in part through research and further refined in practice.* The practitioner and research worker often were one and the same. The context also included continual teaching and publication, and the interacting, cross-fertilizing features were manifold. I chose the term 'client-centred' here because this full confluence applied most distinctly, at least around Rogers, in the university phases of his career. Its character is especially consistent with my own experience in and knowledge of the enormously formative phase at the University of Chicago. The conditions of development under the rubric 'person-centred' have on the whole been less conducive to evolutionary momentum in underlying thought and theory. Recent indications, including the flow of original books and strong development of full training centres in Europe (with resource persons based both in teaching/research and practice settings), imply that another truly developmental phase is building.

Continuities running through the history of this approach are the main topic of these enduring themes. More particular threads from the large canvas of this book might also be discriminated, in (necessarily selective) summary. However, such added distillation does not promise the same furtherance of ideas, and has less appeal to me, than to follow some wavefronts of thought already beckoning. The extensions in my sights are new in their specifics but flow as next steps from features of content and perspective already advanced. I have in this book mostly started new sections with a focus on Rogers, and do so again in suggesting advances.

---

11 Maureen O'Hara, for one, has over a number of years expressed strong concern from within the person-centered movement over the more a-scientific and even evangelistic quality to be found in some contexts of Rogers' later work (O'Hara, 1995). It seems that, after Wisconsin, he lost his faith in the positivistic science prevailing in psychology, and never embraced an alternative systematic approach to testing and refining the ideas that came out of his close personal observation and depths of experience. O'Hara searches into a span of related issues.

The process and reach of engagements: 'growing' our theory

Symmetrical dialogue, and mutual facilitation

As a graduate student and trainee, I (and others with me) found Rogers' leadership style at moments frustrating even though, in sum, enormously affirming and enabling. The frustration aspect had to do with his relative silence, in direct dialogue with us, as to his own reaction, thought or opinion. If he had not also been continually expressing both his viewpoint, new ideas, and his more personal experience in very accessible, highly communicative and often forceful writing, I would not have had contact and known him in vitally important dimensions. His writing was effectively part of our relationship, which otherwise would have been incomplete and unsatisfying in some vital areas. It was a region where he was not immediately listening and making room for the other but holding forth and asserting his own views, meanings, experience. Hearing him at conferences, listening to him on tape, were further avenues. Although a skilled debater, spontaneous back-and-forth symmetrical dialogue was not his forte – nor was it mine, or that of more than a few of his other students.

Arguably, no counselling approach comes close to the person-centred innovation in its contribution to heightened consciousness and understanding around the process of listening. Honest, interested, respecting attention to the immediate experiencing and message of the other clearly can have profound effects. It works (for example) to release expressive sharing, especially of immediate felt meanings, and to enable experienced connection. Yet, one-way listening, of whatever depth and impact, lacks the mutuality found in some complete natural dialogue. A two-way flow in which each closely shares *and* listens, that is, a *symmetrical* dialogue, must involve a somewhat different inner process. This process would seem to depend on an easy fluency in running two closely linked, interweaving channels at once: close listening attention to the other while also forming and expressing one's own thought and feeling; and an inner building toward a next response as one is reading further signals and sensing below the surface of the other and self. There is no fear in easy and full dialogue, either of inability to express and communicate self or of implying any lower valuing of the other when not concentrating on them wholly. To the contrary, valuing and trust is implied in sharing from self and caring to be known.

Person-centred processes have helped to bring complementary dialogue (as between client and therapist, teacher and student, and other relations where positions and purposes differ) to new qualities and depths. The case of symmetrical personal dialogue presents a challenge for further development. Practice in small groups, and in relationship counselling with couples, are just two of the familiar contexts in which its achievement is an implicit or potential goal, such that the process between partners or group members becomes mutually facilitative. In a training context, the achievement of depth and fluency in such dialogue might be considered an advanced stage of learning, building on mastery of component features, especially, empathic listening and capacity for congruent expressive communication. As a concept, symmetrical dialogue is recent in my own thought, and I look forward to the input of reader-colleagues, and its further working out in terms of specific process and application. The common element of facilitative communication is the link to another emergent focus of thought.

Responsibility, and conditions for leadership

Let us ask again the question of *what 'taking responsibility' means positively*, in person-centred counselling and related practice? Does exercise of responsibility lie in what the helper-facilitator does (or seeks to do), or in what s/he purposefully does not do; or are both levels necessarily involved? Much of this book is about what the helper in this approach seeks to do, or does at best. In a word, this could be said to centre on 'living' the therapy/facilitative conditions in relation to the client. Another reply might stress the attitude of being responsible *to* the other and *for* oneself, but not *for* them. It may reasonably be pointed out that it does not facilitate self-agency and empowerment to shelter the other with decisions made for him or her. Or, taking this a little further, literally guiding the other is believed to easily work against, rather than calling forth and facilitating, development of their own resources and internal guidance system.

The approach has been and remains not directive, but where precisely does one draw the line of *not doing*, in the context of wanting to serve clients as a potent ally in their quest and need? By never expressing a reaction except to acknowledge or test one's understanding? (Such extreme constraint would at this stage be a caricature of 'nondirectivity', and inconsistent with helper congruency.) By never offering an opinion as to a course of action, when the client is seeking it? ('Never' is too strong, but the listener's sense of the client's *felt* meaning as they ask for advisory opinion is the most likely first level of response; and one which person-centred therapists tend to feel is least interventionist or leading.)[12] By responding in the same way whatever the client's kind or extremity of desperation and disturbance? (An answer might be 'no' *and* 'yes'; no in specific behaviour, yes in basic attitude.) By never directly inviting the other to try something in a process sense that the counsellor's strong intuition or direct experience suggests would be helpful? (Client/person-centred therapists nowadays would divide on answering this question, but not differ on believing that such suggestions, if given, should be both genuine invitations and interwoven with depth listening.)

What therapist/facilitators in this approach include or emphasize positively, and exclude or believe to be unhelpful, are sensitive issues that call for fine-tuned discrimination. The avoidance of visibly active or 'leading' ways of

---

12 Such response is not directive but it *is leading*, in the sense of inviting and usually drawing the person to further expression and exploration. Its effect is more powerful than a face value answer usually would be.

responding clearly *can* have personal roots. A person may have a general tendency to avoid initiating, or asserting a distinct viewpoint, or stepping into hurtful/damaging situations to try to alter their course. There seems a fine distinction between what one means not to do – and which also allows for more subtle but powerful kinds of 'doing' – and an unchosen passive-avoidant mode. Rogers was not only a skilled debater and luminous writer but a person clearly with great resolve, tenacity, and the capacity for effectively forceful response to opposition from outside his group. Handling anger was an acknowledged difficulty, but it seems safe to say that his own nondirectivity did not arise from an incapacity to respond in confronting or guiding-directive ways. This may be less true of some others of us drawn later to his developed approach, and raises a potential area for self-examination, in training and practice. Similar issues are very relevant in an administrative/organizational leadership context, which is my immediate focus.

When a non-intervening, other-responsive leader style is due more to involuntary disposition than to experience-based choice, the participation of an initiative-taking and trusted unofficial leader (somewhat akin to the 'emotional leader' Beck speaks of (pp. 150–151, and 301) may be crucial for viability. Both in this case and where the person-centred leader's facilitating approach is an evolved outcome of experience-tested learning, the group's composition in terms of member style is also vitally relevant, and success or failure is possible. It appears to me that a fruitful outcome of person-centred group leadership depends on at least three conditions external to the facilitative resources of the leader (the person recognized in and outside the group as having most formal responsibility, perhaps as chairperson, director or manager). These *leadership conditions* are advanced here as propositions – the first with two parts:

1 (i) *The group includes members already inclined toward and capable of engaging associatively in self-starting generative ways*, that is, they are immediately equipped to thrive in this mode, and effectively can assist others to grow toward it. (ii) *The group is not divided from the start, by inclusion of other members having distinctly opposed values and agendas* (with attitudes, for example, of profound mistrust of unfettered motivations, or of open-ended facilitation). I am speaking not of group therapy contexts but of working groups with responsibilities beyond their own well-being and growth. The element of member homogeneity implied in this proposed condition still leaves room for many differences in style, talent and specific problem-solving process.

2 A group's dynamics naturally change in the absence of a leader who has a relationship with each person and a symbolically and substantially vital role in the development of the group. *Thus a second condition is that the 'group-centred' leader remains actively engaged or available, and generally on the job, in his/her facilitative mode.* To assume a self-generating, naturally corrective process that continues reliably with or without the leader's enabling involvement is considered a wishful or over-simplified view.

Rogers tended to underrate his own crucial, even powerful influence in groups he was part of. Although wonderfully successful in some innovative leadership contexts, 'disasters' also occurred. The traumatic instance involving his large research team in Wisconsin, is acknowledged in his autobiography:

> Although I wished the group to be responsible for itself, I did not devote time enough or energy enough to implement this. . . . Consequently, when an important member of the group engaged in behavior which I (and others) regarded as unethical, there was not a solid basis for handling this. The fact that most of the turmoil which then occurred happened while I was away for a year at Palo Alto, multiplied the problems. . . . Because of the emergency I tried to pull back some of the authority, which I had freely given to the group, into my own hands. This was a grave mistake also. The ensuing [crisis] . . . constitutes without doubt the most painful and anguished period in my whole professional life. (1967a: 370–371)

This brief account in print could not fully express the damaging depth and trauma of the crisis; and other crises in other settings have occurred, for reasons both similar and additional to those Rogers touches on.[13] One further reason is that person-centred leadership innovations have tended, at their peril, to treat their special group as though it was self-contained and influenced mostly from the conditions within itself. My belief that this generally is a faulty assumption feeds into the remaining condition.

3 *The official leader and (some) other members are not only highly perceptive within their group but actively look and engage beyond it, acquiring awareness of attitudes of persons and groups in the near environment.*[14] This is a minimal statement of the condition. A stronger expression would include the aspect that the leader and others have a generally developed consciousness and sensitivity to the interwoven, multi-level working of systems of engagement that are part of any larger human relations context. Such consciousness would naturally lead to increased recognition and awareness of interactive relations beyond the group itself. This feature connects with my next focus.

Toward an extended theory of change

Some critics have argued that the 'therapy culture' has tended to work at making people as happy and well-functioning as possible in a seriously ailing

13 I speak from my own personal experience within a 'failed' group, one that I helped to bring into being with promise of interdisciplinary trail-blazing contribution along person-centred lines. As in the case Rogers describes, one member had a pivotal role in the drawn out trauma, but larger problems were also failures in knowing by those most involved in the leadership, including myself. Of the three mentioned conditions, the first was only partially met, and the other two were not met at crucial stages. (In this case, unusual, valuable things happened none the less, for the great majority of the venturesome students involved, over a decade span.)

14 The Roman god, Janus, facing two ways at once – both inward to and outward from the group, in this case – occurred to me as a suggestive symbol for the awareness I am speaking of.

society. Personal therapies have not addressed the systemic problems and, while helping individuals, could even have the effect of deflecting attention from the broader malaise. Alongside this view, is the observation that therapeutic self-discovery is, in significant part, a discovery of the capacity to make a difference in one's world. The client-person is likely to move in the direction of a more active, outreaching stance, a clearer sense of direction, and a perception of choice where this was not experienced before. Discovered agency in regard to one's own self may lead to change in one's sense of responsibility *to* others. But if the liberating movement proceeds only to the point of discovering 'the autonomous self', as occurs in some therapies and clients, the person is still in a separated state. The possibility of coming to a maturity of consciousness of interdependence is unrealized.

It may seem paradoxical that the availability and use of psychotherapy, relationship counselling, and of growth and support groups of varied kinds, could indirectly help an alienating culture to survive with little systemic change. Large police forces and prison systems may also have this survival effect in a deficient culture – although I hesitate to give this example in the same breath. An excellent fire-fighting system might help an urban population to tolerate dangerously decrepit tenement housing. With or without analogy, a view that is both person-centred *and* systems-sensitive opens the way to further distinctions and wider practice. One distinction is that developed problems within the self or personality are simultaneously primary and secondary or symptomatic. They are primary in the sense of having become part of the individual's pattern, and not just a temporary reaction to an immediate environment. They are symptomatic in that the person's disturbance has developed through the impact of conditions working to inhibit or undo, rather than to permit and further, integration and growth. Change within this view depends on a combination of inner and external conditions. The inner aspect includes some active concern and action by the affected individual; the outer one implies need for a sphere of opportunity, including resource availability and relief from stresses feeding conditions of worth or producing other shielding/inhibitory processes.

As therapist helpers, we face the challenge if not the responsibility to truly sensitize ourselves to both primary and secondary features of client problems, perhaps of our own problems to start with, *in their whole potential reach.* From the view that life is lived interactively, through many layers and kinds of interconnecting engagement system, achieving a receptive attunement to the working of these systems requires more than incidental learning. Growth in this capacity can be an intrinsic aspect of assisted discovery, as discussed in the last chapter. I want to add to the thought so far advanced by reconsidering what it means truly to understand and know another person. Several levels of understanding can be distinguished, each depending in some way on true recognition of felt experience and circumstance.

Most familiar in idea is the level of literal (empathic) apprehension of how the other is feeling within and in relation to themselves, especially what they are grappling with or torn about in reference to self. Another level is being in touch with the other around their feelings and meanings in close relationships, including the immediate one between 'client' and therapist/facilitator. But the total orbit of life engagements is much broader still than these two vital realms, and to know a person within the wider human relations habitat of their lives is another major sphere of understanding. A further level consists in awareness of engagements with other kinds of living beings and the natural environment. One could extend the spectrum to include engagements of meaning with the world as designed and built (thus indirectly with the designers/builders), and as imagined or invented. All such engagement spheres have a more or less individualized significance to the person(s) in focus; 'more or less' because some systems can be experienced quite similarly by many people.

The central point of my immediate reasoning can be simply stated. To understand and know a person in a full-bodied way, including but going beyond empathic recognition of immediately felt experience, is to apprehend the scope and qualities of the other's world of engagements. Helper readiness and capacity to do this means that the 'client' person can bring their *life* – as much of it as they wish – to the helping situation. It also means that the helper has or is gaining the knowledge to be advocate and contributor to more healthy human systems and environments. The reader will have seen my efforts and thought toward a more embracing perspective in various parts of this book. A further feature is the envisioning of nine levels of engagement system that apply in most people's lives, in a world of interconnection (Barrett-Lennard, 1993c).[15] Individually, we are very complex 'systems', and the person's self-integration has connection with qualities of relation at other levels (see Seeman, 1989a). The levels I see are as follows:

1 The individual, or person/self system.
2 Twosome relationships – the person's main dyadic systems.
3 Nuclear and other family (-like) relational systems of three persons or more.
4 Small face-to-face groups which the person experiences as a whole as well as member by member and at the level of component relations.
5 Large groups and organizations, where the person has a sense or idea of the whole, and felt relation with their immediate group, but is not in direct contact with all members.
6 Communities of association and belonging.
7 States, nations and transnational systems.
8 Humankind/the human race system.
9 The planetary life system.

---

15 The scheme outlined here distinguishes one plausible, conceptually manageable set of engagement system levels. For the reader interested in looking more broadly and deeply into living systems theory, the pioneers in the area include James and Jessie Miller. 'Community' was a later addition to their former schema of seven (now eight) main levels; from cells to transnational systems. Some twenty 'subsystems' of distinctive function are distinguished, common to virtually all levels of living system – as set forth in an up-to-date account (Miller and Miller, 1995).

The referent person visualized at the apex of this scheme is also present within all other levels, in association with others in the progressively broader groupings. Although the individual is 'within' the engagement systems that are fundamental in their living, none of these is considered inclusive of the person in his or her totality of being. This totality transcends particular levels and includes the person's own active consciousness of his or her world, self, and the relations between them. Accepted as a primary feature of this consciousness is the need to connect diverse realms of experience in some overall system of meaning.

Dyadic personal relationships are engagements clearly of profound importance in human lives, and individuals who lack any close, confident interpersonal bonds would in most cases be living in an extremity of deprivation (Barrett-Lennard, 1997b). Persons tend to have a larger direct role in fashioning their twosome relationships, as compared with their influence in fashioning multi-person systems. Family relationships typically include, besides dyads, interwoven subsystems of three, four and more members, a sense and concept of the whole family, and other features closely explored elsewhere (Barrett-Lennard, 1984). Clearly, there is huge variety in families, structurally and qualitatively, and a person can be 'at their best', or 'their worst', in particular family relations. Other strong family-like groupings (for example, lasting couple-to-couple mini-groups) sometimes compete with literal family relations in strength of influence.

Small face-to-face groups become very consequential from the time a child enters a day-care program, play school or kindergarten. In schools, children are arranged in small groups most of the time, some of these intact for a year or longer. Almost any context of collective human association gives rise to small-group engagements – conducive, detrimental, or of both kinds – with effects on further engagements. Any large organization encompasses small groups and relationships of likely importance in their own right to the members involved in them. These smaller systems affect and are affected by qualities of the host organization, and the more personal bonding in subgroups means there are alternative codes by which members may act – at times, with cruel effect. Self-identity and sense of worth tends to be bound up significantly with one's engagement in work/career organizations; and any personal wounds carried from treatment by an organization can be harder to bear when a standard of personal relationship is applied to this treatment.

Communities may grow (for example) out of tribal, ethnic and linguistic affiliations, common residence and/or interests, and shared religious or other belief. Their diverse origins and often voluntary nature make them more diffuse and variable in their working than organizations. Externally, persons may be more locked into their organizations; internally, bonds with communities of association and belonging tend to run deeper (Barrett-Lennard, 1994). An organization (a work/career setting, say) can also develop qualities of a primary community for many of its members. This overlap extends the range of needs served by the system, but at some risk to the individual due to the great and ramifying impact if membership is lost. The sense of belonging by members is inherent in the meaning of community, as earlier discussed (p. 312ff.), and people define and recognize their own identity in significant part by their communal affiliation(s). Ethnic and cultural sensitivity would seem a vital resource to counsellor-helpers of all kinds working in the multi-cultural environments now commonplace in urban settings.

Most persons feel an identification with their country (nation state), 'native land' or indigenous culture, which contributes to their sense of personal identity. (In the frequent case of migration, individuals often carry as much as possible of their familiar ethos with them, and feel lost or suffer painfully from its absence.) A large part of the impact of national affiliation is mediated through the component smaller systems of membership, with chains of interactive influence that may run from level to level between the person and the national system. In Europe, at present, governments are searching cautiously for a path to an increasing union that can not only deliver economic and security benefits but preserve the distinctive national–cultural identities that are contributing avenues to people knowing who they are.

All of us are members of the human race and world community, and to the extent that one experiences this whole as a great WE fabric of interwoven, interdependent lives, communities and states, it becomes a system of engagement. Much the same thing applies in respect to one's even more ultimate membership in the total life system of our planet. Persons with highly developed ecological consciousness would be distinctly engaged with this system level. Anyone husbanding or with friends among animals, or who experiences kinship with certain other species in the spectrum of life, or who feels a direct sense of union or embrace in certain natural surroundings, is involved directly with other life systems. Many of our interdependent associations, as with micro-organisms, are largely invisible. Not to appreciate this whole level of relation would seem to deprive and put ourselves at risk; to experience it positively is to be more connected in our world, and regardful of the commonality, diversity and wonder of life.[16]

It is evident that one's sense of personal identity can partake of all of these levels of engagement. It is as though we are players, each with many roles, in a multi-layered living theatre. But it is a theatre in which we are always on stage, even when learning (or composing) our parts, and which we never leave. I have discussed the various levels of scene we play in. Persons also interact, both as individuals and from within their engagement systems, with 'outside' systems of others – as these are perceived. Viewed externally, these groups of 'they' and 'them' usually are connected with 'me' or 'we', within a more encompassing system. Ambiguous inside/outside relations include frequent involvements as client or customer, or in another engagement role, with commercial, financial, service, regulatory and other 'bodies'. In principle,

---

16 People who believe deeply in a personal deity, with whom they experience contact and relation, may naturally add this to the important engagement systems in their lives.

the relations are interdependent but between dissimilar partners, especially, person and organization.

When we take seriously the great spectrum of interwoven connections in human life, and see these engagements not just as optional settings but as being at the heart of the process of living, a highly individualist model of change becomes insufficient. An implication is that we need to supplement the core conditions theory, or situate it within a wider model. Thus my intention to bring together principles of an approach to developing an expanded theory-and-practice model. These amount to a distillation of issues and implications from the picture so far drawn.

◇ A first principle is simply the recognition that we *live* interactively. Persons cannot be isolated and understood as complete entities, separate from their many interconnected and lived engagements. These engagements do not merely express us; we are embodied in them. As our engagement processes and systems change, we are different.
◇ The engagements of people in a community or societal system both reflect the qualities of that system and collectively help to create and sustain it. Viewed organically, personal and social system qualities are intricately linked; and no component of the whole is literally without influence, or immune from it.
◇ The therapy/counselling relation is one (temporary) engagement system among the many ongoing systems in an individual's life. Effectively the client mediates the interplay of this system and his/her many other engagements.
◇ If a helping engagement is to have a truly transformative role the person needs not only relief from inner torment or conflict within the self but to advance or refine his/her 'skills of engagement'. This broadly entails further development of personal consciousness of the terrain of one's interactive life *and* added discovery learning of navigational resources, priorities and paths to growth in engagement qualities.
◇ For the therapist/facilitator to have any potency in relation to the broader contexts in which individuals come to grief she/he needs to understand the systemic working of the worlds that clients inhabit, and to seek avenues of contributing involvement additional to counselling. This implies responsibility not only on a healing level but also on a preventive one; thus not only to individual clients but to the working of systems that help to spawn or sustain dysfunctional engagements.
◇ One main level of facilitative social intervention is that of contributing to the preservation and enhancement of experienced working community, in which persons find opportunity for mutual engagement of high personal meaning and social value. This is assisted by the ways we work as helpers, as well as the levels or contexts we work in.
◇ One approach to the actual framing of a more complete model of change would *articulate embracing social conditions necessary for the interpersonal facilitative conditions to be widely available and effective in individual life*. A second, slightly different approach would *place principles of communal/*

social healing in complementary interactive relation to those of personal healing change. Whatever the exact approach, it could also draw from distinctions still to be mentioned.

Conclusion: our clients, our field, and moving forward

Rogers' central contribution was and is a system of psychotherapy. Within a decade or so of his first book on therapy he began to search into the implications and application of his evolving philosophy and helping system in other spheres of human engagement: education, management, family life and relations, group relations and ethnic conflict, and finally, to the level of national and international tensions and his effort to contribute in some way to a more peaceful, less humanly destructive world. His clients at various times ranged from disturbed children and their parents, to war veterans inwardly scarred or 'lost' in the process of coming home, and bright, reflective but troubled adult students. Also included were 'psychotic' mental hospital patients, resourceful individuals seeking deeper meaning or engagement growth through intensive group experience, school-age students and their teachers and administrators. Persons came to large-group events, searching for further paths of connection and meaning, others came ambivalently together to confront racial, ethnic and similar divides; and these levels of work unfolded into the literal efforts to catalyse 'peace processes' within and among groups of varied national affiliation, identity and agenda.

Helper/facilitators of broadly person-centred persuasion between them work with 'clients' over this whole spectrum. Clearly, the kinds of needs to which they/we collectively are responding varies very widely, and could evolve further.[17] A coherent way of portraying the concerns and needs we implicitly address over such a wide range is to group them by the *level of relation and connection involved.* The following levels seem to me quite distinct in their main thrust:

1 Issues of *self relation and integration* are at the heart of psychotherapy as conceived in this approach. A frequent aspect of therapy is the search to find a coherent meaning in confusing, conflictual inner experience. Our clients over the broad span now in view obviously do not all have this level of concern. I have at times treated persons who consulted me about disturbing life engagement difficulties as though *self* concern was central, or would be if my response gave them the opportunity they needed. Usually, in these circumstances, they have not returned or not stayed long.

---

17 Person-centred practitioners have been inclined as helpers to leave possibilities very open so that concerns can unfold and persons find their own direction – a value I largely share. But if we are reluctant to distinguish and prepare ourselves to respond to truly *different kinds* of concern and need, arising in very different contexts, our potential assistance is curtailed.

2 *Self–other relation and connection* issues, in partner, family and/or other close personal relationships may be central. Sometimes client concerns focus on a particular dimension of intimate relations, as in the sexual sphere for example, vital to the client in its own right and possibly a doorway into further relational issues. The client seeking help on this interactive level may come alone or with their involved partner or family members. The person-centred helper, skilled in relationship counselling, is not meeting identical needs, engaging in the same process, or exercising the same balance of resources, as in the case of intensive psychotherapy.

3 *Internal group relations* issues are the distinctive ones when a group seeks or accepts consultation assistance with its own collectivity and working. Here the facilitator's task broadly entails assisting the membership of the group in its interior quality of engagement. Effective assistance may lead to changes such as greater mutual awareness of actual views, attitudes and resources, more inter-member confidence, and a growing quality of joint empowerment, energy and resourcefulness of the group. Such features do not reflect desire for personal group therapy, even though there is a sense in which the *group* is being healed. The consultant's role is as process facilitator in group relations.

4 A further context is that of *community relations development and health*. A community resource person or team working from an expanded person-centred frame of reference faces a very distinctive situation. To start with, partly because an ailing community can rarely speak with one voice, the 'helper' is not likely to enter that situation through choice by all constituencies. Once present, although crucial that he/she/they listen to individuals, it is vital also to tune in to broader currents and gain an informed sense of what the *community* is going through. Becoming aware on such levels, in enabling mode, entails participative communication by many community members in a process potentially as illuminating to them as to any outsider. In practice, a community in difficulty is often divided along factional/group lines, making inter-group relations a significant issue.

5 *Inter-group relations phenomena and issues* may be one focus or *the* focus of concern and desired assistance, the latter more likely where groups are from differing communities. One challenge for the facilitator is to become attuned to the distinct, broadly shared perspectives within each group. However, it might well be that some people in 'opposing' camps actually are closer in outlook to each other than to their main groups; or that certain individuals or subgroups rely on the status quo of opposition and conflict. Intergroup exchange is between people speaking or reacting from within the engagement system of their group, their own role and ambitions in the group, and the subgroup they are most closely associated with. For the larger groups to move to positive and confident engagement, actual change would need to occur in the composition of influences that have sustained the conflictual breach.

6 Responding to *stressed relations or conflict between large people systems* represents the further theatre of potential engagement by suitably prepared person-centred specialists. Each such system, of course, has its own structure, its historical and current outlook, special interests, type of governmental system, and other distinguishing characteristics. Each almost certainly includes persons or groups whose presumed interests or even life meaning are embedded in the conditions or process of conflict. If one thinks, for example, of the former Yugoslavia, of Afghanistan, or of Lebanon not long ago, the warring may appear bizarre as well as tragic in the extreme.[18] UN and other negotiators have struggled long and occasionally succeeded in helping to move such systems toward options other than armed struggle. The possibility exists for person-centred facilitators, *tuned to a wide range of human engagements*, to learn to contribute on such a level; hopefully, before an outbreak of armed combat. The further learning desirably would start from experience in less hardened and dangerous conflict situations. Holding such a possible role in view seems a vital step toward some colleagues actually choosing and finding a way to this level of effective contribution.

All of these levels of relational breakdown and remedial/growth process involve persons who individually have a spectrum of outside engagement systems, as already discussed. I have argued that any and all of these levels can come into the picture in working with an individual. When working primarily at the level of problematic group or system relations, all the other engagements that the whole persons involved bring implicitly within them are important for the helper to be sensitive to. Problems at such other levels may invite attention, but with discriminating response and *care not to shift the whole stage from the level that has produced the call for assistance*, or to construe the difficulty as though it was simply a conflict or communication crisis between free-standing individuals.

So much for the span of our clientele and potential levels of assistance. This range has implications for the identity of our field, which as a whole needs perspectives and expertise beyond the resources of any single discipline, certainly beyond one established speciality. Psychotherapy and counselling, alone, do not 'belong' to any single primary discipline. If our work is to have the extended range envisioned here, even if is to be effective over the wide band to which Rogers personally applied his efforts, we need resources between us that draw from a variety of backgrounds in the human sciences and other fields concerned with human well-being. There is need for special talents among us that would rarely be found in high measure all in the same person when one thinks of areas such as depth psychotherapy, community or group relations facilitation, large-system conflict resolution, social ethics and

18 In Afghanistan, for example, for many young adults life goals and meaning from early childhood evidently have built up around warring struggle, in the name of preserving group identity but against varied opponents. To abandon this struggle without losing self ('who I am') or group ('who we are') identity, strong alternative meanings would somehow have to evolve.

advocacy, theoretical systematizing, and methodology advance in research. We each could be broadly informed and sensitive to the whole range outlined without having the specialist resources to work in all parts of it. Other things help to define our field and approach.

This book has Carl Rogers' name in its title, and the word *journey*. It is about an evolving approach still often called client-centred in reference to therapy, but with 'person-centred' now being the more frequent and broader designation. What then is the core that justifies speaking of 'an approach', one that we name, that courses, workshops and programs are woven around, that a large number of people identify with. I suggest that the core does not lie in any final belief, nor in any one aspect of theory or practice, however pivotal it seems. Many would hold that it is most basically a stance toward the human person, although this is difficult to state without having the ring of a fixed creed. Rogers sought to express it in a paper framed in the sixties and finally published nearly a decade later (1974c). He noted several aspects, saying first that 'a willingness to change, an openness to experience and to research data, has been one of the most distinctive features', and that this element of evolving changingness has set it apart from other therapy orientations (1974c: 9). I earlier quoted his second powerful point of stance, that 'client-centred therapy has seen the unique, subjective, inner person as the honored and valued core of human life'. A related third aspect implied from an early stage is 'the stress on the enormous potential of the individual' (10).

Rogers' other points are mixed in level and I would supplement these three with the essence of most of the enduring features distinguished in the first section of this chapter. Specific theory, which needs to continue to evolve, is not emphasized among those qualitative features nor is it by Rogers in his statement. There is also another, different kind of 'core', compatible, with much that has been presented here, both in terms of major strands *and* the living spectrum of particularities of thought and practice. This core pivots on what it means to be an individual 'qualified' in this approach, and a representative or exponent of it. Surely the most defining feature is that the person has attained a deeply knowing conversance with and engagement in it. Put another way, a background of having strongly searched into the approach at levels of theory and idea, experiential learning and practice application, and areas of investigative work, is I believe what its exponents desirably and most basically have in common. Likely broad effects are a critical appreciation, and depth of individualized understanding and resourcefulness.

For any helping system of thought and practice to remain vividly alive and relevant it must continue to evolve. This book has certainly been a vehicle for me to experience and participate in a searching, living motion of ideas and of their practical expression and investigation. At best, it will add to the momentum of serious, informed advance. If particular aspects of my current thought seem radical, as they may to some with a long history in the approach, so be it. I have gone back to the beginning, to the heart of the thought, practice and research through the formational and school eras of client-centred therapy. Most characteristics of the approach are in motion in my perception; they are not endings. Reaching for the heart of things, and sharing the differentiated picture that ensues, assumes active and rather searching reader-companions, ones who can pass over pedantic elements or points of dispute without losing interest in main themes. I think that forward motion is an almost inevitable consequence of experiencing the enterprise of this system as an absorbing journey not only a place of arrival. This book reflects and is another step in this *larger* journey, a realization that helps me finally to end it.

References

Adams, R.P. (1968). *Faulkner: Myth and motion.* Princeton, New Jersey: Princeton University Press.

Adorno, T.W., Frenkel-Brunswick, E., Levinson, D.J. and Sanford, R.N. (1950). *The authoritarian personality.* New York: Harper.

Agee, J. and Evans, W. (1941). *Let us now praise famous men.* Boston: Houghton Mifflin.

Allen, F.H. (1942/1947). *Psychotherapy with children.* New York: W.W. Norton (1942) and London: Kegan Paul, Trench, Trubner & Co. (1947).

Allen, F.L. (1931). *Only yesterday: An informal history of the nineteen-twenties.* New York: Harper & Row.

Allport, G.W. (1945). The psychology of participation. *Psychological Review, 53,* 117–132.

Anderson, W. (1974). Personal growth and client-centered therapy: an information-processing view. In D.A. Wexler and L.N. Rice (eds), *Innovations in client-centered therapy* (21–48). New York: Wiley.

Anderson, W.A. (1989). Family therapy in the client-centered tradition. *Person-Centered Review, 4,* 295–307.

Auckenthaler, A. (1980). Klientenzentrierte Partnertherapie: Überlegungen zür Gültigkeit des klientenzentrierte Konzeptes für die Psychotherapie mit Paaren. In M. Hautzinger and W. Schulz (eds), *Klinische Psychologie und Psychotherapie. Band 4,* Tübigen, Köln: Steinbauer und Rau.

Axline, V.M. (1947). *Play therapy: the inner dynamics of childhood..* Boston: Houghton Mifflin.

Axline, V.M. (1964). *Dibs: In search of self.* Boston: Houghton Mifflin.

Bakan, D. (1966). *The duality of human existence.* Chicago: Rand McNally.

Bakan, D. (1971). *Slaughter of the innocents: A study of the battered child phenomenon.* San Francisco: Jossey-Bass.

Bales, R.F. (1958). Task roles and social roles in problem-solving groups. In E.E. Maccoby, T.M. Newcomb and L. Hartley (eds), *Readings in social psychology.* New York: Holt, Rinehart & Winston.

Barnard, D. (1984). The personal meaning of illness: client-centered dimensions of medicine and health care. In R.F. Levant and J.M. Shlien (eds), *Client-centered therapy and the person-centered approach: New directions in theory, research and practice* (337–351). New York: Praeger.

Barrett-Lennard, G.T. (1959). Dimensions of perceived therapist response related to therapeutic change. Doctoral dissertation (psychology), University of Chicago.

Barrett-Lennard, G.T. (1962a). Dimensions of therapist response as causal factors in therapeutic change. *Psychological Monographs, 76* (43, Whole No. 562).

Barrett-Lennard, G.T. (1962b). The mature person. *Mental Hygiene, 46,* 98–102.

Barrett-Lennard, G.T. (1963). Significant aspects of a helping relationship. *Mental Hygiene, 47,* 223–227. (Republished in *Canada's Mental Health,* 1965, *13,* July–August issue. Supplement No. 47.)

Barrett-Lennard, G.T. (1965). Professional psychology and the control of human behaviour. *Australian Journal of Psychology, 17,* 24–34. Republished in J.T. Hart and T.M. Tomlinson (eds), *New directions in client-centered therapy* (442–452). Houghton Mifflin, 1970.

Barrett-Lennard, G.T. (1967). Experiential learning in small groups: the basic encounter process.

Proceedings, Canadian Association University Student Personnel Services: The Ottawa Conference. November issue, 2–12.
Barrett-Lennard, G.T. (1972a). Notes on congruence. Privately circulated manuscript, based on a presentation to the Society for Psychotherapy Research.
Barrett-Lennard, G.T. (1972b). Group process analysis from post-session and follow-up data. *Group Process Study Papers*, No. 5. Ontario: University of Waterloo Library.
Barrett-Lennard, G.T. (1973). The intensive group experience: process description and guidelines. *Canada's Mental Health, 21* (1). Supplement No. 73.
Barrett-Lennard, G.T. (1974). Experiential learning groups. *Psychotherapy: Theory, Research and Practice, 11*, 71–75.
Barrett-Lennard, G.T. (1974/1975). Outcomes of residential encounter group workshops: descriptive analysis of follow-up structured questionnaire data. *Interpersonal Development, 5*, 86–93.
Barrett-Lennard, G.T. (1975). Process, effects and structure in intensive groups: a theoretical-descriptive analysis. In C.L. Cooper (ed.), *Theories of group processes* (59–86). London: Wiley. (Preferred source is the *corrected*, soft-cover reprinting, 1976.)
Barrett-Lennard, G.T. (1976). Empathy in human relationships: significance, nature and measurement. *Australian Psychologist, 11*, 173–184.
Barrett-Lennard, G.T. (1978). The Relationship Inventory: later development and adaptations. JSAS *Catalog of Selected Documents in Psychology, 8*, 68. (MS 1732).
Barrett-Lennard, G.T. (1979a). The client-centered system unfolding. In F.J. Turner (ed.), *Social work treatment: Interlocking theoretical approaches* (177–241). New York: Free Press. Second edition.
Barrett-Lennard, G.T. (1979b). A new model of communicational-relational systems in intensive groups. *Human Relations, 32*, 841–849.
Barrett-Lennard, G.T. (1981). The empathy cycle: refinement of a nuclear concept. *Journal of Counseling Psychology, 28*, 91–100.
Barrett-Lennard, G.T. (1984). The world of family relationships: a person-centered systems view. In R.F. Levant and J.M. Shlien (eds), *Client-centered therapy and the person-centered approach: New directions in theory, research and practice* (222–242). New York: Praeger.
Barrett-Lennard, G.T. (1985a). The helping interview in counselling and psychotherapy. *British Journal of Hospital Medicine, 33*, 287–290.
Barrett-Lennard, G.T. (1985b). The helping relationship: crisis and advance in theory and research. *The Counseling Psychologist, 13*, 279–294.
Barrett-Lennard, G.T. (1986a). The Relationship Inventory now: issues and advances in theory, method and use. In L.S. Greenberg and W.M. Pinsof (eds), *The psychotherapeutic process: A research handbook* (439–476). New York: Guilford Press.
Barrett-Lennard, G.T. (1986b). On loneliness. *The Ceshur Connection, 1* (2 and 3), 3–8.
Barrett-Lennard, G.T. (1987a). South Pacific adventure: Carl and Helen Rogers in Australia. *Person-Centered Review, 2*, 299–305.
Barrett-Lennard, G.T. (ed.) (1987b). Writing person to person: letters from Carl. *The Ceshur Connection, 2* (1 and 2 – Carl Rogers Memorial issue). Pp. 3–5 (Introduction); pp. 5–40 (selection of letters. Serial held, e.g., in the Australian National Library, Canberra).
Barrett-Lennard, G.T. (1988). Listening. *Person-Centered Review, 3*, 410–425.
Barrett-Lennard, G.T. (1990). The therapy pathway reformulated. In G. Lietaer, J. Rombauts and R. Van Balen (eds), *Client-centered and experiential psychotherapy in the nineties* (123–153). Leuven, Belgium: Leuven University Press.
Barrett-Lennard, G.T. (1993a). The phases and focus of empathy. *British Journal of Medical Psychology, 66*, 3–14.
Barrett-Lennard, G. T. (1993b). Understanding the person-centered approach to therapy: a 'reply' to questions and misconceptions. In D. Coghlan and E. McIlduff (eds), *The person-centered approach and cross-cultural communication: An international review, Vol. 2* (99–113). Linz: Sandkorn edition – for the Center for Cross-Cultural Communication, Dublin. (Corrected revision privately circulated.)
Barrett-Lennard, G.T. (1993c). Viewing the person in context: a systemic model of change. *Network, 8* (2), 13–25. (Melbourne: Australian Psychological Society.)

Barrett-Lennard, G.T. (1994). Toward a person-centered theory of community. *Journal of Humanistic Psychology, 34* (3), 62–86.
Barrett-Lennard, G.T. (1996a). Therapy and groups in context: a study of developmental episodes in adulthood. In R. Hutterer, G. Pawlowsky, P.F. Schmid and R. Stipsits (eds), *Client-centered and experiential psychotherapy: A paradigm in motion* (185–198). Frankfurt am main: Peter Lang.
Barrett-Lennard, G.T. (1996b). *End-of-meeting group process questionnaire*. Privately printed – available from author.
Barrett-Lennard, G.T. (1997a). The recovery of empathy – toward others and self. In A.C. Bohart and L.S. Greenberg (eds), *Empathy reconsidered: New directions in psychotherapy* (103–121). Washington, DC: APA Books.
Barrett-Lennard, G.T. (1997b). Levels of loneliness. Manuscript submitted for publication.
Barrett-Lennard, G.T., Kwasnik, T.M. and Wilkinson, G.R. (1973/1974). Some effects of participation in encounter group workshops: an analysis of written follow-up reports. *Interpersonal Development, 4*, 35–41.
Barron, F.X. (1950). Psychotherapy as a special case of personal interaction: prediction of its outcome. Unpublished doctoral dissertation, University of California.
Bebout, J. (1974). It takes one to know one: Existential–Rogerian concepts in encounter groups. In D. A. Wexler and L.N. North (eds), *Innovations in client-centered therapy* (367–420). New York: Wiley.
Bebout, J. and Gordon, B. (1972). The value of encounter. In L.N. Solomon and B. Berzon (eds), *New perspectives on encounter groups* (83–118). San Francisco: Jossey Bass.
Beck, A.P. (1974). Phases in the development of structure in therapy and encounter groups. In D.A. Wexler and L.N. Rice (eds), *Innovations in client-centered therapy* (421–463). New York: Wiley.
Beck, A.P. (1981). Developmental characteristics of the system-forming process. In J.E. Durkin (ed.), *Living groups: Group psychotherapy and general system theory* (316–332). New York: Bruner/Mazel.
Beck, A.P., Dugo, J.M., Eng, A.M. and Lewis, C.M. (1986). The search for phases in group development: designing process analysis measures of group interaction. In L.S. Greenberg and W.M. Pinsof (eds), *The psychotherapeutic process: A research handbook* (615–705). New York: Guilford Press.
Beck, A.P., Dugo, J.M., Eng., A.M., Lewis, C.M. and Peters, L.N. (1983). The participation of leaders in the structural development of therapy groups. In R.R. Dies and K.R MacKenzie (eds), *Advances in group psychotherapy: Integrating research and practice*. New York: International Universities Press.
Beck, A.P., Eng., A.M. and Brusa, J.A. (1989). The evolution of leadership during group development. *Group, 13* (3 and 4), 155–164.
Beck, A.P. and Keil, A.V. (1967). Observations on the development of client-centered, time-limited therapy groups. *Counseling Center Discussion Papers, 13* (5). Chicago: University of Chicago Library.
Beck, A.P. and Peters, L.N. (1981). The research evidence for distributed leadership in therapy groups. *International Journal of Group Psychotherapy, 31*, 43–71.
Berzon, B., Pious, C. and Farson, R.E. (1963). The therapeutic event in group psychotherapy: a study of subjective reports by group members. *Journal of Individual Psychology, 19*, 204–212.
Berzon, B. and Solomon, L.N. (1966). The self-directed therapeutic group: three studies. *Journal of Counseling Psychology, 13*, 491–497. (See also the book-published revision and extension of this article by Solomon and Berzon, 1970.)
Berzon, B., Solomon, L.N. and Reisel, R. (1972). Audio-tape programs for self-directed groups. In L.N. Solomon and B. Berzon (eds), *New perspectives on encounter groups* (211–223). San Francisco: Jossey-Bass.
Bills, R.E. (1950). Nondirective play therapy with retarded readers. *Journal of Consulting Psychology, 14*, 140–149.
Bills, R.E. (1952). An investigation of student-centered teaching. *Journal of Educational Research, 46*, 313–319.

Blatt, S.J., Quinlan, D.M., Zuroff, D.C. and Pilkonis, P.A. (1996). Interpersonal factors in brief treatment of depression: further analyses of the National Institute of Mental Health Treatment of Depression Collaborative Research Program. *Journal of Consulting and Clinical Psychology, 64*, 162–171.

Blocksma, D.D. and Porter, E.H. (1947). A short-term training program in client-centered counseling. *Journal of Consulting Psychology, 11*, 55–60.

Boardman, F.W. Jnr (1967). *The thirties: America and the Great Depression*. New York: Henry Z. Walck.

Boettcher, R.E. (1977). Interspousal empathy, marital satisfaction, and marriage counseling. *Journal of Social Service Research, 1*, 105–113.

Bohart, A.C. (1991). Empathy in client-centred therapy: A contrast with psychoanalysis and self-psychology. *Journal of Humanistic Psychology, 31* (1), 34–48.

Bohart, A.C. and Greenberg, L.S. (eds) (1997). *Empathy reconsidered: New directions in psychotherapy*. Washington, DC: APA Books.

Bohart, A.C., O'Hara, M. and Leitner, L.M. (1998). Empirically violated treatments: Disenfranchisement of humanistic and other psychotherapies. *Psychotherapy Research, 8*, 141–147.

Bonner, T.N. (1963). *Our recent past: American civilization in the 20th century*. Englewood Cliffs, NJ: Prentice-Hall.

Bornet, V.D. (1960). *Welfare in America*. Norman: University of Oklahoma Press.

Boukydis, C.F.Z. (1990). Client-centered/experiential practice with parents and infants. In G. Lietaer, J. Rombauts and R. Van Balen (eds), *Client-centered and experiential psychotherapy in the nineties* (797–811). Leuven, Belgium: Leuven University Press.

Bowen, M.C.V-B. (1986). Personality differences and person-centered supervision. *Person-Centered Review, 1*, 291–309.

Bowen, M.V-B. (1987). Special characteristics of the Rust Workshop and their influence on my facilitation process. *Journal of Humanistic Psychology, 27*, 348–363.

Bowen, M., Miller, M., Rogers, C.R. and Wood, J.K. (1980). Learnings in large groups: their implications for the future. In C.R. Rogers, *A way of being* (316–335). Boston: Houghton Mifflin.

Bown, O.H. (1954). An investigation of therapeutic relationship in client-centered psychotherapy. Unpublished doctoral dissertation, University of Chicago.

Bozarth, J.D. (1981). The person-centered approach in the large community group. In G. Gazda (ed.), *Innovations to group psychotherapy* (100–133). Springfield, IL: Thomas. Second edition.

Bozarth, J.D. (1990). The essence of client-centered therapy. In G. Lietaer, J. Rombauts and R. Van Balen (eds), *Client-centered and experiential psychotherapy in the nineties* (59–64). Leuven, Belgium: Leuven University Press.

Bozarth, J.D. and Shanks, A. (1989). Person-centered family therapy with couples. *Person-Centered Review, 4*, 280–294.

Braaten, L.J. (1961a). The main themes of 'existentialism' from the viewpoint of a psychotherapist. *Mental Hygiene, 45* (January), 10–17.

Braaten, L.J. (1961b). The movement from non-self to self in client-centered psychotherapy. *Journal of Counseling Psychology, 8*, 20–24.

Braaten, L.J. (1989a). The effects of person-centered group therapy. *Person-Centered Review, 4*, 183–209.

Braaten, L.J. (1989b). The Self-Development Project list-90: a new instrument to measure positive goal attainment. *Small Group Behavior, 20*, 3–23.

Braaten, L.J. (1991). To what extent do clients discriminate between the person-centered facilitating conditions in group psychotherapy? A factorial model. Presented to the Second International Conference on Client-Centered and Experiential Psychotherapy, Stirling, Scotland. (Full article, as planned for publication, circulated by author.)

Brodley, B.T. (1990). Client-centred and experiential: two different therapies. In G. Lietaer, J. Rombauts and R. Van Balen (eds), *Client-centered and experiential psychotherapy in the nineties* (87–107). Leuven, Belgium: Leuven University Press.

Brodley, B.T. (1992). Empathic understanding and feelings in client-centered therapy. *The Person-Centered Journal, 1* (1), 21–37.

Brodley, B.T. (1994). Some observations of Carl Rogers' behavior in therapy interviews. *The Person-Centered Journal, 1* (2), 37–47.
Brusa, J.A., Stone, M.H., Beck, A.P., Dugo, J.M. and Peters, L.N. (1994). A sociometric test to identify emergent leader and member roles: Phase 1. *International Journal of Group Psychotherapy, 44*, 79–100.
Buber, M. (1947). *Between man and man*. London: Kegan Paul.
Burgess, E.W. and Cottrell, L.S. (1939). *Predicting success or failure in marriage*. New York: Prentice-Hall.
Burns, J.M. (1956). *Roosevelt: The lion and the fox*. New York: Harcourt, Brace & World.
Butler, J.M. (1956). The goals of counseling. *Counseling Centre Discussions Papers, 2*, No. 20. Chicago: University of Chicago Library. (Presented to the American Personnel and Guidance Association, St. Louis, Missouri, 1953.)
Butler, J.M. (1958). Client-centered counselling and psychotherapy. In D. Brower and L.E. Abt (eds), *Progress in clinical psychology*, Vol. 3: *Changing conceptions in psychotherapy*. New York: Grune & Stratton.
Butler, J.M. (1964). Simplest data factors and simple structure in factor analysis. *Educational and Psychological Measurement, 24*, 755–763.
Butler, J.M. (1966). Self-acceptance as a measure of outcome of psychotherapy. *The British Journal of Social Psychiatry, 1*, 51–62.
Butler, J.M. (1968). Self-ideal congruence in psychotherapy. *Psychotherapy: Theory, Research and Practice, 5*, 13–17.
Butler, J.M. (1969). Simple structure reconsidered: distinguishability and invariance in factor analysis. *Multivariate Behavioral Research, 4*, 5–28.
Butler, J.M. (1974). The iconic mode in psychotherapy. In D.A. Wexler and L.N. Rice (eds), *Innovations in client-centered therapy* (171–210). New York: Wiley.
Butler, J.M. and Haigh, G.V. (1954). Changes in the relation between self-concepts and ideal concepts consequent upon client-centered counseling. In C.R. Rogers and R.F. Dymond (eds), *Psychotherapy and personality change* (55–75). Chicago, University of Chicago Press.
Butler, J.M. and Hook, L.H. (1966). Multiple factor analysis in terms of weighted regression. *Educational and Psychological Measurement, 26*, 545–565.
Butler, J.M. and Rice, L.N. (1963). Adience, self-actualization and drive theory. In J.M. Wepman and R.W. Heine (eds), *Concepts of personality* (79–110). Chicago: Aldine.
Butler, J.M., Rice, L.N. and Wagstaff, A.K. (1962). On the naturalistic definition of variables: an analogue of clinical analysis. In H.H. Strupp and L. Luborsky (eds), *Research in psychotherapy*, Vol. 2 (178–205). Washington: APA.
Butler, J.M., Rice, L.N. and Wagstaff, A.K. (1963). *Quantitative naturalistic research*. Englewood Cliffs, NJ: Prentice-Hall.
Byrne, B. (1983). Trainee uses of reciprocal peer supervision and of faculty supervision in psychotherapy training. *Dissertation Abstracts International, 44*, 111A.
Cain, D.J. (1989). From the individual to the family. *Person-Centered Review, 4*, 248–255.
Cantor, N. (1946). *The dynamics of learning*. Buffalo: Foster & Stewart.
Carkhuff, R.R. (1967). *Beyond counseling and therapy*. New York: Holt, Rinehart & Winston.
Carleton, W.G. (1963). Government and health before the New Deal. *Current History, 45*, 71–76.
Carr, A.C. (1949). An evaluation of psychotherapy cases by means of the Rorschach. *Journal of Consulting Psychology, 13*, 196–205.
Cartwright, D.S., Kirtner, W.L. and Fiske, D.W. (1963). Method factors in change associated with psychotherapy. *Journal of Abnormal and Social Psychology, 66*, 164–175.
Cartwright, D.S., Robertson, R.J., Fiske, D.W. and Kirtner, W.L. (1961). Length of therapy in relation to outcome and change in personal integration. *Journal of Consulting Psychology, 25*, 84–88.
Cedar, B. and Levant, R.F. (1990). A meta-analysis of the effects of parent effectiveness training. *The American Journal of Family Therapy, 18*, 373–384.
Chickadonz, G.H. et al. (undated). Master of Science in Nursing program plan (printed brochure). Toledo: Medical College of Ohio.

Chickadonz, G.H., Whitmire, V.M., Lindstrom, C.J. and Utz, S.W. (1986). Creating a person-centered environment for a new graduate nursing program. *Person-Centered Review, 1*, 201–220.
Cilliers, F. (1996). Facilitator training in South Africa. In R. Hutterer, G. Pawlowsky, P.F. Schmid and R. Stipsits (eds), *Client-centered and experiential psychotherapy: A paradigm in motion* (547–555). Frankfurt am Main: Peter Lang.
Clark, C.A. (1990). A comprehensive process analysis of focusing events in experiential therapy. Unpublished doctoral dissertation, University of Toledo.
Clark, J.V. and Culbert, S.A. (1965). Mutually therapeutic perception and self-awareness in a T group. *Journal of Applied Behavioral Science, 1*, 180–194.
Clark, J.V., Culbert, S.A. and Bobele, H.K. (1969). Mutually therapeutic perception and self-awareness under variable conditions. *Journal of Applied Behavioral Science, 5*, 65–72.
Clebsch, W. and Jaekle, C. (1975). *Pastoral care in historical perspective.* New York: Aronson.
Cline, E.W. (1970/1971). Confirming behaviour of school executives. (Doctoral dissertation, University of Florida, 1969). *Dissertation Abstracts, 31*, 1067A.
Cochrane, C.T. and Holloway, A. J. (1974). Client-centered therapy and Gestalt therapy: in search of a merger. In D.A. Wexler and L.N. Rice (eds), *Innovations in client-centered therapy* (259–287). New York: Wiley.
Coghlan, D. and McIlduff, E. (1991). Dublin 1985: perceptions of a cross-cultural communication workshop. In E. McIlduff and D. Coghlan, *The person-centered approach and cross-cultural communication: International Review*, Vol. 1 (43–60). Linz: Sandkorn.
Cooper, C.L. (1969). The influence of the trainer on participant change in T-groups. *Human Relations, 22*, 515–530.
Cooper, C.L. (1973). A follow-up study on the influence of the T-group trainer on participant change. *Journal of European Training, 2*, 181–188.
Coulson, W.R. (1970). Inside a basic encounter group. *The Counseling Psychologist, 2* (2), 1–27.
Coulson, W.R. (1972). *Groups, gimmicks and instant gurus: An examination of encounter groups and their distortions.* New York: Harper & Row.
Coulson, B., Land, D. and Meador, B. (eds) (1977). *The La Jolla experiment: Eight personal views.* La Jolla: Landmark Press.
Counselling Unit, University of Strathclyde (1996). *Course book for diploma students.*
Cramer, D. (1985). Psychological adjustment and the facilitative nature of close personal relationships. *British Journal of Medical Psychology, 58*, 165–168.
Cramer, D. (1987). Self-esteem, advice-giving, and the facilitative nature of close personal relationships. *Person-Centered Review, 2*, 99–110.
Cramer, D. (1989). Self-esteem and the facilitativeness of parents and close friends. *Person-Centered Review, 4*, 61–76.
Cramer, D. (1990a). Disclosure of personal problems, self-esteem, and the facilitativeness of friends and lovers. *British Journal of Guidance and Counselling, 18*, 186–196.
Cramer, D. (1990b). Psychological adjustment, close relationships and personality: a comment on McLennan and Omodei. *British Journal of Medical Psychology, 63*, 341–343.
Cramer, D. (1990c). Self-esteem and close relationships: a statistical refinement. *British Journal of Social Psychology, 29*, 189–191.
Cramer, D. (1994). Self-esteem and Rogers' core conditions in close friends: a latent variable path analysis of panel data. *Counselling Psychology Quarterly, 7*, 327–337.
Dayan, M. (1981) *Breakthrough: A personal account of the Egypt-Israel peace negotiations.* New York: Knopf.
Derogatis, L.R. (1977). *The SCL-90–R: Administration, scoring and procedures manual 1.* Baltimore, MD: Clinical Psychometric Research.
Devonshire, C.M. and Auw, A. (1973). *A cross-cultural communications workshop.* California: College of San Mataeo, and Center for Studies of the Person. (Mimeographed, 2/1973.)
Dewey, J. (1928). Philosophies of freedom. In H. Kallen (ed.), *Freedom in the modern world.* New York: Coward-McCann. Also in Dewey, J. (1960). *On experience, nature, and freedom: Representative selections* (ed., R.J. Bernstein) (261–287). Indianapolis: Bobs-Merrill.
Dierick, P. and Lietaer, G. (1990). Member and therapist's perceptions of therapeutic factors in therapy and growth groups: comments on a category system. In G. Lietaer, J. Rombauts and

R. Van Balen (eds), *Client-centered and experiential psychotherapy in the nineties* (741–770). Leuven, Belgium: Leuven University Press.

Divine, R.A. (1967). *The triumph of internationalism in America during World War II*. New York: Atheneum.

Dorfman, E. (1951). Play therapy. In C.R. Rogers, *Client-centered therapy* (235–277). Boston: Houghton Mifflin.

Dugo, J.M. and Beck, A.P. (1984). A therapist's guide to issues of intimacy and hostility viewed as group-level phenomena. *International Journal of Group Psychotherapy, 34*, 25–45.

Dymond, R.S. (1954a). Adjustment changes over therapy from self-sorts. In C.R. Rogers and R.F. Dymond (eds), *Psychotherapy and personality change* (76–84). Chicago: University of Chicago Press.

Dymond, R.S. (1954b). Adjustment changes over therapy from thematic apperception test ratings. In C.R. Rogers and R.F. Dymond (eds), *Psychotherapy and personality change* (109–120). Chicago: University of Chicago Press.

Eckert, J. and Biermann-Ratjen, E.-M. (1990). Client-centered therapy versus psychoanalytic psychotherapy: reflections following a comparative study. In G. Lietaer, J. Rombauts and R. Van Balen (eds), *Client-centered and experiential psychotherapy in the nineties* (457–468). Leuven, Belgium: Leuven University Press.

Einaudi, M. (1959). *The Roosevelt revolution*. New York: Harcourt Brace.

Ekirch, A.A. Jnr (1969). *Ideologies and utopias: The impact of the New Deal on American thought*. Chicago: Quadrangle Books.

Elkin, I., Shea, M.T., Watkins, J.T., Imber, S.D., Sotsky, S.M., Collins, J.F., Glass, D.R., Pilkonis, P.A., Leber, W.R., Docherty, J.P., Fiester, S.J. and Parloff, M.B. (1989). National Institute of Mental Health treatment of depression collaborative research program: general effectiveness of treatments. *Archives of General Psychiatry, 46*, 971–982.

Ellinwood, C. (1959). Some observations from work with parents in a child therapy program. *Counseling Center Discussion Papers, 5* (18). University of Chicago library.

Ellinwood, C. (1989). The young child in person-centered family therapy. *Person-Centered Review, 4*, 256–262.

Ellinwood, C.G. and Raskin, N.J. (1993). Client-centered/humanistic psychotherapy. In T.R. Kratochwill and R.J. Morris (eds), *Handbook of psychotherapy with children and adolescents* (258–287). Boston: Allyn and Bacon.

Ely, A.L., Guerney, B.G. and Stover, L. (1973). Efficacy of the training phase of conjugal therapy. *Psychotherapy: Theory, Research, and Practice, 10*, 201–207.

Emmerling, F.C. (1961). A study of the relationship between personality characteristics of classroom teachers and pupil perceptions of these teachers. *Dissertation Abstracts, 22*, 1054–1055. (University Microfilms No. 61–3002.)

Ends, E.J. and Page, C.W. (1957). A study of three types of group psychotherapy with hospitalized male inebriates. *Quarterly Journal of Studies in Alcohol, 18*, 263–277.

Ends, E.J. and Page, C.W. (1959). Group psychotherapy and concomitant psychological change. *Psychological Monographs, 73* (10, Whole No. 480).

Esser, U. and Schneider, I. (1990). Client-centered partnership therapy as relationship therapy. In G. Lietaer, J. Rombauts and R. Van Balen (eds), *Client-centered and experiential psychotherapy in the nineties* (829–846). Leuven, Belgium: Leuven University Press.

Etzioni, A. (1972). *The active society: A theory of societal and political processes*. New York: Free Press/London: Collier-Macmillan.

Farson, R. (1972). Self-directed groups and community mental health. In L.N. Solomon and B. Berzon (eds), *New perspectives on encounter groups* (224–232). San Francisco: Jossey-Bass.

Farson, R. (1974a). *Birthrights*. New York: Macmillan.

Farson, R. (1974b). Carl Rogers: quiet revolutionary. *Education, 95*, 197–203.

Fenichel, O. (1945). *The psychoanalytic theory of the neurosis*. New York: Norton.

Fiedler, F.E. (1950a). The concept of an ideal therapeutic relationship. *Journal of Consulting Psychology, 14*, 239–245.

Fiedler, F.E. (1950b). A comparison of therapeutic relationships in psychoanalytic, non-directive and Adlerian therapy. *Journal of Consulting Psychology, 14*, 436–445. (Based on Fiedler, F.E. [1949]. A comparative investigation of early therapeutic relationships created by experts and non-experts of the psychoanalytic, non-directive and Adlerian schools. Doctoral dissertation, University of Chicago.)

Fiedler, F.E. (1953). Quantitative studies on the role of therapists' feelings toward their patients. In O.H. Mowrer (ed.), *Psychotherapy theory and research* (296–315). New York: Ronald Press.

Finke, H. (1947). Changes in the expression of emotionalized attitudes in six cases of play therapy. Unpublished Master's thesis, University of Chicago.

Fiske, D.W., Cartwright, D.S. and Kirtner, W.L. (1964). Are psychotherapeutic changes predictable? *Journal of Abnormal and Social Psychology*, *69*, 418–426.

Fitzsimmons, M.A. (1945). Roosevelt: America's strategist. *Review of Politics*, *7*, 280–296.

Forsyth, G.L. (1979). Exploration of empathy in nurse–client interaction. *Advances in Nursing Science*, *1*, 53–61.

Foster, C.M. and Back, J. (1974) A neighborhood school board: its infancy, its crises, its growth. *Education*, *95*, 145–162.

Freeman, S.C. (1992). C.H. Patterson on client-centered supervision: an interview. *Counselor Education and Supervision*, *31*, 219–226.

Frohburg, I. (1997). Telefax letter to G.T. Barrett-Lennard (June 16).

Frohburg, I. and Auckenthaler, A. (1996). Die Gesprächspsychotherapie in der universitären Ausbulding un Forschung der Bundesrepublik Deutschland. *GwG*, No. 103 (September, 1996), 14–18.

Fuchs, N.P. (1957). Play therapy at home. *Merrill-Palmer Quarterly*, *3*.

Fuller, R.C. (1984). Carl Rogers' impact on pastoral counseling and contemporary religious reflection. In R.F. Levant and J.M. Shlien (eds), *Client-centered therapy and the person-centered approach: New directions in theory, research and practice* (352–369). New York: Praeger.

Fusfeld, D.R. (1959). The New Deal in retrospect. *Challenge*, *7* (June), 65–69.

Ganley, R.M. (1989). The Barrett-Lennard Relationship Inventory (BLRI): current and potential uses with family systems. *Family Process*, *28*, 107–115.

Gaylin, N.L. (1974). On creativeness and a psychology of well-being. In D.A. Wexler and L.N. Rice (eds), *Innovations in client-centered therapy* (339–365). New York: Wiley.

Gaylin, N.L. (1989). The necessary and sufficient conditions for change: individual versus family therapy. *Person-Centered Review*, *4*, 263–279.

Gaylin, N.L. (1990). Family-centered therapy. In G. Lietaer, J. Rombauts and R. Van Balen (eds), *Client-centered and experiential psychotherapy in the nineties* (813–828). Leuven, Belgium: Leuven University Press.

Gaylin, N.L. (1996). Reflections on the self of the therapist. In R. Hutterer, G. Pawlowsky, P.F. Schmid and R. Stipsits (eds), *Client-centered and experiential psychotherapy: A paradigm in motion* (383–393). Frankfurt am Main: Peter Lang.

Gendlin, E.T. (1958). The function of experiencing in symbolisation. Doctoral dissertation, University of Chicago.

Gendlin, E.T. (1961a). Experiencing: a variable in the process of therapeutic change. *American Journal of Psychotherapy*, *15*, 233–245.

Gendlin, E.T. (1961b). Initiating psychotherapy with 'unmotivated' patients. *The Psychiatric Quarterly*, *34* (1), 1–6.

Gendlin, E.T. (1962). Client-centered developments and work with schizophrenics. *Journal of Counseling Psychology*, *9*, 205–211.

Gendlin, E.T. (1963). Subverbal communication and therapist expressivity: trends in client-centered therapy with schizophrenics. *Journal of Existential Psychiatry*, *4*, 105ff. (Initially circulated in *Wisconsin Psychiatric Institute Discussion Papers*, *1*, No. 10–g.)

Gendlin, E.T. (1964/1970). A theory of personality change. In P. Worchel and D. Byrne (eds), *Personality change* (206–247). New York: Wiley. Reprinted in J.T. Hart and T.M. Tomlinson (eds) (1970), *New directions in client-centered therapy* (129–173). Boston: Houghton Mifflin.

Gendlin, E.T. (1966). Existentialism and experiential psychotherapy. In C. Moustakas (ed.), *Existential child therapy* (206–247). New York: Basic Books.

Gendlin, E.T. (1967). A scale for rating the manner of relating. In C.R. Rogers et al. (eds), *The therapeutic relationship and its impact* (603–611 – Appendix C4). Madison: University of Wisconsin Press.

Gendlin, E.T. (1968). The experiential response. In E.F. Hammer (ed.), *The use of interpretation in treatment: Technique and art*. New York: Grune & Stratton.

Gendlin, E.T. (1969). Focusing. *Psychotherapy: Theory, Research and Practice, 6*, 4–15.

Gendlin, E.T. (1974). Client-centered and experiential psychotherapy. In D.A. Wexler and L.N. Rice (eds), *Innovations in client-centered therapy* (211–246). New York: Wiley.

Gendlin, E.T. (1978). *Focusing*. New York: Everest House.

Gendlin, E.T. (1981). *Focusing*. New York: Bantam Books. Revised edition.

Gendlin, E.T. and Beebe, J. (1968). Experiential groups: instructions for groups. In G.M. Gazda (ed.), *Innovations to group psychotherapy*. Springfield, IL: Charles C. Thomas.

Gendlin, E.T., Beebe, J., Cassens, J., Klein, M. and Oberlander, M. (1968). Focusing ability in psychotherapy, personality and creativity. In J.M. Shlien, with H.F. Hunt, J.D. Matarazzo and C. Savage (eds), *Research in Psychotherapy, 3* (217–238). Washington, DC.: American Psychological Association.

Gendlin, E.T., Grindler, D. and McGuire, M. (1984). Imagery, body, and space in focusing. In A.A. Sheikh (ed.), *Imagination and healing* (259–286). Farmingdale, New York: Baywood Pub. Co.

Gendlin, E.T., Jenney, R.H. and Shlien, J.M. (1960). Counselor ratings of process and outcome in client-centered therapy. *Journal of Clinical Psychology, 16* (2), 210–213.

Gendlin, E.T., Tomlinson, T.M., Mathieu, P.L. and Klein, M.H. (1967). A scale for the rating of experiencing. In C.R. Rogers et al. (eds), *The therapeutic relationship and its impact* (589–592 – Appendix C1). Madison: University of Wisconsin Press. (Scale prepared by Gendlin and Tomlinson, and as revised by Mathieu and Klein.)

Gendlin, E.T. and Zimring, F. (1955). The qualities or dimensions of experiencing and their change. *Counseling Center Discussion Papers, 1* (3). University of Chicago Library. (Republished, 1994, in *The Person-Centered Journal, 1* (2), 55–67.)

Giesekus, U. and Mente, A. (1986). Client empathic understanding in client-centered therapy. *Person-Centered Review, 1*, 163–171.

Gilmour-Barrett, K.C. (1973). Managerial systems and interpersonal treatment processes in residential centres for disturbed youth. Unpublished doctoral dissertation, University of Waterloo, Ontario.

Goetze, H. (ed.) (1981). *Personenzentrierte Spieltherapie* [Person-centered play therapy]. Göttingen: Hogrefe.

Gomes, W.B. (1981). The communicational-relational system in two forms of family group composition. Unpublished Master's thesis, Southern Illinois University.

Goodman, G. (1970). Companionship as therapy: the use of non-professional talent. In J.T. Hart and T.M. Tomlinson (eds), *New directions in client-centered therapy* (348–371). Boston: Houghton Mifflin.

Goodman, G. (1972). *Companionship therapy: Studies in structured intimacy*. San Francisco: Jossey-Bass.

Goodman, G. (1984). SASHAtapes: expanding options for help-intended communication. In D. Larson (ed.), *Teaching psychological skills: Models for giving psychology away* (271–286). Monterey, CA: Brooks-Cole.

Goodman, G. (April 1996). Personal communication to G. Barrett-Lennard.

Goodman, G. and Dooley, G. (1976). A framework for help-intended communication. *Psychotherapy: Theory, Research and Practice, 13* (2), 106–117.

Goodman, G. and Esterly, G. (1988). *The talk book: The intimate science of communicating in close relationships*. Emmaus, PA: Rodale Press.

Gordon, T. (1951). Group-centered leadership and administration. In C.R. Rogers, *Client-centered therapy* (320–383). Boston: Houghton Mifflin.

Gordon, T. (1955). *Group-centered leadership*. Boston: Houghton Mifflin.

Gordon, T. (1970a). A theory of healthy relationships and a program of parent effectiveness training. In J.T. Hart and T.M. Tomlinson (eds), *New directions in client-centered therapy* (407–425). Boston: Houghton Mifflin.

Gordon, T. (1970b). *P.E.T. Parent effectiveness training*. New York: P.H. Wyden.

Gordon, T. (1977). *Leader effectiveness training, L.E.T.* New York: Wyden Books. Republished in Bantam Books, 1980. (Page citations are from Bantam edition.)

Gordon, T. (1988). The case against disciplining children at home or in school. *Person-Centered Review, 3*, 59–85.

Gordon, T. (1989). *Teaching children self-discipline*. New York: Times Books.

Gordon, T. and Burch, N. (1974). *T.E.T. Teacher effectiveness training*. New York: P.H. Wyden.

Gordon, T. and Cartwright, D. (1954). The effect of psychotherapy upon certain attitudes towards others. In C.R. Rogers and R.F. Dymond (eds), *Psychotherapy and personality change* (167–195). Chicago, University of Chicago Press.

Gorlow, L., Hoch, E.L. and Telschow, E.F. (1952). *The nature of non-directive group psychotherapy*. New York: Bureau of Publications, Teachers College, Columbia University.

Greenberg, L.S., Elliot R. and Lietaer, G. (1994). Research on experiential psychotherapies. In A.E. Bergin and S.L. Garfield (eds), *Handbook of psychotherapy and behavior change* (509–539). New York: Wiley. Fourth edition.

Greenberg, L.S. and Pinsof, W.M. (eds) (1986). *The psychotherapeutic process: A research handbook*. New York: Guilford Press.

Greenberg, L.S., Rice, L.N. and Elliot R. (1993). *Facilitating emotional change: The moment-by-moment process*. New York: Guilford.

Griffin, E.J. (1978). A study of effects of a curriculum-centered college reading course and an affectively oriented curriculum-centered course on reading achievement and attitude toward reading. *Dissertation Abstracts International, 38*, 6496A.

Gross, W.F., Curtin, M.E. and Moore, K.B. (1970). Appraisal of a milieu therapy environment by treatment team and patients. *Journal of Clinical Psychology, 26*, 541–545.

Grummon, D.L. (1954). Design, procedures, and subjects for the first block. In C.R. Rogers and R.F. Dymond (eds), *Psychotherapy and personality change* (35–52). Chicago, University of Chicago Press.

Grummon, D.L. and John, E.S. (1954). Changes over client-centered therapy evaluated on psychoanalytically based Thematic Apperception Test scales. In C.R. Rogers and R.F. Dymond (eds), *Psychotherapy and personality change* (121–144). Chicago, University of Chicago Press.

Guerney, B.G. (1964). Filial therapy: description and rationale. *Journal of Consulting Psychology, 28*, 304–310.

Guerney, B.G. (1977). *Relationship enhancement: Skill-training programs for therapy, problem prevention, and enrichment*. San Francisco: Jossey-Bass.

Guerney, B.G. (1984). Contributions of client-centered therapy to filial, marital, and family relationship enhancement therapies. In R.F. Levant and J.M. Shlien (eds), *Client-centered therapy and the person-centered approach: New directions in theory, research, and practice* (261–277). New York: Praeger.

Guerney, B.G., Coufal, J. and Vogelsong, E. (1981). Relationship enhancement versus a traditional approach to therapeutic/preventative/enrichment parent–adolescent programs. *Journal of Consulting and Clinical Psychology, 49*, 927–939.

Guerney, B. and Guerney, L. (1989). Child relationship enhancement: family therapy and parent education. *Person-Centered Review, 4*, 344–357.

Guerney, B.G., Guerney, L.F. and Andronica, M.P. (1970). Filial therapy. In J.T. Hart and T.M. Tomlinson (eds), *New directions in client-centered therapy* (372–386). Boston: Houghton Mifflin.

Guerney, L.F. (1976). Filial therapy program. In D.H.L. Olson (ed.), *Treating relationships* (67–91). Lake Mills, Iowa: Graphic Publishing.

Gurman, A.S. (1977). The patient's perception of the therapeutic relationship. In A.S. Gurman and A.M. Razin (eds), *Effective psychotherapy: A handbook of research* (503–543). Oxford: Pergamon.

Hackney, H. and Goodyear, R.K. (1984). Carl Roger's client-centered approach to supervision. In R.F. Levant and J.M. Shlien (eds), *Client-centered therapy and the person-centered approach: New directions in theory, research and practice* (278–296). New York: Praeger.

Haigh, G. (1949). Defensive behaviour in client-centered therapy. *Journal of Consulting Psychology, 13*, 181–189.

Haimowitz, N.R. and Haimowitz, M.L. (1952). Personality changes in client-centered therapy. In W. Wolff (ed.), *Success in psychotherapy* (ch. 3). New York: Grune & Stratton.

Halkides, G. (1958). An experimental study of four conditions necessary for therapeutic change. Unpublished doctoral dissertation, University of Chicago.
Hall, C.S. and Lindzey, G. (1957). *Theories of personality*. New York: Wiley.
Handley, P. (1982). Relationship between supervisors' and trainees' cognitive style and the supervision process. *Journal of Counseling Psychology, 29*, 508–515.
Hart, J.T. and Tomlinson, T.M. (eds) (1970). *New directions in client-centered therapy*. Boston: Houghton Mifflin.
Hartley, M.W. (1951). A Q-technique study of changes in the self-concept during psychotherapy. Unpublished doctoral dissertation, University of Chicago.
Harvey, L.V. (1964). The use of non-professional auxiliary counselors in staffing a counseling service. *Journal of Counseling Psychology, 11*, 348–351.
Hatch, A.P. (1948). *Citizen of the world: Franklin D. Roosevelt*. London: Skeffington & Son.
Hayashi, S., Kuno, T., Osawa, M., Shimizu, M. and Suetake, Y. (1992). The client-centered therapy and person-centered approach in Japan: historical development, current status, and perspectives. *Journal of Humanistic Psychology, 32*, 115–136.
Heine, R.W. (1953). A comparison of patients' reports on psychotherapeutic experience with psychoanalytic, nondirective and Adlerian therapists. *Psychotherapy, 7*, 16–23. (Based on author's doctoral dissertation, of same title, University of Chicago, 1950.)
Hemingway, E. (1937). *To have and have not*. New York: Charles Scribner.
Hemingway, E. (1940). *For whom the bell tolls*. New York: Charles Scribner.
Heppner, P.P., Rogers, M.E. and Lee, L.A. (1984). Carl Rogers: reflections on his life. *Journal of Counseling and Development, 63* (Sept.), 14–20.
Hill-Hain, A. and Rogers, C.R. (1988). A dialogue with Carl Rogers: cross-cultural challenges of facilitating person-centered groups in South Africa. *Journal for Specialists in Group Work, 13*, 62–69.
Hiltner, S. (1958). *Preface to pastoral theology*. New York: Abingdon.
Hobbs, N. (1951). Group-centered psychotherapy. In C.R. Rogers, *Client-centered therapy* (278–319). Boston: Houghton Mifflin.
Hobbs, N. (1963). A psychologist in the Peace Corps. *American Psychologist, 18*, 47–55.
Hobbs, N. (1966). Helping disturbed children: psychological and ecological strategies. *American Psychologist, 21*, 1105–1115.
Hobbs, N. and Pascal, G. (1946). A method for the quantitative analysis of group psychotherapy. *American Psychologist, 1*, 297.
Höder, J., Tausch, R. and Weber, A. (1979). Die Qualität der Schülerbeiträge im Unterricht und ihr Zusammenhang mit 3 personenzentrierten Haltungen ihrer Lehrer. *Zeitschrift f. Entwicklungspsychologie und Pädagogische Psychologie, 11* (3), 232–243.
Hoffman, A.E. (1949). A study of reported behavior changes in counseling. *Journal of Consulting Psychology, 13*, 190–195.
Hofstader, R. (1966). *Anti-intellectualism in American life*. New York: Random House (Vintage Books).
Hogan, R. (1952). The development of a measure of client defensiveness in a counseling relationship. In W. Wolff and J.A. Precker (eds), *Success in psychotherapy* (112–142). New York: Grune & Stratton.
Holdstock, L. (1990). Can client-centered therapy transcend its monocultural roots? In G. Lietaer, J. Rombauts and R. Van Balen (eds), *Client-centered and experiential psychotherapy in the nineties* (109–121). Leuven, Belgium: Leuven University Press.
Holdstock, L. (1993). Can we afford not to revision the person-centred concept of self? In D. Brazier (ed.), *Beyond Carl Rogers* (229–252). London: Constable.
Holland, D.A. (1976). The Relationship Inventory–Experimental Form OS-S-42: a validity study. Unpublished honours BA thesis (psychology), University of Waterloo, Ontario.
Hollenbeck, G.P. (1965). Conditions and outcomes in the student–parent relationship. *Journal of Consulting Psychology, 29*, 237–241.
Hutterer, R. (1993). Eclecticism: An identity crisis for person-centred therapists. In D. Brazier (ed.), *Beyond Carl Rogers* (274–284). London: Constable.
Hutterer, R., Pawlowsky, G., Schmid, P.F. and Stipsits, R. (eds) (1996). *Client-centered and experiential psychotherapy: A paradigm in motion*. Frankfurt am Main: Peter Lang.

Iberg, J.R. (1990). Ms. C's focusing and cognitive functions. In G. Lietaer, J. Rombauts and R. Van Balen (eds), *Client-centered and experiential psychotherapy in the nineties* (173–203). Leuven, Belgium: Leuven University Press.

Jacobs, M.K. and Goodman, G. (1989). Psychology and self-help groups: predictions on a partnership. *American Psychologist*, *44*, 536–545.

Jaeger, T.K. (1989). Principal/teacher interpersonal relations and school climate. *Dissertation Abstracts International*, *49*, 3571A.

Jahoda, M. (1958). *Current concepts of positive mental health.* (Report to the Joint Commission on Mental Illness and Health.) New York: Basic Books.

Johnson, B. L. (1980). Empathy in nursing: its effect on patient satisfaction and adherence. Unpublished Master's thesis, Yale University.

Jonietz, A.K. (1950). A study of the phenomenological changes in perception after psychotherapy as exhibited in the content of Rorschach percepts. Unpublished doctoral dissertation, University of Chicago.

Katon, W. and Kleinman, A. (1981). Doctor–patient negotiation and other social science strategies in patient care. In L. Eisenberg and A. Kleinman (eds), *The relevance of social science for medicine*. Dordrecht, Holland: Reidel.

Keil, W.W. (1996). Training therapy in the client-centered approach. In R. Hutterer, G. Pawlowsky, P.F. Schmid and R. Stipsits (eds), *Client-centered and experiential psychotherapy: A paradigm in motion* (413–425). Frankfurt am Main: Peter Lang.

Kelly, G.A. (1955). *The psychology of personal constructs*. New York: Norton.

Kiesler, D.J., Mathieu, P.L. and Klien, M.H. (1967). Process movement in therapy and sampling interviews. In C.R. Rogers et al. (eds), *The therapeutic relationship and its impact* (221–250). Madison: University of Wisconsin Press.

Kinget, M.G. and Rogers, C.R. (1959). *Psychotherapie en menselijke verhoudingen*. Utrecht/ Antwerpen: Uitgeverij Het Spectrum.

Kirschenbaum, H. (1979). *On becoming Carl Rogers*. New York: Delacorte.

Kirschenbaum, H. and Henderson, V.L. (eds) (1989a). *The Carl Rogers reader*. Boston: Houghton Mifflin.

Kirschenbaum, H. and Henderson, V.L. (eds) (1989b). *Carl Rogers: Dialogues*. Boston: Houghton Mifflin.

Kirtner, W.L. and Cartwright, D.S. (1958). Success and failure in client-centered therapy as a function of initial in-therapy behavior. *Journal of Consulting Psychology*, *22*, 329–333.

Klein, M.H., Mathieu-Coughlan, P. and Kiesler, D.J. (1986). The experiencing scales. In L.S. Greenberg and W.M. Pinsof (eds), *The psychotherapeutic process: A research handbook* (21–71). New York: Guilford Press.

Knutson, J.N. (1972). *The human basis of polity: A psychological study of political men*. Chicago: Aldine-Atherton.

Kramer, R. (1995). The birth of client-centered therapy: Carl Rogers, Otto Rank, and 'The beyond'. *Journal of Humanistic Psychology*, *35* (4), 54–110.

Kristal-Anderson, B. (1975). Intercultural communication encounter groups. *Invandrar Rapport*, *3* (7).

Krutch, J.W. (1929). *The modern temper: A study and a confession*. New York: Harcourt, Brace & World.

Kurtz, R.R. and Grummon, D.L. (1972). Different approaches to the measurement of therapist empathy and their relationship to therapy outcomes. *Journal of Consulting and Clinical Psychology*, *37*, 106–115.

Laing, R.D. (1967). *The politics of experience*. Harmondsworth: Penguin Books. (Also republished by Ballantine Books [Random House, New York], 1968.)

La Jolla Program: 1977 Summer Institute (1977). La Jolla, California: Center for Studies of the Person. (Printed announcement.)

Landisberg, S. and Snyder, W.U. (1946) Non-directive play therapy. *Journal of Clinical Psychology*, *2*, 203–213.

Lecky, P. (1945). *Self-consistency: A theory of personality*. New York: Island Press.

Leijssen, M. (1990). On focusing and the necessary conditions of therapeutic personality change. In G. Lietaer, J. Rombauts and R. Van Balen (eds), *Client-centered and experiential psychotherapy in the nineties* (225–250). Leuven, Belgium: Leuven University Press.

Leijssen, M. (1996). Focusing processes in client-centered/experiential psychotherapy. Doctoral dissertation, Katholieke Universiteit te Leuven, Belgium. (Original in Dutch. Summary in English translation, provided by the investigator.)

Leuchtenburg, W.E. (1963). *Franklin D. Roosevelt and the New Deal, 1932–1940*. New York: Harper & Row.

Levant, R.F. (1978). Family therapy: a client-centered perspective. *Journal of Marriage and Family Counseling*, *4*, 35–42.

Levant, R.F. (1982). Client-centered family therapy. *American Journal of Family Therapy*, *10*, 72–75.

Levant, R.F. (1984). From person to system: two perspectives. In R.F. Levant and J.M. Shlien (eds), *Client-centered therapy and the person-centered approach: New directions in theory, research and practice* (243–260). New York: Praeger.

Levant, R.F. and Haffey, N.A. (1981). Toward an integration of child and family therapy. *International Journal of Family Therapy*, Summer issue, 130–143.

Levant, R.F. and Shlien, J.M. (eds) (1984). *Client-centered therapy and the person-centered approach: New directions in theory, research and practice*. New York: Praeger.

Lietaer, G. (1976). Nederlandstalige revisie van Barrett-Lennard's Relationship Inventory voor individueel-terapeutische relaties. *Psychologica Belgica*, *16* (1), 73–94.

Lietaer, G. (1979). De beleving van de relatie door client en therapeut in client-centered en psychoanalytisch georienteerde therapie. Een empirische bijdrage. *Tijdschrift voor Psychotherapie*, *5*, 141–160.

Lietaer, G. (1980). Goals of personal therapy for trainees, considered from a client-centered or existential viewpoint. In W. de Moor and H.R. Wijnngaarden (eds), *Psychotherapy: Research and training*. Elsevier/North-Holland Biomedical Press.

Lietaer, G. (1990). The client-centered approach after the Wisconsin project: a personal view of its evolution. In G. Lietaer, J. Rombauts and R. Van Balen (eds), *Client-centered and experiential psychotherapy in the nineties* (19–45). Leuven, Belgium: Leuven University Press.

Lietaer, G. (1992). Helping and hindering processes in client-centered/experiential psychotherapy: a content analysis of client and therapist postsession perceptions. In S.G. Toukmanian and D.L. Rennie (eds), *Psychotherapy process research: Theory-guided and phenomenological research strategies*. Beverly Hills, CA: Sage Publications.

Lietaer, G. (1993). Authenticity, congruence and transparency. In D. Brazier (ed.), *Beyond Carl Rogers* (17–46). London: Constable.

Lietaer, G. (1995). Carl Rogers' verbale interventies in 'On anger and hurt': een kwantitatieve en kwalitatieve analyse. In G. Lietaer and M. Van Kalmthout (eds), *Praktijkboek gesprekstherapie: Psychopathologie en experiëentiële procesbevordering* (69–91). Utrecht: De Tijdstroom.

Lietaer, G. and Dierick, P. (1996). Client-centered group psychotherapy in dialogue with other orientations: commonality and specificity. In R. Hutterer, G. Pawlowsky, P.F. Schmid and R. Stipsits (eds), *Client-centered and experiential psychotherapy: A paradigm in motion* (563–583). Frankfurt am Main: Peter Lang.

Lietaer, G. and Neirinck, M. (1986). Client and therapist perceptions of helping processes in client-centered/experiential psychotherapy. *Person-Centered Review*, *1*, 436–455.

Lietaer, G., Rombauts, J. and Van Balen, R. (eds) (1990). *Client-centered and experiential psychotherapy in the nineties*. Leuven, Belgium: Leuven University Press.

Lippman, W. (1929). *A preface to morals*. New York: Macmillan.

Luckey, E.B. (1960). Implications for marriage counseling of self perceptions and spouse perceptions. *Journal of Counselıng Psychology*, *7*, 3–9.

Lynd, R.S. and Lynd, H.M. (1937). *Middletown in transition: A study in cultural conflicts*. New York: Harcourt, Brace & Company.

McCormick, A.O'H. (1936, June 21). Still a little left of centre. *New York Times Magazine*, 2–3.

McGaw, W.H., Rogers, C.R. and Rice, C.P. (1973). *The steel shutter* (16 mm film). La Jolla, California: Center for Studies of the Person. (Filmed encounter group of Irish Catholic and Protestant members.)

McIlduff, E. and Coghlan, D. (1989). Process and facilitation in a cross-cultural communication workshop. *Person-Centered Review, 4*, 77–98.
McKeachie, W.G. (1954). Student-centered versus instructor-centered instruction. *Journal of Educational Psychology, 45*, 143–150.
MacLeish, A. (1935). *Panic: A play in verse*. Boston: Houghton Mifflin.
MacLeish, A. (1937). *The fall of the city: A verse play for radio*. New York: Farrar & Rinehart.
McLennan, J. and Omodei, M.M. (1988). Psychological adjustment, close personal relationships and personality. *British Journal of Medical Psychology, 61*, 285–290.
McLeod, J. (1994). *Doing counseling research*. London: Sage.
MacMillan, M. and Lago, C. (1993). Large groups: critical reflections and some concerns. In E. McIlduff and D. Coghlan (eds), *The person-centered approach and cross-cultural communication: An international review*, vol. 2 (35–53). Linz: Sandkorn edition for the Center for Cross-Cultural Communication, Dublin.
MacMillan, M. and Lago, C. (1996). The facilitation of large groups: participants' experiences of facilitative moments. In R. Hutterer, G. Pawlowsky, P.F. Schmid and R. Stipsits (eds), *Client-centered and experiential psychotherapy: A paradigm in motion* (599–609). Frankfurt am Main: Peter Lang.
Madrid, M. (1993). Psychological type among nurses' and patients' perception of received empathy. Doctoral dissertation, New York University.
Mantaro, C.A. (1972). An investigation of the relationship between the inter-personal relation perceived by a pupil that exists between himself and his reading teacher and (1) his reading achievement and (2) his self-concept. *Dissertation Abstracts International, 32*, 4245A.
Marques-Teixeira, J., Pires de Carvalho, M.M., Moreira, A.M. and Pinho, C. (1996). 'Group Effect?' Implementation of the Portuguese translation of the Barrett-Lennard Inventory on five individual group types. In R. Hutterer, G. Pawlowsky, P.F. Schmid and R. Stipsits (eds), *Client-centered and experiential psychotherapy: A paradigm in motion* (585–598). Frankfurt am Main: Peter Lang.
Maslow, A.H. (1962). *Toward a psychology of being*. Princeton, NJ: Van Nostrand.
Meador, B.D. (1971). Individual process in a basic encounter group. *Journal of Counseling Psychology, 18*, 70–76.
Mearns, D. (1991). On being a supervisor. In W. Dryden and B. Thorne (eds), *Training and supervision for counselling in action* (116–128). London: Sage.
Mearns, D. (1996). Working at relational depth with clients in person-centred therapy. *Counselling, 7* (4), 306–311.
Mearns, D. (1997a). Achieving the personal development dimension in professional counsellor training. *Counselling, 8* (2), 113–120.
Mearns, D. (1997b). *Person-centred counselling training*. London: Sage.
Mearns, D. (1997c). Personal communications regarding programs (29 April and 3 July, 1997).
Mearns, D. et al. (*c.* 1996). Counselling Unit, University of Strathclyde – Jordanhill Campus: Printed brochure on training programs and services.
Mearns, D. and McLeod, J. (1984). A person-centred approach to research. In R.F. Levant and J.M. Shlien (eds), *Client-centered therapy and the person-centered approach: New directions in theory, research and practice* (370–389). New York: Praeger.
Mearns, D. and Thorne, B. (1988). *Person-centred counselling in action*. London: Sage.
Mente, A. and Spittler, H.-D. (1980). *Erlebnisorientierte Gruppenpsychotherapie: Eine wirksame methode der klienten-zentrierten behandlung von verhaltensstörungen* [Experience-oriented group psychotherapy: an effective method of client-centred handling of behavioural disturbances]. Vol. 2. Paderborn: Junfermann.
Merrill, C. and Andersen, S. (1990). Person-centred expressive therapy: an outcome study. In D. Brazier (ed.), *Beyond Carl Rogers* (109–128). London: Constable.
Merry, T. (1996). An analysis of ten demonstration interviews by Carl Rogers: implications for the training of client-centred counsellors. In R. Hutterer, G. Pawlowsky, P.F. Schmid and R. Stipsits (eds), *Client-centered and experiential psychotherapy: A paradigm in motion* (273–283). Frankfurt am Main: Peter Lang.
Merry, T. (1997). Counselling and creativity: an interview with Natalie Rogers. *British Journal of Guidance & Counselling, 25*, 263–273.

Meyer, A.E., Stuhr, U., Wirth, U. and Ruester, P. (1988). Twelve-year follow-up study of the Hamburg short psychotherapy experiment: an overview. *Psychotherapy and Psychosomatics*, *50*, 192–200.
Miller, J.L. and Miller, J.G. (1995). Greater than the sum of its parts III: information processing subsystems. *Behavioral Science*, *40*, 171–269.
Mitchell, K.M., Bozarth, J.D. and Krauft, C.C. (1977). A reappraisal of the therapeutic effectiveness of accurate empathy, nonpossessive warmth and genuineness. In A.S. Gurman and A.M. Razin (eds), *Effective psychology: A handbook of research* (482–502). Oxford: Pergamon.
Moos, R. H. (1972). Assessment of the psychosocial environments of community-oriented psychiatric treatment programs. *Journal of Abnormal Psychology*, *79*, 9–18.
Moustakas, C.E. (1953). *Children in play therapy*. New York: McGraw-Hill.
Moustakas, C.E. (1959). *Psychotherapy with children: The living relationship*. New York: Harper & Row. (Republished by Ballantine, New York, 1970.)
Mowrer, O.H. (1953). *Psychotherapy theory and research*. New York: Ronald Press.
Muench, G.A. (1947). An evaluation of nondirective psychotherapy by means of the Rorschach and other tests. *Applied Psychology Monographs*, *13*, 1–163.
Murayama, S. and Nakata, Y. (1996). Fukuoka human relations community: a network approach to developing human potential. *Journal of Humanistic Psychology*, *36* (1), 91–103.
Murayama, S. and Shin, E. (1986). Person-centered group approach in Japan – interim survey. Fukuoka: Department of Educational Psychology, Kyusyu University.
Myers, S.A. (1995). Contextualizing empathy: a relational study. Unpublished [to 1997] doctoral dissertation, Harvard University.
Nash, G.D. (1971). *The great transition: A short history of twentieth-century America*. Boston, MA: Allyn and Bacon.
Natiello, P. (1990). The person-centered approach, collaborative power, and cultural transformation. *Person-Centered Review*, *5*, 268–286.
Natiello, P. (1997). Private communication (May–June); and training program brochure (with C. Graf) titled 'Healing through connection in the therapeutic relationship'.
Neville, B. (1989). *Educating Psyche: Emotion, imagination and the unconscious in learning*. Melbourne: Collins Dove.
Novak, A.L. and van der Veen, F. (1970). Family concepts and emotional disturbance in the families of disturbed adolescents with normal siblings. *Family Process*, *9*, 157–171.
Odets, C. (1935a). *Waiting for lefty* and *Till the day I die: Two plays*. New York: Covici-Friede. Also in *Six plays of Clifford Odets*; Modern Library, 1939 (and in *Waiting for lefty, and other plays*; NY: Grove-Atlic, 1993).
Odets, C. (1935b). *Awake and sing*. Published ca. 1935. Reprinted 1963, with *Golden boy* and *The big knife*. Harmondsworth: Penguin.
ÖGWG (*c*. 1996). *Klientenzentrierte Fachspezifikum*. Client-centred program syllabus (under translation into English).
O'Hara, M.M. (1984). Person-centered Gestalt: toward a holistic synthesis. In R.F. Levant and J.M. Shlien (eds), *Client-centered therapy and the person-centered approach: New directions in theory, research and practice* (182–221). New York: Praeger.
O'Hara, M.M. (1986). Heuristic inquiry as psychotherapy: The client-centered approach. *Person-Centered Review*, *1*, 172–184.
O'Hara, M. (1995). Carl Rogers: scientist and mystic. *Journal of Humanistic Psychology*, *35*, No. 4, 40–53.
O'Leary, C.J. (1989). The person-centered approach and family therapy: a dialogue between two traditions. *Person-Centered Review*, *4*, 308–323.
Osgood, C.E. (1962). *An alternative to war or surrender*. Urbana: University of Illinois Press.
Patterson, C.H. (1964). Supervising students in the counseling practicum. *Journal of Counseling Psychology*, *11*, 47–53.
Patterson, C.H. (1983). A client-centered approach to supervision. *The Counseling Psychologist*, *11* (1), 21–25.
Pearl, D. (1950). Ethnocentrism and the concept of self. Unpublished doctoral dissertation, University of Chicago.

Pentony, P. (1970). Persons as teams: an analogy. *Comparative Group Studies*, *2*, 211–268.
Pentony, P. (1981). *Models of influence in psychotherapy*. New York: Free Press/Macmillan.
Pentony, P. (1994). A discussion of contributions by Gregory Bateson and Carl Rogers via an analysis of two seminal papers. *The Person-Centered Journal*, *1* (3), 43–55.
Peres, H. (1947). An investigation of nondirective group therapy. *Journal of Consulting Psychology*, *11*, 159–172.
Perkins, F. (1947). *The Roosevelt I knew*. London: Hammond, Hammond & Co.
Pfeiffer, W.M. and Ripke, T. (1990). Reflections on a person-centered approach to medicine. In G. Lietaer, J. Rombauts and R. Van Balen (eds), *Client-centered and experiential psychotherapy in the nineties* (683–696). Leuven, Belgium: Leuven University Press.
Porter, E.H. (1941). The development and evaluation of a measure of counseling interview procedures. Doctoral thesis, Ohio State University. (Published in two parts in *Educational and Psychological Measurement*, 1943, *3*, 105–126 and 215–238.)
Porter, E.H. (1950). *An introduction to therapeutic counseling*. Boston: Houghton Mifflin.
Powers, W.T., McFarland, R.I. and Clark, R.K. (1957). A general feedback theory of human behavior. *Counseling Center Discussion Papers*, *3* (18): University of Chicago Library.
Prilleltensky, I. (1997). Values, assumptions, and practices: assessing the moral implications of psychological discourse and action. *American Psychologist*, *52*, 517–535.
Prouty, G.F. (1990). Pre-therapy: a theoretical evolution in the person-centered/experiential psychotherapy of schizophrenia and retardation. In G. Lietaer, J. Rombauts and R. Van Balen (eds), *Client-centered and experiential psychotherapy in the nineties* (645–658). Leuven, Belgium: Leuven University Press.
Prouty, G.F. (1994). *Theoretical evolutions in person-centered/experiential therapy: Applications to schizophrenic and retarded psychoses*. Westport, CT: Praeger.
Quinn, R.D. (1950). Psychotherapists' expressions as an index to the quality of early therapeutic relationships established by representatives of the non-directive, Adlerian and psychoanalytic schools. Unpublished doctoral dissertation, University of Chicago. (Source used is author's 13-page duplicated 'abstract' of Sept., 1950 – same title.)
Raimy, V.C. (1943). The self-concept as a factor in counseling and personality organization. Unpublished doctoral dissertation, Ohio State University.
Raimy, V.C. (1948). Self-reference in counseling interviews. *Journal of Consulting Psychology*, *12*, 153–163.
Rank, O. (1936/1945). *Will therapy* and *Truth and reality*. (Single-volume edition.) New York: Knopf.
Ranney, E.C. (1995). The relationship between childhood sexual abuse and empathy levels in late adolescent and adult women. Unpublished doctoral disseration, St. Louis University.
Raskin, N.J. (1948). The development of non-directive psychotherapy. *Journal of Consulting Psychology*, *12*, 92–110.
Raskin, N.J. (1949a). An analysis of the six parallel studies of the therapeutic process. *Journal of Consulting Psychology*, *13*, 206–219.
Raskin, N.J. (1949b). The development of the 'parallel studies' project. *Journal of Consulting Psychology*, *13*, 154–156.
Raskin, N.J. (1952). Client-centered counseling and psychotherapy. In D. Brower and L.E. Abt (eds), *Progress in clinical psychology*, Vol. 1 (236–248). New York: Grune & Stratton.
Raskin, N.J. (1974). Studies of psychotherapeutic orientation: ideology and practice. *AAP Research Monograph*, No. 1. Orlando, FL: American Academy of Psychotherapists.
Raskin, N.J. (1985). Client-centered therapy. In S.J. Lynn and J.P. Garske (eds), *Contemporary psychotherapies: Models and methods* (155–190). Columbus, OH: Charles E. Merrill.
Raskin, N.J. and van der Veen, F. (1970). Client-centered family therapy: some clinical and research perspectives. In J.E. Hart and T.M. Tomlinson (eds), *New directions in client-centered therapy* (387–406). Boston: Houghton Mifflin. (Initially in *Institute for Juvenile Research Report*, *4* (14), 1967.)
Rauch, B. (1963). *The history of the New Deal, 1933–1938*. New York, Capricorn Books.
Reader, N. (1948). An investigation into some personality changes occurring in individuals undergoing client-centered therapy. Unpublished doctoral thesis, University of Chicago.

Redfield, R. (1960). *The little community*. Chicago: University of Chicago Press. (Phoenix Edition, including *Peasant society and culture*, in same volume.)

Rennie, D.L. (1990). Toward a representation of the client's experience of the psychotherapy hour. In G. Lietaer, J. Rombauts and R. Van Balen (eds), *Client-centered and experiential psychotherapy in the nineties* (155–172). Leuven, Belgium: Leuven University Press.

Rennie, D.L. (1994). Storytelling in psychotherapy: the client's subjective experience. *Psychotherapy*, *31*, 234–243.

Rice, L.N. (1974). The evocative function of the therapist. In D.A. Wexler and L.N. Rice (eds), *Innovations in client-centered therapy* (289–311). New York: Wiley.

Rice, L.N. (1980). A client-centered approach to the supervision of psychotherapy. In A.K. Hess (ed.), *Psychotherapy supervision: Theory, research, and practice* (136–147). New York: Wiley.

Rice, L.N. and Greenberg, L.S. (eds) (1984). *Patterns of change: Intensive analysis of psychotherapy process*. New York: Guilford Press.

Rice, L.N. and Kerr, G.P. (1986). Measures of client and therapist vocal quality. In L.S. Greenberg and W.M. Pinsof (eds), *The psychotherapeutic process: A research handbook* (73–105). New York: Guilford Press.

Rice, L.N. and Saperia, E.L. (1984). Task analysis of the resolution of problematic reactions. In L.N. Rice and L.S. Greenberg (eds), *Patterns of change: Intensive analysis of psychotherapy process* (29–66). New York: Guilford Press.

Rice, L.N. and Wagstaff, A.K. (1967). Client voice quality and expressive style as indexes of productive psychotherapy. *Journal of Consulting Psychology*, *31*, 557–563.

Rogers, C.R. (1931a). Measuring personality adjustment in children nine to thirteen. New York: Teachers College, Columbia University, Bureau of Publications.

Rogers, C.R. (1931b). *A test of personality adjustment*. New York: Association Press.

Rogers, C.R. (1937). Three surveys of treatment measures used with children. *American Journal of Orthopsychiatry*, *7*, 48–57.

Rogers, C.R. (1939). *The clinical treatment of the problem child.* Boston: Houghton Mifflin.

Rogers, C.R. (1942a). *Counseling and psychotherapy: Newer concepts in practice*. Boston: Houghton Mifflin.

Rogers, C.R. (1942b). The use of electrically recorded interviews in improving psychotherapeutic techniques. *American Journal of Orthopsychiatry*, *12*, 429–434.

Rogers, C.R. (1943). Therapy in guidance clinics. *Journal of Abnormal and Social Psychology*, *38*, 284–289.

Rogers, C.R. (1943/1987). Letter to N.R. *The Ceshur Connection*, *2* (1 and 2), 5–6. (Carl Rogers Memorial Issue).

Rogers, C.R. (1944a). The development of insight in a counseling relationship. *Journal of Consulting Psychology*, *8*, 331–341.

Rogers, C.R. (1944b). Psychological adjustments of discharged service personnel. *Psychological Bulletin*, *41*, 689–696.

Rogers, C.R. (1945a). Counseling with the returned serviceman and his wife. *Marriage and Family Living*, *7*, 82–84.

Rogers, C.R. (1945b). The non-directive method as a technique for social research. *American Journal of Sociology*, *50*, 279–283.

Rogers, C.R. (1946). Significant aspects of client-centered therapy. *American Psychologist*, *1*, 415–422.

Rogers, C.R. (1947). Some observations on the organization of personality. *American Psychologist*, *2*, 358–368.

Rogers, C.R. (1949a) The attitude and orientation of the counselor in client-centered therapy. *Journal of Consulting Psychology*, *13*, 82–94.

Rogers, C.R. (1949b). A coordinated research in psychotherapy: a non-objective introduction. *Journal of Consulting Psychology*, *13*, 149–153.

Rogers, C.R. (1951). *Client-centered therapy*. Boston: Houghton Mifflin.

Rogers, C.R. (1952a). 'Client-centered' psychotherapy. *Scientific American*, *187*, 66–76. (Also in D.E. Dulaney et al. [eds] [1958]. *Contributions to modern psychology*. New York: Oxford University Press.)

Rogers, C.R. (1952b). Personal thoughts on teaching and learning. Presented at the conference

'Classroom Approaches to Influencing Human Behaviour', Harvard University. (Also in *Improving College and University Teaching*, 1958 [Winter issue: 3–4], and in C.R. Rogers, *On becoming a person* [273–278]. Boston: Houghton Mifflin, 1961.)
Rogers, C.R. (1953). Some directions and end points in therapy. In O.H. Mowrer (ed.), *Psychotherapy: Theory and research* (44–68). New York: Ronald.
Rogers, C.R. (1953/1961). The implications of client-centered therapy for family life. Paper presented in April, 1953 to the International Society for General Semantics, Chicago chapter. In C.R. Rogers (1961), *On becoming a person* (314–328). Boston: Houghton Mifflin.
Rogers, C.R. (1954a). Changes in the maturity of behavior related to therapy. In C.R. Rogers and R.F. Dymond (eds), *Psychotherapy and personality change* (215–237). Chicago: University of Chicago Press.
Rogers, C.R. (1954b). The case of Mrs. Oak: a research analysis. In C.R. Rogers and R.F. Dymond (eds), *Psychotherapy and personality change* (259–348). Chicago: University of Chicago Press.
Rogers, C.R. (1954c). The case of Mr. Bebb: the analysis of a failure case. In C.R. Rogers and R.F. Dymond (eds), *Psychotherapy and personality change* (349–409). Chicago: University of Chicago Press.
Rogers, C.R. (1955). Persons or science: a philosophical question. *American Psychologist*, *10*, 267–278.
Rogers, C.R. (1956). Client-centered therapy: a current view. In F. Fromm-Reichmann and J.L. Moreno (eds), *Progress in Psychotherapy*, Vol. 1 (199–209). New York: Grune & Stratton.
Rogers, C.R. (1957a). The necessary and sufficient conditions of therapeutic personality change, *Journal of Consulting Psychology*, *21*, 95–103.
Rogers, C.R. (1957b). A therapist's view of the good life. *The Humanist*, *17*, 291–300.
Rogers, C.R. (1957c). A tentative formulation of a general law of interpersonal relationships. Mimeographed article, University of Chicago. (Also in C.R. Rogers [1961], *On becoming a person* (338–346). Boston: Houghton Mifflin.)
Rogers, C.R. (1957d). Training individuals to engage in the therapeutic process. In C.R. Strother (ed.), *Psychology and mental health*. Washington, DC: American Psychological Association.
Rogers, C.R. (1958a). The characteristics of a helping relationship. *Personnel and Guidance Journal*, *37*, 6–16.
Rogers, C.R. (1958b). The growing power of the behavioral sciences. *Counseling Center Discussion Papers*, *4* (4). (Also in C.R. Rogers [1961], *On becoming a person* (364–383). Boston: Houghton Mifflin.)
Rogers, C.R. (1958c). A process conception of psychotherapy. *American Psychologist*, *13*, 142–149.
Rogers, C.R. (1959a). A theory of therapy, personality, and interpersonal relationships as developed in the client-centered framework. In S. Koch (ed.), *Psychology: A study of a science*, Vol 3: *Formulations of the person and the social context* (184–256). New York: McGraw-Hill.
Rogers, C.R. (1959b). A tentative scale for the measurement of process in psychotherapy. In E.A. Rubinstein and M.B. Parloff (eds), *Research in psychotherapy* (96–107). Washington, DC: American Psychological Association.
Rogers, C.R. (1959c). Significant learning: in therapy and in education. *Educational Leadership*, *16*, 232–242. (Also in C.R. Rogers [1961], *On becoming a person* (279–296). Boston: Houghton Mifflin.)
Rogers, C.R. (1961a). *On becoming a person: A therapist's view of psychotherapy*. Boston: Houghton Mifflin.
Rogers, C.R. (1961b). The process equation of psychotherapy. *American Journal of Psychotherapy*, *15*, 27–45.
Rogers, C.R. (1961c). A theory of psychotherapy with schizophrenics and a proposal for its empirical investigation. In J.G. Dawson, H.K. Stone and N.P. Dellis (eds), *Psychotherapy with schizophrenics* (3–19). Baton Rouge: Louisiana State University Press.
Rogers, C.R. (1961d). The place of the person in the new world of the behavioral sciences. *Personnel and Guidance Journal*, *40*, 442–451.
Rogers, C.R. (1962). The interpersonal relationship: the core of guidance. *Harvard Educational Review*, *32*, 416–429.

Rogers, C.R. (1963a). The actualizing tendency in relation to 'motives' and to consciousness. In M.R. Jones (ed.), *Nebraska Symposium on Motivation*, Vol 11 (1–24). Lincoln: University of Nebraska Press.

Rogers, C.R. (1963b). The concept of the fully functioning person. *Psychotherapy: Theory, Research and Practice, 1*, 17–26.

Rogers, C.R. (1963c). Learning to be free. In S. Farber and R.H.L. Wilson (eds), *Conflict and creativity: Control of the mind.* New York: McGraw-Hill.

Rogers, C.R. (1963d). Psychotherapy today, or, Where do we go from here? *American Journal of Psychotherapy, 17*, 5–16.

Rogers, C.R. (1963e). Personal communication to Godfrey Barrett-Lennard (July 16 letter).

Rogers, C.R. (1964a). Freedom and commitment. *The Humanist, 24* (2), 37–40.

Rogers, C.R. (1964b). Toward a modern approach to values: the valuing process in the mature person. *Journal of Abnormal and Social Psychology, 68*, 160–167.

Rogers, C.R. (1964c). Toward a science of the person. In T.W. Wann (ed.), *Behaviorism and phenomenology* (109–140). Chicago: University of Chicago Press (Phoenix Books).

Rogers, C.R. (1965a). Dealing with psychological tensions. *Journal of Applied Behavioral Science, 1*, 6–24.

Rogers, C.R. (1965b). Client-centered therapy (16 mm film of interview with 'Gloria'). In E. Shostrom (ed.), *Three approaches to psychotherapy.* Santa Ana, California: Psychological Films, Inc.

Rogers, C.R. (1965c). Some thoughts regarding the current philosophy of the behavioral sciences. *Journal of Humanistic Psychology, 5*, 182–194.

Rogers, C.R. (1965d). The therapeutic relationship: recent theory and research. *Australian Journal of Psychology, 17*, 95–108.

Rogers, C.R. (1966a). Client-centered therapy. In S. Arieti (ed.), *American Handbook of Psychiatry* (183–200). New York: Basic Books.

Rogers, C.R. (1966b). To facilitate learning. In M. Provus (ed.), *Innovations for time to teach.* Washington, DC: National Education Association.

Rogers, C.R. (1966c). Privately circulated 'travel' letters of April 27 and May 13, 1966 (also in *The Ceshur Connection, 2* [1 and 2: Carl Rogers Memorial Issue: 37–40], 1987).

Rogers, C.R. (1967a). Autobiography. In E.G. Boring and G. Lindzey (eds), *A history of psychology in autobiography*, Vol. 5. New York: Appleton-Century-Crofts.

Rogers, C.R. (1967b). The facilitation of significant learning. In L. Siegel (ed.), *Contemporary theories of instruction* (37–54). San Francisco: Chandler Publishing Corp.

Rogers, C.R. (1967c). The interpersonal relationship in the facilitation of learning. In R. Leeper (ed.), *Humanizing education.* Washington, DC: National Education Association.

Rogers, C.R. (1967d). A plan for self-directed change in an educational system. *Educational Leadership, 24*, 717–731.

Rogers, C.R. (1967e). The process of the basic encounter group. In J.F.T. Bugental (ed.), *The challenges of humanistic psychology* (261–278). New York: McGraw-Hill.

Rogers, C.R. (1967f). A silent young man. In C.R. Rogers et al. (eds), *The therapeutic relationship and its impact* (401–416). Madison: University of Wisconsin Press.

Rogers, C.R. (1967g). Some learnings from a study of psychotherapy with schizophrenics. In C.R. Rogers and B. Stevens, *Person to person: The problem of being human* (181–192). Lafayette, CA: Real People Press.

Rogers, C.R. (1969a). *Freedom to learn.* Columbus, OH: Charles E. Merrill.

Rogers, C.R. (1969b). The increasing involvement of the psychologist in social problems: some comments, positive and negative. *Journal of Applied Behavioral Science, 5*, 3–7.

Rogers, C.R. (1970). *Carl Rogers on encounter groups.* New York: Harper & Row.

Rogers, C.R. (1972a). *Becoming partners: Marriage and its alternatives.* New York: Delacorte Press.

Rogers, C.R. (1972b). Some social issues which concern me. *Journal of Humanistic Psychology, 12* (Fall issue), 45–60.

Rogers, C.R. (1972c). The person of tomorrow. *Colorado Journal of Educational Research, 12* (1). Greeley: University of Northern Colorado.

Rogers, C.R. (1972d). Personal communication to G.T. Barrett-Lennard (letter of April 30).

Rogers, C.R. (undated). Personal adjustment – set of audio cassette tapes, numbered 1 to 10. Chicago: Instructional Dynamics, *c.* 1972. (Personal talks, on a spectrum of life topics.)

Rogers, C.R. (1973a). Some new challenges. *American Psychologist, 28*, 370–387.

Rogers, C.R. (1973b). My philosophy of interpersonal relationships and how it grew. *Journal of Humanistic Psychology, 13* (2), 3–15.

Rogers, C.R. (1974a). Can learning encompass both ideas and feelings? *Education, 95*, 103–114.

Rogers, C.R. (1974b). The project at Immaculate Heart: an experiment in self-directed change. *Education, 95*, 172–189.

Rogers, C.R. (1974c). Remarks on the future of client-centered therapy. In D.A. Wexler and L.N. Rice (eds), *Innovations in client-centered therapy* (7–13). New York: Wiley. (Based on presentations in an APA conference symposium, Sept., 1964.)

Rogers, C.R. (1974d). In retrospect: forty-six years. *American Psychologist, 29* (2), 115–123.

Rogers, C.R. (1975). Empathic: an unappreciated way of being. *The Counseling Psychologist, 5* (2), 2–11. Also in C.R. Rogers (1980), *A way of being* (137–163). Boston: Houghton Mifflin.

Rogers, C.R. (1977a). *Carl Rogers on personal power*. New York: Delacorte Press.

Rogers, C.R. (1977b). A person-centered workshop: its planning and fruition. In *Carl Rogers on personal power* (143–185). New York: Delacorte Press.

Rogers, C.R. (1977c). Resolving intercultural tensions: a beginning. In *Carl Rogers on personal power* (115–140). New York: Delacorte Press.

Rogers, C.R. (1978). The formative tendency. *Journal of Humanistic Psychology, 18*, 23–26.

Rogers, C.R. (1979a). Groups in two cultures. *Personnel and Guidance Journal, 38* (1), 11–15.

Rogers, C.R. (1979b). Memo from Carl Rogers. La Jolla: CSP, Sept. 13, 1979.

Rogers, C.R. (1980a). *A way of being*. Boston: Houghton Mifflin.

Rogers, C.R. (1980b). The foundations of a person-centered approach. In C.R. Rogers, *A way of being* (113–136). Boston: Houghton Mifflin.

Rogers, C.R. (1980c). Growing older: or older and growing. In C.R. Rogers, *A way of being* (70–95). Boston: Houghton Mifflin.

Rogers, C.R. (1980d). Client-centered psychotherapy. In H.I. Kaplan, B.J. Sadock and A.M. Freedman (eds), *Comprehensive textbook of psychiatry* (Chapter 30.3). Baltimore: Williams & Wilkins. Third edition.

Rogers, C.R. (1982). A psychologist looks at nuclear war. *Journal of Humanistic Psychology, 22* (4), 9–20. And in H. Kirschenbaum and V.L. Henderson (eds) (1989a), *The Carl Rogers reader* (445–456). Boston: Houghton Mifflin.

Rogers, C.R. (1983). *Freedom to learn for the 80's*. Columbus, OH: Charles E. Merrill.

Rogers, C.R. (1986a). The Rust workshop: a personal overview. *Journal of Humanistic Psychology, 26* (3), 23–45. And in H. Kirschenbaum and V.L. Henderson (eds) (1989). *The Carl Rogers reader* (457–477). Boston: Houghton Mifflin.

Rogers, C.R. (1986b). The dilemmas of a South African white. *Person-Centered Review, 1*, 15–35.

Rogers, C.R. (1986c). Journal of South African trip, and covering 'letter to family and friends'. Unpublished manuscript.

Rogers, C.R. (1986/1993). A client-centered, person-centered approach to therapy. In I.L. Kutash and A. Wolf (eds), *Psychotherapist's casebook: Theory and technique in practice* (197–208). 1986, San Francisco: Jossey-Bass. 1993, Northvale, NJ: Aronson.

Rogers, C.R. (1987). Inside the world of the soviet professional. *Journal of Humanistic Psychology, 27* (3), 277–304. And in H. Kirschenbaum and V.L. Henderson (eds) (1989). *The Carl Rogers reader* (478–501). Boston: Houghton Mifflin.

Rogers, C.R. and Dymond, R.F. (eds) (1954). *Psychotherapy and personality change*. Chicago: University of Chicago Press.

Rogers, C.R. and Farson, R.E. (1957). *Active listening*. University of Chicago: Industrial Relations Center (and University Library).

Rogers, C.R., with Gendlin, E.T., Kiesler, D.J. and Truax, C.B. (eds). (1967). *The therapeutic relationship and its impact: A study of psychotherapy with schizophrenics*. Madison: University of Wisconsin Press.

Rogers, C.R., McGaw, W. and Farson, R.E. (1968). *Journey into self* (16 mm film). La Jolla, California: Western Behavioral Sciences Institute. (From an encounter group.)

Rogers, C.R. and Roethlisberger, F.J. (1952). Barriers and gateways to communication. *Harvard Business Review, 30* (4), 46–52.
Rogers, C.R. and Rose, A. (facilitators) (1971). *Because that's my way* (16 mm film). Lincoln, Nebraska: Great Plains Instructional Television Library, University of Nebraska. (Portrays encounter group with drug-involved, mixed race membership.)
Rogers, C.R. and Ryback, D. (1984). One alternative to nuclear planetary suicide. *The Counseling Psychologist, 12* (2), 3–12. Also in R.F. Levant and J.M. Shlien (eds), *Client-centered therapy and the person-centered approach: New directions in theory, research, and practice* (400–422). New York: Praeger.
Rogers, C.R. and Sanford, R. (1987). Reflections on our South African experience (January–February, 1986). *Counseling and Values, 32* (1), 17–20. (Journal issue is titled *Carl R. Rogers and the person-centered approach to peace.*)
Rogers, C.R. and Skinner, B.F. (1956). Some issues concerning the control of human behavior. *Science, 124*, 1057–1066.
Rogers, C.R. and Skinner, B.F. (1962/1989). Education and the control of human behavior. Dialogue held at the University of Minnesota, Duluth, June 11–12, 1962 (audiotaped). Published in H. Kirschenbuam and V.L. Henderson (eds), *Carl Rogers: Dialogues* (82–152). Boston: Houghton Mifflin, 1989.
Rogers, C.R. and Wallen, J.L. (1946). *Counseling with returned servicemen.* New York: McGraw-Hill.
Rogers, C.R. and Wood, J.K. (1974). Client-centered theory: Carl R. Rogers. In A. Burton (ed.), *Operational theories of personality* (211-258). New York: Brunner/Mazel.
Rogers, C.R., Wood, J.K., Rogers, N. et al. (1975). *A person-centered approach: The process of individual growth and its social implications.* La Jolla, California: Center for Studies of the Person. (Mimeographed workshop announcement.)
Rogers, N. (1993). *The creative connection: Expressive arts as healing.* Palo Alto, CA: Science and Behavior Books.
Rogers, W.R. (1974). Client-centered and symbolic perspectives on social change: a schematic model. In D.A. Wexler and L.N. Rice (eds), *Innovations in client-centered therapy* (465–496). New York: Wiley.
Rogers, W.R. (1984). Person-centered administration in higher education. In R.F. Levant and J.M. Shlien (eds), *Client-centered therapy and the person-centered approach: New directions in theory, research and practice* (317–336). New York: Praeger.
Rombauts, J. and Devriendt, M. (1990). Conjoint couple therapy in client-centered practice. In G. Lietaer, J. Rombauts and R. Van Balen (eds), *Client-centered and experiential psychotherapy in the nineties* (847–863). Leuven, Belgium: Leuven University Press.
Rosen, H.H. (1961) Dimensions of the perceived parent-relationship as related to juvenile delinquency. Unpublished Master's thesis, Auburn University, Alabama.
Rudikoff, E.C. (1954). A comparative study of the changes in the concepts of the self, the ordinary person, and the ideal in eight cases. In C.R. Rogers and R.F. Dymond (eds), *Psychotherapy and personality change* (85–98). Chicago: University of Chicago Press.
Rudolph, J., Langer, I. and Tausch, R. (1980). Prüfung der psychischen Auswirkungen und Bedingungen von personenzentriertier Einzel-Psychotherapie (An investigation of the psychological effects and conditions of person-centered individual psychotherapy). *Zeitschrift für Klinische Psychologie, 9*, 23–33.
Sanford, R. (1984). The beginning of a dialogue in South Africa. *The Counseling Psychologist, 12* (2), 3–14.
Scheuer, A.L. (1971). The relationship between personal attributes and effectiveness in teachers of the emotionally disturbed. *Exceptional Children, 38*, 723–731.
Seeman, J. (1949). A study of the process of nondirective therapy. *Journal of Consulting Psychology, 13*, 157–168.
Seeman, J. (1954). Counselor judgements of therapeutic process and outcome. In C.R. Rogers and R.F. Dymond (eds), *Psychotherapy and personality change* (99–108). Chicago: University of Chicago Press.
Seeman, J. (1959). Toward a concept of personality integration. *American Psychologist, 14*, 633–637.

Seeman, J. (1983). *Personality integration: Studies and reflections.* New York: Human Sciences Press.
Seeman, J. (1984). The fully functioning person: theory and research. In R.F. Levant and J.M. Shlien (eds), *Client-centered therapy and the person-centered approach: New directions in theory, research and practice* (131–152). New York: Praeger.
Seeman, J. (1989a). Toward a model of positive health. *American Psychologist, 44,* 1099–1109.
Seeman, J. (1989b) Experiential supervision: case illustrations. In L.J. Bradley (ed.), *Counselor supervision* (375–397). Muncie, IN: Accelerated Development, Inc.
Seeman, J., Barry, E. and Ellinwood, C. (1957). The process and outcomes of play therapy. *Counseling Center Discussion Papers, 3* (No. 14). University of Chicago Library.
Seeman, J., Barry, E. and Ellinwood, C. (1963). Personality integration as a criterion of therapy outcome. *Psychotherapy: Theory, research and practice, 1,* 14–16.
Seeman, J. and Raskin, N.J. (1953). Research perspectives in client-centered therapy. In O.H. Mowrer (ed.), *Psychotherapy: Theory and research.* New York: Ronald Press.
Segrera, A.S. (1997). Personal communication (information on training programs; June 30, 1977).
Sheerer, E.T. (1949). An analysis of the relationship between acceptance of and respect for self, and acceptance of and respect for others, in ten counseling cases. *Journal of Consulting Psychology, 13,* 169–175.
Shlien, J.M. (1961). A client-centered approach to schizophrenia: first approximation. In A. Burton (ed.), *Psychotherapy of the psychoses* (285–317). New York: Basic Books.
Shlien, J.M. (1962). Toward what level of abstraction in criteria? In H.H. Strupp and L. Luborsky (eds), *Research in psychotherapy,* Vol. 2 (142–154). Washington: APA.
Shlien, J.M. (1963). Phenomenology and personality. In J.M. Wepman and R.W. Heine (eds), *Concepts of personality* (291–330). Chicago: Aldine.
Shlien, J.M. (1965). Cross-theoretical criteria in time-limited therapy. In *Selected Lectures, 6th International Congress of Psychotherapy.* Basel/New York: S. Karger.
Shlien, J.M. (1987). A countertheory of transference. *Person-Centered Review, 2,* 15–49. (Initially in R.F. Levant and J.M. Shlien (eds) (1984), *Client-centered therapy and the person-centered approach: New directions in theory, research and practice* (153–181). New York: Praeger. London: Sage.)
Shlien, J.M., Mosak, H.H. and Dreikers, R. (1962). Effect of time limits: a comparison of two psychotherapies. *Journal of Counseling Psychology, 9,* 31–34.
Shohet, R. and Wilmot, J. (1991). The key issue in the supervision of counsellors: the supervisory relationship. In W. Dryden and B. Thorne (eds), *Training and supervision for counselling in action* (87–98). London: Sage.
Siegel, S. (1956). *Nonparametric statistics for the behavioral sciences.* New York: McGraw-Hill.
Skinner, B.F. (1953). *Science and human behavior.* New York: Free Press.
(See also listings under 'Rogers, C.R. and Skinner, B.F. – name order alphabetical.)
Snyder, M. (1989). The relationship enhancement model of couple therapy: an integration of Rogers and Bateson. *Person-Centered Review, 4,* 358–383.
Snyder, W.U. (1945). An investigation of the nature of non-directive psychotherapy. *Journal of General Psychology, 33,* 193–223.
Snyder, W.U. (1947a). *Casebook of non-directive counseling.* Boston: Houghton Mifflin.
Snyder, W.U. (1947b). The present status of psychotherapeutic counseling. *Psychological Bulletin, 44,* 297–386.
Snygg, D. and Combs, A.W. (1949). *Individual psychology: A new frame of reference for psychology.* New York: Harper. (Also published in revised edition by Combs & Snygg: Harper, 1959.)
Soldwisch, S.S. (1990). An examination of the association between caring in nursing and Erikson's epigenetic theory. Unpublished doctoral dissertation, University of Wisconsin.
Solomon, L.N. (1987). International tension reduction through the person-centered approach. *Journal of Humanistic Psychology, 27,* 337–347.
Solomon, L.N. (1990). Carl Rogers' efforts for world peace. *Person-Centered Review, 5,* 39–56.
Solomon, L.N. and Berzon, B. (1970). The self-directed group: a new direction in personal growth learning. In J.T. Hart and T.M. Tomlinson (eds), *New directions in client-centered therapy*

(314–347). Boston: Houghton Mifflin. (This article is a revision and extension of the listed 1966 report by Berzon and Solomon.)
Solomon, L.N. and Berzon, B. (eds) (1972). *New perspectives on encounter groups*. San Francisco: Jossey-Bass.
Spain, A. (1977/1978). Quality of supervision and effectiveness of interns as a function of supervisor–intern psychotherapeutic orientations. *Dissertation Abstracts International, 38*, 5046B.
Spence, S.A. (1989). The presence of and relationships between helping elements and task steps in post-observation supervisory conferences. *Dissertation Abstracts International, 49A*, 2887–888.
Spiro, M.E. (1970). *Kibbutz: Venture in utopia*. New York: Schocken Books. Augmented edition.
Standal, S. (1954). The need for positive regard. A contribution to client-centered theory. Unpublished doctoral dissertation, University of Chicago.
Standal, S.W. and van der Veen, F. (1957). Length of therapy in relation to counselor estimates of personal integration and other case variables. *Journal of Consulting Psychology, 21*, 1–9.
Steinbeck, J. (1936). *In dubious battle*. New York: Covici-Friede. (Also, New York: Modern Library, 1939.)
Steinbeck, J. (1937). *Of mice and men*. New York: Heinemann.
Steinbeck, J. (1939). *The grapes of wrath*. New York: Viking Press.
Stephenson, W. (1953). *The study of behavior: Q-technique and its methodology*. Chicago: University of Chicago Press.
Stephenson, W. (1980). Newton's fifth rule and Q methodology: application to educational psychology. *American Psychologist, 35*, 882–889.
Stetler, C.B. (1977). Relationship of perceived empathy to nurses' communication. *Nursing Research, 26*, 432–438.
Stock, D. (1949). An investigation into the interrelations between the self concept and feelings directed toward other persons and groups. *Journal of Consulting Psychology, 13*, 176–180.
Sundaram, D.K. (1977). Psychological adjustment as a function of interpersonal relationships: a field study. *Dissertation Abstracts International, 37*, 5380–5381B.
Swenson, G.L. (1987). When personal and political processes meet: the Rust Workshop. *Journal of Humanistic Psychology, 27*, 309–332.
Taft, J. (1933). *The dynamics of therapy in a controlled relationship*. New York: Macmillan.
Tassinari, M.C. (1995/1997). The history of the person-centered approach in Brazil. Electronically circulated manuscript, supplemented by private communication (in 1997).
Tausch, R. (1960). *Das psychotherapeutische Gespräch: Erwachsenen-Psychotherapie in nicht-directiver Orientierung*. Göttingen: Hogrefe. Revised, with A-M. Tausch, and reissued under the main title *Gesprächpsychotherapie* in eight further editions from 1968 to 1990.
Tausch, R. (1978). Facilitative dimensions in interpersonal relations: verifying the theoretical assumptions of Carl Rogers in school, family education, client-centered therapy, and encounter groups. *College Student Journal, 12*, 2–11.
Tausch, R. (1988). The relationship between emotions and cognitions: implications for therapist empathy. *Person-Centered Review, 3*, 277–291.
Tausch, R. (1990). The supplementation of client-centered communication therapy with other validated therapeutic methods: a client-centered necessity. In G. Lietaer, J. Rombauts and R. Van Balen (eds), *Client-centered and experiential psychotherapy in the nineties* (447–455). Leuven, Belgium: Leuven University Press.
Tausch, R. and Tausch, A-M. (1956). *Kinderpsychotherapie in nicht-directivem Verfahren*. Göttingen. Hogrefe.
Taylor, J.A. (1953). A personality scale of manifest anxiety. *Journal of Abnormal and Social Psychology, 48*, 285–290.
Terkel, S. (1970). *Hard times: An oral history of the Great Depression*. New York: Random House (Pantheon Books). (Also published in Pocket Books – Quokka edition: New York, 1978.)
Thorne, B. (1988). The person-centred approach to large groups. In M. Aveline and W. Dryden (eds), *Group therapy in Britain*. Milton Keynes (UK), and Philadelphia: Open University Press.
Thorne, B. (1991). *Person-centred counselling: Therapeutic and spiritual dimensions*. London: Whurr.
Thorne, B. (1992). *Carl Rogers*. London: Sage.

Thorne, B. and Lambers, E. (eds) (1998). *Person-Centred Therapy: A European perspective*. London: Sage.
Thornton, B.M. (1960). Dimensions of perceived relationship as related to marital adjustment. Unpublished Master's thesis, Auburn University, Alabama.
Tomlinson, T.M. and Hart, J.T. (1962). A validation study of the process scale. *Journal of Consulting Psychology*, *26*, 74–78. Reprinted in J.T. Hart and T.M. Tomlinson (eds) (1970), *New directions in client-centered therapy* (206–213). Boston: Houghton Mifflin.
Tougas, R.R. (1954). Ethnocentrism as limiting factor in verbal therapy. In C.R. Rogers and R.F. Dymond (eds), *Psychotherapy and personality change* (196–214). Chicago: University of Chicago Press.
Toukmanian, S.G. (1986). A measure of client perceptual processing. In L.S. Greenberg and W.M. Pinsof (eds), *The psychotherapeutic process: A research handbook* (107–130). New York: Guilford Press.
Townsend, M.E. (1988). Self-disclosure and psychological adjustment: Towards an understanding. Unpublished honours Bachelor thesis (psychology), Monash University, Melbourne.
Trattner, W.I. (1974). *From poor law to welfare state: A history of social welfare in America*. New York: Free Press.
Truax, C.B. (1961). The process of group psychotherapy: relationships between hypothesised therapeutic conditions and intrapersonal exploration. *Psychological Monographs*, *75* (7, Whole No. 511).
Truax, C.B. and Carkhuff, R.R. (1967). *Toward effective counseling and psychotherapy: Training and practice*. Chicago: Aldine.
Tscheulin, D. (1990). Confrontation and non-confrontation as differential techniques in client-centered therapy. In G. Lietaer, J. Rombauts and R. Van Balen (eds), *Client-centered and experiential psychotherapy in the nineties* (327–336). Leuven, Belgium: Leuven University Press.
Van Belle, H.A. (1980). *Basic intent and therapeutic approach of Carl R. Rogers*. Toronto: Wedge Publishing Foundation.
van der Veen, F. (1967). The effects of the therapist and the patient on each other. In C.R. Rogers et al. (eds), *The therapeutic relationship and its impact* (353–366). Madison: University of Wisconsin Press.
van der Veen, F. (1970). Client perception of therapist conditions as a factor in psychotherapy. In J.T. Hart and T.M. Tomlinson (eds), *New directions in client-centered therapy* (214–222). Boston: Houghton Mifflin.
van der Veen, F., Huebner, B., Jorgens, B. and Neja, P. (1964). Relationships between the parents' concept of the family and family adjustment. *American Journal of Orthopsychiatry*, *34*, 45–55.
van der Veen, F. and Novak, A.L. (1971). Perceived parental attitudes and family concepts of disturbed adolescents, normal siblings and normal controls. *Family Process*, *10*, 327–343.
van der Veen, F. and Olson, R.E. (1983). Manual and Handbook for the Family Concept Assessment Method. Encinitas, CA: Circulated manuscript.
van der Veen, F. and Tomlinson, T.M. (1967). A scale for the rating of problem expresson. In Rogers, C.R. et al. (eds), *The therapeutic relationship and its impact* (599–601 – Appendix C3). Madison: University of Wisconsin Press.
Vansteenwegen, A. (1979). Residentiële partnerrelatie-therapie: Een evaluatie-onderzoek. *Tijdschrift voor Psychiatrie*, *21*, 426–440. (As 'Residential couple-therapy: a controlled outcome study', presented at the Society for Psychotherapy Research annual meeting in Oxford, England, 1979.)
Vansteenwegen, A. (1982). Intensive psycho-educational couple therapy: therapeutic program and outcome research results. *Cahiers des Sciences Familiales et Sexologiques*, No. 5 de L'Université Catholique de Louvain, Belgium.
Vansteenwegen, A. (1990). Het effect van partner-relatietherapie na zeven jaar: individuele en relationele veranderingen. *Directieve Therapie*, *10*, 44–62. (English version 'The outcome of marital therapy after seven years: individual and relational changes', in A. Vansteenwegen, F.A. Van Assche and P. Nijs (eds), *Human sexuality and family health sciences*. Louvain: Peeters Press.)

Vargas, M.J. (1954). Changes in self-awareness during client-centered therapy. In C.R. Rogers and R.F. Dymond (eds), *Psychotherapy and personality change* (145–166). Chicago, University of Chicago Press.
Verwaaijen, A.A.G. (1990). Therapist behaviour in process: Therapist behaviour in treatment of adolescent girls at risk of placement. Unpublished doctoral dissertation, Catholic University, Nijmegen, Netherlands. (Dissertation in English.)
Volpe, E.L. (1974). *A reader's guide to William Faulkner*. New York: Octagon Books.
Walker, A., Rablen, R. and Rogers, C.R. (1960). Development of a scale to measure process changes in psychotherapy. *Journal of Clinical Psychology*, *16*, 79–85.
Wampler, K.S. and Powell, G.S. (1982). The Barrett-Lennard Relationship Inventory as a measure of marital satisfaction. *Family Relations*, *31*, 139–145.
Wampler, K.S. and Sprenkle, D.H. (1980). The Minnesota Couple Communication Program: a follow-up study. *Journal of Marriage and the Family*, *42*, 577–584.
Wargo, D.G. and Meek, V.C. (1970/1971). The Relationship Inventory as a measure of milieu perception in rehabilitation center students. *Rehabilitation Counseling Bulletin*, *14*, 42–48.
Warner, M.S. (1989). Empathy and strategy in the family system. *Person-Centered Review*, *4*, 324–343.
Watson, N. (1984). The empirical status of Rogers' hypothesis of the necessary and sufficient conditions for effective psychotherapy. In R.F. Levant and J.M. Shlien (eds), *Client-centered therapy and the person-centered approach: New directions in theory, research and practice* (17-40). New York: Praeger.
Wexler, D.A. (1974). A cognitive theory of experiencing, self-actualization and therapeutic process. In D.A. Wexler and L.N. Rice (eds), *Innovations in client-centered therapy* (49–116). New York: Wiley.
Wexler, D.A. (1975). A scale for the measurement of client and therapist expressiveness. *Journal of Clinical Psychology*, *31*, 486–489.
Wexler, D.A. and Butler, J.M. (1976). Therapist modification of client expressiveness in client-centered therapy. *Journal of Consulting and Clinical Psychology*, *44*, 261–265.
Wexler, D.A. and Rice, L.N. (eds) (1974). *Innovations in client-centered therapy*. New York: Wiley.
White, R.W. (1959). Motivation reconsidered: the concept of competence. *Psychological Review*, *66*, 297–333.
Wilkinson, G.R. (1972). The application of differentiated small group processes to developmental learning in an educational setting. Unpublished doctoral dissertation, University of Waterloo, Ontario. (Appendix C [115–126] is titled 'Interpersonal intensity of group interaction at three levels – Manual for group leaders'.)
Willoughby, R.R. (1931). A scale of emotional maturity. *Journal of Social Psychology*, *3*, 3–36.
Wiseman, H. and Rice, L.N. (1989). Sequential analysis of therapist–client interaction during change events: a task-focused approach. *Journal of Consulting and Clinical Psychology*, *57*, 281–286.
Wish, H. (1966). *Contemporary America: The national scene since 1900* (Fourth edition). New York: Harper & Row.
Wood, J.K. (1977). Shadows of surrender: first notes on person-centered approaches. La Jolla, California: Center for Studies of the Person (circulated manuscript).
Wood, J.K. (1982). Person-centered group therapy. In G. Gazda (ed.), *Basic approaches to group psychotherapy and group counseling* (235–275). Springfield, IL: Thomas.
Wood, J.K. (1984). Communities for learning: a person-centered approach. In R.F. Levant and J.M. Shlien (eds), *Client-centered therapy and the person-centered approach: New directions in theory, research and practice* (297–336). New York: Praeger.
Wood, J.K. (1994). The person-centered approach's greatest weakness: not using it's strength. *The Person-Centered Journal*, *1* (2), 96–105.
Zevin, B.C. (ed.) (1946). *Nothing to fear: The selected addresses of Franklin Delano Roosevelt, 1932–1945*. Boston: Houghton Mifflin.
Zilbach, J.J. (1986). *Young children in family therapy*. New York: Brunner/Mazel.
Zimring, F.M. (1974). Theory and practice of client-centered therapy: a cognitive view. In D.A. Wexler and L.N. Rice (eds), *Innovations in client-centered therapy* (117–137). New York: Wiley.

Zimring, F.M. (1990a). Cognitive processes as a cause of psychotherapeutic change: self-initiated processes. In G. Lietaer, J. Rombauts and R. Van Balen (eds), *Client-centered and experiential psychotherapy in the nineties* (361–380). Leuven, Belgium: Leuven University Press.

Zimring, F. (1990b). A characteristic of Rogers' response to clients. *Person-Centered Review, 5*, 433–448.

Zucconi, A. (1987). Thoughts about Carl Rogers. *Person-Centered Review, 2*, 438–440.

Zucconi, A. (1997). Personal communication (on training programs; June 30, 1997).

Subject Index

Name Index